Irene C. Fountas & Gay Su Pinnell

The Reading Minilessons Book

Your Every Day Guide for Literacy Teaching

GRADE 5

HEINEMANN
Portsmouth, NH

Heinemann
361 Hanover Street
Portsmouth, NH 03801–3912
www.heinemann.com

Offices and agents throughout the world

The author and publisher wish to thank those who have generously given permission to reprint borrowed material: Please see the Credits section beginning on page 647.

Library of Congress Cataloging-in-Publication Data is on file at the Library of Congress.
ISBN: 978-0-325-09866-1

Editor: Sue Paro
Production: Cindy Strowman
Cover and interior designs: Ellery Harvey
Illustrator: Sarah Snow
Typesetter: Sharon Burkhardt
Manufacturing: Erin St. Hilaire

Printed in the United States of America on acid-free paper

1 2 3 4 5 6 7 WC 24 23 22 21 20 19
June 2019 Printing

CONTENTS

Introduction

1 Management

2 Literary Analysis

Fiction and Nonfiction

General

Messages and Themes

Style and Language

Illustrations

Book and Print Features

Nonfiction

Genre

Organization

Topic

Illustration/Graphics

Book and Print Features

Fiction

Genre

Plot

Character

Style and Language

3 Strategies and Skills

4 Writing About Reading

Chapter 1 The Role of Reading Minilessons in Literacy Learning

THE GOAL OF ALL READING is the joyful, independent, and meaningful processing of a written text. As a competent reader, you become immersed in a fiction or nonfiction text; you read for a purpose; you become highly engaged with the plot, the characters, or the content. Focused on the experience of reading the text, you are largely unconscious of the thousands of actions happening in your brain that support the construction of meaning from the print that represents language. And, this is true whether the print is on a piece of paper or an electronic device. Your purpose may be to have vicarious experiences via works of fiction that take you to places far distant in time and space—even to worlds that do not and cannot exist! Or, your purpose may be to gather fuel for thinking (by using fiction or nonfiction) or it may be simply to enjoy the sounds of human language via literature and poetry. Most of us engage in the reading of multiple texts every day—some for work, some for pleasure, and some for practical guidance—but what we all have in common as readers is the ability to independently and simultaneously apply in-the-head systems of strategic actions that enable us to act on written texts.

Young readers are on a journey toward efficient processing of any texts they might like to attempt, and it is important every step of the way that they have successful experiences in independently reading those texts that are available at each point in time. In a literacy-rich classroom with a multitext approach, readers have the opportunity to hear written texts read aloud through interactive read-aloud, and so they build a rich treasure chest of known stories and nonfiction books that they can share as a classroom community. They understand and talk about these shared texts in ways that extend comprehension, vocabulary, and knowledge of the ways written texts are presented and organized. They participate with their classmates in the shared or performance reading of a common text so that they understand more and know how to act on written language. They experience tailored instruction in small guided reading groups using leveled texts precisely matched to their current abilities and needs for challenge. They stretch their thinking as they discuss a variety of complex texts in book clubs. They process fiction and nonfiction books with expert teacher support—always moving in the direction of more complex texts that will lift their reading abilities. *But it is in independent reading that they apply everything they have learned across all of those instructional contexts.* So the goal of all the reading instruction is to enable the reader to engage in effective, efficient, and meaningful processing of written text *every day* in the classroom. This is what it means to grow up literate in our schools.

Independent reading involves choices based on interests and tastes. Competent, independent readers are eager to talk and write about the books they have chosen and read on their own. They are gaining awareness of themselves as readers with favorite authors, illustrators, genres, and topics; their capacity for self-regulation is growing. The key to this kind of independent reading is making an explicit connection between all other instructional contexts—interactive read-aloud, shared reading, guided reading, and book clubs—and the reader's own independent work. Making these explicit links is the goal of minilessons. All teaching, support, and confirmation lead to the individual's successful, independent reading.

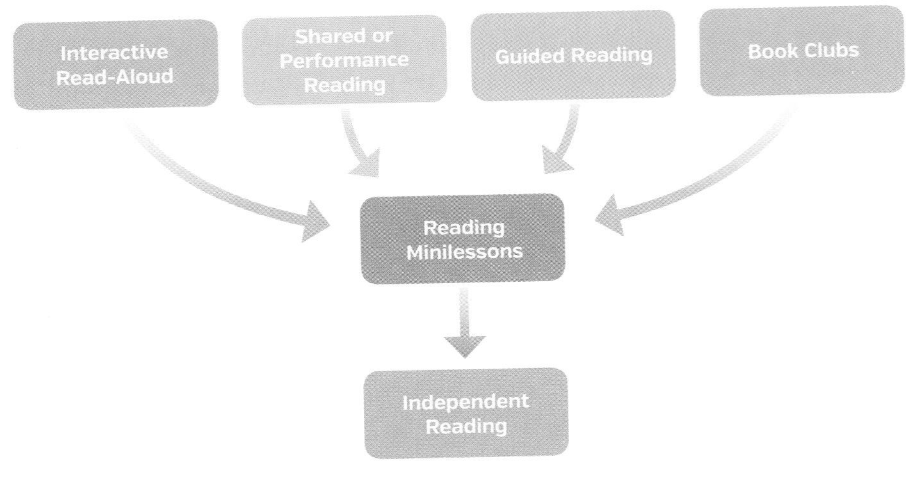

Figure 1-1: Various reading experiences supported by explicit instruction in reading minilessons lead to independent reading.

What Is a Reading Minilesson?

A reading minilesson is a concise and focused lesson on any aspect of effective reading that is important for students to explicitly understand at a particular point in time. It is an opportunity to build on all of the students' literacy experiences, make one important understanding visible, and hold learners accountable for applying it consistently in reading. These explicit minilessons place a strong instructional frame around independent reading.

A minilesson takes only a few minutes and usually involves the whole class. Because it builds on shared literary experiences that the students in your class have experienced prior to the lesson, you can quickly bring these shared texts to mind as powerful examples. Usually, you will teach only one focused lesson each day, but minilessons are logically organized to build on each other. Each minilesson is designed to engage your students in an inquiry process that leads to the discovery and understanding of a general principle that they can immediately apply. Most of the time, interactive read-aloud books that students have already heard serve as **mentor texts** from which they generalize the understanding. In this way, the reading minilesson provides a link between students' previous experience and their own independent reading (see Figure 1-1). The reading minilesson plays a key role in systematic, coherent teaching, all of which is directed toward each reader's developing competencies.

To help students connect ideas and develop deep knowledge and broad application of **principles**, related reading minilessons are grouped under **umbrella** concepts (see Chapter 3). An umbrella is the broad category within which several lessons are linked to each other and all of which contribute to the understanding of the umbrella concept. Within each umbrella, the lessons build on each other (see Figure 1-2). In each lesson, you will create an **anchor chart** with the students. This visual representation of the principle will be a useful reference tool as students learn new routines, encounter new texts, and draw and write about their reading in a reader's notebook.

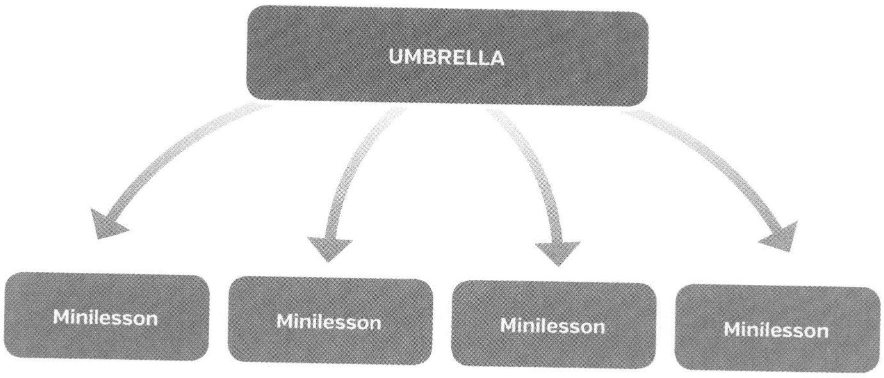

Figure 1-2: Each minilesson focuses on a different aspect of the larger umbrella concept.

Four Types of Reading Minilessons

In this book, you will find 225 minilessons that are organized into four types:

Management	Page 83
Literary Analysis	Page 125
Strategies and Skills	Page 485
Writing About Reading	Page 561

Figure 1-3: The minilessons in this book are organized into four sections.

Management Minilessons. These lessons include routines that are essential to the smooth functioning of the classroom and student-centered, independent literacy learning. The Management minilessons are designed to support students' development of independence and self-regulatory behavior. The Management minilessons for fifth graders help students learn to be respectful members of a classroom community of readers who share book recommendations, talk together about books, and write about reading on a regular basis. You'll also find minilessons that support students in reading independently at school and at home and that prepare them for living a reading life by developing their reading interests and preferences, challenging themselves to stretch and grow as readers, and dedicating time to read at home. Most of your minilessons at the beginning of the school year will focus on management. You will want to repeat any of the lessons as needed across the year. A guiding principle: teach a minilesson on anything that prevents the classroom from running smoothly and feeling like a strong community.

Literary Analysis Minilessons. These lessons build students' awareness of the characteristics of various genres and of the elements of fiction and nonfiction texts. Most of the mentor texts used to illustrate the principles are interactive read-aloud books that you have read previously to the class. However, a few mentor texts are independent reading books or guided reading books. When using these books, make sure that you have read them aloud to the whole class before the minilesson. Through these lessons, students learn how to apply new thinking to their independent reading; they also learn how to share their thinking with others.

Strategies and Skills Minilessons. Readers need to develop a robust body of in-the-head strategic actions for the efficient processing of texts. For example, they need to monitor their reading for accuracy and understanding, solve words (simple and complex), read fluently with phrasing, and constantly construct meaning. And, as they encounter more complex books in fifth grade, they need to use a variety of effective techniques when approaching texts that are difficult for them to read. The lessons not only support your students in monitoring their comprehension but also address the importance of focus and persistence in reading difficult texts. Teaching related to processing texts (decoding words, parsing language, and reading with accuracy and fluency) will best take place in guided reading and independent reading conferences. The general lessons included in this volume reinforce broad principles that every reader in your class may need to be reminded of from time to time. Included in Section Three: Strategies and Skills is Umbrella 7: Reading in Digital Environments, which is designed to help you teach students to effectively find online the information they need, evaluate its relevance and credibility, and stay focused while doing so. At fifth grade, when many students begin to spend more time reading in digital environments, these lessons provide essential teaching for the digital age. Also included are lessons on navigating a difficult text.

Writing About Reading Minilessons. Throughout the fifth-grade year, students will have opportunities to use a reader's notebook to respond to

Figure 1-4: Characteristics of effective minilessons

Characteristics of Effective Minilessons

Effective Minilessons . . .

- have a **clear rationale and a goal** to focus meaningful teaching
- are **relevant to the specific needs of readers** so that your teaching connects with the learners
- are **brief, concise, and to the point** for immediate application
- use **clear and specific language** to avoid talk that clutters learning
- stay **focused on a single idea** so students can apply the learning and build on it day after day
- **build one understanding on another** across several days instead of single isolated lessons
- use an **inquiry approach** whenever possible to support constructive learning
- often include **shared, high-quality mentor texts** that can be used as examples
- are **well paced** to engage and hold students' interest
- are **grouped into umbrellas** to foster depth in thinking and coherence across lessons
- provide time for students to **"try out" the new concept** before independent application
- engage students in **summarizing the new learning** and thinking about its application to their own work
- build **academic vocabulary** appropriate to the grade level
- help students become **better readers and writers**
- **foster community** through the development of shared language
- **can be assessed** as you observe students in authentic literacy activities to provide feedback on your teaching
- help **students understand what they are learning** how to do and how it helps them as readers

what they read. These lessons introduce *Reader's Notebook: Advanced* (Fountas and Pinnell 2011) and help students use this important tool for independent literacy learning. Fifth graders will use a reader's notebook to keep track of their reading and writing (which will include new genres and forms of writing), keep a record of the principles taught in minilessons, write a weekly letter about the books they are reading, and write regularly about the thinking they do while reading.

The goal of all minilessons is to help students to think and act like readers and to build effective processing strategies while reading continuous text independently. Whether you are teaching Management lessons, Literary Analysis lessons, Strategies and Skills lessons, or Writing About Reading lessons, the characteristics of effective minilessons, listed in Figure 1-4, apply.

Constructing Anchor Charts for Effective Minilessons

Anchor charts are an essential part of each minilesson in this book (see Figure 1-5). They provide a way for you to capture the students' thinking during the lesson and reflect on the learning at the end. When you think about a chart, it helps you think through the big, important ideas and the language you will use in the minilesson. It helps you think about the sequence and your efficiency in getting down what is important.

Each minilesson in this book provides guidance for adding information to the chart. Read through each lesson carefully to know whether any parts of the chart should be prepared ahead or whether the chart is constructed during the lesson or at the end. After the lesson, the charts become resources for your students to use for reference throughout the day and on following days. They can revisit these charts as they apply the principles in reading, talking, and writing about books, or as they try out new routines in the classroom. You can refer to them during interactive read-aloud, shared and performance reading, reading conferences, guided reading, and book clubs. Anchor charts are a resource for students who need a visual representation of their learning.

Though your charts will be unique because they are built from the ideas your students share, you will want to consider some of the common characteristics among the charts we have included in this book. We have created one example in each lesson, but vary it as you see fit. When you create charts with students, consider the following:

- **Make your charts simple, clear, and organized.** The charts you create with your students should be clearly organized. Regardless of grade, it is important to keep them simple without a lot of dense text. Provide white space and write in dark, easy-to-read colors. You will notice that some of the sample charts are more conceptual. The idea is conveyed through a few words and a visual representation. Others use a grid to show how the principle is applied specifically across several texts.

- **Make your charts visually appealing and useful.** Many of the minilesson charts for fifth grade contain visual support, and this is especially helpful to English language learners. For example, you will see book covers, symbols, and drawings. Some students will benefit from the visuals to help them in reading the words on the chart and in understanding the concept. The drawings are intentionally simple to give you a quick model to draw yourself. English language learners might need to rely heavily on a graphic representation of the principle ideas. You might find it helpful to prepare these drawings on separate pieces of paper or sticky notes ahead of the lesson and tape or glue them on the chart as the students construct their understandings. This time-saving tip can also make the charts look more interesting and colorful, because certain parts stand out for the students.

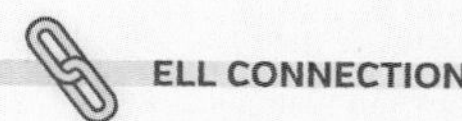

When you teach English language learners, you must adjust your teaching—not more teaching, but different teaching—to assure effective learning. Look for this symbol to see ways to support English language learners.

- **Make your charts colorful.** Though the sample minilesson charts are colorful for the purpose of engagement or organization, be careful about the amount and types of color that you use. You may want to use color for specific purposes. For example, color can help you point out particular parts of the chart ("Look at the purple word on the chart") or support English language learners by providing a visual link to certain words or ideas. However, color can also be distracting if overused. Be thoughtful about when you choose to use colors to highlight an idea or a word on a chart so that students are supported in reading continuous text. Text that is broken up by a lot of different colors can be very distracting for readers. You will notice that the minilesson principle is usually written in black or another dark color across the top of the chart so that it stands out and is easily recognized as the focus of the lesson.

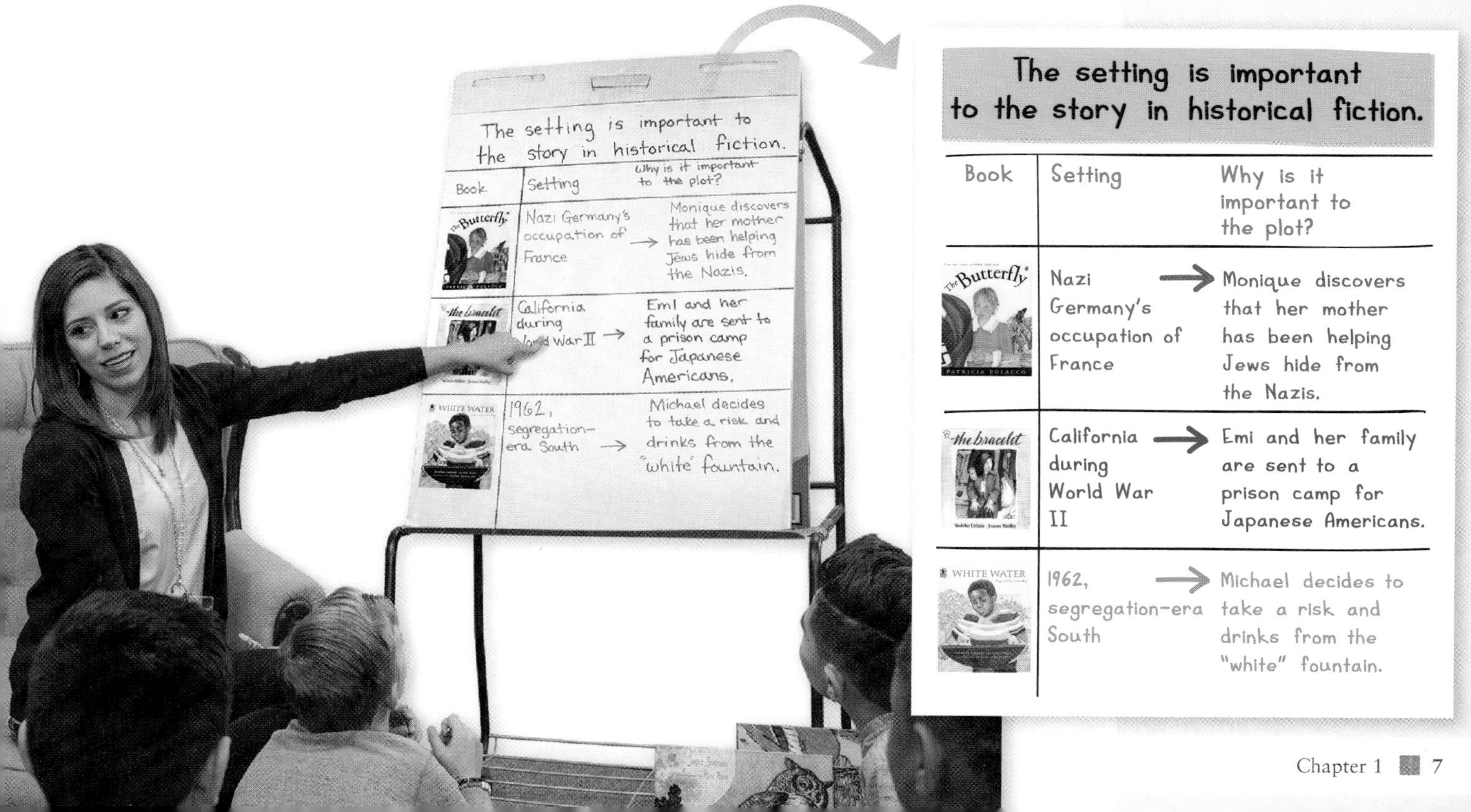

Figure 1-5: Constructing anchor charts with your students provides verbal and visual support for all learners.

The setting is important to the story in historical fiction.

Book	Setting	Why is it important to the plot?
The Butterfly	Nazi Germany's occupation of France →	Monique discovers that her mother has been helping Jews hide from the Nazis.
The bracelet	California during World War II →	Emi and her family are sent to a prison camp for Japanese Americans.
White Water	1962, segregation-era South →	Michael decides to take a risk and drinks from the "white" fountain.

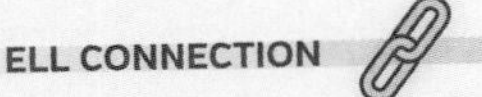

ELL CONNECTION

Anchor charts support language growth in all students, and especially in English language learners. Conversation about the minilesson develops oral language and then connects that oral language to print when you write words on the chart and provide picture support. By constructing an anchor chart with your students, you provide print that is immediately accessible to them because they helped create it and have ownership of the language. After a chart is finished, revisit it as often as needed to reinforce not only the ideas but also the printed words.

Balancing Time and Inquiry

Most minilessons in this book follow an inquiry-based approach in which students discover and construct understandings of the minilesson principle. Constructing ideas through inquiry can take a lot of time if not properly structured and supported. Notice that most of the minilessons in this book start right away with focused examples from mentor texts rather than a general review of the books. Time can be lost by reviewing each mentor text used in a minilesson. Avoid starting the lesson by asking "Do you remember what this book is about?" or "What happened in this story?" Instead, choose examples from books your students know really well. Following are some helpful time-saving tips:

- Teach students to listen to one another to avoid wasting time by repeating the same information during the minilesson.
- Avoid repeating every student response yourself. Repeat (or ask the student to repeat) only if clarification is needed.
- Take a few responses and move on; you don't need to hear from everyone who has raised a hand. Over time, assure everyone a chance to respond.
- Don't be afraid to ask a student to hold a thought for another time if it is not related or is only tangentially related. A lot of time can be lost when students share personal stories or go far away from the focus. Stay focused on building understanding of the minilesson principle and invite the sharing of personal experiences only when it is applicable to understanding the principle.
- Make sure the mentor text examples you choose are short and to the point. Usually you will not need to read more than a paragraph or a few sentences out of the mentor texts to conduct the inquiry.
- Assess your students' talk as they participate in the inquiry and omit examples you do not need. Each minilesson section generally has two or three examples. They are there if you need them, but you should judge from your students' participation whether you need to share every example or whether you can simply move on and ask students to have a try.

Using Reading Minilessons with Fifth-Grade Students

A minilesson brings to students' conscious attention a focused principle that will assist them in developing an effective, independent literacy processing system. It provides an opportunity for students to do the following:

- Respond to and act on a variety texts
- Become aware of and be able to articulate understandings about texts
- Engage in further inquiry to investigate the characteristics of texts
- Search for and learn to recognize patterns and characteristics of written texts
- Build new ideas on known ideas
- Think critically about the quality, authenticity, and credibility of texts
- Learn how to think about effective actions as they process texts
- Learn to manage their own reading lives
- Learn how to work together well in the classroom
- Learn to talk to others to share their thinking about books
- Learn how to write to communicate their thinking about books

Reading minilessons help readers build in-the-head processing systems. In the following chapters, you will explore how minilessons support students in using integrated systems of strategic actions for thinking *within*, *beyond*, and *about* many different kinds of texts and also how to use minilessons to build a community of readers who demonstrate a sense of agency and responsibility. You will also look in more depth at how minilessons fit within a design for literacy learning and within a multitext approach.

We conclude this chapter with some key terms we will use as we describe minilessons in the next chapters (see Figure 1-6). Keep these in mind so you can develop a common language to talk about the minilessons you teach.

Figure 1-6: Important terms used in *The Reading Minilessons Book*

Key Terms When Talking About Reading Minilessons	
Umbrella	A group of minilessons, all of which are directed at different aspects of the same larger understanding.
Principle	A concise statement of the understanding students will need to learn and apply.
Mentor Text	A fiction or nonfiction text that offers a clear example of the principle toward which the minilesson is directed. Students will have previously heard and discussed the text.
Text Set	A group of fiction or nonfiction texts or a combination of fiction and nonfiction texts that, taken together, support a theme or exemplify a genre. Students will have previously heard all the texts referenced in a minilesson and had opportunities to make connections between them.
Anchor Chart	A visual representation of the lesson concept, using a combination of words and images. It is constructed by the teacher and students to summarize the learning and is used as a reference tool by the students.

Chapter 2 Using *The Literacy Continuum* to Guide the Teaching of Reading Minilessons

We believe schools should be places where students read, think, talk, and write every day about relevant content that engages their hearts and minds. Learning deepens when students engage in thinking, talking, reading, and writing about texts across many different learning contexts and in whole-group, small-group, and individual instruction. Students who live a literate life in their classrooms have access to multiple experiences with texts throughout a day. As they participate in interactive read-aloud, shared and performance reading, guided reading, book clubs, and independent reading, they engage in the real work of reading and writing. They build a network of systems of strategic actions that allow them to think deeply within, beyond, and about text.

The networks of in-the-head strategic actions are inferred from observations of proficient readers, writers, and speakers. We have described these networks in *The Fountas & Pinnell Literacy Continuum: A Tool for Assessment, Planning, and Teaching* (Fountas and Pinnell 2017b). This volume presents detailed text characteristics and behaviors and understandings to notice, teach, and support for prekindergarten through middle school across eight instructional reading, writing, and language contexts. In sum, *The Literacy Continuum* describes proficiency in reading, writing, and language as it changes over grades and over levels.

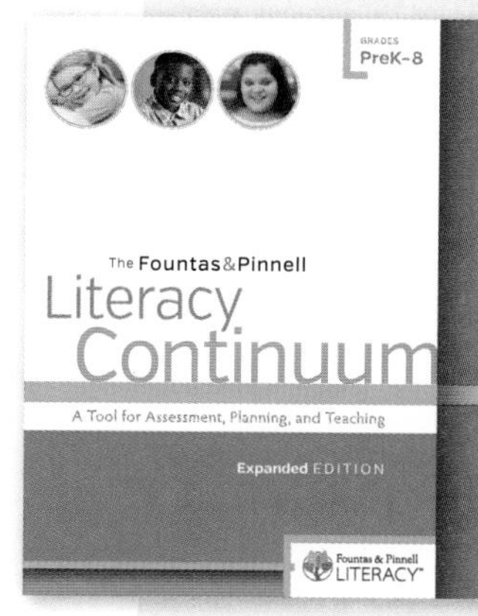

Figure 2-1: Minilesson principles are drawn from the observable behaviors of proficient students as listed in *The Literacy Continuum*.

	INSTRUCTIONAL CONTEXT	BRIEF DEFINITION	DESCRIPTION OF THE CONTINUUM
1	Interactive Read-Aloud and Literature Discussion	Students engage in discussion with one another about a text that they have heard read aloud or one they have read independently.	• Year by year, grades PreK–8 • Genres appropriate to grades PreK–8 • Specific behaviors and understandings that are evidence of thinking within, beyond, and about the text
2	Shared and Performance Reading	Students read together or take roles in reading a shared text. They reflect the meaning of the text with their voices.	• Year by year, grades PreK–8 • Genres appropriate to grades PreK–8 • Specific behaviors and understandings that are evidence of thinking within, beyond, and about the text
3	Writing About Reading	Students extend their understanding of a text through a variety of writing genres and sometimes with illustrations.	• Year by year, grades PreK–8 • Genres/forms for writing about reading appropriate to grades PreK–8 • Specific evidence in the writing that reflects thinking within, beyond, and about the text
4	Writing	Students compose and write their own examples of a variety of genres, written for varying purposes and audiences.	• Year by year, grades PreK–8 • Genres/forms for writing appropriate to grades PreK–8 • Aspects of craft, conventions, and process that are evident in students' writing, grades PreK–8
5	Oral and Visual Communication	Students present their ideas through oral discussion and presentation.	• Year by year, grades PreK–8 • Specific behaviors and understandings related to listening and speaking, presentation
6	Technological Communication	Students learn effective ways of communicating and searching for information through technology; they learn to think critically about information and sources.	• Year by year, grades PreK–8 • Specific behaviors and understandings related to effective and ethical uses of technology
7	Phonics, Spelling, and Word Study	Students learn about the relationships of letters to sounds as well as the structure and meaning of words to help them in reading and spelling.	• Year by year, grades PreK–8 • Specific behaviors and understandings related to nine areas of understanding related to letters, sounds, and words, and how they work in reading and spelling
8	Guided Reading	Students read a teacher-selected text in a small group; the teacher provides explicit teaching and support for reading increasingly challenging texts.	• Level by level, A to Z • Genres appropriate to grades PreK–8 • Specific behaviors and understandings that are evidence of thinking within, beyond, and about the text • Specific suggestions for word work (drawn from the phonics and word analysis continuum)

Figure 2-2: From *The Literacy Continuum* (Fountas and Pinnell 2017b, 3)

Systems of Strategic Actions

The systems of strategic actions are represented in the wheel diagram shown in Figure 2-3 and on the inside back cover of this book. This model helps us think about the thousands of in-the-head processes that take place simultaneously and largely unconsciously when a competent reader processes a text. When the reader engages the neural network, he builds a literacy processing system over time that becomes increasingly sophisticated. Teaching in each instructional context is directed toward helping every reader expand these in-the-head networks across increasingly complex texts.

Four sections of *The Literacy Continuum* (Fountas and Pinnell 2017b)—Interactive Read-Aloud and Literature Discussion, Shared and Performance Reading, Guided Reading, and Writing About Reading—describe the specific competencies or goals of readers, writers, and language users:

Within the Text (literal understanding achieved through searching for and using information, monitoring and self-correcting, solving words, maintaining fluency, adjusting, and summarizing) The reader gathers the important information from the fiction or nonfiction text.

Beyond the Text (predicting; making connections with personal experience, content knowledge, and other texts; synthesizing new information; and inferring what is implied but not stated) The reader brings understanding to the processing of a text, reaching for ideas or concepts that are implied but not explicitly stated.

About the Text (analyzing or critiquing the text) The reader looks at a text to analyze, appreciate, or evaluate its construction, logic, literary elements, or quality.

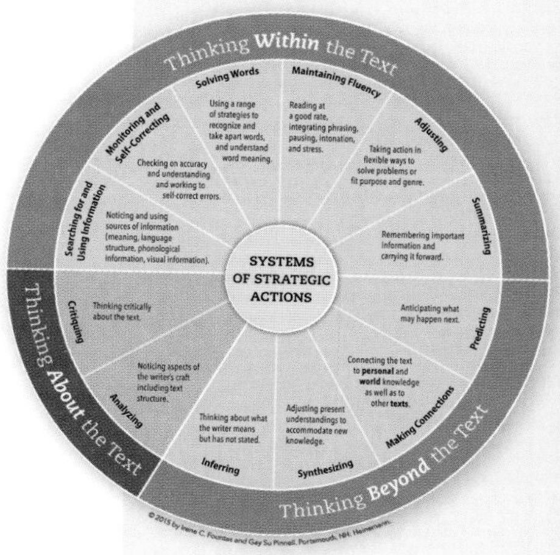

Figure 2-3: All of your teaching will be grounded in support of each reader's development of the systems of strategic actions (see the inside back cover for a larger version of the Systems of Strategic Actions wheel).

The Literacy Continuum is the foundation for all the minilessons. The minilesson principles come largely from the behaviors and understandings in the Interactive Read-Aloud continuum, but some are selected from the Shared and Performance Reading, Writing About Reading, Oral and Visual Communication, Technological Communication, and Guided Reading continua. In addition, we have included minilessons related to working together in a classroom community to assure that effective literacy instruction can take place. In most lessons, you will see a direct link to the goals from *The Literacy Continuum* called Continuum Connection.

As you ground your teaching in support of each reader's development of the systems of strategic actions, it is important to remember that these actions are never applied one at a time. A reader who comprehends a text engages these actions rapidly and simultaneously and largely without conscious attention. Your intentional talk and conversations in the various instructional contexts should support students in engaging and building their processing systems while they respond authentically as readers and enjoy the text.

Relationship of Intentional Talk to Reading Minilessons

Intentional talk refers to the language you use that is consciously directed toward the goal of instruction. We have used the term *facilitative talk* to refer to the language that the teacher uses to support student learning in specific ways. When you plan for intentional talk in your interactive read-aloud and shared and performance reading experiences, think about the meaning of the text and what your students will need to think about to fully understand and enjoy the story. You might select certain pages where you want to stop and have students turn and talk about their reading so they can engage in sharing their thinking with each other. The interactive read-aloud and shared and performance reading sections of *The Literacy Continuum* can help you plan what to talk about. For example, when you read a book like *The Raft,* you would likely invite talk about the characters' feelings and traits, discuss the importance of the setting to the plot, and predict the outcome of the story (see Figure 2-4). When you read a text set of expository nonfiction, you might invite students to comment on why the author wrote a book about the topic, how the author organized the information, and what they think is the theme of the book.

As you talk about texts together, embed brief and specific teaching in your read-aloud lessons while maintaining a focus on enjoyment and support for your students in gaining the meaning of the whole text. In preparation, mark a few places with sticky notes and a comment or question to invite thinking. Later, when you teach explicit minilessons about concepts such as theme, the importance of the setting, and text organization, your students will already have background knowledge to bring to the minilesson and will be ready to explore how the principle works across multiple texts.

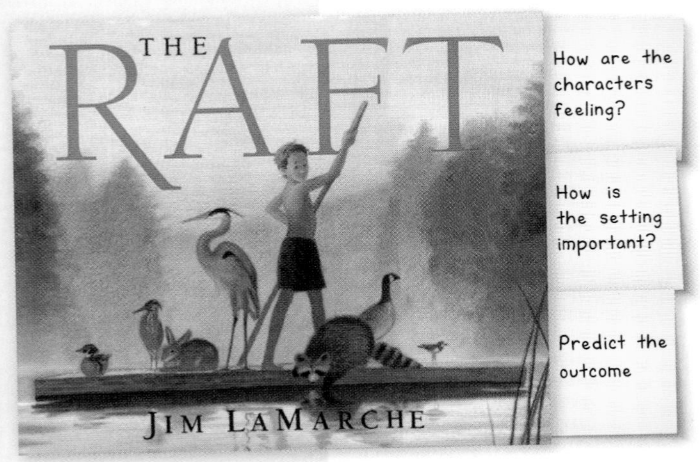

Figure 2-4: Mark a few pages to invite students to think about during interactive read-aloud. Later, you might teach an explicit minilesson on one of the concepts introduced during the interactive read-aloud.

In reading minilessons, you explicitly teach the principles you have already embedded in the students' previous experiences with text in these different instructional contexts. Intentional talk within each context prepares a foundation for this explicit focus. Through each interactive read-aloud and shared or performance reading experience, you build a large body of background knowledge, academic vocabulary, and a library of shared texts to draw on as you explore specific literary principles. You will read more about this multitext approach in Chapter 9.

Chapter 3 Understanding the Umbrellas and Minilessons

MINILESSONS IN THIS BOOK ARE organized into conceptual groups, called "umbrellas," in which groups of principles are explored in sequence, working toward larger concepts. Within each section (Management, Literary Analysis, etc.), the umbrellas are numbered in sequence and are often referred to by *U* plus the number, for example, U1 for the first umbrella. A suggested sequence of umbrellas is presented in Figure 8-2 to assist you in planning across the year, but the needs of your students always take priority.

Umbrella Front Page

Each umbrella has an introductory page on which the minilessons in the umbrella are listed and directions are provided to help you prepare to present the minilessons within the umbrella (see Figure 3-1). The introductory page is designed to provide an overview of how the umbrella is organized and the texts from *Fountas & Pinnell Classroom™ Interactive Read-Aloud Collection, Independent Reading Collection, Guided Reading Collection,* and *Book Clubs Collection* that are suggested for the lessons (Fountas and Pinnell 2020). In addition, we provide types of texts you might select if you are not using the books referenced in the lessons. Understanding how the umbrella is designed and how the minilessons fit together will help you keep your lessons focused, concise, and brief. Using familiar mentor texts that you have previously read and enjoyed with your students will help you streamline the lessons in the umbrella. You will not need to spend a lot of time rereading large sections of the texts because the students will already know them well.

ELL CONNECTION

When you teach lessons in an umbrella, you help students make connections between concepts and texts and help them develop deeper understandings. A rich context such as this one is particularly helpful for English language learners. Grouping lessons into umbrellas supports English language learners in developing shared vocabulary and language around a single and important area of knowledge.

Following the umbrella front page, you will see a series of two-page lesson spreads that include several parts.

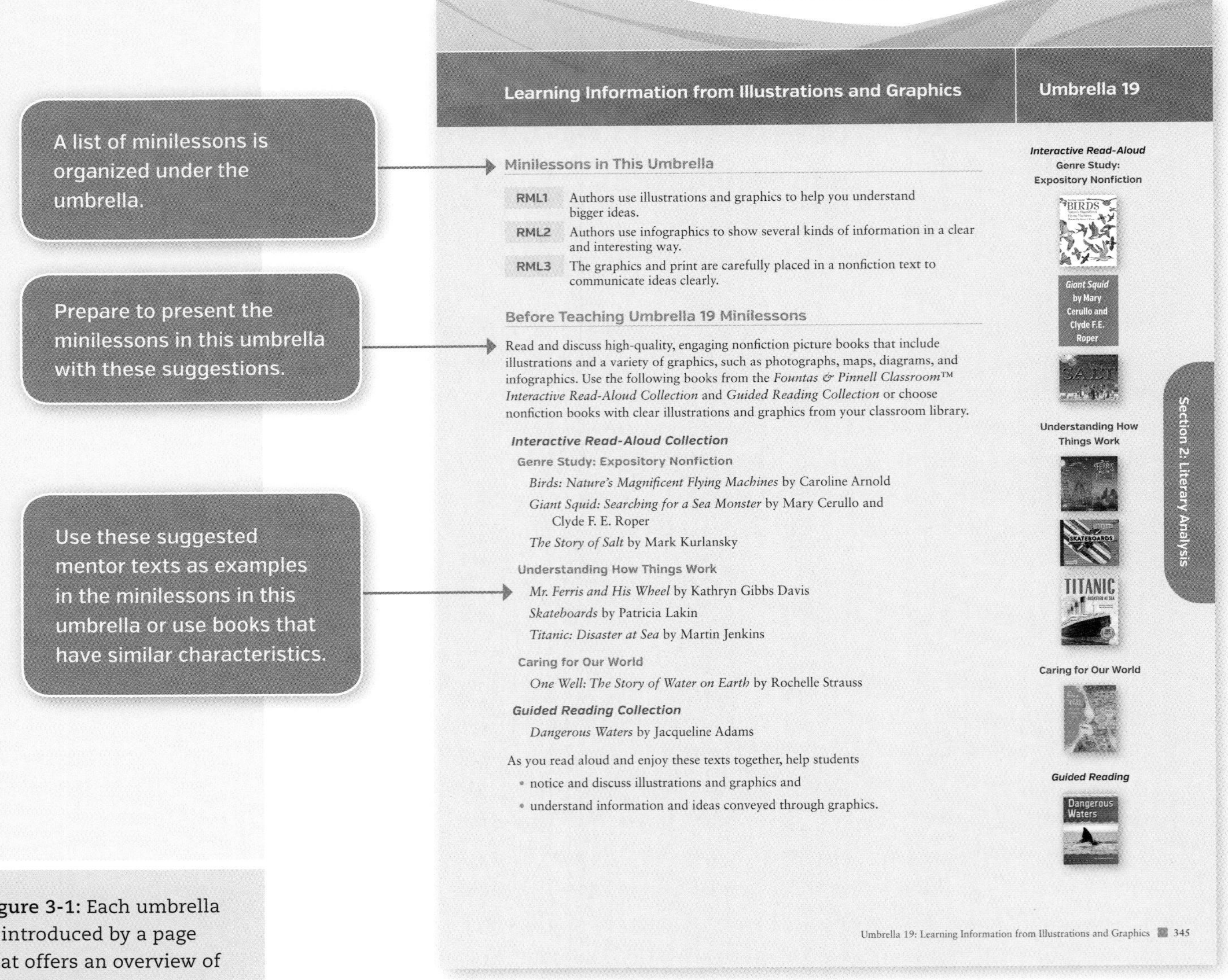
A list of minilessons is organized under the umbrella.
Prepare to present the minilessons in this umbrella with these suggestions.
Use these suggested mentor texts as examples in the minilessons in this umbrella or use books that have similar characteristics.

Learning Information from Illustrations and Graphics | Umbrella 19

Minilessons in This Umbrella

RML1	Authors use illustrations and graphics to help you understand bigger ideas.
RML2	Authors use infographics to show several kinds of information in a clear and interesting way.
RML3	The graphics and print are carefully placed in a nonfiction text to communicate ideas clearly.

Before Teaching Umbrella 19 Minilessons

Read and discuss high-quality, engaging nonfiction picture books that include illustrations and a variety of graphics, such as photographs, maps, diagrams, and infographics. Use the following books from the *Fountas & Pinnell Classroom*™ *Interactive Read-Aloud Collection* and *Guided Reading Collection* or choose nonfiction books with clear illustrations and graphics from your classroom library.

Interactive Read-Aloud Collection

Genre Study: Expository Nonfiction

Birds: Nature's Magnificent Flying Machines by Caroline Arnold

Giant Squid: Searching for a Sea Monster by Mary Cerullo and Clyde F. E. Roper

The Story of Salt by Mark Kurlansky

Understanding How Things Work

Mr. Ferris and His Wheel by Kathryn Gibbs Davis

Skateboards by Patricia Lakin

Titanic: Disaster at Sea by Martin Jenkins

Caring for Our World

One Well: The Story of Water on Earth by Rochelle Strauss

Guided Reading Collection

Dangerous Waters by Jacqueline Adams

As you read aloud and enjoy these texts together, help students

- notice and discuss illustrations and graphics and
- understand information and ideas conveyed through graphics.

Interactive Read-Aloud Genre Study: Expository Nonfiction

Giant Squid by Mary Cerullo and Clyde F.E. Roper

Understanding How Things Work

Caring for Our World

Guided Reading

Section 2: Literary Analysis

Umbrella 19: Learning Information from Illustrations and Graphics ■ 345

Figure 3-1: Each umbrella is introduced by a page that offers an overview of the umbrella.

Two-Page Minilesson Spread

Each minilesson includes a two-page spread that consists of several parts (see Figure 3-2). The section (for example, Literary Analysis), umbrella number (for example, U1), and minilesson number (for example, RML1) are listed at the top to help you locate the lesson you are looking for. Accordingly, the code LA.U1.RML1 identifies the first minilesson in the first umbrella of the Literary Analysis section.

Principle, Goal, Rationale

The **Principle** describes the understanding the students will need to learn and apply. The idea of the principle is based on *The Literacy Continuum* (Fountas and Pinnell 2017b), but the language of the principle has been carefully crafted to be precise, focused on a single idea, and accessible to students. We have placed the principle at the top of the lesson on the left-hand page so you have a clear idea of the understanding you will help students construct through the example texts used in the lesson. Although we have crafted the language to make it appropriate for the age group, you may shape the language in a slightly different way to reflect the way your students use language. Be sure that the principle is stated simply and clearly and check for understanding. Once that is accomplished, say it the same way every time.

The **Goal** of the minilesson is stated in the top section of the lesson, as is the **Rationale**, to help you understand what this particular minilesson will do and why it may be important for the students in your classroom. In this beginning section, you will also find suggestions for specific behaviors and understandings to observe as you assess students' learning during or after the minilesson.

Minilesson

In the **Minilesson** section of the lesson, you will find an example lesson for teaching the understanding, or principle. The example includes suggestions for teaching and the use of precise language and open-ended questions to engage students in a brief, focused inquiry. Effective minilessons include, when possible, the process of inquiry so students can actively construct their understanding from concrete examples, because *telling* is not *teaching*. Instead of simply being told what they need to know, students get inside the understanding by engaging in the thinking themselves. In the inquiry process, invite students to look at a group of texts that were read previously (for example, stories in which characters change). Choose the books carefully so they represent the characteristics students are learning about. They will have knowledge of these texts because they have previously experienced them. Invite them to talk about what they notice across all the books. As students

A Closer Look at a Reading Minilesson

The **Goal** of the minilesson is clearly identified, as is the **Rationale**, to support your understanding of what this particular minilesson is and why it may be important for the students in your classroom.

The Reading Minilesson Principle—a brief statement that describes the understanding students will need to learn and apply.

This code identifies this minilesson as the third reading minilesson (RML3) in the nineteenth umbrella (U19) in the Literary Analysis (LA) section.

Specific behaviors and understandings to observe as you assess students' learning after presenting the minilesson.

Academic Language and **Important Vocabulary** that students will need to understand in order to access the learning in the minilesson.

Suggested language to use when teaching the minilesson principle.

RML3
LA.U19.RML3

Reading Minilesson Principle
The graphics and print are carefully placed in a nonfiction text to communicate ideas clearly.

Learning Information from Illustrations and Graphics

You Will Need

- two or three familiar nonfiction books that have pages with multiple graphics and text elements, such as the following:
  - *Giant Squid* by Mary Cerullo and Clyde F. E. Roper and *The Story of Salt* by Mark Kurlansky, from Text Set: Genre Study: Expository Nonfiction
  - *Skateboards* by Patricia Lakin, from Text Set: Understanding How Things Work
- chart paper and markers

Academic Language / Important Vocabulary

- graphics
- text
- nonfiction
- placed
- communicate

Continuum Connection

- Understand that graphics and text are carefully placed in a nonfiction text so that ideas are communicated clearly (p. 75)

Goal

Understand that graphics and print are carefully placed in a nonfiction text so that ideas are communicated clearly.

Rationale

When students think about how the graphics and print are placed in nonfiction books, they understand that they work together to communicate ideas. They also understand that people who work on creating books (e.g., editors, designers) need to make decisions about how best to place the graphics and the print.

Assess Learning

Observe students when they read and talk about nonfiction books and notice if there is evidence of new learning based on the goal of this minilesson.

- Can students infer why the graphics and print are placed on the page in a certain way?
- Do they use vocabulary such as *graphics, text, nonfiction, placed,* and *communicate?*

Minilesson

To help students think about the minilesson principle, engage them in a discussion about the placement of graphics and print. Here is an example.

- Show the cover of *Giant Squid* and read the title. Display pages 16–17 and read the text aloud, pointing to each section as you read it.

  What do you notice about how the graphics and the print are placed, or arranged, on these pages?

- As needed, prompt the conversation with further questions such as the following:
  - *Why is a squid's tail placed above the section titled "Ocean Detective on the Chase"?*
  - *Why is the print in this section shaped like a question mark? Why is there a magnifying glass? Why is the background in this section black?*
  - *Why is the print that says "ARCHITEUTHIS 'The Chief Squid'" placed here?*
- Show the cover of *The Story of Salt* and read the title. Read and display page 7.

  What do you notice about how the graphics and print are placed on this page?

  Why do you think they are placed in this way?

350 ■ *The Reading Minilessons Book, Grade 5*

Figure 3-2: All the parts of a single minilesson are contained on a two-page spread.

Suggestions for students to practice the new thinking from the minilesson, usually with a partner.

Create **anchor charts** as a useful reference tool and reinforcement of the principle for students during independent reading and writing.

RML3
LA.U19.RML3

Have a Try

Invite the students to talk with a partner about the placement of graphics and text in *Skateboards*.

- Show the cover of *Skateboards* and read the title. Then read and display pages 22–23.

  Turn and talk to your partner about what you notice about how the graphics and print are placed on these pages. Why do you think they are placed in this way?

- After students turn and talk, invite a few pairs to share their thinking.

The graphics and print are carefully placed in a nonfiction text to communicate ideas clearly.

- Graphics are placed near the print that they relate to.

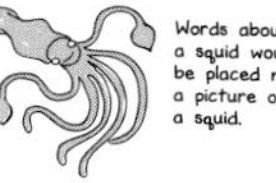
Words about a squid would be placed near a picture of a squid.

- The print may be placed in a certain shape to communicate an idea.

- The graphics may be placed in a certain order to indicate a process or sequence.

Step 1
Step 2
Step 3

Summarize and Apply

Summarize the learning and remind students to notice the placement of graphics and print in nonfiction books.

What did you notice today about the placement of the graphics and text in nonfiction books?

- Record students' responses on chart paper and write the principle at the top of the chart.

If you read a nonfiction book today, notice how the graphics and text are placed on the pages, and think about why they might be placed in that way. If you find a page that has the graphics and print placed in an interesting way, bring your example to share when we come back together.

A **summary** of the minilesson principle to help you guide the students to **apply** what they have learned to their independent reading.

Share

Following independent reading time, gather students together in the meeting area to talk about their reading.

Did anyone find an example of a page in a nonfiction book that has the graphics and print placed in an interesting way?

Why do you think the graphics and print are placed in that way?

After independent reading, it is important for students to have a chance to **share** learning, which gives you feedback on the learning students took on.

Extend the Lesson (Optional)

After assessing students' understanding, you might decide to extend the learning.

- When students write their own nonfiction texts, encourage them to think about how best to place the print and graphics on a page. Teach them how to place graphics and print in interesting ways using word-processing or page-layout software.

Umbrella 19: Learning Information from Illustrations and Graphics ■ 351

Optional suggestions for extending the learning of the minilesson over time or in other contexts.

explore the text examples using your questions and supportive comments as a guide, co-construct the anchor chart, creating an organized and visual representation of the students' noticings and understandings. (See the section on anchor charts in Chapter 1 for more information on chart creation.) From this exploration and the discussion surrounding it, students derive the principle, which is then written at the top of the chart.

Throughout this book, you will find models and examples of the anchor charts you will co-construct with students. Of course, the charts you create will be unique because they reflect your students' thinking. Learning is more powerful and enjoyable for students when they actively search for the meaning, find patterns, talk about their understandings, and share in the co-construction of the chart. Students need to form networks of understanding around the concepts related to literacy and to be constantly looking for connections for themselves.

ELL CONNECTION 

Creating a need to produce language is an important principle in building language, and reading minilessons provide many opportunities for students to express their thoughts in language and to communicate with others. The inquiry approach found in these lessons invites more student talk than teacher talk, and that can be both a challenge and an opportunity for you as you work with English language learners. In our previous texts, we have written that Marie Clay (1991) urges us to be "strong minded" about holding meaningful conversations even when they are difficult. In *Becoming Literate,* she warns us that it is "misplaced sympathy" to do the talking for those who are developing and learning language. Instead, she recommends "concentrating more sharply, smiling more rewardingly and spending more time in genuine conversation." Building talk routines, such as turn and talk, into your reading minilessons can be very helpful in providing these opportunities for English language learners in a safe and supportive way.

When you ask students to think about the minilesson principle across several texts that they have previously listened to and discussed, they are more engaged and able to participate because they know these texts and can shift their attention to a new way of thinking about them. Using familiar texts is particularly important for English language learners. When you select examples for a reading minilesson, choose texts that you know were particularly engaging for the English language learners in your classroom. Besides choosing accessible, familiar texts, it is important to provide plenty of wait and think time. For example, you might say, "Let's think about that for a minute" before calling for responses.

When working with English language learners, value partially correct responses. Look for what the child knows about the concept instead of focusing on faulty grammar or language errors. Model appropriate language use in your responses, but do not correct a child who is attempting to use language to learn it. You might also provide an oral sentence frame to get the student response started. Accept variety in pronunciation and intonation, remembering that the more students speak, read, and write, the more they will take on the understanding of grammatical patterns and the complex intonation patterns that reflect meaning in English.

Have a Try

Because students will be asked to apply the new thinking on their own during independent literacy work, it is important to give students a chance to apply it with a partner or a small group while still in the whole-group setting. **Have a Try** is designed to be brief, but it offers you an opportunity to gather information on how well students understand the minilesson principle. In many minilessons, students are asked to apply the new thinking to another concrete example from a familiar book. In Management lessons, students quickly practice the new routine that they will be asked to do independently. You will often add further thinking to the chart after the students have had the chance to try out their new learning.

The Have a Try portion of the reading minilesson is particularly important for English language learners. Besides providing repetition and allowing for the gradual release of responsibility, it gives English language learners a safe place to try out the new idea before sharing it with the whole group. These are a few suggestions for how you might support students during the Have a Try portion of the lesson:

- Pair students with specific partners in a way that will allow for a balance of talk between the two.
- Spend time teaching students how to turn and talk. (In Section One: Management, MGT.U2.RML2, addresses the turn and talk routine.) Teach students how to provide wait time for one another, invite the other partner into the conversation, and take turns.
- Provide concrete examples to discuss so that students are clear about what they need to talk about and are able to stay grounded in the text. English language learners will feel more confident if they are able to talk about a text that they know really well.
- Observe partnerships involving English language learners and provide support as needed.
- When necessary, you might find it helpful to provide the oral language structure or language stem for how you want your students to share. For example, ask them to start with the phrase "I think the character feels . . ." and to rehearse the language structure a few times before turning and talking.

Summarize and Apply

This part of the lesson consists of two parts: summarizing the learning and applying the learning to independent reading.

The **summary** is a brief but essential part of the lesson. It provides a time to bring together all of the learning that has taken place through the inquiry and to help students think about its application and relevance to their own learning. It is best to involve the students in constructing the minilesson principle with you. Ask them to reflect on the chart you have created together and talk about what they have learned that day. In simple, clear language, shape the suggestions. Other times, you may decide to help summarize the new learning to keep the lesson short and allow enough time for the students to apply it independently. Whether you state the principle or co-construct it with your students, summarize the learning in a way that makes the principle generative and applicable to future texts the students will read.

After the summary, the students **apply** their new understandings to their independent reading. However, before students begin their independent reading, let them know what you expect them to discuss or bring for the group sharing session so they can think about it as they read. This way, they know they are accountable for trying out the new thinking in their own books and are expected to share upon their return.

Students engaged in independent reading will choose books from the classroom library. These are genuine choices based on their interests and previous experiences. Book levels are not used in the classroom library. Some teachers choose to have students shop for books in the library at specific times and have them keep selected books in their personal literacy boxes. When you designate certain times for browsing, you maximize students' time spent on reading and are able to carve out time to assist with book selection. When needed, plan to supply independent reading books that will provide opportunities to apply the principle. For example, if you teach the umbrella on studying biographies, make sure students have access to biographies. You will notice that in some of the lessons, students are invited to read from a certain basket of books in the classroom library to ensure that there are opportunities to apply their new learning.

We know that when students first take on new learning, they often overgeneralize or overapply the new learning at the exclusion of some of the other things they have learned. The best goal when students are reading any book is to enjoy it, process it effectively, and gain its full meaning. Always encourage meaningful and authentic engagement with text. You don't want students so focused and determined to apply the minilesson principle that they make superficial connections to text that actually distract from their understanding of the book. You will likely find the opportunity in many reading conferences, guided reading lessons, or book club meetings to reinforce the minilesson understanding.

In our professional book, *Teaching for Comprehending and Fluency: Thinking, Talking, and Writing About Reading, K–8* (Fountas and Pinnell 2006), we write, "Whenever we instruct readers, we mediate (or change) the meaning they derive from their reading. Yet we must offer instruction that helps readers expand their abilities. There is value in drawing readers' attention to important aspects of the text that will enrich their understanding, but we need to understand that using effective reading strategies is not like exercising one or two muscles at a time. The system must always work together as an integrated whole." The invitation to apply the new learning must be clear enough to have students try out new ways of thinking, but "light" enough to allow room for readers to expand and express their own thinking. The application of the minilesson principle should not be thought of as an exercise or task that needs to be completed but instead as an invitation to a deeper, more meaningful response to the events or ideas in a text.

While students are reading independently, you may be meeting with small groups for guided reading or book clubs, rotating to observe students working independently, or conferring with individuals. If you have a reading conference, you can take the opportunity to reinforce the minilesson principle. We have provided two conferring record sheets (choose whichever form suits your purpose) for you to download from the online resources (see Figure 3-3) so that you can make notes about your individual conferences with students. You can use your notes to plan the content of future minilessons.

Teacher Mr. Viruez Grade 5 Week of April 3

Conferring Record 1

Minilesson Focus Thinking About Themes (LA U9)

Student	Monday	Tuesday	We
Colin			
Rachel	Reading Jacques Cousteau. Has read several biographies; encouraged to try historical fiction.		
Amelia		Yang the Third and Her Impossible Family. Talked about the themes of the book.	
Farhan			Ways Gets Stran Provic evider chara traits
Raúl			

Teacher Ms. Locust Grade 5 Week of 2/4–2/8

Conferring Record 2

Minilesson Focus LA U14 Studying Expository Nonfiction

Student	Comments/Observations
Robbie	Magyc. Loving the series; plans to read another; talked about the characteristics of fantasy.
Jessie	Life in a Castle. Discussed some of the facts learned from illustrations.
Raye	Malala Yousafzai. Talked about Malala's personality traits; Raye provided evidence for her opinions.
Lila	Roller Girl. Talked about speech bubbles; going to try an expository text next.
Luck	Kids Who Are Changing the World. Easily identified messages and themes and provided evidence.
Marcos	Mad Scientists. Talked about how the book works. Needs more instruction in identifying NF text structures.
Siddu	The Science of a Tornado. Made connections to science weather unit. Compared information in the book to what he had read on the internet.
Saliim	Quarterback Season. Discussed looking at some NF books about sports. Has read very little NF this year so made this a goal.
Amelia	Puppies, Dogs, and Blue Northers. Discussed narrative nonfiction and how she is learning facts through the story. Plans to read expository NF about dogs.
Rohan	The Mighty Mars Rovers. Read a portion aloud. Needs support with phrasing and intonation.
Roshon	The Peculiar. Discussed whether the characters are believable within the fantasy world. Strong understanding of the elements of fantasy.
Ava	Marie Curie. Loves biographies. Talked about what the author included/omitted compared to another book she read about Curie.

Figure 3-3: Choose one of these downloadable forms to record your observations of students' behaviors and understandings during reading conferences. Visit **resources.fountasandpinnell.com** to download this and all other online resources.

Share

At the end of the independent work time, students come together and have the opportunity to **share** their learning with the entire group. Group share provides an opportunity for you to revisit, expand, and deepen understanding of the minilesson principle as well as to assess learning. In Figure 3-2, you will notice that in the Share section we provide suggestions for how to engage students in sharing their discoveries. Often, students are asked to bring a book to share and to explain how they applied the minilesson principle in their independent reading. Sometimes we suggest sharing with the whole group, but other times we suggest that sharing take place among pairs, triads, or quads. As you observe and talk to students engaged in independent reading, shared and performance reading, guided reading, or book clubs, you can assess whether they are easily able to apply the minilesson principle. Use this information to inform how you plan to share. If only a few students were able to apply the minilesson to their reading (for example, if the minilesson applies to a particular book feature or genre characteristic that not all students came across in their books during independent reading), you might ask only a few students to share. Whereas if you observe most of the class applying the principle, you might have them share in pairs or small groups.

As a general guideline, in addition to revisiting the reading minilesson principle at the end of independent reading time, you might also ask students to share what they thought or wrote about their reading that day. For example, a student might share part of a letter he wrote about his reading. Another student might share a memorable line from a book or celebrate reaching the goal of trying a book in a different genre. The Share is a wonderful way to bring the community of readers and writers back together to expand their understandings and celebrate their learning at the end of the workshop time.

There are some particular accommodations you might want to consider to support English language learners during sharing:

- Ask English language learners to share in pairs before sharing with the whole group.
- Use individual conferences and guided reading to help students rehearse the language structure they might use to share their application of the minilesson principle to the text they have read.
- Teach the entire class respectful ways to listen to peers and model how to give their peers time to express their thoughts. Many of the minilessons in the Management section will be useful for developing a peaceful, safe and supportive community of readers and writers.

Extending the Lesson

At the end of each lesson we offer suggestions for **extending** the learning of the principle. Sometimes extending the learning involves repeating the lesson over time with different examples. Fifth graders might need to experience some of the concepts more than once before they are able to transfer actions to their independent reading. Using the questions in the Assess Learning section will help you to determine if you need to repeat the lesson, move on, or revisit the lesson (perhaps in a slightly different way) in the future. Other suggestions for extending the lesson include applying the minilesson concept within other contexts, performing readers' theater, or writing and drawing in response to reading. In several cases, the suggestions will refer to a reader's notebook (see Chapter 7 for more information about writing about reading and Section Four: Writing About Reading for minilessons that teach ways to use a reader's notebook).

Umbrella Back Page

Assessment and Link to Writing

Following the minilessons in each umbrella, you will see the final umbrella page that includes **Assessment**, sometimes **Link to Writing**, and **Reader's Notebook**. The last page of each umbrella, shown in Figure 3-4, provides suggestions for assessing the learning that has taken place through the minilessons in the entire umbrella. The information you gain from observing what the students can already do, almost do, and not yet do will help inform the selection of the next umbrella you teach. (See Chapter 8 for more information about assessment and the selection of umbrellas.) In many umbrellas, this last page also provides a Link to Writing. In some cases, this section provides further suggestions for writing about reading in a reader's notebook. However, in most cases, the Link to Writing provides ideas for how students might try out some of the new learning in their own writing. For example, after learning about text features in nonfiction, you might want to teach students how to include one or more of the features, such as an infographic or sidebar, in their own nonfiction writing.

You will also find a section titled Reader's Notebook, which describes how to access and print a copy of the minilesson principles for your students to glue in a reader's notebook to refer to as needed.

Gain important information by **assessing** students' understandings as they apply and share their learning of a minilesson principle. Observe and then follow up with individuals or address the principle during guided reading.

Umbrella 19 | Learning Information from Illustrations and Graphics

Assessment

After you have taught the minilessons in this umbrella, observe students as they talk and write about their reading across instructional contexts: interactive read-aloud, independent reading, guided reading, shared reading, and book club. Use *The Literacy Continuum* (Fountas and Pinnell 2017) to observe students' reading and writing behaviors.

- What evidence do you have of new understandings related to learning information from illustrations and graphics?
  - Do students talk about what they learned from illustrations and other graphics in nonfiction books?
  - Can they explain how a graphic can communicate a bigger idea?
  - Do they know how to read infographics?
  - Can they infer why the graphics and print are placed a certain way?
  - Do they use academic language, such as *illustration, photograph, graphic, author, illustrator, diagram*, and *infographic*?
- In what other ways, beyond the scope of this umbrella, are students talking about nonfiction?
  - Have they noticed that there are different genres of nonfiction?
  - Are they noticing different ways that nonfiction authors organize information?

Use your observations to determine the next umbrella you will teach. You may also consult Minilessons Across the Year (pp. 61–64) for guidance.

Wrap up the umbrella by engaging students in an activity that uses their expanded understanding of the umbrella concept.

Link to Writing

After teaching the minilessons in this umbrella, help students link the new learning to their own writing:

- Give students numerous opportunities to write their own nonfiction texts. Let them decide whether to include illustrations, photographs, infographics, or other types of graphics, and help them find or create relevant images. Remind them to use graphics that help the reader understand bigger ideas and to think about how to place the images on the page.

Reader's Notebook

When this umbrella is complete, provide a copy of the minilesson principles (see resources.fountasandpinnell.com) for students to glue in the reader's notebook (in the Minilessons section if using *Reader's Notebook: Advanced* [Fountas and Pinnell 2011]), so they can refer to the information as needed.

352 ■ *The Reading Minilessons Book, Grade 5*

Figure 3-4: The final page of each umbrella offers ways to wrap up new learning from the umbrella: questions to use in assessing students' learning, suggestions for linking new learning to writing, and a reference to online resources for downloading the umbrella's principles.

Online Resources for Planning

We have provided examples in this book of how to engage your fifth-grade students in developing the behaviors and understandings of competent readers, as described in *The Literacy Continuum* (Fountas and Pinnell 2017b). Remember that you can modify the suggested lesson or construct new lessons using the goals of the continuum as needed for your particular students. The form shown in Figure 3-5 will help you plan each part of a new minilesson. For example, you can design a minilesson that uses a different set of example texts from the ones suggested in this book or you can teach a concept in a way that fits the current needs of your students. The form shown in Figure 3-6 will help you plan which minilessons to teach over a period of time so as to address the goals that are important for your students. You can find both forms at **resources.fountasandpinnell.com.**

Teacher Mrs. James Grade 5 Year

Planning a Minilesson

Umbrella:	LA U8 Thinking About the Author's Message
Minilesson Principle:	The author gives a message in fiction and nonfiction books.
Continuum Goal(s):	Infer the message in a work of fiction (p. 69); Infer the larger (main) ideas or messages in a nonfiction text (p. 74).
Minilesson:	Examples: Show Desmond and the Very Mean Word. What do you think the author wants you to learn? Evidence? Message—Forgiveness is powerful. Two wrongs don't make a right. Show One Well. Ask: What do you think is the author's message? Message—Need to take care of the world's water because it is all Chart: Principle — Book / Message / How is it revealed?
Have a Try	
Summarize and Apply	
Share	

Figure 3-5: Use this downloadable form to plan your own minilessons.

Teacher Mr. Jackson Grade 5 Year

Curriculum Plan: Reading Minilessons

Month November	Umbrella/Minilesson	Comments/Observations	✓ or Date
Week 1	LA U11: Understanding the Craft of Poetry RML1: line breaks and white space RML2: imagery RML3: repetition RML4: alliteration and assonance RML5: onomatopoeia	• U11: Students quite engaged; finding poems to share and providing strong examples after each minilesson	11/5 11/6 11/7 11/8 11/9
Week 2	SAS U2: Using Context and Word Parts to Understand Vocabulary RML1: author defines word within the text RML2: author uses word in the sentence that is similar or opposite to the meaning of a word RML3: author gives example RML4: word parts RML5: Greek and Latin roots	• RML5: Need more support with Latin roots	11/12 11/13 11/14 11/15 11/16
Week 3	LA U27: Understanding Plot RML1: plot—beginning, problem, series of events, high point, solution, ending RML2: more than one problem RML3: flashbacks, flash-forwards, story-within-a-story RML4: plot and subplot	• RML4: Check in with Maggie, Yonjin, and Jack about subplots	11/19 11/20 11/21 11/22
Week 4	LA U27: Understanding Plot (continued) RML5: plot predictions RML6: writers end stories in different ways LA U26 Thinking About the Setting in Fiction Books RML1: poetic and descriptive language to describe setting	• U27 RML6: Students brought lots of background info from writing	11/22 11/23

Figure 3-6: Use this downloadable form to make notes about specific minilessons for future planning.

Chapter 4 Management Minilessons: Building a Literacy Community

Management minilessons focus on routines for thinking and talking about reading and working together in the classroom. Good management allows you to teach effectively and efficiently; use these lessons to create an orderly, busy classroom in which students know what is expected as well as how to behave responsibly and respectfully in a community of learners. They learn how the classroom library is organized, how to choose books and return them, how to use their voices in the classroom, and how to engage in independent reading. You can use these minilessons to teach your students the routines for independent reading, how to use and return materials, and how to solve problems independently. Classroom management is important in implementing a multitext approach to literacy learning. You want your students to grow in the ability to regulate their own behavior and to sustain reading and writing for increasing periods of time.

Altogether, there are seventeen minilessons in the Management section for your use. Teach the Management minilessons in the order that fits your class, or consult the suggested sequence in Figure 8-2. You may need to reteach some Management minilessons across the year, especially as students encounter more complex situations and routines. Sometimes when there is a schedule change or other disruption in classroom operations, a refresher Management minilesson will be needed. Any management problem in your classroom should be addressed through a Management minilesson.

The Physical Space

Before students enter your classroom, prepare the physical space in a way that provides maximum support for learning (see Figure 4-1). Remember that this relatively small room must support the productive work of some 20 to 30 people, 6 or 7 hours a day, 180-plus days a year. Each Management umbrella will help your students become acquainted with different parts of the classroom, which will make them feel secure and at home. Make sure that the classroom is:

- **Welcoming and Inviting.** Pleasing colors and a variety of furniture will help. There is no need for commercially published posters or slogans. The room can be filled with the work that students have produced beginning on day one. They see signs of their learning everywhere—shared writing, charts, drawings of various kinds, and their names. The classroom library should be as inviting as a bookstore or a public library. Place books in baskets and tubs on shelves to make the front covers of books visible and accessible for easy browsing. Clear out old, dated, poor-quality, or tattered books that students never choose. Clearly label (or, even better, have students label) the tub or basket with the topic, author, series, genre, or illustrator. Add new books to the library all year and retire books that are no longer of interest or that perpetuate stereotypes and inaccuracies. Once you have taught LA.U5.RML1, you can use the list to evaluate the classroom library collection for diversity and fair representation.

- **Organized for Easy Use.** The first thing you might want to do is to take out everything you do not need. Clutter increases stress and noise. Using scattered and hard-to-find materials increases student dependence on the teacher. Consider keeping supplies for reading, writing, and word study in designated areas. For example, some teachers designate a writing area where they keep paper, highlighters, staplers, etc. Every work area

Figure 4-1: The classroom is organized to support students' learning. Here, students gather in the meeting area to learn together.

should be clearly organized with necessary, labeled materials and nothing else. The work that takes place in each area should be visible at a glance; all materials needed for the particular activity should be available. See Figure 4-2 for a list of some suggested materials to keep accessible in the different areas in your classroom.

- **Designed for Whole-Group, Small-Group, and Individual Instruction.** Minilessons are generally provided as whole-class instruction and typically take place at an easel in a meeting space that is comfortable and large enough to accommodate all students in a group or circle. It will be helpful to have a colorful rug with some way of helping students find an individual space to sit without crowding one another. Often, the meeting space is adjacent to the classroom library so books are handy. The teacher usually has a larger chair or seat next to an easel or two so that he can display the mentor texts, make anchor charts, do shared writing, or place materials for shared or performance reading. This space is available for all whole-group instruction; for example, the students come back to it for group share. In addition to the group meeting space, there should be designated tables and spaces in the classroom for small-group reading instruction. The guided reading table is best located in a quiet corner of the room that keeps the group focused on reading, talking, and listening and at the same time allows you to scan the room to identify students who may need help staying on task independently. The table (round or horseshoe) should be positioned so the students in the group are turned away from the activity in the classroom. You might also designate a place to meet with book clubs. Provide a space that allows everyone to comfortably see one another and engage in conversation (ideally a circle of chairs). Students also need tables and spaces throughout the classroom where they can work independently and where you can easily set a chair next to a student for a brief, individual conference.

Figure 4-2: Adapted from *Guided Reading: Responsive Teaching Across the Grades* (Fountas and Pinnell 2017c)

Classroom Areas	Materials
Classroom Library	Organize books by topic, author, illustrator, genre, and series. Spaces for students to read comfortably and independently.
Writing Materials	Pencils, different types of paper for first and final drafts, markers, stapler, scissors, glue, sticky notes, colored pencils, and highlighters.
Word Work Materials	Blank word cards; magnetic letters; games; folders for Look, Cover, Write, Check; word study principles; place for students' individualized lists.
Listening Area or Media Center	Computers, audio players (e.g., iPod®, iPhone®, tablet), clear sets of directions for the activity and/or technology, multiple copies of books organized in boxes or plastic bags.

- **Respectful of personal space.** Fifth-grade students do not necessarily need an individual desk. Desks can be pushed together to make tables. But they do need a place to keep a personal box, including items such as their book of choice (or several that they plan to read) and a reader's notebook. These containers can be placed on a shelf and labeled for each student. A writer's notebook, writing folder, and word study folder may be stored in the same place or in groups by themselves to be retrieved easily. If students have personal poetry books (colorfully decorated by them and growing out of the shared reading of poetry and poetry workshop), they can be placed face out on a rack for easy retrieval. Artifacts like these add considerably to the aesthetic quality of the classroom.

A Peaceful Atmosphere for a Community of Readers and Writers

The minilessons in this book will help you establish a classroom environment where students can become confident, self-determined, and kind members of the community. They are designed to contribute to an ambiance of peaceful activity and shared responsibility in the fifth-grade classroom. Through the Management minilessons, students will make agreements, or set norms, about working together as a community of readers and writers. They will learn how to find help when the teacher is busy, listen to and show empathy for one another, and make everyone feel included. The lessons in this section are designed to help you develop a community of readers and writers who use multiple resources to find interesting and enjoyable books, are excited to share book recommendations, and challenge themselves and one another to stretch and grow in their reading tastes, preferences, and goals. The overall tone of every classroom activity is respectful. Fifth-grade students who enter your classroom for the first time will benefit from learning your expectations and being reminded of how to work with twenty to thirty others in a small room day after day. These minilessons are designed to help you establish the atmosphere you want. Everything in the classroom reflects the students who work there; it is their home for the year.

Figure 4-3: A readers' workshop structure as shown in *Guided Reading: Responsive Teaching Across the Grades* (Fountas and Pinnell 2017c, 565)

Structure of Readers' Workshop		
	Book Talks and Minilessons	5–15 minutes
Students: • Independent Reading • Writing in a Reader's Notebook	Teacher: • Guided Reading Groups (about 20–25 minutes each) • Book Clubs (about 20–25 minutes each) • Individual Conferences (3–5 minutes each)	45–50 minutes
	Group Share	5 minutes

Getting Started with Independent Reading: A Readers' Workshop Structure

Many of the minilessons in the Management section will be the ones that you address early in the year to establish routines that students will use to work at their best with one another and independently. In Umbrella 2: Getting Started with Independent Reading, you will teach students the routines and structure for independent reading. We recommend a readers' workshop structure for grade 5 in which students move from a whole-class meeting, to individual reading and small-group work, and back to a whole-class meeting (see Figure 4-3). The minilessons in this book are designed with this structure in mind, providing a strong instructional frame around independent reading and regular opportunities for students to share their thinking with each other. Your use of time will depend on the amount of time you have for the entire class period. As we explain in Chapter 23 of *Guided Reading: Responsive Teaching Across the Grades* (Fountas and Pinnell 2017c), ideally you will have seventy-five to ninety minutes, though many teachers have only sixty minutes. You will need to adjust accordingly. The minilessons in this umbrella are focused on promoting independence and supporting students in making good book choices for independent reading, including knowing when to abandon a book. Students also learn how to keep their materials for independent reading organized and ready to use. It is possible that you will spend several days reviewing the minilessons in this umbrella until you feel students are able to choose books and read independently for a sustained period of time. It's worth the effort and will benefit the learning community all year. At the beginning of the year, make independent reading time relatively short and circulate around the room to help students select books, write about their reading, and stay engaged. As students become more self-directed, you can increase independent reading time, and this should happen quickly with fifth graders. When you determine that students can sustain productive independent behavior, you can begin to meet with guided reading groups.

Figure 4-4: Readers' workshop begins with a minilesson and, often, a book talk.

Book Talks and Minilessons

The minilessons in the Management section will help you establish routines for your students that they will use throughout the year. In addition to these lessons, you will want to teach the students to sit in a specific place during book talks and reading minilessons. They might sit on a carpet or in chairs. Be sure everyone can see the chart and hear you and each other. Teachers with larger classes sometimes find it helpful to have a smaller circle sitting on the carpet and the remaining students sitting behind them in chairs. Be sure each student has sufficient personal space. Everyone should have enough space so as not to distract others. Most importantly, make it a comfortable place to listen, view, and talk.

Teachers often start readers' workshop with a few short book talks. Book talks are an effective way to engage students' interest in books, enriching independent reading. Consider giving two or three very short book talks before your reading minilesson a few times a week. Students can write titles in their notebooks for later reference (see Writing About Reading minilessons). Book talks are an important part of creating a community of readers and writers who talk about and share books. Once you have set the routines for book talks, you can turn this responsibility over to the students. Minilessons in Management Umbrella 3: Living a Reading Life are designed to teach students how to craft an interesting book talk.

Whether you are engaging your students in a reading minilesson, a book talk, or another whole-group instruction, you will need to teach them how to listen and talk when the entire class is meeting. Management minilessons lay the foundation for this whole-group work.

Figure 4-5: While some students read and write independently, you can work with small groups or hold individual conferences.

Independent Reading, Individual Conferences, and Small-Group Work

After the reading minilesson, work with students individually and in small groups (e.g., in guided reading and book clubs) while other students are engaged in independent reading and writing in the reader's notebook. To establish this as productive independent time, spend time on the minilessons in Management Umbrella 1: Being a Respectful Member of the Classroom Community and Umbrella 2: Getting Started with Independent Reading. Independent reading and the reader's notebook, while highly beneficial in themselves, also act as your management system. Students are engaged in reading and writing for a sustained period of time, freeing you to have individual conferences and to meet with small groups. You will find minilessons in Section Four: Writing About Reading to help you introduce and use the reader's notebook.

Students will have plenty of time during the share and small-group work to express their thinking about books. During independent reading time, there should be limited opportunity for distraction. The only voices heard should be your individual conferences with students and your work with small groups. In MGT.U1.RML2, students have the opportunity to establish agreements or norms for working together, including using the appropriate voice level during readers' workshop.

Consider the space in your classroom and position yourself during small-group work in a way that you can scan the room frequently. This thoughtful positioning will allow you to identify problems that arise and make notes to use in individual conferences. However, if you spend the time to set and practice these routines and expectations, students will learn to self-regulate and change inappropriate behavior with little intervention. When they are taught to make good book choices and are members of a community that share and recommend books with one another, they look forward to this quiet time of the day to read books of their own choosing.

When you first start readers' workshop, you will spend all or most of your time engaging in individual conferences to get to know your students. Conferences allow you time to evaluate whether they are making good book choices and help them become self-managed. Students who have persistent difficulty in selecting books might benefit from working with a limited selection of just-right books, which you can assemble in a temporary basket for this purpose.

Sharing Time

The readers' workshop ends with the community of readers and writers coming together for a short time to share discoveries made during independent reading time. Whatever is taught in the minilesson (management routines, literary analysis, strategies and skills, or writing about reading) guides the independent work time and is revisited during group share. Besides using sharing time to revisit the minilesson principle, you can use this time for your students to self-evaluate how the whole class is working together. The charts you create together during Management minilessons can be a source for self-evaluation. For example, you might ask students to review the list of agreements they made for working together and evaluate the class's behavior based on the chart criteria.

In addition to evaluating independent work time, you might also ask students to evaluate the quality of their sharing time. Is everyone able to see and hear each other? Does everyone transition well from turning and talking with a partner back to the whole group? Is everyone using an appropriate voice level? Do enough students have an opportunity to share their thinking?

In *Guided Reading: Responsive Teaching Across the Grades* (Fountas and Pinnell 2017c), we wrote the following: "The readers' workshop brings together both individual interests and the shared experiences of a literate community. Students read at a sharper edge when they know they will be sharing their thoughts with peers in their classroom. They are personally motivated because they have choice. In addition to providing an excellent management system, the workshop engages students in massive amounts of daily reading and in writing about reading" (p. 571). The Management minilessons in this book are designed to set a management system in motion in which choice and independence are guiding principles. Students develop into a community of readers and writers that respect and look forward to listening to and responding to each other's ideas.

Chapter 5 Literary Analysis Minilessons: Thinking and Talking About Books

Literary Analysis minilessons support students in a growing awareness of the elements of literature and the writer's and illustrator's craft. Use these lessons to help students learn how to think analytically about texts and identify the characteristics of fiction and nonfiction genres. Invite them to notice characters and how they change, critique whether a story's plot is believable, and analyze how nonfiction writers present and organize information as well as how they use graphics and other nonfiction features. Prior to each Literary Analysis minilesson, students will have listened to texts read aloud or will have experienced them through shared or performance reading. You will have read the texts aloud and taught specific lessons that encourage students to discuss and explore concepts and to respond in writing, art, or drama. This prior knowledge will be accessed as they participate in the minilesson and will enable them to make the understanding explicit. They then can apply the concepts to their own reading and share what they have learned with others.

Organization of Literary Analysis Umbrellas and the Link to *The Literacy Continuum*

There are 148 Literary Analysis minilessons in Section Two of this book. These minilessons are divided into categories according to *The Literacy Continuum* (Fountas and Pinnell 2017b), and the order of presentation in this book follows that of *The Literacy Continuum*. The categories of fiction and nonfiction are listed below.

- Fiction and Nonfiction
  - General
  - Genre
  - Messages and Themes
  - Style and Language
  - Illustrations
  - Book and Print Features
- Nonfiction
  - Genre
  - Organization
  - Topic
  - Illustration/Graphics
  - Book and Print Features
- Fiction
  - Genre
  - Setting
  - Plot
  - Character
  - Style and Language

As you can tell from the suggested sequence in Minilessons Across the Year (Figure 8-2), you will want to use simpler concepts (such as recognizing that characters have feelings and motivations) before more sophisticated concepts (such as critiquing a character's authenticity).

Echoes of the Literary Analysis minilessons reverberate across all the instruction for the year in instructional contexts for reading (interactive read-aloud, shared and performance reading, guided reading, book clubs, and independent reading) as well as for writing. The students continue to develop their understanding of the characteristics of fiction and nonfiction texts.

Genre Study

Within the Literary Analysis section you will find five umbrellas that bring students through a process of inquiry-based study of the characteristics of a particular genre. Genre study gives students the tools they need to navigate a variety of texts with deep understanding. When readers understand the characteristics of a genre, they know what to expect when they begin to read a text. They use their knowledge of the predictable elements within a genre as a road map to anticipate structures and elements of the text. They make increasingly more sophisticated connections between books within the same genre and build on shared language for talking about genre. In our professional book *Genre Study: Teaching with Fiction and Nonfiction Books* (Fountas and Pinnell 2012c), we designed a six-step approach for learning about a variety of genres. The six broad steps are described in Figure 5-1. For this book, we have designed specific minilessons based on our *Genre Study* book to help you engage your students in the powerful process of becoming knowledgeable about a range of genres.

The first two steps of the genre study process take place before and during interactive read-aloud. Steps 3–5 are accomplished through reading minilessons. Step 6 is addressed on the last page of each genre study umbrella. In fifth grade, we suggest five genre studies to help students expand their understanding of genre. Figure 5-3 is an overview of how we categorize various fiction and nonfiction genres. As students progress through the grades, they will revisit some genres to gain a deeper understanding and be introduced to new genres. In grade 5, we feature genre studies about expository nonfiction, biography, historical fiction, and two genres of traditional literature: legends and tall tales. Tall tales are categorized as a type of folktale (a subcategory of traditional literature) along with beast tales, cumulative tales,

Figure 5-1: Adapted from *Genre Study* (Fountas and Pinnell 2012c)

Steps in the Genre Study Process	
1	**Collect** books in a text set that represent good examples of the genre you are studying.
2	**Immerse.** Read aloud each book using the lesson guidelines. The primary goal should be enjoyment and understanding of the book.
3	**Study.** After you have read these mentor texts, have students analyze characteristics or "noticings" that are common to the texts, and list the characteristics on chart paper.
4	**Define.** Use the list of characteristics to create a short working definition of the genre.
5	**Teach** specific minilessons on the important characteristics of the genre.
6	**Read and Revise.** Expand students' understanding by encouraging them to talk about the genre in appropriate instructional contexts (book club, independent reading conferences, guided reading lessons, and shared or performance reading lessons) and revise the definition.

Tall Tales

Noticings:

Always	Often
• Are a type of folktale, handed down over many years	• Describe how something came to be
• Have characters, settings, and events that are exaggerated	• Have characters that do not change or develop
• Tell about a person with extraordinary qualities and abilities	• Reflect something important about the culture or place they come from
• Describe unbelievable things as factual or true	

Figure 5-2: On this anchor chart, the teacher has recorded what the students noticed was always or often true about several tall tales that they had read.

porquoi tales, trickster tales, noodlehead (or fool) tales, and realistic tales. Though tall tales and legends provide entertaining reading, they also present significant themes for students to think and talk about. Because modern fantasy is rooted in traditional literature, the same themes, ideas, or subjects, called motifs (e.g., the struggle between good and evil, the presence of magic, and the concept of a hero's quest), are found in both.

These motifs are often embedded in one's mind as part of a cultural experience. Students who are not familiar with traditional European motifs may, however, be familiar with others.

It is important to make connections between straightforward traditional literature and the more challenging literature that students will be expected to understand later on. Early experiences with these motifs in traditional literature provide a strong foundation for understanding the more complex types of fantasy, such as high fantasy and science fiction. The steps in the genre study process allow students to discover these characteristics through inquiry.

The first step in the genre study process, **Collect**, involves collecting a set of texts. The genre study minilessons in this book draw on texts sets from the

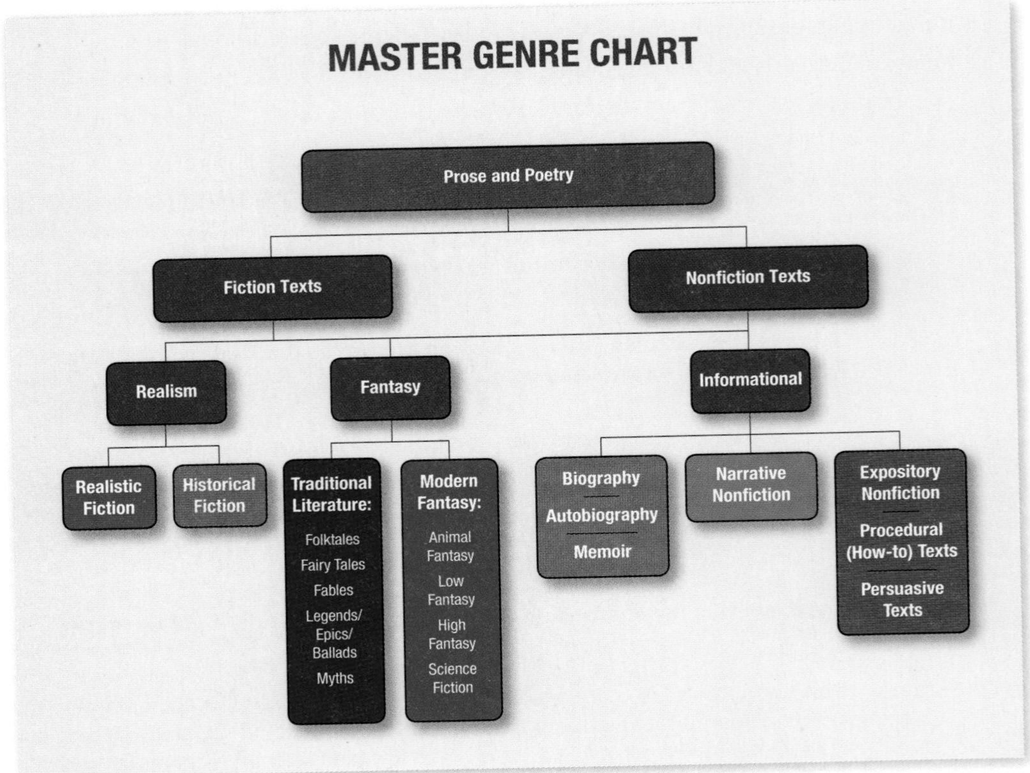

Figure 5-3: Master Genre Chart from *Genre Study: Teaching with Fiction and Nonfiction Books* (Fountas and Pinnell 2012c)

Fountas & Pinnell Classroom™ *Interactive Read-Aloud Collection* (Fountas and Pinnell 2020). Use these texts if you have them, but we encourage you to collect additional texts within each genre to immerse your students in as many texts as possible. Students will enjoy additional examples of the genre placed in a bin in the classroom library. You can use the texts listed in the Before Teaching section of each umbrella as a guide to making your own genre text set if you do not have access to the *Interactive Read-Aloud Collection.*

As you engage students in step 2 of the genre study process, **Immerse,** be sure that the students think and talk about the meaning of each text during the interactive read-aloud. The imperative is for students to enjoy a wonderful book, so it is important for them to respond to the full meaning of the text before focusing their attention on the specific characteristics of the genre.

After immersing students in the books through interactive read-aloud, it is time to teach minilessons in the appropriate genre study umbrella. The first minilesson in each genre study umbrella addresses step 3 in the process, **Study.** During this initial minilesson, help students notice characteristics that are common across all of the texts. As students discuss and revisit books in the genre, list their noticings on chart paper. Distinguish between what is *always* true about the genre and what is *often* true about the genre.

The second minilesson in each genre study umbrella addresses step 4 in the process, **Define.** Use shared writing to co-construct a working definition of the genre based on the students' previous noticings. Help students understand that you will revisit and revise this definition as they learn more about the genre over the next few days.

Next, as part of step 5, **Teach,** provide specific minilessons related to each of your students' noticings about the genre. In each genre study umbrella, we offer minilessons that we think would develop out of most fifth graders' noticings. Pick and choose the lessons that match your own students' noticings or use these lessons as a model to develop your own minilessons. In the minilessons and throughout a genre study, support your teaching with prompts for thinking, talking, and writing about reading. Prompts and definitions for each genre are included in *Fountas & Pinnell Genre Prompting Guide for Fiction* (2012a) and *Fountas & Pinnell Genre Prompting Guide for Nonfiction, Poetry, and Test Taking* (2012b).

At the end of the umbrella, work with the students to **Read and Revise** the class definition of the genre based on the minilessons that have been taught. Using shared writing, make changes to the definition so it reflects your students' understanding of the genre.

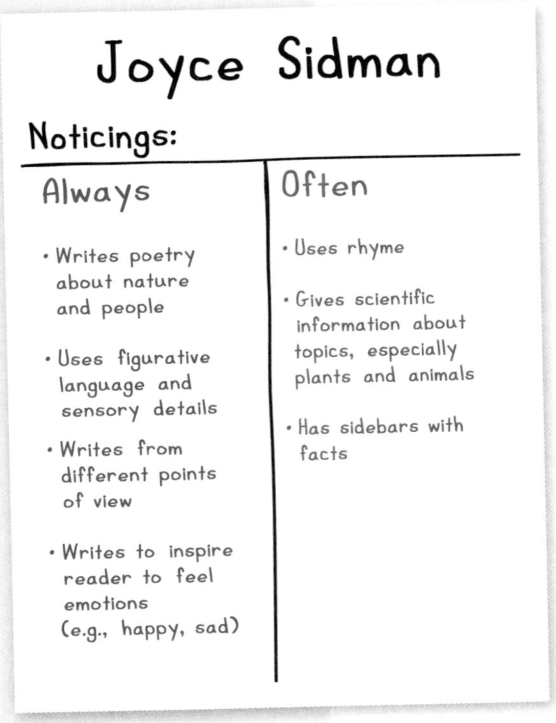

Joyce Sidman

Noticings:

Always	Often
• Writes poetry about nature and people • Uses figurative language and sensory details • Writes from different points of view • Writes to inspire reader to feel emotions (e.g., happy, sad)	• Uses rhyme • Gives scientific information about topics, especially plants and animals • Has sidebars with facts

Figure 5-4: This chart shows what students noticed about the work of poet Joyce Sidman.

Author and Illustrator Studies

Section Two: Literary Analysis also includes two umbrellas of minilessons for conducting inquiry-based author and illustrator studies. They are Umbrella 3: Studying Authors and Their Processes and Umbrella 12: Studying Illustrators and Analyzing an Illustrator's Craft. Author and illustrator studies allow students to make connections to the people behind the books they love. For an author or illustrator study, be sure that the students think and talk about the full meaning of each text in interactive read-aloud before identifying characteristics specific to the author or illustrator.

Students will need plenty of opportunities to explore the texts during read-aloud time, on their own, or in groups or pairs. As they become more familiar with the steps in an author or illustrator study, they learn how to notice characteristics common to a particular author's or illustrator's work. The steps in an author/illustrator study are described in Figure 5-5.

In the first minilesson in Umbrella 3: Studying Authors and Their Processes, you provide a demonstration of step 3 by working with your students to create a chart of noticings about an author or illustrator. In this lesson, we model a study of Joyce Sidman from the *Fountas & Pinnell Classroom™ Interactive Read-Aloud Collection* (Fountas and Pinnell 2020). For this author study, we have chosen an author who is a poet. You might choose to study authors who are also illustrators or simply authors your students are familiar with and love. The other minilessons in this umbrella address why authors choose their topics, how authors engage in research, and how they often revisit the same themes, topics, or settings. We recommend teaching the lessons in this umbrella across the year as

Figure 5-5: Minilessons address step 3 of an author/illustrator study.

Steps in an Author/Illustrator Study	
1	Gather a set of books and read them aloud to the class over several days. The goal is for students to enjoy the books and discuss the full meaning.
2	Take students on a quick tour of all the books in the set. As you reexamine each book, you might want to have students do a brief turn and talk with a partner about what they notice.
3	Have students analyze the characteristics of the author's or illustrator's work, and record their noticings on chart paper.
4	You may choose to read a few more books by the author and compare them to the books in this set, adding to the noticings as needed.

you conduct author or illustrator studies, instead of consecutively (see Minilessons Across the Year, Figure 8-2). Simply collect books by a particular author or illustrator and follow the steps listed in Figure 5-5. Use the same language and process modeled in the minilessons in these umbrellas, but substitute the authors and illustrators of your choice.

Developing Critical Thinking

In the age of social media and biased media views, it is imperative for students to be able to evaluate the accuracy, authenticity, and quality of the information they read. They need to be able to identify the sources of the information they read in both digital and print forms and evaluate an author's credibility and expertise. Throughout the Literary Analysis umbrellas, you will find several minilessons designed to foster the deep analysis of text and to develop the ability of students to think critically. For example, Umbrella 14: Studying Expository Nonfiction and Umbrella 15: Exploring Persuasive Texts both have lessons that help students evaluate the accuracy and quality of texts, consider an author's qualifications and sources, and notice both overt and subtle persuasive techniques. In Umbrella 18: Reading and Evaluating Multiple Sources, students learn how to cross-check information in more than one source and begin to notice that authors carefully select the facts they include in their nonfiction texts. Through inquiry, they develop a foundational understanding of how to use multiple texts to compare and contrast information to answer a larger research questions.

It is also important for students to be able to critique texts for bias, stereotyping, and representation (or omission) of race, gender, socioeconomic levels, disability, and different family structures. In Umbrella 5: Thinking Critically About the Ways People Are Represented in Texts, students are taught to evaluate how characters are portrayed in fiction, critique how different groups of people are represented in illustrations and graphics, and think about how stories are affected by an author's choice of a character's gender, race/culture, and socioeconomic status.

In the next section on Strategies and Skills, you will read more about teaching students to apply these critical thinking skills in meeting the challenges of reading in digital environments.

Chapter 6

Strategies and Skills Minilessons: Teaching for Effective Processing

STRATEGIES AND SKILLS minilessons will help students continue to strengthen their ability to process print by searching for and using information from the text, self-monitoring their reading, self-correcting their errors, and solving multisyllable words. You'll notice the students engaging in these behaviors in your interactive read-aloud, shared or performance reading, and guided reading lessons. Strategies and skills are taught in every instructional context for reading, but guided reading is the most powerful one. The text is just right to support the learning of all the readers in the group, enabling them to learn how to solve words and engage in the act of problem solving across a whole text.

The Strategies and Skills minilessons in this book may serve as reminders and be helpful to the whole class. They can be taught any time you see a need. For example, as students engage in independent reading, they may need to realize that a reader

- uses context to understand vocabulary,
- breaks apart a new word to read it,
- understands how connectives work in sentences, and
- applies different techniques to monitor comprehension when reading a difficult text.

The minilessons in Section Three: Strategies and Skills are designed to bring a few important strategies to temporary, conscious attention so that students are reminded to think in these ways as they problem solve in independent reading. By the time students participate in these minilessons, they should have engaged these strategic actions successfully in shared or guided reading. In the minilessons, they will recognize the strategic actions; bring them to brief, focused attention; and think about applying them consistently in independent reading. Some Strategies and Skills minilessons require students to see the print from a page of text. For these lessons, we recommend you use a document camera or write the word, sentence, or phrase from the text on a piece of chart paper.

Through the reading of continuous text, students develop an internal sense of in-the-head actions; for example, monitoring and checking, searching for and using information, and using multiple sources of information to solve words. They have a sense of how to put words together in phrases and use intonation to convey meaning. They are thinking more deeply about how a character would speak the dialogue. And, they are learning to check their comprehension by summarizing the most important parts and the big ideas and messages of a fiction or nonfiction text. The minilesson, the application, and the share help them better understand what they do and internalize effective and efficient reading behaviors.

Figure 6-1: Students are able to see and follow print and punctuation when you write on chart paper or use a projector.

Reading in Digital Environments

Fifth graders increasingly use the internet to research topics they are investigating, read reviews, participate in online communities, and compare information from multiple sources. A 2015 report by Common Sense Media, (https://www.commonsensemedia.org/sites/default/files/uploads/research/census_researchreport.pdf, 21) found that eight- to twelve-year-old children spend about two and a half hours per day using digital media (e.g., computers, tablets, and smart phones) outside of school. It is important for students to learn to navigate digital environments safely and critically. Umbrella 7: Reading in Digital Environments is designed to provide an overview of some of these crucial skills; however, we encourage you to become informed about the safety features and policies that your school district uses to safeguard students as they navigate the digital world. The minilessons in this umbrella help students learn how to use search engines efficiently and effectively, evaluate the credibility and sources of the information they find, and stay focused in a reading environment that provides link after link to related and sometimes unrelated information. Students need to learn to be critical readers of *all* information, but the seemingly anonymous nature of many websites requires students to be active in seeking out, identifying, and evaluating the sources of the digital information they are reading.

Students also need teaching to efficiently use search engines to find information and evaluate the results of their searches. In a study at the University of Maryland, a team of researchers found that children (ages seven through eleven) in their sample group showed an inability to construct queries requiring more than one search step (http://www.cs.umd.edu/hcil/trs/2009-04/2009-04.pdf). This limitation

Figure 6-2: Minilessons on reading in digital environments help students learn how to search for information online and to stay focused while reading it.

created frustration for students involved in the search process because they couldn't find exactly what they were looking for. The study also showed that when students *did* successfully execute a search, they focused primarily on the first few items on the results page and ignored the rest of the information. The first two lessons in Umbrella 7 offer techniques for searching effectively and evaluating which search results seem relevant and worthy of further investigation. We hope this umbrella will get you started in establishing critical reading within a digital environment and inspire you and your students to learn more about navigating this challenging, yet rewarding, world of information.

Chapter 7 Writing About Reading Minilessons: The Reading-Writing Connection

THROUGH DRAWING/WRITING ABOUT READING, students reflect on their understanding of a text. For example, a story might have a captivating character or characters or a humorous sequence of events. A nonfiction text might have interesting information or call for an opinion. Two kinds of writing about reading are highly effective with fifth-grade students.

- **Shared Writing.** In shared writing (see Figure 7-1) you offer the highest level of support to the students. You act as scribe while the students participate fully in the composition of the text. You help shape the text, but the students supply the language and context.

> - The astronomers were all curious, so we can be more curious in our lives.
> - We can stay open to new points of view, like the scientists did when they decided Pluto was no longer a planet.
> - Like Clyde Tombaugh, we can keep looking and looking until we find a reasonable answer.
> - We can try to make sense of new information, like the astronomers did when they saw Pluto's strange orbit.

Figure 7-1: In shared writing, the teacher acts as scribe.

- **Independent Writing.** After you have introduced and modeled different forms of writing about reading, fifth graders begin trying these different ways independently (see Figure 7-2). Occasionally, it may be helpful to teach students how to use graphic organizers to bring structure to their writing about both fiction and nonfiction books (see Umbrella 4: Using Graphic Organizers to Share Thinking About Books in the Writing About Reading section). Fifth graders also enjoy writing independently about their reading in a weekly letter to you (see Figure 7-6). Keep good examples of different writing on hand (possibly in a scrapbook) for students to use as models.

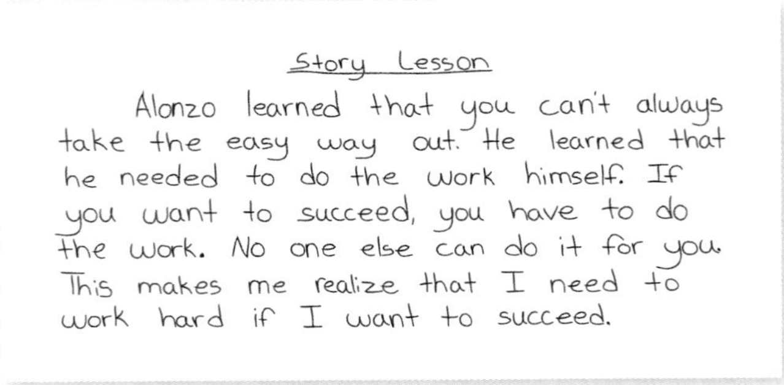

Story Lesson

Alonzo learned that you can't always take the easy way out. He learned that he needed to do the work himself. If you want to succeed, you have to do the work. No one else can do it for you. This makes me realize that I need to work hard if I want to succeed.

Figure 7-2: The independent writing in response to reading minilessons will reflect students' thinking about their reading.

In most Literary Analysis lessons, you will find a suggestion for extending the learning using shared or independent writing. In whatever way students write, they are exposed to different ways of thinking about their reading. You can expect fifth graders to accurately spell a significant number of high-frequency words as well as words with patterns that you have introduced in phonics and word study lessons; however, they will try many others using their growing vocabulary and knowledge about the way words work. You want them to move beyond "safe" words they know and try new vocabulary, using tools to achieve standard spelling. You will notice that in Umbrella 3: Writing Letters to Share Thinking About Books, we have provided a lesson for students to evaluate the qualities of a good letter. In this lesson, students learn to proofread and evaluate the use of standard conventions as one aspect of writing quality letters.

The students' independent writing about reading will be in a reader's notebook. The first two umbrellas in Section Four provide inquiry-based lessons for exploring the reader's notebook and establish routines for writing about reading. Some of these routines include keeping lists of books read and books "to be read," maintaining a section of minilesson notes, and tallying the types of writing about reading that have been attempted and completed. This section also includes inquiry-based lessons to help students learn different genres and forms for responding to their reading in independent writing. The minilessons in Umbrella 5: Introducing Different Genres and Forms for Responding to Reading provide examples of how to use a particular genre or form to explore an aspect of literary analysis. For example, in RML5, students participate in analyzing an example of a short write in which the writer critiques the author's ability to persuade about a particular topic. The extension to the lesson provides a list of other types of literary analysis that might also be addressed using a short write. Other suggestions for using the form or genre are included in online resources. You can find a comprehensive list of different genres and forms for fifth grade in the Writing About Reading section of *The Literacy Continuum* (Fountas and Pinnell 2017b).

Like Management minilessons, the lessons in the Writing About Reading umbrellas need not be taught consecutively within the umbrella; instead, they can be paired with the Literary Analysis lessons that support the concept students are being asked to write about. For example, if you have just completed Literary Analysis minilessons about plot (Umbrella 27: Understanding Plot), you might decide it would be an appropriate time to teach students how write a summary of a fiction book. After writing a few summaries as a whole class through shared writing and teaching the summary lesson in Writing About Reading (WAR.U5.RML3), students will be able to write a summary independently. Through this gradual release of responsibility, students learn how to transition to writing about their reading independently as they learn how to use each section of the notebook. A reader's notebook is an important tool to support student independence and response to books. It becomes a rich collection of thinking across the years.

ELL CONNECTION

For English language learners, a reader's notebook is a safe place to practice a new language. It eventually becomes a record of their progress not only in content and literary knowledge but in acquiring a new language. However, they may do as much drawing as writing depending on where they

Figure 7-3: Occasionally ask students to reflect on their understanding of a text by writing independently about their reading.

are in acquiring English. Drawing is key because it provides a way to rehearse ideas. Use this opportunity to ask students to talk about what they have drawn, and then help them compose labels for their artwork so they begin to attach meaning to the English words. In some cases, you might choose to pull together small groups of students and engage them in interactive writing, in which the teacher and students compose together and share the pen. This might be particularly helpful with English language learners who might still be learning English letter and sound correlations. Students who struggle with spelling and phonics can also benefit from interactive writing in small groups.

Eventually, the students will do more writing, but you can support the writing by providing a chance for them to rehearse their sentences before writing them and encouraging students to borrow language from the texts they are writing about. The writing in a reader's notebook is a product they can read because they have written it. It is theirs. They can read and reread it to themselves and to others, thereby developing their confidence in the language.

Using a Reader's Notebook in Fifth Grade

A reader's notebook is a place where students can collect their thinking about books. They draw and write to tell about themselves and respond to books and to keep a record of their reading lives. A reader's notebook includes

- a section for students to list the title, author, and genre of the books they have read and write a one-word response to show their reaction to the book,
- a section for helping students choose and recommend books, including a place to list books to read in the future,

Figure 7-4: Students write to share their thinking about reading in a reader's notebook.

- a section to write or glue in reading minilesson principles to refer to as needed (see Figure 7-5), and
- a section for students to respond to books they have read or listened to.

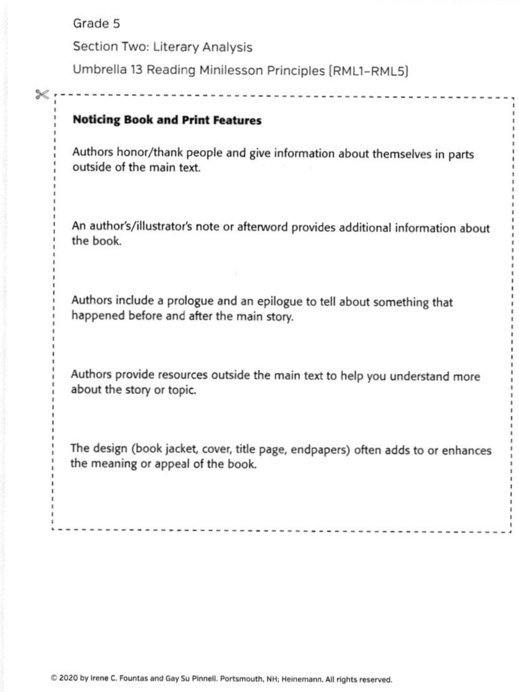

Grade 5

Section Two: Literary Analysis

Umbrella 13 Reading Minilesson Principles (RML1–RML5)

Noticing Book and Print Features

Authors honor/thank people and give information about themselves in parts outside of the main text.

An author's/illustrator's note or afterword provides additional information about the book.

Authors include a prologue and an epilogue to tell about something that happened before and after the main story.

Authors provide resources outside the main text to help you understand more about the story or topic.

The design (book jacket, cover, title page, endpapers) often adds to or enhances the meaning or appeal of the book.

Figure 7-5: At the end of each umbrella, download the umbrella's principles, like the sample shown here. Students can glue the principles in the reader's notebook to refer to as needed. Encourage students to make notes or sketches to help remember the principles. To download the principles, go to **resources.fountasandpinnell.com**.

With places for students to make a record of their reading and respond to books in a variety of ways using different kinds of writing (including charts, webs, short writes, and letters), a reader's notebook thus represents a rich record of progress. To the student, the notebook represents a year's work to reflect on with pride and share with family. Students keep their notebooks in their personal boxes, along with their bags of book choices for independent reading time. We provide a series of minilessons in Section Four: Writing About Reading for teaching students how to use a reader's notebook. As described previously, reading minilessons in the Writing About Reading section focus on writing in response to reading.

If you do not have access to the preprinted *Reader's Notebook: Advanced* (Fountas and Pinnell 2011), simply give each student a plain notebook (bound if possible). Glue in sections and insert tabs yourself to make a neat, professional notebook that can be cherished.

Writing Letters About Reading: Moving from Talk to Writing

In fifth grade, we continue the routine of having students write a weekly letter about their reading in the past week. In most cases, they address these letters to you, the teacher, although occasionally they may write to other readers in the classroom or school. Letter writing is an authentic way to transition from oral conversation to written conversation about books. Students have had rich experiences talking about books during interactive read-aloud, guided reading, book clubs, and reading conferences. Writing letters in a reader's notebook allows them to continue this dialogue in writing and provides an opportunity to increase the depth of reader response.

Figure 7-6: Weekly letters about reading allow you and your students to participate in a written dialogue to share thinking about the books the class has read together or books the students have read on their own.

Dear Ms. Zylstra,

I just finished the book Bridge to Teribithea. It was a book that I started in fourth grade that I was never able to finish. Everyone was telling me how good it was so I really wanted to try to read it again.

It really made me think about my friends and to what level they would go to for me. And that just made me think about how close to my friends I am in general. To what level they would go to for me. To what level would I go to for them? I think it is preatty crazy how a book can make you do that and make you question what you always took for granted.

The main charchater Jesse really grew in the couple of months the story takes place. In the beginign of Bridge to Teribithea Jess was just wanted to be the fastest runner in the fifth grade. Jess was the only boy in between a family of sisters. Jess didn't have any friends he just had a hippie music teacher that he could show his drawings to. He was just being an average kid and wanted to be as average as posible. In the end he was still an average kid in school and on the outside but had a friend and he had courage and he had patience, and he had tolerance. He was a bold and caring kid.

In the end when tragedy struck he didn't stop being all those things that he wanted to be for his friend and instead was all of those things for the people that he should have been kind and caring and thoughtful to everyday.

Sincerley,
Rowan

Dear Rowan,

Bridge to Terabithia had a strong impact on me too. I agree that Jesse and Leslie's friendship really makes us think about our own friendships. I wonder if Katherine Paterson had that purpose in mind when she wrote it. You point out an important reason why we read—to learn more about ourselves and our world.

You mention that Jesse wanted to be bold and caring for his friend. Can you say more about this? What do you mean? How do you think their friendship impacted Jesse?

We have been talking a lot about symbolism in class lately. I am wondering if Paterson uses any symbolism in this book. What you think Terabithia symbolizes? I can't wait to hear what you think.

Sincerely,
Mrs. Zylstra

By using the Writing About Reading section of *The Literacy Continuum* (Fountas and Pinnell 2017b) and carefully analyzing students' letters, you can systematically assess students' responses to the texts they are reading independently. The *Fountas & Pinnell Prompting Guide, Part 2, for Comprehension: Thinking, Talking, and Writing* (2009b) is a useful resource for choosing the language to prompt the thinking you want to see in a student's response. A weekly letter from you offers the opportunity to respond in a timely way to address students individually, differentiating instruction by asking specific questions or making comments targeted at the strengths and needs of each student's individual processing system.

Letters about reading also provide you with the opportunity to model your own thinking about reading. This reader-to-reader dialogue helps students learn more about what readers do when they actively respond to a text. The depth of their oral discussions will increase as students experience writing letters over time. Just as the discussions in your classroom set the stage for readers to begin writing letters, the writing of letters about reading will in turn enrich the discussions in your classroom.

Umbrella 3: Writing Letters to Share Thinking About Books, in Section Four, provides minilessons for getting dialogue letters started in your classroom. Through inquiry-based lessons, students learn the format of a letter, the routines involved in writing a weekly letter, and the qualities of a strong response. They learn to identify the different types of thinking they might include in a letter and how to integrate evidence to support their thinking.

We recommend that you teach these minilessons over two or three weeks. For example, you might teach the first minilesson in this umbrella in the first week to introduce the format and content of a letter. You can then ask students to apply these new understandings to writing their first letter. After responding to their letters, use RML2 to introduce the second round of writing letters. This minilesson teaches students how to respond to your questions in their next letter. Lastly, you may decide to wait until the third week as students embark on the third letter to provide an inquiry lesson on the qualities of a strong letter (RML3). They can use these characteristics to evaluate the quality of their own reading letters. When you teach these minilessons over time, you give students the opportunity to gain experience writing letters about their reading before introducing another new principle.

Managing Letters About Reading

Before introducing dialogue letters, think about how you will manage to read and respond to your students in a timely way. Some teachers assign groups of students to submit their letters on particular days of the week as shown in Figure 7-7. Many teachers find it more manageable to respond to five or six letters a day versus responding to the whole class at once. As the students write letters about reading, collect samples of quality letters that you might be able to share as examples in subsequent years to launch the writing of letters in your classroom.

We recommend that students work on their weekly letters during independent reading time. They can write their letters all at one time or over the course of two or three days. Monitor how long students are spending on writing versus reading to make sure they are dedicating enough time to both. However you choose to organize and manage this system, you will want to make sure it is feasible for both you and your students. It is critical that you are able to respond to the letters in a timely manner because students will quickly move on to new books and ask new questions about their reading.

You will find several other suggestions for helping students write thoughtful letters in Chapter 27 of *Teaching for Comprehending and Fluency* (Fountas and Pinnell 2006).

Figure 7-7: To make reading and responding to students' letters manageable, set up a schedule so that only a few letters are due each day.

Letters Due

Monday	Tuesday	Wednesday	Thursday
Kaliyah	Isla	Mia	Henry
Liam	Evelyn	Charlotte	Dafcar
Noah T.	Jack	Olivia M.	Emma
Olivia B.	Oliver	Ethan	Harper
Ava	Logan	Nayelisse	Avery
Ibn	Noah S.	Mason	Matthew
Luke			

Name Rowan Date ______

Assessment of Letters in Reader's Notebook

Does the student share his personal response to the book?

- Shared her own personal response by making connections to her own life and friends.
- Recognized the fact that books can make you reflect on your own life.
- Noticed the change in the main character.
- Needs support in providing evidence for character change.
- Alluded to the cause of change but didn't provide clear evidence.

Does the student incorporate new ways of thinking about books from reading minilessons that have been taught?

- Showed some evidence of incorporating new thinking from minilessons about character change.
- Alluded to author's message and the impact on her own life and friendships. Could use support with writing about the author's message more explicitly.
- Invited her to look for symbolism in the book; look to see if she addresses it in her next letter.

Does the student use standard writing conventions expected at this time in fifth grade (e.g., title and author's name spelled correctly, capitals, punctuation, spelling, legible handwriting)?

- Rowan underlined the title.
- Appropriate beginning and end punctuation consistently used.
- Needs to reference author.
- Needs support spelling high-frequency words: character, pretty, instead, sincerely.
- Needs to learn to identify run-on sentences and use more sophisticated sentence constructions.
- Work with her on varying sentence structures using appropriate punctuation.

Does the student use the format of a friendly letter for the response (date, greeting, body, closing, signature)?

- Consistently used format of letter including paragraphing.

Figure 7-8: Use questions such as these to evaluate students' letters about their reading. To download the questions, visit **resources.fountasandpinnell.com.**

Chapter 8 Putting Minilessons into Action: Assessing and Planning

As noted in Chapter 2, the minilessons in this book are examples of teaching that address the specific bullets that list the behaviors and understandings to notice, teach for, and support in *The Literacy Continuum* (Fountas and Pinnell 2017b) for fifth grade. We have drawn from the sections on Interactive Read-Aloud, Shared and Performance Reading, Guided Reading, Writing About Reading, Technological Communication, and Oral and Visual Communication to provide a comprehensive vision of what students need to become aware of, understand, and apply to their own literacy and learning. With such a range of important goals, how do you decide what to teach and when?

Deciding Which Reading Minilessons to Teach

To decide which reading minilessons to teach, first look at the students in front of you. Teach within what Vygotsky (1978) called the "zone of proximal development"—the zone between what the students can do independently and what they can do with the support of a more expert other. Teach on the cutting edge of students' competencies. Select topics for minilessons that address the needs of the majority of students in your class.

Think about what will be helpful to most readers based on your observations of their reading and writing behaviors. Here are some suggestions and tools to help you think about the students in your classroom:

- **Use *The Literacy Continuum*** (Fountas and Pinnell 2017b) to assess your students and observe how they are thinking, talking, and writing/drawing about books. Think about what they can already do, almost do, and not yet do to select the emphasis for your teaching. Look at the Selecting Goals pages in each section to guide your observations.
- **Use the Interactive Read-Aloud and Literature Discussion section.** Scan the Selecting Goals in this section and think about the ways you have noticed students thinking and talking about books.
- **Use the Writing About Reading section** to analyze how students are responding to texts in their drawing and writing. This analysis will help you determine possible next steps. Talking and writing about reading provides concrete evidence of students' thinking.
- **Use the Oral and Visual Communication continuum** to help you think about some of the routines your students might need for better communication between peers. You will find essential listening and speaking competencies to observe and teach.
- **Use the Technological Communication section** to help you assess your students' technological skills and plan teaching that will help them improve their computer literacy and their ability to read digital texts.
- **Look for patterns in your anecdotal records.** Review the anecdotal notes you take during reading conferences, shared and performance reading, guided reading, and book clubs to notice trends in students' responses and thinking. Use *The Literacy Continuum* to help you analyze the records and determine strengths and areas for growth across the classroom. Your observations will reveal what students know and what they need to learn next as they build knowledge over time. Each goal becomes a possible topic for a minilesson.
- **Consult district and state standards as a resource.** Analyze the skills and areas of knowledge specified in your local and state standards. Align these standards with the minilessons suggested in this text to determine which might be applicable within your frameworks (see fountasandpinnell.com/resourcelibrary for an alignment of *The Literacy Continuum* with Common Core Standards).
- **Use the Assessment section after each umbrella.** Take time to assess student learning after the completion of each umbrella. Use the guiding questions on the last page of each umbrella to determine strengths and next steps for your students. This analysis can help you determine what minilessons to reteach if needed and what umbrella to teach next.

A Suggested Sequence

The suggested sequence of umbrellas, Minilessons Across the Year, shown in Figure 8-2 (also downloadable from the online resources for record keeping), is intended to help you establish a community of independent readers and writers early in the year and work toward more sophisticated concepts across the year. Learning in minilessons is applied in many different situations and so is reinforced daily across the curriculum. Minilessons in this sequence are timed so they occur after students have had sufficient opportunities to build some explicit understandings as well as a great deal of implicit knowledge of aspects of written texts through interactive read-aloud and shared and performance reading texts. In the community of readers, they have acted on texts through talk, writing, and extension through writing and art. These experiences have prepared them to fully engage in the reading minilesson and move from this shared experience to the application of the concepts in their independent reading.

The sequence of umbrellas in Minilessons Across the Year follows the suggested sequence of text sets in *Fountas & Pinnell Classroom™ Interactive Read-Aloud Collection* (Fountas and Pinnell 2020). If you are using this collection, you are invited to follow this sequence of texts. If you are not using it, the first page of each umbrella describes the types of books students will need to have read before you teach the minilessons. The text sets are grouped together by theme, topic, author, and genre, not by skill or concept. Thus, in many minilessons, you will use books from several different text sets, and you will see the same books used in more than one umbrella.

We have selected the most concrete and instructive examples from the recommended books. The umbrellas draw examples from text sets that have been read and enjoyed previously. In most cases, the minilessons draw on text sets that have been introduced within the same month or at least in close proximity to the umbrella. However, in some cases, minilessons taught later, for example in month eight, might draw on texts introduced earlier in the year. Most of the time, students will have no problem recalling the events of these early books because you have read and discussed them thoroughly as a class and sometimes students have responded to them through writing or art. However, in some cases, you might want to quickly reread a book or a portion of it before teaching the umbrella so it is fresh in the students' minds.

If you are new to these minilessons, you may want to follow the suggested sequence, but remember to use the lessons flexibly to meet the needs of the students you teach:

- Omit lessons that you think are not necessary for your students (based on assessment and your experiences with them in interactive read-aloud).

- Repeat some lessons that you think need more time and instructional attention (based on observation of students across reading contexts).
- Repeat some lessons using different examples for a particularly rich experience.
- Move lessons around to be consistent with the curriculum that is adopted in your school or district.

The minilessons are here for your selection according to the instructional needs of your class, so do not be concerned if you do not use them all within the year. Record or check the minilessons you have taught so that you can reflect on the work of the semester and year. You can do this simply by downloading the minilessons record form (see Figure 8-1) from online resources (resources.fountasandpinnell.com).

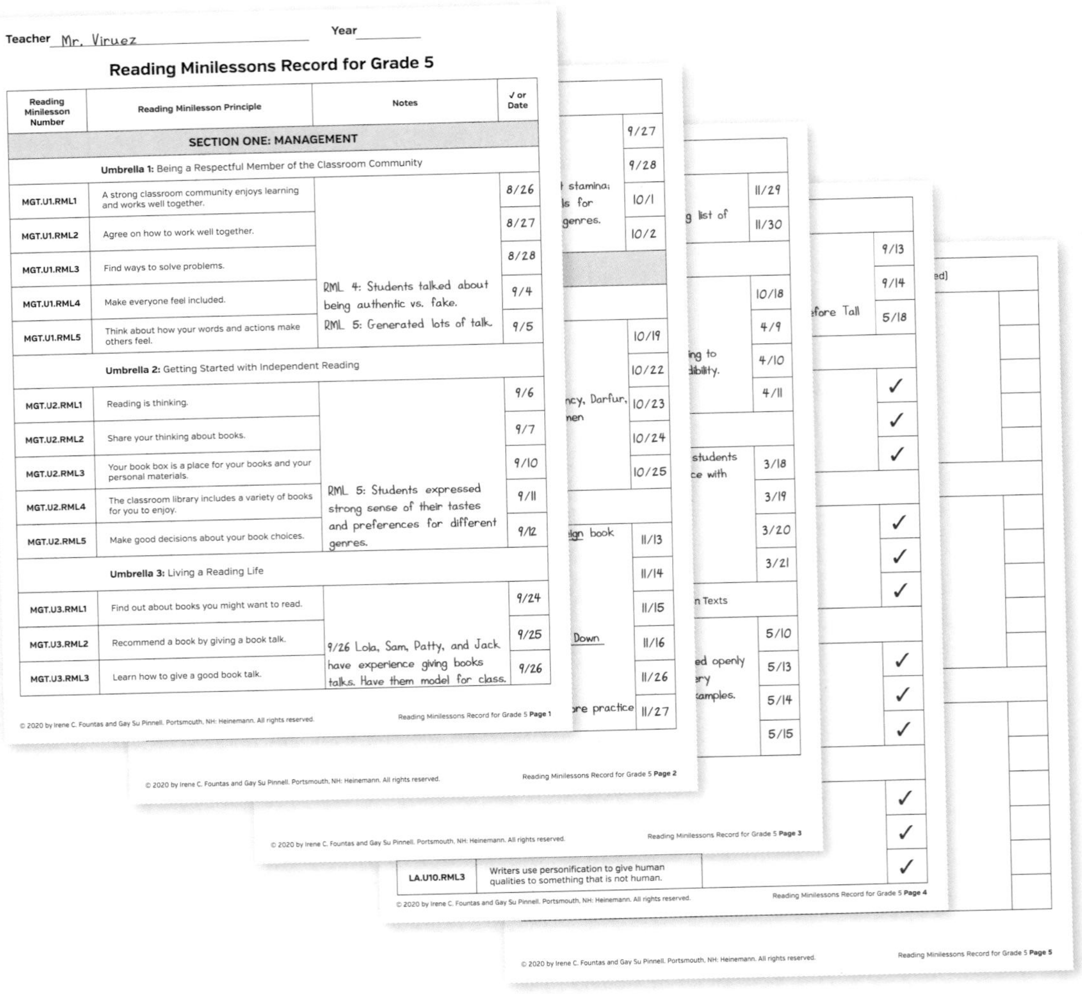

Teacher Mr. Viruez Year

Reading Minilessons Record for Grade 5

Reading Minilesson Number	Reading Minilesson Principle	Notes	✓ or Date
	SECTION ONE: MANAGEMENT		
	Umbrella 1: Being a Respectful Member of the Classroom Community		
MGT.U1.RML1	A strong classroom community enjoys learning and works well together.		8/26
MGT.U1.RML2	Agree on how to work well together.		8/27
MGT.U1.RML3	Find ways to solve problems.		8/28
MGT.U1.RML4	Make everyone feel included.	RML 4: Students talked about being authentic vs. fake.	9/4
MGT.U1.RML5	Think about how your words and actions make others feel.	RML 5: Generated lots of talk.	9/5
	Umbrella 2: Getting Started with Independent Reading		
MGT.U2.RML1	Reading is thinking.		9/6
MGT.U2.RML2	Share your thinking about books.		9/7
MGT.U2.RML3	Your book box is a place for your books and your personal materials.		9/10
MGT.U2.RML4	The classroom library includes a variety of books for you to enjoy.	RML 5: Students expressed strong sense of their tastes and preferences for different genres.	9/11
MGT.U2.RML5	Make good decisions about your book choices.		9/12
	Umbrella 3: Living a Reading Life		
MGT.U3.RML1	Find out about books you might want to read.		9/24
MGT.U3.RML2	Recommend a book by giving a book talk.	9/26 Lola, Sam, Patty, and Jack have experience giving books talks. Have them model for class.	9/25
MGT.U3.RML3	Learn how to give a good book talk.		9/26

Reading Minilessons Record for Grade 5 **Page 1**

Figure 8-1: Download this record-keeping form to record the minilessons that you have taught and to make notes for future reference.

MINILESSONS ACROSS THE YEAR

Month	Recommended Umbrellas	Approximate Time
Month 1	**MGT U1:** Being a Respectful Member of the Classroom Community	1 week
	MGT U2: Getting Started with Independent Reading	1 week
	LA U6: Understanding Fiction and Nonfiction Genres	0.5 week
	WAR U1: Introducing a Reader's Notebook	1 week
	MGT U3: Living a Reading Life	1.5 weeks
Month 2	**WAR U2:** Using a Reader's Notebook	1 week
	LA U3: Studying Authors and Their Processes (RML1) *Note: We recommend teaching this minilesson as part of an author study. The lesson can be repeated each time an author is studied. If you are using the* Fountas & Pinnell Classroom™ Interactive Read-Aloud Collection, *the first author study is Joyce Sidman.*	1 day
	LA U1: Getting Started with Book Clubs	1 week
	WAR U3: Writing Letters to Share Thinking About Books (RML1)	1 day
	SAS U1: Solving Multisyllable Words	1 week
	WAR U3: Writing Letters to Share Thinking About Books (RML2)	1 day
	LA U7: Exploring Different Kinds of Poetry	0.5 week
Month 3	**LA U11:** Understanding the Craft of Poetry	1 week
	WAR U3: Writing Letters to Share Thinking About Books (RML3)	1 day
	LA U2: Learning Conversational Moves in Book Club	1.5 weeks
	LA U27: Understanding Plot	1.5 weeks
	LA U26: Thinking About the Setting in Fiction Books (RML1-RML2)	2 days
	SAS U5: Summarizing (RML1)	1 day

KEY

MGT	Section One	Management Minilessons
LA	Section Two	Literary Analysis Minilessons
SAS	Section Three	Strategies and Skills Minilessons
WAR	Section Four	Writing About Reading Minilessons

Figure 8-2: Use this chart as a guideline for planning your year with minilessons.

MINILESSONS ACROSS THE YEAR (CONT.)

Month	Recommended Umbrellas	Approximate Time
Month 4	**WAR U5:** Introducing Different Genres and Forms for Responding to Reading (RML1–RML3)	0.5 week
	LA U28: Understanding Characters' Feelings, Motivations, and Intentions	0.5 week
	LA U29: Understanding a Character's Traits and Development	1 week
	LA U30: Thinking Critically About Characters	0.5 week
	LA U31: Analyzing Perspective and Point of View	0.5 week
	WAR U7: Responding Creatively to Reading (RML1–RML2)	2 days
	LA U21: Understanding Realistic Fiction	0.5 week
	SAS U4: Maintaining Fluency	0.5 week
Month 5	**LA U16:** Studying Biography	2 weeks
	WAR U4: Using Graphic Organizers to Share Thinking About Books (RML1)	1 day
	WAR U5: Introducing Different Genres and Forms for Responding to Reading (RML4)	1 day
	SAS U5: Summarizing (RML2)	1 day
	WAR U7: Responding Creatively to Reading (RML3)	1 day
	LA U3: Studying Authors and Their Processes (RML1) *Note: We recommend teaching this minilesson as part of an author study. The lesson can be repeated each time an author is studied. If you are using the* Fountas & Pinnell Classroom™ Interactive Read-Aloud Collection, *the second author study is Ted and Betsy Lewin. You can also use this text set for an illustrator study.*	1 day
	LA U14: Studying Expository Nonfiction	1.5 weeks
	SAS U5: Summarizing (RML3)	1 day
Month 6	**SAS U6:** Monitoring Comprehension of Difficult Texts	1 week
	SAS U2: Using Context and Word Parts to Understand Vocabulary	1 week
	SAS U3: Understanding Connectives	1 week
	SAS U7: Reading in Digital Environments	1 week
	LA U13: Noticing Book and Print Features	1 week

MINILESSONS ACROSS THE YEAR (CONT.)

Month	Recommended Umbrellas	Approximate Time
Month 7	**LA U17:** Noticing How Nonfiction Authors Choose to Organize Information	1.5 weeks
	LA U19: Learning Information from Illustrations and Graphics	0.5 week
	LA U20: Using Text Features to Gain Information	1 week
	WAR U4: Using Graphic Organizers to Share Thinking About Books (RML2)	1 day
	LA U15: Exploring Persuasive Texts	1 week
	WAR U5: Introducing Different Genres and Forms for Responding to Reading (RML5)	1 day
	WAR U6: Writing About Reading to Persuade	0.5 week
Month 8	**LA U25:** Studying Historical Fiction	1.5 weeks
	LA U8: Thinking About the Author's Message	0.5 week
	LA U9: Thinking About Themes	0.5 week
	WAR U4: Using Graphic Organizers to Share Thinking About Books (RML3)	1 day
	LA U18: Reading and Evaluating Multiple Sources	1 week
	LA U10: Reading Like a Writer: Analyzing the Writer's Craft	1 week
	WAR U5: Introducing Different Genres and Forms for Responding to Reading (RML6)	1 day
	LA U3: Studying Authors and Their Processes (RML1–RML3) *Note: We recommend teaching one or more of these minilessons as part of an author study. If you are using the* Fountas & Pinnell Classroom™ Interactive Read-Aloud Collection, *the third author study is Andrea Davis Pinkney. You can also use this text set as an illustrator study.*	0.5 week
Month 9	**LA U12:** Studying Illustrators and Analyzing an Illustrator's Craft *Note: We recommend teaching the minilessons in this umbrella as part of an illustrator study. If you are using the* Fountas & Pinnell Classroom™ Interactive Read-Aloud Collection, *one illustrator study is Brian Pinkney.*	1 .5 weeks
	LA U5: Thinking Critically About the Ways People Are Represented in Texts	1 week
	LA U4: Reading Graphic Texts	1 week
	LA U22: Understanding Fantasy	1 week

MINILESSONS ACROSS THE YEAR (CONT.)

Month	Recommended Umbrellas	Approximate Time
Month 10	**LA U26:** Thinking About the Setting in Fiction Books (RML3–RML4)	2 days
	LA U24: Studying Tall Tales	1.5 weeks
	LA U23: Studying Legends	1.5 weeks
	WAR U4: Using Graphic Organizers to Share Thinking About Books (RML4)	1 day
	WAR U7: Responding Creatively to Reading (RML4)	1 day
	LA U3: Studying Authors and Their Processes (RML1, RML4) *Note: We recommend teaching these minilessons as part of an author study. If you are using the* Fountas & Pinnell Classroom™ Interactive Read-Aloud Collection, *the last author study is Demi. You can also use this text set as an illustrator study.*	2 days
	WAR U4: Using Graphic Organizers to Share Thinking About Books (RML5)	1 day

*Note: Minilessons Across the Year offers general guidance as to the time of year you might teach a particular umbrella and is aligned with the *Fountas & Pinnell Classroom™ Interactive Read-Aloud Collection* sequence. However, because there are 225 reading minilessons in *The Reading Minilessons Book, Grade 5,* it would not be possible to teach every one of these lessons in a normal 180-day school year. You will need to make choices about which minilessons will benefit your students. The minilessons are designed for you to pick and choose what your students need at a particular point in time based on your careful observation of students' reading behaviors.

Chapter 9 Reading Minilessons Within a Multitext Approach to Literacy Learning

THIS COLLECTION OF 225 LESSONS for fifth grade is embedded within an integrated set of instructional approaches that build an awareness of classroom routines, literary characteristics, strategies and skills, and ways of writing about texts. In Figure 9-8, this comprehensive, multitext approach is represented, along with the central role of minilessons. Note that students' processing systems are built across instructional contexts so that students can read increasingly complex texts independently. *The Literacy Quick Guide: A Reference Tool for Responsive Literacy Teaching* (Fountas and Pinnell 2018) provides concise descriptions of these instructional contexts. In this chapter, we will look at how the reading minilessons fit within this multitext approach and provide a balance between implicit and explicit teaching that allows for authentic response and promotes the enjoyment of books.

Throughout this chapter we describe how to build the shared literary knowledge of your classroom community, embedding implicit and explicit teaching with your use of intentional conversation and specific points of instructional value to set a foundation for explicit teaching in reading minilessons. All of the teaching in minilessons is reinforced in shared and performance reading, guided reading, and book clubs, with all pathways leading to the goal of effective independent reading.

Let's look at the range of research-based instructional contexts that constitute an effective literacy design.

Interactive Read-Aloud

Interactive read-aloud provides the highest level of teacher support for students as they experience a complex, grade-appropriate text. In this instructional context, you carefully select sets of high-quality student literature, fiction and nonfiction, and read them aloud to students. We use the word *interactive* because talk is a salient characteristic of this instructional context. You do the reading but pause to invite student discussion in pairs, in triads, or as a whole group at selected points. After the reading, students engage in a lively discussion. Finally, you invite students to revisit specific points in the text for deeper learning and may provide further opportunities for responding to the text through writing, drama, movement, or art.

We recommend that you read aloud from high-quality, organized text sets that you use across the year. A text set contains several titles that are related in some conceptual way, such as the following categories:

- Author
- Illustrator
- Genre
- Topic
- Theme or big idea
- Format (such as graphic texts)

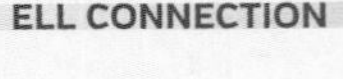

ELL CONNECTION

When you use books organized in text sets, you can support students in making connections across a related group of texts and in engaging in deeper thinking about texts. All students benefit from the use of preselected sets, but these connected texts are particularly supportive for English language learners. Text sets allow students to develop vocabulary around a particular theme, genre, or topic. This shared collection of familiar texts and the shared vocabulary developed through the talk provide essential background knowledge that all students will be able to apply during subsequent reading minilessons.

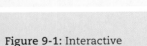

Figure 9-1: Interactive read-aloud in a fifth-grade class

The key to success with reading minilessons is providing the intentional instruction in interactive read-aloud that will, first, enable the students to enjoy and come to love books and, second, build a foundation of shared understandings about texts within a community of readers and writers.

If you are using *Fountas & Pinnell Classroom*™ (Fountas and Pinnell 2020), you will notice that we have used examples from the *Interactive Read-Aloud Collection* as the mentor texts in the minilessons. If you do not have the texts from *Fountas & Pinnell Classroom*™, select read-aloud texts with the same characteristics (described at the beginning of each umbrella) to read well ahead of the minilessons and then use the lessons as organized and presented in this book. Simply substitute the particular texts you selected. You can draw on any texts you have already read and discussed with your students as long as the genre is appropriate for the set of minilessons and the ideas can be connected. For example, if you are going to teach a set of minilessons about characters, pull examples from fiction stories rather than nonfiction books and include engaging characters. If you are reading rich literature in various genres to your students, the chances are high that many of the types of reading behaviors or understandings you are teaching for in reading minilessons can be applied to those texts.

At the beginning of each umbrella (set of related minilessons), you will find a section titled Before Teaching Minilessons that offers guidance in the use of interactive read-aloud as a prelude to teaching the explicit minilessons in the umbrella. It is important to note that the texts in a text set can be used for several different umbrellas. In general, text sets are connected with each other in particular ways so students can think about concepts across texts and notice literary characteristics during read-aloud lessons. But the texts have multiple uses. When you have finished reading the books in a set, you will have provided students with a rich, connected set of literacy

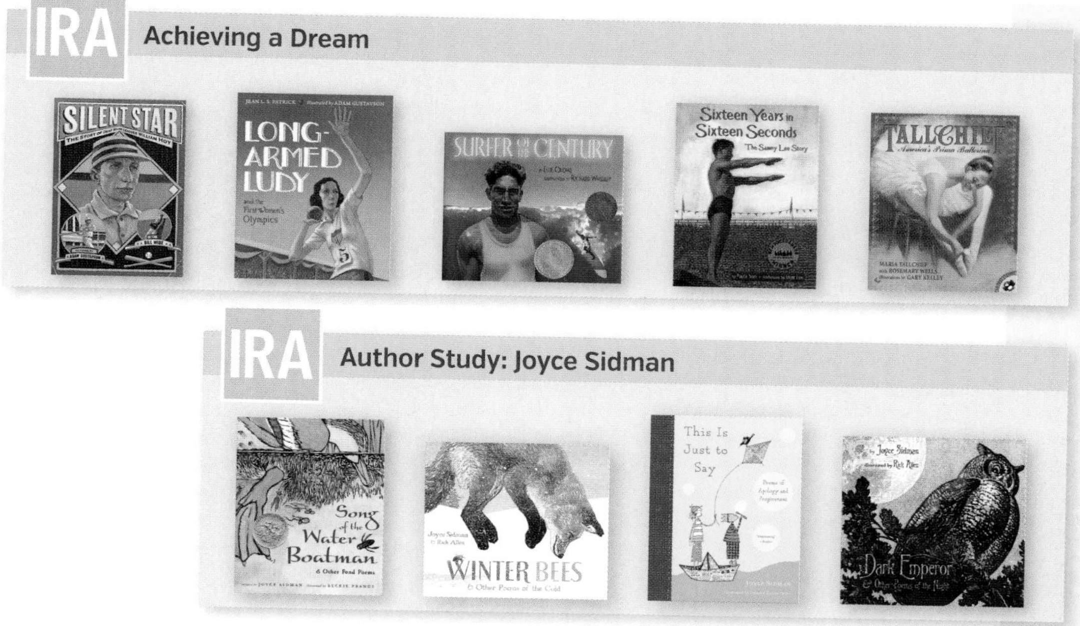

Figure 9-2: Examples of preselected text sets from *Fountas & Pinnell Classroom™ Interactive Read-Aloud Collection*

Books We Have Shared

Mrs. Katz and Tush by Patricia Polacco
My Man Blue by Nikki Grimes
The Crane Girl by Curtis Manley
Shooting at the Stars by John Hendrix
The Lion Who Stole My Arm by Nicola Davies
This Is the Rope by Jacqueline Woodson
The Treasure Box by Margaret Wild
Richard Wright and the Library Card by William Miller
The Storyteller by Evan Turk
Under the Quilt of Night by Deborah Hopkinson
Brian's Winter by Gary Paulsen
Coraline by Neil Gaiman

Figure 9-3: Keep a list of books that you have shared with your students as a record of shared literary knowledge.

experiences that include both explicitly taught and implicitly understood concepts. Then, you have a rich resource from which you can select examples to use as mentor texts in minilessons. We have selected examples across sets. Rich literary texts can be used for multiple types of lessons, so you will see many of the same familiar texts referenced throughout the reading minilessons. Each time a text is used for a different focus, students have a chance to view it with new eyes and see it differently. Usually, texts are not reread in entirety during a minilesson. They are already known because of the rich and deep experiences in your classroom. The result is shared literary knowledge for the class. In minilessons, they are revisited briefly with a particular focus. It is most powerful to select examples from texts that students have heard in their *recent* experience. But, you can always revisit favorites that you read at the very beginning of the year. In fact, reading many picture books at the beginning of the year will quickly build students' repertoire of shared texts, providing you with a variety of choices for mentor texts for your minilessons. When texts have been enjoyed and loved in interactive read-aloud, students know them deeply and can remember them over time. It is helpful to keep an ongoing list of books read during interactive read-aloud so you and your students can refer to them throughout the year (see Figure 9-3). Some of the books in the *Interactive Read-Aloud Collection* are novels, and you are apt to include novels in text sets you assemble yourself as well. This is appropriate for readers in fifth grade. It is important, however, to remember the power of shorter picture books to expose students to a wide variety of genres, authors, and themes. When you continue to read aloud age-appropriate picture books while working through a longer novel, you expose your students to different authors and genres while developing some of the deeper understandings a novel can offer. It is also important to note that you can use familiar novels as mentor texts in your minilesson examples in the same way that you use picture books.

Here are some steps to follow for incorporating your own texts into the minilessons:

1. Identify a group of read-aloud texts that will be valuable resources for use in the particular minilesson. (These texts may be from the same text set, but usually they are drawn from several different sets. The key is their value in teaching routines, engaging in literary analysis, building particular strategies and skills, or writing about reading.)

2. The mentor texts you select will usually be some that you have already read to and discussed with the students, but if not, read and discuss them with the goal of enjoyment and understanding. The emphasis in interactive read-aloud is not on the minilesson principle but on enjoying and deeply understanding the text, appreciating the illustrations and design, and constructing an understanding of the deeper messages of the text.
3. Teach the reading minilesson as designed, substituting the texts you have chosen and read to the students.

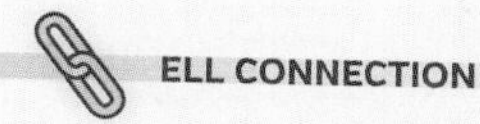

Interactive read-aloud will greatly benefit your English language learners. In *Fountas & Pinnell Classroom*™ (Fountas and Pinnell 2020), we have selected the texts with English language learners in mind and recommend that you do the same if you are selecting texts from your existing resources. In addition to expanding both listening and speaking vocabularies, interactive read-aloud provides constant exposure to English language syntax. Stories read aloud provide "ear print" for the students. Hearing grammatical structures of English over and over helps English language learners form an implicit knowledge of the rules. Here are some other considerations for your English language learners:

- Increase the frequency of your interactive read-alouds.
- Choose books that have familiar themes and concepts and take into account the cultural backgrounds of all the students in your classroom.
- Be sure that students can see themselves as well as the diversity of the world in a good portion of the texts you read.
- Reread texts that your English language learners enjoy. Rereading texts that students especially enjoy will help them acquire and make use of language that goes beyond their current understanding.
- Choose texts that are simple and have high picture support. This will allow you to later revisit concrete examples from these texts during reading minilessons.
- Seat English language learners in places where they can easily see, hear, and participate in the text.
- Preview the text with English language learners by holding a small-group discussion before reading the book to the entire class. As they hear it the second time, they will understand more and will have had the experience of talking. This will encourage the students to participate more actively during the discussion.

When you provide a rich and supportive experience through interactive read-aloud, you prepare English language learners for a successful experience in reading minilessons. They will bring the vocabulary and background knowledge developed in interactive read-aloud to the exploration of the reading minilesson principle. These multiple layers of support will pave the road to successful independent reading.

Shared and Performance Reading

In the early grades, shared reading of big books and enlarged texts plays a vital role in helping students understand how to find and use information from print—directional movement, one-to-one correspondence, words and letters, and the whole act of reading and understanding a story or nonfiction text. As readers become more proficient, shared reading and performance reading (see Figure 9-4) continue to offer opportunities for more advanced reading work than students can do independently. In fact, a form of shared reading can be used at every grade level and is especially supportive to English language learners, who can benefit greatly from working with a group of peers.

For students in grade 5 and above, you can use the level of support that shared reading affords to develop readers' competencies in word analysis, vocabulary, fluency, and comprehension. You'll want to provide regular opportunities for shared and performance reading not only of fiction and nonfiction books, but of poems, readers' theater scripts, plays, speeches, and primary source documents as well. Select a page or pages from a text and use a document camera to enlarge it so that students can see the features you are asking them to discuss. If you have a class set of novels, you might distribute them to focus on a particular section or chapter as a shared reading experience. Of course, you would want to choose a section that would be meaningful on its own without having to have the context of the entire novel.

Like the books read aloud, the texts you select for shared and performance reading should offer students the opportunity to discuss characters, events, concepts, and ideas. Read the text to the students and then invite them to read all or a portion of it in unison. Having students reread the text several times until they know it well, gives you the option of revisiting it for different purposes; for example, to locate content words, practice fluency, or use inflection to convey the author's meaning. If you want, you can then extend the meaning through writing, art, or drama.

Here are some steps to follow for incorporating shared and performance reading as part of your classroom activities:

1. Display an enlarged text or provide individual copies. The text may be one that the students have previously read.

2. Engage students in a shared reading of the text. Plan to reread it several times. (Use your own judgment. Sometimes two or three readings are sufficient.) Remember, the focus at this point is on understanding and enjoying the enlarged text, not on a specific principle.
3. Revisit the text to do some specific teaching toward any of the systems of strategic actions listed in *The Literacy Continuum* (Fountas and Pinnell 2017b). If the text you've selected is a choral reading, script, poem, or speech, encourage students to perform it, using their voices and inflection to convey the writer's meaning.
4. If you plan to use a shared reading text in a reading minilesson, implement the lesson as designed using the texts you have used in teaching.

On the occasions that you use a shared reading text in a minilesson, students have had opportunities to notice print and how it works and to practice fluent reading. They have located individual words and noticed the use of bold and italicized words. They have learned how to use the meaning, language, and print together to process the text fluently and may have used performance techniques to amplify the writer's intent. In addition, here, too, they have noticed characteristics of the genre, the characters, and the message anchors.

Shared and performance reading can also be important in reinforcing students' ability to apply understandings from the minilesson. You can revisit the texts to remind students of the minilesson principle and invite them to notice text characteristics or engage strategic actions to process them. When you work across texts, you help students apply understandings in many contexts.

Figure 9-4: Performance reading (readers' theater) in a fifth-grade class

ELL CONNECTION

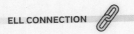

Shared and performance reading provide a supportive environment for English language learners to both hear and produce English language structures and patterns. Familiar shared reading texts often have repeated or rhythmic text, which is easy to learn. Using shared reading texts to teach Strategies and Skills minilessons can be particularly supportive for English language learners because they have had the opportunity to develop familiarity with the meaning, the vocabulary, and the language structures of the text. They can focus on exploring the minilesson principle because they are not working so hard to read and understand the text. Shared reading gives them the background and familiarity with text that makes it possible to easily learn the minilesson principle.

Shared reading is a context that is particularly supportive to English language learners because of the enjoyable repetition and opportunity to "practice" English syntax with the support of the group. Shared reading can be done in a whole-group or small-group setting. Following are some suggestions you can use to support English language learners:

- Use enlarged texts, projected texts, or an individual copy of the text for every student.
- Select texts with easy-to-say refrains, often involving rhyme and repeating patterns.
- Reread the text as much as needed to help students become confident in joining in.
- Use some texts that lend themselves to inserting students' names or adding repetitive verses.

Guided Reading

Guided reading is small-group instruction using an appropriately selected leveled text that is at students' instructional level. This means that the text is more complex than the students can process independently, so it offers appropriate challenge.

Supportive and precise instruction with the text enables the students to read it with proficiency, and in the process they develop in-the-head strategic actions that they can apply to the reading of other texts. Guided reading involves several steps:

1. Assess students' strengths through the analysis of oral reading behaviors as well as the assessment of comprehension—thinking within, beyond, and about the text. This knowledge enables you to determine an appropriate reading level for instruction.
2. Bring together a small group of students who are close enough to the same level that it makes sense to teach them together. (Ongoing assessment takes place in the form of running records or reading records

so that the information can guide the emphasis in lessons and groups may be changed and reformed as needed.)

3. Based on assessment, select a text that is at students' instructional level and offers opportunities for new learning.
4. Introduce the text to the students in a way that will support reading and engage them with the text.
5. Have students read the text individually. (In fifth grade, this usually means reading silently without pointing to the words. You may choose to hear several students read softly to you so you can check on their processing.) Support reading through quick interactions that use precise language to support effective processing.
6. Invite students to engage in an open-ended discussion of the text and use some guiding questions or prompts to help them extend their thinking.
7. Based on previous assessment and observation during reading, select a teaching point.
8. Engage students in quick word work that helps them flexibly apply principles for solving words that have been selected based on information gained from the analysis of oral reading behaviors and reinforcement of principles explored in phonics minilessons (see *The Fountas & Pinnell Comprehensive Phonics, Spelling, and Word Study Guide* [2017a] and *Fountas & Pinnell Word Study System, Grade 5* [2021]).
9. As an option, you may have students engage in writing about the book to extend their understanding, but it is not necessary—or desirable—to write about every book.

Guided reading texts are not usually used as examples in minilessons because they are not texts that are shared by the entire class. However, on occasion, you might find a guided reading book that perfectly illustrates a minilesson

Figure 9-5: Guided reading in a fifth-grade class

principle. In this case, you will want to introduce the book to the entire class as an interactive read-aloud before using it as a mentor text. You can also take the opportunity to reinforce the minilesson principle across the guided reading lesson at one or more points:

- In the introduction to the text, refer to a reading minilesson principle as one of the ways that you support readers before reading a new text.
- In your interactions with students during the reading of the text, remind them of the principle from the reading minilesson.
- In the discussion after the text, reinforce the minilesson principle when appropriate.
- In the teaching point, reinforce the minilesson principle.

In small-group guided reading lessons, students explore aspects of written texts that are similar to the understandings they discuss in interactive read-aloud and shared and performance reading. They evaluate the authenticity of characters, analyze character change, talk about the significance of the setting, talk about the problem in the story and the ending, and discuss the theme or message of the story. They talk about information they learned and questions they have, they notice genre characteristics, and they develop phonics knowledge and word-solving strategies. So, guided reading also gives readers the opportunity to apply what they have learned in reading minilessons.

ELL CONNECTION 

When you support readers in applying the minilesson principle within a guided reading lesson, you give them another opportunity to talk about text with this new thinking in mind. It is particularly helpful to English language learners to have the opportunity to try out this new thinking in a small, safe setting. Guided reading can provide the opportunity to talk about the minilesson principle before the class comes back together to share. Often, students feel more confident about sharing their new thinking with the whole group because they have had this opportunity to practice talking about their book in the small-group setting.

Book Clubs

For a book club meeting, bring together a small group of students who have chosen the same book to read and discuss with their classmates. The book can be one that you have read to the group or one that the students can either read independently or listen to and understand from an audio recording.

The implementation of book clubs follows these steps:

1. Preselect about four books that offer opportunities for deep discussion. These books may be related in some way (for example, they might be by the same author or feature stories around a theme). Or, they might just be a group of titles that will give students good choices.

2. Give a book talk about each of the books to introduce them to students. A book talk is a short "commercial" for the book.
3. Have students read and prepare for the book club discussion. (If the student cannot read the book, prepare an audio version that can be used during independent reading time.) Each reader marks a place or places that he wants to discuss with a sticky note.
4. Convene the group and facilitate the discussion.
5. Have students self-evaluate the discussion.

Book clubs provide students the opportunity for deep, enjoyable talk with their classmates about books. Minilessons in two umbrellas are devoted to teaching the routines of book clubs. Literary Analysis Umbrella 1: Getting Started with Book Clubs focuses on the routines for getting started and takes students through the process of choosing books, marking pages they want to discuss, and participating in the discussion in meaningful ways. Umbrella 2: Learning Conversational Moves in Book Club teaches students how to enter a conversation, invite others to participate, build on other people's ideas, and change the focus when necessary.

A discussion among four or five diverse fifth-grade students can go in many directions, and you want to hear all of their ideas! *Prompting Guide, Part 2, for Comprehension: Thinking, Talking, and Writing* (Fountas and Pinnell 2009b) is a helpful tool. The section on book discussions contains precise teacher language for getting a discussion started, asking for thinking, affirming thinking, agreeing and disagreeing, changing thinking, clarifying thinking, extending thinking, focusing on the big ideas, making connections, paraphrasing, questioning and hypothesizing, redirecting, seeking evidence, sharing thinking, and summarizing.

Figure 9-6: Book club in a fifth-grade class

Before teaching several of the book club minilessons, we suggest holding a fishbowl observation of a book club discussion. To do this, prepare a small book group ahead of time and help them mark pages in the book they want to discuss. During the minilesson, have the small group sit in a circle with the remaining students sitting outside the circle to observe. Lead the conversation as needed, having book club members talk about their thinking for a few minutes. Encourage them to invite others in the group to talk, ask each other questions, and agree or disagree with one another in a respectful way. In some cases, the lesson suggests observing students with a particular lens. In others, they will be asked to make general observations. In either case, the prepared group models what a book club meeting should look like.

ELL CONNECTION 

Book clubs offer English language learners the unique opportunity to enter into conversations about books with other students. If they have listened to an audio recording many times, they are gaining more and more exposure to language. The language and content of the book lifts the conversation and gives them something to talk about. They learn the conventions of discourse, which become familiar because they do it many times. They can hear others talk and respond with social language, such as "I agree with ___________ because ___________."

Independent Reading

In independent reading, students have the opportunity to apply all they have learned in minilessons. To support independent reading, assemble a well-organized classroom library with a range of engaging fiction and nonfiction books. Although you will take into account the levels students can read independently to assure a range of options, we do *not* suggest that you arrange the books by level. It is not productive and can be destructive

Figure 9-7: The goal of all literacy teaching is effective independent reading.

for the students to choose books by "level." Instead, create tubs or baskets by author, topic, genre, and so forth. There are minilessons in Section One: Management to help you teach fifth graders how to choose books for their own reading (see MGT.U2.RML5). Consider the following as you prepare students to work independently.

- **Personal Book Boxes.** A personal book box is where students keep their materials (e.g., reader's notebook, writer's notebook, writing folder, books to read) all together and organized. A magazine holder or cereal box works well. Students can label the boxes with their names and decorate them. Management minilesson MGT.U2.RML3 provides guidance on setting up the box and keeping it organized. Keep these boxes in a central place so that students can retrieve them during independent reading time.
- **Classroom Library.** The classroom library is filled with baskets or tubs of books that fifth-grade students will love. Books are organized by topic, theme, genre, series, or author. Have students help you organize the books so that they share some ownership of the library. In some minilessons, there is a direction to guide students to read from a particular basket in the classroom library so that they have the opportunity to apply the reading minilesson to books that include the characteristics addressed in the minilesson. For example, you might have them read from a basket of fantasy books or a basket of poetry books.

ELL CONNECTION

Becoming independent as a reader is an essential life skill for all students. English language learners need daily opportunities to use their systems of strategic actions on text that is accessible, meaningful, and interesting to them. Here are some suggestions for helping English language learners during independent reading:

- Make sure your classroom library has a good selection of books at a range of levels. If possible, provide books in the first language of your students as well as books with familiar settings and themes.
- During individual conferences, help students prepare—and sometimes rehearse—something that they can share with others about the text during group share. When possible, ask them to think about the minilesson principle.
- Provide opportunities for English language learners to share with partners before being asked to share with the whole group.

Combining Implicit and Explicit Teaching for Independent Reading

You are about to embark on a highly productive year of literacy lessons. We have prepared these lessons as tools for your use as you help students engage with texts, making daily shifts in learning. When students participate in a classroom that provides a multitext approach to literacy learning, they are exposed to textual elements in a variety of instructional contexts. As described in Figure 9-8, all of these instructional contexts involve embedding literary and print concepts into authentic and meaningful experiences with text. A powerful combination of many concepts is implicitly understood as students engage with books, but the explicit teaching brings them to conscious awareness and supports students' ability to articulate the concepts using academic language.

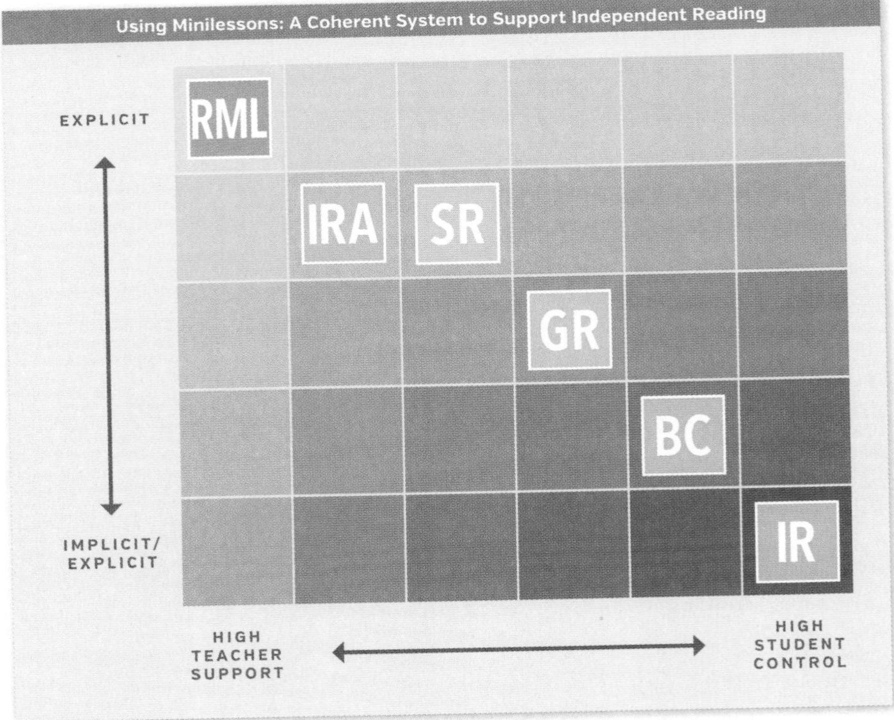

Figure 9-8: Text experiences are supported and developed by implicit and explicit teaching in all instructional contexts, including interactive read-aloud, shared reading, guided reading, book clubs, and independent reading conferences. Reading minilessons provide explicit teaching that makes learning visible and is reinforced in the other contexts.

In interactive read-aloud, students are invited to respond to text as they turn and talk and participate in lively discussions after a text is read. You will be able to support your students in thinking within, beyond, and about the text because you will have used *The Literacy Continuum* (Fountas and Pinnell 2017b) to identify when you will pause and invite these conversations and how you will ask questions and model comments to support the behaviors you have selected. In response, your students will experience and articulate deeper thinking about texts.

In shared and performance reading, students learn from both implicit and explicit teaching. For example, when they work on performing a reader's theater script, they read and discuss the text several times, enjoying the story and discussing aspects of the text that support their thinking within, beyond, and about the text. As they prepare to perform the script, the teacher might provide explicit teaching for fluency (e.g., interpreting a character's dialogue using appropriate intonation and stress). The embedded, implicit teaching, as well as some of the more explicit teaching that students experience in shared and performance reading, lays the groundwork for the explicit teaching that takes place in reading minilessons. Reading minilessons become the bridge from these shared and interactive whole-group reading experiences to independent reading.

Figure 9-9: A rich array of books provides the basis of shared literary knowledge for the community of readers in your classroom.

Guided reading and book clubs scaffold the reading process through a combination of implicit and explicit teaching that helps students apply the reading minilesson principles across a variety of instructional-level texts. The group share reinforces the whole process. Reading minilessons do not function in the absence of these other instructional contexts; rather, they all work in concert to build processing systems for students to grow in their ability to independently read increasingly complex texts over time.

The minilessons in this book serve as a guide to a meaningful, systematic approach to joyful literacy learning across multiple reading contexts. Students acquire a complex range of understandings. Whole-class minilessons form the "glue" that connects all of this learning, makes it explicit, and turns it over to the students to apply to their own independent reading and writing. You will find that the talk and learning in those shared experiences will bring your class together as a community with a shared knowledge base. We know that you and your students will enjoy the rich experiences as you engage together in thinking, talking, and responding to a treasure chest of beautiful books. Students deserve these rich opportunities—every child, every day.

Works Cited

Clay, Marie. 2015 [1991]. *Becoming Literate: The Construction of Inner Control*. Auckland, NZ: Global Education Systems.

Fountas, Irene C., and Gay Su Pinnell. 2006. *Teaching for Comprehending and Fluency: Thinking, Talking, and Writing About Reading, K–8*. Portsmouth, NH: Heinemann.

———. 2009a. *Fountas & Pinnell Prompting Guide, Part 1, for Oral Reading and Early Writing*. Portsmouth, NH: Heinemann.

———. 2009b. *Fountas & Pinnell Prompting Guide, Part 2, for Comprehension: Thinking, Talking, and Writing*. Portsmouth, NH: Heinemann.

———. 2011. *Reader's Notebook: Advanced*. Portsmouth, NH: Heinemann.

———. 2012a. *Fountas & Pinnell Genre Prompting Guide for Fiction*. Portsmouth, NH: Heinemann.

———. 2012b. *Fountas & Pinnell Genre Prompting Guide for Nonfiction, Poetry, and Test Taking*. Portsmouth, NH: Heinemann.

———. 2012c. *Genre Study: Teaching with Fiction and Nonfiction Books*. Portsmouth, NH: Heinemann.

———. 2017a. *The Fountas & Pinnell Comprehensive Phonics, Spelling, and Word Study Guide*. Portsmouth, NH: Heinemann.

———. 2017b. *The Fountas & Pinnell Literacy Continuum: A Tool for Assessment, Planning, and Teaching*. Portsmouth, NH: Heinemann.

———. 2017c. *Guided Reading: Responsive Teaching Across the Grades*. Portsmouth, NH: Heinemann.

———. 2018. *The Literacy Quick Guide: A Reference Tool for Responsive Literacy Teaching*. Portsmouth, NH: Heinemann.

———. 2020. *Fountas & Pinnell Classroom™*. Portsmouth, NH: Heinemann.

———. 2021. *Fountas & Pinnell Word Study System, Grade 5*. Portsmouth, NH: Heinemann.

LaMarche, Jim. 2012. *The Raft*. New York: HarperCollins.

Vygotsky, Lev. 1978. *Mind in Society: The Development of Higher Psychological Processes*. Cambridge, MA: Harvard University Press.

Section 1 Management

Management minilessons focus on routines for thinking and talking about reading and working together in the classroom. These lessons allow you to teach effectively and efficiently. They are directed toward the creation of an orderly, busy classroom in which students know what is expected as well as how to behave responsibly and respectfully within a community of learners. Most of the minilessons at the beginning of the school year will focus on management.

1 Management

Being a Respectful Member of the Classroom Community

Minilessons in This Umbrella

RML1	A strong classroom community enjoys learning and works well together.
RML2	Agree on how to work well together.
RML3	Find ways to solve problems.
RML4	Make everyone feel included.
RML5	Think about how your words and actions make others feel.

Before Teaching Umbrella 1 Minilessons

The purpose of this umbrella is to help students identify as a community of readers and writers who work and learn together. You can support this concept by creating an inviting and well-organized classroom in which students can take ownership of their space and materials, and by giving students plenty of opportunities to choose, read, and talk about books.

Read books about friendship, inclusivity, fitting in, empathy, and conflict resolution to help students understand what it means to be part of a caring and considerate community. The minilessons in this umbrella use books from the following *Fountas & Pinnell Classroom™ Interactive Read-Aloud Collection* text sets, but you can use books more closely related to your students' experiences and interests.

Conflict Resolution

Shooting at the Stars: The Christmas Truce of 1914 by John Hendrix

Desmond and the Very Mean Word by Archbishop Desmond Tutu and Douglas Carlton Abrams

Thirty Minutes Over Oregon: A Japanese Pilot's World War II Story by Marc Tyler Nobleman

Empathy

Mrs. Katz and Tush by Patricia Polacco

My Man Blue by Nikki Grimes

Family

Keeping the Night Watch by Hope Anita Smith

This Is the Rope by Jacqueline Woodson

Conflict Resolution

Empathy

Family

Keeping the Night Watch by Hope Anita Smith

RML1
MGT.U1.RML1

Reading Minilesson Principle

A strong classroom community enjoys learning and works well together.

Being a Respectful Member of the Classroom Community

You Will Need

- classroom set up with areas to support students in reading and writing activities (e.g., classroom library; writing-supply area; areas for small-group, whole-group, and independent work)
- chart paper and markers

Academic Language / Important Vocabulary

- community
- respectful
- organized

Continuum Connection

- Actively participate in conversation during whole- and small-group discussion (p. 339)

Goal

Learn what a classroom community is and how the members behave toward one another.

Rationale

To create a healthy and positive classroom community, all students need to take responsibility for treating each other with respect and doing what they can to support each other. In addition to social and emotional responsibility, students also need to care for the environment, the materials, and other physical aspects of the communal space.

Assess Learning

Observe students when they work and learn together and notice if there is evidence of new learning based on the goal of this minilesson.

- Do students understand their individual roles in fostering a positive classroom community?
- Do they treat each other and the classroom respectfully?
- Do they understand and use the terms *community, respectful,* and *organized*?

Minilesson

To help students think about the minilesson principle, engage them in a discussion about what responsibilities the members of a community have in creating a positive place for working and learning together. Here is an example.

> Here in this room, we are members of a classroom community. What does that mean? What is a community?
>
> For each of us to enjoy learning and do our best work together in the classroom, we need to build a strong community. Let's talk about what you can do to make everyone feel good about being part of the classroom community. What are your ideas? Turn and talk about that.

- Use the following prompts as needed to support the conversation:
    - *How can the members of a community make everyone feel part of it?*
    - *How can the members of a community support each other in their learning?*
- After time for discussion, ask students to share their thinking. Make a list of how each student can support the work of the community.
- Record responses on the chart.

Have a Try

Invite the students to talk with a partner about being a member of the classroom community.

What is something you can do to make a classmate feel welcome and included?

- After time for discussion, ask students to share.

Summarize and Apply

Summarize the learning by reviewing the chart.

- Write the principle at the top.

Keep the items on the chart in mind as you go through the day. Later, we will meet to share. Be ready to talk about something you did to make our classroom community strong.

A strong classroom community enjoys learning and works well together.

- Treat others with respect.
- Make everyone feel welcome and included.
- Listen to what others have to say.
- Share ideas honestly and respectfully.
- Ask others for help and give help to others.
- Work on your own or in groups.

Share

Following independent reading time, gather students together in the meeting area.

Who would like to share what you did to help build a strong community?

Extend the Lesson (Optional)

After assessing students' understanding, you might decide to extend the learning.

- Have regular whole-class meetings to discuss how well the class is working as a learning community and to allow students to voice concerns or suggest ways to improve.

RML 2

MGT.U1.RML2

Reading Minilesson Principle

Agree on how to work well together.

Being a Respectful Member of the Classroom Community

You Will Need

- chart paper and markers

Academic Language / Important Vocabulary

- community
- agreement
- norms

Continuum Connection

- Listen respectfully and responsibly (p. 339)
- Speak at an appropriate volume (p. 339)
- Use respectful turn-taking conventions (p. 339)

Goal

Create norms and agreements for a classroom community to follow.

Rationale

When students understand that in a successful community people work well together and that they can create a classroom agreement to establish norms, they learn to take ownership of their classroom and behaviors so that a positive classroom environment can be maintained.

Assess Learning

Observe students when they construct and follow a classroom agreement and notice if there is evidence of new learning based on the goal of this minilesson.

- Do students contribute ideas for the ways they can learn and work well together?
- Do they exhibit the behaviors the class has decided will make collaborative learning possible?
- Do they understand the terms *community, agreement,* and *norms*?

Minilesson

To help students think about the minilesson principle, engage them in discussing and creating a community agreement or a set of norms for working together. Here is an example.

We have talked about what the members of a classroom community can do to make everyone feel a part of the community. When community members agree on ways to work together well, they create a set of classroom norms, or expectations, for the way each person should behave.

What are the norms we can agree upon to make it possible for everyone to enjoy working and learning together? Let's make a list.

- As needed, support the conversation with prompts such as the following:
  - *When you are reading or writing, how can you do your best work?*
  - *How can you make the classroom a place where everyone can learn?*
  - *How can you participate positively when you are working in a group?*
  - *How should you care for the resources and materials in the classroom?*
- After time for discussion, record students' ideas on chart paper.

This chart will remind us of how we have agreed to work and learn together.

Have a Try

Invite the students to talk with a partner about the community agreement.

> Do you have any additional ideas for the chart? Turn and talk to your partner about that. You can also talk about why the ideas we have written on the chart are important.

- After time for discussion, ask a few students to share ideas. Discuss whether any new items should be added to the classroom agreement.

Our Classroom Norms

- Use an appropriate voice level.
- Focus on our work.
- Take turns talking.
- Help each other feel safe taking risks.
- Listen carefully.
- Be respectful of what others say.
- Help each other learn.
- Keep the classroom organized.
- Take good care of materials.

Kashvi Trinity Jasmine Chloe Luis Shun Josiah Luciano Rosamie Dylan Kevin Alex Hansh Lilibeth Kennedy Jordan Lan Rohan Mia Ethan Santiago Mateo Riley Oliver

Summarize and Apply

Summarize the learning and remind students to think about the community agreement.

> Today we made a community agreement. Why is this important for our classroom?
>
> Today, take a moment to think about our agreement and how it will help you as a reader and writer. Why is it important? What things will you do to follow each part of the agreement? After you have thought about these things, come up and sign the agreement at the bottom. Be ready to share your thinking when we come back together.

Share

Following independent reading time, gather students together in the meeting area to discuss the classroom agreement.

> Take a look at our list of classroom norms. What do you think? Is there anything we should change or add?

Extend the Lesson (Optional)

After assessing students' understanding, you might decide to extend the learning.

- Keep the norms posted in the classroom and have new discussions from time to time to evaluate whether any changes should be made.
- Point out that the physical classroom arrangement (e.g., a place for the whole group to meet, places for reading and writing independently, a classroom library, organized storage for material) supports the classroom community members' ability to do their best work.

RML 3

MGT.U1.RML3

Reading Minilesson Principle

Find ways to solve problems.

Being a Respectful Member of the Classroom Community

You Will Need

- chart paper and markers

Academic Language / Important Vocabulary

- classroom community
- problem
- solution

Goal

Solve problems independently.

Rationale

When you teach students problem-solving strategies, they become independent and confident, allowing time for you to work with small groups or individual students.

Assess Learning

Observe students when they try to solve problems and notice if there is evidence of new learning based on the goal of this minilesson.

- Can students talk about ways to solve problems?
- Do they try to solve problems independently?
- Do they use the terms *classroom community, problem,* and *solution*?

Minilesson

To help students think about the minilesson principle, engage them in a discussion about how to solve problems independently. Here is an example.

- Have students sit in the meeting area.

  Think about the different problems you might have while working in our classroom and the different ways you can solve them. Also think about which problems you can solve on your own and which problems you would need my help to solve. Turn and talk about that.

- After time for discussion, ask students to share ideas. As students provide ideas, create a two-column chart for classroom problems and solutions. Encourage students to consider multiple solutions for each type of problem.

  Why is it important for you to solve most of your problems independently?

- Support a conversation about why independent problem solving is important. As new ideas emerge, add to the chart.

Have a Try

Invite the students to talk in groups of three about problem solving.

> What is another problem you might have in class? How would you solve it? Turn and talk with your group about that.

- After students turn and talk, ask a couple of students to share their ideas with the class. Add new ideas to the chart.

Find ways to solve problems.

Problem	Solution
Finish work early	• Review your work • Read independently • Finish other work • Select a choice time activity
Have a conflict with someone in class	• Talk directly and kindly to the person and try to find a solution • Compromise
Don't understand directions	• Reread directions • Think about how you have done a similar assignment • Ask someone in the class
Run out of something like paper, staples, glue, pencil	• Look in the class writing area • Ask to borrow from another student
Book is too difficult	• Select a different book
Emergency, like sick, bleeding, or injured	• Tell the teacher right away

Summarize and Apply

Summarize the learning and remind students to try to solve problems independently.

> How can solving problems independently help create a positive classroom community?

- Add the principle to the chart.

> When you have a problem, try to solve it on your own before you ask for help, unless it is an emergency. Refer to the chart if you are unsure of a possible solution.

Share

Following independent reading time, gather students together in the meeting area to discuss problem solving.

> Did anyone have a problem today that you solved independently?
>
> What might be another way to solve this problem?

Extend the Lesson (Optional)

After assessing students' understanding, you might decide to extend the learning.

- Recognize when students solve problems independently and provide positive reinforcement for their efforts.
- Keep the chart posted in the classroom and continue to discuss problems and solutions as they arise. Add new ideas to the chart.

RML 4
MGT.U1.RML4

Reading Minilesson Principle

Make everyone feel included.

Being a Respectful Member of the Classroom Community

You Will Need

- several fiction books that have examples of getting to know one another and including each other, such as the following:
  - *Shooting at the Stars* by John Hendrix, from Text Set: Conflict Resolution
  - *Mrs. Katz and Tush* by Patricia Polacco, from Text Set: Empathy
  - *Keeping the Night Watch* by Hope Anita Smith and *This Is the Rope* by Jacqueline Woodson, from Text Set: Family
- chart paper and markers
- sticky notes

Academic Language / Important Vocabulary

- classroom community
- conversation
- unique
- diverse
- inclusive

Continuum Connection

- Learn from vicarious experiences with characters in stories (p. 71)
- Respect the age, gender, position, and cultural traditions of the speaker (p. 339)

Goal

Value the unique identities of others and take actions that make them feel included.

Rationale

When students learn words and actions to get to know one another, to invite others to join in, and to value the unique identities of others and embrace diversity, they create a rich, interesting, and safe environment in which all classroom community members feel valued.

Assess Learning

Observe students as they interact with classmates and notice if there is evidence of new learning based on the goal of this minilesson.

- Are students taking steps to include others?
- Do they understand the terms *classroom community, conversation, unique, diverse,* and *inclusive*?

Minilesson

To help students think about the minilesson principle, engage them in a discussion about getting to know one another and inclusion. Here is an example.

- Show pages 21 and 25–26 from *Shooting at the Stars.*

  Remember in *Shooting at the Stars* when the British and German soldiers first met? Think about what they did.

- Show pages 1–2, 3, and 8 from *Mrs. Katz and Tush.*

  Think about how Larnel got to know Mrs. Katz.

- Show page 55 from *Keeping the Night Watch.*

  Think about how C.J. and Maya got to know one another.

  How can you get to know someone? Turn and talk about that.

- After time for discussion, ask students to share ideas. Begin a list on chart paper.
- Revisit pages 13–14 of *This Is the Rope.* Then revisit page 52, lines 1–7 from *Keeping the Night Watch.*

  Think about how the narrator's mom felt when she moved to a new neighborhood. Think about how C.J. felt when he didn't have anyone to sit by in the lunchroom. What did they want others to do? What can you say to be inclusive, or to make others feel wanted?

- Ask students to share a few ideas. Write the ideas on chart paper.

Have a Try

Invite the students to talk with a partner about being inclusive.

Why is it important to do things to get to know others and why is it important to be inclusive? Turn and talk about that.

- After time for discussion, briefly discuss new ideas. Add responses to the chart.

Make everyone feel included.

Get to Know Someone	Be Inclusive

• Help a new person get to know the classroom.
• Make a graphic organizer or poster that shows information about yourself.
• Talk about favorite books.
• Share something about yourself.
• See if you can help with anything.
• Ask questions:
  • Who is in your family?
  • What do you like to do when you're not at school?
  • What is your favorite music or favorite sport?
  • What pets do you have?
  • What is your favorite food?
	• What do you think about that?
	• What is your opinion?
	• Can I help you with that?
	• Would you like to join us?
	• Do you want to sit with me/us at lunch?
	• Do you want to join our game?

Summarize and Apply

Summarize the learning and remind students to think about ways they can include others.

Think about the different ideas posted on the chart and try to use these ideas in the classroom or around the school.

- Write the minilesson principle at the top of the chart paper.

When you read today, notice examples of how characters get to know each other, when they are inclusive, or when they make someone feel left out. Place a sticky note on the page with the example. Bring the book when we meet so you can share.

Share

Following independent reading time, gather students in the meeting area.

Did you find any examples of characters who got to know each other, who included others, or who did not include others? Share the examples that you noticed.

Extend the Lesson (Optional)

After assessing students' understanding, you might decide to extend the learning.

- Have students create graphic organizers, modeled after a character web, to share information about themselves so that other students can get to know them better.
- **Writing About Reading** Have students write about a character who made another character feel included or excluded. Encourage them to also write about how they felt when they read that part of the book.

RML 5

MGT.U1.RML5

Reading Minilesson Principle

Think about how your words and actions make others feel.

Being a Respectful Member of the Classroom Community

You Will Need

- several familiar fiction books that encourage thinking about empathy, such as the following:
  - *Desmond and the Very Mean Word* by Archbishop Desmond Tutu and Douglas Carlton Abrams, from Text Set: Conflict Resolution
  - *My Man Blue* by Nikki Grimes, from Text Set: Empathy
  - *Thirty Minutes Over Oregon* by Marc Tyler Nobleman, from Text Set: Conflict Resolution
- chart paper and markers
- sticky notes

Academic Language / Important Vocabulary

- classroom community
- empathy

Continuum Connection

- Learn from vicarious experiences with characters in stories (p. 71)

Goal

Show empathy towards others.

Rationale

When students reflect on how their words and actions affect classmates, they develop empathy and concern for others, both of which contribute to a positive learning environment.

Assess Learning

Observe students as they discuss empathy and interact with others. Notice evidence of new learning based on the goal of this minilesson.

- Do students talk about how someone's words or actions make another person feel?
- Are they able to infer how their own words and actions make others feel?
- Do they understand the terms *classroom community* and *empathy*?

Minilesson

To help students think about the minilesson principle, use familiar texts with examples of empathy to help them think about how words and actions make others feel. Here is an example.

- Revisit pages 3–6 from *Desmond and the Very Mean Word.*

  Think about how the boys were treating Desmond. How did that make him feel? How do you know? Turn and talk about that.

- As students share ideas, create a two-column chart. On the left side, write things that the characters say and do. On the right side, write how those words or actions make the main character feel.
- Revisit pages 19–20 and then pages 23–24, pausing after each spread to ask students to notice empathy and add ideas to the chart.
- Revisit pages 5–6 and then pages 7–8 from *My Man Blue.*

  What did you notice about how the words and actions of Blue made Damon feel?

- Add examples to the chart.
- Revisit page 23 from *Thirty Minutes Over Oregon* and repeat the activity.

  Trying to understand how others feel is called empathy. Thinking about how your words and actions make others feel is one part of empathy.

Have a Try

Invite the students to talk with a partner about empathy.

> Think of a time when someone's words or actions made you feel good or feel bad. Turn and talk to your partner about that.

- Make sure the discussions don't name individuals in a negative way. Keep them general. After students turn and talk, ask a couple of pairs to share their ideas. Add ideas to the chart.

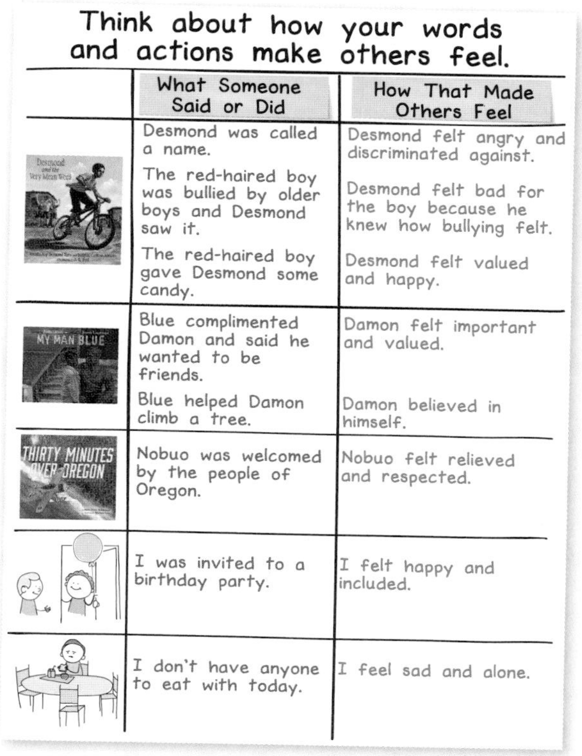

Think about how your words and actions make others feel.

	What Someone Said or Did	How That Made Others Feel
Desmond and the Very Mean Word	Desmond was called a name.	Desmond felt angry and discriminated against.
	The red-haired boy was bullied by older boys and Desmond saw it.	Desmond felt bad for the boy because he knew how bullying felt.
	The red-haired boy gave Desmond some candy.	Desmond felt valued and happy.
My Man Blue	Blue complimented Damon and said he wanted to be friends.	Damon felt important and valued.
	Blue helped Damon climb a tree.	Damon believed in himself.
Thirty Minutes Over Oregon	Nobuo was welcomed by the people of Oregon.	Nobuo felt relieved and respected.
	I was invited to a birthday party.	I felt happy and included.
	I don't have anyone to eat with today.	I feel sad and alone.

Summarize and Apply

Summarize the learning and remind students to think about how their words and actions affect others.

> Think about the different ideas on the chart and how you can use words and actions that make others feel good.

- Write the minilesson principle at the top of the chart paper.

> When you read today, notice examples of characters who show empathy toward others, or notice when one character understands how another character feels. Place a sticky note on any pages with examples. Bring the book when we meet so you can share.

Share

Following independent reading time, gather students together in the meeting area to discuss examples of empathy.

> Did you find any examples of characters who used words or actions to make others feel good or bad? Share what you noticed.

Extend the Lesson (Optional)

After assessing students' understanding, you might decide to extend the learning.

- Have students write about examples from their own lives of how the words or actions of others made them feel, what others could have said or done to show more empathy, or about times when they were empathetic toward another person.
- Notice when students practice empathy in the classroom and point out the specific examples to show how it helps build a positive community of learners, readers, and writers.

Assessment

After you have taught the minilessons in this umbrella, observe students as they learn and interact with others in the classroom.

- What evidence do you have of new understandings related to being respectful members of the classroom community?
    - Are students developing skills to work and learn together as a community?
    - Do they take care of the classroom and the materials they use?
    - Do they try to get to know one another?
    - Do they participate in making and honoring classroom agreements?
    - Do students use an appropriate voice level in the classroom?
    - Can they find ways to solve problems on their own?
    - Are they inclusive of others?
    - Do they think about how their words and actions make others feel?
    - Do they use terms such as *community, agreement, problem, solution,* and *unique* when they talk about the classroom community?
- What other minilessons might you teach to help students grow and function as members of a community of readers and writers?
    - Are students able to find books to read and books to recommend to others?
    - Are they able to share their thinking with others during turn and talk or during a book club meeting?

Use your observations to determine the next umbrella you will teach. You may also consult Minilessons Across the Year (pp. 61–64) for guidance.

Reader's Notebook

When this umbrella is complete, provide a copy of the minilesson principles (see resources.fountasandpinnell.com) for students to glue in the reader's notebook (in the Minilessons section if using *Reader's Notebook: Advanced* [Fountas and Pinnell 2011]), so they can refer to the information as needed.

Minilessons in This Umbrella

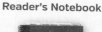

RML1	Reading is thinking.
RML2	Share your thinking about books.
RML3	Your book box is a place for your books and your personal materials.
RML4	The classroom library includes a variety of books for you to enjoy.
RML5	Make good decisions about your book choices.

Reader's Notebook

Before Teaching Umbrella 2 Minilessons

The purpose of the minilessons in this umbrella is to help students learn about what to do during the time set aside for independent reading and writing. Students learn that reading and writing are both important parts of this time, discover the importance of keeping their personal materials organized, and explore how the classroom library system makes finding books easier. Taking the time to establish independent reading routines will be worth the effort. While students are engaged in reading and writing, you will be able to offer small-group instruction or individual reading conferences. Before teaching the minilessons in this umbrella, decide whether you will organize the library ahead of time or whether you will engage students in the process of categorizing the books. Give students plenty of opportunities to choose, read, and talk about books. Also, decide where students will do their reading and writing during independent reading time. Here are some suggestions for preparing for introducing independent reading time:

- Organize (or have students help you organize) books in the classroom library into baskets in a way that allows students to see the front covers and that provides easy access for browsing.
- In each basket, display high-quality, diverse, and interesting books that offer a range of difficulty levels and are grouped by category.
- Label (or have students label) baskets with the topic, author, illustrator, series, genre, or theme.
- Give each student a personal book box for keeping books and other literacy materials.

RML 1

MGT.U2.RML1

Reading Minilesson Principle

Reading is thinking.

Getting Started with Independent Reading

You Will Need

- chart paper and markers

Academic Language / Important Vocabulary

- independent reading

Continuum Connection

- Give reasons (either text-based or from personal experience) to support thinking (pp. 69, 73)

Goal

Understand that reading is thinking and that independent reading time should be quiet and focused.

Rationale

When students understand that reading is thinking and understand the expectations for independent reading time, they spend this time reading silently, allowing themselves to do their best thinking about their reading.

Assess Learning

Observe students during independent reading time and notice if there is evidence of new learning based on the goal of this minilesson.

- Do students read silently during independent reading time?
- Do they understand and use the term *independent reading*?

Minilesson

To help students think about the minilesson principle, engage them in a discussion about how to work during independent reading time. Here is an example.

- Write *Reading Is Thinking* on chart paper.

  Reading is thinking. What are some of the things you might think about when you are reading?

- Record students' responses on the chart.

  What kind of classroom will help you to do your best thinking while you read?

  During independent reading time, read silently so everyone can do their best thinking.

Have a Try

Invite the students to talk with a partner about their reading.

> Think about a book that you are reading or that you read recently. What are some of the things you thought about while reading it? Turn and talk to your partner about the book.

- After students turn and talk, invite a few students to share their thinking.

Summarize and Apply

Summarize the learning and remind students to read silently during independent reading time.

> What will you do during independent reading time?
>
> Why is it important that you read silently?
>
> During independent reading time today, read a book silently. When we come back together, you will have the chance to share your thinking about your reading.

Reading Is Thinking

- characters
- setting
- author's message
- author's writing style
- something that surprised you
- something interesting you learned
- what might happen next
- your opinion about the book

Share

Following independent reading time, gather students together in the meeting area to talk about their books.

> Turn and talk to your partner about what you were thinking about the book you read today.

Extend the Lesson (Optional)

After assessing students' understanding, you might decide to extend the learning.

- Revisit the chart from time to time and invite students to add other things they have thought about while reading.

RML 2

MGT.U2.RML2

Reading Minilesson Principle

Share your thinking about books.

Getting Started with Independent Reading

You Will Need

- chart paper and markers
- a reader's notebook

Academic Language / Important Vocabulary

- independent reading
- turn and talk
- reader's notebook

Continuum Connection

- Give reasons (either text-based or from personal experience) to support thinking (pp. 69, 73)
- Engage actively in conversational routines (e.g., turn and talk) (p. 339)

Goal

Share thinking through talking and writing about reading.

Rationale

When you encourage students to share their thinking about books, they develop their identities as readers and deepen their understanding and appreciation of texts. They also strengthen their interpersonal and communication skills.

Assess Learning

Observe students when they share their thinking about books and notice if there is evidence of new learning based on the goal of this minilesson.

- Do students share their thinking about books both orally and in writing?
- Do they follow the turn and talk routine?
- Do they understand the terms *independent reading, turn and talk*, and *reader's notebook*?

Minilesson

To help students think about the minilesson principle, discuss different ways to share thinking about books. Here is an example.

> You know that during independent reading time, you will read a book silently and think about your reading. You will also share your thinking about books with your classmates and teacher. One way to share your thinking is by talking about your reading.

- Write the heading *Turn and Talk* on chart paper.

> When you turn and talk with a partner about your thinking, what would be important?

- Record students' responses under the heading.

> Another way to share your thinking about your reading is by writing about your thinking.

- Write the heading *Write About Your Thinking* on the chart.

> This year, you will learn how to write about your thinking in many ways. One place to write about your thinking is in your reader's notebook.

- Show a reader's notebook.

Have a Try

Invite the students to talk with a partner about their reading.

> Turn and talk to your partner about the book you are reading now or the last book you read. Look at what we wrote on the chart under Turn and Talk, and remember to do these things.

- After students turn and talk, invite several students to evaluate their discussion, using the chart for guidance.

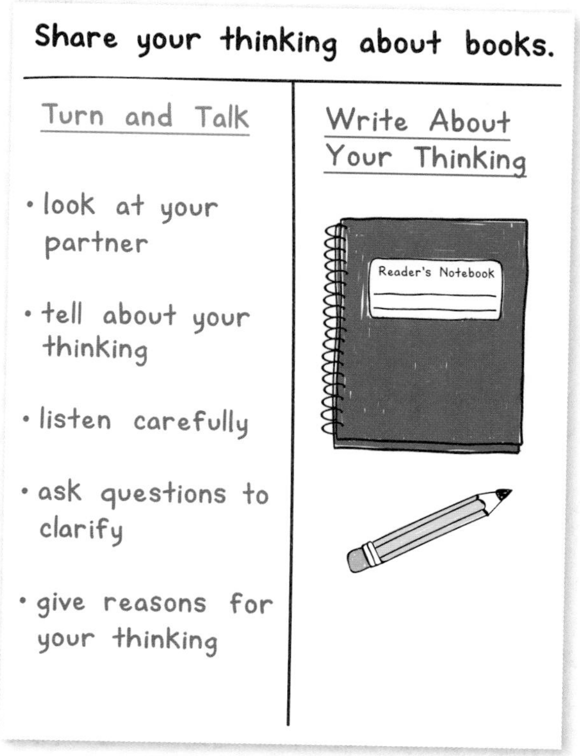

Share your thinking about books.

Turn and Talk	Write About Your Thinking
• look at your partner • tell about your thinking • listen carefully • ask questions to clarify • give reasons for your thinking	Reader's Notebook

Summarize and Apply

Summarize the learning and remind students to share their thinking about books.

- Write the principle at the top of the chart.

> When you read today, remember to read the book silently. When we come back together, you will have the opportunity to talk about what you were thinking as you read. Sometimes, you will also write about your thinking about your reading in a reader's notebook.

Share

Following independent reading time, gather students together in the meeting area to talk about their reading.

> Turn and talk to a partner and share your thinking about the book you read today. Remember to follow the guidelines on our chart.

Extend the Lesson (Optional)

After assessing students' understanding, you might decide to extend the learning.

- **Writing About Reading** Teach the minilessons in Section Four: Writing About Reading to formally introduce the reader's notebook and familiarize students with different ways of writing about reading.

RML 3

MGT.U2.RML3

Reading Minilesson Principle

Your book box is a place for your books and your personal materials.

Getting Started with Independent Reading

You Will Need

- for each student, a book box and materials to go inside (a book from the classroom library, a reader's notebook, a writer's notebook, a writing folder, a word study folder, and a poetry notebook)
- chart paper and markers

Academic Language / Important Vocabulary

- book box
- personal materials
- organized
- reader's notebook
- writer's notebook
- writing folder

Goal

Keep books and materials organized for use during independent reading time.

Rationale

When students understand that a book box is a place for personal literacy materials, know where to find it, and know how to keep it organized, they spend less time searching for materials and more time reading, writing, and learning.

Assess Learning

Observe students when they use their book boxes and notice if there is evidence of new learning based on the goal of this minilesson.

- Can students explain the purpose of a book box and the importance of keeping it organized?
- Do they keep their book boxes organized?
- Do they understand and use the terms *book box, personal materials, organized, reader's notebook, writer's notebook,* and *writing folder*?

Minilesson

To help students think about the minilesson principle, help them become familiar with their personal book boxes and engage them in a discussion about how to organize materials in a book box. Here is an example.

- Display a book box and the materials (not in the box) so that everyone can see them.

  Here are the materials that I would need during the time for independent reading and writing. I can throw them all in the box, but is there a better way to store them?

  How can I make sure that I have all my materials and can find them easily?

- Lead students to understand that if the materials are organized and kept in order, they will always be able to access what they need quickly and easily.

  Here's how I will organize my box. I will put in the book I am reading and maybe the one I want to read next because that's what I will want to get most often. Then I will put in my reader's notebook because I will use that often, too. Next, I'll put in my writer's notebook, writing folder, word study folder, and poetry notebook. What do you think?

- Record the order of materials on chart paper.

Have a Try

Invite the students to organize their own book boxes.

Get a book box and the materials that belong in it. Label the box with your name. Then put the materials in the order we listed on the chart.

Summarize and Apply

Summarize the learning and remind students to keep their book boxes organized.

At the beginning of the time for reading every day, go to your book box and get your book and your reader's notebook so you are prepared for your work.

- Write the principle at the top of the chart.

Today, read the book in your book box. If you want a different book, you can choose one from the classroom library. After you read, remember to put your book back in your box in the right place and be sure your materials are in order.

Your book box is a place for your books and your personal materials.

1. One or two books from the classroom library
2. Reader's notebook
3. Writer's notebook
4. Writing folder
5. Word study folder
6. Poetry notebook

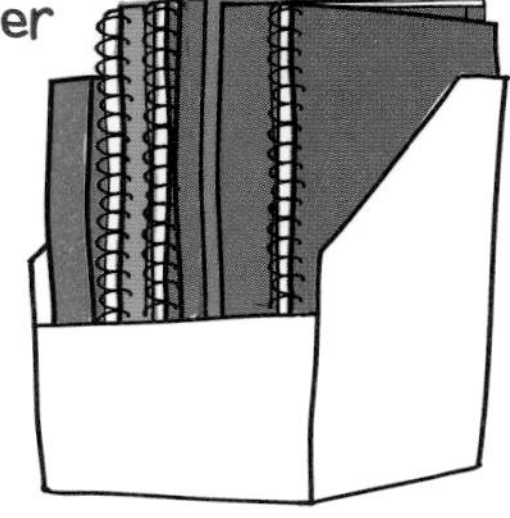

Share

Following independent reading time, gather students together in the meeting area to talk about their book boxes.

How did you use your book box today? Was it easy for you to find what you needed?

Extend the Lesson (Optional)

After assessing students' understanding, you might decide to extend the learning.

- You might have students add items to their book boxes throughout the school year. As you introduce each new item, discuss its purpose and remind students to keep their boxes organized.

RML 4

MGT.U2.RML4

Reading Minilesson Principle

The classroom library includes a variety of books for you to enjoy.

Getting Started with Independent Reading

You Will Need

- an organized, inviting classroom library
- several selected books from your classroom library (see Have a Try)
- sticky notes
- chart paper and markers

Academic Language / Important Vocabulary

- classroom library
- organized
- topic
- genre
- theme
- series

Goal

Understand that the classroom library is organized by illustrator, author, genre, series, theme, and topic to make finding books easier.

Rationale

When you teach students how the classroom library is organized, they are better able to find and select books that they will enjoy reading. As an alternative to the process suggested in this lesson, you could have your students sort books, create categories, and label the baskets with you.

Assess Learning

Observe students when they select books from the classroom library and notice if there is evidence of new learning based on the goal of this minilesson.

- Can students explain how and why the classroom library is organized?
- Do they use their understanding of the organization of the classroom library to choose books to read?
- Do they use the terms *classroom library*, *organized*, *topic*, *genre*, *theme*, and *series*?

Minilesson

To help students think about the minilesson principle, have them gather in the classroom library and engage them in a discussion about the organization of the books. Here is an example.

> Take a moment to look around and see what you notice about our classroom library.
>
> What do you notice about how the books in our classroom library are organized?

- Help students notice the specific ways the books are organized by asking questions such as the ones below. Alter the questions to reflect the specific categories of books available in your own classroom library, but try to include all the ways the books are organized (author, illustrator, genre, series, theme, topic, etc.).
  - *Where should I look if I want to read a book by S. D. Nelson?*
  - *What kind of books are in this basket?*
  - *Who can help me find the next book in the Anastasia Krupnik series?*
  - *Where can I look for books about achieving a dream?*
  - *Where can I look if I want to read nonfiction books?*
- Record each category of books that students notice (and an example of that category) on the chart paper.

Have a Try

Invite the students to talk with a partner about how to organize books in the classroom library.

- Divide students into small groups, and give each group a small stack of books from your classroom library. Each book should clearly correspond with a basket in your classroom library.

  Turn and talk to your group about where you think each of your books should go. Then write your decision on a sticky note and stick it on the front cover of the book.

- After students turn and talk, invite groups to share and explain their decisions.

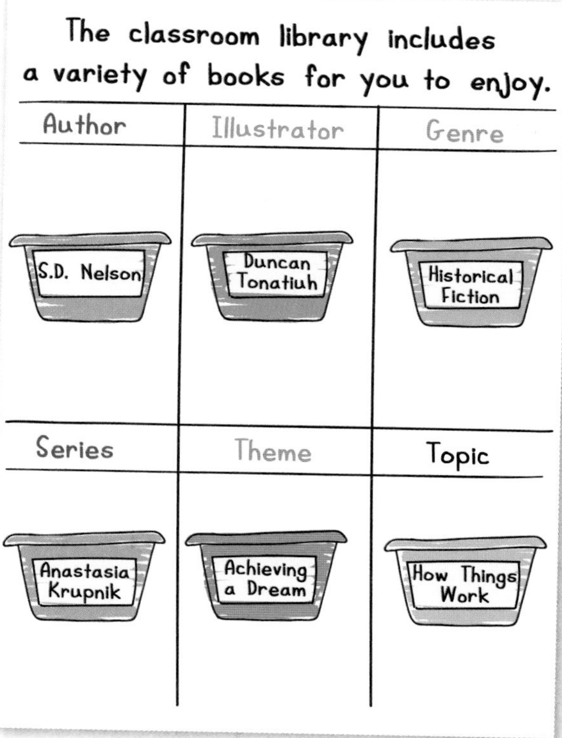

The classroom library includes a variety of books for you to enjoy.
Author
Illustrator
Genre
S.D. Nelson
Duncan Tonatiuh
Historical Fiction
Series
Theme
Topic
Anastasia Krupnik
Achieving a Dream
How Things Work

Summarize and Apply

Summarize the learning and remind students to use the organization of the classroom library to help them find and select books.

What did you notice about our classroom library?

- Write the principle at the top of the chart.

  Before you choose a book to read today, think about what kind of book you'd like to read. Maybe you would like to read a book from a particular genre or a book by your favorite author. Use what you learned today about our classroom library to help you find the kind of book that you want to read.

Share

Following independent reading time, gather students together in the meeting area to talk about the books they chose.

Turn and talk to your partner about the book you chose and where you found it.

How did the way our classroom library is organized help you find a book?

Extend the Lesson (Optional)

After assessing students' understanding, you might decide to extend the learning.

- Regularly rotate the books and categories of books available in your classroom library. Involve students in choosing new categories and in organizing new books.
- Give regular books talks about books you are adding to your classroom library or that you want to highlight.

RML 5
MGT.U2.RML5

Reading Minilesson Principle

Make good decisions about your book choices.

Getting Started with Independent Reading

You Will Need

- chart paper and markers

Academic Language / Important Vocabulary

- choice
- decision
- independent reading
- recommendation
- genre
- abandon

Continuum Connection

- Express tastes and preferences in reading and support choices with descriptions and examples of literary elements: e.g., genre, setting, plot, theme, character, style, and language (pp. 559, 569, 581)

Goal

Make good book choices for independent reading.

Rationale

When you teach students to be aware of the ways they choose books and to make good decisions about their reading, they spend more time reading books they enjoy. They also become more independent and confident, and they develop their interests and identities as readers. They are more likely to love reading and to become lifelong readers.

Assess Learning

Observe students when they choose books and talk about books they have chosen. Notice if there is evidence of new learning based on the goal of this minilesson.

- Can students explain why they chose a particular book?
- Do they vary their book choices in terms of genre, topic, and difficulty level?
- Do they give books a good try before abandoning them?
- Do they understand the terms *choice, decision, independent reading, recommendation, genre,* and *abandon*?

Minilesson

To help students think about the minilesson principle, engage them in a discussion about how to choose books. Here is an example.

With so many books available to choose from, sometimes it can be hard to choose the right book. One of the ways I choose books is by reading book reviews. What are some of the ways you choose books to read?

- Record responses on chart paper.

Also think about whether a book is easy, just right, or difficult for you. How do you know when you have picked a book that is just right for you?

- Record students' responses on the chart.

Sometimes readers choose to read books that are easy or a bit difficult. When might you decide to read an easy book?

When might you choose a book that is difficult?

- Record responses on the chart.

Sometimes you might want to read an easy book because you want to relax. Sometimes you might choose a book that is difficult because it is about something you really want to learn about. It is a good idea to choose a book that you can read with some challenges but not so many that you can't enjoy it.

Have a Try

Invite the students to talk with a partner about a book they chose recently.

Think about either the book you're reading now or the last book you read. Turn and talk to your partner about why you chose that book.

- After students turn and talk, invite a few students to share. Add any new ways to choose books to the chart.

Now turn and talk about whether the book you chose was a good choice for you. Be sure to explain the reasons why or why not.

- Ask a few students to share their thinking.

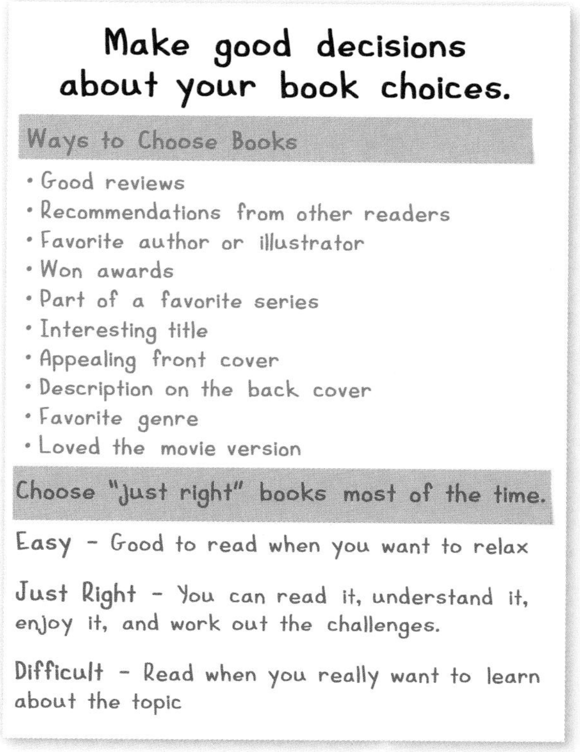

Make good decisions about your book choices.

Ways to Choose Books

- Good reviews
- Recommendations from other readers
- Favorite author or illustrator
- Won awards
- Part of a favorite series
- Interesting title
- Appealing front cover
- Description on the back cover
- Favorite genre
- Loved the movie version

Choose "just right" books most of the time.

Easy - Good to read when you want to relax

Just Right - You can read it, understand it, enjoy it, and work out the challenges.

Difficult - Read when you really want to learn about the topic

Summarize and Apply

Summarize the learning and remind students to make good decisions about book choices.

What did you learn today about choosing books?

Sometimes you may surprise yourself by loving a book that is different from what you usually read! However, sometimes you might start a book and find that it is not a good choice for you. If that happens, you can abandon it after you've given it a good try.

- Write the principle at the top of the chart.

If you choose a new book to read today, try to choose a book that you think you'll enjoy and that is just right for you. Be ready to share why you chose your book.

Share

Following independent reading time, gather students together in the meeting area to discuss the books they are reading.

Based on what you've read so far, do you think your book was a good choice for you? Why or why not?

Extend the Lesson (Optional)

After assessing students' understanding, you might decide to extend the learning.

- **Writing About Reading** Have students list in a reader's notebook books they have read and assess whether each book was a good choice (see WAR.U1.RML2).

Assessment

After you have taught the minilessons in this umbrella, observe students as they use classroom spaces and materials. Use *The Literacy Continuum* (Fountas and Pinnell 2017) to observe students' reading and writing behaviors.

- What evidence do you have of new understandings related to independent reading?
  - Are students able to find and select books?
  - Are they making good decisions about book choices?
  - Do they read silently during independent reading time?
  - Do they share their thinking about books both orally and in writing?
  - Do they understand that a book box is a place for their books and personal materials?
  - How well do they keep their personal materials organized in their book boxes?
  - Do they use terms such as *independent reading*, *book box*, *organized*, and *classroom library*?
- What other minilessons might you teach to help students grow and function as readers and as members of the classroom community?
  - Do students treat each other respectfully and inclusively?
  - Do they incorporate reading into their daily lives and make good choices about their reading?

Use your observations to determine the next umbrella you will teach. You may also consult Minilessons Across the Year (pp. 61–64) for guidance.

Reader's Notebook

When this umbrella is complete, provide a copy of the minilesson principles (see resources.fountasandpinnell.com) for students to glue in the reader's notebook (in the Minilessons section if using *Reader's Notebook: Advanced* [Fountas and Pinnell 2011]), so they can refer to the information as needed.

Minilessons in This Umbrella

RML1	Find out about books you might want to read.
RML2	Recommend a book by giving a book talk.
RML3	Learn how to give a good book talk.
RML4	Think about who influences your reading and whose reading you influence.
RML5	Reflect on your reading habits.
RML6	Challenge yourself to grow or stretch as a reader.
RML7	Dedicate time to read outside of school.

Independent Reading

Before Teaching Umbrella 3 Minilessons

The importance of literacy instruction extends far beyond the classroom. It is not enough to simply teach students the skills to comprehend what they read. Students who love reading, dedicate time to reading, and consider themselves readers have the greatest chance of success in school and beyond. The purpose of this umbrella is to help students develop lifelong reading habits. The minilessons guide students to dedicate time to reading both in school and outside of school, to reflect on their reading habits, and to develop their identities and preferences as readers. Before teaching this umbrella, provide students with several opportunities to choose, read, enjoy, share, and talk about books. For this umbrella, use the following books from the *Fountas & Pinnell Classroom™ Independent Reading Collection* or select books that your students will find engaging.

Independent Reading Collection

Deadly! The Truth About the Most Dangerous Creatures on Earth by Nicola Davies

Flora & Ulysses: The Illuminated Adventures by Kate DiCamillo

RML1
MGT.U3.RML1

Reading Minilesson Principle
Find out about books you might want to read.

Living a Reading Life

You Will Need

- chart paper and markers

Academic Language / Important Vocabulary

- recommendation
- review
- book talk

Continuum Connection

- Express tastes and preferences in reading and support choices with descriptions and examples of literary elements: e.g., genre, setting, plot, theme, character, style, and language (pp. 559, 581)

Goal

Find books using different resources both inside and outside of the classroom.

Rationale

When students learn about the many resources for finding books, they expand the book choices that they have available to them. They are therefore more likely to find books that they enjoy reading.

Assess Learning

Observe students when they talk about how they find out about books and notice if there is evidence of new learning based on the goal of this minilesson.

- Do students find out about books in a variety of ways?
- Do they talk about the different ways they find out about books?
- Do they use terms such as *recommendation*, *review*, and *book talk*?

Minilesson

To help students think about the minilesson principle, discuss different ways to find out about books. Here is an example.

Think about the book you are reading now or the last book you read. How did you find out about that book?

- List students' responses on chart paper.

What are some other ways that you can find out about books that you might like to read?

- Add responses to the chart. If necessary, use questions such as the following to encourage students to name ways to find out about books both inside and outside of school:
    - *What are some places in our school where you can find out about books?*
    - *What are some places outside of school where you can find out about books?*

Have a Try

Invite the students to talk with a partner about ways to find out about books.

> Turn and talk to your partner about which of these ways to find out about books you have already tried. Tell which you would like to try in the future. If you have any other ideas, share them with your partner as well.

- After students turn and talk, invite a few students to share their thinking.

Summarize and Apply

Summarize the learning and remind students to take advantage of these different ways to find out about books.

> Today you thought about different ways to find out about books you might want to read.

- Write the principle at the top of the chart.

> When you read today, take a moment to think about a way that you like to find out about new books to read. Be ready to share how that way of finding out about books is helpful when we come back together.

Find out about books you might want to read.

- classroom, school, or public library
- book talks by teacher or classmates
- librarian's recommendations
- recommendations from friends or family members
- bookstores (special displays and recommendations from booksellers)
- lists of books that have won awards
- book reviews in magazines or online
- websites about books
- online reading communities
- online bookstores
- blogs
- online videos
- author websites

Share

Following independent reading time, gather students together in the meeting area to share their thinking.

> Turn and talk to your partner about how you find out about books to read.
>
> What are you going to do next time you need a new book to read? Is anybody going to try something new?

Extend the Lesson (Optional)

After assessing students' understanding, you might decide to extend the learning.

- Use a section of your classroom library to feature books recommended by you or by particular students. Each recommended book should have a notecard explaining why it is recommended and the signature of the person who recommended it.
- Guide students in using various websites (e.g., Amazon, Goodreads) for finding out about new books to read. Encourage them to also use local resources, such as librarians at the school and public libraries.

RML 2

MGT.U3.RML2

Reading Minilesson Principle

Recommend a book by giving a book talk.

Living a Reading Life

You Will Need

- a book that most of your students haven't read, such as *Deadly!* by Nicola Davies, from *Independent Reading Collection*
- chart paper and markers

Academic Language / Important Vocabulary

- book talk
- recommend

Continuum Connection

- Express tastes and preferences in reading and support choices with descriptions and examples of literary elements: e.g., genre, setting, plot, theme, character, style, and language (pp. 559, 581)

Goal

Learn that a book talk is a short talk about a book (or series of books) and its purpose is to get others interested in reading it.

Rationale

Book talks give students the opportunity to share their enthusiasm for certain books with other readers. They also offer listeners a valuable opportunity for finding out about books that they might like to read.

Assess Learning

Observe students when they discuss book talks and notice if there is evidence of new learning based on the goal of this minilesson.

- Can students explain the features and purpose of a book talk?
- Do they use the terms *book talk* and *recommend*?

Minilesson

To help students think about the minilesson principle, give a model book talk about a book students have not read. Here is an example.

- Give a book talk about a book that all or most of your students haven't read. The example below uses *Deadly! The Truth About the Most Dangerous Creatures on Earth* by Nicola Davies. As you give the book talk, show a few appealing pages.

  Lions and tigers and bears . . . oh my! In this fascinating nonfiction book, author Nicola Davies shows that the natural world is not just sunshine and rainbows . . . sometimes it's nasty, brutal, and shocking. From snakes that spit poison to insects with exploding bottoms to killer cats with two-inch claws, this book has it all! And, the illustrations are hilarious. If you're curious about the dark side of the animal world, you're going to devour *Deadly! The Truth About the Most Dangerous Creatures on Earth.*

  What did you notice about how I talked about this book? What did I share about it?

  I gave a book talk about this book. What do you think a book talk is?

  What do you think is the purpose of a book talk?

- Record students' responses on chart paper.

Have a Try

Invite the students to talk with a partner about book talks.

> Why might you want to listen to someone giving a book talk? How can listening to book talks help you? Turn and talk to your partner about what you think.

- After students turn and talk, invite a few students to share their thinking. Record responses on the chart.

Summarize and Apply

Summarize the learning and remind students to use book talks to share book recommendations.

> What did you learn about book talks today?

- Write the principle at the top of the chart.

> You will have opportunities to give book talks this year. Today, start thinking about a book that you'd like to recommend. Think about what you might say about your book to get people excited. Be ready to share your thinking with a partner when we come back together.

Recommend a book by giving a book talk.

A book talk . . .

- is a short talk about a book.
- includes the title and the author's name.
- gives some information about the book without giving too much.
- explains why the speaker liked the book.
- gets others interested in the book.
- helps people find out about books that they might like to read.

Share

Following independent reading time, gather students in pairs to share their thinking.

> Turn and talk to your partner about the book that you'd like to recommend in a book talk. Tell at least one thing that you would say about this book in a book talk.

Extend the Lesson (Optional)

After assessing students' understanding, you might decide to extend the learning.

- **Writing About Reading** Tell students that they can write the titles of books they hear about in book talks on the Books to Read page in a reader's notebook (see WAR.U2.RML1).

RML 3
MGT.U3.RML3

Reading Minilesson Principle

Learn how to give a good book talk.

Living a Reading Life

You Will Need

- a book that is likely to be of interest to your students, such as *Flora & Ulysses* by Kate DiCamillo, from *Independent Reading Collection*
- a few notes about the book and some sticky notes in the book
- chart paper and markers
- notecards and sticky notes

Academic Language / Important Vocabulary

- book talk
- prepare
- present

Continuum Connection

- Speak at an appropriate volume (p. 341)
- Communicate interest in and enthusiasm about a topic (p. 342)
- Speak with confidence and in a relaxed manner (p. 342)

Goal

Prepare and present the book confidently, clearly, and enthusiastically.

Rationale

When students learn how to give a good book talk, they are better able to share their enthusiasm for books with other readers and they learn public speaking skills. They develop their identities as readers and foster a community where readers share and talk about books.

Assess Learning

Observe students when they give book talks and notice if there is evidence of new learning based on the goal of this minilesson.

- Do students prepare for giving engaging and effective book talks?
- Do they use the terms *book talk*, *prepare*, and *present*?

Minilesson

To help students think about the minilesson principle, provide a model book talk and then discuss the characteristics that make it effective. Here is an example.

- Prior to the lesson, make note of a few important ideas about *Flora & Ulysses: The Illuminated Adventures* on a notecard and place sticky notes on a few pages to share in the book talk.

  This is a superhero book unlike any other superhero book! After Ulysses the squirrel has an unfortunate run-in with a vacuum cleaner, his ten-year-old neighbor, Flora Bell, rushes over to save him. The girl and the squirrel become the best of friends and have all sorts of crazy adventures with a cast of wacky characters. This hilarious, bestselling book even won the Newbery Medal. The funny illustrations and comic strips make this book fun to read. If you're looking for a unique, laugh-out-loud funny story, *Flora & Ulysses: The Illuminated Adventures* by Kate DiCamillo is the book for you!

  What did you notice about how I gave my book talk?

- As needed, prompt the conversation with questions such as the following:
  - *What do you think I did to prepare for the book talk?*
  - *How did I position my body and use my hands?*
  - *How did I use my voice?*
  - *What information did I share?*
  - *How long was my book talk?*
- Record students' responses on chart paper.

Have a Try

Invite the students to talk with a partner about how to give a good book talk.

Turn and talk to your partner about what you think are the most important things to remember when giving a book talk. What do you absolutely have to do in order to give a good book talk?

- After students turn and talk, invite a few pairs to share their thinking. Add any new suggestions to the list.

Learn how to give a good book talk.

- Use an exciting introduction to get your audience interested in the book.
- Tell the title and author of the book.
- Write important words or phrases on a notecard or sticky note.
- Mark pages that you want to talk about.
- Practice your book talk.
- Hold the book so everyone can see it.
- Stand up straight and look at the audience.
- Be enthusiastic.
- Speak clearly and loudly.
- Tell why people should read the book.
- Keep it short.

Summarize and Apply

Summarize the learning and remind students to use the techniques they learned for giving a good book talk.

- Write the principle at the top of the chart.

What did you learn today about how to give a good book talk?

Today, choose a book that you've read and enjoyed and that you think your classmates might enjoy reading. Prepare to give a book talk about this book. When we come back together, you will present your book talk to a small group.

Share

Following independent reading time, gather students in small groups to present their book talks.

- Have each student present a book talk to the group.
- After students have presented, bring the whole class back together.

What worked well for you when you gave your book talk?

What will you do differently next time?

Extend the Lesson (Optional)

After assessing students' understanding, you might decide to extend the learning.

- Refer students to How to Give a Book Talk in *Reader's Notebook: Advanced* (Fountas and Pinnell 2011).
- Give book talks frequently to keep students' interest in reading good books high. For example, give a book talk when you introduce a new book to the classroom library or when you want to highlight a particular book.

RML 4

MGT.U3.RML4

Reading Minilesson Principle

Think about who influences your reading and whose reading you influence.

Living a Reading Life

You Will Need

- chart paper and markers

Academic Language / Important Vocabulary

- influence

Goal

Notice and identify the people or reading communities that influence reading choices.

Rationale

When students think about how they influence and are influenced by other readers, they begin to understand the importance of being part of a reading community. Students who develop reading relationships with other people are more likely to enjoy reading, to be confident about talking about their reading, and to become lifelong readers.

Assess Learning

Observe students when they talk about their reading influences and notice if there is evidence of new learning based on the goal of this minilesson.

- Can students identify other readers who influence them and whom they influence?
- Can they explain how they are influenced by and influence other readers?
- Do they understand the term *influence*?

Minilesson

To help students think about the minilesson principle, engage them in a discussion about reading influences. Here is an example, but use your own personal story.

> I just finished reading a great book that was recommended to me by my sister. My sister and I are always talking about books and recommending books to each other. She is one of the people who influences my reading, or has an effect on what I choose to read. Who are the people who influence your reading the most?
>
> How do they influence your reading?

- Use students' responses to create on chart paper a list of influential people and a list of ways readers influence other readers.

Have a Try

Invite the students to talk with a partner about whose reading they influence.

> Now I'd like you to think about whose reading you influence and how. Take a moment to think about this. Then turn and talk to your partner about how you influence the reading of other people.

- After students turn and talk, invite a few students to share. Add new ideas to the chart.

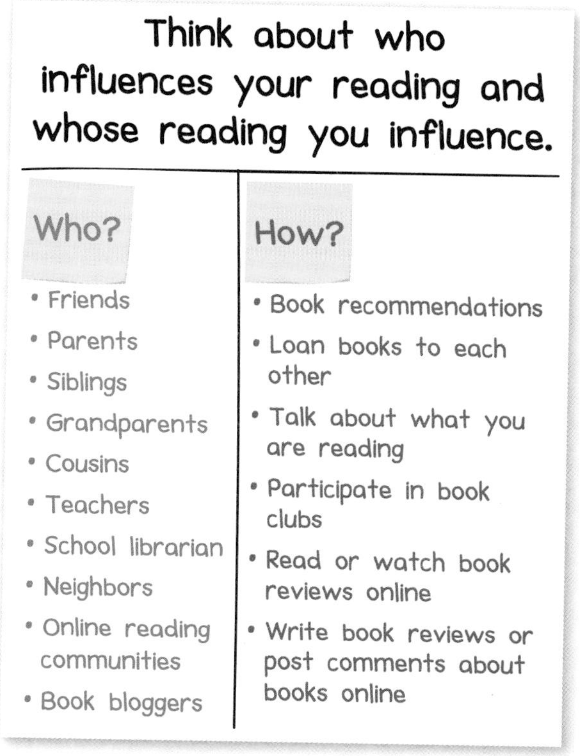

Think about who influences your reading and whose reading you influence.

Who?	How?
• Friends • Parents • Siblings • Grandparents • Cousins • Teachers • School librarian • Neighbors • Online reading communities • Book bloggers	• Book recommendations • Loan books to each other • Talk about what you are reading • Participate in book clubs • Read or watch book reviews online • Write book reviews or post comments about books online

Summarize and Apply

Summarize the learning and remind students to think about their relationships with other readers.

- Write the principle at the top of the chart.

> Why do you think it's important to influence and be influenced by other readers? How does this help you as a reader?
>
> Today, take five or ten minutes to write about how you influence other readers and they influence you. Give specific examples. Be ready to share your thinking when we come back together.

Share

Following independent reading time, gather students together in the meeting area to talk about their reading influences.

> Would anyone like to share something they wrote or thought about how they influence or are influenced by other readers?

Extend the Lesson (Optional)

After assessing students' understanding, you might decide to extend the learning.

- When you hold individual reading conferences, ask students who or what influenced their decision to read a particular book.

RML 5

MGT.U3.RML5

Reading Minilesson Principle

Reflect on your reading habits.

Living a Reading Life

You Will Need

- chart paper and markers

Academic Language / Important Vocabulary

- reflect
- reading habits

Goal

Reflect on reading habits including text selection, commitment, engagement level, etc.

Rationale

When students reflect on their reading habits, they get to know themselves as readers. They develop their identities as readers and identify potential areas for growth. They become more engaged readers and are more likely to become lifelong readers.

Assess Learning

Observe students when they reflect on their reading habits and notice if there is evidence of new learning based on the goal of this minilesson.

- Do students reflect on their reading habits (text selection, commitment, engagement level, etc.)?
- Can they identify areas where they might change or strengthen their reading habits?
- Do they use the terms *reflect* and *reading habits*?

Minilesson

To help students think about the minilesson principle, engage them in a discussion about how to reflect on their reading habits. Here is an example.

> We've been talking about how to find books you want to read and how other people influence your reading choices. When you thought about these things, you were reflecting on your reading. What does it mean to reflect?
>
> When you reflect on something, you think seriously and carefully about it. Take a moment to think about yourself as a reader. Would you say that you are successful at choosing books to read? Why or why not?

- Invite a few students to share. Then continue the conversation with a few more questions such as the following:
  - *Do you read across a variety of genres? Why or why not?*
  - *Do you stay committed when you choose a book to read, or do you abandon books easily? If you often abandon books, why do you think that is?*
  - *Are you excited or bored by most of the things you read? If you are often bored, why do you think that is?*
- Write each question that you discuss on chart paper.

Have a Try

Invite the students to reflect on their reading habits with a partner.

How much time do you spend reading in a typical day? Is that enough or not enough time? If it's not enough, what prevents you from reading? Turn and talk to your partner about your answers.

- After students turn and talk, invite a few students to share their thinking.

Summarize and Apply

Summarize the learning and remind students to reflect on their reading habits.

What are some of the things you can think about when you reflect on your reading habits?

Why is it important to reflect on your reading habits?

- Write the principle at the top of the chart.

When you read today, take a few minutes to reflect on your reading habits in your reader's notebook (or on a sheet of paper). You might choose to write about one of the questions on our list, or you can think of your own question to respond to. Be ready to share your thinking when we come back together.

Reflect on your reading habits.

- Are you successful at choosing books to read?
- Do you read across a variety of genres?
- Are you committed to your reading?
- Are you excited by your reading?
- How much time do you dedicate to reading?
- Do you talk to others about your reading?

Share

Following independent reading time, gather students together in the meeting area to share their thinking.

How did you reflect on your reading habits today? What did you think and write about?

Extend the Lesson (Optional)

After assessing students' understanding, you might decide to extend the learning.

- Refer students to Tips for Choosing Books in *Reader's Notebook: Advanced* (Fountas and Pinnell 2011).
- **Writing About Reading** Have students keep a list in a reader's notebook of the books they have read (see WAR.U1.RML2). Encourage them to briefly reflect on one or two of their reading choices (e.g., how they chose the book, their reaction to it, was it a good choice).

RML 6
MGT.U3.RML6

Reading Minilesson Principle

Challenge yourself to grow or stretch as a reader.

Living a Reading Life

You Will Need

- chart paper and markers

Academic Language / Important Vocabulary

- reading plan
- goal
- challenge

Goal

Make reading plans to stretch and grow as a reader.

Rationale

When students make plans for their reading, they are more likely to maintain their reading habits and develop their competencies and identities as readers. Examples of reading plans include reading more books, spending more time reading at home, reading more challenging books, and reading different genres of books.

Assess Learning

Observe students when they set, work toward, and discuss their reading plans and notice if there is evidence of new learning based on the goal of this minilesson.

- Do students make personalized reading plans that are challenging but realistic?
- Do they stay committed to their reading plans? If not, do they reflect on the reasons and adjust their reading plans as appropriate?
- Do they use the terms *reading plan*, *goal*, and *challenge*?

Minilesson

To help students think about the minilesson principle, engage them in a discussion about their reading goals and plans. Here is an example.

With so many wonderful books to choose from, sometimes it's hard to decide what to read next! One thing that I like to do is keep a list of the books that I want to read. When I finish a book on my list, I cross it off and choose another. Do you keep a list of books you'd like to read? What books do you plan to read?

Thinking about what books you want to read in the future is a type of reading plan. A plan is a list of your goals. A reading plan can be just one goal or a few more, but don't set so many goals that you can't accomplish them. Having a plan for what to read next helps you grow as a reader. In what other ways can you challenge yourself to grow as a reader?

- Record students' responses on chart paper. Use questions such as the following to prompt the conversation, as needed:
  - *What goal could I set to read more outside of school?*
  - *If I only read nonfiction books, how could I challenge myself to read other kinds of books?*
  - *If the books I read are too easy for me, and I get bored while reading them, what reading plan might I make?*

Have a Try

Invite the students to talk with a partner about what book they would like to read next.

> Turn and talk to your partner about one book or type of book that you'd like to read soon.

- After students turn and talk, invite a few students to share with the class.

Summarize and Apply

Summarize the learning and remind students to always have a plan for challenging themselves as readers.

> Why is it important to have a reading plan?

- Write the principle at the top of the chart.

> Today, take about ten minutes to think about how you are going to challenge yourself to grow or stretch as a reader this year. What reading plans would you like to make for yourself? Write down at least one way that you are going to challenge yourself this year.

Challenge yourself to grow or stretch as a reader.

Examples of reading plans:

- Read Winter Frost by Michelle Houts next.
- Read 50 books this year.
- Read for at least an hour every day.
- Try reading books that are more challenging.
- Read the whole Anastasia Krupnik series.
- Read 10 biographies this year.
- Read more fiction books.

Share

Following independent reading time, gather students together in the meeting area to discuss their reading plans.

> Who made a reading plan for themselves that they would like to share?

Extend the Lesson (Optional)

After assessing students' understanding, you might decide to extend the learning.

- Consider using the Reading Requirements page in *Reader's Notebook: Advanced* (Fountas and Pinnell 2011) as a way for students to set goals for reading different kinds of books.
- At the end of the school year, encourage students to set goals for summer reading.
- **Writing About Reading** Have students make lists in a reader's notebook of books they want to read or other reading goals that they have set for themselves.

RML 7
MGT.U3.RML7

Reading Minilesson Principle

Dedicate time to read outside of school.

Living a Reading Life

You Will Need

- chart paper and markers

Academic Language / Important Vocabulary

- classroom library
- personal reading

Goal

Find more time to read outside of school.

Rationale

Students who spend time reading outside of school on a regular basis do better in school and are more likely to love reading and become lifelong readers. Many people, adults and children, find it challenging to find time to read, and this minilesson offers suggestions for carving out more reading time.

Assess Learning

Observe students when they talk about their reading habits and notice if there is evidence of new learning based on the goal of this minilesson.

- Do students report that they read outside of school on a regular basis?
- Do they use the terms *classroom library* and *personal reading*?

Minilesson

To help students think about the minilesson principle, engage them in a discussion about reading outside of school. Here is an example.

> When you read books that you choose, that means you are in charge of yourself as a reader. You are independent. You are making personal choices, and you'll be doing this all your life. Your choices are not only about the book to read; you also choose where and when you will read. Does anyone have a special place outside of school where you like to read? Why do you like that place?

- Record students' responses on chart paper.

> Sometimes it is hard to find enough time to read all the books we want to read.
>
> One way that I've found to have more time to read is to bring a book with me everywhere I go. For example, if I am on a trip in a car or airplane, I make sure to bring a book along. If you always have a book with you, you can spend a few minutes reading whenever you have a little bit of spare time. Does anyone else have any tips for finding time to read?

Have a Try

Invite the students to talk with a partner about their reading habits.

> Turn and talk to your partner about whether finding time to read outside of school is easy or challenging for you. Be sure to explain the reasons why.

- After time for discussion, invite several students to share. If some students express obstacles to reading outside of school, collectively brainstorm ways to overcome them.

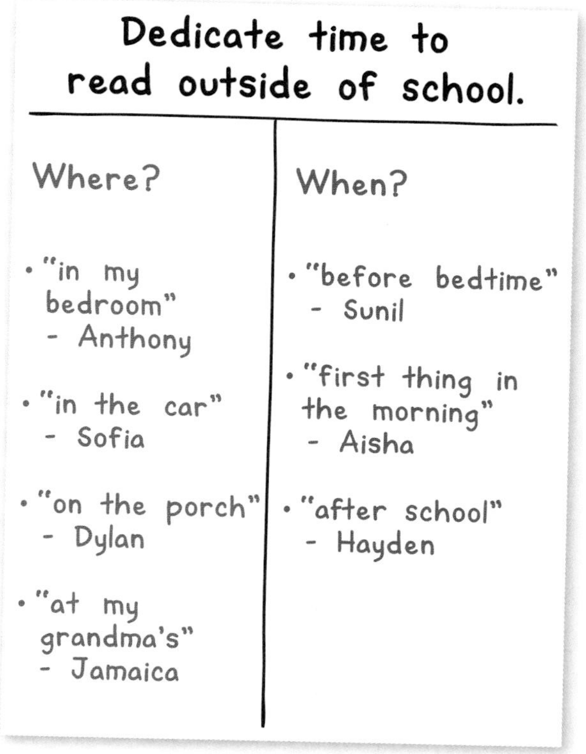

Summarize and Apply

Summarize the learning and remind students to dedicate time to reading outside of school.

> We talked about when and where you like to read and about ways to find more time to read. What are some of the ways we talked about?

- Write the principle at the top of the chart.

> Today, take about ten minutes to think and write about your reading time outside of school. You might write about your favorite time and place to read. You may also write about ways that you could find more time to read.

Dedicate time to read outside of school.

Where?	When?
• "in my bedroom" - Anthony	• "before bedtime" - Sunil
• "in the car" - Sofia	• "first thing in the morning" - Aisha
• "on the porch" - Dylan	• "after school" - Hayden
• "at my grandma's" - Jamaica	

Share

Following independent reading time, gather students together in the meeting area to discuss their plans for reading outside of school.

> What ideas do you have for how you could find more time to read outside of school?

Extend the Lesson (Optional)

After assessing students' understanding, you might decide to extend the learning.

- Regularly invite students to talk about the books they read outside of school.
- During individual reading conferences with students, discuss their reading habits and, if applicable, make a plan for overcoming obstacles to reading outside of school.

Assessment

After you have taught the minilessons in this umbrella, observe students as they talk about their reading. Use *The Literacy Continuum* (Fountas and Pinnell 2017) to guide the observation of students' reading and writing behaviors.

- What evidence do you have of new understandings related to living a reading life?
    - Do students actively seek out new books they might want to read?
    - Do they recommend books to classmates, sometimes in a book talk?
    - Do they think about who influences their reading and whose reading they influence?
    - Do they reflect on their reading habits?
    - Do they make reading plans that help them grow and stretch as readers?
    - Do they view themselves as readers?
    - Do they regularly spend time reading outside of school?
    - Do they use terms such as *classroom library, personal reading, recommend, book talk, influence*, and *reading habits*?
- What other minilessons might you teach to maintain and grow independent reading habits?
    - Do students know how to find books that interest them in the classroom library?
    - Do they keep their personal literacy materials organized?

Use your observations to determine the next umbrella you will teach. You may also consult Minilessons Across the Year (pp. 61–64) for guidance.

Reader's Notebook

When this umbrella is complete, provide a copy of the minilesson principles (see resources.fountasandpinnell.com) for students to glue in the reader's notebook (in the Minilessons section if using *Reader's Notebook: Advanced* [Fountas and Pinnell 2011]), so they can refer to the information as needed.

Section 2 Literary Analysis

Literary Analysis minilessons support students' growing awareness of the elements of literature and the writer's and illustrator's craft. The minilessons help students learn how to think analytically about texts and to identify the characteristics of fiction and nonfiction genres. The books that you read during interactive read-aloud can serve as mentor texts when applying the principles of literary analysis.

2 Literary Analysis

Fiction and Nonfiction

Nonfiction

Fiction

Minilessons in This Umbrella

RML1	Choose a book you would like to read and talk about.
RML2	Mark places you want to talk about.
RML3	Talk about your thinking in book clubs.
RML4	Ask questions to clarify understanding.
RML5	Give directions to help everyone get to a specific place in the book quickly.

Before Teaching Umbrella 1 Minilessons

The minilessons in this umbrella are designed to help you introduce and teach procedures and routines to establish book clubs in your classroom. Book clubs (pp. 74–76) are meetings facilitated by the teacher with about six students of varying reading abilities who come together to discuss a common text. The goal is for students to share their thinking with each other and build a richer meaning than one reader could gain alone. You may want to conduct a fishbowl lesson to demonstrate how a book club discussion works, either before selected minilessons as a model or afterward as a reflection. This umbrella will take students through the first set in the *Book Clubs Collection*. Based on RML1, students will choose a book club book. Then, after each lesson, you can meet with a different book club. The minilessons in this umbrella use the following books from the *Fountas & Pinnell Classroom™ Book Clubs Collection* and *Interactive Read-Aloud Collection* text sets; however, you can use other book sets from your classroom. Refer to the *Book Clubs Collection* cards for book summaries to use for book talks and additional discussion ideas.

Book Clubs Collection

Empathy

A Handful of Stars by Cynthia Lord

The Gift-Giver by Joyce Hansen

Save Me a Seat by Sarah Weeks and Gita Varadarajan

Amina's Voice by Hena Khan

Interactive Read-Aloud Collection

Empathy

My Man Blue by Nikki Grimes

Book Clubs Collection

Empathy

Interactive Read-Aloud

Empathy

RML 1

LA.U1.RML1

Reading Minilesson Principle

Choose a book you would like to read and talk about.

Getting Started with Book Clubs

You Will Need

- prepared book talks for four books students have not read or heard, such as the following from the *Book Clubs Collection* Text Set: Empathy:
  - *A Handful of Stars* by Cynthia Lord
  - *The Gift-Giver* by Joyce Hansen
  - *Save Me a Seat* by Sarah Weeks and Gita Varadarajan
  - *Amina's Voice* by Hena Khan
- chart paper and markers
- sticky notes
- a slip of paper for each student that has the four book club titles written on it
- To download the following online resource visit **resources.fountasandpinnell.com**: Book Talks

Academic Language / Important Vocabulary

- book club
- title
- author
- illustrator
- choice
- preference

Continuum Connection

- Form and express opinions about a text and support with rationale and evidence (pp. 69, 73)

Goal

Make a good book choice for book club meetings.

Rationale

When students make their own choices about what to read, they are more engaged and motivated to read. This contributes to a positive book club experience and increases the possibility of a lifelong love of reading.

Assess Learning

Observe students when they choose books for book club meetings and notice if there is evidence of new learning based on the goal of this minilesson.

- Are students able to identify information that will help them select a book they want to read?
- Do they express and reflect on the reasons they choose particular books to read?
- Do they use the terms *book club, title, author, illustrator, choice,* and *preference*?

Minilesson

To help students think about the minilesson principle, demonstrate the process of choosing a book for book club and help students reflect on that process. Here is an example.

> Think about your interest in each of these four books as I tell you a little about them.

- Show the cover of *A Handful of Stars*.

> Lily's blind dog, Lucky, disappears into a huge blueberry field. Salma, a migrant family member, is able to catch him. The girls strike up a friendship despite the fact that in their small community residents and migrant workers don't usually associate with one another. But, when Salma decides to enter the Blueberry Queen pageant, normally reserved only for local residents, the girls have to question the true meaning of their friendship.

- Turn through a few pages.

> What are some reasons why this book about Lucky the dog, Lily, and Salma might be enjoyable to read?

- Continue giving short book talks for the other three books (use your own book talks or the prepared book talks in online resources).

> You have now listened to a book talk about four different books. Think about your preferences.

Have a Try

Invite the students to talk with a partner about which book interests them.

> Turn and talk to a partner about your first and second choices.

- After time for discussion, ask student to share their thinking.

Summarize and Apply

Summarize the learning for students.

> We talked about different reasons you might choose a book for your book club meeting.
>
> During reading today, fill out the sheet of paper to show your preferences for a book club book. Number the books in the order you want to read them. Number one will be your first choice. Be sure to put your name on the paper.

- While students are reading, collect the numbered slips of paper and create four book clubs. Make a chart to show when each club will meet.

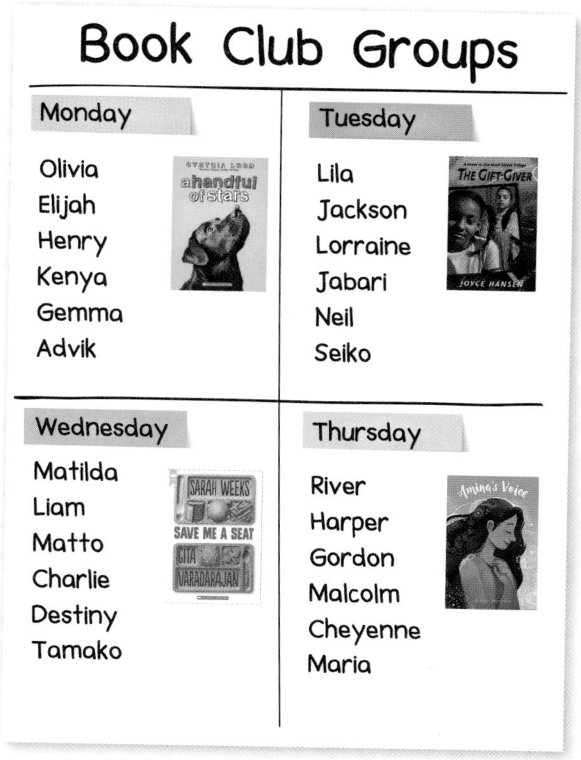

Book Club Groups

Monday	Tuesday
Olivia Elijah Henry Kenya Gemma Advik (Cynthia Lord, *a handful of stars*)	Lila Jackson Lorraine Jabari Neil Seiko (*The Gift-Giver*, Joyce Hansen)

Wednesday	Thursday
Matilda Liam Matto Charlie Destiny Tamako (Sarah Weeks, Gita Varadarajan, *Save Me a Seat*)	River Harper Gordon Malcolm Cheyenne Maria (*Amina's Voice*)

Share

Following independent reading time, gather students in the meeting area.

> This chart shows which group you will be in for the first book club of the year. It also shows when your book club will meet. Turn and talk to a partner about what you think you will enjoy about the book.
>
> Between now and your first book club meeting, read the book and think of something to ask or talk about.

Extend the Lesson (Optional)

After assessing students' understanding, you might decide to extend the learning.

- After the first round of book club meetings, use the same set of books for a second round, asking students to choose a different book. Use the opportunity to explain that not everyone will get to read their first choice every time.

RML2

LA.U1.RML2

Reading Minilesson Principle

Mark places you want to talk about.

Getting Started with Book Clubs

You Will Need

- a familiar book, such as the following:
    - *My Man Blue* by Nikki Grimes, from *Interactive Read-Aloud Collection* Text Set: Empathy
- chart paper and markers
- sticky notes prepared with page numbers and a few words indicating discussion topics, placed on corresponding pages in *My Man Blue*
- document camera (optional)
- set of book club books

Academic Language / Important Vocabulary

- book club
- sticky notes

Continuum Connection

- Form and express opinions about a text and support with rationale and evidence (pp. 69, 73)

Goal

Identify the important information to discuss in preparation for a book club.

Rationale

When students learn to note parts of a book they want to discuss, they think critically about the book and develop a process for preparing for a discussion.

Assess Learning

Observe students when they discuss the books they are reading and notice if there is evidence of new learning based on the goal of this minilesson.

- Do students understand the purpose of noting pages in a book?
- Are they able to identify and mark relevant pages in a book to prepare for a book club meeting?
- Do they understand the terms *book club* and *sticky notes*?

Minilesson

To help students think about the minilesson principle, use a familiar book to model how to prepare for a book club meeting by marking pages with sticky notes. Here is an example.

- Show the cover of *My Man Blue* with the sticky notes showing.

    Imagine that this book you know, *My Man Blue*, is the book I am reading for book club. While I was reading the book, I thought of some things I'd like to talk about in a book club meeting.

- Show page 5 with the first sticky note.

    On page 5, I placed a sticky note on which I wrote: *Page 5, Blue's motivation for being friends*. I wrote this note to remember to talk about the fact that Blue lost his own son, so he is trying to make up for it by being a mentor for another boy. The note helps me remember the page and what I want to talk about on the page.

- Place the sticky note on the chart. Below, write *insight into characters* to show that this is a type of information that would be interesting to discuss in a book club meeting.
- Continue discussing the other sticky notes in the book, placing them on the chart and adding a general term for the type of information that can be discussed.

Have a Try

Invite the students to talk with a partner about using sticky notes to prepare for book club meetings.

> Turn and talk about the kinds of interesting information a sticky note can help you remember in a book.

- After time for discussion, ask students to share ideas. Add new ideas to the chart list.

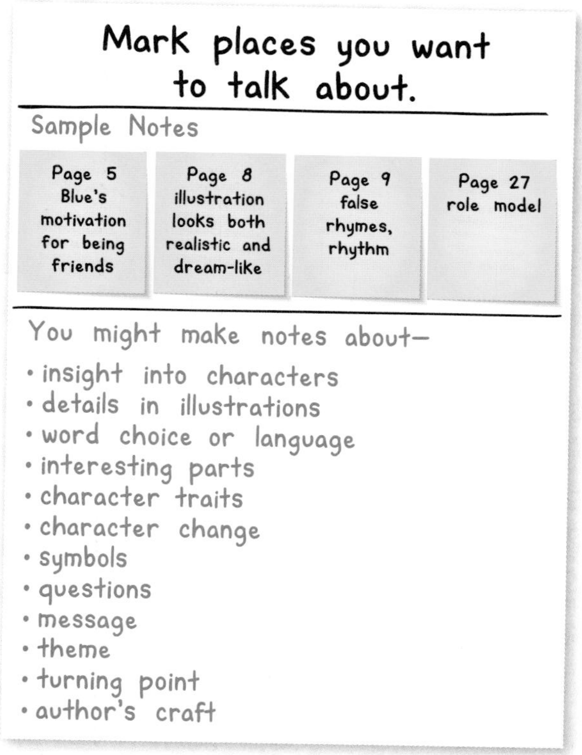

Summarize and Apply

Summarize the learning and remind students to use sticky notes to prepare for book club discussions.

> What did you learn about preparing for a book club discussion?

- Add the principle to the top of the chart.

> When you read today, use a few sticky notes to prepare for your book club meeting. Remember to add the page number in case the sticky note falls off. Write just a few words on the note, like the examples you see on the chart. Bring the book when we meet so you can share.

- During independent reading time, meet with one of the book club groups.

Mark places you want to talk about.

Sample Notes

Page 5 Blue's motivation for being friends	Page 8 illustration looks both realistic and dream-like	Page 9 false rhymes, rhythm	Page 27 role model

You might make notes about—

- insight into characters
- details in illustrations
- word choice or language
- interesting parts
- character traits
- character change
- symbols
- questions
- message
- theme
- turning point
- author's craft

Share

Following independent reading time, gather students in pairs.

> Share the pages that you marked with a sticky note. Tell your partner why you wanted to remember that page.

Extend the Lesson (Optional)

After assessing students' understanding, you might decide to extend the learning.

- As an alternative to using sticky notes, teach the students how to use a Thinkmark (visit resources.fountasandpinnell.com). Students can fill in a Thinkmark for books they have read and want to talk about in a book club or a conference.

RML 3

LA.U1.RML3

Reading Minilesson Principle

Talk about your thinking in book clubs.

Getting Started with Book Clubs

You Will Need

- students' book club books
- a book that you are reading yourself
- chart paper and markers

Academic Language / Important Vocabulary

- author
- illustrator
- book club
- discussion

Continuum Connection

- Form and express opinions about a text and support with rationale and evidence (pp. 69, 73)
- Identify and discuss interesting, surprising, and important information in a text (p. 73)

Goal

Brainstorm different ways of talking about books during book club.

Rationale

When students learn to share ideas in a book club, the activity expands comprehension, creates enthusiasm for reading, and contributes to rich conversations. You may wish to have one group of students model how to hold a book club by staging a fishbowl discussion (p. 76).

Assess Learning

Observe students when they meet for book club and notice if there is evidence of new learning based on the goal of this minilesson.

- Are students expressing opinions about books?
- Are they trying out new ways to talk about books?
- Do they use the terms *author, illustrator, book club,* and *discussion*?

Minilesson

To help students think about the minilesson principle, help them think about what they might want to talk about in book club. Here is an example.

- Show a fiction book that you are reading yourself. (Adjust language for a nonfiction book.)

  Here is the book that I am reading. I really enjoy the characters and the setting. If I meet with friends who also are reading this book, what do you think I might talk about?

- Create a chart to write ideas about what to talk about in book club. Add the ideas you shared.

  Think about the book you have been reading for your book club. What are some of the things you find interesting to talk about in book club about the book?

- As students share ideas, add to the list. Prompt the conversation as needed.

Have a Try

Invite the students to talk with a partner about book club discussion ideas.

> Turn and talk about the book you are reading for your book club. What would you like to talk about with your book club members?

- After time for discussion, ask students to share. Add new ideas to the chart.

Talk about your thinking in book clubs.

- title, author, illustrator
- characters' behaviors and thoughts
- dialogue
- setting
- plot
- high point
- flashbacks
- an illustration
- a part that is interesting, funny, confusing, exciting, or surprising
- the genre
- words or phrases that you like
- symbolism
- predictions
- social issues
- author's message
- theme
- author's point of view
- topic
- organizational structure

Summarize and Apply

Summarize the learning and remind students to think about what they might talk about in book club meetings.

> Today you talked about a range of topics you might discuss in book club meetings.
>
> As you read your book club book today, think about what you would like to talk about and whether there is anything else to add to the chart. I will be meeting with one book club, and those students will be sharing about their book during our class meeting.

- During independent reading time, meet with one of the book club groups.

Share

Following independent reading time, gather students in the meeting area. Have the book club members you met with share the things they discussed in their book club. Then invite the class to talk about new ideas.

> Is there anything that you want to add to the chart based on what the book club members shared with you?

Extend the Lesson (Optional)

After assessing students' understanding, you might decide to extend the learning.

- **Writing About Reading** Have students glue a list of items (visit resources.fountasandpinnell.com) they can reflect on into a reader's notebook as a reference for thinking and writing about books.

RML 4
LA.U1.RML4

Reading Minilesson Principle
Ask questions to clarify understanding.

Getting Started with Book Clubs

You Will Need

- four students who have written prepared questions about a book club book on sticky notes
- the book club selection that students will be sharing, such as the following:
  - *Save Me a Seat* by Sarah Weeks and Gita Varadarajan, from *Book Clubs Collection* Text Set: Empathy
- students' book club selections
- sticky notes
- chart paper and markers

Academic Language / Important Vocabulary

- book club
- questions
- phrase
- clarify

Continuum Connection

- Monitor own understanding of others' comments and ask for clarification and elaboration (p. 339)

Goal

Ask questions to clarify understandings about the book and about one another's thinking.

Rationale

When students learn to ask questions to clarify understanding, they learn how to engage in rich conversations about books and to converse with others to understand their thinking.

Assess Learning

Observe students during book club meetings and notice if there is evidence of new learning based on the goal of this minilesson.

- Are students asking relevant, thoughtful questions during book club meetings?
- Do they understand the terms *book club, questions, phrase,* and *clarify*?

Minilesson

To help students think about the minilesson principle, engage them in a discussion about how to ask genuine questions to clarify the understanding and interpretation of a book. Here is an example.

- Gather students in the meeting area so they can all view the chart.

  Today, several book club members are going to share the questions they prepared for their book club selection, *Save Me a Seat.*

- Have the book club members read their questions aloud one at a time and, as they do, add sticky notes with the questions across the top of the chart.

  What do you notice about the book club members' questions?

  These are some questions that your classmates had when they read *Save Me a Seat*. Sometimes there is something in a book that doesn't quite make sense, or you want to know more about something. You can ask questions like these in a book club meeting. The questions help you to think together about the book's meaning. Let's look at how these questions were formed.

- Guide students to notice that they, too, can start questions in a similar way. Make a list on the chart of question and wonderings starters.

  When someone asks a question to understand the book better, you can respond. What are some ways that you might start a response to questions that start like the ones in our list?

- Guide students to come up with response frames that they can refer to in their next book club meetings. Record on the chart.

Have a Try

Invite the students to ask questions about their book club books in small groups.

> In your small group, practice asking a question or wondering about something in the book club book you are reading. Some of you can ask a question and some of you can practice responding.

- After time for discussion, ask students to share what they shared with their group members. Write additional responses on the chart.

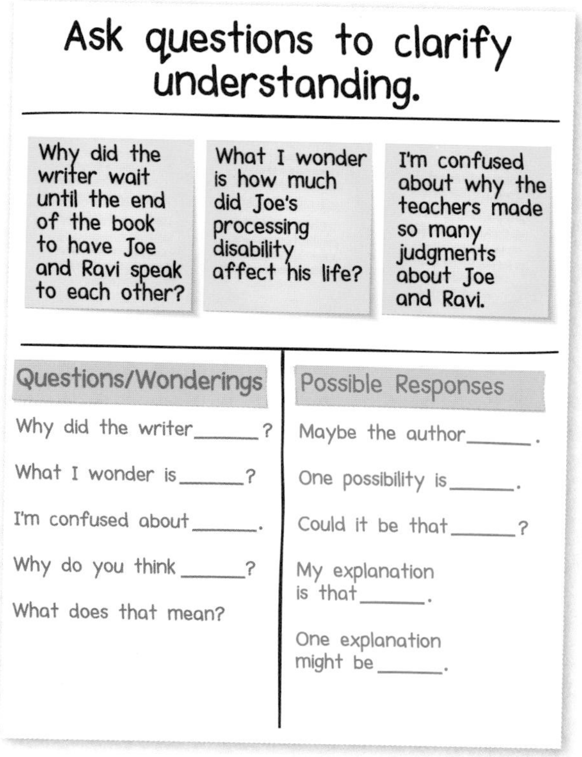

Ask questions to clarify understanding.

Why did the writer wait until the end of the book to have Joe and Ravi speak to each other?	What I wonder is how much did Joe's processing disability affect his life?	I'm confused about why the teachers made so many judgments about Joe and Ravi.

Questions/Wonderings	Possible Responses
Why did the writer_____?	Maybe the author_____.
What I wonder is_____?	One possibility is_____.
I'm confused about_____.	Could it be that_____?
Why do you think_____?	My explanation is that_____.
What does that mean?	One explanation might be_____.

Summarize and Apply

Summarize the learning and remind students to think about questions they want to ask during book club meetings.

- Add the principle to the top of the chart. Remind students to refer to the chart during their book club meetings.

> If you are reading your book club selection today and you get confused or wonder about something, write it on a sticky note. You can phrase it like one of the questions on the chart. If you are meeting with me today for book club, bring any questions you have about the book so we can talk about them.

- During independent reading time, meet with one of the book club groups.

Share

Following independent reading time, gather students in the meeting area to talk about asking questions during a book club meeting.

> Why is your book club meeting a good place to talk about the questions you might have about what you read?

- Guide the conversation so students understand the value of getting multiple perspectives.

Extend the Lesson (Optional)

After assessing students' understanding, you might decide to extend the learning.

- Introduce higher-level questions as students become more proficient with asking questions during book club. If you have *Fountas & Pinnell Prompting Guide, Part 2, for Comprehension: Thinking, Talking, and Writing* (Fountas and Pinnell 2009), refer to Section IV: Prompts for Book Discussions.

RML 5

LA.U1.RML5

Reading Minilesson Principle

Give directions to help everyone get to a specific place in the book quickly.

Getting Started with Book Clubs

You Will Need

- chart paper prepared with a sketch of an open book, or a book and document camera
- markers
- students' book club books

Academic Language / Important Vocabulary

- directions
- specific place
- line
- paragraph
- caption
- panel

Goal

Understand how to give directions for everyone to locate the same section of a text.

Rationale

When students learn to use precise language to ensure that everyone can locate the same section of a text, they improve their conversational skills and their ability to talk about books with specific evidence.

Assess Learning

Observe students when they talk about books to notice evidence of new learning based on the goal of this minilesson.

- Can students follow and use specific language to identify sections of a text?
- Do they use the terms *directions, specific place, line, paragraph, caption,* and *panel*?

Minilesson

To help students think about the minilesson principle, help them practice using directional language to ensure they can locate a specific place in a book quickly. Here is an example.

- Display the prepared chart or use a document camera to project the pages of a book. (If you use a book and document camera, make a list of the specific language on chart paper.)

  Today we are going to talk about how you can get everyone to a specific place in the book you are talking about.

- Point to page 2.

  If I want to talk about this page, what words can I use to direct you to the page?

- Write the label *page 2* on the sketch.
- Point to the third sentence.

  What words can I use to help you locate a specific place on the page?

- Add a label based on students' responses.
- Repeat the activity with other features (e.g., words, paragraphs, lines, captions, graphic panels) and ask students to talk about words they could use to help others locate that feature. Add ideas to the chart.

Have a Try

Invite the students to talk with a partner about ways to help others find a specific place in a book.

- Have students sit with book club groups and book club books. Each person in the group should have a copy of the same book.

  Practice using directions to help each other find a specific place in your book.

- After time for discussion, ask students to share directional words they used. Add new ideas to the chart.

Summarize and Apply

Summarize the learning and remind students to think about how to be sure that everyone is in a specific place during book club meetings.

  What did you learn today about how to help each other locate the specific place you want to talk about quickly?

- Add the principle to the top of the chart.

  During book club, use words to make sure everyone is at the specific place in the book. I will meet with a book club today and they will be able to try this out. Then they will share what they noticed when we come together for our class meeting.

- During independent reading time, meet with a book club group.

Share

Following independent reading time, gather students in the meeting area. Ask the group that met in book club to share.

  What words did you use to make sure everyone was looking at the same place when you talked about the book?

- Add new ideas to the chart.

Extend the Lesson (Optional)

After assessing students' understanding, you might decide to extend the learning.

- **Writing About Reading** Have students use Ways to Have a Good Book Club Discussion on the inside back cover of *Reader's Notebook: Advanced* (Fountas and Pinnell 2011) to reflect on their book club meetings.

Assessment

After you have taught the minilessons in this umbrella, observe students as they talk and write about their reading across instructional contexts: interactive read-aloud, independent reading, guided reading, shared reading, and book club. Use *The Literacy Continuum* (Fountas and Pinnell 2017) to observe students' reading and writing behaviors.

- What evidence do you have of new understandings related to the way students engage with book clubs?
  - Are students able to choose an appropriate book for book club and explain why they chose it?
  - Do they mark the pages and make notes about what they want to talk about?
  - Can they articulate their thinking in book clubs?
  - Are they asking questions to clarify understanding?
  - Do they use clear directions to make sure everyone is at the same place in the book they are discussing?
  - Do they understand terms such as *book club, preference, clarify,* and *discussion*?
- In what other ways, beyond the scope of this umbrella, are students talking about books?
  - Are students showing an interest in specific authors or illustrators?
  - Do they notice elements of an author's craft?

Use your observations to determine the next umbrella you will teach. You may also consult Minilessons Across the Year (pp. 61–64) for guidance.

Link to Writing

After teaching the minilessons in this umbrella, help students link the new learning to their own writing:

- Encourage students to write book reviews and recommendations that can be displayed in the classroom and used by others when choosing books.

Reader's Notebook

When this umbrella is complete, provide a copy of the minilesson principles (see resources.fountasandpinnell.com) for students to glue in the reader's notebook (in the Minilessons section if using *Reader's Notebook: Advanced* [Fountas and Pinnell 2011]), so they can refer to the information as needed.

Minilessons in This Umbrella

RML1	Be a strong listener and a strong speaker.
RML2	Recognize appropriate times to take a turn.
RML3	Monitor your participation and encourage others to participate.
RML4	Invite each other to provide evidence.
RML5	Value and encourage diverse perspectives.
RML6	Add on to the important ideas to extend the thinking of the group.
RML7	Change the topic and refocus the discussion as needed.
RML8	Reflect on and evaluate your book club discussion.

Before Teaching Umbrella 2 Minilessons

Once students have begun to participate in book club meetings, you can teach these minilessons to help them learn conversational moves that will improve the quality of the discussions. During book club meetings, the teacher plays a key role in facilitating the group to assure new levels of understanding, so even if students are taught to start the discussion, you are still part of the group to lift the conversation as needed. You might want to take students through one set of book club meetings (see Umbrella 1: Getting Started with Book Clubs) prior to teaching these minilessons so that they have a basic understanding of how a book club meeting goes.

Several lessons suggest doing a fishbowl observation (p. 76) right before teaching the minilesson. For additional prompts and to learn more, please see *Fountas & Pinnell Prompting Guide, Part 2, for Comprehension: Thinking, Talking, and Writing*, Section IV: Prompts for Book Discussions (Fountas and Pinnell 2009, 61–78) because this umbrella reflects some of the language from that section. To start the discussion, a few language prompts are suggested below.

- *Who wants to get us started?*
- *What does this book make you wonder about?*
- *What is important about this story (or book)?*
- *Let's think together about* ___________.
- *Turn and talk to your neighbor and share your first thoughts about this book.*

RML1

LA.U2.RML1

Reading Minilesson Principle

Be a strong listener and a strong speaker.

Learning Conversational Moves in Book Club

You Will Need

- chart paper and markers
- students' book club books

Academic Language / Important Vocabulary

- book club
- listener
- speaker

Continuum Connection

- Actively participate in conversation by listening and looking at the person speaking (p. 339)
- Refrain from speaking over others (p. 339)
- Use conventions of respectful conversation (p. 339)
- Listen to and speak to a partner about a given idea, and make a connection to the partner's idea (p. 339)

Goal

Understand the verbal and nonverbal ways to demonstrate committed listening and strong, clear speaking skills.

Rationale

When students think about what it means to be a strong listener and a strong speaker during a book club meeting, they learn to attend to their interactions with other classmates, notice the messages their body language is sending, and learn more about the text through balanced, rich discussions. This lays the foundation for becoming a good communicator and engaged member of the class.

Assess Learning

Observe students when they communicate with classmates and notice if there is evidence of new learning based on the goal of this minilesson.

- Do students actively listen to their classmates by making eye contact and turning their bodies toward the speaker?
- Do they speak at an appropriate level, refrain from speaking over others, and take turns talking?
- Do they use the terms *book club, listener,* and *speaker*?

Minilesson

To help students think about the minilesson principle, help them notice verbal and nonverbal cues and the kind of behaviors they might demonstrate as strong listeners and speakers. Here is an example.

- Before teaching this lesson, make sure students have had a recent book club experience to reflect on, whether it is a fishbowl demonstration (p. 76) or their own book club meeting.

  To be an active member of a book club, it is important to be a strong listener and a strong speaker.

  What does it look like to be a strong listener?

  What does it sound like?

- Prompt students' thinking by asking about where their eyes are looking, how their bodies are positioned, or how they might respond when they are the listener. Record students' responses on chart paper.

  What does it look like to be a strong speaker?

  What does it sound like?

- Prompt students' thinking by asking about what they are doing and how their voices sound when they are the speaker. Record responses on the chart.

Have a Try

Invite the students to talk in a small group and demonstrate what it means to be a strong listener and speaker.

Talk in your group about the book you are reading. When you listen, show what it looks like and sounds like to be a strong listener. When you speak, show what it looks like and sounds like to be a strong speaker. Take turns being the speaker in the group while the others listen.

- After time for discussion, ask students to share what they noticed. Add new ideas to the chart.

Be a strong listener and a strong speaker.

	Looks Like	Sounds Like
Strong Listener	• Makes eye contact with the speaker • Body is turned toward the speaker • Might nod at the speaker	• Can you say that in a different way? • Responds to ideas before changing the subject • Doesn't talk over speaker • I see why you might say that, but did you think about_____? • So, you mean_____. • In other words,_____.
Strong Speaker	• Takes turns • Makes eye contact with everyone in the group • Might nod or gesture to someone in the group	• Uses appropriate volume • Does not talk over the speaker • Asks questions • Adds on to comment

Summarize and Apply

Summarize the learning and remind students to be a strong listener and a strong speaker during book club meetings.

You learned some ways to be a strong listener and a strong speaker during your book club meeting.

- Add the principle to the top of the chart.

Today I will meet with one book club group. Later when we all meet to share, I will ask the book club members to share what they noticed about listening and speaking.

Share

Following independent reading time, gather students in the meeting area. Ask the group that met in book club to share.

What did you notice about listening and speaking when you met in book club today?

- After book club members respond, ask the whole group to reflect.

Why is it important to be a good listener and a good speaker?

Extend the Lesson (Optional)

After assessing students' understanding, you might decide to extend the learning.

- If you have *Fountas & Pinnell Prompting Guide, Part 2, for Comprehension: Thinking, Talking, and Writing*, refer to the prompts that support strong listening and thinking in Section IV: Prompts for Book Discussions (Fountas and Pinnell 2009).

RML 2

LA.U2.RML2

Reading Minilesson Principle

Recognize appropriate times to take a turn.

Learning Conversational Moves in Book Club

You Will Need

- chart paper and markers
- students' book club books

Academic Language / Important Vocabulary

- book club
- lull
- respect
- appropriate

Continuum Connection

- Demonstrate balance in conversation by taking turns (p. 339)
- Refrain from speaking over others (p. 339)
- Enter a conversation appropriately (p. 339)
- Use conventions of respectful conversation (p. 339)
- Understand the role of nonverbal language and use it effectively (p. 339)

Goal

Understand verbal and nonverbal cues for knowing when to enter a conversation at the appropriate time.

Rationale

When students learn how to take turns speaking during book club discussions by looking for verbal and nonverbal cues, they can share their ideas, comment on and extend one another's thoughts, and learn more about the text they are reading. This skill extends beyond book clubs to other conversations and discussions inside and outside of the classroom.

Assess Learning

Observe students when they converse with classmates and notice if there is evidence of new learning based on the goal of this minilesson.

- Can students recognize appropriate times to speak during a discussion?
- Do they invite others to share their thinking?
- Do they use nonverbal cues to signal that they have something to say?
- Do they understand the terms *book club, lull, respect,* and *appropriate*?

Minilesson

To help students think about taking turns in a book club discussion, engage them in an interactive lesson on how to look for verbal and nonverbal clues. Here is an example.

- Before teaching this lesson, be sure that students have had a recent book club experience to reflect on, whether it is a fishbowl demonstration (p. 76) or their own book club meeting.

  Think about the book club discussions you have seen or participated in. What did you notice about how everyone took turns speaking? Turn and talk about that.

- As needed, provide several prompts to encourage the conversation.
  - *What did people do when they had something to add to the conversation?*
  - *How did you know when it was your turn to speak?*
  - *Did you, or anyone else, say something to encourage others to take a turn sharing?*
- After time for discussion, bring the group back together and ask students to share their thinking about how to know when it is an appropriate time to speak. Make a list of responses on chart paper.

Have a Try

Invite the students to talk in a small group about identifying when it is time to take a turn speaking.

Talk in your group about a book you are currently reading. Take turns sharing and adding on to what your classmates have said.

- After time for discussion, ask students to share what they noticed about taking turns. Add new ideas to the chart.

Why is it important for you to know how to respectfully take turns in a conversation?

Recognize appropriate times to take a turn.

- Wait for a natural break, pause, or lull in the conversation.
- Make eye contact with the speaker.
- Notice if the speaker is looking around for someone to add to the conversation.
- Lean in to show you have something to say.

Summarize and Apply

Summarize the learning and remind students to think about book club discussions.

What did you learn about taking turns speaking during a discussion?

- Add the principle to the top of the chart.

Today I will meet with one book club group. Later when we come together to share, I will ask them to talk about what they observed about taking turns in a discussion.

Share

Following independent reading time, gather students in the meeting area. Ask the group that met in book club to share.

What are some examples of how you took turns talking?

What did you remember to do when you wanted to add to the conversation?

Extend the Lesson (Optional)

After assessing students' understanding, you might decide to extend the learning.

- Knowing when to enter a conversation is useful in many contexts, not just book club meetings. Remind students to use the same techniques when they speak in other settings.

RML 3
LA.U2.RML3

Reading Minilesson Principle

Monitor your participation and encourage others to participate.

Learning Conversational Moves in Book Club

You Will Need

- chart paper and markers

Academic Language / Important Vocabulary

- book club
- participation
- monitor
- encourage

Continuum Connection

- Use conventional techniques that encourage others to talk (e.g., "What do you think?" "Do you agree? Why or why not?") (p. 339)
- Evaluate one's own part in a group discussion as well as the effectiveness of the group (p. 339)
- Facilitate a group discussion by ensuring that everyone has a chance to speak (p. 339)

Goal

Monitor your own participation and learn language for encouraging others to participate.

Rationale

When students are aware of their own level of participation in a book club discussion, they are better prepared to adjust their behavior to either add more to the conversation or contribute less so that others have an opportunity to share.

Assess Learning

Observe students when they are participating in a book club discussion and notice if there is evidence of new learning based on the goal of this minilesson.

- Do students participate in the discussion in a balanced way?
- Can they evaluate whether they are talking too much or too little?
- Do they use the terms *book club, participation, monitor,* and *encourage*?

Minilesson

To help students think about the minilesson principle, engage them in a discussion about how to self-monitor their participation in a book club meeting. Here is an example.

- Before teaching this lesson, be sure that students have had a recent book club experience to reflect on, whether it is a fishbowl demonstration or their own book club meeting.

  What does it mean to monitor your participation in a book club discussion? It means to check how you are taking part in the group. Turn and talk to a partner about what questions you can ask yourself to monitor your participation.

- After time for discussion, invite students to share. Prompt the conversation as needed. Record student ideas on the chart.

  Now think about how you can invite others to talk during a book club meeting. What are some ways you could encourage someone to participate?

- Make a list of questions for inviting others to talk on the chart.

  Look back at the questions on the chart. Why is it important to check your participation and include others during a book club discussion?

- Prompt the conversation as needed.

Have a Try

Invite the students to talk with a small group about how they can invite others to participate.

> Turn and talk about any other questions you might ask yourself and language you might use to monitor your participation during book clubs.

- After a short time for discussion, ask students to share. Add new ideas to the chart.

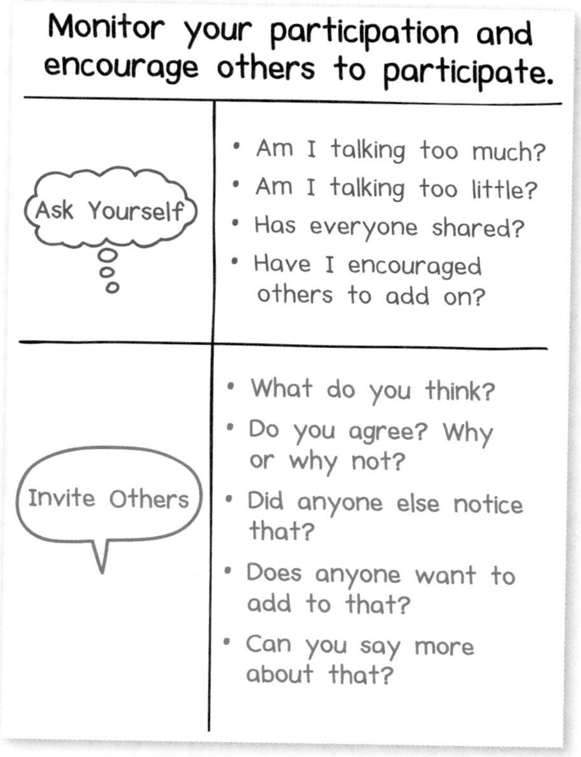

Monitor your participation and encourage others to participate.

Ask Yourself	• Am I talking too much? • Am I talking too little? • Has everyone shared? • Have I encouraged others to add on?
Invite Others	• What do you think? • Do you agree? Why or why not? • Did anyone else notice that? • Does anyone want to add to that? • Can you say more about that?

Summarize and Apply

Summarize the learning and remind students to monitor themselves and to invite others to talk during book club discussions.

> What did you learn about monitoring yourself during book club discussions?

- Add the principle to the top of the chart. Ask a volunteer to read the questions on the chart.

> Use the chart when you meet with your book club. The book club members that meet with me today will share about their book club when we have our class meeting.

Share

Following independent reading time, gather students in the meeting area. Have the book club members you met with share with the whole group.

> How well did you monitor your participation and support the participation of other book club members?

Extend the Lesson (Optional)

After assessing students' understanding, you might decide to extend the learning.

- If you have *Fountas & Pinnell Prompting Guide, Part 2, for Comprehension: Thinking, Talking, and Writing*, refer to the prompts that support participation in Section IV: Prompts for Book Discussions (Fountas and Pinnell 2009).

RML 4

LA.U2.RML4

Reading Minilesson Principle

Invite each other to provide evidence.

Learning Conversational Moves in Book Club

You Will Need

- chart paper and markers
- students' book club books

Academic Language / Important Vocabulary

- book club
- clarify
- evidence

Continuum Connection

- Use evidence from the text to support statements about the text (pp. 69, 73)

Goal

Develop language to give evidence and invite others to provide evidence for their thinking.

Rationale

When students learn to provide evidence for their thinking, they learn to clarify their thinking, clear up potential misconceptions, develop more sophisticated conversation skills, monitor their understanding, and share new insights with classmates.

Assess Learning

Observe students during book club meetings to notice evidence of new learning based on the goal of this minilesson.

- Do students provide evidence for their thinking from personal experience and/or the book during book club meetings?
- Can they identify when more information is needed and know how to ask for it?
- Do they use the terms *book club, clarify,* and *evidence*?

Minilesson

To help students think about the minilesson principle, engage them in a discussion using evidence from the text during book club meetings. Here is an example.

- Right before teaching this minilesson, conduct a fishbowl observation (p. 76) of a book club meeting. Ask students to focus on how the group members provide evidence for their thinking or ask each other for evidence for their opinions. (You may want to prepare the book club members being observed beforehand with some of the language represented in the chart, and you can also model this language.) Ask students to record their observations. Once the observation is complete, engage students in a reflective discussion to help them think about the minilesson principle.

  What did you notice about some of the ways group members invited each other to add evidence?

- As students share ideas, generalize their thinking to create two lists, one for *Give Evidence* and one for *Ask for Evidence*. Add responses to the appropriate section. Prompt the conversation as needed:
  - *Why is it important to provide evidence from the book for your thinking during book club?*
  - *How can you make sure you are specific with your evidence?*

Have a Try

Invite the students to talk about how they might give evidence or ask for evidence during book club.

- Have students sit with one or more members of their current book club. Each person in the group should have a copy of the same book.

  Practice giving evidence or asking for evidence about your book club book.

- After a brief time for practice, ask students to share the types of things they said to give or ask for evidence. Add new ideas to the chart.

Invite each other to provide evidence.

Give Evidence

- An example of that is on page_______.
- I think_______because_______.
- On page_______, paragraph_______, the writer says_______, so_______.
- One place I noticed this is on page_______.
- I used this quote because_______.

Ask for Evidence

- What makes you think that?
- Can you provide some details?
- How do you know that?
- What part of the story led you to that conclusion?
- Help me understand why you thought that.

Summarize and Apply

Summarize the learning and remind students to think about how to give or ask for evidence during book club meetings.

Today you learned about giving and asking for evidence for your thinking.

- Add the principle to the top of the chart.

  Think about using the chart when you have book club discussions. Today, I will meet with one book club. Later, when we have our class meeting, the book club members will share how they provided evidence in their discussion.

Share

Following independent reading time, gather students in the meeting area. Ask the group that met in book club to share.

In what ways did you give evidence or ask for evidence?

- Add new ideas to the chart. After the group members have shared, ask others in the class to reflect on providing evidence during book club meetings.

  Why is it important to share evidence for your thinking and to ask others to share evidence for their thinking?

Extend the Lesson (Optional)

After assessing students' understanding, you might decide to extend the learning.

- If you have *Fountas & Pinnell Prompting Guide, Part 2, for Comprehension: Thinking, Talking, and Writing*, refer to the prompts for giving and seeking evidence in Section IV: Prompts for Book Discussions (Fountas and Pinnell 2009).

RML 5

LA.U2.RML5

Reading Minilesson Principle

Value and encourage diverse perspectives.

Learning Conversational Moves in Book Club

You Will Need

- chart paper and markers

Academic Language / Important Vocabulary

- book club
- diverse
- perspective

Continuum Connection

- Use conventions of respectful conversation (p. 339)
- Listen and respond to a partner by agreeing, disagreeing, or adding on, and explain reasons (p. 339)

Goal

Learn to share different perspectives, agree and disagree respectfully, and provide reasons for opinions.

Rationale

When students share new and different ideas about a text, they are expanding and deepening their classmates' understandings of the text and working to ensure that a book club discussion is a safe place for everyone to share ideas.

Assess Learning

Observe students during book club discussions to notice evidence of new learning based on the goal of this minilesson.

- Do students show that they value perspectives that differ from their own by respectfully responding to their classmates?
- Are they sharing a variety of ideas during book club meetings?
- Do they use the terms *book club, diverse,* and *perspective*?

Minilesson

To help students think about the minilesson principle, engage them in a discussion about how to encourage and value diverse opinions. Here is an example.

- Right before teaching this lesson, conduct a fishbowl observation (p. 76) of one book club group discussing their book. Ask students to notice ways members show that they are valuing each other's opinions. Prepare students in the book club with some of the language in the chart.

  Think about a time during a book club discussion when people had different, or diverse, ideas about aspects of the book. Why is it important to hear a variety of ideas, or diverse perspectives?

- Prompt the conversation as needed.

  Now think about respectful language you can use when you hear an idea that is different from yours or when you disagree with an idea. Also think about ways you can invite others to share their ideas, which might be different from yours. Turn and talk about that.

- After time for discussion, ask volunteers to suggest ways to discuss diverse ideas. Create two lists on chart paper, one for ways to respond to diverse ideas and one for ways to ask for diverse ideas.

Have a Try

Invite the students to talk in small groups about what they can say to share or encourage diverse perspectives during book club meetings.

> Think about a book we have recently read aloud together in class. Have a conversation about the book and practice sharing opinions using words that show you are listening. You can look to the chart for ideas if you wish.

- After time for a brief discussion, ask students to share about the experience. Add new ideas to the chart.

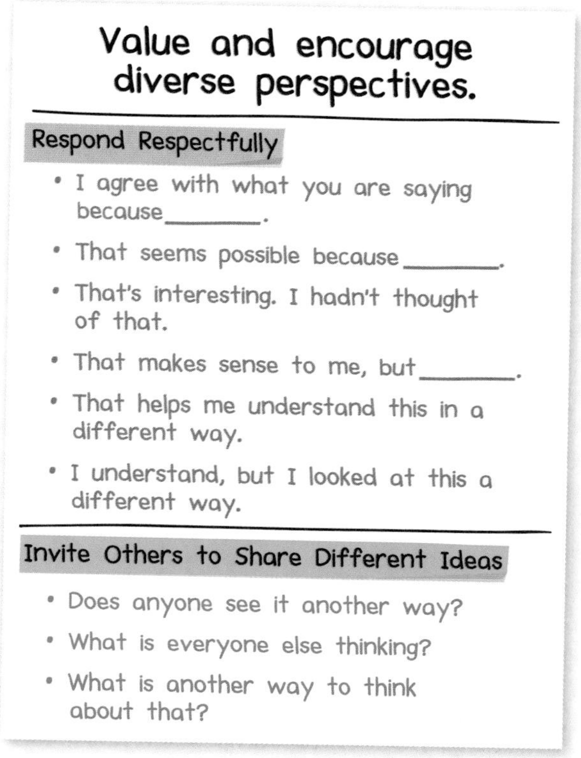

Value and encourage diverse perspectives.

Respond Respectfully

- I agree with what you are saying because_______.
- That seems possible because_______.
- That's interesting. I hadn't thought of that.
- That makes sense to me, but_______.
- That helps me understand this in a different way.
- I understand, but I looked at this a different way.

Invite Others to Share Different Ideas

- Does anyone see it another way?
- What is everyone else thinking?
- What is another way to think about that?

Summarize and Apply

Summarize the learning and remind students to think about how to share and ask for diverse perspectives.

> Today you learned how to respond to classmates who have new or different ideas. You also learned how to ask your classmates to share different ideas.

- Add the principle to the top of the chart.

> Use the chart when you meet with your book club. Today I will meet with one book club. When we have our class meeting, they will share their thinking about the book club discussion.

Share

Following independent reading time, gather students in the meeting area. Ask the group that met in book club to share.

> Think about your book club meeting. In what ways did you respond to your classmates' ideas? How did you show that you value their ideas? How did you invite others to share their perspective? Talk about that.

Extend the Lesson (Optional)

After assessing students' understanding, you might decide to extend the learning.

- If you have *Fountas & Pinnell Prompting Guide, Part 2, for Comprehension: Thinking, Talking, and Writing*, refer to the prompts for supporting diverse viewpoints in Section IV: Prompts for Book Discussions (Fountas and Pinnell 2009).

RML 6
LA.U2.RML6

Reading Minilesson Principle

Add on to the important ideas to extend the thinking of the group.

Learning Conversational Moves in Book Club

You Will Need

- chart paper and markers

Academic Language / Important Vocabulary

- book club
- focus
- restate

Continuum Connection

- Listen and respond to a partner by agreeing, disagreeing, or adding on, and explain reasons (p. 339)
- Sustain a discussion by staying on the main topic and requesting or signaling a change of topic (p. 339)

Goal

Add on to important ideas to build a deeper understanding.

Rationale

When students learn how to add on to an important idea and invite others to extend their thinking, they gain a deeper understanding of the text. Some teachers use hand signals for students to indicate when they plan to add on to a topic versus changing the subject. This lesson is designed to move students past using hand signals and to recognize language they can use to have an extended discussion on one idea.

Assess Learning

Observe students in book club discussions to notice evidence of new learning based on the goal of this minilesson.

- Can students identify the important ideas in a discussion?
- Can they determine how to appropriately refocus or add on?
- Do they use the terms *book club, focus, and restate*?

Minilesson

To help students think about the minilesson principle, engage them in a discussion about how to focus on main ideas and move on. Here is an example.

- Right before you plan to teach this minilesson, have your students participate in a fishbowl observation (p. 76) of a book club group. You can prepare the book club members ahead of time by teaching them some of the language on the chart and by modeling it yourself. Ask students to record some of the things the book club members say to stay focused and add on to an important idea. After the fishbowl is completed, engage them in reflective discussion about how to add on to an idea to extend the group's thinking.

  What did you notice about some of the ways group members added on to each other's ideas?

- Support the conversation as needed. Some suggested prompts are below.
  - *What are some other ways you might add on to a conversation?*
  - *Did you notice the book club members inviting each other to add on to the conversation?*
  - *What were some of the ways they invited each other to add on to an idea?*
- Write the headings *Add On* and *Invite Others to Add On* and record responses in the appropriate category

  When you feel that an idea has been fully discussed, then it is time to move on.

Have a Try

Invite the students to talk with a partner about book club discussions.

Look back at the chart. Turn and talk about any other ways you can add on to a discussion or invite others in.

- After time for discussion, ask students to share. Add new ideas to the chart.

Summarize and Apply

Summarize the learning and remind students to think about how to focus, add on to, and restate ideas during book club meetings.

Why is it important to add on to the conversation in a respectful way?

- Add the principle to the top of the chart.

Use the chart when you meet with your book club. Today I will meet with one book club. When we have our class meeting, they will share what they learned about their book club discussion.

Add on to the important ideas to extend the thinking of the group.

Add On +

- I would like to add that ________.
- Building on what ________ said, I think ________.
- To add on, ________.
- I also think ________.
- Now I'm thinking ________.
- You made me think ________.
- I'm changing my thinking because you ________.
- And this part of the text makes me think ________.

Invite Others to Add On

- Say more about that.
- Did anyone else want to add to that?
- What else does that make you think of?
- Say more about what you mean about ________.
- Did anyone else notice that?
- What do others think about that?
- Can anyone add on to ________'s comment/idea?
- Let's reread that paragraph to notice more.

Share

Following independent reading time, gather students in the meeting area. Ask the group that met in book club to share.

Share what you noticed about your book club discussion. How did group members add on to or restate what others said?

- Add new ideas to the chart. After book club members have responded, ask the class to reflect on book club discussions and provide any new ideas for the chart.

Extend the Lesson (Optional)

After assessing students' understanding, you might decide to extend the learning.

- If you have *Fountas & Pinnell Prompting Guide, Part 2, for Comprehension: Thinking, Talking, and Writing*, refer to the prompts for adding on and restating in Section IV: Prompts for Book Discussions (Fountas and Pinnell 2009).

RML 7
LA.U2.RML7

Reading Minilesson Principle
Change the topic and refocus the discussion as needed.

Learning Conversational Moves in Book Club

You Will Need

- chart paper and markers

Academic Language / Important Vocabulary

- book club
- refocus
- discussion

Continuum Connection

- Suggest new lines of discussion when appropriate (p. 339)
- Demonstrate effectiveness as a group leader (p. 339)
- Sustain a discussion by staying on the main topic and requesting or signaling a change of topic (p. 339)

Goal

Learn language to change or refocus a discussion and identify when it is appropriate to use it.

Rationale

The teacher plays a key role in facilitating the group to ensure new levels of understanding. When students learn to change or refocus a book club discussion, they learn to take responsibility for themselves by keeping a conversation moving forward and gain opportunities to think more deeply about the text. You may eventually teach students to start the discussion, but that doesn't mean you aren't part of the group to observe and lift the conversation as needed.

Assess Learning

Observe students when they are in book club meetings and notice if there is evidence of new learning based on the goal of this minilesson.

- Do students recognize when the discussion needs to be changed or refocused and use appropriate language to do so?
- Do they use the terms *book club, refocus,* and *discussion*?

Minilesson

To help students think about the minilesson principle, engage them in a discussion about noticing when a book club discussion needs to change or be refocused. Here is an example.

- Right before you plan to teach this minilesson, have students participate in a fishbowl observation (p. 76) of a book club group. Prepare the members ahead of time by teaching them some of the language on the chart. Ask students to record some of the things the book club members say to change and refocus the discussion. After they have completed the fishbowl observation, engage them in reflective discussion.

  Some ways to get the conversation in book club meeting started might be to ask: Who wants to get us started? Or, what do you think would be important to talk about today? But what about when you might want to move the discussion in a new direction? What are some ways you noticed the book club group members doing that?

- As needed, provide prompts to support the conversation.
  - *What might you say to the group to respectfully change the topic?*
  - *If a conversation gets off course, what could you say to bring the conversation back to the topic?*
- On chart paper, list ideas for changing and refocusing the discussion.

Have a Try

Invite the students to talk with a partner about book club discussions.

When you feel that an idea has been fully discussed, then it is time to move on. Turn and talk about what else you could say to change or refocus a discussion during a book club meeting.

- After a brief time for discussion, ask students to share ideas. Add to chart.

Change the topic and refocus the discussion as needed.

Change

- If everyone is finished with that idea, I'd like to change the topic.
- Let's think together about ________.
- Who has another idea they want us to think about?
- What else would be important for us to talk about?
- Take us to another part of the story you want us to think about.

Refocus

- Another way to say that is ________.
- I'd like to return to our discussion of ________.
- Where are we now with this idea?
- We were talking about ________.
- We're getting far away from the book.

Summarize and Apply

Summarize the learning and remind students to think about ways to start, change, or refocus the conversation during book club meetings.

Why is it important to talk about more than one idea during a book club discussion?

- Add the principle to the top of the chart.

Use the chart when you meet with your book club. Today I will meet with one book club. When we meet later, they will share their thinking about their discussion.

Share

Following independent reading time, gather students in the meeting area. Ask the group that met in book club to share.

How did your book club discussion go? What did you do to have a good discussion?

- Add new ideas to the chart. After book club members have responded, ask the class to reflect on book club discussions.

Why is it important to notice when a book club conversation needs to change or be refocused?

Extend the Lesson (Optional)

After assessing students' understanding, you might decide to extend the learning.

- If you have *Fountas & Pinnell Prompting Guide, Part 2, for Comprehension: Thinking, Talking, and Writing*, refer to the prompts for changing or refocusing the topic in Section IV: Prompts for Book Discussions (Fountas and Pinnell 2009).

RML 8
LA.U2.RML8

Reading Minilesson Principle

Reflect on and evaluate your book club discussion.

Learning Conversational Moves in Book Club

You Will Need

- chart paper and markers
- charts from previous minilessons in this umbrella

Academic Language / Important Vocabulary

- book club
- reflect
- assess
- evaluate

Continuum Connection

- Evaluate one's own part in a group discussion as well as the effectiveness of the group (p. 339)

Goal

Develop guidelines to self-assess book club meetings.

Rationale

When students reflect on a book club meeting, they begin to consider how their preparation and participation help the group better understand the text. Their evaluation process improves their self-assessment skills and increases their ownership and engagement of their work.

Assess Learning

Observe students during book club meetings to notice evidence of new learning based on the goal of this minilesson.

- Do students reflect on their participation so that they can identify what went well and what they can improve upon?
- Do they use the terms *book club, reflect, assess,* and *evaluate*?

Minilesson

To help students think about the minilesson principle, engage them in a reflection of a recent book club discussion. Here is an example.

- Before teaching this lesson, all students should have participated in at least one book club meeting. Post the charts from the previous minilessons in this umbrella.

  Here are the charts we made about ways to have a good book club meeting.

- Ask students to quickly review the charts.

  At the end of a book club meeting, you can reflect on what went well for you and your peers and what things you would like to work on so that your next book club meeting is even better.

  Let's create a list of what you can do to ensure a good book club meeting.

- Ask students for suggestions. As they respond, generalize their thinking and write statements on the chart paper. Prompt the conversation as needed.

  After your next meeting, you can use the list to evaluate how well your meeting went.

Have a Try

Invite the students to talk with a partner about ways to reflect on and evaluate a book club discussion.

> Turn and talk with a partner about something on the list that went well in your last book club meeting. What made it go well?

- After time for discussion, ask students to share ideas. Add to chart.

Reflect on and evaluate your book club discussion.

- [ ] We came prepared with pages marked and ideas to talk about.
- [ ] We took turns talking.
- [ ] We added on to each other's ideas.
- [ ] We invited others to participate.
- [ ] We stayed on topic.
- [ ] We supported our ideas with evidence from the text or personal experience.
- [ ] We respected everyone's ideas, including those we didn't agree with.
- [ ] We asked questions when we wanted to know more or didn't understand something.

Summarize and Apply

Summarize the learning and remind students to reflect after book club meetings.

> Today you created a list to help you think about your book club meetings.

- Add the principle to the top of the chart.

> Think about the things on this list after your next book club meeting. Think about what went well and decide on something that you can make better the next time.

- Meet with a book club while the other students engage in independent reading.

Share

Following independent reading time, gather students in the meeting area. Ask the group that met in book club to share.

> What went well in your book club discussion?
>
> What is something you would like to improve for next time?
>
> How did the checklist help you evaluate your book club meeting?

Extend the Lesson (Optional)

After assessing students' understanding, you might decide to extend the learning.

- Have students write in a reader's notebook a way to improve their next book club discussion and what steps they might take to do that.

Assessment

After you have taught the minilessons in this umbrella, observe students as they listen and speak about their reading across instructional contexts: interactive read-aloud, independent reading, guided reading, shared reading, and book club. Use *The Literacy Continuum* (Fountas and Pinnell 2017) to observe students' reading and writing behaviors.

- What evidence do you have of new understandings related to the way students engage with book clubs?
    - Are students effectively using conversation skills and effective language in book club discussions?
    - Do they know when to continue addressing one topic or when to move the discussion in a new direction?
    - Do they demonstrate that they value everyone's ideas and opinions?
    - Are they monitoring their own participation and encouraging others to share?
    - Do they use terms such as *book club, listener, speaker, respect, discussion,* and *reflect*?
- In what other ways, beyond the scope of this umbrella, are students talking about books?
    - Are students talking about author's craft?
    - Do they write in response to what they have read?

Use your observations to determine the next umbrella you will teach. You may also consult Minilessons Across the Year (pp. 61–64) for guidance.

Link to Writing

After teaching the minilessons in this umbrella, help students link the new learning to their own writing:

- Encourage students to write in a reader's notebook about ways in which a book club discussion has enhanced and deepened their understanding.

Reader's Notebook

When this umbrella is complete, provide a copy of the minilesson principles (see resources.fountasandpinnell.com) for students to glue in the reader's notebook (in the Minilessons section if using *Reader's Notebook: Advanced* [Fountas and Pinnell 2011]), so they can refer to the information as needed.

Studying Authors and Their Processes

Umbrella 3

Minilessons in This Umbrella

RML1	Study authors to learn about their craft.
RML2	Hypothesize the author's reasons for choosing a topic or idea.
RML3	Authors engage in research for their writing.
RML4	Authors often revisit the same themes, topics, or settings across their books.

Before Teaching Umbrella 1 Minilessons

During an author study (pp. 42–43), students learn that authors repeatedly make decisions as part of the authoring process. Author study supports students in noticing and appreciating elements of an author's craft as well as understanding the kind of research an author engages in to create an authentic and accurate book. Teach one or more of these lessons throughout the year as you conduct an author study or as students think about an author's decisions.

The first step in studying authors is to collect a set of mentor texts for students to read and enjoy. Use the following books from the *Fountas & Pinnell Classroom™ Interactive Read-Aloud Collection* text sets, along with these complete text sets: Author Study: Joyce Sidman, Author/Illustrator Study: Ted and Betsy Lewin, and Author/Illustrator Study: Demi. However, you can use books by a single author or authors that your students have read.

Genre Study: Expository Fiction

Giant Squid: Searching for a Sea Monster by Mary Cerullo and Clyde F. E. Roper

Family

This Is the Rope: A Story from the Great Migration by Jacqueline Woodson

Genre Study: Historical Fiction

The Butterfly by Patricia Polacco

Author Study: Andrea Davis Pinkney

Duke Ellington: The Piano Prince and His Orchestra

Martin and Mahalia: His Words, Her Song

As you read aloud and enjoy these texts together, help students

- look across texts to learn about authors and their craft, and
- think about the research an author needs to do in order to make a book authentic.

Genre Study: Expository Fiction

Giant Squid by Mary Cerullo and Clyde F. E. Roper

Family

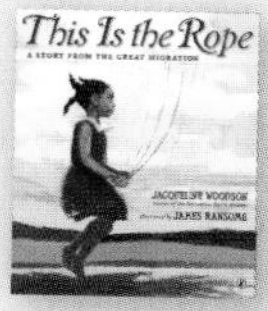

Genre Study: Historical Fiction

Author Study: Andrea Davis Pinkney

Duke Ellington by Andrea Davis Pinkney
Martin and Mahalia by Andrea Davis Pinkney

RML1
LA.U3.RML1

Reading Minilesson Principle

Study authors to learn about their craft.

Studying Authors and Their Processes

You Will Need

- multiple books by the same author, such as the following from Text Set: Author Study: Joyce Sidman:
  - *Dark Emperor and Other Poems of the Night*
  - *Winter Bees and Other Poems of the Cold*
  - *Song of the Water Boatman and Other Pond Poems*
  - *This Is Just to Say: Poems of Apology and Forgiveness*
- chart paper and markers
- large sticky notes

Academic Language / Important Vocabulary

- author
- characteristics
- style
- craft

Continuum Connection

- Connect text by a range of categories: e.g., content, theme, message, genre, author/illustrator, character, setting, special forms, text structure, or organization (pp. 69, 73)
- Recognize some authors by the style of their illustrations, their topics, characters they use, or typical plots (p. 71)
- Recognize some authors by the topics they choose or the style of their illustrations (p. 74)

Goal

Understand that an author usually writes several books and that there are often recognizable characteristics across the books.

Rationale

When students analyze the characteristics of an author's work, they begin to appreciate that writing is a process of decision making and that artistry is involved. Recognizing an author's patterns or style can heighten anticipation, enjoyment, and depth of understanding because familiarity has been established. Note that this lesson format can be used for future author studies.

Assess Learning

Observe students when they talk about authors and notice if there is evidence of new learning based on the goal of this minilesson.

- Do students recognize similar characteristics across books by the same author?
- Are they able to ascertain whether characteristics *always* or *often* occur in books by the same author?
- Do they use the terms *author, characteristics, style,* and *craft*?

Minilesson

To help students think about the minilesson principle, engage them in noticing characteristics of an author's style. Here is an example.

- Show the covers of multiple books by an author, for example, Joyce Sidman.

  Think about these books you have been reading by Joyce Sidman. What are some things you have noticed about her writing?

  Which of these ideas are *always* true of Joyce Sidman's books and which of these ideas are *often* true?

- On chart paper, write the author's name at the top, with *Noticings* underneath. Create separate columns with the headings *Always* and *Often*. Record the students' ideas in the appropriate column on the chart. (You might want to write the ideas on sticky notes so that they can be moved from column to column as students read more books and learn more about the author.)
- Read or show pages from *Dark Emperor and Other Poems of the Night, Winter Bees and Other Poems of the Cold,* and *Song of the Water Boatman and Other Pond Poems* to prompt the conversation. Make additions to the chart.

  Each thing you notice in Joyce Sidman's writing is the result of a decision she made.

Have a Try

Invite the students to talk with a partner about one of Joyce Sidman's books.

- Show the cover of *This Is Just to Say: Poems of Apology and Forgiveness* and show a few pages.

  Turn and talk about Joyce Sidman's writing in this book. Do you see any of the characteristics on this chart? Is there anything else that should be added?

- After time for discussion, ask a few students to share. Add new ideas to the chart.

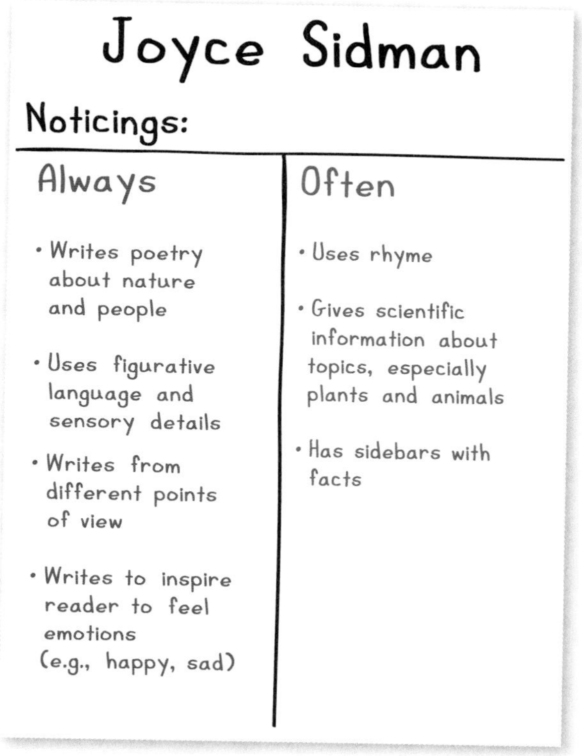

Joyce Sidman

Noticings:

Always	Often
• Writes poetry about nature and people • Uses figurative language and sensory details • Writes from different points of view • Writes to inspire reader to feel emotions (e.g., happy, sad)	• Uses rhyme • Gives scientific information about topics, especially plants and animals • Has sidebars with facts

Summarize and Apply

Summarize the learning and remind students to think about the characteristics of an author's writing when reading independently.

Today you learned that if you look closely at several books by the same author you begin to notice the decisions the author has made and to recognize the characteristics of that author's writing. This is called the author's craft.

When you read today, you can choose a book by Joyce Sidman, or you can choose to read a book by an author whose books you have read before. Place a sticky note on pages that show characteristics of that author's craft. Bring the book when we meet so you can share.

Share

Following independent reading time, gather students in the meeting area.

Did anyone read a book by Joyce Sidman or another author whose books you know? Share what you noticed.

Extend the Lesson (Optional)

After assessing students' understanding, you might decide to extend the learning.

- See LA.U12.RML1 for a comparable lesson to study illustrators and their work.
- **Writing About Reading** After conducting several author studies, have students fill in a graphic organizer to compare the work of the authors they have studied (see resources.fountasandpinnell.com). They can glue the organizer into a reader's notebook.

RML 2

LA.U3.RML2

Reading Minilesson Principle

Hypothesize the author's reasons for choosing a topic or idea.

Studying Authors and Their Processes

You Will Need

- several familiar texts that provide information or clues about where authors get ideas for writing, such as the following:
  - *This Is Just to Say: Poems of Apology and Forgiveness* by Joyce Sidman, from Text Set: Author Study: Joyce Sidman
  - *The Butterfly* by Patricia Polacco, from Text Set: Genre Study: Historical Fiction
  - *Giant Squid* by Mary Cerullo and Clyde F. E. Roper, from Text Set: Genre Study: Expository Nonfiction
  - *This Is the Rope* by Jacqueline Woodson, from Text Set: Family
- chart paper and markers
- document camera (optional)

Academic Language / Important Vocabulary

- hypothesize
- author
- dedication page
- author's note
- author's page

Continuum Connection

- Use evidence from the text to support statements about it (pp. 69, 73)
- Understand that a writer has a purpose in writing a fiction text (p. 69)
- Form and state the basis for opinions about authors and illustrators (pp. 69, 73)

Goal

Use different parts of the book (e.g., dedication, author's note, biographical information) to hypothesize why the author chose the idea or topic of the text.

Rationale

When students learn to use parts of a book to learn about an author, they realize that an author gets ideas for books from many places. Students begin to think about topics or ideas they might write about using experiences and connections from their own lives.

Assess Learning

Observe students when they talk about where authors get ideas for writing and notice if there is evidence of new learning based on the goal of this minilesson.

- Are students reading beyond the body of the text to learn more about the author?
- Do they notice different ways authors get writing ideas?
- Do they use academic vocabulary, such as *hypothesize, author, dedication page, author's note,* and *author's page*?

Minilesson

To help students think about the minilesson principle, engage them in discovering how authors use their life experiences to get ideas for books. Here is an example.

- Show the cover of *This Is Just to Say: Poems of Apology and Forgiveness.*

  Where do you think Joyce Sidman got her ideas to write this book?

  Where are some places we could look in the book to find out about this?

- Guide students to think about places to look to find out more about an author. Then show (or project) and read the author's bio on the inside back cover and the dedication page.

  What information do you learn about Joyce Sidman and where she found ideas for this book?

- As students share ideas, create a chart that shows where they can find information in the book. Ask them for ideas about other places to find out more about the author and add to chart.

  How do you see this information about Joyce Sidman being used in this book?

- Add responses to the chart.
- Repeat the activity with several other books by different authors, such as *The Butterfly* by Patricia Polacco and *Giant Squid* by Mary Cerullo and Clyde F. E. Roper.

Have a Try

Invite the students to talk with a partner about where another author got her ideas for writing.

Turn and talk about where Jacqueline Woodson got her idea for writing *This Is the Rope*.

- After time for discussion, ask students to share their thinking. Read or project the dedication page and author's note if needed. Add to chart.

Author and Title	Where can you find out about why the author chose the topic or idea?	How did the author find ideas to write about?
Joyce Sidman *This Is Just to Say*	• inside back cover • dedication page • other books • author website • author interviews	• The author wrote an apology poem to her mom and received a forgiving response. • Poems from her students • One of her teachers
Patricia Polacco *The Butterfly*	• author's note • author's page • dedication • author website • author interviews	• The book is based on the lives of the author's aunt and great-aunt.
Mary M. Cerullo and Clyde F.E. Roper *Giant Squid*	• author's note • author's page • online resources • book reviews	• The authors are both scientists who research facts about the ocean. • A marine educator in Maine shared stories with one of the authors.
Jacqueline Woodson *This Is the Rope*	• dedication • author's note • online resources	• The author's mother and grandmother both left the south for a better life. • The rope in the book title represents hope to her family.

Hypothesize the author's reasons for choosing a topic or idea.

Summarize and Apply

Summarize the learning and remind students to think about where authors get ideas.

When you take what you learn about the author and make a good guess about how the author got the idea to write the book, you hypothesize the author's reasons for writing.

- Add the principle to the chart.

When you read today, look for places where you might find additional information about where authors find ideas for the book you are reading. You also can hypothesize, or make an informed guess, based on what you know about the book and author. Bring the book when we meet so you can share.

Share

Following independent reading time, gather students in the meeting area.

Did anyone find information or hypothesize about where an author got an idea for writing? What is the connection between the author's life and the book?

Extend the Lesson (Optional)

After assessing students' understanding, you might decide to extend the learning.

- Encourage students to use ideas from their own lives as they write stories.
- Talk about how knowing where an author gets ideas for writing helps in appreciating the book (e.g., the characters are more empathetic, the story feels more authentic, the story becomes more engaging).

RML3
LA.U3.RML3

Reading Minilesson Principle

Authors engage in research for their writing.

Studying Authors and Their Processes

You Will Need

- several familiar nonfiction or historical fiction books, such as the following:
  - *Duke Ellington* and *Martin and Mahalia* by Andrea Davis Pinkney, from Text Set: Author Study: Andrea Davis Pinkney
  - *Gorilla Walk* and *Elephant Quest* by Ted and Betsy Lewin, from Text Set: Author/Illustrator Study: Ted and Betsy Lewin
- document camera (optional)
- chart paper and markers
- sticky notes

Academic Language / Important Vocabulary

- author
- research
- source
- accurate
- authentic

Continuum Connection

- Notice and evaluate the accuracy of the information presented in the text and across texts (p. 75)

Goal

Understand that authors engage in research for their writing.

Rationale

When you teach students to think about what an author needs to research before writing a book, they learn to appreciate the work involved in writing a book and to evaluate the authenticity and accuracy of the writing. They understand that research is an essential part of writing.

Assess Learning

Observe students when they discuss the research authors do and notice if there is evidence of new learning based on the goal of this minilesson.

- Can students locate information in a book that shows that authors have researched a topic?
- Do they think critically about how an author gains expertise on a topic?
- Do they use the terms *author, research, source, accurate,* and *authentic*?

Minilesson

To help students think about the minilesson principle, engage them in discovering how authors conduct research prior to writing. Here is an example.

- Show the cover of *Duke Ellington.*

  What types of things did Andrea Davis Pinkney need to learn before writing this book about Duke Ellington?

- Record their examples on a chart.

  Sometimes books provide information about the research the author conducted. Let's look at a few pages in this book to see what we can learn.

- Read and show (or project) the sources information at the end of the book.

  What are some sources the author used for research?

  What other places do you think she might have looked to learn about Duke Ellington?

- Record responses.
- Repeat with *Martin and Mahalia* (using the acknowledgments and bibliography) and *Gorilla Walk* (using the introduction and dedication page). Record responses.

  When you think about the sources an author uses to research a topic before writing, you determine whether the book is accurate and authentic.

Have a Try

Invite the students to talk with a partner about an author's research.

- Read and show (or project) the dedications in *Elephant Quest.*

  Think about what topics Ted and Betsy Lewin had to research before writing this book and what sources they used to learn about African elephants. Turn and talk about that.

- After students turn and talk, ask a few students to share ideas. Add to the chart.

Summarize and Apply

Summarize the learning and remind students to think about the research that authors conduct before writing.

What can you say about what an author does before writing about a topic?

- Add the principle to the top of the chart.

  When you read today, look outside the main part of the book to see if there is information that tells you about the author's research. Use sticky notes to mark pages you want to remember. Bring the book when we meet so you can share.

Authors engage in research for their writing.

Author and Title	What did the author need to learn to write this book?	Resources the Author Used
Andrea Davis Pinkney Duke Ellington	• Information about Duke Ellington's life and accomplishments	• books • videos • museums exhibitions
Andrea Davis Pinkney Martin and Mahalia	• Information about Martin Luther King Jr.'s life and accomplishments • Information about Mahalia Jackson's life and accomplishments	• audio recordings • books • libraries • museums
Ted and Betsy Lewin Gorilla Walk	• Information about gorillas (where and how they live) • Details about how to visit the gorillas • How to prepare for a difficult expedition	• in-the-field research • Wildlife Conservation Society • International Gorilla Conservation Programme • African Wildlife Foundation • guides in the park • books about gorillas
Ted and Betsy Lewin Elephant Quest	• Information about African elephants • Details about how to visit the elephants • How to prepare for the journey	• in-the-field research • staff at the camp • Wildlife Conservation Society • books about African elephants

Share

Following independent reading time, gather students in pairs to talk about the author's research.

Share with your partner what you learned about the author's research. Talk about what the author needed to learn before writing and what sources the author used.

Extend the Lesson (Optional)

After assessing students' understanding, you might decide to extend the learning.

- Help students engage in research about a nonfiction topic before writing about it.
- **Writing About Reading** Have students use a reader's notebook to write about the research an author had to do before writing a book. The book can be fiction or nonfiction.

RML 4
LA.U3.RML4

Reading Minilesson Principle

Authors often revisit the same themes, topics, or settings across their books.

Studying Authors and Their Processes

You Will Need

- several sets of books by the same authors, such as the following:
  - Text Set: Author/Illustrator Study: Ted and Betsy Lewin
  - Text Set: Author/Illustrator Study: Demi
- chart paper and markers
- sticky notes
- sticky notes labeled *Settings, Topics,* and *Themes*

Academic Language / Important Vocabulary

- author
- setting
- topic
- theme
- characteristics
- style
- recognize

Continuum Connection

- Recognize some authors by the style of their illustrations, their topics, characters they use, or typical plots (p. 71)
- Recognize some authors by the topics they choose or the style of their illustrations (p. 74)

Goal

Understand that authors often write about the same settings, topics, or themes in their books.

Rationale

When you teach students to see patterns across texts written by the same author, they learn to think in depth about an author's style, interests, values, and ideas, as well as anticipate similarities as they read books by the same author. Students need to be familiar with themes for this minilesson (see Umbrella 9: Thinking About Themes in this section).

Assess Learning

Observe students when they talk about authors and notice if there is evidence of new learning based on the goal of this minilesson.

- Can students discuss similarities across books by the same author?
- Do they understand that authors can be identified by their style?
- Do they use the terms *author, setting, topic, theme, characteristics, style,* and *recognize*?

Minilesson

To help students think about the minilesson principle, engage them in thinking about similarities across texts by the same author. Here is an example.

- Ahead of time, gather the books by Ted and Betsy Lewin and by Demi. Cover the authors' names with sticky notes and display the covers.
- Hold up *Top to Bottom Down Under.* Read and show the illustrations from several pages.

  Based on what you have noticed in other books, who wrote this book? How do you know?

- Reveal the authors' names. Show the other books by Ted and Betsy Lewin.

  The similarities help you recognize books by Ted and Betsy Lewin. What are some of the characteristics of these books that let you know they are by Ted and Betsy Lewin?

- Guide the conversation so students notice the similarities in types of themes, topics, or settings. Fill in a chart with students' responses.

Have a Try

Invite the students to talk with a partner about the style of an author.

- Show the covers and a few pages from several of the books by Demi.

  Turn and talk about the author of these books. What are the characteristics of her writing style?

- After students turn and talk, add responses to the chart.

Authors often revisit the same themes, topics, or settings across their books.

	Ted and Betsy Lewin	Demi
Themes	Benefits of learning about new animals and cultures	Power of the human spirit Learning from ancient and wise teachers
Topics	Animals, cultures, environments	Chinese culture Achievements of people from other cultures
Settings	Natural habitats of animals Places that are far from where they live	Ancient China

Summarize and Apply

Summarize the learning and remind students to notice the style of the author when they read.

Today you looked at multiple books by the same authors and realized that you can recognize an author's work by noticing similarities in settings, topics, and themes.

- Add the principle to the top of the chart.

  When you read today, you might choose a book by an author you have read before. If you do, use sticky notes to mark similarities between the books. Bring the book when we meet so you can share.

Share

Following independent reading time, gather students in the meeting area.

Did anyone read a book by an author you have read before? How is it helpful to think about things that are similar across books by the same author? Share your thoughts.

Extend the Lesson (Optional)

After assessing students' understanding, you might decide to extend the learning.

- **Writing About Reading** Have students write about the characteristics of an author whose books they have read.
- **Writing About Reading** Have students compare books by the same illustrator and write about their noticings in a reader's notebook.

Assessment

After you have taught the minilessons in this umbrella, observe students as they talk and write about their reading across instructional contexts: interactive read-aloud, independent reading, guided reading, shared reading, and book club. Use *The Literacy Continuum* (Fountas and Pinnell 2017) to observe students' reading and writing behaviors.

- What evidence do you have of new understandings related to authors and their work?
- Do students understand that studying an author will help them learn about the author's craft?
- Are they thinking about how an author came up with a topic or idea?
- Do they understand and think about the ways authors do research before writing?
- Are they aware that authors often write about similar themes, topics, or settings in their books?
- Are they using academic language, such as *characteristics, style, craft, author's note, author's page, dedication page, research, authentic, theme, topic,* and *setting*?

- In what other ways, beyond the scope of this umbrella, are students thinking about authors and illustrators?
  - Are they noticing and talking about the illustrator's craft?

Use your observations to determine the next umbrella you will teach. You may also consult Minilessons Across the Year (pp. 61–64) for guidance.

Link to Writing

After teaching the minilessons in this umbrella, help students link the new learning to their own writing:

- Students can write books in the style of an author they enjoy.
- Students can include an author bio, author's note, or dedication page in their own writing that shares information about their craft.

Reader's Notebook

When this umbrella is complete, provide a copy of the minilesson principles (see resources.fountasandpinnell.com) for students to glue in the reader's notebook (in the Minilessons section if using *Reader's Notebook: Advanced* [Fountas and Pinnell 2011]), so they can refer to the information as needed.

Minilessons in This Umbrella

RML1	Study the illustrations closely to understand what is happening in the text.
RML2	Notice the text features the author/illustrator uses to help you follow the action.
RML3	Notice the text features the author/illustrator uses to create narration, sound, and dialogue.
RML4	Notice how the author/illustrator uses color and lines to show setting, mood, and motion.

Independent Reading

Before Teaching Umbrella 4 Minilessons

Though not a genre, graphic texts are a popular text format. They can be fiction or nonfiction. Studying graphic texts with students prepares them to read and understand graphic texts independently. When reading fiction graphic texts together, encourage students to pay close attention to the illustrations because they carry much of the action. Introduce the various features of graphic texts. For example, panels in graphic texts function like paragraphs and are read left to right and top to bottom. They hold the pictures and the speech and thought bubbles, and they carry the narrative. Gutters, or the spaces between the panels, sometimes show time passing. The reader must infer action between panels.

Before introducing this umbrella, create a basket of graphic texts in a variety of genres for use during independent reading time. You may choose to use the texts from the *Fountas & Pinnell Classroom™ Independent Reading Collection* listed below, but also collect other graphic texts from your own library that engage students' intellectual curiosity and emotions, making sure the texts have content, themes, and ideas that are appropriate for your students' cognitive development, emotional maturity, and life experience.

Independent Reading Collection

Bluffton: My Summers with Buster by Matt Phelan

The Sinking of the Titanic by Matt Doeden

As you read aloud and enjoy these texts together, help students

- notice that the illustrations carry most of the action,
- read the text and study the text features for meaning, and
- notice an author/illustrator's color and line choices.

RML1
LA.U4.RML1

Reading Minilesson Principle

Study the illustrations closely to understand what is happening in the text.

Reading Graphic Texts

You Will Need

- two or three graphic texts students are reading, such as the following from *Independent Reading Collection*:
  - *Bluffton* by Matt Phelan
  - *The Sinking of the Titanic* by Matt Doeden
- document camera (optional)
- chart paper and markers
- sticky notes

Academic Language / Important Vocabulary

- graphic text
- action

Continuum Connection

- Follow a complex plot with multiple events, episodes, or problems (p. 70)
- Notice how illustrations and graphics go together with the text in a meaningful way (p. 72)
- Understand that graphics provide important information (p. 75)

Goal

Study the illustrations closely to understand what is happening in the text.

Rationale

Graphic texts have both illustrations and printed text, and the illustrations carry a good deal of the information. Students must learn to follow the story and infer characters' feelings and traits from the illustrations. This will ensure they understand what they are reading.

Assess Learning

Observe students when they read graphic texts. Notice if there is evidence of new learning based on the goal of this minilesson.

- Can students describe what they see in the illustrations?
- Do they use the illustrations to understand the story?
- Are they using language such as *graphic text* and *action*?

Minilesson

To help students understand the minilesson principle, engage them in a discussion about the role of the illustrations in a graphic text. Use a document camera, if available, to support viewing the illustrations. Here is an example.

- Show the cover of *Bluffton*. Display a few pages, stopping on page 9.

  Bluffton is an example of a graphic text. How is this book different from other kinds of books that you have read?

  There are more illustrations than words. Look at the illustrations on this page while I read it to you. What do you see in the illustrations? How does that help you understand the story?

- Record noticings about how the illustrations help a reader to understand the story.
- Repeat this process with pages 31–32.

  In a graphic text, you look at both the words and the illustrations, but the illustrations carry at least as much—often more—information as the words.

Have a Try

Invite the students to talk with a partner about some illustrations from *The Sinking of the Titanic.*

- Have students study the illustrations on pages 8–9 and then 22–23.

  Turn and talk to your partner. What do the illustrations show? How do they help you understand the story?

- After they turn and talk, ask a few students to share. Record responses on the chart.

Study the illustrations closely to understand what is happening in the text.

Title	What do you see in the illustrations?	What does that help you understand in the story?
 BLUFFTON	• Henry and Sally talking to each other	Action Characters
	• Old-fashioned clothes	Setting
	• Pictures of different vaudeville acts	Shows what is meant by vaudeville acts
 TITANIC	• People dancing	Characters
	• A telegraph operator	Setting
	• Orchestra playing	Setting
	• The ship cracking and sinking	Action

Summarize and Apply

Summarize the learning and remind students to study the illustrations in a graphic text.

Take a look at the chart we created. What do you need to do to understand a graphic text?

- Write the principle at the top of the chart.

  When you read today, you might choose to read a graphic text. If you do, mark with a sticky note an illustration that helps you understand what is happening in the book. Bring the book when we meet so you can share.

Share

Following independent reading time, gather students in the meeting area to talk about their reading.

Tell what you learned from the illustrations on a page in your book.

- Display a page on a document camera, if possible, so that everyone can see.

Extend the Lesson (Optional)

After assessing students' understanding, you might decide to extend the learning.

- As students gain experience with graphic texts, add examples to the chart.
- **Writing About Reading** Encourage students to write in a reader's notebook about a graphic text they have read and why the format is particularly suited to the content.

RML 2

LA.U4.RML2

Reading Minilesson Principle

Notice the text features the author/illustrator uses to help you follow the action.

Reading Graphic Texts

You Will Need

- two or three graphic texts with which the students are familiar, such as the following from *Independent Reading Collection*:
- *Bluffton* by Matt Phelan
- *The Sinking of the Titanic* by Matt Doeden
- document camera (optional)
- chart paper and markers

Academic Language / Important Vocabulary

- panels
- gutters
- illustrations

Continuum Connection

- Notice how illustrations and graphics go together with the text in a meaningful way (p. 72)
- Understand that graphics and text are carefully placed in a nonfiction text so that ideas are communicated clearly (p. 75)

Goal

Notice and understand the function of the panels, gutters, and pictures in a graphic text and the author/illustrator's craft in creating them.

Rationale

Studying the function of panels and gutters within graphic texts, and how an author/illustrator uses these text features, allows students to successfully read graphic texts and appreciate the author/illustrator's craft.

Assess Learning

Observe students when they read graphic texts. Notice if there is evidence of new learning based on the goal of this minilesson.

- Do students read all the panels to follow the action in a story?
- Can they talk about how the panels and gutters help them understand a story?
- Are they using language such as *panels, gutters,* and *illustrations*?

Minilesson

To help students understand more about the minilesson principle, use familiar texts to engage them in a discussion about the text features in a graphic text. Use a document camera, if available, so that everyone can see the books. Here is an example.

- Show the cover of *Bluffton*. Display a few pages, stopping on page 47.

  Follow along as I read aloud from *Bluffton*. How does the placement of the illustrations help you read this graphic text?

- Read page 47, pointing to the panels as you read.

  These boxes are called panels. The blank spaces between the boxes are called gutters.

- Turn to page 5 and point to the gutters.

  Why is having this blank space here important?

- Record noticings on a chart. As necessary, prompt students to expand upon their thinking about how the author and illustrator show what is happening in the story:
  - *Why did the author and illustrator use panels?*
  - *What did they include in the panels?*
  - *In what order should you read the panels?*
- Continue to record noticings on the chart.

Have a Try

Invite the students to talk with a partner about the panels in *The Sinking of the Titanic*.

- Show pages 16 and 17, reviewing what is happening on these pages.

  Turn and talk to your partner. Think about why the illustrator drew panels of different sizes on these pages.

- After time to turn and talk, ask a few students to share. Record responses on the chart.

Notice the text features the author/illustrator uses to help you follow the action.

Panels

- Help the reader follow the action
- Read left to right and top to bottom

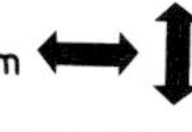

- Contain speech bubbles
- Panels within panels changes the reader's focus
- Different sized boxes show the importance of the action

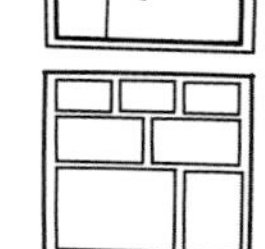

Gutters

- Blank spaces between panels
- Separate events
- Different sizes
- Help reader know time has passed between boxes

Summarize and Apply

Summarize the learning and remind students to use the panels and gutters to understand the action of the text.

- Review the chart and write the principle at the top.

  When you read today, you might choose to read a graphic text. As you read, notice how the panels and gutters help you understand what is happening in the story. Bring the book when we meet so you can share.

Share

Following independent reading time, gather students in the meeting area to talk about their reading.

Who read a graphic text today? Talk about how you used the panels and gutters to help you follow the action of the story.

- Display a page on a document camera, if possible, so that everyone can see.

Extend the Lesson (Optional)

After assessing students' understanding, you might decide to extend the learning.

- If you have not already displayed graphic texts in the classroom library, enlist several students to create a display.
- Use this lesson as a model for teaching students to use text features to gather information in nonfiction graphic texts and/or graphic text biographies.
- **Writing About Reading** Encourage students to create a response to their book in a reader's notebook using a few panels and gutters to show their thinking.

RML 3
LA.U4.RML3

Reading Minilesson Principle

Notice the text features the author/illustrator uses to create narration, sound, and dialogue.

Reading Graphic Texts

You Will Need

- a graphic text with which students are familiar, such as *The Sinking of the Titanic* by Matt Doeden, from *Independent Reading Collection*
- document camera (optional)
- chart paper and markers
- sticky notes

Academic Language / Important Vocabulary

- speech bubbles
- thought bubbles
- narrative boxes
- sound words

Continuum Connection

- Notice how illustrations and graphics go together with the text in a meaningful way (p. 72)

Goal

Notice and understand the use of speech and thought bubbles, lettering, narrative boxes, and sound words to create narration, sound, and dialogue in a graphic text.

Rationale

Teaching students to notice and use text features in a graphic text (e.g., speech and thought bubbles, lettering, narrative boxes, and sound words)—and understand how they create narration, sound, and dialogue—helps them create a story in the mind and supports them in understanding.

Assess Learning

Observe students when they read graphic texts. Notice if there is evidence of new learning based on the goal of this minilesson.

- Do students use and understand the features authors and illustrators use in graphic texts to show the action in the story?
- Are they using language such as *speech bubbles, thought bubbles, narrative boxes,* and *sound words*?

Minilesson

To demonstrate the minilesson principle, use a familiar graphic text to engage them in a discussion about text features that show narration, sound, and dialogue. Use a document camera, if available. Here is an example.

- Read aloud and display pages 20–21 from *The Sinking of the Titanic.*

  Look at the words on these pages. What do you notice about the print?

  Some words look like they could have been written by hand. Other words are in regular print, like what you would see in most books. Why do you think there are two different kinds of print?

  In this book, the handwriting print is in the speech bubbles and shows what the characters say. The regular print is in the rectangular boxes, called narrative boxes, and gives background information about what is happening.

- Record noticings on a chart. Then display pages 24–25.

  Look closely at the print in the speech bubbles on page 25. Which words look different? How are they different?

  The words *Someone help us!* are bigger and bolder than the other print. That shows the desperation of the person who is speaking those words.

- Record responses on the chart.

Have a Try

Invite the students to talk with a partner about more text features in *The Sinking of the Titanic*.

- Display pages 22 and 23.

  What do you see on this page that is different from the other pages? Turn and talk about what it is and why it's there.

- After time to turn and talk about the sound word, ask a few students to share. Record responses on the chart.

Notice the text features the author/illustrator uses to create narration, sound, and dialogue.

Speech Bubbles	Narrative Boxes	Lettering	Sound Words
• Tell what characters are saying • Point to the character who is talking • Sometimes there are double speech bubbles. What will happen now?	• Tell what is happening • Are written in third person • Act like a narrator in a play On April 10, 1912, . . .	• ALL CAPITAL LETTERS draw your attention • **Bold** letters can mean yelling • Small letters can mean whispering **Someone help us!**	• Tell the sound you would hear if it was a movie • Various sizes tell how loud or soft the sound would be CRAACK!

Summarize and Apply

Summarize the learning and remind students to notice text features when they read graphic texts.

Take a look at the chart we created. What can you say about the features authors and illustrators use in graphic texts?

- Review the chart and write the principle at the top.

  When you read today, if you choose a graphic text to read, mark with a sticky note one or two features that the author or illustrator used to create narration, sound, and/or dialogue. Bring the book when we meet so you can share.

Share

Following independent reading time, gather students in the meeting area to talk about their reading.

What text features did you notice in your reading? How did they help you understand that part of the story?

- Ask a few students to share with the class and add to the chart as necessary.

Extend the Lesson (Optional)

After assessing students' understanding, you might decide to extend the learning.

- Some graphic novels have thought bubbles to show a character's inner thoughts. Point them out and discuss with students how they differ from speech bubbles in appearance and purpose.
- **Writing About Reading** Ask students to create a response in a reader's notebook using narrative boxes, speech and thought bubbles, lettering, and sound words.

RML 4

LA.U4.RML4

Reading Minilesson Principle

Notice how the author/illustrator uses color and lines to show setting, mood, and motion.

Reading Graphic Texts

You Will Need

- two or three graphic texts with which students are familiar, such as the following from *Independent Reading Collection*:
  - *The Sinking of the Titanic* by Matt Doeden
  - *Bluffton* by Matt Phelan
- document camera (optional)
- chart paper and markers
- sticky notes

Academic Language / Important Vocabulary

- illustrator
- illustration
- mood

Continuum Connection

- Notice how illustrations and graphics go together with the text in a meaningful way (p. 72)
- Notice and infer how illustrations contribute to mood in a fiction text (p. 72)

Goal

Notice how the author/illustrator uses color and lines.

Rationale

Encouraging students to notice and understand how illustrators use and make decisions about color and lines in graphic texts supports students in gaining deeper meaning from their reading and in developing an understanding of the illustrator's craft.

Assess Learning

Observe students when they read graphic texts. Notice if there is evidence of new learning based on the goal of this minilesson.

- Are students able to discuss why an illustrator made certain color choices?
- Can they talk about how an illustrator uses lines in illustrations?
- Do they use academic language, such as *illustrator*, *illustration*, and *mood* when they talk about graphic texts?

Minilesson

To help students think about the minilesson principle, use a familiar graphic text to engage them in discussion about an illustrator's use of color and lines. Here is an example.

- Display pages 8–9 and then 26–27 from *The Sinking of the Titanic*.

  What do you notice about the illustrators' use of color on these two spreads? Think about how each makes you feel.

  The second spread has only a few colors, and they are dull. That shows a contrast between the joyful mood, or feeling, of the first spread and the mood of despair of the second one.

- Record noticings on a chart.

  Look again at page 9. What do you see near the telegraph operator's hand?

  Why do you think the illustrator used those lines?

- Record noticings on the chart.

Have a Try

Invite the students to talk about color and lines in *Bluffton*.

What do you notice about the illustrator's use of color in this book? What does that tell you? Turn and talk to your partner about that.

- After time to turn and talk, ask a few students to share. Record responses on the chart. Then turn to page 3 and ask about the lines near the falling apple.

Summarize and Apply

Summarize the learning and remind students to notice how authors/illustrators use color and lines in graphic texts.

- Review the chart and write the principle at the top.

Today, you might choose a graphic text to read. If you do, notice the author/illustrator's use of color and lines. Bring the book when we meet so you can share.

Notice how the author/illustrator uses color and lines to show setting, mood, and motion.

	The Sinking of the TITANIC	BLUFFTON (MATT PHELAN)	Color and Lines Show
Color	Bright colors at the beginning show a joyful time Few colors at the end show the tragedy	Soft colors make the story feel like it happened a long time ago	Setting Mood
Line	Lines near the telegraph key		Motion

Share

Following independent reading time, gather students in the meeting area to talk about their reading.

What did you notice about color and lines in the book you read today? Why do you think the author/illustrator made these choices?

Extend the Lesson (Optional)

After assessing students' understanding, you might decide to extend the learning.

- Continue collecting and offering graphic texts to students for independent reading. Add to the chart as necessary.
- **Writing About Reading** Ask students to write a letter in a reader's notebook about how the author/illustrator used color and lines in a graphic text.

Assessment

After you have taught the minilessons in this umbrella, observe students as they talk and write about their reading across instructional contexts: interactive read-aloud, independent reading, guided reading, shared reading, and book club. Use *The Literacy Continuum* (Fountas and Pinnell 2017) to guide observation of students' reading and writing behaviors.

- What evidence do you have of new understandings related to graphic texts?
  - Do students understand that the illustrations carry much of the meaning?
  - Do they read panels and text left to right and top to bottom?
  - Do they understand and use text features to support their understanding of the text (e.g., panels, gutters, narrative boxes, speech bubbles, thought bubbles, sound words)?
  - Do they notice and discuss an illustrator's decisions about color and lines?
  - Are they using vocabulary such as *graphic texts*, *illustrations*, *panels*, *gutters*, *narrative boxes*, *speech bubbles*, *thought bubbles*, *lettering*, and *sound words*?
- In what other ways, beyond the scope of this umbrella, are students talking about the decisions authors and illustrators make?
  - Do students notice the decisions authors make about the language they use?
  - Do they notice the decisions illustrators make about what to draw?

Use your observations to determine the next umbrella you will teach. You may also consult Minilessons Across the Year (pp. 61–64) for guidance.

Link to Writing

After teaching the minilessons in this umbrella, help students link the new learning to their own writing:

- Provide students with time to work on writing their own graphic texts. Encourage them to include text features.

Reader's Notebook

When this umbrella is complete, provide a copy of the minilesson principles (see resources.fountasandpinnell.com) for students to glue in the reader's notebook (in the Minilessons section if using *Reader's Notebook: Advanced* [Fountas and Pinnell 2011]), so they can refer to the information as needed.

Thinking Critically About the Ways People Are Represented in Texts

Umbrella 5

Minilessons in This Umbrella

RML1	Critique books for representation and omission.
RML2	Evaluate how different groups of people are represented in illustrations and graphics.
RML3	Evaluate how characters are portrayed in books.
RML4	Think about how a story is affected by an author's choice of characters (e.g., gender, race/culture, socioeconomic status).

Before Teaching Umbrella 5 Minilessons

All students, regardless of background, benefit from exposure to a broad range of literature that represents the heterogeneous world in which we live. This is important so that all students can learn in a culturally relevant environment, which includes having access to materials in which they can see themselves and feel valued. In addition, it is crucial that they have opportunities to learn about a wide diversity of people and places in order to develop rich and expansive relationships and understandings.

The first minilesson provides a framework for critiquing the classroom library (or other book collection) to ensure that books represent people from many backgrounds—including race, religion, gender, socioeconomic levels, age, family dynamics, varied geographic settings, and disabilities to name just a few. It is also important to include books that show people as they exist today, rather than older stereotypical representations or just a narrow segment of a particular population. Use the entire text set Achieving a Dream as well as the books listed below from the *Fountas & Pinnell Classroom™ Interactive Read-Aloud Collection* or suitable books from your classroom library.

Grit and Perseverance

Ada's Violin by Susan Hood

Nim and the War Effort by Milly Lee

Illustrator Study: Duncan Tonatiuh

Danza! by Duncan Tonatiuh

Exploring Literary Language

Hoops by Robert Burleigh

Problem Solving/Resourcefulness

Destiny's Gift by Natasha Anastasia Tarpley

Family

Morning on the Lake by Jan Bourdeau Waboose

Empathy

Mrs. Katz and Tush by Patricia Polacco

Genre Study: Historical Fiction

The Bracelet by Yoshiko Uchida

As you read aloud and enjoy these texts together, help students

- think and talk about the people who are represented in books they read, and
- analyze illustrations and content for the way characters are represented.

Grit and Perseverance

Illustrator Study: Duncan Tonatiuh

Exploring Literary Language

Problem Solving/ Resourcefulness

Family

Empathy

Genre Study: Historical Fiction

RML1

LA.U5.RML1

Reading Minilesson Principle

Critique books for representation and omission.

Thinking Critically About the Ways People Are Represented in Texts

You Will Need

- one set of books that shows diversity in representation, such as books in Text Set: Achieving a Dream
- chart paper and markers
- small sticky notes
- classroom library books, divided into random sets (one per group)

Academic Language / Important Vocabulary

- critique
- representation
- diversity
- race
- gender
- socioeconomic

Continuum Connection

- Share opinions about a written text and/or about illustrations and give rationales and examples (pp. 559, 569, 581)

Goal

Evaluate the diversity of representation in books.

Rationale

When students learn to critique whether books are culturally responsive and diverse, they learn to value and embrace reading about a wide range of people that resemble the heterogeneous world in which we live, as well as to see themselves represented and valued in the classroom through literature.

Assess Learning

Observe students when they critique sets of books and notice if there is evidence of new learning based on the goal of this minilesson.

- Are students able to analyze sets of books and notice similarities and differences in representation?
- Do they understand the terms *critique, representation, diversity, race, gender,* and *socioeconomic*?

Minilesson

To help students think about the minilesson principle, engage them in thinking about how to critique sets of books for representation. Here is an example.

> Think about the world we live in and all of the different types of people and different backgrounds there are. Today let's think a bit about whether the books we have in the classroom reflect that diversity. In other words, who is represented in and who is missing from our books?

- Display the books from Text Set: Achieving a Dream.

> If we want to look at this set of books, one question we might ask is whether people from different races are represented. What are some other questions we might ask to notice whether different types of people are represented? Turn and talk about that.

- After time for discussion, ask students to share ideas and begin a list on chart paper. Introduce academic vocabulary that defines their thinking (e.g., if students say *rich or poor,* introduce the term *socioeconomic)*.

> Take a look at the list of questions and think about this set of books. Let's try to answer these questions about who is represented and who is missing.

- Depending on the experiences of your students with this topic, you may need to model the initial critique.

> Why is it important that we have a diverse range of books available to read?

Have a Try

Invite the students to critique a set of books.

- Have students sit in groups, each with a set of books randomly selected from the classroom library.

  Take a look at the questions we have written on the chart. With your group, critique the set of books. Talk about whether the books represent a wide range of people. Ask yourselves who is represented and who is missing. You can place a sticky note on books with notes about your findings.

- After time for discussion, have groups share their noticings. Add new questions to the chart.

Critique books for representation and omission.

Are there books that include or are about people—

- ☐ of different races
- ☐ of different genders
- ☐ in non-stereotypical roles
- ☐ from different socioeconomic backgrounds
- ☐ with disabilities
- ☐ from a variety of cultures and countries
- ☐ who practice diverse religions
- ☐ from different backgrounds interacting
- ☐ of different ages and generations
- ☐ who speak languages other than English
- ☐ who are from different types of families

Who is represented in the books?
Who is missing in the books?

Summarize and Apply

Summarize the learning and remind students to think critically about representation in books.

  What did you learn to do today?

- Write the principle on the top of chart.

  When you read today, think about who is represented in the book you are reading. Bring the book when we meet so you can share.

Share

Following independent reading time, gather students in the meeting area in a circle to talk about books.

- Ask each student to briefly describe the main character(s) or subject(s) in the book. After all students have shared, ask them to talk about the kinds of people who are in the books and the kinds of people who are not in the books.

Extend the Lesson (Optional)

After assessing students' understanding, you might decide to extend the learning.

- Have students meet with the librarian to talk about the library collection and how the librarian goes about choosing books to purchase for the library.
- Ask students to research books about people who are not represented in the school or classroom library and compile a list of titles that would be worthwhile purchases for the school. Ask them to also consider funding sources (e.g., present the list at PTA/PTO meeting, hold a fundraising event).

RML 2
LA.U5.RML2

Reading Minilesson Principle

Evaluate how different groups of people are represented in illustrations and graphics.

Thinking Critically About the Ways People Are Represented in Texts

You Will Need

- several books that show illustrations of diverse people, such as the following:
  - *Ada's Violin* by Susan Hood, from Text Set: Grit and Perseverance
  - *Danza!* by Duncan Tonatiuh, from Text Set: Illustrator Study: Duncan Tonatiuh
  - *Hoops* by Robert Burleigh, from Text Set: Exploring Literary Language
  - *Destiny's Gift* by Natasha Anastasia Tarpley, from Text Set: Problem Solving/ Resourcefulness
  - *Morning on the Lake* by Jan Bourdeau Waboose, from Text Set: Family
- document camera (optional)
- books or online resources that show modern photographs of people (optional)
- chart paper and markers
- sticky notes
- basket of books with illustrations of people

Academic Language / Important Vocabulary

- diversity
- depicted
- representation
- stereotype

Continuum Connection

- Share opinions about a written text and/or about illustrations and give rationales and examples (pp. 559, 569, 581)

Goal

Evaluate how different groups of people are represented in illustrations and graphics.

Rationale

When students think critically about the way people are represented in illustrations, they not only see themselves accurately and feel valued, but they also experience realistic depictions of people outside their community in order to develop empathy and a broader worldview.

Assess Learning

Observe students as they discuss illustrations in the books they read and notice if there is evidence of new learning based on the goal of this minilesson.

- Do students think and talk about the way people are depicted in illustrations?
- Are they using language such as *diversity, depicted, representation,* and *stereotype*?

Minilesson

To help students think about the minilesson principle, engage them in a discussion about the way people are depicted in illustrations. Here is an example.

- If possible, project pages so that students can see illustrations in detail or provide time before the lesson for students to look closely at illustrations. You may be able to gather current photographs from books or online that show young people from Paraguay and Mexico, especially those who live in cities, so that the diversity within the culture is evident.

  Think about the way people are depicted (shown) in illustrations. Sometimes they are accurate, and sometimes they show stereotypes.

- Show several illustrations of people from *Ada's Violin* and *Danza!* and, if available, current photographs of children from Paraguay and Mexico.

  Compare the illustrations in these books that show people from Paraguay and Mexico to the way people really look. Turn and talk about that.

- After discussion, ask students to note whether the illustrations look realistic and to support their opinions with evidence from the illustrations and photographs. Record responses on the chart paper.
- Show a few illustrations from *Hoops*.

  What do you notice about these illustrations and the way people are depicted? Do they look realistic?

- Add to chart. Repeat with *Destiny's Gift* and *Morning on the Lake*.

Have a Try

Invite the students to talk in small groups about the way people are represented in books.

- Provide each group with one or two books that show illustrations of people. Try to include a diversity of people in the books so that the follow-up conversation will be rich and diverse.

  In your group, talk about how people are depicted in the illustrations. Do you think the illustrations are accurate, or do they show stereotypes? Is there a range in the way people look that is realistic, or do they all look the same?

- After time for discussion, ask students to share their thinking.

Evaluate how different groups of people are represented in illustrations and graphics.

	Are people represented realistically?	Reasons
 *Ada's Violin*	Yes	The people have unique features and are different ages.
 *¡Danza!*	No	The illustrator uses a pre-Columbian art style, reflecting his Mexican American heritage.
	Yes	Each person has unique features.
 *Destiny's Gift*	No	Facial features are not realistic, but people do look different (skin tones, facial features).
 *Morning on the Lake*	Yes	The characters look Native American. Each has unique features.

Summarize and Apply

Summarize the learning and remind students to evaluate the way people are depicted in illustrations.

Today you learned that you can evaluate how different groups of people are represented in illustrations and graphics.

- Write the principle at the top of the chart.

  If you read a book with illustrations of people, notice how they are shown in the illustrations. Place a sticky note on any pages you want to remember. Bring the book when we meet so you can share your noticings.

Share

Following independent reading time, gather students in the meeting area.

What did you notice about the way people are depicted in illustrations? Show an example that supports your thinking.

Extend the Lesson (Optional)

After assessing students' understanding, you might decide to extend the learning.

- Have students compare the illustrations in an older book to the illustrations in a recent book and talk about how awareness of the importance to accurately depict people has changed the way illustrations are done.
- Encourage students to consider the background of the author and illustrator as they critique the illustrations in books.

RML 3

LA.U5.RML3

Reading Minilesson Principle

Evaluate how characters are portrayed in books.

Thinking Critically About the Ways People Are Represented in Texts

You Will Need

- several books with a variety of human characters, such as the following:
  - *Morning on the Lake* by Jan Bourdeau Waboose, from Text Set: Family
  - *Mrs. Katz and Tush*, by Patricia Polacco, from Text Set: Empathy
  - *The Bracelet* by Yoshiko Uchida, from Text Set: Genre Study: Historical Fiction
- chart paper and markers
- basket of fiction books with human characters

Academic Language / Important Vocabulary

- represented
- portrayed
- authentic
- stereotypes

Continuum Connection

- Share opinions about a written text and/or about illustrations and give rationales and examples (pp. 559, 569, 581)

Goal

Evaluate the way characters are portrayed in books, including critiquing for stereotyping and overgeneralizations of different groups of people.

Rationale

When students think critically about how characters are portrayed in books, they begin to notice the perpetuation of stereotypes and will begin to understand how an author can accurately and respectfully reflect people from different races, cultures, genders, or abilities.

Assess Learning

Observe students when they talk about characters and notice if there is evidence of new learning based on the goal of this minilesson.

- Do students discuss how characters are portrayed in the books they read?
- Do they notice whether characters are portrayed in a stereotypical way?
- Are they using language such as *represented, portrayed, authentic,* and *stereotypes*?

Minilesson

To help students think about the minilesson principle, engage them in a thoughtful discussion about evaluating how characters are portrayed. Here is an example.

- Revisit a few pages from *Morning on the Lake.*

  Think about Noshen and his grandfather, Mishomis. How would you describe them?

- Guide the conversation to help students focus on their background (Ojibway).

  How are Noshen and Mishomis portrayed? Do they seem like authentic people, or are they portrayed as stereotypes? Turn and talk about that.

- After time for discussion, have students share their opinions about the way Noshen and Mishomis are portrayed and the reasons for their opinions. Record responses on chart paper.
- Repeat the activity with *Mrs. Katz and Tush*, focusing on the diversity in race, age, and religion of the two main characters and the way that both Mrs. Katz and Larnel have unique personalities.

  What are some questions you might ask yourself when you evaluate how characters are portrayed in books?

- Guide the conversation and make a list of questions on the chart.

Have a Try

Invite the students to evaluate the way a character is portrayed in a story.

- Revisit pages 5–8 from *The Bracelet.*

  Think about Emi in *The Bracelet.* Take a look at the questions on the chart and talk with a partner about the way Emi is portrayed.

- After time for discussion, ask students to share their thinking. Guide the conversation as needed. Add to the chart.

Summarize and Apply

Summarize the learning and remind students to think about how characters are portrayed in books.

You talked about some ways you can evaluate how characters are portrayed in books.

- Write the principle on the chart.

  When you read today, evaluate the characters in your book. Mark any pages you want to remember with a sticky note. Bring the book when we meet so you can share.

Evaluate how characters are portrayed in books.

Title	How Characters Are Portrayed	
Morning on the Lake	Not stereotypes	Mishomis shares his wisdom and respect for nature with Noshen.
Patricia Polacco, Mrs. Katz and Tush	Not stereotypes	The main characters are very different from each other (different ages, races, religions), but they become friends and have a genuine friendship.
the bracelet	Not stereotypes	Emi and Laurie are from different races and have a true friendship. Emi has a unique personality.

Questions to Ask About How Characters Are Portrayed

- Do characters reflect diverse groups fairly and accurately?
- Do characters show diversity within a group?
- Do characters show a variety of characteristics or just stereotypes?

Share

Following independent reading time, gather students in the meeting area in groups of two or three to talk about how they evaluated characters.

Talk with your group about what you noticed in the way characters are portrayed in the book you are reading.

Extend the Lesson (Optional)

After assessing students' understanding, you might decide to extend the learning.

- Have students critique texts for stereotypes and misrepresentations. If appropriate for your class, you might provide books that have these negative attributes to small groups so students can think critically about the impact the misrepresentations have on the reader. Guide students to understand that stereotypical characters are often simple and one-dimensional. When characters are rounder and more complex, they are less likely to seem like a stereotype of a certain group.

RML 4
LA.U5.RML4

Reading Minilesson Principle

Think about how a story is affected by an author's choice of characters (e.g., gender, race/culture, socioeconomic status).

Thinking Critically About the Ways People Are Represented in Texts

You Will Need

- several familiar fiction texts with diverse characters, such as the following:
  - *Morning on the Lake* by Jan Bourdeau Waboose, from Text Set: Family
  - *Hoops* by Robert Burleigh, from Text Set: Exploring Literary Language
  - *Destiny's Gift* by Natasha Anastasia Tarpley, from Text Set: Problem Solving/ Resourcefulness
  - *Nim and the War Effort* by Milly Lee, from Text Set: Grit and Perseverance
- chart paper and markers
- sticky notes

Academic Language / Important Vocabulary

- impact
- gender
- race
- culture
- socioeconomic status

Continuum Connection

- Share opinions about a written text and/or about illustrations and give rationales and examples (pp. 559, 569, 581)

Goal

Notice how the author's choice of a character's gender, race, etc., influences a story.

Rationale

When students think about how culture, race, gender, location, historical time period, political environment, and/or socioeconomic status impact a story, they develop empathy for people and an awareness of inequalities, unfairness, and misrepresentation of people now and in the past.

Assess Learning

Observe students as they discuss characters and notice if there is evidence of new learning based on the goal of this minilesson.

- Do students notice how a character's race, gender, or socioeconomic status impacts a story?
- Can they talk about how the story would be different if the character's race, gender, or socioeconomic status were different?
- Are they using language such as *impact, gender, race, culture,* and *socioeconomic status*?

Minilesson

To help students think about the minilesson principle, engage them in a discussion about how a character's gender, race/culture, or socioeconomic status affects the story. Here is an example.

- Show the cover of *Morning on the Lake*.

  Think about this story. In what ways do the types of characters chosen by the author have an impact on the story?

  How would the story be different if the characters were not Native American and not from different generations?

- Record responses on the chart.
- Continue the conversation with the books *Hoops* and *Destiny's Gift*.

  Sometimes a story is not affected by the race of a character or whether a character is male or female. Does thinking about this help you understand characters better? How?

Have a Try

Invite the students to talk about how the gender, race/culture, or socioeconomic status of a character impacts a story.

- Show the cover of *Nim and the War Effort*.

  How does Nim's race, culture, or gender impact this story? Turn and talk about that.

- Invite a few students to share. Record responses on the chart.

Title	What impact does the character choice have on the story?
Morning on the Lake	If the story were about a non-Native American boy and grandpa, they would have had different experiences, although the boy would probably still learn a lot from his grandpa.
Hoops	Race and gender do not impact this story.
Destiny's Gift	Race and gender do not impact this story.
Nim and the War Effort	Nim's race and possibly gender impact this story. This character shows how some Americans were unfairly treated due to their race and culture.

Think about how a story is affected by an author's choice of characters (e.g., gender, race/culture, socioeconomic status).

Summarize and Apply

Summarize the learning and remind students to think about the ways that an author's character choice does or does not impact a story.

What have you noticed today about characters?

- Review the chart and write the principle at the top.

  When you read today, think about how the choice of the characters' gender, race, culture, or socioeconomic status impacts the story. Bring the book when we meet so you can share your noticings.

Share

Following independent reading time, gather students in small groups.

Share how the story is impacted by the characters' race, culture, gender, or socioeconomic background. How does this help you to better understand the characters and the story?

Extend the Lesson (Optional)

After assessing students' understanding, you might decide to extend the learning.

- Suggest that students think critically about the characters in the movies or television shows that they watch in the same way they have been thinking about the characters in books.
- **Writing About Reading** Have students write in a reader's notebook about how a character's race, culture, gender, or socioeconomic status influences, or does not influence, a story they are reading.

Thinking Critically About the Ways People Are Represented in Texts

Assessment

After you have taught the minilessons in this umbrella, observe students as they talk and write about their reading across instructional contexts: interactive read-aloud, independent reading, guided reading, shared reading, and book club. Use *The Literacy Continuum* (Fountas and Pinnell 2017) to observe students' reading and writing behaviors.

- What evidence do you have of new understandings related to the way people are represented in texts?
  - Are students able to critique books for fair representation of people?
  - Can they evaluate how different groups of people are represented in illustrations and graphics?
  - Are they able to analyze how characters are portrayed in books?
  - Do they think about how the story is affected by an author's choice of gender, race/culture, or socioeconomic status of a character?
  - Are they using the terms *critique, representation, diversity, race, gender, socioeconomic, evaluate,* and *portrayed*?
- In what other ways, beyond the scope of this umbrella, are students thinking about representation?
  - Are students beginning to self-select books that show a broader diversity of people, including people from backgrounds that are both similar to and different from their own?

Use your observations to determine the next umbrella you will teach. You may also consult Minilessons Across the Year (pp. 61–64) for guidance.

Link to Writing

After teaching the minilessons in this umbrella, help students link the new learning to their own writing:

- Encourage students to write about what they notice about representation as they read books, including both positive and negative examples.

Reader's Notebook

When this umbrella is complete, provide a copy of the minilesson principles (see resources.fountasandpinnell.com) for students to glue in the reader's notebook (in the Minilessons section if using *Reader's Notebook: Advanced* [Fountas and Pinnell 2011]), so they can refer to the information as needed.

Minilessons in This Umbrella

RML1	There are different genres of fiction books.
RML2	There are different genres of nonfiction books.
RML3	There are several types of traditional literature.

Before Teaching Umbrella 6 Minilessons

Before teaching these minilessons, read and discuss fiction and nonfiction books from a range of genres. Make a Books We Have Shared chart (p. 68) and add to it as you read books together.

The minilessons in this umbrella support students in understanding that there are different genres of books (p. 40) and that each one has specific characteristics. We recommend teaching the first two minilessons early in the year to provide students with a framework for thinking about fiction and nonfiction texts. The third minilesson should ideally be taught later in the year, when students have had exposure to several different types of traditional literature and have a deeper understanding of the genre. Use the following suggested books from the *Fountas & Pinnell Classroom™ Interactive Read-Aloud Collection* or choose examples of fiction, nonfiction, and traditional literature from your classroom library.

Interactive Read-Aloud Collection

Empathy

Mrs. Katz and Tush by Patricia Polacco

The Poet's Dog by Patricia MacLachlan

The Crane Girl by Curtis Manley

Conflict Resolution

Shooting at the Stars by John Hendrix

Thirty Minutes Over Oregon by Marc Tyler Nobleman

The Power of Knowledge

Seeker of Knowledge: by James Rumford

Genre Study: Expository Nonfiction

The Cod's Tale by Mark Kurlansky

Caring for Our World

Cycle of Rice, Cycle of Life by Jan Reynolds

Genre Study: Legends

Merlin and the Dragons by Jane Yolen

Author/Illustrator Study: Demi

The Emperor's New Clothes by Demi

Independent Reading Collection

Look Up! by Annette LeBlanc Cate

As you read aloud and enjoy books together, help students notice defining characteristics of the different genres of fiction and nonfiction.

Interactive Read-Aloud

Empathy

Conflict Resolution

The Power of Knowledge

Expository Nonfiction

Caring for Our World

Legends

Demi

Independent Reading

RML1
LA.U6.RML1

Reading Minilesson Principle

There are different genres of fiction books.

Understanding Fiction and Nonfiction Genres

You Will Need

- seven notecards, each with one of the following labels: *Fiction, Fantasy, Realism, Realistic Fiction, Historical Fiction, Modern Fantasy, Traditional Literature*
- a variety of types of fiction books, such as the following:
  - *Mrs. Katz and Tush* by Patricia Polacco, from Text Set: Empathy
  - *Shooting at the Stars* by John Hendrix, from Text Set: Conflict Resolution
  - *The Poet's Dog* by Patricia MacLachlan and *The Crane Girl* by Curtis Manley, and from Text Set: Empathy
- chart paper and markers
- glue stick or tape

Academic Language / Important Vocabulary

- genre
- fiction
- fantasy
- realism
- realistic fiction
- historical fiction

Continuum Connection

- Understand that there are different types of texts and that they have different characteristics (p. 69)
- Notice and understand the characteristics of some specific fiction genres: e.g., realistic fiction, historical fiction, folktale, fairy tale, fractured fairy tale, fable, myth, legend, epic, ballad, fantasy including science fiction, hybrid text (p. 69)

Goal

Understand that there are different genres of fiction texts (e.g., realistic fiction, historical fiction, traditional literature, and fantasy) that fall within the broader categories of realism or fantasy.

Rationale

Studying the characteristics of fiction genres–e.g., realistic, historical, traditional, and fantasy–helps students know what to expect when reading and increases their comprehension.

Assess Learning

Observe students when they read and talk about books and notice if there is evidence of new learning based on the goal of this minilesson.

- Can students name different fiction genres and describe the characteristics?
- Do they use academic vocabulary, such as *genre, fiction, fantasy, realism, realistic fiction,* and *historical fiction*?

Minilesson

To help students think about the minilesson principle, engage them in discussing and categorizing the different genres of fiction. Here is an example.

- Display and review as necessary these books: *Mrs. Katz and Tush*, *Shooting at the Stars*, *The Crane Girl*, and *The Poet's Dog*.

  Are these books fiction or nonfiction? What makes you think that?

  These books are fiction. They are stories made up by the author. But each is a different kind of fiction.

- Attach the Fiction card to the top of the chart paper. Attach the Fantasy and Realism cards underneath the Fiction card and draw lines connecting them.

  Which of these books are examples of realism—stories that the author made up but that could happen? What kinds of fiction are they?

- Add the cards for Realistic Fiction (*Mrs. Katz and Tush*) and Historical Fiction (*Shooting at the Stars*) to the chart. Provide brief definitions of each genre as necessary (a story that could be real but is made up; a story based on a real person, place, and/or event).

- Repeat the process for fantasy. *The Poet's Dog* is modern fantasy (a story written by a known author and could never happen in real life). *The Crane Girl* is traditional literature (a story passed down from generation to generation that could never happen in real life).

Have a Try

Invite the students to talk with a partner about fiction books.

Think of a fiction book you have read recently or that we have read in class. Turn and talk to your partner about where it fits on the chart.

- After students turn and talk, invite a few pairs to share their thinking.

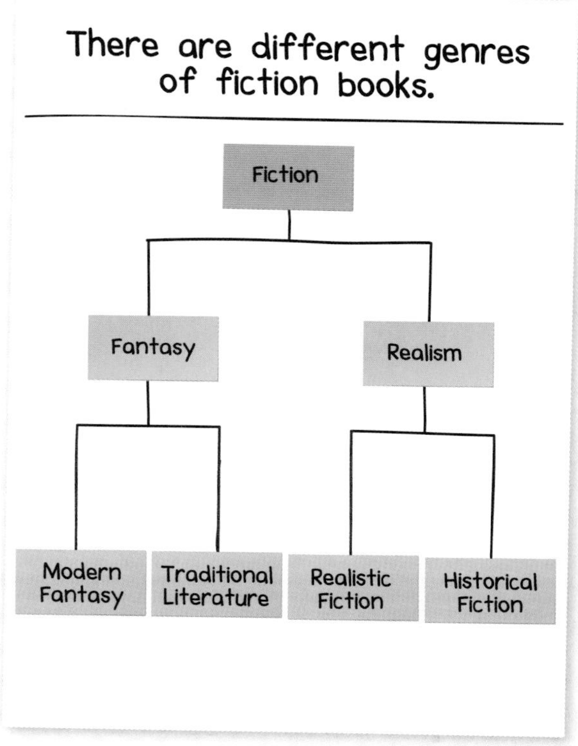

Summarize and Apply

Summarize the learning and remind students to notice different genres of fiction books.

What does this diagram show?

- Write the principle at the top of the chart.

If you read a fiction book today, think about which genre of fiction it is. Be ready to share your thinking when we come back together.

Share

Following independent reading time, gather students together in the meeting area to talk about their reading.

Who read a fiction book today?

What genre of fiction did you read? How could you tell which genre it was?

Extend the Lesson (Optional)

After assessing students' understanding, you might decide to extend the learning.

- Point out the genre chart on the orange tab in *Reader's Notebook: Advanced* (Fountas and Pinnell 2011).
- There are different forms of modern fantasy, including animal fantasy, low fantasy, high fantasy, and science fiction. Umbrella 22: Understanding Fantasy in this section includes a lesson on science fiction. We recommend teaching low and high fantasy starting in Grade 6, but you may choose to do this sooner if you feel your students are ready.

RML2

LA.U6.RML2

Reading Minilesson Principle

There are different genres of nonfiction books.

Understanding Fiction and Nonfiction Genres

You Will Need

- eleven notecards, each printed with one of the following labels: *Nonfiction, Told Like a Story, Not Told Like a Story, Biographical Texts, Procedural/How-to Texts, Narrative Nonfiction, Expository Texts, Persuasive Texts, Biography, Autobiography, Memoir*
- a variety of types of nonfiction books, such as the following:
  - *Seeker of Knowledge* by James Rumford, from Text Set: The Power of Knowledge
  - *Thirty Minutes Over Oregon* by Marc Tyler Nobleman, from Text Set: Conflict Resolution
  - *The Cod's Tale* by Mark Kurlansky, from Text Set: Expository Nonfiction
  - *Look Up!* by Annette LeBlanc Cate, from *Independent Reading Collection*
  - *Cycle of Rice, Cycle of Life* by Jan Reynolds, from Text Set: Caring for Our World
- chart paper and markers
- glue stick or tape

Academic Language / Important Vocabulary

- genre
- nonfiction
- biographical
- narrative nonfiction
- expository
- procedural

Continuum Connection

- Notice and understand the characteristics of some specific nonfiction (p. 73)

Goal

Understand that there are different genres of nonfiction texts (e.g., biography, autobiography, informational, memoir, and narrative nonfiction).

Rationale

Studying the characteristics of different nonfiction genres–e.g., narrative nonfiction, expository, and procedural–helps students know what to expect when reading and increases their comprehension.

Assess Learning

Observe students when they read and talk about nonfiction books and notice if there is evidence of new learning based on the goal of this minilesson.

- Can students name different nonfiction genres and describe their basic characteristics?
- Do they use academic vocabulary, such as *genre, nonfiction, biographical, narrative nonfiction, expository,* and *procedural*?

Minilesson

To help students think about the minilesson principle, engage them in discussing and categorizing the different genres of nonfiction. Here is an example.

- Attach the Nonfiction card to the top of the chart paper. Display and review as necessary these books: *Seeker of Knowledge, Thirty Minutes Over Oregon, The Cod's Tale, Look Up!,* and *Cycle of Rice, Cycle of Life.*

  These books are nonfiction. They are not stories made up by an author. They give information. But each is a different kind of nonfiction.

- Attach the Told Like a Story and Not Told Like a Story cards underneath Nonfiction and draw lines connecting them.

  In which of these books is the information written like a story with a beginning, middle, and end?

  Do you know what kinds of nonfiction they are?

- Add the cards for Biographical Texts (*Seeker of Knowledge*) and Narrative Nonfiction (*Thirty Minutes Over Oregon*) to the chart. Provide brief definitions of each genre as necessary (books written about people's lives; information written in such a way as to seem like a story).
- Repeat the process for Not Told Like a Story. *The Cod's Tale* is an expository text (written solely to give information). *Look Up!* is a procedural/how-to text (telling how to do something, often in order). *Cycle of Rice, Cycle of Life,* particularly in the foreword and the author's note, is a persuasive text (seeks to convince the reader to agree with the author's point).

Have a Try

Invite the students to talk with a partner about biographical texts.

- Show the cards for Biography, Autobiography, and Memoir.

  Turn and talk to your partner about biographies, autobiographies, and memoirs. Share what you know about these genres and, with your partner, decide where they should go.

- After time for discussion, invite a few pairs to share their thinking, and add the cards to complete the diagram.

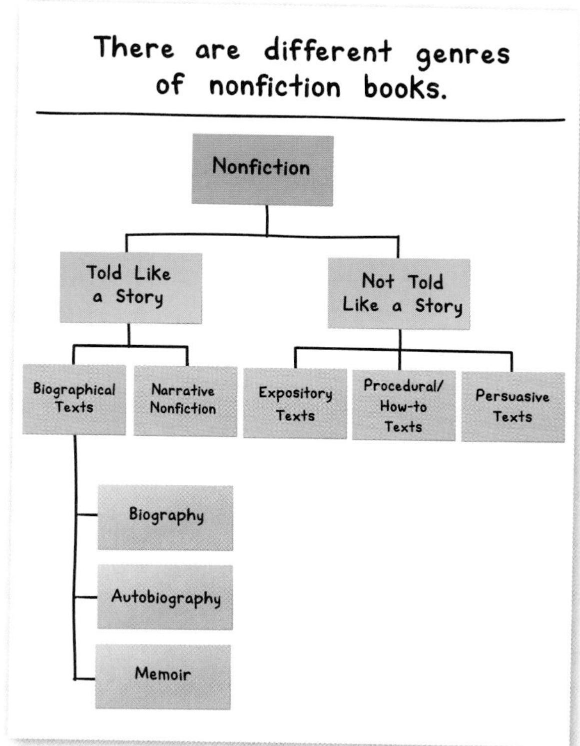

Summarize and Apply

Summarize the learning and remind students to notice different genres of nonfiction books.

What does the diagram show?

- Write the principle at the top of the chart.

  If you read a nonfiction book today, think about which genre of nonfiction it is. Be ready to share your thinking when we come back together.

Share

Following independent reading time, gather students together in the meeting area to talk about their reading.

Who read a nonfiction book today?

What genre of nonfiction did you read? How could you tell which genre it was?

Extend the Lesson (Optional)

After assessing students' understanding, you might decide to extend the learning.

- Point out the genre chart on the orange tab in *Reader's Notebook: Advanced* (Fountas and Pinnell 2011).
- Have students use the categories to organize the classroom library.

RML3

LA.U6.RML3

Reading Minilesson Principle
There are several types of traditional literature.

Understanding Fiction and Nonfiction Genres

You Will Need

- at least two or three familiar books that represent different types of traditional literature (folk tales, fables, legends, etc.), such as the following:
    - *The Crane Girl* by Curtis Manley, from Text Set: Empathy
    - *Merlin and the Dragons* by Jane Yolen, from Text Set: Genre Study: Legends
    - *The Emperor's New Clothes* by Demi, from Text Set: Author/Illustrator Study: Demi
- chart paper and markers

Academic Language / Important Vocabulary

- traditional literature
- folktale
- myth
- legend
- fairy tale
- fable

Continuum Connection

- Notice and understand the characteristics of some specific fiction genres: e.g., realistic fiction, historical fiction, folktale, fairy tale, fractured fairy tale, fable, myth, legend, epic, ballad, fantasy including science fiction, hybrid text (p. 69)
- Identify elements of traditional literature and fantasy: e.g., the supernatural; imaginary and otherworldly creatures; gods and goddesses; talking animals, toys, and dolls; heroic characters; technology or scientific advances; time travel; aliens or outer space (p. 69)

Goal

Understand that there are different types of traditional literature (e.g., folktales, fairy tales, legends, and fables).

Rationale

Studying the characteristics of traditional literature helps students know what to expect when reading and increases comprehension.

Assess Learning

Observe students when they read and talk about traditional literature and notice if there is evidence of new learning based on the goal of this minilesson.

- Can students describe the basic characteristics of traditional literature?
- Do they use academic vocabulary, such as *traditional literature*, *folktale*, *myth*, *legend*, *fairy tale*, and *fable*?

Minilesson

To help students think about the minilesson principle, engage them in a discussion of different types of traditional literature. Here is an example.

- Show the cover of *The Crane Girl.*

  The Crane Girl is a kind of traditional literature called a folktale. What do you know about folktales? What makes this book a folktale?

- Record students' responses on chart paper. Then show the cover of *Merlin and the Dragons.*

  This book is a type of traditional literature called a legend. Legends are stories about a person that may or may not have been real. Some people think Merlin is based on a historical character and some think he isn't.

- Record features of legends on the chart. Then hold up *The Emperor's New Clothes.*

  This book is a fairy tale, which is another kind of traditional literature. What other fairy tales do you know? What makes a fairy tale a fairy tale?

- Record responses on the chart.

  Myths are another type of traditional literature. You may have read or heard of the myths of Hercules, Persephone, King Midas, or Pandora's box. Myths are very old stories that people imagined to explain why people behaved in certain ways or to explain natural phenomena, such as the seasons.

- Record features of myths on the chart.

Have a Try

Invite the students to talk with a partner about fables.

> Fables are also a type of traditional literature. You are probably familiar with "The Boy Who Cried Wolf" and "The Tortoise and the Hare," which are both fables. Turn and talk to your partner about the characteristics of fables.

- After students turn and talk, invite several pairs to share their thinking. Record responses on the chart.

There are several types of traditional literature.

Type of Traditional Literature	Example(s)	Characteristics
Folktale		• Stories about ordinary people • Handed down over many years • Simple plot and characters
Legend		• Tells the story of a hero (often with exaggerated qualities) • Often involves a quest • May have imaginary creatures
Fairy tale		• Characters with magical abilities • Good and bad characters • Good wins over evil
Myth	Myths about Hercules, Persephone, King Midas, Pandora	• Explains something (e.g., beginning of the world, something in nature, human behavior) • Often involves gods and goddesses
Fable	"The Boy Who Cried Wolf" "The Tortoise and the Hare"	• Very short • Teaches a moral or lesson • Animals who talk and act like people

Summarize and Apply

Summarize the learning and remind students to read different kinds of traditional literature.

> What did you notice about traditional literature today?

- Write the principle at the top of the chart.

> When you read today, you may want to choose a traditional literature story. If you do, think about what type of traditional literature it is. Be ready to share your thinking when we come back together.

Share

Following independent reading time, gather students together in the meeting area to talk about their reading.

> Who read an example of traditional literature today?
>
> What kind of traditional literature was the book you read? How do you know?

Extend the Lesson (Optional)

After assessing students' understanding, you might decide to extend the learning.

- Introduce students to additional types of traditional literature, such as epics and ballads or different types of folktales (beast tales, cumulative tales, trickster tales, etc.).

Understanding Fiction and Nonfiction Genres

Assessment

After you have taught the minilessons in this umbrella, observe students as they talk and write about their reading across instructional contexts: interactive read-aloud, independent reading, guided reading, shared reading, and book club. Use *The Literacy Continuum* (Fountas and Pinnell 2017) to observe students' reading and writing behaviors.

- What evidence do you have of new understandings related to fiction and nonfiction genres?
  - Are students able to describe the characteristics of specific fiction genres, such as realistic fiction, historical fiction, science fiction, and fantasy?
  - Are they able to describe the characteristics of specific nonfiction genres, such as biography, autobiography, memoir, expository, and narrative nonfiction?
  - Can they describe the characteristics of specific traditional literature, such as fairy tales, fables, and folktales?
  - Do they use academic language, such as *fiction*, *nonfiction*, *folktale*, and *memoir*?
- In what other ways, beyond the scope of this umbrella, are students talking about fiction and nonfiction?
  - Are students thinking about theme and author's message?
  - Are they analyzing writer's and illustrator's craft?
  - Are they noticing book and print features?

Use your observations to determine the next umbrella you will teach. You may also consult Minilessons Across the Year (pp. 61–64) for guidance.

Link to Writing

After teaching the minilessons in this umbrella, help students link the new learning to their own writing:

- Give students numerous opportunities to write their own texts in various genres. Before they write a text in a particular genre, review the characteristics of that genre and remind students to implement them in their own writing.

Reader's Notebook

When this umbrella is complete, provide a copy of the minilesson principles (see resources.fountasandpinnell.com) for students to glue in the reader's notebook (in the Minilessons section if using *Reader's Notebook: Advanced* [Fountas and Pinnell 2011]), so they can refer to the information as needed.

Minilessons in This Umbrella

RML1	A lyrical poem is a songlike poem that has rhythm and sometimes rhyme.
RML2	A free verse poem doesn't have to rhyme or have rhythm.
RML3	A limerick is a rhyming poem that is usually surprising, funny, and sometimes nonsensical.

Author Study: Joyce Sidman

Before Teaching Umbrella 7 Minilessons

"Poetry is compact writing characterized by imagination and artistry and imbued with intense meaning" (Fountas and Pinnell 2012c, 19). Studying poetry helps students to understand the role poetry plays in their lives as readers. Looking closely at and discussing the characteristics of different kinds of poems prepares students to understand the range of emotions poetry can make one feel. However, before students study poems or identify characteristics of certain types of poetry, they need to have the experience of enjoying individual poems.

Select poems that your students will enjoy and that represent the characteristics of different kinds of poetry (lyrical, free verse, limerick). Choose some poems that have rhythm, rhyme, or descriptive or figurative language. Use the following books from the *Fountas & Pinnell Classroom™ Interactive Read-Aloud Collection* or choose poetry texts from your own library to support students in studying poetry.

Author Study: Joyce Sidman

Song of the Water Boatman and Other Pond Poems

Winter Bees and Other Poems of the Cold

This Is Just to Say: Poems of Apology and Forgiveness

As you read aloud and enjoy these poems together, help students

- enjoy each poem,
- think and talk about the meaning of each poem, and
- notice and generalize the characteristics of poetry.

RML1

LA.U7.RML1

Reading Minilesson Principle

A lyrical poem is a songlike poem that has rhythm and sometimes rhyme.

Exploring Different Kinds of Poetry

You Will Need

- several familiar lyrical poems, such as the following by Joyce Sidman, from Text Set: Author Study: Joyce Sidman:
  - "Listen for Me" from *Song of the Water Boatman and Other Pond Poems*
  - "Snake's Lullaby" and "What Do the Trees Know?" from *Winter Bees and Other Poems of the Cold*
- chart paper and markers
- document camera (optional)
- two sticky notes, one that says *Rhythm* and one that says *Rhyme*
- sticky notes
- basket of poetry books

Academic Language / Important Vocabulary

- lyrical
- rhythm
- rhyme

Continuum Connection

- Recognize and understand some specific types of poetry: e.g., lyrical poetry, free verse, limerick, haiku, narrative poetry, ballad, epic/saga, concrete poetry (pp. 69, 73)

Goal

Recognize and understand the characteristics of a lyrical poem.

Rationale

Once students have read, enjoyed, and talked about poems, they can begin to understand the characteristics of different kinds of poems. This minilesson will help them know what to expect when reading a lyrical poem.

Assess Learning

Observe students when they read and discuss poetry. Notice if there is evidence of new learning based on the goal of this minilesson.

- Can students recognize a lyrical poem?
- Are they able to describe the characteristics of a lyrical poem?
- Do they use the words *lyrical, rhythm,* and *rhyme*?

Minilesson

To help students think about the minilesson principle, engage them in noticing the characteristics of familiar lyrical poems. Here is an example.

- Display a lyrical poem, such as "Listen for Me" from *Song of the Water Boatman and Other Pond Poems*. Read it aloud, emphasizing the rhythmic qualities.

  What do you notice about how the lines of the poem sound?

  What do they make you feel like doing?

- Lead students to notice the rhythm of the poem. Record responses on chart paper.

  Sometimes the poet chooses words for a poem that make you feel a beat. A word for language that sounds like that is *rhythm*.

- Have a student place the sticky note for *Rhythm* on the chart.
- Display "Snake's Lullaby" from *Winter Bees and Other Poems of the Cold*. Read it aloud, emphasizing the rhyme.

  What do you notice about how some of the words in this poem sound?

- Record rhyming words that students name on the chart. Have a student place the sticky note for *Rhyme* on the chart.

  Poems like the ones you just heard could easily be set to music. They have songlike qualities. These are lyrical poems.

Have a Try

Invite the students to talk with a partner about the qualities of a lyrical poem.

- Ask a student to read aloud "What Do the Trees Know?" from *Winter Bees and Other Poems of the Cold.*

  Turn and talk to your partner. What do you notice about the lines and words in this poem?

- After time for discussion, ask a few students to share their thinking. Record responses on the chart.

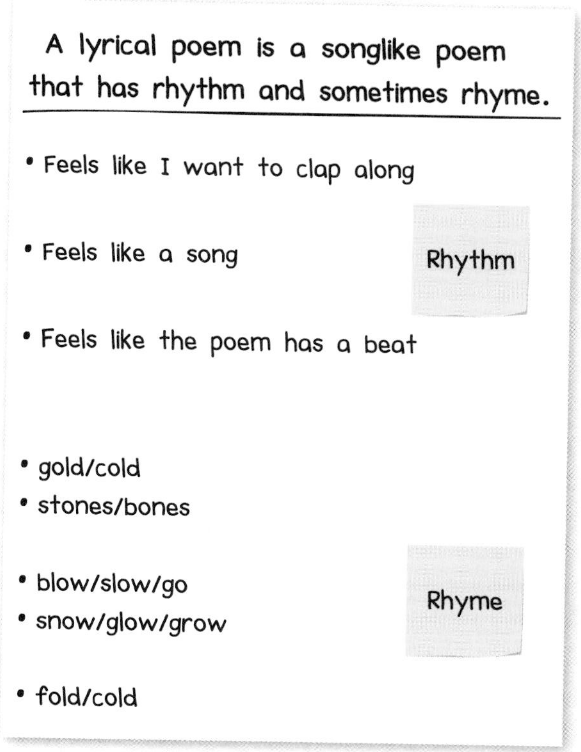

A lyrical poem is a songlike poem that has rhythm and sometimes rhyme.

- Feels like I want to clap along
- Feels like a song
- Feels like the poem has a beat

Rhythm

- gold/cold
- stones/bones
- blow/slow/go
- snow/glow/grow
- fold/cold

Rhyme

Summarize and Apply

Summarize the learning and remind students to notice rhythm and rhyme in lyrical poems.

Today you read some lyrical poems. How can you describe a lyrical poem?

- Invite responses and write the principle at the top of the chart.

Today when you read, choose a book of poetry from this basket. Read and enjoy several poems. Notice if one of the poems you read has rhythm or rhyme. If it does, mark it with a sticky note and bring it to share when we meet.

Share

Following independent reading time, gather students together in groups of three or four to discuss the poems they read.

Is the poem you read today a lyrical poem? How can you tell that it is or isn't?

Extend the Lesson (Optional)

After assessing students' understanding, you might decide to extend the learning.

- As students become more confident in understanding the characteristics of lyrical poems, you might decide to introduce additional types of poetry, such as haiku.
- Encourage students to write and illustrate poems that have rhythm and rhyme.
- **Writing About Reading** Have students write in a reader's notebook their thoughts about a poem they have read. Invite them to comment on the rhythm, rhyme, topic, or other aspects of the poem.

RML 2
LA.U7.RML2

Reading Minilesson Principle

A free verse poem doesn't have to rhyme or have rhythm.

Exploring Different Kinds of Poetry

You Will Need

- several familiar, free verse poems such as the following by Joyce Sidman, from Text Set: Author Study: Joyce Sidman:
  - "I Got Carried Away" from *This Is Just to Say: Poems of Apology and Forgiveness*
  - "Dream of the Tundra Swan" from *Winter Bees and Other Poems of the Cold*
  - "Diving Beetle's Food-Sharing Rules" from *Song of the Water Boatman and Other Pond Poems*
- chart paper prepared to make a word web (oval in center, spokes)
- markers
- sticky notes
- basket of poetry books

Academic Language / Important Vocabulary

- free verse
- rhythm
- rhyme
- characteristic

Continuum Connection

- Recognize and understand some specific types of poetry: e.g., lyrical poetry, free verse, limerick, haiku, narrative poetry, ballad, epic/saga, concrete poetry (pp. 69, 73)

Goal

Recognize and understand the characteristics of free verse poetry.

Rationale

Once students have read, enjoyed, and talked about poems, they can begin to understand the characteristics of different kinds of poems. This minilesson will help them understand that free verse poems do not need to rhyme and include a variety of poetic techniques.

Assess Learning

Observe students when they read and discuss poetry. Notice if there is evidence of new learning based on the goal of this minilesson.

- Can students describe what they notice about the poems they read?
- Do they talk about free verse poems not needing to have rhyme or rhythm?
- Do they use the words *free verse, rhythm, rhyme,* and *characteristic*?

Minilesson

To help students think about the minilesson principle, use familiar free verse poems to engage them in noticing the characteristics. Here is an example.

- Read a free verse poem, such as "I Got Carried Away" from *This Is Just to Say: Poems of Apology and Forgiveness.*

  What do you notice about this poem? Is it similar to or different from other poems you have read? How?

- Record responses around the center oval on the chart.
- Repeat this process with "Dream of the Tundra Swan" from *Winter Bees and Other Poems of the Cold.*

  What are you noticing about these poems, especially as compared with other poems you have read?

  These poems don't have to have the "usual" characteristics of poetry, such as rhythm and rhyme, though they might. These poems are free of any poetic "have-to's," so they are called free verse.

Have a Try

Invite the students to talk with a partner about a free verse poem.

- Ask a student to read aloud "Diving Beetle's Food-Sharing Rules" from *Song of the Water Boatman and Other Pond Poems.*

  Turn and talk to your partner. Is this a free verse poem, or another type of poem? How do you know?

- Record responses on the chart.

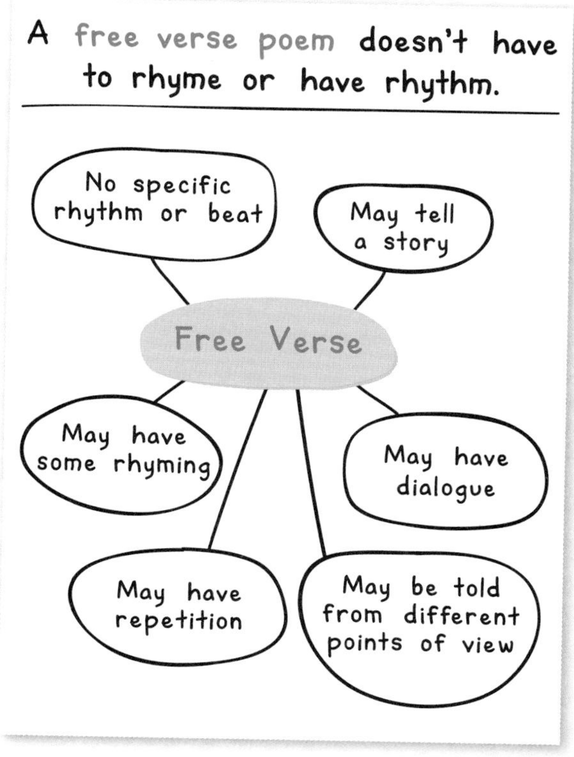

Summarize and Apply

Summarize the learning and remind students to think about how free verse poems are different from other types of poetry.

Look at the chart we made today. What can you say about free verse poems?

- Write the principle at the top of the chart.

  Today when you read, choose a book of poetry from this basket and enjoy several poems. Decide if the poem you read is free verse. If it is, mark it with a sticky note and bring it to share when we meet.

Share

Following independent reading time, gather students together in groups of three or four to discuss the poems they read.

Did you read a free verse poem today? How did you know it was a free verse poem?

Extend the Lesson (Optional)

After assessing students' understanding, you might decide to extend the learning.

- As students become more confident in noticing how an author uses poetic techniques in free verse poems, you might decide to introduce concrete poems, which are shaped to show what the poem is about.
- Encourage students to write and illustrate free verse poems.
- **Writing About Reading** Ask students to describe in a reader's notebook their opinion of a free verse poem they read.

RML3

LA.U7.RML3

Reading Minilesson Principle

A limerick is a rhyming poem that is usually surprising, funny, and sometimes nonsensical.

Exploring Different Kinds of Poetry

You Will Need

- chart paper prepared in advance with two limericks, chosen from your own library, written by students, or provided here
- markers
- basket of poetry books, some including limericks
- sticky notes

Academic Language / Important Vocabulary

- limerick
- rhyming
- nonsensical

Continuum Connection

- Recognize and understand some specific types of poetry: e.g., lyrical poetry, free verse, limerick, haiku, narrative poetry, ballad, epic/saga, concrete poetry (pp. 69, 73)

Goal

Recognize and understand the characteristics of limericks.

Rationale

Once students have read, enjoyed, and talked about poems, they can begin to understand the characteristics of different kinds of poems. This minilesson will help them understand the uniquely recognizable form of poetry, the limerick.

Assess Learning

Observe students when they read and discuss poetry. Notice if there is evidence of new learning based on the goal of this minilesson.

- Can students recognize a limerick?
- Are they able to explain why a particular poem is a limerick?
- Do they use the words *limerick, rhyming*, and *nonsensical*?

Minilesson

To help students think about the minilesson principle, use a limerick to engage students in noticing the characteristics. Here is an example.

- Display the limericks, written in advance on chart paper.

  Today I will share with you some limericks written by one of my prior students.

- Read the first limerick.

  What do you notice about this poem?

- If necessary, prompt students to notice the rhyme and rhythm patterns of lines 1, 2, and 5 and of lines 3 and 4.
- List responses on chart paper.

  This poem is a limerick. It has a pattern of rhyme and rhythm that is easy to recognize and is very different from other poems. It is a little bit silly, too.

Have a Try

Invite the students to talk with a partner about another limerick, such as the second example provided.

- Read aloud the second limerick on the chart.

  Turn and talk to your partner. Is this poem a limerick? How can you tell?

Summarize and Apply

Summarize the learning and remind students to notice the characteristics of limericks.

Today you learned about a kind of poem called a limerick.

- Write the principle at the top of the chart.

  Today choose a book of poetry from this basket and enjoy several poems. Think about what the poet is trying to say and notice the characteristics of the poems you read. If you read a limerick, mark it with a sticky note and bring it to share when we meet.

Share

Following independent reading time, gather students together in groups of three or four to discuss the poems they read.

Did anyone read a limerick today? How did you know it was a limerick? If no one in your group read a limerick, talk about the characteristics of the poem you did read.

A Puppy Named Moe
by Ella G.

I once had a puppy named Moe.
He did not do anything slow.
He ate every last slipper,
And was a constant nipper
'Til the day he heard me shout, "NO!"

Pickle
by Ella G.

I once bit right into a pickle.
The juice gave my chin quite a tickle!
I spit it right out,
Turned my mouth to a pout.
If you try one, I'll give you a nickel!

A limerick is a rhyming poem that is usually surprising, funny, and sometimes nonsensical.

Limerick

- Has 5 lines
- Lines 1, 2, and 5 rhyme
- Lines 1, 2, and 5 have the same rhythm
- Lines 3 and 4 rhyme
- Lines 3 and 4 have the same rhythm
- Funny
- Doesn't really make sense

Extend the Lesson (Optional)

After assessing students' understanding, you might decide to extend the learning.

- Encourage students to continue reading poetry. Add titles of limericks to the chart.
- Encourage students to write and illustrate a limerick. Have them read their poems aloud.
- **Writing About Reading** Ask students to respond in a reader's notebook to a limerick or other poem.

Assessment

After you have taught the minilessons in this umbrella, observe students as they talk and write about their reading across instructional contexts: interactive read-aloud, independent reading, guided reading, shared reading, and book club. Use *The Literacy Continuum* (Fountas and Pinnell 2017) to observe students' reading and writing behaviors.

- What evidence do you have of new understandings related to different kinds of poetry?
    - Do students understand and discuss different kinds of poetry—lyrical, free verse, and limerick?
    - Can they talk about the characteristics of each different kind of poetry?
    - Do they use vocabulary words such as *rhythm*, *rhyme*, *free verse*, *limerick*, and *nonsensical*?
- In what other ways, beyond the scope of this umbrella, are students talking about the poetry they read?
    - Are students discussing why a poet chose certain words?
    - Can they compare and contrast two poems written about the same topic?
    - Are they able to compare and contrast two different types of poems?

Use your observations to determine the next umbrella you will teach. You may also consult Minilessons Across the Year (pp. 61–64) for guidance.

Link to Writing

After teaching the minilessons in this umbrella, help students link the new learning to their own writing:

- When students write their own poetry, encourage them to try out different forms. Encourage them to try writing a poem about the same topic using a different form of poetry. Have them choose which type of poem fits best with the topic of their poem.

Reader's Notebook

When this umbrella is complete, provide a copy of the minilesson principles (see resources.fountasandpinnell.com) for students to glue in the reader's notebook (in the Minilessons section if using *Reader's Notebook: Advanced* [Fountas and Pinnell 2011]), so they can refer to the information as needed.

Minilessons in This Umbrella

RML1	The author gives a message in fiction and nonfiction books.
RML2	Authors use symbolism to communicate a message.
RML3	Think about what the message means to you, to society, or to the world.

Before Teaching Umbrella 8 Minilessons

The minilessons in this umbrella are designed to help students think about and discuss the author's message in both fiction and nonfiction.

It is important to note the difference between purpose, theme, and message. Purpose is the author's intent in writing the book, while theme is a big, universal idea or larger aspect of human existence explored in a literary work (e.g., courage, kindness). The message is a specific aspect of the theme. For example, in a book that expresses the theme of courage, the message might be "You can conquer fears by facing them." If the theme is kindness, the message might be "Treat others as you would like to be treated." After teaching this umbrella, you may want to follow it with Umbrella 9: Thinking About Themes to help your students broaden their thinking about messages and consider the more general or universal idea of the book.

To prepare for these minilessons, read and discuss a variety of engaging fiction and nonfiction books with clear messages and symbolism. Use the following texts from the *Fountas & Pinnell Classroom*™ *Interactive Read-Aloud Collection* text sets or choose books from your classroom library.

Hope and Resilience

Malala: A Brave Girl from Pakistan/Iqbal: A Brave Boy from Pakistan by Jeanette Winter

Freedom

Wall by Tom Clohosy Cole

The Power of Knowledge

Richard Wright and the Library Card by William Miller

Genre Study: Historical Fiction

White Water by Michael S. Bandy and Eric Stein

The Butterfly by Patricia Polacco

As you read aloud and enjoy these texts together, help students

- infer and discuss the author's message(s),
- notice and discuss symbols, and
- think about how to apply the lessons in the books to their own lives.

Hope and Resilience

Freedom

The Power of Knowledge

Genre Study: Historical Fiction

RML1

LA.U8.RML1

Reading Minilesson Principle

The author gives a message in fiction and nonfiction books.

Thinking About the Author's Message

You Will Need

- two or three familiar fiction and nonfiction books with clear messages, such as the following:
  - *Wall* by Tom Clohosy Cole, from Text Set: Freedom
  - *Malala/Iqbal* by Jeanette Winter, from Text Set: Hope and Resilience
  - *Richard Wright and the Library Card* by William Miller, from Text Set: The Power of Knowledge
- chart paper and markers

Academic Language / Important Vocabulary

- message
- author
- fiction
- nonfiction

Continuum Connection

- Infer the messages in a work of fiction (p. 69)
- Infer the larger (main) ideas or messages in a nonfiction text (p. 74)
- Understand that there can be different interpretations of the meanings of a text (p. 74)
- Understand that a nonfiction text can have more than one message or big idea (p. 74)

Goal

Infer messages in works of fiction and nonfiction.

Rationale

Authors often write books to convey one or more messages to their readers. When students think about what the author is really trying to say, they are able to think more deeply about the meaning and learn from it.

Assess Learning

Observe students when they read and talk about books and notice if there is evidence of new learning based on the goal of this minilesson.

- Can students infer the author's message in both fiction and nonfiction books?
- Can they support their interpretation of the author's message with evidence from the text?
- Do they understand that a book can have more than one message?
- Do they use academic vocabulary, such as *message*, *author*, *fiction*, and *nonfiction*?

Minilesson

To help students think about the minilesson principle, use familiar fiction and nonfiction books to discuss the author's message. Here is an example.

- Show the cover of *Wall* and read the title. Then read the last six pages.

  What do you think the author wants you to learn or understand?

  What makes you think that?

- Record students' responses on chart paper.

  Beyond writing a good story, some authors want you to learn or understand an important idea. This is the author's message. Different readers may have different ideas about what the author's message is. Does anyone else have any other ideas about the author's message in this story?

- Show the two covers of *Malala/Iqbal* and read the titles. Read page 13 of the *Malala* section.

  In addition to giving you facts about a topic, nonfiction authors also try to communicate a message, or big idea, that they want you to understand. What big idea do you think the author of this book wants you to understand?

  How does the author reveal her message on this page?

  Does anybody have any other ideas about the author's message?

- Record responses on the chart.

Have a Try

Invite the students to talk with a partner about the author's message.

- Show the cover of *Richard Wright and the Library Card* and read the final page of the story.

  Turn and talk to your partner about what you think the author's message is in this story. Talk about how the author reveals his message on this page.

- After time for discussion, invite a few students to share their thinking. Record responses on the chart.

The author gives a message in fiction and nonfiction books.

Book	Message	Evidence
 WALL	• Family members should not be separated. • People should have freedom.	• "He said nothing should come between a father and his family."
 MALALA / IQBAL	• One person can change the world. • It is important to speak out against injustice. • Every child has the right to an education.	• "One child, one teacher, one pen, can change the world." • "She speaks out again, stronger than before."
 RICHARD WRIGHT AND THE LIBRARY CARD	• Books can change your life and give you a sense of freedom. • Everyone has the right to knowledge. • Everyone is equal and deserves the same rights.	• "Every page was a ticket to freedom, to the place where he would always be free."

Summarize and Apply

Summarize the learning and remind students to think about the author's message when they read.

What did you notice about the books we talked about today?

Authors of both fiction and nonfiction can give a message. A book can have more than one message, and different readers can have different opinions about what the message is.

- Write the principle at the top of the chart.

  When you read today, think about the author's message. Beyond the details of the story or the information, what does the author want you to know? Be ready to share your thinking when we come back together.

Share

Following independent reading time, gather students in the meeting area to talk about their reading.

Turn and talk to your partner about the author's message in the book you read today. Be sure to give evidence for your thinking.

Extend the Lesson (Optional)

After assessing students' understanding, you might decide to extend the learning.

- Help students notice when two or more books communicate the same message, and discuss how the different authors communicate the same message in different ways.
- **Writing About Reading** Have students write about and reflect on an author's message in a reader's notebook. Encourage them to make connections to their own lives, current events, and/or other books.

RML 2

LA.U8.RML2

Reading Minilesson Principle

Authors use symbolism to communicate a message.

Thinking About the Author's Message

You Will Need

- two familiar fiction books that use obvious symbolism to help communicate a message, such as the following:
  - *Richard Wright and the Library Card* by William Miller, from Text Set: The Power of Knowledge
  - *The Butterfly* by Patricia Polacco, from Text Set: Genre Study: Historical Fiction
- chart from RML1
- chart paper and markers

Academic Language / Important Vocabulary

- message
- author
- symbol
- symbolism
- fiction

Continuum Connection

- Recognize and understand symbolism in a text and illustrations (p. 70)

Goal

Understand that authors sometimes use symbolism to communicate a message.

Rationale

When you teach students to notice and think about symbolism in stories, they think more deeply about a story's meaning and can appreciate the author's message.

Assess Learning

Observe students when they read and talk about fiction books and notice if there is evidence of new learning based on the goal of this minilesson.

- Can students identify symbols in stories and tell what they represent?
- Do they use academic vocabulary, such as *message, author, symbol, symbolism,* and *fiction*?

Minilesson

To help students think about the minilesson principle, use familiar fiction books to engage them in a discussion of symbolism and author's message. Here is an example.

- Show the cover of *Richard Wright and the Library Card.*

  The library card in this story is not *just* a card that allows someone to take books out from the library. What does the library card mean to Richard?

  To Richard, the library card stands for knowledge and freedom. It gives him the freedom to access the knowledge that he had never been allowed to have as a black boy growing up under segregation. The library card is a symbol. A symbol is something that stands for something else—usually a big idea, like freedom.

- Display the chart from RML1. Point to the messages for *Richard Wright and the Library Card.*

  Which of the author's messages does the library card help communicate?

  How does the library card do that?

- Record the symbol, what it represents, and the relevant author's message on a new sheet of chart paper.
- Show the cover of *The Butterfly* and read the title. Then read pages 21 and 39.

  What is an important symbol in this story?

  What do the butterflies represent?

- Record students' responses on the chart. If students give multiple answers, emphasize that different readers can have different interpretations of a symbol's meaning.

Have a Try

Invite the students to talk with a partner about the author's message in *The Butterfly*.

Think about why the author uses the butterfly as a symbol in this story. How does the author use a butterfly to deliver her message? Turn and talk to your partner about that.

- After students turn and talk, invite a few pairs to share their thinking. Record responses on the chart.

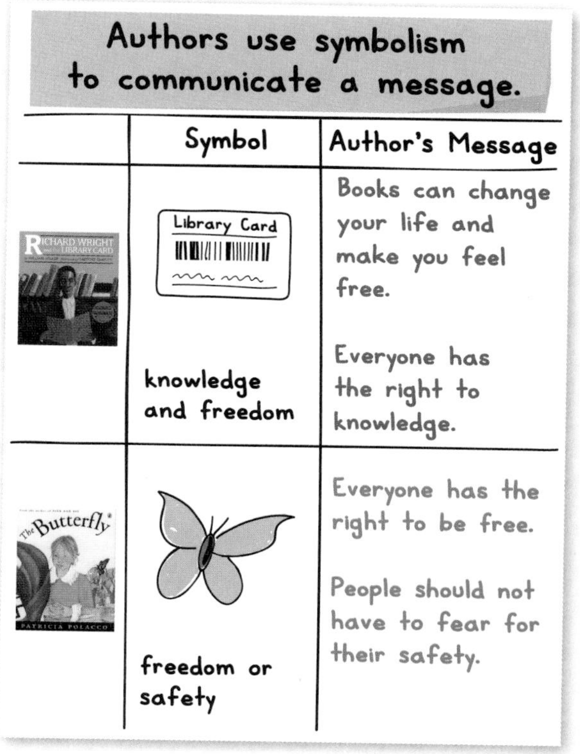

Authors use symbolism to communicate a message.

	Symbol	Author's Message
Richard Wright and the Library Card	Library Card knowledge and freedom	Books can change your life and make you feel free. Everyone has the right to knowledge.
The Butterfly, Patricia Polacco	freedom or safety	Everyone has the right to be free. People should not have to fear for their safety.

Summarize and Apply

Summarize the learning and remind students to notice and think about symbolism.

What does the chart show about an author's message?

You noticed that fiction authors sometimes use symbols, or things that stand for something else, to communicate a message. The use of symbols is called symbolism.

- Write the principle at the top of the chart.

If you read a fiction book today, notice if there are any symbols in your story. If so, think about what the symbols mean and how they help communicate the author's message. Be ready to share your thinking when we come back together.

Share

Following independent reading time, gather students in the meeting area to talk about their reading.

Did anybody find any examples of symbolism in the book you read today?

What symbols are in your story? What do the symbols represent? How do they help communicate the author's message?

Extend the Lesson (Optional)

After assessing students' understanding, you might decide to extend the learning.

- During interactive read-aloud, point out that sometimes the title of a book can give a clue about the author's message.
- **Writing About Reading** Have students write in a reader's notebook about the meaning of a symbol and how it helps communicate the author's message.

RML 3
LA.U8.RML3

Reading Minilesson Principle

Think about what the message means to you, to society, or to the world.

Thinking About the Author's Message

You Will Need

- two familiar fiction and nonfiction books with clear messages, such as the following:
  - *Malala/Iqbal* by Jeanette Winter, from Text Set: Hope and Resilience
  - *Wall* by Tom Clohosy Cole, from Text Set: Freedom
- chart from RML1 (optional)
- chart paper and markers

Academic Language / Important Vocabulary

- author
- message
- society

Continuum Connection

- Understand that the messages or big ideas in fiction texts can be applied to their own lives or to other people and society (p. 69)
- Relate the messages in a nonfiction text to one's own life (p. 73)

Goal

Understand that the messages or big ideas can be applied to their own lives or to other people and society.

Rationale

When you teach students to think about how an author's message can be applied in real life, they understand the power of the written word. They learn that something they write might someday influence how other people think and act.

Assess Learning

Observe students when they read and talk about books and notice if there is evidence of new learning based on the goal of this minilesson.

- Can students identify the author's message in fiction and nonfiction books?
- Can they explain how an author's message can be applied to their own lives, to society, or to the world?
- Do they use the terms *author*, *message*, and *society*?

Minilesson

To help students think about the minilesson principle, engage them in a discussion about author's message. Here is an example.

- Show the cover of *Malala/Iqbal*. (Display the chart from RML1 if you have it.)

  Even though this book is about children who lived in a different country and had very different lives from yours, you can still learn important lessons from it and use these lessons in your own life. You noticed that one of the author's messages is "It is important to speak out against injustice." What does this message mean to you? How could you learn from this message and apply it to your own life?

  You can also think about what an author's message means to society. A society is a group of people who live together in a community. For example, all the people in our town, state, country, or even the world are members of a society. How could our society use this message? What could members of our society do differently?

- Record students' responses on chart paper.

Have a Try

Invite the students to talk with a partner about the author's messages in another book.

- Show the cover of *Wall*.

  You noticed that two of the author's messages in this book are "Family members should not be separated" and "People should have freedom." Turn and talk to your partner about how one or both of these messages could be applied to real life.

- After time for discussion, invite several students to share their thinking. Record responses on the chart.

Think about what the message means to you, to society, or to the world.

Book		
 MALALA / IQBAL "It is important to speak out against injustice."	• You	• Speak up when a classmate is being bullied.
	• Society	• Speak up when certain groups of people are being mistreated.
	• The World	• National leaders can speak about countries that mistreat their citizens.
 WALL "Family members should not be separated." "People should have freedom."	• You	• Don't tell other people what to do. Respect their decisions.
	• Society	• Don't build walls that separate people.
	• The World	• Governments should protect the human rights of all the people they represent.

Summarize and Apply

Summarize the learning and remind students to think about the author's message when they read.

> Today you thought about what the author's message means to you and how the message could be applied to your own life, to society, or to the world.

- Write the principle at the top of the chart.

  When you read today, think about the author's message. Then think about what the message means to you and how you could use it in your own life or how society could use it. Be ready to share your thinking when we come back together.

Share

Following independent reading time, gather students together in the meeting area to talk about their reading.

> What is the author's message in the book you read today?
>
> How could this message be applied to your own life, to society, or to the world?

Extend the Lesson (Optional)

After assessing students' understanding, you might decide to extend the learning.

- Continue to discuss the author's message as you read more books aloud. Discuss specific ways that students can act on each message, such as organizing a fundraiser or volunteering in the community.
- **Writing About Reading** Have students write in a reader's notebook about how the author's message in a book could be applied to their own lives, to society, or to the world.

Assessment

After you have taught the minilessons in this umbrella, observe students as they talk and write about their reading across instructional contexts: interactive read-aloud, independent reading, guided reading, shared reading, and book club. Use *The Literacy Continuum* (Fountas and Pinnell 2017) to guide the observation of students' reading and writing behaviors.

- What evidence do you have of new understandings related to the author's message?
  - Can students infer the author's message in both fiction and nonfiction books?
  - Do they understand that a book can have more than one message?
  - Can they identify symbols and explain what they represent?
  - Do they talk about ways to apply an author's message to real life?
  - Do they use academic vocabulary, such as *author's message* and *symbolism*?
- In what other ways, beyond the scope of this umbrella, are students talking about fiction and nonfiction books?
  - Are students talking about the theme of books?
  - Are they noticing different genres of fiction and nonfiction?

Use your observations to determine the next umbrella you will teach. You may also consult Minilessons Across the Year (pp. 61–64) for guidance.

Link to Writing

After teaching the minilessons in this umbrella, help students link the new learning to their own writing:

- When students write both fiction and nonfiction texts, remind them to think about the message they want to convey to readers and how they want to convey it. Encourage them to use symbolism to help communicate their message.

Reader's Notebook

When this umbrella is complete, provide a copy of the minilesson principles (see resources.fountasandpinnell.com) for students to glue in the reader's notebook (in the Minilessons section if using *Reader's Notebook: Advanced* [Fountas and Pinnell 2011]), so they can refer to the information as needed.

Minilessons in This Umbrella

RML1	The theme of a fiction book is what the book is really about.
RML2	The theme of a nonfiction book is more than the topic of the book.
RML3	Books often have themes that address human challenges and social issues.

Before Teaching Umbrella 9 Minilessons

These minilessons are designed to help students think about and discuss themes in fiction and nonfiction books. We strongly recommend that you teach Umbrella 8: Thinking About the Author's Message before teaching the minilessons in this umbrella.

Theme and message are related, but there is a difference. Theme is the big, universal idea or larger aspect of human existence explored in a literary work (e.g., courage, kindness). The message is a specific aspect of the theme—a directive or special understanding for the reader. The message in a book that explores the theme of courage might be "You can conquer fears by facing them." If the theme is kindness, the message might be "Treat others as you would like to be treated." Teaching Umbrellas 8 and 9 consecutively will help your students broaden their thinking about messages and think about the more general or universal ideas communicated by the writers.

To prepare for these minilessons, read and discuss a variety of engaging fiction and nonfiction books with clear themes. Use the following texts from the *Fountas & Pinnell Classroom™ Interactive Read-Aloud Collection* text sets or choose books from your classroom library.

Empathy

Mrs. Katz and Tush by Patricia Polacco

Hope and Resilience

Let the Celebrations Begin! A Story of Hope for the Liberation by Margaret Wild

Malala: A Brave Girl from Pakistan / Iqbal: A Brave Boy from Pakistan by Jeanette Winter

Grit and Perseverance

Ira's Shakespeare Dream by Glenda Armand

Caring for Our World

One Well: The Story of Water on Earth by Rochelle Strauss

Can We Save the Tiger? by Martin Jenkins

Genre Study: Historical Fiction

White Water by Michael S. Bandy and Eric Stein

The Butterfly by Patricia Polacco

As you read aloud and enjoy these texts together, help students

- think about the big ideas explored in each book, and
- discuss the authors' treatment of human challenges and social issues.

Empathy

Hope and Resilience

Grit and Perseverance

Caring for Our World

Genre Study: Historical Fiction

Section 2: Literary Analysis

RML 1
LA.U9.RML1

Reading Minilesson Principle

The theme of a fiction book is what the book is really about.

Thinking About Themes

You Will Need

- two or three familiar fiction books with clear themes, such as the following:
  - *Mrs. Katz and Tush* by Patricia Polacco, from Text Set: Empathy
  - *Let the Celebrations Begin!* by Margaret Wild, from Text Set: Hope and Resilience
  - *Ira's Shakespeare Dream* by Glenda Armand, from Text Set: Grit and Perseverance
- chart paper and markers

Academic Language / Important Vocabulary

- theme
- author
- fiction
- empathy
- resilience
- perseverance

Continuum Connection

- Notice and infer the importance of ideas relevant to their world: e.g., becoming independent; valuing change in self and others; empathizing with others; valuing differences; connecting past, present, and future; overcoming challenges; following your dreams; learning from the lives of others; social justice; exploring artistic expression and appreciation (p. 70)
- Notice and understand themes that are close to their own experience and also themes that are beyond them: e.g., imagination, courage, fears, sharing, friendship, family relationships, self, nature, growing, behavior, community, responsibilities, diversity, belonging, peer relationships, loss (p. 70)

Goal

Infer the major themes of a fiction book.

Rationale

A theme is a big, universal idea or concept explored in a book or other artistic work. Thinking about the themes in a story helps students relate to the story on a personal level, which keeps them engaged. It also helps them to think more broadly about the characters and plot and to apply the lessons in a story to their own lives.

Assess Learning

Observe students when they read and talk about fiction books and notice if there is evidence of new learning based on the goal of this minilesson.

- Can students infer the theme(s) of a story?
- Do they use academic vocabulary, such as *theme, author, fiction, empathy, resilience,* and *perseverance*?

Minilesson

To help students think about the minilesson principle, use familiar fiction books to engage them in a discussion about theme. Here is an example.

- Show the cover of *Mrs. Katz and Tush* and read the title.

  This story is about an African American boy who develops a special friendship with his neighbor, an elderly Jewish woman. But that's not *all* that it's about.

- Read page 16.

  What big idea does the author want you to think about?

  The theme of a story is what it is really about. It is a big idea. One of the themes of this story is empathy. How does the author reveal, or show, this theme on this page?

  Does anybody have any other ideas about what the theme of this book is?

- Record students' responses on chart paper and ask students to justify their responses with evidence from the story (e.g., dialogue, a character's actions, story outcomes). Explain that a book can have more than one theme and that different readers can have different ideas about what the theme is.
- Repeat the process with *Let the Celebrations Begin!*
- Record responses on the chart.

Have a Try

Invite the students to talk with a partner about the theme in a book.

- Show the cover of *Ira's Shakespeare Dream* and review the story.

  Turn and talk to your partner about what you think is the theme of this story. What is the big idea that it is *really* about? Be sure to talk about how the author reveals the theme.

- After students turn and talk, invite several students to share their thinking. Record all reasonable responses on the chart.

The theme of a fiction book is what the book is really about.
Patricia Polacco
Mrs. Katz and Tush
• empathy
• accepting others
• kindness
• friendship
Let the Celebrations Begin!
• hope
• survival
• memory
• resilience
• perseverance
• following dreams
• empathy
• fighting injustice

Summarize and Apply

Summarize the learning and remind students to think about theme when they read fiction.

Today you thought about the theme of a few fiction books. The theme is what the book is really about. Authors reveal the theme or themes through the plot, the setting, and what the characters do and say. Why do you think fiction authors write stories with themes? Why are themes important?

- Write the principle at the top of the chart.

  If you read a fiction book today, think about the theme of your book. Be ready to share your thinking when we come back together.

Share

Following independent reading time, gather students in the meeting area to talk about their reading.

Did you read a fiction book today?

What do you think is the theme of the story you read?

Extend the Lesson (Optional)

After assessing students' understanding, you might decide to extend the learning.

- Help students notice that more than one book may have the same theme. Talk about how this shows the importance of these themes in people's lives.
- **Writing About Reading** Have students write about the theme of a fiction book in a reader's notebook. They should state the theme and provide evidence from the text that supports their interpretation.

RML 2
LA.U9.RML2

Reading Minilesson Principle
The theme of a nonfiction book is more than the topic of the book.

Thinking About Themes

You Will Need

- two or three familiar nonfiction books with clear themes, such as the following:
  - *One Well* by Rochelle Strauss, from Text Set: Caring for Our World
  - *Malala/Iqbal* by Jeanette Winter, from Text Set: Hope and Resilience
  - *Can We Save the Tiger?* by Martin Jenkins, from Text Set: Caring for Our World
- chart paper and markers

Academic Language / Important Vocabulary

- theme
- topic
- author
- nonfiction

Continuum Connection

- Understand themes and ideas that are mature issues and require experience to interpret (p. 74)

Goal

Infer the major themes of a nonfiction book.

Rationale

Thinking about themes in nonfiction books helps students understand that a nonfiction book is more than just a collection of facts. They develop an understanding of the big ideas that nonfiction authors explore in their work.

Assess Learning

Observe students when they read and talk about nonfiction books and notice if there is evidence of new learning based on the goal of this minilesson.

- Can they differentiate between the theme and the topic of a nonfiction book?
- Do they understand that a nonfiction book can have more than one theme and that different readers may interpret the theme(s) differently?
- Do they use academic vocabulary, such as *theme*, *topic*, *author*, and *nonfiction*?

Minilesson

To help students think about the minilesson principle, use familiar nonfiction books to engage them in a discussion about topic and theme. Here is an example.

- Show the cover of *One Well* and read the title.

  What is the topic of this book?

- Record responses on chart paper.

  This book is about water, but that's not *all* it's about. What do you think is the theme, or big idea, of the book? What makes you think that?

- Record all reasonable responses on the chart, emphasizing that a nonfiction book can have more than one theme and that different readers can have different interpretations of the theme.

  The theme of a nonfiction book is more than the topic of the book. It is what the book is *really* about.

- Show the cover of *Malala* and read the title.

  What is the topic of this book?

  What do you think is the theme of the book?

- Record responses on the chart.

Have a Try

Invite the students to talk with a partner about the theme of *Can We Save the Tiger?*

- Show the cover of *Can We Save the Tiger?* and read the title.

  Remember this book about extinct and endangered animals? Turn and talk to your partner about what you think is the theme, or big idea, of this book.

- After time for discussion, invite a few pairs to share their thinking. Record all reasonable responses on the chart.

The theme of a nonfiction book is more than the topic of the book.

Nonfiction Book	Topic	Theme: BIG Idea
 One Well	water	• protecting the planet • conservation • creating change
 MALALA / IQBAL	Malala	• courage • freedom
 can we save the tiger?	extinct and endangered animals	• protecting the planet • the impact of human actions

Summarize and Apply

Summarize the learning and remind students to think about theme when they read nonfiction.

Today you thought about the topic and theme of a few nonfiction books we have read together. How are the topic and the theme of a book different?

- Write the principle at the top of the chart.

  If you read a nonfiction book today, be sure to think about the theme or themes of your book. Be ready to share your thinking when we come back together.

Share

Following independent reading time, gather students together in the meeting area to talk about their reading.

Who read a nonfiction book today?

What is the theme of the book you read?

Extend the Lesson (Optional)

After assessing students' understanding, you might decide to extend the learning.

- Help students notice that different books have the same theme, and discuss how different authors approach the theme differently.
- **Writing About Reading** Have students write about the theme of a nonfiction book in a reader's notebook.

RML 3

LA.U9.RML3

Reading Minilesson Principle

Books often have themes that address human challenges and social issues.

Thinking About Themes

You Will Need

- two or three familiar books that explore human challenges or social issues, such as the following:
  - *White Water* by Michael S. Bandy and Eric Stein, from Text Set: Genre Study: Historical Fiction
  - *Malala/Iqbal* by Jeanette Winter, from Text Set: Hope and Resilience
  - *The Butterfly* by Patricia Polacco, from Text Set: Genre Study: Historical Fiction
- chart paper and markers

Academic Language / Important Vocabulary

- theme
- topic
- human challenge
- social issue
- discrimination

Continuum Connection

- Notice and infer the importance of ideas relevant to their world: e.g., becoming independent; valuing change in self and others; empathizing with others; valuing differences; connecting past, present, and future; overcoming challenges; following your dreams; learning from the lives of others; social justice; exploring artistic expression and appreciation (p. 70)
- Notice and understand themes that are close to their own experience and also themes that are beyond them: e.g., imagination, courage, fears, sharing, friendship, family relationships, self, nature, growing, behavior, community, responsibilities, diversity, belonging, peer relationships, loss (p. 70)

Goal

Notice and understand themes reflecting important human challenges and social issues.

Rationale

When students notice and think about themes reflecting human challenges and social issues, they learn about important ideas and values (e.g., equality, compassion, justice) and think about how to apply them to their lives. They are more likely to become engaged, active, and compassionate members of society.

Assess Learning

Observe students when they read and talk about books and notice if there is evidence of new learning based on the goal of this minilesson.

- Do students notice and discuss themes that address human challenges and social issues?
- Do they use vocabulary such as *theme, topic, human challenge, social issue,* and *discrimination*?

Minilesson

To help students think about the minilesson principle, use familiar books to engage them in a discussion about theme. Here is an example.

- Show the cover of *White Water* and read the title.

  What problem does Michael have in this story?

  What do you think is the theme, or big idea, of this story?

  What makes you think that?

- Record all reasonable responses on chart paper.
- Show the two covers of *Malala/Iqbal*.

  What do Malala and Iqbal have in common?

  What do you think is the theme of this book? What big ideas does the author want you to think about?

- Record responses on the chart.

Have a Try

Invite the students to talk with a partner about the theme of *The Butterfly*.

- Show the cover of *The Butterfly*.

  Turn and talk to your partner about what you think is the theme of this story.

- After students turn and talk, invite several students to share their thinking. Record all reasonable responses.

Books often have themes that address human challenges and social issues.

	• equality • courage
	• speaking out • courage • freedom • human rights • creating change
	• protecting others • fighting injustice • courage • empathy • friendship

Summarize and Apply

Summarize the learning and remind students to notice themes addressing human challenges and social issues.

Look at the chart. How would you describe these themes?

Human challenges and social issues are problems or challenges that affect people, particularly problems having to do with living together in a society. Discrimination against a particular group of people is an example of this.

- Write the principle at the top of the chart.

  When you read today, think about the theme or themes of your book. If your book has themes addressing human challenges or social issues, bring it to share when we come back together.

Share

Following independent reading time, gather students together in the meeting area to talk about the themes in the books they read.

What challenge or social issue did the characters or people in your book face?

What do you think is the theme of your book?

Extend the Lesson (Optional)

After assessing students' understanding, you might decide to extend the learning.

- **Writing About Reading** Have students write in a reader's notebook about a book with a theme that addresses human challenges or social issues. They should identify the theme(s) of the book, explain how the book approaches the theme, and give their opinion about the theme (e.g., why it is important).

Thinking About Themes

Assessment

After you have taught the minilessons in this umbrella, observe students as they talk and write about their reading across instructional contexts: interactive read-aloud, independent reading, guided reading, shared reading, and book club. Use *The Literacy Continuum* (Fountas and Pinnell 2017) to guide the observation of students' reading and writing behaviors.

- What evidence do you have of new understandings related to thinking about themes?
  - Can students infer the theme(s) of both fiction and nonfiction books?
  - How well do they notice and discuss themes related to human challenges and social issues?
  - Do they use academic language, such as *theme*, *message*, and *topic*?
- In what other ways, beyond the scope of this umbrella, are students talking about books?
  - Are students able to infer the author's message in a book?
  - Are they able to think critically about characters or the way people are represented in texts?

Use your observations to determine the next umbrella you will teach. You may also consult Minilessons Across the Year (pp. 61–64) for guidance.

Link to Writing

After teaching the minilessons in this umbrella, help students link the new learning to their own writing:

- When students write their own fiction and nonfiction texts, remind them to think about the theme(s) they want to communicate in their work.
- Have students choose a theme represented in two or more of the books they have read and write about how they see that theme in their own lives.

Reader's Notebook

When this umbrella is complete, provide a copy of the minilesson principles (see resources.fountasandpinnell.com) for students to glue in the reader's notebook (in the Minilessons section if using *Reader's Notebook: Advanced* [Fountas and Pinnell 2011]), so they can refer to the information as needed.

Reading Like a Writer: Analyzing the Writer's Craft

Umbrella 10

Minilessons in This Umbrella

RML1	Writers use poetic or descriptive language to appeal to the five senses.
RML2	Writers use similes and metaphors to compare one thing to another.
RML3	Writers use personification to give human qualities to something that is not human.
RML4	Writers choose language to fit the setting.
RML5	Writers choose precise words to create a mood.
RML6	Writers choose specific words to express their attitude or feelings toward a subject.
RML7	Writers use different techniques to create humor.
RML8	Writers use specific fonts to communicate ideas.

Freedom

Writer's Craft

Ted and Betsy Lewin

Problem Solving/ Resourcefulness

Genre Study: Biography (Musicians)

Hope and Resilience

Understanding How Things Work

Before Teaching Umbrella 10 Minilessons

The lessons in this umbrella do not need to be taught consecutively but can be taught when you observe a need. Once students have enjoyed the texts as readers, have them look at the texts as writers, noting elements of the writer's craft. Use the following books from the *Fountas & Pinnell Classroom™ Interactive Read-Aloud Collection* or choose other books that will engage your class.

Freedom

- *Under the Quilt of Night* by Deborah Hopkinson

Writer's Craft

- *Eliza's Freedom Road* by Jerdine Nolen
- *Letters from Rifka* by Karen Hesse
- *Firebird* by Misty Copeland
- *Black Dog* by Levi Pinfold
- *Encounter* by Jane Yolen

Author/Illustrator Study: Ted and Betsy Lewin

- *Elephant Quest*
- *Balarama: A Royal Elephant*
- *Gorilla Walk*
- *Top to Bottom Down Under*

Problem Solving/Resourcefulness

- *Finding the Music* by Jennifer Torres

Genre Study: Biography (Musicians)

- *I and I: Bob Marley* by Tony Medina

Hope and Resilience

- *Malala: A Brave Girl from Pakistan / Iqbal: A Brave Boy from Pakistan* by Jeanette Winter

Understanding How Things Work

- *Mr. Ferris and His Wheel* by Kathryn Gibbs Davis

As you read aloud and enjoy these texts together, help students notice and appreciate how writers use language.

RML1

LA.U10.RML1

Reading Minilesson Principle

Writers use poetic or descriptive language to appeal to the five senses.

Reading Like a Writer: Analyzing the Writer's Craft

You Will Need

- two or three familiar texts with examples of language that appeals to the five senses, such as the following from Text Set: Writer's Craft:
  - *Letters from Rifka* by Karen Hesse
  - *Firebird* by Misty Copeland
- chart paper prepared with three columns and pictures to represent the five senses (optional)
- markers
- sticky notes

Academic Language / Important Vocabulary

- appeal
- language
- five senses

Continuum Connection

- Notice when a fiction writer uses poetic or descriptive language to show the setting, appeal to the five senses, or to convey human feelings such as loss, relief, or anger (p.71)

Goal

Notice how authors use poetic or descriptive language to appeal to the five senses.

Rationale

Writers sometimes use language that appeals to a reader's five senses to help the reader connect with a story. When you teach students to notice the use of poetic or descriptive language, it leads to a deeper understanding of their reading. Students may then try to use sensory language in their writing, using high-quality texts as models.

Assess Learning

Observe students when they discuss writer's craft. Notice if there is evidence of new learning based on the goal of this minilesson.

- Do students notice how authors use poetic or descriptive language?
- Can they talk about the sense the language appeals to?
- Do they use the language *appeal*, *language*, and *five senses*?

Minilesson

To help students think about the minilesson principle, use familiar texts with examples of poetic or descriptive language that appeals to the five senses. Here is an example.

- Read pages 14–15 from *Letters from Rifka*.

  What do you notice about the words the author chose to use on these pages?

  Think about your five senses: sight, smell, hearing, taste, and touch. What sense(s) do you think the writer is trying to appeal to on this page?

- Record responses on a chart.
- Repeat this process with page 18.
- Then repeat this process by reading and showing the illustrations on pages 10–11 from *Firebird*.

  What word do you hear repeated in this part of the story?

  The repetition sounds like poetry. Why do you think the author chose to do this? What sense(s) does this appeal to?

  What sense(s) does the illustration appeal to?

- Record responses on the chart.

Have a Try

Invite the students to talk with a partner about why and how writers use descriptive or poetic language.

- From *Letters from Rifka*, read page 83.

  Turn and talk to your partner. What words do you notice? What sense(s) do they appeal to?

- Invite a few students to share, and add to the chart.

Writers use poetic or descriptive language to appeal to the five senses.

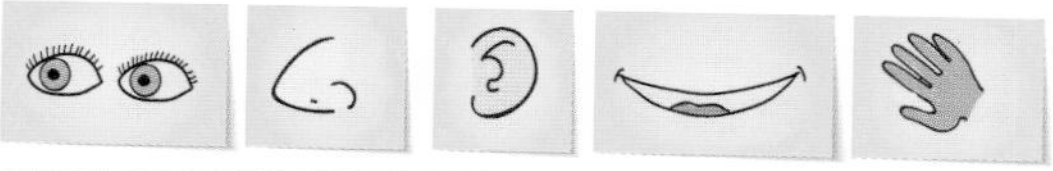

Title	Author's Words	Appeal to which of the five senses?
Letters from Rifka	"Scrambled" "Sprawling"	Sight: seeing how Rifka got on the train
	"Stank of vomit" "Breath choked my throat." "I thought I would be sick."	Smell: all of the distinct, bad smells Taste: tasting the bad smell in her throat
Firebird	"before" Illustration of experienced dancer touching hand of new dancer	Hearing: repeated word draws the reader's attention Sight/Touch: hands pressed together as if in a mirror, shows how similar they are to each
Letters from Rifka	"shivering" "taste blood in my mouth and smell it in my nose." "cold, metallic taste"	Touch: feel fear when you shiver Taste: blood

Summarize and Apply

Summarize the learning and remind students to notice word choice.

Take a look at the chart. What do you notice writers sometimes do?

- Write the principle at the top of the chart.

  As you read today, look for examples of descriptive or poetic language that appeals to the senses. Place a sticky note on the pages and be prepared to share when we come back together.

Share

Following independent reading time, gather students together in the meeting area to share examples of poetic and descriptive language in groups of three or four.

Did anyone find an example of descriptive or poetic language that appeals to the senses? Why did the author choose to do that?

Extend the Lesson (Optional)

After assessing students' understanding, you might decide to extend the learning.

- Have several students make a class poster of exemplary words or phrases that stand out in the books they read to provide inspiration when they write.
- Find a picture (e.g., photograph, painting) of a setting. Have students write a brief description of the setting that appeals to one or more of the senses.

RML 2

LA.U10.RML2

Reading Minilesson Principle

Writers use similes and metaphors to compare one thing to another.

Reading Like a Writer: Analyzing the Writer's Craft

You Will Need

- two or three familiar texts or poems with similes and metaphors, such as the following from Text Set: Writer's Craft:
  - *Firebird* by Misty Copeland
  - *Letters from Rifka* by Karen Hesse
- chart paper and markers
- document camera (optional)
- three sticky notes labeled *simile*, one sticky note labeled *metaphor*
- sticky notes for students to use
- basket of familiar texts containing metaphors or similes

Academic Language / Important Vocabulary

- simile
- metaphor
- compare
- comparison

Continuum Connection

- Notice and understand how the author uses idioms and literary language, including metaphors, similes, symbolism, and personification (p. 71)
- Understand the writer's meaning when words are used in figures of speech or idioms (p. 145)

Goal

Notice and understand how the author uses similes and metaphors.

Rationale

Writers use metaphors and similes to make abstract ideas more concrete and to prompt readers to use their imagination to create lasting images. Students can think about how they might use figurative language in their own writing.

Assess Learning

Observe students when they talk about the writer's craft. Notice if there is evidence of new learning based on the goal of this minilesson.

- Do students notice similes and metaphors in books they hear read aloud or read independently?
- Can they describe what the similes or metaphors mean?
- Do they use the terms *simile*, *metaphor*, *compare*, and *comparison*?

Minilesson

To help students think about the minilesson principle, use familiar texts to discuss similes and metaphors. If a document camera is available, consider projecting the pages to provide visual support. Here is an example.

- Hold up *Firebird* and read page 5.

  How do you feel if you are as "gray as rain"?

  What does the author mean by "heavy as naptime" and "low as a storm pressing on rooftops"?

- Make three columns on the chart paper and record responses. Then repeat the process with page 3.

  Whose feet are "swift as sunlight"?

  Why does the author say that?

  The author decided to compare dancing to something you know—sunlight. When an author compares two things using the words *like* or *as*, it is called a simile.

- Have a volunteer underline the word *as* or *like* in each example. Have another volunteer add a sticky note labeled *simile* next to each example.

  When you read the words *like* or *as*, think about the simile, or what the author is comparing.

- Repeat this process using page 82 from *Letters from Rifka*.

Have a Try

Invite the students to talk about how writers compare one thing to another.

- Hold up *Firebird* and read the first line of page 3 again.

  How does the author describe the girl?

  When a writer makes a direct comparison by saying that one thing *is* something else, it is called a metaphor.

- Record responses on the chart and have a volunteer underline *are* and place the sticky note labeled *metaphor*.

Writers use similes and metaphors to compare one thing to another.

Title	Comparison	Purpose/Meaning
Firebird	"I'm gray as rain, heavy as naptime, low as a storm" simile	• Describes how sad she is
	"your feet are swift as sunlight" simile	• Describes how quickly and gracefully she dances • Feels light and bright like the sun
Letters from Rifka	"the sky was a sickly yellow, like an old bruise" simile	• Describes the sky • Bruises are ugly.
Firebird	"you are the clouds and sky and air" metaphor	• Describes the girl dancing • Her dancing is light and full of movement all around.

Summarize and Apply

Summarize the learning and remind students to think about how writers use similes and metaphors.

How do writers use similes and metaphors?

- Write the principle at the top of the chart.

  You may choose a book from this basket to read today. As you are reading, notice whether the author uses any metaphors or similes. Mark the page with a sticky note and bring the book when we meet so you can share.

Share

Following independent reading time, gather students together in the meeting area to talk about figurative language.

Tell us about a simile or metaphor you found in your reading. What did it help you to understand?

Extend the Lesson (Optional)

After assessing students' understanding, you might decide to extend the learning.

- Have students help you collect examples of metaphors and similes on a large poster to display so that students can be inspired to use language in creative and evocative ways when they do their own writing.
- **Writing About Reading** When students write letters about books they have read in a reader's notebook, encourage them to share similes and metaphors they have found and describe how the authors used the comparisons.

RML 3
LA.U10.RML3

Reading Minilesson Principle

Writers use personification to give human qualities to something that is not human.

Reading Like a Writer: Analyzing the Writer's Craft

You Will Need

- several familiar texts with personification, such as the following:
  - *Under the Quilt of Night* by Deborah Hopkinson, from Text Set: Freedom
  - *Eliza's Freedom Road* by Jerdine Nolen and *Letters from Rifka* by Karen Hesse, from Text Set: Writer's Craft
- chart paper and markers
- sticky notes

Academic Language / Important Vocabulary

- personification

Continuum Connection

- Notice and understand how the author uses idioms and literary language, including metaphors, similes, symbolism, and personification (p. 71)
- Understand the writer's meaning when words are used in figures of speech or idioms (p. 145)

Goal

Notice and understand how the author uses personification.

Rationale

Personification brings nonhuman things to life and helps a reader connect with an object. This creates a clear image in readers' minds and leads to a deeper understanding of their reading. Students may then experiment with using personification in their own writing.

Assess Learning

Observe students when they discuss writer's craft. Notice if there is evidence of new learning based on the goal of this minilesson.

- Do students recognize personification in their reading?
- Can they describe what is being personified and how?
- Do they understand and use the word *personification*?

Minilesson

To help students think about the minilesson principle, use familiar texts to engage them in a discussion of personification. Here is an example.

- Hold up *Under the Quilt of Night* and read pages 10 and 15.

  What do you notice about the way the author writes about the stars and the dark sky? What do the stars and dark sky do?

- Record the actions of the stars and sky on chart paper.
- Read page 32 from *Eliza's Freedom Road.*

  What do you notice about how the ground is described?

- Record the action attributed to the ground. Then draw attention to the chart.

  Are these things that the stars, sky, and ground can really do?

  When an author writes about an object that does something that only a human can do, it is called personification. Notice that the word *person* is in *personification.* What does the personification show in these books?

Have a Try

Invite the students to talk with a partner about why writers use personification.

- Read page 82 of *Letters from Rifka*.

  Turn and talk to your partner. Where does the author use personification? How does this help you understand the story?

- Invite a few students to share. Record responses on the chart.

Summarize and Apply

Summarize the learning and remind students to notice how writers use personification.

- Review the chart and write the principle at the top.

  Writers use personification to make their writing interesting and to help readers understand the story even better. Today when you read, be on the lookout for personification. If you find an example, mark it with a sticky note and bring the book back when we meet so you can share.

Writers use personification to give human qualities to something that is not human.

Title	Human Quality	What the Personification Shows
Under the Quilt of Night	• Stars "hearing" • Stars "hurry out to guide our way"	• Shows stars as helpers or guides
Eliza's Freedom Road	• Ground "walking"	• Shows how unsteady and undependable the ground is
Letters from Rifka	• Ship "shivering" • Ocean "acting hateful"	• Helps you feel the dread • Describes the harshness of the surroundings

Share

Following independent reading time, gather students together in the meeting area to talk about their reading.

Who marked a page in your reading that shows personification?

What is the human action the author used? How did it help you understand that part of the story?

Extend the Lesson (Optional)

After assessing students' understanding, you might decide to extend the learning.

- Poems often contain examples of figurative language, such as personification. Share poems with examples of personification with your class.
- **Writing About Reading** When students write letters about their reading, encourage them to share examples of personification.

RML 4
LA.U10.RML4

Reading Minilesson Principle

Writers choose language to fit the setting.

Reading Like a Writer: Analyzing the Writer's Craft

You Will Need

- two or three familiar texts, such as the following:
  - *Finding the Music* by Jennifer Torres, from Text Set: Problem Solving/ Resourcefulness
  - *I and I: Bob Marley* by Tony Medina, from Text Set: Genre Study: Biography (Musicians)
  - *Malala/Iqbal* by Jeanette Winter, from Text Set: Hope and Resilience
- chart paper and markers

Academic Language / Important Vocabulary

- author
- language
- setting
- grammar
- dialect

Continuum Connection

- Notice and think critically about a writer's word choice (p. 71)
- Notice a writer's use of regional or historical vocabulary or features of dialect included for literary effect (p. 71)
- Notice a writer's use of some words from languages other than English (p. 71)

Goal

Notice how a writer chooses language to fit the setting.

Rationale

Writers often shape their language to fit the setting, for example, by using unconventional grammar, dialects, and words from foreign languages. These choices serve to make the setting seem more authentic. When students notice these language choices, they become more aware of the myriad choices that writers must make when writing a book, and they are more likely to make similar decisions in their own writing process.

Assess Learning

- Observe students when they talk about the setting of a book. Notice if there is evidence of new learning based on the goal of this minilesson.
- Can students explain how a writer's language choices fit the setting?
- Do they use academic vocabulary, such as *author, language, setting, grammar,* and *dialect*?

Minilesson

To help students think about the minilesson principle, guide them in noticing how writers choose language to fit the setting. Here is an example.

- Read the title and page 1 of *Finding the Music*. Display the illustration.

  What is the setting for this part of the story? How can you tell?

  The author uses Spanish words like *vihuela*, *abuelito*, and *mariachi* to fit the setting. Mariachi is a style of music that started in Mexico.

- Record the setting and the Spanish words on the chart paper.
- Turn to the poem titled "Reggae" in *I and I: Bob Marley* and read it aloud.

  What is the setting of this book? Where was Bob Marley from?

- Reread the lines "Rita shake her hips / I and I light step my feet."

  How is this language different from the language that you usually read in books?

- Help students, if necessary, notice the unconventional grammar ("Rita shake," "light step") and use of dialect ("I and I"). Briefly explain what a dialect is and that Rastafarians in Jamaica have their own dialect. (The copyright page in *I and I: Bob Marley* provides a brief explanation about the meaning and origin of "I and I.")

Have a Try

Invite the students to talk with a partner about the language used in *Malala/Iqbal*.

- Show the cover of *Malala/Iqbal* (*Iqbal* side) and read the title and page 7.

  What do you notice about how the writer of this book chooses language to fit the setting? Turn and talk to your partner.

- After students turn and talk, invite a volunteer to share. Record the word *Peshgi* on the chart.

Writers choose language to fit the setting.

Book	Setting	Language Choices
	A Mexican restaurant	Spanish words: • vihuela • abuelito • mariachi
	Jamaica	Dialect and unconventional grammar: • "Rita shake her hips" • "I and I light step my feet"
	Pakistan	Hindustani word: • Peshgi

Summarize and Apply

Summarize the learning and remind students to notice how writers choose language to fit the setting.

What did you notice today about how writers choose language to fit the setting?

- Write the principle at the top of the chart.

  When you read today, notice if the author of your book makes any interesting language choices to fit the setting of the book—for example, by using non-English words, unconventional grammar, or dialects. If you find an example, bring your book to share when we come back together.

Share

Following independent reading time, gather students together to talk about their reading.

Did anyone find an example of an author choosing language to fit the setting?

How did the author of your book shape the language to fit the setting?

Extend the Lesson (Optional)

After assessing students' understanding, you might decide to extend the learning.

- Encourage students to choose language to fit the setting in their own writing.
- Discuss how writers choose language to fit the characters (e.g., their cultural background, age, personality), especially in dialogue.

RML 5
LA.U10.RML5

Reading Minilesson Principle
Writers choose precise words to create a mood.

Reading Like a Writer: Analyzing the Writer's Craft

You Will Need

- three or four familiar fiction books, such as the following from Text Set: Writer's Craft:
  - *Eliza's Freedom Road* by Jerdine Nolen
  - *Firebird* by Misty Copeland
  - *Encounter* by Jane Yolen
- chart paper and markers
- document camera (optional)
- sticky notes

Academic Language / Important Vocabulary

- mood
- feeling

Continuum Connection

- Notice language that conveys an emotional atmosphere (mood) in a text, affecting how the reader feels: e.g., tension, sadness, whimsicality, joy (p. 74)
- Notice how a writer uses language to convey a mood (p. 147)

Goal

Notice how a writer's word choices create the mood.

Rationale

Writers choose words to create a mood or feeling in their writing, which helps readers connect to the characters and the plot. When you support students in noticing these language choices, you engage them in their reading and make books more enjoyable. You also help them think about how to learn from writers to enhance their own writing.

Assess Learning

Observe students when they talk about the writer's craft. Notice if there is evidence of new learning based on the goal of this minilesson.

- Can students identify when an author uses language to help the reader experience a feeling?
- Do they point out a writer's use of language during individual reading conferences, book clubs, or small-group guided reading?
- Do they understand how the words *mood* and *feeling* are used in this lesson?

Minilesson

To help students think about the minilesson principle, help them notice the author's use of language. If a document camera is available, consider projecting the pages to provide visual support. Here is an example.

- From *Eliza's Freedom Road,* show and read page 78.

  What do these sentences tell you about the situation Eliza is in?

  How does that make you feel?

  What is some of the language that makes you feel that way?

- Record words on the chart paper.

  Writers choose words very carefully when they write. When a writer uses certain words to create a certain feeling, she creates a mood.

- Repeat this process with page 98 of *Eliza's Freedom Road.*

  How does the writer's language make you feel?

  Which words create that mood?

- If time allows, repeat this process with page 1 of *Firebird.*

Have a Try

Invite the students to talk with a partner about the words writers choose to create a mood.

- Show *Encounter* and read page 1.

  Turn and talk to your partner. What mood does the writer create? How does she do it?

- Ask a couple of students to share. Record the language that creates the mood.

Writers choose precise words to create a mood.

Title	Mood	Author's Words
Eliza's Freedom Road	• fear • dread • weakness • chaos	• "my insides turned weak" • "my legs did not hold me" • "like an earthquake"
	• overwhelmed • grief • heartache • alone	• "loud roar of sadness" • "first time I felt how deep inside I hurt" • "leaving with no goodbyes"
Firebird	• hopeless • discouraged • lonely	• "space between you and me is longer than forever"
Encounter	• fear • foreboding • danger	• "voices like thunder • "sharp, white, teeth"

Summarize and Apply

Summarize the learning and remind students to notice how writers choose words to create a mood.

How do writers create a mood in their writing?

- Write the principle at the top of the chart.

  As you read today, be on the lookout for words the author uses to create a mood. Use a sticky note to mark the pages. Bring your book when we come back together so you can share.

Share

Following independent reading time, gather students together in small groups to talk about mood.

If you marked a page that helped you notice the mood of a story, share that with your group. What mood did the author's words create?

- Choose a few students to share with the class.

Extend the Lesson (Optional)

After assessing students' understanding, you might decide to extend the learning.

- Many of the words authors use to create a mood describe the setting. During interactive read-aloud, talk with students about how the setting impacts the mood of a story.

RML 6

LA.U10.RML6

Reading Minilesson Principle

Writers choose specific words to express their attitude or feelings toward a subject.

Reading Like a Writer: Analyzing the Writer's Craft

You Will Need

- three or four familiar texts, such as the following:
  - *Firebird* by Misty Copeland and *Eliza's Freedom Road* by Jerdine Nolan, from Text Set: Writer's Craft
  - *Elephant Quest* by Ted and Betsy Lewin, from Text Set: Author/Illustrator Study: Ted and Betsy Lewin
- chart paper and markers
- document camera (optional)
- sticky notes

Academic Language / Important Vocabulary

- mood
- attitude
- feelings
- tone

Continuum Connection

- Notice language that expresses the author's attitude or feelings toward a subject reflected in the style of writing (tone): e.g., lighthearted, ironic, earnest, affectionate, formal (p. 71)
- Notice and think critically about a writer's word choice (p. 71)

Goal

Notice how writers choose words that express their feelings or attitude toward a subject (tone).

Rationale

Tone is an author's attitude toward or feelings about a subject. The tone is revealed in part through the author's carefully chosen language. When you support students in noticing language that indicates tone, you deepen their understanding. You also help them think about how to learn from writers to support their own writing.

Assess Learning

Observe students when they talk about the writer's craft. Notice if there is evidence of new learning based on the goal of this minilesson.

- Can students identify language that reveals the author's tone?
- Do they understand how the words *mood, attitude, feelings,* and *tone* are used in this lesson?

Minilesson

To help students think about the minilesson principle, help them notice a writer's use of language. If a document camera is available, consider projecting the pages to provide visual support. Here is an example.

- From *Firebird,* show and read page 28.

  How do you think the author, Misty Copeland, feels about becoming an accomplished dancer?

  What are some of the words that make you think that?

- Record the words on the chart paper.

  Writers choose words very carefully when they write. When a writer uses specific words to express her feelings or attitude toward a subject, like dancing, she creates a tone.

  What word could you use to describe her tone?

- Repeat this process with pages 138–139 of *Eliza's Freedom Road.*

  How does the writer feel about the subject of learning to read and write?

  How would you describe the tone of the writing?

  Which words create that tone?

Have a Try

Invite the students to talk with a partner about the words writers choose to create a tone.

- Show *Elephant Quest* and read page 16.

  Turn and talk to your partner. What tone do the writers create? How do they do it?

- Ask a couple of students to share. Record the language that creates the tone.

Summarize and Apply

Summarize the learning and remind students to notice how writers choose words to create a tone.

How do writers create a tone in their writing?

- Write the principle at the top of the chart.

  As you read today, be on the lookout for words the author uses to create a tone. Use a sticky note to mark the pages. Bring your book when we come back together so you can share.

Writers choose specific words to express their attitude or feelings toward a subject.

Title	Author's Words	Author's Tone
Firebird	• "the space between you and me is longer than forever" • "I will show them that forever is not so far away."	• Direct: The distance between a beginning dancer and an accomplished dancer is huge. • Determined: She knows she can achieve her dream.
Eliza's Freedom Road	• "my gift" • "your inheritance" • "share in the broad light of day, not a secret" • "I will remind them each day of the kind regard I have for them to learn"	• Passionate: Compares education to things that are treasured • Enthusiastic: Eager to share • Compassionate: Teaching is a kindness.
Elephant Quest	• "we stare intently" • "But it's not the one we're after" • "We worry about the lion cubs and marvel at . . . the kudu."	• Excited • Disappointed • Loving: Shows concern and care for the animals

Share

Following independent reading time, gather students together in small groups to talk about the author's tone.

If you marked a page that helped you notice the tone in a story, share that with your group. What feelings or attitude did it help you understand that the author had toward their subject?

- Choose a few students to share with the class.

Extend the Lesson (Optional)

After assessing students' understanding, you might decide to extend the learning.

- During interactive read-aloud, talk with students about the tone of the author's writing. Notice how the tone impacts the mood of a story.

RML 7
LA.U10.RML7

Reading Minilesson Principle

Writers use different techniques to create humor.

Reading Like a Writer: Analyzing the Writer's Craft

You Will Need

- three or four familiar texts or poems with clear examples of humor, such as the following by Ted and Betsy Lewin, from Text Set: Author/Illustrator Study: Ted and Betsy Lewin:
  - *Balarama*
  - *Elephant Quest*
  - *Gorilla Walk*
  - *Top to Bottom Down Under*
- chart paper and markers
- sticky notes

Academic Language / Important Vocabulary

- humor
- humorous

Continuum Connection

- Notice that words have specific qualities, such as musical or pleasing sound, dramatic impact, or humor (p. 71)
- Recognize how a writer creates humor: e.g., dialogue; effective descriptions of characters' actions, words, behavior, and feelings; surprising metaphors and similes; ironic expressions (p. 71)
- Appreciate or critique fiction texts that utilize subtle or whimsical humor (p. 71)

Goal

Recognize how a writer creates humor.

Rationale

Humorous stories may feel abstract to students. It is challenging to determine what makes a story humorous because humor is personal. But when students learn to recognize how writers create humor, stories become more enjoyable. They also learn to create humor in their own stories.

Assess Learning

Observe students when they talk about the writer's craft. Notice if there is evidence of new learning based on the goal of this minilesson.

- Can students identify places in a story that they found funny?
- Can they talk about how a writer made a story humorous?
- Do they understand and use the words *humor* and *humorous*?

Minilesson

To help students think about the minilesson principle, discuss familiar books that bring in an element of humor that is tangible and concrete. Here is an example.

- Show *Balarama* and read page 10.

  What do you think about this page?

  What is humorous, or funny, here?

  What did the writers do to create humor, or make you laugh?

- Record responses on a chart.

  The writers said that the young elephant is "a little handful of mischief." Could you really hold an 800-pound elephant in your hand? Of course not!

- Repeat the process with page 8 from *Elephant Quest*.
- Repeat the process again by reading page 8 from *Gorilla Walk*.

Have a Try

Invite the students to notice with a partner how writers create humor.

- Read page 5 of *Top to Bottom Down Under* and show the illustrations.

  Turn and talk to your partner. What makes this part humorous?

- Ask a couple of students to share. Record responses.

Summarize and Apply

Summarize the learning and remind students to notice how writers create humor.

What does the chart show you?

- Write the principle at the top of the chart.

  When you read today, notice places in your book that you find humorous and mark them with a sticky note. Bring the book when we meet so you can share.

Writers use different techniques to create humor.

Title	Humorous Part	What makes it humorous?
 Balarama: A Royal Elephant	"He's already a little handful of mischief."	Opposite idea: Elephants are huge.
 Elephant Quest	"In the middle of the river is the resident hippo." "This part of the river is his."	Unexpected idea: The hippo "owns" the river.
 Gorilla Walk	"Ah, you're going to visit those people in the forest."	Silly idea: It's amusing to think of gorillas as people.
 Top to Bottom	"There's a bird that lives in a hole and swims like a fish, but it can't fly."	Surprise: Illustrations show surprising and unexpected animals.

Share

Following independent reading time, gather students together in the meeting area to talk about humor.

Who read something humorous today? What did the writer do to create humor?

Extend the Lesson (Optional)

After assessing students' understanding, you might decide to extend the learning.

- Take time during interactive read-aloud for students to respond to and critique a writer's use of humor in fiction and nonfiction books.
- **Writing About Reading** Encourage students to share in their weekly letters about reading (see Umbrella 3: Writing Letters to Share Thinking About Books, found in Section Four: Writing About Reading) humorous parts of their books and to explain how the writer created humor.

RML 8

LA.U10.RML8

Reading Minilesson Principle

Writers use specific fonts to communicate ideas.

Reading Like a Writer: Analyzing the Writer's Craft

You Will Need

- three or four familiar books or poems with interesting use of fonts, such as the following:
  - *Black Dog* by Levi Pinfold, from Text Set: Writer's Craft
  - *Finding the Music* by Jennifer Torres, from Text Set: Problem Solving/ Resourcefulness
  - *Mr. Ferris and His Wheel* by Kathryn Gibbs Davis, from Text Set: Understanding How Things Work
- document camera (optional)
- chart paper and markers
- sticky notes

Academic Language / Important Vocabulary

- font
- italics
- features
- indicate

Continuum Connection

- Make connections between texts, illustrations, and book and print features (p. 147)
- Talk about illustrations and book and print features and evaluate whether they help readers understand information and add interest (p. 147)

Goal

Notice the different ways writers use fonts to communicate ideas.

Rationale

Typically, writers use a consistent font throughout their writing. Sometimes, however, they use a change of font (such as italics, boldface, or large or small fonts) to communicate additional meaning. When you encourage students to notice how and why different fonts are used, you help them appreciate the writer's craft and gain a better understanding of the text. They also learn possibilities for their own writing.

Assess Learning

Observe students when they talk about the writer's craft. Notice if there is evidence of new learning based on the goal of this minilesson.

- Do students notice interesting uses of fonts?
- Can they discuss an author's decisions about fonts and what the author is using print to convey?
- Can they use the words *font, italics, features,* and *indicate*?

Minilesson

To help students think about the minilesson principle, use enlarged texts that they can see easily. Write words on chart paper or, if a document camera is available, project the pages. Here is an example.

- Show and read pages 5 and 14 from *Black Dog*.

  What unique font do you see on these pages? Why do you think the author chose to use that font here? What does it indicate?

- Record responses on a chart.
- Repeat the process with page 21.
- Repeat the process with page 1 from *Finding the Music*.

  How does the author use the font to help you to figure out what the words mean?

Have a Try

Invite the students to notice with a partner how writers use font to communicate ideas.

- Read and show one or two of the two-page spreads from *Mr. Ferris and His Wheel*, changing the tone and speed of your voice to indicate the storyline versus the supporting facts.

  Turn and talk to your partner. Why did the writer choose to use different fonts here?

- Ask a couple of students to share. Record responses.

Writers use specific fonts to communicate ideas.

Book	Font	What does the font choice indicate?
BLACK DOG	*Italics* *Italics* CAPITAL letters	• Emphasis to show humor • A song • An exclamation • Excitement • Triumph
Finding the Music	*Italics*	• A language other than English • Indicates you should look at the illustrations and surrounding words for the meaning of the non-English words
Mr. Ferris and His Wheel	Larger Smaller and darker	• The words in the larger font tell the story. • The words in the smaller font give supporting details.

Summarize and Apply

Summarize the learning and remind students to notice how writers use fonts.

What did you learn about how writers use fonts?

- Write the principle at the top of the chart.

  When you read today, notice how the writer uses fonts in the book. If you notice a different font, mark the page with a sticky note. What does the font choice indicate? Bring the book when we come back together so you can share.

Share

Following independent reading time, gather students together in the meeting area to talk about the fonts in the books they read.

Who found an interesting example of font choice in your reading today? Why do you think the author chose to do that?

Extend the Lesson (Optional)

After assessing students' understanding, you might decide to extend the learning.

- As you read aloud or as students read independently, notice how authors use fonts to communicate meaning. Add examples to the chart.
- Notice how authors use fonts to communicate meaning in poetry. Add examples to the chart.

Assessment

After you have taught the minilessons in this umbrella, observe students as they talk and write about their reading across instructional contexts: interactive read-aloud, independent reading, guided reading, shared reading, and book club. Use *The Literacy Continuum* (Fountas and Pinnell 2017) to guide the observation of students' reading and writing behaviors.

- What evidence do you have of new understandings related to analyzing the writer's craft?
  - Do students understand writers' use of poetic, descriptive, or figurative language?
  - Do they notice and discuss an author's choice of words to create a mood or tone?
  - Are they able to talk about different ways writers use humor?
  - Can they share examples of fonts used to communicate an idea?
  - Do they use vocabulary such as *language, five senses, simile, metaphor, compare, personification, mood, tone, humor* and *font?*
- In what other ways, beyond the scope of this umbrella, are students talking about writer's craft?
  - Do students talk about the decisions that writers of various genres must make?
  - Are they aware of craft moves that poets use?

Use your observations to determine the next umbrella you will teach. You may also consult Minilessons Across the Year (pp. 61–64) for guidance.

Link to Writing

After teaching the minilessons in this umbrella, help students link the new learning to their own writing:

- As students do their own writing, encourage them to explore elements of writer's craft by choosing words that create a particular mood and tone; using fonts to communicate ideas; adding humorous or figurative language; and choosing poetic or descriptive words to appeal to the five senses.

Reader's Notebook

When this umbrella is complete, provide a copy of the minilesson principles (see resources.fountasandpinnell.com) for students to glue in a reader's notebook (in the Minilessons section if using *Reader's Notebook: Advanced* [Fountas and Pinnell 2011]), so they can refer to the information as needed.

Minilessons in This Umbrella

RML1	Poets use line breaks and white space to show you how to read the poem.
RML2	Poets use imagery to make you see, hear, and feel things.
RML3	Poets use repetition to draw attention or create rhythm.
RML4	Poets use alliteration and assonance to create rhythm and make the poem interesting.
RML5	Poets use onomatopoeia to help you make an image with sound.

Author Study: Joyce Sidman

Before Teaching Umbrella 11 Minilessons

Poetry is not a genre, but a "broad, overarching category of language of writing that can appear in any genre. . . . Poetry is compact writing characterized by imagination and artistry and imbued with intense meaning" (Fountas and Pinnell 2012c, 19). Studying the craft of poetry allows students to understand the characteristics of poetry and to think about applying the craft to their own writing.

Before beginning this umbrella, give students the opportunity to hear, read, and enjoy many different poems. Read poems that encompass a variety of forms (lyrical, free verse, haiku, limerick, etc.) and topics. Read poems that tell stories, poems that convey information, and poems that explore emotions and ideas. Read poems that highlight the poet's craft and that play with sound, language, space, and imagery. Use the following books from the *Fountas & Pinnell Classroom™ Interactive-Read-Aloud Collection* text set listed below or choose poetry texts from your own library.

Author Study: Joyce Sidman

Dark Emperor and Other Poems of the Night

Winter Bees and Other Poems of the Cold

Song of the Water Boatman and Other Pond Poems

As you read aloud and enjoy these texts together, help students

- notice and discuss the physical characteristics of poetry, such as line breaks and white space, and
- notice and discuss the characteristics of the language of poetry, such as imagery, repetition, alliteration, assonance, and onomatopoeia.

RML1
LA.U11.RML1

Reading Minilesson Principle
Poets use line breaks and white space to show you how to read the poem.

Understanding the Craft of Poetry

You Will Need

- two familiar poems with multiple stanzas, such as the following from *Dark Emperor and Other Poems of the Night* by Joyce Sidman, from Text Set: Author Study: Joyce Sidman:
  - "Oak After Dark"
  - "Cricket Speaks"
- chart paper and markers
- document camera (optional)

Academic Language / Important Vocabulary

- poem
- poet
- line break
- white space

Continuum Connection

- Notice and understand some elements of poetry: e.g., figurative language, rhyme, repetition, onomatopoeia, layout/line breaks (shape), imagery, alliteration, assonance (p. 69)
- Notice and understand some elements of poetry when they appear in nonfiction: e.g., figurative language, rhyme, repetition, onomatopoeia, layout/line breaks (shape), imagery, alliteration, assonance (p. 73)

Goal

Learn how to read the line breaks and white space of a poem.

Rationale

Poets intentionally use line breaks and white space to construct the rhythm of a poem and to group ideas thematically. When you teach students to notice this, they are better able to think about the structure and meaning of poetry.

Assess Learning

Observe students when they read and talk about poetry. Notice if there is evidence of new learning based on the goal of this minilesson.

- When students read poetry aloud, do they pause at appropriate points?
- Can they talk about how and why poets use line breaks and white space?
- Do they use vocabulary such as *poem, poet, line break*, and *white space* when talking about poetry?

Minilesson

To help students think about the minilesson principle, use a familiar poem to engage them in a discussion about line breaks and white space. Here is an example.

- Display the poem "Oak After Dark" so all students can see it (projected, if possible).
- Read the poem aloud. Then reread it, emphasizing the line breaks.

  What did you notice about how I read these lines?

  How did I know when to pause?

  How would I read these sentences differently if this were a paragraph instead of a poem?

  When you're reading a paragraph, pause when you reach the end of a sentence. When you're reading a poem, pause slightly when you reach the end of a line. The end of a line in a poem is called a line break. Poets choose where to put the line breaks. How do you think poets decide where to put line breaks?

  How do line breaks help you when you read poetry?

- Point to the space between the two stanzas of the poem.

  When I was reading the poem aloud, what did I do when I got to this part?

  This is called white space. White space is a place in a poem where there are no words. Why do you think the poet put white space here?

  How will the white space help you read the poem?

Have a Try

Invite the students to talk with a partner about line breaks and white space in a poem.

- Display another familiar poem, such as "Cricket Speaks."

  Read this poem aloud with your partner. Remember to pay attention to the line breaks and white space. After you read it, turn and talk about how and why the poet used line breaks and white space.

- After students read and discuss the poem in pairs, ask a few students to share their thinking with the class.

Poets use line breaks and white space to show you how to read the poem.

Line breaks
- Group certain words together
- Tell you to pause slightly
- Make the poem sound a certain way

White space
- Separates different parts of the poem
- Tells you to pause a little longer

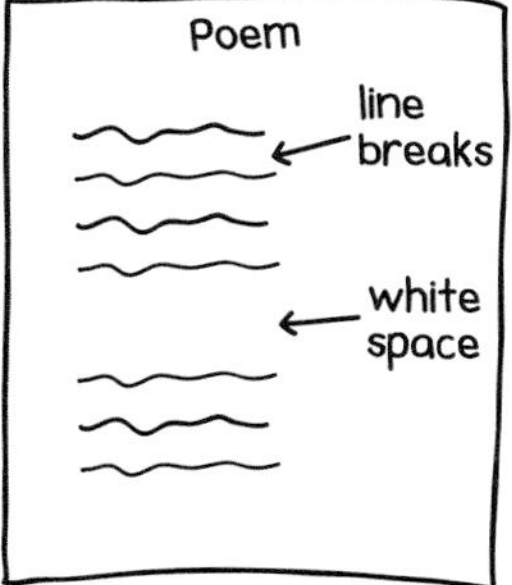

Summarize and Apply

Summarize the learning and remind students to pay attention to line breaks and white space when they read poetry.

Why do poets use line breaks?

Why do poets use white space?

- Record students' responses on chart paper, grouping the lines to look like lines and stanzas of a poem. Write the principle at the top of the chart.

  If you read poetry today, pay attention to how the poet used line breaks and white space. Bring one poem that you would like to share when we come back together.

Share

Following independent reading time, gather students together in the meeting area to talk about poetry.

Who would like to share a poem that you read today? What did you notice about the poem?

Extend the Lesson (Optional)

After assessing students' understanding, you might decide to extend the learning.

- Have students recite poems to the class to give them practice in observing line breaks and white space.
- Encourage students to think about how to effectively use line breaks and white space when they write their own poems.

RML 2
LA.U11.RML2

Reading Minilesson Principle

Poets use imagery to make you see, hear, and feel things.

Understanding the Craft of Poetry

You Will Need

- two or three familiar poems that contain imagery, such as the following by Joyce Sidman, from Text Set: Author Study: Joyce Sidman:
  - "Welcome to the Night" and "Snail at Moonrise" from *Dark Emperor and Other Poems of the Night*
  - "Snowflake Wakes" from *Winter Bees and Other Poems of the Cold*
- chart paper and markers
- document camera (optional)
- sticky notes

Academic Language / Important Vocabulary

- poet
- poem
- poetry
- imagery

Continuum Connection

- Notice and understand some elements of poetry: e.g., figurative language, rhyme, repetition, onomatopoeia, layout/line breaks (shape), imagery, alliteration, assonance (p. 69)
- Notice and understand some elements of poetry when they appear in nonfiction: e.g., figurative language, rhyme, repetition, onomatopoeia, layout/line breaks (shape), imagery, alliteration, assonance (p. 73)

Goal

Notice and understand how poets use imagery to appeal to the senses—sight, sound, touch, smell, and taste.

Rationale

When you teach students to recognize imagery in poetry, they are better able to understand the poem's meaning and appreciate the poet's craft.

Assess Learning

Observe students when they read and talk about poetry and notice if there is evidence of new learning based on the goal of this minilesson.

- Do students notice imagery in poems?
- Do they understand and talk about how the use of imagery helps convey the meaning of the poem?
- Do they use vocabulary such as *poet, poem, poetry,* and *imagery*?

Minilesson

To help students think about the minilesson principle, use familiar poems to engage them in a discussion about imagery in poetry. Here is an example.

- Ask students to close their eyes; then, read the poem "Welcome to the Night."

  What did you imagine while I read this poem?

  Which senses did the poet address?

- Then display the poem so all students can see and refer to it.

  Which words help form an image with your senses?

- Record responses on chart paper.

  Now close your eyes again and listen carefully as I read another poem.

- Read "Snail at Moonrise."

  What did you see in your mind while I read this poem?

  What texture did the poet help you feel?

- Display the poem.

  How did the poet help you imagine seeing or touching something?

- Record responses on the chart.

Have a Try

Invite the students to talk with a partner about imagery.

- Display "Snowflake Wakes" and read it aloud.

  What did you imagine seeing, hearing, or touching while I read this poem? What did the poet do to create images in your mind? Turn and talk to your partner about the imagery the poet created.

- After students turn and talk, ask a few students to share. Record responses on the chart.

Poets use imagery to make you see, hear, and feel things.

Poem	Imagery	What the Poet Did to Create Imagery
"Welcome to the Night"	• Sights: owl's flexible head • Sounds: insects and animals in the night • Touch: bark and leaves	• Used sound words buzz, chirp, hoot, peep • Used describing words rough and leathered
"Snail at Moonrise"	• Sights: a shiny trail, a long log • Touch: rough tongue	• Described the trail as slick and silver • Compared the log to a horizon • Compared the snail's tongue to sandpaper
"Snowflake Wakes"	• Sights: snowflakes flying through the air • Sounds: quiet • Touch: warm, cozy, soft	• Compared a snowflake to a pinwheel • Used word silently • Described a snowflake being tucked in its own blanket

Summarize and Apply

Summarize the learning and remind students to notice and think about imagery in poetry.

Poets use certain words and phrases to help you see, hear, smell, taste, or touch things in your mind. This is called imagery. Every decision the poet makes, like to use imagery, is the poet's craft.

- Write the principle at the top of the chart.

  If you read poetry today, notice if the poet used imagery to help you see, hear, or feel things in your mind. If you find an example of imagery, mark it with a sticky note and bring your book to share when we come back together.

Share

Following independent reading time, gather students together in the meeting area to share examples of imagery.

Who found an example of imagery in a poem today?

Read aloud the example you found. What did you imagine while you read the poem? How did the imagery help you better understand or enjoy the poem?

Extend the Lesson (Optional)

After assessing students' understanding, you might decide to extend the learning.

- Help students think about creating imagery by showing a particular image (e.g., a sunset) or by playing a sound (e.g., a thunderstorm). Have students write phrases that could help readers imagine the image or sound.
- **Writing About Reading** Have students write a response to an image in a poem they have read. They should describe what the imagery helped them imagine and explain how the imagery helped them better understand or appreciate the poem.

RML 3

LA.U11.RML3

Reading Minilesson Principle

Poets use repetition to draw attention or create rhythm.

Understanding the Craft of Poetry

You Will Need

- two familiar poems that use repetition, such as the following by Joyce Sidman, from Text Set: Author Study: Joyce Sidman:
  - "Diving Beetle's Food-Sharing Rules" from *Song of the Water Boatman and Other Pond Poems*
  - "Welcome to the Night" from *Dark Emperor and Other Poems of the Night*
- chart paper and markers
- document camera (optional)

Academic Language / Important Vocabulary

- poem
- poet
- poetry
- repetition

Continuum Connection

- Notice and understand some elements of poetry: e.g., figurative language, rhyme, repetition, onomatopoeia, layout/line breaks (shape), imagery, alliteration, assonance (p. 69)
- Notice and understand some elements of poetry when they appear in nonfiction: e.g., figurative language, rhyme, repetition, onomatopoeia, layout/line breaks (shape), imagery, alliteration, assonance (p. 73)

Goal

Notice and understand a poet's use of repetition.

Rationale

Repetition in poetry can create rhythm, emphasize certain ideas, or make a poem memorable. When you teach students to notice repetition in poetry, they are better able to understand the poet's craft in creating an experience for the reader, which could help them when writing their own poems.

Assess Learning

Observe students when they read and discuss poetry and notice if there is evidence of new learning based on the goal of this minilesson.

- Do students notice when a poet uses repetition?
- Do they understand how repetition helps convey the meaning and enjoyment of a poem?
- Do they use vocabulary such as *poem, poet, poetry,* and *repetition*?

Minilesson

To help students think about the minilesson principle, use familiar poems to engage them in noticing repetition in poetry. Here is an example.

- Display "Diving Beetle's Food-Sharing Rules" so all students can see it.

  As I read this poem aloud, listen carefully and notice how the poet used words.

- Read the poem aloud, emphasizing the repeated word *mine*.

  What did you notice about how this poem sounds?

  What word did you hear repeated?

  How does repeating the word *mine* help you to know something about diving beetles?

  When something is repeated, it is called repetition. Part of this poet's craft is repetition.

- Record students' responses on chart paper.

Have a Try

Invite the students to talk with a partner about repetition in a poem.

- Display the poem "Welcome to the Night" and read it aloud, emphasizing its repetition.

  Turn and talk to your partner about what you noticed about this poem. Why do you think the author chose to use repetition?

- After students turn and talk, invite several pairs to share their thinking. Record their responses on the chart.

Poets use repetition to draw attention or create rhythm.

Poem	Repetition	Effects
"Diving Beetle's Food-Sharing Rules"	• Word – "mine"	• Tells you that the diving beetle is greedy and eats anything • Makes the poem enjoyable to read
"Welcome to the Night"	• Phrase – "welcome to the night"	• Helps you feel the excitement the night animals feel • Creates a rhythm

Summarize and Apply

Summarize the learning and remind students to notice repetition when they read poetry.

How do poets use repetition?

- Write the principle at the top of the chart.

  If you read poetry today, notice if the author used repetition of a word or phrase. If you read a poem that has repetition, bring it to share when we come back together.

Share

Following independent reading time, gather students together in the meeting area to talk about repetition in poetry.

Who read a poem with an interesting use of repetition today?

Read the poem aloud. How did the repetition help you to understand the poem, or better enjoy it?

Extend the Lesson (Optional)

After assessing students' understanding, you might decide to extend the learning.

- Use poems with repetition, such as "Spelling Bomb" from *This Is Just to Say: Poems of Apology and Forgiveness* and "In the Depths of the Summer Pond" from *Song of the Water Boatman & Other Pond Poems* by Joyce Sidman, from Text Set: Author Study: Joyce Sidman, for performance reading.
- **Writing About Reading** Have students write in a reader's notebook about how an author uses repetition in a poem. Encourage them to discuss how the repetition draws attention to an idea or creates a rhythm.

RML 4

LA.U11.RML4

Reading Minilesson Principle

Poets use alliteration and assonance to create rhythm and make the poem interesting.

Understanding the Craft of Poetry

You Will Need

- three or four familiar poems that contain alliteration and/or assonance, such as the following by Joyce Sidman from Text Set: Author Study: Joyce Sidman:
  - "Snowflake Wakes" and "Dream of the Tundra Swan" from *Winter Bees and Other Poems of the Cold*
  - "Cricket Speaks" and "Oak After Dark" from *Dark Emperor and Other Poems of the Night*
- chart paper and markers
- document camera (optional)

Academic Language / Important Vocabulary

- repetition
- vowel
- consonant
- alliteration
- assonance

Continuum Connection

- Notice and understand some elements of poetry: e.g., figurative language, rhyme, repetition, onomatopoeia, layout/line breaks (shape), imagery, alliteration, assonance (p. 69)
- Notice and understand some elements of poetry when they appear in nonfiction: e.g., figurative language, rhyme, repetition, onomatopoeia, layout/line breaks (shape), imagery, alliteration, assonance (p. 73)

Goal

Notice when poets use alliteration and assonance.

Rationale

Alliteration and assonance can create a rhythm, lend coherence to poems, or make them interesting and enjoyable for the reader or listener. Teaching students to notice alliteration and assonance is likely to deepen their appreciation of poetry. It also encourages them to think about the decisions poets make when writing poetry, which helps them when writing their own poems.

Assess Learning

Observe students when they read and talk about poetry and notice if there is evidence of new learning based on the goal of this minilesson.

- Do students notice alliteration and assonance in poetry?
- Can they define *alliteration* and *assonance*?
- Do they use vocabulary such as *repetition, vowel, consonant, alliteration,* and *assonance*?

Minilesson

To help students think about the minilesson principle, use familiar poems to help them notice alliteration and assonance in poetry. Here is an example.

- Display "Snowflake Wakes" so all students can see it. Read the poem aloud, emphasizing the alliteration.

  What do you notice about the first two words in the second stanza?

  The first two words both start with the letter *l*. This is called alliteration. Alliteration is when two or more words close together start with the same consonant sound. Where else do you see alliteration in this poem?

- Display "Cricket Speaks" and read it aloud.

  Who can find an example of alliteration in this poem?

- Write the definition and examples of alliteration on chart paper.
- Display "Oak After Dark" and read it aloud.

  What do you notice about the words *feeding, leaves,* and *sealing*?

  These three words have the same vowel sound. When a vowel sound is repeated in words close together, it's called assonance.

  Who can find another example of assonance in this poem?

- Write the definition of assonance and the examples on the chart.

Have a Try

Invite the students to talk with a partner about alliteration and assonance in a poem.

- Display "Dream of the Tundra Swan" and read it aloud.

  With your partner, look for examples of repeated sounds in this poem. Talk about whether they are alliteration or assonance.

- After students turn and talk, invite a few pairs to share their thinking. Record examples on the chart.

Poets use alliteration and assonance to create rhythm and make the poem interesting.

	Definition	Examples
Alliteration	The repetition of consonant sounds at the beginning of words	"leaps," "laughing" "suddenly soft" "stars spinning silently" "drifts down" "cold came creeping"
Assonance	The repetition of vowel sounds	"feeding leaves" "sealing" "remain" "same" "pale wafer"

Summarize and Apply

Summarize the learning and remind students to notice alliteration and assonance when they read poetry.

Why do you think poets use alliteration and assonance?

When poets make the decision to use alliteration or assonance, that is part of their craft.

- Write the principle at the top of the chart.

  If you read poetry today, notice if the poet used alliteration or assonance. If you find examples, bring them to share when we come back together.

Share

Following independent reading time, gather students together in the meeting area to share examples of alliteration and assonance.

Did anyone find examples of alliteration or assonance in a poem today?

Share the examples you found. Why do you think the poet chose to use those words?

Extend the Lesson (Optional)

After assessing students' understanding, you might decide to extend the learning.

- Encourage students to write or find poems that use alliteration or assonance to share with the class. You might have several students use the poems for performance reading.

RML 5

LA.U11.RML5

Reading Minilesson Principle

Poets use onomatopoeia to help you make an image with sound.

Understanding the Craft of Poetry

You Will Need

- three or four familiar poems that contain onomatopoeia, such as the following from Text Set: Author Study: Joyce Sidman:
  - "Welcome to the Night" and "Dark Emperor" from *Dark Emperor and Other Poems of the Night*
  - "Spring Splashdown" from *Song of the Water Boatman and Other Pond Poems*
- chart paper and markers
- document camera (optional)

Academic Language / Important Vocabulary

- poem
- poet
- poetry
- onomatopoeia

Continuum Connection

- Notice and understand some elements of poetry: e.g., figurative language, rhyme, repetition, onomatopoeia, layout/line breaks (shape), imagery, alliteration, assonance (p. 69)
- Notice and understand some elements of poetry when they appear in nonfiction: e.g., figurative language, rhyme, repetition, onomatopoeia, layout/line breaks (shape), imagery, alliteration, assonance (p. 73)

Goal

Notice when and why poets use onomatopoeia.

Rationale

Poets use onomatopoeia to help the reader create a sound image in the mind, which makes poems enjoyable. Teaching students to notice onomatopoeia is likely to deepen their appreciation of poetry. It also encourages them to think about the decisions poets make when writing poetry, which helps them when writing their own poems.

Assess Learning

Observe students when they read and talk about poetry and notice if there is evidence of new learning based on the goal of this minilesson.

- Do students notice onomatopoeia in poetry?
- Can they explain why a poet might use onomatopoeia?
- Do they use vocabulary such as *poem, poet, poetry,* and *onomatopoeia*?

Minilesson

To help students think about the minilesson principle, use familiar poems to provide an inquiry-based lesson about onomatopoeia in poetry. Here is an example.

I'm going to read a poem to you. As I read, I want you to close your eyes, listen carefully, and use the words to make a picture in your mind.

- Read "Welcome to the Night" aloud, emphasizing the onomatopoetic words.

That poem made an image in your mind. What did you hear?

Which words in the poem helped you hear those sounds?

Those words imitate the sound the object or animal makes. This is called onomatopoeia. For example, the word *hoot* imitates the sound an owl makes. Say onomatopoeia slowly with me: /on/uh/mat/uh/PEE/uh.

- Repeat this process with "Dark Emperor."
- Write the definition of *onomatopoeia* on chart paper. Then ask students for examples of onomatopoeia from the poems. List them on the chart.

Have a Try

Invite the students to talk with a partner about onomatopoeia in a poem.

- Display "Spring Splashdown" and read it aloud.

  With your partner, find examples of onomatopoeia in this poem. Why do you think the author chose to use those words?

- After students turn and talk, invite a few pairs to share their thinking. Record examples on the chart.

Poets use onomatopoeia to help you make an image with sound.

Definition	Examples	
When a word imitates the sound an object or animal makes	buzz chirp hoot peep	
	squeaks skitters rustles	
	peck crackle	

Summarize and Apply

Summarize the learning and remind students to notice onomatopoeia when they read poetry.

You noticed that poets use words that imitate sounds to engage your sense of hearing and that this technique is called onomatopoeia.

- Write the principle at the top of the chart.

  If you read poetry today, notice if the poet used onomatopoeia. If you find examples, bring them to share when we come back together.

Share

Following independent reading time, gather students together in the meeting area to share examples of onomatopoeia.

Did anyone find examples of onomatopoeia in the poems you read today?

Share the examples you found. How did the sound words help you understand or enjoy the poem?

Extend the Lesson (Optional)

After assessing students' understanding, you might decide to extend the learning.

- Have students prepare a performance of some poetry that uses onomatopoeia.
- **Writing About Reading** Have students write in a reader's notebook about examples of onomatopoeia, what they add to the poem, and how the poem would be different without onomatopoeia.

Understanding the Craft of Poetry

Assessment

After you have taught the minilessons in this umbrella, observe students as they talk and write about their reading across instructional contexts: interactive read-aloud, independent reading, guided reading, shared reading, and book club, as well as their poetry writing in writers' workshop. Use *The Literacy Continuum* (Fountas and Pinnell 2017) to guide the observation of students' reading and writing behaviors.

- What evidence do you have of new understandings related to the craft of poetry?
    - Do students pay attention to line breaks and white space when reading poetry?
    - Do they notice and understand imagery in poetry?
    - Do they notice and enjoy repetition in certain poems?
    - Do they notice when and why poets use alliteration, assonance, and onomatopoeia?
    - Do they use academic language, such as *poetry, imagery, repetition, alliteration, assonance,* and *onomatopoeia*?
- In what other ways, beyond the scope of this umbrella, are students talking about poetry?
    - Are students interested in reading different kinds of poetry?
    - Do they write poetry in response to their reading?

Use your observations to determine the next umbrella you will teach. You may also consult Minilessons Across the Year (pp. 61–64) for guidance.

Link to Writing

After teaching the minilessons in this umbrella, help students link the new learning to their own writing:

- Invite students to write a poem about a topic that describes an idea or emotion, tells a story, or gives information. Alternatively, they may want to write a poem that is a response to or inspired by another poem. Remind them that they should use line breaks and white space to show the reader how to read the poem. They also may want to experiment with imagery, repetition, alliteration, assonance, and/or onomatopoeia.

Reader's Notebook

When this umbrella is complete, provide a copy of the minilesson principles (see resources.fountasandpinnell.com) for students to glue in the reader's notebook (in the Minilessons section if using *Reader's Notebook: Advanced* [Fountas and Pinnell 2011]), so they can refer to the information as needed.

Studying Illustrators and Analyzing an Illustrator's Craft

Umbrella 12

Minilessons in This Umbrella

RML1	Study illustrators to learn about their craft.
RML2	Illustrators create art to add to the meaning of the text.
RML3	Illustrators create art to show the mood.
RML4	Illustrators use perspective in their art to communicate an idea or a feeling.
RML5	Illustrators use symbols or color to reflect the theme of the book.
RML6	Illustrators create art that reflects the author's feelings or attitude (tone) toward the subject of the text.

Before Teaching Umbrella 12 Minilessons

Read and discuss books with strong illustration support and that engage students' intellectual curiosity and emotions. The minilessons in this umbrella use the following books from the *Fountas & Pinnell Classroom™ Interactive Read-Aloud Collection* text sets; however, you can use books that have strong illustration support and are based on the experiences and interests of the students in your class.

Author Study: Andrea Davis Pinkney

Sit-In: How Four Friends Stood Up by Sitting Down

Boycott Blues: How Rosa Parks Inspired a Nation

Duke Ellington: The Piano Prince and His Orchestra

Martin and Mahalia: His Words, Her Song

Problem Solving/Resourcefulness

Destiny's Gift by Natasha Anastasia Tarpley

Understanding How Things Work

Mr. Ferris and His Wheel by Kathryn Gibbs Davis

Genre Study: Historical Fiction

The Butterfly by Patricia Polacco

White Water by Michael S. Bandy and Eric Stein

Baseball Saved Us by Ken Mochizuki

Achieving a Dream

Surfer of the Century: The Life of Duke Kahanamoku by Ellie Crowe

Sixteen Years in Sixteen Seconds: The Sammy Lee Story by Paula Yoo

Author/Illustrator Study: Ted and Betsy Lewin

Elephant Quest

As you read aloud and enjoy these texts together, help students look closely at the illustrations to understand and appreciate the many decisions an illustrator makes about how to support the text.

Author Study: Andrea Davis Pinkney

Sit-In by Andrea Davis Pinkney

Boycott Blues by Andrea Davis Pinkney

Duke Ellington by Andrea Davis Pinkney

Martin and Mahalia by Andrea Davis Pinkney

Problem Solving/ Resourcefulness

Understanding How Things Work

Genre Study: Historical Fiction

Achieving a Dream

Author/Illustrator Study: Ted and Betsy Lewin

RML1
LA.U12.RML1

Reading Minilesson Principle
Study illustrators to learn about their craft.

Studying Illustrators and Analyzing an Illustrator's Craft

You Will Need

- a variety of books by the same illustrator, such as Brian Pinkney from Text Set: Author Study: Andrea Davis Pinkney
- chart paper and markers
- sticky notes
- document camera (optional)

Academic Language / Important Vocabulary

- illustrator
- perspective
- distance
- angle
- craft
- authentic

Continuum Connection

- Notice how illustrations and graphics can reflect the theme or the writer's tone (p. 72)
- Notice and infer how illustrations contribute to mood in a fiction text (p. 72)

Goal

Understand that an illustrator might illustrate several books and that there are often recognizable characteristics across the books.

Rationale

By studying the characteristics of an illustrator's work, students begin to appreciate that illustrating books is a process of decision-making involving meaning (of the text) and artistry. Students become aware of the illustrator's craft and how it enhances the meaning of the book. Note that this lesson format can be used to study an author, illustrator, or author/illustrator.

Assess Learning

Observe students when they talk about an illustrator's craft and notice if there is evidence of new learning based on the goal of this minilesson.

- Do students recognize similar characteristics among different books with the same illustrator?
- Do they understand the terms *illustrator*, *perspective*, *distance*, *angle*, *craft*, and *authentic*?

Minilesson

To help students think about the minilesson principle, use familiar books to engage them in a discussion of an illustrator's craft. Here is an example.

Let's look closely at illustrations by Brian Pinkney and talk about them. What do you notice?

- As the conversation progresses, show several books illustrated by Brian Pinkney, such as *Sit-In*, *Boycott Blues*, and *Duke Ellington*.

Think about what you *always* notice in Brian Pinkney's illustrations and what you *often* notice in his illustrations.

- The following prompts can be used to support the conversation:
  - *How do the illustrations add to the meaning of the story?*
  - *How does the illustrator use color?*
  - *How does the perspective of the illustration help you understand the story or characters?*
  - *How do the illustrations make the characters and backgrounds seem real and authentic?*
- On chart paper, create a noticings chart with the headings *Always* and *Often*. Add student responses to the chart.

Have a Try

Invite the students to talk in small groups about a familiar illustrator's work.

- Provide each group with a book by Brian Pinkney.

  Talk about what you notice about Brian Pinkney's illustrations. How do they help you understand more about the story?

- After time for discussion, ask students to share. Add to chart.

Brian Pinkney

Noticings:

Always	Often
• Bright colors show movement and mood changes: threatening/alarming to hopeful/joyful. • Dark brushstrokes in facial expressions and clothing create texture and movement. • Colors and shapes in backgrounds create sound and energy.	• Illustrations on scratchboard tinted with vibrant colors • Single-color backgrounds make the characters or places the focus. • Draws intangible things, such as music • Draws illustrations across two pages

Summarize and Apply

Summarize the learning and remind students to think about an illustrator's craft.

Today you learned that when you read many books that are illustrated by the same person, you begin to notice decisions that illustrators make. Each choice they make is part of their craft.

When you read today, select a book illustrated by Brian Pinkney or by another illustrator whose books you enjoy. As you read, think about the decisions the illustrator had to make. Use sticky notes to mark pages you want to remember. Bring the book when we meet so you can share.

Share

Following independent reading time, gather students in the meeting area to discuss an illustrator's craft.

Who would like to share what you noticed about an illustrator's craft? Share any illustrations that show what you are thinking.

Extend the Lesson (Optional)

After assessing students' understanding, you might decide to extend the learning.

- During interactive read-aloud, stop at an illustration. Ask students to talk about the decisions the illustrator had to make for that illustration (e.g., what exactly to show in the illustration, how to portray a character, what colors to use).

RML2
LA.U12.RML2

Reading Minilesson Principle
Illustrators create art to add to the meaning of the text.

Studying Illustrators and Analyzing an Illustrator's Craft

You Will Need

- several familiar fiction books with illustrations that add to the meaning of the text, such as the following from Text Set: Genre Study: Historical Fiction:
  - *The Butterfly* by Patricia Polacco
  - *White Water* by Michael S. Bandy and Eric Stein
  - *Baseball Saved Us* by Ken Mochizuki
- chart paper and markers
- sticky notes
- document camera (optional)

Academic Language / Important Vocabulary

- illustrations
- details
- meaning

Continuum Connection

- Notice how illustrations and graphics go together with the text in a meaningful way (p. 72)
- Notice how illustrations and graphics help to communicate the writer's message (p. 75)

Goal

Gain new information from the illustrations and understand that illustrations can be interpreted in different ways.

Rationale

When students know that illustrators have to thoroughly understand a text so that they can visualize how it can look in illustrations, they develop a deeper understanding of the illustrator's craft. Teaching students that illustrations can be interpreted in different ways increases students' understandings and enhances the conversations students have about books.

Assess Learning

Observe students when they discuss illustrations and notice if there is evidence of new learning based on the goal of this minilesson.

- Do students notice information in illustrations that helps them understand the text?
- Are they able to discuss different interpretations of the same illustration?
- Do they use the terms *illustrations, details,* and *meaning*?

Minilesson

To help students think about the minilesson principle, use familiar books to engage them in a discussion about how illustrations enhance the meaning of a text. Here is an example.

Think about the illustrations in *The Butterfly*.

- Show the cover of *The Butterfly*. Read and show the illustrations on pages 7–8 ("The tall shining boots"), the last paragraph on page 16 ("Suddenly the air grew still"), and pages 29–30 ("It seemed that Monique").

  How does the art add to the meaning of the story?

- As students provide ideas, create a chart that shows what the illustrations help a reader understand. Ask students to provide specific text examples and add to the chart.

  Now think about the art in *White Water*.

- Show the cover of *White Water*. Read pages 11–12 ("I was so thirsty"), 31–32 ("I ran as fast as I could"), 35–36 ("I was startled"), and 37–38 ("The signs over the fountains"), and show the corresponding illustrations.

  What other meanings do the illustrations add?

- Add students' ideas to the chart.

Have a Try

Invite the students to talk with a partner about the meaning illustrations add to a text.

- Show and read an example from *Baseball Saved Us*, such on pages 9–10. Turn and talk about how the illustrations on these pages help you understand the story.
- After time for discussion, ask students to share. Add to chart.

Illustrators create art to add to the meaning of the text.

Title	What the Art Helps You Understand	Examples
 *The Butterfly* (Patricia Polacco)	The characters' feelings and reaction to events	The illustrations of a large fist in front of the child's face and the mother and children hiding in shadows show fear but also standing together.
 *White Water*	A character's imagination and response to that time in history	Illustration on the last page shows how Michael is thinking beyond segregation to his future.
 *Baseball Saved Us*	How life was desolate and hard for the characters, but they worked together to make the best of it	The illustrations show everyone looking serious but determined. The colors are brown and barren.

Summarize and Apply

Summarize the learning and remind students to think about how illustrations add meaning to what they read.

What does the chart tell you about why illustrators create art?

- Write the principle at the top of the chart.

When you read today, choose a book with illustrations and think about how they add to the meaning of the story or nonfiction book. Place a sticky note on a page you would like to share. Bring the book when we meet.

Share

Following independent reading time, gather students in the meeting area to talk about illustrations. Ask several volunteers to share.

Who noticed an illustration that added to the meaning of the book? Show us the illustration and share your thinking about it.

Extend the Lesson (Optional)

After assessing students' understanding, you might decide to extend the learning.

- **Writing About Reading** Encourage students to write about how an illustration adds to the meaning of a book they are reading.

RML 3

LA.U12.RML3

Reading Minilesson Principle

Illustrators create art to show the mood.

Studying Illustrators and Analyzing an Illustrator's Craft

You Will Need

- several familiar fiction and nonfiction books that show clear examples of illustrations that support the mood of the story, such as the following:
  - *The Butterfly* by Patricia Polacco, from Text Set: Genre Study: Historical Fiction
  - *Destiny's Gift* by Natasha Anastasia Tarpley, from Text Set: Problem Solving/ Resourcefulness
  - *Duke Ellington* by Andrea Davis Pinkney, from Text Set: Author Study: Andrea Davis Pinkney
- chart paper and markers
- sticky notes
- document camera (optional)

Academic Language / Important Vocabulary

- illustrations
- physical space
- texture
- mood

Continuum Connection

- Notice and infer how illustrations contribute to mood in a fiction text (p 72)

Goal

Understand that illustrators create and change the mood using different techniques.

Rationale

Illustrators use color, size, and physical space to create and change the mood of a story. When students notice these techniques, they can better understand the mood that the author and illustrator want to convey.

Assess Learning

Observe students when they talk about illustrations and notice if there is evidence of new learning based on the goal of this minilesson.

- Are students able to identify examples of an illustrator's use of color, size, and physical space to create and change the mood of a story?
- Do they use the terms *illustrations, physical space, texture,* and *mood*?

Minilesson

To help students think about the minilesson principle, provide an interactive lesson about the impact an illustrator has on mood. If you have access to a projector, project the illustrations. Here is an example.

- Ensure that your students understand what is meant by the term *mood*.

  Illustrators think very carefully about their artistic choices and how they support and expand upon the writing. When an illustrator uses a certain color, size, or technique to create a feeling, she creates a mood.

- Show and read pages 21–22 ("Tears began to fill") from *The Butterfly* and discuss how the color shows the mood.

  Describe what you see in this illustration.

  How does the illustrator want you to feel? What is the mood?

- Record students' responses about the illustration and mood on chart paper.
- Show and read pages 27–28 ("The girls watched as Marcelle") and discuss how the characters' facial expressions and gestures contribute to mood.

  Describe what you see in this illustration.

  What mood does the illustrator create here?

- Record responses.

  Compare the two illustrations we just looked at. How are they different?

- Repeat the process with *Destiny's Gift*, showing and reading pages 21–22 ("Even with all the signs").

Have a Try

Invite the students to talk with a partner about how illustrators show mood.

- From *Duke Ellington*, show and read pages 25–26 ("With the tunes that he and Billy wrote").

  Turn and talk about how these illustrations create or change the mood of the book.

- As needed, prompt student conversations to notice how size and color create mood.
- After time for discussion, ask a few students to share. Add to the chart.

Illustrators create art to show the mood.

Title	Description of the Art	Mood
The Butterfly	• pale colors, butterfly, open window • peaceful expressions on characters' faces	• hopeful • happy
	• adults rushing, alarmed and scared expressions • focused on arms and hands working quickly	• anxious • scared • urgent
Destiny's Gift	• Mom comforting daughter • facial expressions look sad and worried	• worry • concern
Duke Ellington	• many colors swirl out of the instruments • large swirls fill the page	• energetic • lively • exciting

Summarize and Apply

Summarize the learning and remind students to think about mood in illustrations when they read.

Look at the chart. What is one of the decisions illustrators have to make about the art?

- Add the principle to the chart.

  When you read today, notice illustrations that create or change the mood. You might find examples beyond color and size. Place a sticky note on each page you want to remember. Bring the book when we meet so you can share.

Share

Following independent reading time, gather students in small groups to talk about mood in illustrations.

With your group, talk about how the art creates or changes the mood.

- After time for discussion, ask a few students to share. If you have access to a projector, you can project the illustrations that students share.

Extend the Lesson (Optional)

After assessing students' understanding, you might decide to extend the learning.

- Have students look for examples of an illustrator's use of physical space (e.g., empty space, proximity) and texture (e.g., sharp and rounded edges) and talk about how this affects mood.
- **Writing About Reading** Encourage students to write about an example of how an illustrator creates or changes the mood in their response to books.

RML 4

LA.U12.RML4

Reading Minilesson Principle

Illustrators use perspective in their art to communicate an idea or a feeling.

Studying Illustrators and Analyzing an Illustrator's Craft

You Will Need

- several familiar fiction and nonfiction books, such as the following:
  - *Destiny's Gift* by Natasha Anastasia Tarpley, from Text Set: Problem Solving/ Resourcefulness
  - *Surfer of the Century* by Ellie Crowe and *Sixteen Years in Sixteen Seconds* by Paula Yoo, from Text Set: Achieving a Dream
  - *Elephant Quest* by Ted and Betsy Lewin, from Text Set: Author/Illustrator Study: Ted and Betsy Lewin
- chart paper and markers
- sticky notes
- document camera (optional)

Academic Language / Important Vocabulary

- perspective
- communicate
- zoom
- close-up
- distance

Continuum Connection

- Understand that there can be different interpretations of the meaning of an illustration (p. 72)
- Notice how illustrations and graphics help to communicate the writer's message (p. 75)

Goal

Understand that illustrators use perspective to communicate an idea or feeling.

Rationale

Helping students notice perspective in illustrations teaches them to consider what an illustrator might be bringing to their attention at that point in the text. Illustrators might zoom in on a central image or place an image in the distance to create a feeling of space. Illustrators make decisions about the position of images to evoke certain feelings in a reader.

Assess Learning

Observe students when they talk about perspective in illustrations and notice if there is evidence of new learning based on the goal of this minilesson.

- Are students able to identify when an illustrator uses perspective to communicate an idea or a feeling (e.g., zooming in on images, placing them far away, or putting distance between them)?
- Do they use language such as *perspective, communicate, zoom, close-up,* and *distance*?

Minilesson

To help students think about the minilesson principle, engage them in a discussion about perspective in illustrations. If you have access to a projector, you can project the illustrations. Here is an example.

- From *Destiny's Gift*, show pages 25–26 ("The next morning I finished writing").

  Notice how the illustration is from the perspective of being in the store, looking at Destiny looking in. I wonder why the illustrator decided to present it that way. What do you think about that? Does it give you a certain feeling?

- On chart paper, record student responses in two columns, one for the illustration perspective example and one for the idea or feeling it supports.

  Now think about an illustration in *Surfer of the Century*.

- Show the first page.

  What do you notice about this illustration?

- As needed, provide a prompt such as this: *Why did the illustrator choose to use this perspective?*
- Record student responses on the chart.
- Repeat this process with *Sixteen Years in Sixteen Seconds*, showing and reading pages 23–24 ("For his final dive").

Have a Try

Invite the students to talk in groups of three about perspective in illustrations.

- Show and read pages 40–41 from *Elephant Quest* (the elephant charging the truck).

  Talk in your group about the feeling or idea that the illustrator creates. How does the illustrator do that?

- Prompt the conversation so students discuss perspective. After time for discussion, record student responses.

Illustrators use perspective in their art to communicate an idea or a feeling.

Title	Perspective of the Illustration	Idea or Feeling
 Destiny's Gift	From inside the store, looking at Destiny looking in	• sadness • worry • disappointment
 Surfer of the Century	A surfer, who looks quite small inside a large, curling wave	• power and size of the wave • surfer's calmness and confidence
 Sixteen Years in Sixteen Seconds	Overhead view of diver on the tall platform, looking down	• intense pressure • danger • confidence
 Elephant Quest	Large elephant charging at a truck	• alarm • powerful, protective animals • awe

Summarize and Apply

Summarize the learning and remind students to think about perspective in illustrations when they read fiction or nonfiction books.

Look back at the chart. What can you say about how illustrators use perspective?

- Add the principle to the chart.

When you read today, notice if the illustrator used perspective in the art to communicate a feeling or idea. Mark any pages that you would like to share with a sticky note. Bring the book when we meet.

Share

Following independent reading time, gather students in the meeting area to discuss illustrations.

Did anyone notice an example of an illustrator's use of perspective to show a feeling or an idea? Share what you noticed.

- As a few volunteers share, you might choose to project the illustrations so students can see the details.

Extend the Lesson (Optional)

After assessing students' understanding, you might decide to extend the learning.

- Encourage students to think of how they could use perspective effectively to show a scene when they illustrate a story.
- **Writing About Reading** Encourage students to use a reader's notebook to write about the idea or feeling they get when looking at an illustration. Ask them to think about the perspective from which the illustration is created and respond to it.

RML 5

LA.U12.RML5

Reading Minilesson Principle

Illustrators use symbols or color to reflect the theme of the book.

Studying Illustrators and Analyzing an Illustrator's Craft

You Will Need

- several familiar fiction books, such as the following:
  - *The Butterfly* by Patricia Polacco, from Text Set: Genre Study: Historical Fiction
  - *Martin and Mahalia* by Andrea Davis Pinkney, from Text Set: Author Study: Andrea Davis Pinkney
- chart paper and markers
- sticky notes
- document camera (optional)

Academic Language / Important Vocabulary

- symbols
- theme
- color
- reflect

Continuum Connection

- Interpret some illustrations with symbolic characteristics: e.g., use of color or symbols (p. 72)
- Notice how illustrations and graphics go together with the text in a meaningful way (p. 72)
- Notice how illustrations and graphics can reflect the theme or the writer's tone (p. 72)

Goal

Understand that illustrators use symbols or color to reflect the theme of a book.

Rationale

Illustrators make careful choices about how to reflect the theme in their illustrations, sometimes with color and other times with symbols. Understanding the choices that illustrators make about their illustrations is a window into the illustrator's craft. For this minilesson, students need to be familiar with theme (see LA.U9.RML1).

Assess Learning

Observe students when they talk about an illustrator's use of color or symbols to reflect theme and notice if there is evidence of new learning based on the goal of this minilesson.

- Do students recognize an illustrator's use of symbols and color to reflect or highlight the theme of a book?
- Do they use the terms *symbols, theme, color,* and *reflect*?

Minilesson

To help students think about the minilesson principle, use familiar books to engage them in a discussion about how illustrators use symbols or color in illustrations. If you have access to a projector, you can project the illustrations. Here is an example.

- From *The Butterfly*, show and read pages 21–22 ("Tears began to fill") and the last page of the story.

  A symbol is one thing that represents another. What is a symbol in this book?

  Why is the butterfly a good choice for a symbol in this book?

  The theme is what a book is really about. Sometimes a book has more than one theme. What is the theme of *The Butterfly*?

  Do you think butterflies represent the theme? What makes you think that?

- On chart paper, record students' responses.

  Now think about the theme and the illustrations in another book, *Martin and Mahalia*.

- Show and read pages 1–4.

  What do you notice about the illustrator's use of color on these pages?

  What is the theme of *Martin and Mahalia*?

  How has Brian Pinkney used color to help you understand the theme of this book?

Have a Try

Invite the students to talk with a partner about color and symbols in illustrations.

- Show the cover and then turn slowly through pages 1–12 of *Martin and Mahalia*.

  Turn and talk to a partner about colors or symbols in the illustrations that reflect the theme.

- After time for discussion, ask students to share. Record responses.

Illustrators use symbols or color to reflect the theme of the book.

Book	Symbol or Color	Theme
The Butterfly	• Butterfly flying out of the window • Many butterflies flying around	• Freedom • Friendship 
Martin and Mahalia	• Martin: bright blues and greens • Mahalia: bold reds and oranges • Both: magenta—a combination of the colors	• The power of the voice to inspire change
	• Dove flying through each page	• Hope • Peace 

Summarize and Apply

Summarize the learning and remind students to think about how illustrators use color and symbols to reflect the theme of a book.

How do illustrators show a book's theme in their illustrations?

- Add the principle to the chart.

  When you read today, choose a book with illustrations. Notice symbols or colors the illustrator used to reflect the theme of the book. Place a sticky note on each page you want to remember. Bring the book when we meet so you can share.

Share

Following independent reading time, gather students in small groups to talk about the relationship of the illustrations and the theme.

Who would like to share how the illustrator used color or symbols to reflect the book's theme?

- Ask a few volunteers to share. You may want to project the illustrations to help students notice details.

Extend the Lesson (Optional)

After assessing students' understanding, you might decide to extend the learning.

- Have students add examples of illustrators' use of color or symbols to the chart as they read and listen to more books.
- **Writing About Reading** Encourage students to use a reader's notebook to respond to how well an illustrator reflected the theme in the illustrations.

RML 6
LA.U12.RML6

Reading Minilesson Principle

Illustrators create art that reflects the author's feelings or attitude (tone) toward the subject of the text.

Studying Illustrators and Analyzing an Illustrator's Craft

You Will Need

- several familiar texts that show clear examples of illustrations reflecting the tone of a story, such as the following:
  - *Mr. Ferris and His Wheel* by Kathryn Gibbs Davis, from Text Set: Understanding How Things Work
  - *Destiny's Gift* by Natasha Anastasia Tarpley, from Text Set: Problem Solving/ Resourcefulness
  - *Martin and Mahalia* by Andrea Davis Pinkney, from Text Set: Author Study: Andrea Davis Pinkney
- chart paper and markers
- sticky notes
- document camera (optional)

Academic Language / Important Vocabulary

- attitude
- analyze
- tone

Continuum Connection

- Notice how illustrations and graphics can reflect the theme or the writer's tone (p. 72)

Goal

Understand that illustrators reflect the author's feelings or attitude (tone) toward the subject of the text.

Rationale

Illustrators make choices about their illustrations to support or enhance an author's tone—an author's attitude or feelings toward a subject. When you support students in noticing how an illustrator reflects an author's tone, you engage them in critical reading and make reading more engaging. For a minilesson on how authors use words to convey tone, see LA.U10.RML6.

Assess Learning

Observe students when they talk about illustrations and tone and notice if there is evidence of new learning based on the goal of this minilesson.

- Do students understand how illustrations can reflect an author's feelings or attitude toward a subject?
- Can they identify specific illustrations that reflect tone?
- Are they using language such as *attitude, analyze,* and *tone*?

Minilesson

To help students think about the minilesson principle, guide them to notice how illustrators reflect authors' tone. If you have access to a projector, project the illustrations. Here is an example.

- Ensure first that your students understand what is meant by the term *tone*.

  Illustrators think very carefully about their artistic choices and how they reflect the tone of a book. Tone is the author's feelings or attitude toward a subject.

  Think about the illustrations on a few pages from *Mr. Ferris and His Wheel.*

- Show and read pages 15–16 ("George and his brave workers"), 19–20 ("Finally, with only two months left"), and 24 ("George blew the golden whistle").

  As you look at these pages, how do you think the author feels about the Ferris wheel?

  How do the illustrations help you understand that?

- Record students' responses about the illustration and tone on chart paper.
- Repeat this process using *Destiny's Gift*, reading and showing pages 11–12 ("Then one Saturday everything was different"), 15 ("When I got home"), and 21–22 ("Even with all the signs").

Have a Try

Invite the students to talk with a partner about how an illustrator reflects an author's tone.

- From *Martin and Mahalia*, show and read pages 7–8 ("As he grew"), 9–10 ("As she grew"), 23–24 ("Martin's voice had a force"), and 29–30 ("This was a day").

  As you look at these pages, think about the author's attitude or feelings toward Martin and Mahalia. Turn and talk to a partner about how the illustrations reflect the author's tone.

- After time for discussion, ask a few students to share. Add to chart.

Illustrators create art that reflects the author's feelings or attitude (tone) toward the subject of the text.

Title	Tone	Illustration
Mr. Ferris and His Wheel	• awestruck • amazed	• shows size and complexity of the project • people marveling at the Ferris wheel
Destiny's Gift	• concern • compassion	• main characters looking worried • characters comforting each other
Martin and Mahalia	• celebratory • awestruck • optimistic	• powerful words in the illustrations • ripples moving outward in circles from Martin and Mahalia • bright colors

Summarize and Apply

Summarize the learning and remind students to think about how illustrations reflect an author's tone.

What does the chart show about the role of the illustrator in helping you understand tone?

- Add the principle to the chart.

  When you read today, notice how the illustrations show the author's feelings or attitudes toward the subject. Place a sticky note on those pages. Bring the book when we meet so you can share.

Share

Following independent reading time, gather students in small groups to talk about illustrations.

With your group, talk about any illustrations you found that reflected the tone of the writing.

- After time for discussion, ask a few students to share. If you have access to a projector, you can project the illustrations that students share.

Extend the Lesson (Optional)

After assessing students' understanding, you might decide to extend the learning.

- Have students look for examples of illustrations that reflect an author's tone. Add examples to the chart.
- **Writing About Reading** Encourage students to use a reader's notebook to write about examples they find of illustrations that reflect the writer's tone.

Assessment

After you have taught the minilessons in this umbrella, observe students as they talk and write about illustrations across instructional contexts: interactive read-aloud, independent reading, guided reading, shared reading, and book club. Use *The Literacy Continuum* (Fountas and Pinnell 2017) to guide the observation of students' reading and writing behaviors.

- What evidence do you have of new understandings related to studying illustrations?
    - Do students discuss an illustrator's style?
    - Can they discuss how illustrations add to the meaning of the text?
    - Do they notice how illustrators create and change mood?
    - Are they able to discuss how illustrators make decisions about using perspective, symbols, or color?
    - Can they discuss how illustrators reflect authors' feelings or attitude (tone) toward the subject of a text?
    - Do they use terms such as *illustrations, perspective, mood,* and *tone*?
- In what other ways, beyond the scope of this umbrella, are students demonstrating an understanding of illustrations?
    - Do students look at illustrations in expository texts to get more information about the topic?
    - Do they use other graphics and text features to gain knowledge?

Use your observations to determine the next umbrella you will teach. You may also consult Minilessons Across the Year (pp. 61–64) for guidance.

Link to Writing

After teaching the minilessons in this umbrella, help students link the new learning to their own writing:

- Encourage students to experiment with some of the artistic techniques they have learned about (e.g., create and change mood, use perspective to communicate an idea or feeling, support a theme, or reflect the tone of the writing).

Reader's Notebook

When this umbrella is complete, provide a copy of the minilesson principles (see resources.fountasandpinnell.com) for students to glue in the reader's notebook (in the Minilessons section if using *Reader's Notebook: Advanced* [Fountas and Pinnell 2011]), so they can refer to the information as needed.

Minilessons in This Umbrella

RML1	Authors honor/thank people and give information about themselves in parts outside of the main text.
RML2	An author's/illustrator's note or afterword provides additional information about the book.
RML3	Authors include a prologue and an epilogue to tell about something that happened before and after the main story.
RML4	Authors provide resources outside the main text to help you understand more about the story or topic.
RML5	The design (book jacket, cover, title page, endpapers) often adds to or enhances the meaning or appeal of the book.

Before Teaching Umbrella 13 Minilessons

The minilessons in this umbrella help students understand the peritext—the text resources outside the body of the text—and how those resources provide further information about the book and/or the author. Read and discuss engaging fiction and nonfiction books that have peritext resources, such as a dedication, acknowledgments, or an author's note, from the following *Fountas & Pinnell Classroom*™ *Interactive Read-Aloud Collection* text sets and *Independent Reading Collection* or from your classroom library.

Interactive Read-Aloud Collection

Grit and Perseverance

Brian's Winter by Gary Paulsen

Conflict Resolution

The Lion Who Stole My Arm by Nicola Davies

Genre Study: Biography (Musicians)

I and I: Bob Marley by Tony Medina

The Legendary Miss Lena Horne by Carole Boston Weatherford

Esquivel! Space-Age Sound Artist by Susan Wood

Strange Mr. Satie: Composer of the Absurd by M. T. Anderson

Achieving a Dream

Silent Star: The Story of Deaf Major Leaguer William Hoy by Bill Wise

Caring for Our World

Cycle of Rice, Cycle of Life: A Story of Sustainable Farming by Jan Reynolds

Independent Reading Collection

Tales from the Odyssey, Part One by Mary Pope Osborne

As you read aloud and enjoy these texts together, help students notice and discuss peritext resources.

Interactive Read-Aloud

Grit and Perseverance

Conflict Resolution

The Lion Who Stole My Arm by Nicola Davies

Genre Study: Biography (Musicians)

Achieving a Dream

Caring for Our World

Independent Reading

RML1

LA.U13.RML1

Reading Minilesson Principle

Authors honor/thank people and give information about themselves in parts outside of the main text.

Noticing Book and Print Features

You Will Need

- at least two familiar books that contain a dedication, acknowledgments, and/or author information, such as the following:
  - *Cycle of Rice, Cycle of Life* by Jan Reynolds, from Text Set: Caring for Our World
  - *Strange Mr. Satie* by M. T. Anderson, from Text Set: Genre Study: Biography (Musicians)
- chart paper and markers

Academic Language / Important Vocabulary

- author
- dedication
- acknowledgments
- author page

Continuum Connection

- Notice and use and understand the purpose of some text resources outside the body (peritext): e.g., dedication, acknowledgments, author's note, illustrator's note, endpapers, foreword, prologue, pronunciation guide, footnote, epilogue, appendix, endnote, references (pp. 72, 74)

Goal

Notice, use, and understand the purpose of the dedication, acknowledgments, and author's page.

Rationale

When you teach students to notice and read peritext resources, such as the dedication, acknowledgments, and author page, they understand that behind every book is a real person who was helped, inspired, and influenced by many others. Depending on the specific resource, they may gain insight into the author's creative process, who or what inspired the author to write the book, and/or who helped the author write the book.

Assess Learning

Observe students when they read and talk about books and notice if there is evidence of new learning based on the goal of this minilesson.

- Do students notice and read peritext resources, such as the dedication, acknowledgments, and author page?
- Can they explain the purpose of each resource?
- Do they use academic vocabulary, such as *author, dedication, acknowledgments,* and *author page*?

Minilesson

To help students think about the minilesson principle, use familiar books to engage them in noticing and understanding the purpose of peritext resources. Here is an example.

- Show the cover of *Cycle of Rice, Cycle of Life* and read the title. Turn to the copyright page and point to the dedication. Read it aloud.

  What is this part of the book called?

  What do you notice about Jan Reynolds' dedication?

  Why do you think she dedicated the book to Professor Stephen Lansing?

- Point to the acknowledgments and read them aloud.

  What are acknowledgments?

  Who does the author of this book thank and why?

- Read the dedications and acknowledgments in one or two other books. Ask students what they notice about them, and then ask them to come up with what the dedication and acknowledgments are and their purposes. Record responses on chart paper.

Have a Try

Invite the students to talk with a partner about the author information in *Strange Mr. Satie.*

- Turn to the final page of *Strange Mr. Satie* and read aloud the information about the author.

  Turn and talk to your partner about this part of the book. What kind of information does the author give on this page?

- After students turn and talk, ask a few pairs to share their thinking. Help students come up with a definition of *author page* and add it to the chart.

Authors honor/thank people and give information about themselves in parts outside of the main text.

	What	Why
Dedication	A message usually at the beginning of the book in which the author honors someone	To honor a person or the people who inspired the author or whom the author has strong feelings for, like a parent or teacher
Acknowledgments	A message to thank people for their help	To thank people who helped the author, such as those who helped with research, provided photographs, or read the first draft
Author Page	A page that gives information about the person who wrote the book	To give information about the author, for example, where the author lives, her hobbies, her reason for writing the book

Summarize and Apply

Summarize the learning and remind students to read peritext resources.

Today we looked at some parts of books that are outside the main body of the text. What did you notice about these parts?

- Write the principle at the top of the chart.

  When you read today, notice if your book has a dedication, acknowledgments, or an author page. If so, be sure to read them. Be ready to share what you learned from these parts of your book when we come back together.

Share

Following independent reading time, gather students together in the meeting area to talk about their reading.

What did you learn from the dedication, acknowledgments, or author page in the book you read today?

Extend the Lesson (Optional)

After assessing students' understanding, you might decide to extend the learning.

- When students write their own books, encourage them to include a dedication, acknowledgments, and/or an author page.

RML2
LA.U13.RML2

Reading Minilesson Principle

An author's/illustrator's note or afterword provides additional information about the book.

Noticing Book and Print Features

You Will Need

- two or three familiar books that contain an author's and/or illustrator's note or an afterword, such as the following:
  - *Cycle of Rice, Cycle of Life* by Jan Reynolds, from Text Set: Caring for Our World
  - *Esquivel!* by Susan Wood, from Text Set: Genre Study: Biography (Musicians)
  - *Silent Star* by Bill Wise, from Text Set: Achieving a Dream
- chart paper and markers

Academic Language / Important Vocabulary

- author's note
- illustrator's note
- afterword

Continuum Connection

- Notice and use and understand the purpose of some text resources outside the body (peritext): e.g., dedication, acknowledgments, author's note, illustrator's note, endpapers, foreword, prologue, pronunciation guide, footnote, epilogue, appendix, endnote, references (pp. 72, 74)

Goal

Notice and understand that authors and illustrators often give important information in the author's/illustrator's note.

Rationale

An author's or illustrator's note may reveal the inspiration for writing or illustrating a book or offer important contextual information. An afterword might give further information about the topic. When students read and think about the author's or illustrator's note or the afterword, they gain a deeper understanding of the book and of the process and purpose behind the creation of the book.

Assess Learning

Observe students when they read and talk about books and notice if there is evidence of new learning based on the goal of this minilesson.

- Do students understand the purpose of an author's/illustrator's note and an afterword?
- Do they use academic language, such as *author's note*, *illustrator's note*, and *afterword*?

Minilesson

To help students think about the minilesson principle, use familiar books to engage students in noticing and understanding the purpose of an author's/illustrator's note and an afterword. Here is an example.

- Show the cover of *Cycle of Rice, Cycle of Life* and read the title.

  The author of this book wrote a special page at the end of the book that I'd like to share with you.

- Turn to the author's note and read it aloud.

  What do you notice about the author's note? Why do you think she included it in her book?

- Record students' responses, generalizing them as necessary, on chart paper.
- Show the cover of *Esquivel!* and read the title. Then read the illustrator's note.

  What did you learn from the illustrator's note in this book?

- Record students' responses on the chart.

Have a Try

Invite the students to talk with a partner about the afterword in *Silent Star*.

- Show the cover of *Silent Star* and read the title. Turn to the afterword.

  At the end of this book is a special section called an afterword. Why do you think it has that name?

- Read the afterword aloud.

  Turn and talk to your partner about what you noticed about and learned from the afterword.

- After time for discussion, invite a few pairs to share their thinking. Record their responses on the chart.

  An afterword is similar to an author's note. Often, it is written by someone other than the author.

Author's Note
Illustrator's Note
Afterword

- More information about the topic, the subject, the setting, or the story
- What the author wants you to understand (author's message)
- How you can apply the author's message in your own life
- Why the topic of the book is important
- What inspired the author/illustrator to write/illustrate the book
- How the author/illustrator wrote/illustrated the book

Summarize and Apply

Summarize the learning and remind students to read author's or illustrator's notes and afterwords.

What did you learn today?

When you read today, notice if your book has an author's note, illustrator's note, or afterword. If so, be sure to read it. Be ready to share what you learned from it when we come back together.

Share

Following independent reading time, gather students together in the meeting area to talk about their reading.

Who read an author's note, an illustrator's note, or an afterword today?

What did you learn from it?

Extend the Lesson (Optional)

After assessing students' understanding, you might decide to extend the learning.

- Encourage students to include an author's note, illustrator's note, and/or afterword when they write and illustrate their own books.

RML 3
LA.U13.RML3

Reading Minilesson Principle

Authors include a prologue and an epilogue to tell about something that happened before and after the main story.

Noticing Book and Print Features

You Will Need

- two or three familiar fiction books that have a prologue and/or an epilogue, such as the following:
  - *Tales from the Odyssey, Part One* by Mary Pope Osborne, from *Independent Reading Collection*
  - *Brian's Winter* by Gary Paulsen, from Text Set: Grit and Perseverance
  - *The Lion Who Stole My Arm* by Nicola Davies, from Text Set: Conflict Resolution
- chart paper and markers

Academic Language / Important Vocabulary

- fiction
- author
- prologue
- epilogue

Continuum Connection

- Notice and use and understand the purpose of some text resources outside the body (peritext): e.g., dedication, acknowledgments, author's note, illustrator's note, endpapers, foreword, prologue, pronunciation guide, footnote, epilogue, appendix, endnote, references (pp. 72, 74)

Goal

Notice and understand the purpose of prologues and epilogues.

Rationale

When students read a prologue or an epilogue, they gain a fuller understanding of the characters and plot of a story. A prologue may set the context for the rest of the story. A prologue or an epilogue may also help show how the characters have changed or developed over a long period of time.

Assess Learning

Observe students when they read and talk about fiction books and notice if there is evidence of new learning based on the goal of this minilesson.

- Do students read prologues and epilogues?
- Can they explain the purpose of prologues and epilogues?
- Do they use academic vocabulary, such as *fiction, author, prologue,* and *epilogue*?

Minilesson

To help students think about the minilesson principle, use familiar fiction books to discuss prologues and epilogues. Here is an example.

- Show the cover of *Tales from the Odyssey* and read the title. Then read the prologue.

  Where in a book would you find a prologue?

  What does the prologue in this book tell you?

  What is the purpose of a prologue?

- Record students' responses on chart paper.
- Show the cover of *Brian's Winter* and read the title. Turn to page 131 and read the beginning of the epilogue.

  Where in a book would you find an epilogue?

  What happens in the epilogue of this book?

  What is the purpose of an epilogue?

- Add students' responses to the chart.

Have a Try

Invite the students to talk with a partner about the epilogue in *The Lion Who Stole My Arm*.

- Read the epilogue on pages 79–81 of *The Lion Who Stole My Arm*, but do not display it or identify it as the epilogue.

  Is what I just read a prologue or an epilogue? How do you know? Turn and talk to your partner about what you think.

- After students turn and talk, invite a few pairs to share their thinking.

Authors include a prologue and an epilogue to tell about something that happened before and after the main story.

Prologue Before the story . . .	• Before the beginning of a story • May tell about something that happened before the main story • May introduce the story or give background information about it
Epilogue . . . After the story	• At the end of the book • Tells about something that happened after the main story

Summarize and Apply

Summarize the learning and remind students to read prologues and epilogues.

What did you notice about a prologue and an epilogue today?

- Write the principle at the top of the chart.

  If you read a fiction book today, notice if your book has a prologue or an epilogue. If so, be sure to read it. Be ready to share your thinking about the prologue or epilogue when we come back together.

Share

Following independent reading time, gather students together in the meeting area to talk about their reading.

Who read a prologue or an epilogue today?

How did the prologue or epilogue add to your understanding or enjoyment of the story?

Extend the Lesson (Optional)

After assessing students' understanding, you might decide to extend the learning.

- Explain that *prologue* comes from Greek words that mean "speech before" and *epilogue* comes from Greek words that mean "words attached." Often in nonfiction, the terms *foreword* and *afterword* are used instead.
- **Writing About Reading** Ask students to imagine what happened before or after a story they have read and write their own prologue or epilogue for it.

RML4

LA.U13.RML4

Reading Minilesson Principle

Authors provide resources outside the main text to help you understand more about the story or topic.

Noticing Book and Print Features

You Will Need

- two or three familiar books that contain footnotes, a glossary, an appendix, and/or a pronunciation guide, such as the following:
  - *I and I: Bob Marley* by Tony Medina, from Text Set: Genre Study: Biography (Musicians)
  - *Cycle of Rice, Cycle of Life* by Jan Reynolds, from Text Set: Caring for Our World
- chart paper and markers
- document camera (optional)

Academic Language / Important Vocabulary

- footnotes
- glossary
- appendix
- pronunciation guide
- body

Continuum Connection

- Notice and use and understand the purpose of some other text resources: e.g. glossary, index (pp. 72, 74)

Goal

Notice, use, and understand the purpose of footnotes, glossary, appendix, and pronunciation guide.

Rationale

When students notice and read footnotes and appendixes, they learn more about the topic of the book. When they know how to use a glossary and pronunciation guide, they are better equipped to determine the meaning and pronunciation of unfamiliar words while reading independently.

Assess Learning

Observe students when they read and talk about books and notice if there is evidence of new learning based on the goal of this minilesson.

- Are students able to use and explain the purpose of text resources?
- Do they use academic vocabulary, such as *footnotes*, *glossary*, *appendix*, *pronunciation guide*, and *body*?

Minilesson

To help students think about the minilesson principle, discuss how to use footnotes, a glossary, an appendix, and a pronunciation guide. Here is an example.

- Turn to the section at the back of *I and I: Bob Marley* titled Notes for I and I, Bob Marley. Point to and read several of the subheadings and the paragraph underneath the first subheading.

  What do you notice about this section of the book?

  What is the purpose of this part of the book?

- Record students' responses on chart paper.

  A section like this at the end of a nonfiction book is called an appendix.

- Show the author's note of *Cycle of Rice, Cycle of Life*. Point to and read aloud the sentence in the second paragraph that begins with "America's estimated food waste."

  What do you notice at the end of this sentence? What does this mean?

- Point out the first footnote and read it aloud.

  This small text at the bottom of the page is called a footnote. Why do you think it's called that?

  What is the purpose of this footnote?

- Record students' responses on chart paper.

Sometimes authors use footnotes to tell where they found a piece of information, to give more information about something in the body of the text, or to define difficult words.

Have a Try

Invite the students to talk with a partner about a glossary and pronunciation guide.

- Turn to the glossary and pronunciation guide in *Cycle of Rice, Cycle of Life*. Read the heading, introduction, and the first few entries.

  Turn and talk to your partner about the purpose of a glossary and a pronunciation guide.

- Invite a few students to share their thinking. Record their responses on the chart.

Authors provide resources outside the main text to help you understand more about the story or topic.

Appendix Facts about . . .	• A section at the end of a nonfiction book • Gives additional information
Footnotes[1] [1] This is what a footnote looks like.	• May tell where the author found a piece of information • May give additional information or define difficult words • Are numbered
Glossary Bali—an island in Indonesia	• Gives the definition of important or difficult words in the book • May contain words from another language
Pronunciation Guide (BAH-lee)	• Tells how to pronounce challenging words • May contain words from another language

Summarize and Apply

Summarize the learning and remind students to use text resources.

Why do authors include the kinds of resources we talked about today?

- Write the principle at the top of the chart.

  When you read today, notice if your book has an appendix, footnotes, glossary, or pronunciation guide. If so, think about how it helps you. Bring your book to share when we come back together.

Share

Following independent reading time, gather students together in the meeting area to talk about text resources.

Who read a book that has an appendix, footnotes, glossary, or pronunciation guide?

What did you learn from it?

Extend the Lesson (Optional)

After assessing students' understanding, you might decide to extend the learning.

- If students notice other resources (e.g., tables of contents, indexes, sidebars), teach one or more minilessons in Umbrella 20: Using Text Features to Gain Information.
- **Writing About Reading** Have students create a glossary and/or pronunciation guide for a book that does not already have one.

RML 5

LA.U13.RML5

Reading Minilesson Principle

The design (book jacket, cover, title page, endpapers) often adds to or enhances the meaning or appeal of the book.

Noticing Book and Print Features

You Will Need

- three or four familiar books that have a book jacket, cover, title page, and/or endpapers that add to or enhance the meaning of the book, such as the following:
  - *Strange Mr. Satie* by M. T. Anderson, *I and I* by Tony Medina, and *The Legendary Miss Lena Horne* by Carole Boston Weatherford, from Text Set: Genre Study: Biography (Musicians)
  - *Silent Star* by Bill Wise, from Text Set: Achieving a Dream
- chart paper and markers

Academic Language / Important Vocabulary

- design
- book jacket
- cover
- title page
- endpapers

Continuum Connection

- Notice and understand other features of the peritext that have symbolic or cultural significance or add to aesthetic enjoyment (p. 72)
- Appreciate artistry in text design: e.g., book jacket, cover, end pages, title page, margins, chapter headings, illumination (p. 72)
- Notice and understand other features of the peritext that have symbolic value, add to aesthetic enjoyment, or add meaning (p. 75)
- Appreciate artistry in text design: e.g., book jacket, cover, end pages, title page (peritext) (p. 75)

Goal

Understand and appreciate that the design of the peritext often adds to the meaning of the text and sometimes has cultural or symbolic significance.

Rationale

The book jacket, cover, title pages, and endpapers are part of the art of the book and add to or enhance its meaning. When you encourage students to notice the design of these features and to think about how they relate to the meaning of the book, they develop an appreciation for the thought and care that went into creating the book.

Assess Learning

Observe students when they read and talk about books and notice if there is evidence of new learning based on the goal of this minilesson.

- Can students explain how the design of the book jacket, cover, title pages, and/or endpapers adds to or enhances the meaning of a book?
- Do they use academic language, such as *design*, *book jacket*, *cover*, *title page*, and *endpapers*?

Minilesson

To help students think about the minilesson principle, use familiar books to talk about the design of the peritext. Here is an example.

- Show the cover of *Strange Mr. Satie* and read the title and subtitle.

  What does the cover illustration help you understand about Mr. Satie?

- Record students' responses on chart paper. Then show the front cover, back cover, and finally the title page of *I and I*.

  What do you notice about the colors on the front cover, back cover, and title page of this book?

- Record responses on the chart.

  Why do you think the colors red, yellow, and green appear in all three places? Does anyone know why these colors are important?

- Explain that they are the colors of the Rastafarianism movement to which Bob Marley belonged (see the notes under "I Am a Rasta Man" in the appendix).
- Display the front and back flaps of *The Legendary Miss Lena Horne*.

  What do you notice about the design of the book jacket?

  How does this design relate to the meaning of the book?

- Record responses.

Have a Try

Invite the students to talk with a partner about the endpapers in *Silent Star*.

- Turn to the endpaper that is opposite the afterword in *Silent Star*.

  How does the design of the endpaper relate to the meaning of the book? Turn and talk to your partner about what you think.

- After time for discussion, invite a few students to share their thinking. Record their responses on the chart.

The design (book jacket, cover, title page, endpapers) often adds to or enhances the meaning or appeal of the book.			
Title	Resource	The Design	Why Important
 Strange Mr. Satie	Front cover	• Shows random objects flying out of Erik Satie's piano	• Erik Satie was a "composer of the absurd".
	Both covers and title page	• The colors red, yellow, and green are repeated.	• the colors of the Rastafarianism movement, which Bob Marley belonged to
 The Legendary Miss Lena Horne	Book jacket	• Illustrations of records	• Lena Horne was a singer.
 Silent Star	Endpapers	• Quote about William Hoy from a newspaper and a photo of a baseball that he signed	• William Hoy was an important baseball player.

Summarize and Apply

Summarize the learning and remind students to notice the design of the peritext when they read.

Today you looked at the cover, the title page, the endpapers, and the book jacket of a few books. What did you notice about their designs?

- Write the principle at the top of the chart.

  When you read today, take a few minutes to look at the design of parts of your book outside the main text, such as the cover, title page, endpapers, and book jacket. Think about how their design adds to the meaning of your book. Bring your book to share when we come back together.

Share

Following independent reading time, gather students together in the meeting area to share what they noticed about the design of the peritext in their book.

Turn and talk to your partner about how the design of the book jacket, cover, title pages, or endpapers adds to or relates to the meaning of your book.

Extend the Lesson (Optional)

After assessing students' understanding, you might decide to extend the learning.

- You may want to teach a lesson on asking students to evaluate the layout and design of a book.

Assessment

After you have taught the minilessons in this umbrella, observe students as they talk and write about their reading across instructional contexts: interactive read-aloud, independent reading, guided reading, shared reading, and book club. Use *The Literacy Continuum* (Fountas and Pinnell 2017) to observe students' reading and writing behaviors.

- What evidence do you have of new understandings related to book and print features?
  - Do students read and understand the purpose of peritext resources?
  - Do they read prologues and epilogues?
  - Do they use peritext resources, such as footnotes and glossaries?
  - Do they notice the design of the book jacket, the cover, the title page, and/or the endpapers? Can they explain how they add to the meaning of the book?
  - Do they use academic language related to text resources, such as *dedication, acknowledgments, author's note,* and *glossary*?
- In what other ways, beyond the scope of this umbrella, are students talking about books?
  - Are students noticing and using text features, such as headings, sidebars, and indexes?
  - Are they noticing the different ways nonfiction books are organized?

Use your observations to determine the next umbrella you will teach. You may also consult Minilessons Across the Year (pp. 61–64) for guidance.

Link to Writing

After teaching the minilessons in this umbrella, help students link the new learning to their own writing:

- Encourage students to create text resources when they write their own books.

Reader's Notebook

When this umbrella is complete, provide a copy of the minilesson principles (see resources.fountasandpinnell.com) for students to glue in the reader's notebook (in the Minilessons section if using *Reader's Notebook: Advanced* [Fountas and Pinnell 2011]), so they can refer to the information as needed.

Studying Expository Nonfiction

Umbrella 14

Minilessons in This Umbrella

RML1	Expository nonfiction books are alike in many ways.
RML2	The definition of expository nonfiction is what is always true about it.
RML3	Works of expository nonfiction have at least one main topic with information to support it.
RML4	Authors include different tools to help you find and gain information.
RML5	Authors include different types of graphics and illustrations to provide information in a clear way.
RML6	Evaluate the accuracy and quality of expository texts.

Genre Study: Expository Nonfiction

Giant Squid by Mary Cerullo and Clyde F. E. Roper

Before Teaching Umbrella 14 Minilessons

Genre study supports students in having expectations for the characteristics of a text they read. It helps students develop an understanding of the distinguishing characteristics of the genre and gives students the tools they need to navigate a variety of texts. There are six broad steps in a genre study, which are described on pages 39–41.

The first step in any genre study is to collect a set of mentor texts. For this genre study, collect a variety of high-quality expository nonfiction books. Before guiding students to look for genre characteristics, be sure that they first become immersed in the books, thinking and talking about the information in each text. Use the following books from the *Fountas & Pinnell Classroom™ Interactive Read-Aloud Collection* text sets or choose expository nonfiction books with which your students are familiar.

Genre Study: Expository Nonfiction

Birds: Nature's Magnificent Flying Machines by Caroline Arnold

Giant Squid: Searching for a Sea Monster by Mary Cerullo and Clyde F. E. Roper

The Cod's Tale by Mark Kurlansky

The Story of Salt by Mark Kurlansky

As you read aloud and enjoy these texts together, help students

- notice similarities between them,
- identify the topic of each text and supporting information,
- discuss what they learned from each text, and
- notice and discuss graphics and text features.

RML 1

LA.U14.RML1

Reading Minilesson Principle

Expository nonfiction books are alike in many ways.

Studying Expository Nonfiction

You Will Need

- a collection of familiar expository nonfiction books, such as those in Text Set: Genre Study: Expository Nonfiction
- chart paper prepared with the headings *Expository Nonfiction* and *Noticings* and sections for *Always* and *Often*
- markers

Academic Language / Important Vocabulary

- expository nonfiction
- author
- information
- topic
- categories
- subcategories
- body
- organized

Continuum Connection

- Notice and understand the characteristics of some specific nonfiction genres: e.g., expository, narrative, procedural and persuasive texts, biography, autobiography, memoir, hybrid text (p. 73)

Goal

Notice and understand the characteristics of expository nonfiction as a genre.

Rationale

When students study expository nonfiction books through the inquiry process, they gain a deeper understanding of individual books and of the genre as a whole. When they develop an understanding of the genre they will know what to expect when they encounter books of that genre (see pages 39–41 for more about genre study).

Assess Learning

Observe students when they read and talk about expository nonfiction books and notice if there is evidence of new learning based on the goal of this minilesson.

- Are students able to identify and discuss the characteristics of expository nonfiction books?
- Can they determine whether a book is expository nonfiction and explain how they know?
- Do they use academic vocabulary, such as *expository nonfiction, author, information, topic, categories, subcategories, body,* and *organized*?

Minilesson

To help students think about the minilesson principle, use familiar expository nonfiction books to help students notice the characteristics of the genre. Here is an example.

- Divide students into small groups and give each group several expository nonfiction books.

  Take a few minutes to look through the books I gave you. Then turn and talk with your group about the ways all the books are alike.

  What did you notice about how your expository nonfiction books are alike?

- As students share their thinking, prompt them, as necessary, with questions such as the following:
  - *What are expository nonfiction books about?*
  - *How is the information organized?*
  - *What tools help you find specific information?*
  - *Besides the main body of text, what else provides information?*
  - *Why do authors write expository nonfiction books?*
- Help students decide whether each noticing is *always* or *often* a characteristic of expository nonfiction by asking other groups if their books also have the same characteristic.
- Record students' noticings on chart paper.

Have a Try

Invite the students to talk with a partner about the characteristics of expository nonfiction.

> Think about the last nonfiction book that you read or heard read aloud. Was it an expository nonfiction book? How do you know? Turn and talk to your partner about what you think.

- After students turn and talk, invite a few students to share their thinking.

Summarize and Apply

Summarize the learning and remind students to think about the characteristics of expository nonfiction when they read.

> What did you notice about the expository nonfiction books you looked at today?

- Review the noticings chart.

> When you read today, think about whether the book you are reading is expository nonfiction. If it is, bring it to share when we come back together.

Expository Nonfiction

Noticings:

Always	Often
• The author provides facts about a topic. • The information is organized into a clear structure. • The information is not told like a story. • The book has a major topic and supporting information. • The book has a larger message.	• The book has information organized by categories or subcategories. • There are tools to help you find or gain information (table of contents, headings, index, glossary, etc.). • The book includes illustrations or other graphics.

Share

Following independent reading time, gather students together in the meeting area to talk about the books they read.

> Who read an expository nonfiction book today?
>
> How could you tell that your book is expository nonfiction?

Extend the Lesson (Optional)

After assessing students' understanding, you might decide to extend the learning.

- Continue to add to the noticings chart as students read more expository nonfiction books and notice more about the genre.
- Discuss the differences between expository nonfiction and other types of nonfiction (e.g., narrative, persuasive).
- Have students set up a display of student-recommended expository nonfiction books in the classroom library.

RML 2

LA.U14.RML2

Reading Minilesson Principle

The definition of expository nonfiction is what is always true about it.

Studying Expository Nonfiction

You Will Need

- a familiar expository nonfiction book, such as *The Cod's Tale* by Mark Kurlansky, from Text Set: Genre Study: Expository Nonfiction
- the noticings chart from RML1
- chart paper and markers

Academic Language / Important Vocabulary

- expository nonfiction
- definition
- fact
- information
- topic
- organized

Continuum Connection

- Notice and understand the characteristics of some specific nonfiction genres: e.g., expository, narrative, procedural and persuasive texts, biography, autobiography, memoir, hybrid text (p. 73)

Goal

Construct a working definition for expository nonfiction.

Rationale

Writing a definition is part of the genre study process. When you work with students to construct the definition of a genre, you help them analyze and then summarize the most important characteristics. Over time, the students can revise the definition as they read more examples of that genre.

Assess Learning

Observe students when they read and talk about expository nonfiction books and notice if there is evidence of new learning based on the goal of this minilesson.

- Do students discuss what they notice about expository nonfiction books?
- Can they explain whether a particular book fits the definition of expository nonfiction?
- Do they use academic vocabulary, such as *expository nonfiction, definition, fact, information, topic,* and *organized*?

Minilesson

Guide students in writing a definition of expository nonfiction. Here is an example of how to do so.

- Display and review the noticings chart created during the previous minilesson.

  You thought about how expository nonfiction books are alike. Now we are going to use what you noticed to write a definition of expository nonfiction.

- Write the words *Expository nonfiction books* on chart paper.

  Turn and talk to your partner about how you would finish this sentence to write a definition of expository nonfiction. Use our noticings chart to help you.

  How would you finish this sentence?

- Combine students' responses to construct a whole-class definition. Write the rest of the definition on the chart paper.

Have a Try

Invite the students to talk with a partner about a familiar expository nonfiction book.

- Show the cover of *The Cod's Tale*. Briefly review the book to remind students of its contents.

  Turn and talk to your partner about whether this book fits our definition of expository nonfiction. If so, how does it fit? If not, why not?

- After students turn and talk, invite a few pairs to share their thinking.

Expository Nonfiction

Expository nonfiction books provide facts and supporting information about a topic. They are organized using a clear structure. They often include graphics and text features that help you find or gain information.

Summarize and Apply

Summarize the learning and remind students to think about the definition of expository nonfiction.

Today we wrote a definition of expository nonfiction books. The definition tells what is always true about the genre of expository nonfiction.

When you read today, think about whether the book you are reading fits our definition. Be ready to share your thinking when we come back together.

Share

Following independent reading time, gather students together in the meeting area to talk about the books they read.

Turn and talk to your partner about whether the book you read today fits our definition of expository nonfiction. Be sure to give reasons for your thinking.

Extend the Lesson (Optional)

After assessing students' understanding, you might decide to extend the learning.

- During interactive read-aloud, help students evaluate books against the definition of expository nonfiction to determine whether each book is expository nonfiction.

RML 3
LA.U14.RML3

Reading Minilesson Principle

Works of expository nonfiction have at least one main topic with information to support it.

Studying Expository Nonfiction

You Will Need

- two familiar expository nonfiction books, such as the following from Text Set: Genre Study: Expository Nonfiction:
  - *Birds* by Caroline Arnold
  - *The Story of Salt* by Mark Kurlansky
- chart paper and markers

Academic Language / Important Vocabulary

- expository nonfiction
- author
- information
- topic
- support

Continuum Connection

- Recognize that informational texts may present a larger topic with many subtopics (p. 74)
- Notice the topic of a text and that subtopics are related to the main topic (p. 74)

Goal

Understand that works of expository nonfiction have at least one main topic with information to support it.

Rationale

When students understand that all expository nonfiction books have a main topic and information that supports it, they understand that a common thread unites all the information in an expository nonfiction book.

Assess Learning

Observe students when they read and talk about expository nonfiction books and notice if there is evidence of new learning based on the goal of this minilesson.

- Can students identify the main topic in an expository nonfiction book and information that supports it?
- Can they explain how a particular piece of information in an expository nonfiction book is related to the main topic?
- Do they use academic vocabulary, such as *expository nonfiction, author, information, topic,* and *support*?

Minilesson

To help students think about the minilesson principle, help them notice the organization of information in expository nonfiction books. Here is an example.

- Show the cover of *Birds* and read the title.

  What is the topic of this expository nonfiction book?

- Write *Birds' ability to fly* in a circle in the center of a sheet of chart paper.
- Turn to page 3. Read the heading and the second paragraph.

  What is the information on this page about?

  How does this information relate to the main topic of the book?

- Add a spoke from the center circle and add the supporting information in its own circle.
- Turn to page 8. Read the heading and the first paragraph.

  What does the information on this page have to do with the main topic of the book?

- Add responses to the chart. Then continue in a similar manner with page 13.
- Complete the web diagram illustrating how all the information in the book relates to the main topic.

Have a Try

Invite the students to talk with a partner about *The Story of Salt*.

- Read page 18 of *The Story of Salt*.

  Turn and talk to your partner about the main topic and how the information on this page relates to the main topic.

- After students turn and talk, invite a few pairs to share their thinking.

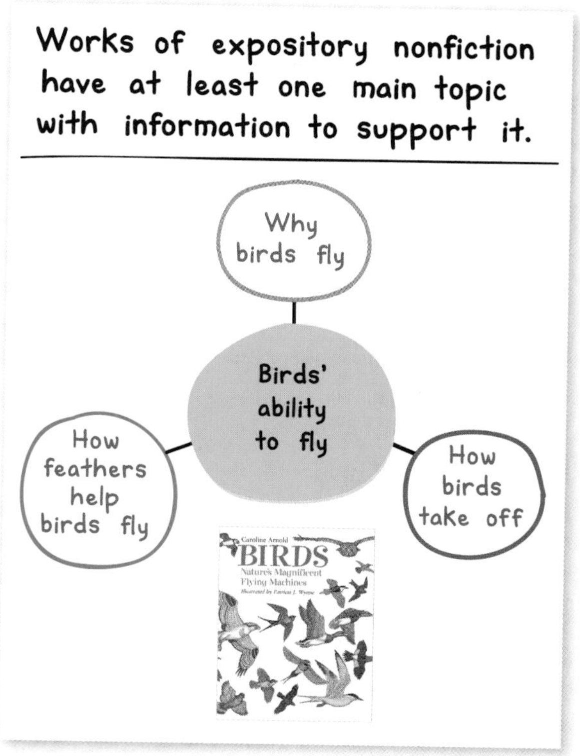

Works of expository nonfiction have at least one main topic with information to support it.

Birds' ability to fly

- Why birds fly
- How feathers help birds fly
- How birds take off

BIRDS Nature's Magnificent Flying Machines

Summarize and Apply

Summarize the learning and remind students to notice how all the information in an expository nonfiction book supports the main topic.

What did you notice about the information in expository nonfiction books?

- Write the principle at the top of the chart.

  If you read an expository nonfiction book today, think about the main topic of the book and notice how the information in the book relates to this topic. Bring your book to share when we come back together.

Share

Following independent reading time, gather students together in the meeting area to talk about their reading.

Who read an expository nonfiction book today?

What is the main topic of your book?

Can you give some examples of information you learned from your book? How does that information relate to the main topic?

Extend the Lesson (Optional)

After assessing students' understanding, you might decide to extend the learning.

- Teach Umbrella 17: Noticing How Nonfiction Authors Choose to Organize Information to help students explore in more detail the different ways information is organized in nonfiction books.
- **Writing About Reading** Have students make a web diagram to show how the information in an expository nonfiction book is related to the main topic (see WAR.U4.RML3).

RML 4

LA.U14.RML4

Reading Minilesson Principle

Authors include different tools to help you find and gain information.

Studying Expository Nonfiction

You Will Need

- a collection of familiar expository nonfiction books containing a variety of text features and organizational tools (e.g., index, table of contents, headings and subheadings, sidebars), such as those in Text Set: Genre Study: Expository Nonfiction
- chart paper and markers

Academic Language / Important Vocabulary

- expository nonfiction
- author
- information
- index
- table of contents
- heading
- sidebar
- glossary

Continuum Connection

- Notice and use and understand the purpose of some organizational tools: e.g., title, table of contents, chapter title, heading, subheading (p. 75)

Goal

Understand that authors of expository nonfiction include different tools to locate information.

Rationale

When students notice and understand how to use the various text features and organizational tools provided in expository nonfiction books, they can find and gain information more easily. They also can see the organization of the book.

Assess Learning

Observe students when they read and talk about expository nonfiction books and notice if there is evidence of new learning based on the goal of this minilesson.

- Can students identify various text features and organizational tools (e.g., index, table of contents, headings and subheadings, sidebars)?
- Do they use these tools to find and gain information?
- Do they use academic vocabulary, such as *expository nonfiction, author, information, index, table of contents, heading,* and names of text features (e.g., *sidebar, glossary*)?

Minilesson

To help students think about the minilesson principle, engage them in a discussion about text features and organizational tools. Here is an example.

- Divide students into small groups and give each group at least one expository nonfiction book.

  Take a few minutes to look through the book I gave you. See what you notice about the tools the author provides to help you find and gain information.

  What did you notice about how the author of your book helps you find or gain information? What tools does he use? Are there headings, an index, or any other tools?

- Ask students to show an example of each tool they found. Make a list of the tools they found on chart paper.

  How are these tools helpful when you read expository nonfiction?

- Discuss how some tools help you find information in the book and other tools offer more information.

Have a Try

Invite the students to talk with their groups about a specific organizational tool or text feature.

> With your group, choose one of the tools you found in your book and talk about how to use it to help you find or gain information.

- After time for discussion, invite groups to share their thinking.

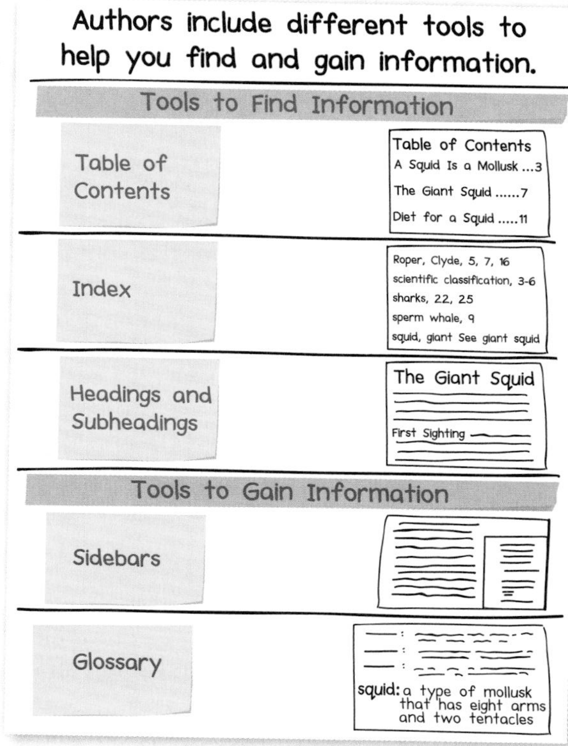

Summarize and Apply

Summarize the learning and remind students to notice and use text features and organizational tools.

> What did you notice about how authors of expository nonfiction books help you find or gain information?

- Write the principle at the top of the chart.

> If you read an expository nonfiction book today, notice the kinds of tools the author includes to help you find or gain information. Read or use these tools, and think about how they help you learn more about the topic of your book.

Share

Following independent reading time, gather students together in the meeting area to talk about their reading.

> Who read an expository nonfiction book today?
>
> What tools does the author of your book include to help you find information? How did the tools help you find information?

- Add additional tools to the list.

Extend the Lesson (Optional)

After assessing students' understanding, you might decide to extend the learning.

- Teach the minilessons in Umbrella 20: Using Text Features to Gain Information to help students explore each type of text feature in more detail.

RML 5
LA.U14.RML5

Reading Minilesson Principle

Authors include different types of graphics and illustrations to provide information in a clear way.

Studying Expository Nonfiction

You Will Need

- a collection of familiar expository nonfiction books containing a variety of types of illustrations and graphics (diagrams, maps, infographics, etc.), such as those in Text Set: Genre Study: Expository Nonfiction
- chart paper and markers

Academic Language / Important Vocabulary

- expository nonfiction
- author
- information
- illustration
- graphic

Continuum Connection

- Understand that graphics provide important information (p. 75)

Goal

Understand that authors include different types of graphics and illustrations to provide information in a clear way.

Rationale

When students notice and think about illustrations and graphics in expository nonfiction books, they acquire information and better understand the topic of the book. They also understand that there are many different ways to communicate information and that authors must make decisions about how best to do so.

Assess Learning

Observe students when they read and talk about expository nonfiction books and notice if there is evidence of new learning based on the goal of this minilesson.

- Do students notice and think about illustrations and graphics in expository nonfiction books?
- Can they explain what they learned from an illustration or graphic?
- Can they identify different types of graphics (e.g., photographs, maps, diagrams)?
- Do they use academic vocabulary, such as *expository nonfiction, author, information, illustration,* and *graphic*?

Minilesson

To help students think about the minilesson principle, engage them in a discussion about illustrations and graphics in expository nonfiction books. Here is an example.

- Divide students into small groups, and give each group at least one expository nonfiction book.

  Look through the expository nonfiction book I've given you and talk about the images. What kinds of pictures are there in your book? Are there illustrations, photographs, or other kinds of graphics?

- After students have had time to look through their books, invite them to share the graphics they found. Ask them to show an example of each kind of graphic they found. List their responses on chart paper.

  Would the information be as clear if the author told you in words instead of using a graphic or illustration?

Have a Try

Invite the students to talk with their groups about a specific illustration or graphic.

> With your group, choose one illustration or graphic in your book and talk about what information it provides. What did you learn from the image? Why did the author include this illustration or graphic in the book?

- After time for discussion, invite groups to share their thinking.

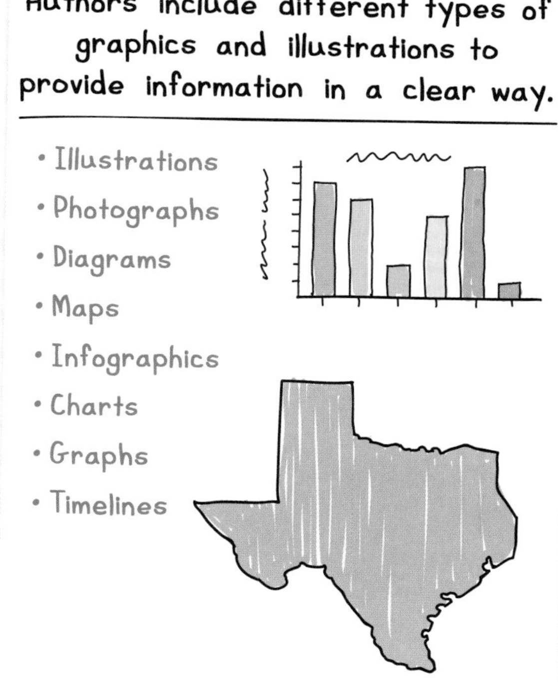
Authors include different types of graphics and illustrations to provide information in a clear way.
• Illustrations
• Photographs
• Diagrams
• Maps
• Infographics
• Charts
• Graphs
• Timelines

Summarize and Apply

Summarize the learning and remind students to notice illustrations and graphics when they read expository nonfiction books.

> Why do authors of expository nonfiction include illustrations and graphics in their books?

- Write the principle at the top of the chart.

> If you read an expository nonfiction book today, remember to look at the illustrations and graphics. Notice the kinds of images that the author included in your book and think about what you are learning from them.

Share

Following independent reading time, gather students together in the meeting area to talk about their reading.

> Who read an expository nonfiction book today?
>
> What kinds of illustrations or graphics did you see in your book? What did you learn from them?

Extend the Lesson (Optional)

After assessing students' understanding, you might decide to extend the learning.

- Teach the minilessons in Umbrella 19: Learning Information from Illustrations and Graphics to help students explore the use of illustrations and graphics in nonfiction in more detail.
- **Writing About Reading** Have students write in a reader's notebook about the information provided in a specific illustration or graphic.

RML 6
LA.U14.RML6

Reading Minilesson Principle

Evaluate the accuracy and quality of expository texts.

Studying Expository Nonfiction

You Will Need

- two familiar expository nonfiction books, such as the following from Text Set: Genre Study: Expository Nonfiction:
    - *Giant Squid* by Mary Cerullo and Clyde F. E. Roper
    - *The Cod's Tale* by Mark Kurlansky
- another reliable source of information (book or website) about the topic of the first book you are using
- chart paper and markers

Academic Language / Important Vocabulary

- expository nonfiction
- information
- accuracy
- quality

Continuum Connection

- Critically examine the quality or accuracy of the text, citing evidence for opinions (p. 74)
- Notice and evaluate the accuracy of the information presented in the text and across texts (p. 75)

Goal

Evaluate the accuracy and quality of expository texts.

Rationale

Students who learn to evaluate the quality and accuracy of expository texts read with a critical eye. They understand that although expository nonfiction books are based in fact, they are not necessarily perfect sources of information. Students then understand the importance of reading multiple sources of information to learn about a topic.

Assess Learning

Observe students when they read and talk about expository nonfiction books and notice if there is evidence of new learning based on the goal of this minilesson.

- Do students understand the importance of evaluating the accuracy and quality of expository nonfiction books?
- Do they use academic vocabulary, such as *expository nonfiction, information, accuracy,* and *quality*?

Minilesson

To help students think about the minilesson principle, model evaluating the quality and accuracy of a familiar expository nonfiction book. Here is an example.

- Show the cover of *Giant Squid*. Read aloud the first sentence on page 16.

    I wonder if it's true that there are more than 500 species of squid.

- Display another reliable source of information about squids. Explain how you know it is a good source of information.

    This website says that there are more than 300 species of squid. I'm not sure if the information in the book or on the website is correct. I need to do more research to know for sure.

    What did you notice about my thinking?

    I evaluated the accuracy of some of the information in this book. When you evaluate the accuracy of information, you think about whether it's correct. You can use other books or websites to check.

    I still think this is a high-quality book. It contains a lot of interesting information about squids. It also has a lot of illustrations and graphics that helped me learn more about squids.

    That is my opinion about the quality of this book. Quality is how well done something is. What did you notice about how I talked about the quality of this book?

Have a Try

Invite the students to talk with a partner about another book.

- Show the cover of *The Cod's Tale* and read the title.

  Turn and talk to your partner about how you could evaluate the accuracy of the information in this book.

- Invite a few students to share. Record their suggestions on chart paper.

  Turn and talk with your partner about questions you can ask to determine the quality of a book.

- After time for discussion, list suggestions on the chart.

Evaluate the accuracy and quality of expository texts.

Accuracy	Quality
• Check the credentials of the author.	• What is my opinion about the author's writing style?
• Check the research the author has done on the topic.	• Is the book interesting and enjoyable?
• Read other books or websites about the topic.	• Does the book make me want to learn more about the topic?
• Compare the information in the book to the information in other sources.	• Does the book have high-quality photographs, illustrations, or other graphics?

Summarize and Apply

Summarize the learning and remind students to evaluate the accuracy and quality of expository nonfiction books.

How should you evaluate the nonfiction books you read?

- Write the principle at the top of the chart.

  If you read an expository nonfiction book today, remember to evaluate the quality and accuracy of the book. You can look for other sources if you want to verify that the information in your book is accurate. Be ready to share your opinion about the quality and accuracy of your book when we come back together.

Share

Following independent reading time, gather students together in the meeting area to talk about their reading.

Who read an expository nonfiction book today?

What is your opinion about the quality and accuracy of the book you read?

Extend the Lesson (Optional)

After assessing students' understanding, you might decide to extend the learning.

- Discuss how to determine if a website is a reliable source of information. Explain that web addresses that end in .edu or .gov are usually good resources (see SAS.U7.RML4).
- **Writing About Reading** Teach students how to write book reviews in which they evaluate the quality and accuracy of expository nonfiction books they've read.

Assessment

After you have taught the minilessons in this umbrella, observe students as they talk and write about their reading across instructional contexts: interactive read-aloud, independent reading, guided reading, shared reading, and book club. Use *The Literacy Continuum* (Fountas and Pinnell 2017) to observe students' reading and writing behaviors.

- What evidence do you have of new understandings related to expository nonfiction?
  - Are students able to identify and describe expository nonfiction books?
  - Do they understand that an expository nonfiction book is about at least one topic and has information to support the topic?
  - Do they use text features and organizational tools and learn from graphics and illustrations?
  - Can they evaluate the accuracy and quality of expository nonfiction books?
  - Do they use vocabulary such as *expository nonfiction, information, topic, organized,* and *accuracy*?
- In what other ways, beyond the scope of this umbrella, are students talking about nonfiction books?
  - Are they noticing different ways nonfiction books are organized?

Use your observations to determine the next umbrella you will teach. You may also consult Minilessons Across the Year (pp. 61–64) for guidance.

Read and Revise

After completing the steps in the genre study process, help students read and revise their definition of the genre based on their new understandings.

- **Before:** Expository nonfiction books provide facts and supporting information about a topic. They are organized using a clear structure. They often include graphics and text features that help you find or gain information.
- **After:** Expository nonfiction books organize information about a main topic into a non-storylike structure. They often include different kinds of graphics and text features to help you learn more about the topic.

Reader's Notebook

When this umbrella is complete, provide a copy of the minilesson principles (see resources.fountasandpinnell.com) for students to glue in the reader's notebook (in the Minilessons section if using *Reader's Notebook: Advanced* [Fountas and Pinnell 2011]), so they can refer to the information as needed.

Minilessons in This Umbrella

RML1	Authors write to persuade you to believe or do something.
RML2	Authors use evidence to support an argument.
RML3	Notice the difference between fact and opinion.
RML4	Notice the techniques authors use to persuade you.
RML5	Consider an author's qualifications and sources when you read a persuasive text.

Caring for Our World

Before Teaching Umbrella 15 Minilessons

Students should be familiar with recognizing an author's opinion or message (see LA.U8.RML1) before you begin this umbrella. Read and discuss high-quality, engaging nonfiction books that present a variety of topics and viewpoints. Explore and discuss the notes and resources found at the end of nonfiction books. Focus on persuasive texts, most of which are nonfiction. Consider collecting and reading shorter persuasive texts, such as news articles and essays. Use the following books from the *Fountas & Pinnell Classroom™ Interactive Read-Aloud Collection* or choose books from your classroom library.

Caring for Our World

One Well: The Story of Water on Earth by Rochelle Strauss

Cycle of Rice, Cycle of Life: A Story of Sustainable Farming by Jan Reynolds

Can We Save the Tiger? by Martin Jenkins

As you read aloud and enjoy these texts together, help students

- notice what the author is persuading them to believe or do, and how,
- discuss evaluating evidence and the difference between fact and opinion, and
- understand the author's qualifications to write on the topic.

RML1

LA.U15.RML1

Reading Minilesson Principle

Authors write to persuade you to believe or do something.

Exploring Persuasive Texts

You Will Need

- a collection of familiar persuasive texts, such as the following from Text Set: Caring for Our World:
  - *One Well* by Rochelle Strauss
  - *Can We Save the Tiger?* by Martin Jenkins
  - *Cycle of Rice, Cycle of Life* by Jan Reynolds
- chart paper

Academic Language / Important Vocabulary

- persuade

Continuum Connection

- Notice and understand the characteristics of some specific nonfiction genres: e.g., expository, narrative, procedural and persuasive texts, biography, autobiography, memoir, hybrid text (p. 73)
- Infer a writer's purpose in a nonfiction text (p. 74)

Goal

Understand that sometimes authors write books or articles to persuade you to believe or do something.

Rationale

When students learn to notice an author's intent in a persuasive text (book or article), they can draw conclusions about the author's purpose and consider their own new beliefs or actions. Students should already have an understanding of author's purpose.

Assess Learning

Observe students when they read and discuss persuasive texts. Notice if there is evidence of new learning based on the goal of this minilesson.

- Can students identify persuasive texts?
- Are they able to identify what an author is trying to persuade readers to believe or do?
- Do they understand and use the term *persuade*?

Minilesson

To help students think about the minilesson principle, use familiar persuasive texts to engage them in noticing how authors persuade the reader. Here is an example.

- Show and read page 23 of *One Well*.

  What do you think the author wants you to believe about water?

- Now show and read page 26.

  What does the author want you to believe or do? How does the author convey that idea?

- Record responses on chart paper.

  The author gives you information about how everything on Earth depends upon water. There is a limited amount of water on Earth, though, which the author explains so that you will understand the problem. Then the author gives you some actions that people can take to conserve water and do something about the problem.

- Repeat this process with pages 50–51 of *Can We Save the Tiger?*

Have a Try

Invite the students to talk with a partner about what the author is trying to persuade them to believe or do in *Cycle of Rice, Cycle of Life*.

- Review in general the information about sustainable farming in the foreword and the author's note.

    Turn and talk to your partner. What does the author want you to believe about farming? What does the author want you to do?

- Invite a few students to share with the class. Record responses on the chart.

Summarize and Apply

Summarize the learning and remind students to think about the author's message in a persuasive text.

> Look at the chart. Why do authors write books like the ones we looked at today?

- Review the chart and write the principle at the top.

    Choose a nonfiction book to read today. Notice whether or not it is a persuasive text. If it is, be ready to share what you think the author is persuading you to believe or do when we come back together.

Authors write to persuade you to believe or do something.

Book	What the Author Wants You to Believe or Do
One Well	Water is important to every living thing on Earth, but it is a limited resource, so people should conserve water.
Can We Save the Tiger?	Tigers are an endangered species because of changes that affect their habitat, but we should not give up on trying to save them if we want a world with a diversity of animals.
	Sustainable farming, the way the people of Bali grow rice, takes care of people and the planet. It is a good way to farm.

Share

Following independent reading time, gather students together in the meeting area to talk about their reading.

> Who read a persuasive book today? What did the author try to persuade you to believe or do?

Extend the Lesson (Optional)

After assessing students' understanding, you might decide to extend the learning.

- Introduce your students to Genre Thinkmarks for persuasive texts (visit resources.fountasandpinnell.com to download this resource). A Genre Thinkmark is a tool that guides readers to note certain elements of a genre. Once students can identify persuasive texts, they can use this resource to note points the author is arguing as well as supporting details.
- **Writing About Reading** After they have read a persuasive text, have students write in a reader's notebook about what the author was persuading them to believe or do.

RML2

LA.U15.RML2

Exploring Persuasive Texts

You Will Need

- a collection of familiar persuasive texts, such as the following from Text Set: Caring for Our World:
  - *One Well* by Rochelle Strauss
  - *Cycle of Rice, Cycle of Life* by Jan Reynolds
- chart from RML1 (optional)
- chart paper and markers
- sticky notes
- basket of persuasive texts

Academic Language / Important Vocabulary

- persuade
- argument
- evidence

Continuum Connection

- Evaluate the way the writer of an argument supports statements with evidence (p. 75)

Reading Minilesson Principle

Authors use evidence to support an argument.

Goal

Identify the evidence authors use to support an argument.

Rationale

To persuade readers, an author presents an argument and supports it with evidence. When you teach students to read texts with a critical eye, they notice an author's argument and the supporting evidence and can begin to evaluate it and form their own opinions.

Assess Learning

Observe students when they read and discuss persuasive texts. Notice if there is evidence of new learning based on the goal of this minilesson.

- Can students identify what an author wants them to believe or do?
- Are they able to find the evidence for the author's argument?
- Do they understand and use the terms *persuade, argument,* and *evidence*?

Minilesson

To help students think about the minilesson principle, use familiar persuasive texts to engage them in noticing how authors use evidence to support an argument. Here is an example.

- Show *One Well* or refer to the chart from the previous minilesson.

  What is the author's argument in *One Well*? What does the author want you to think about?

- Record responses in the center circle of a web on chart paper.

  The author's main argument is that water must be conserved. Let's look back through the book. What evidence do you notice to support the argument that it is important to save water?

- Review a few key pages with the students. Record findings in categories of who or what needs water and why in the arms of the web.

Have a Try

Invite the students to talk with a partner about how the author shows scientists using evidence to support their argument to the Indonesian government in *Cycle of Rice, Cycle of Life*.

- Read the first two paragraphs on the page that begins "To Lansing and Kremer, the ancient water temple system."

  Turn and talk to your partner. What is the author trying to do on this page? How does she use evidence to support her argument?

- Invite a few students to share with the class.

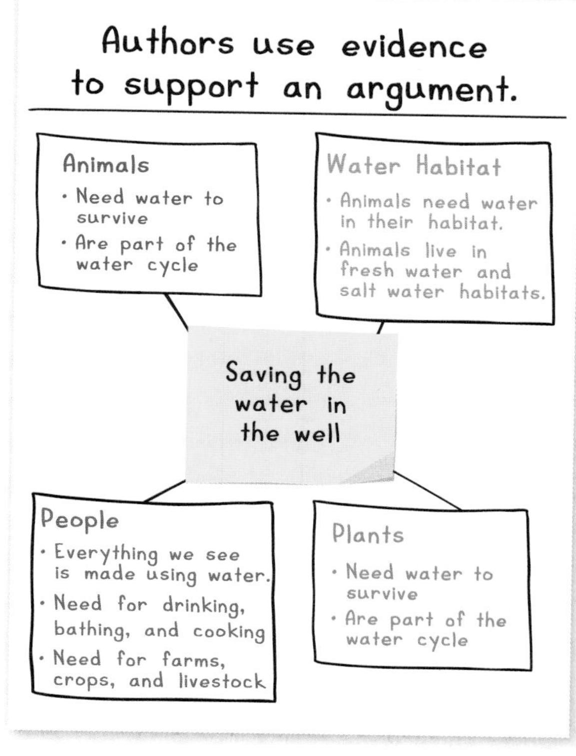

Summarize and Apply

Summarize the learning and remind students to think about how authors use evidence to support an argument.

What should you look for when you read a persuasive text?

- Write the principle at the top of the chart.

  Choose a persuasive text or essay from the basket to read today. Use sticky notes to mark pages where the author explains his or her argument. Then mark the evidence the author uses to support the argument. Be ready to share when we come back together.

Share

Following independent reading time, gather students together in the meeting area to talk about their persuasive texts.

What did the author want to persuade you to think, believe, or do? Share the evidence the author used to support the argument.

Extend the Lesson (Optional)

After assessing students' understanding, you might decide to extend the learning.

- Read aloud or have students read independently other persuasive texts. Ask students to evaluate whether the writer provided evidence to support the argument.
- **Writing About Reading** After reading a persuasive text, have students write in a reader's notebook about the author's argument and the evidence (or lack thereof) the author provides to support the argument.

RML3

LA.U15.RML3

Reading Minilesson Principle

Notice the difference between fact and opinion.

Exploring Persuasive Texts

You Will Need

- a collection of familiar persuasive texts, such as the following from Text Set: Caring for Our World:
  - *Can We Save the Tiger?* by Martin Jenkins
  - *One Well* by Rochelle Strauss
- chart paper and markers
- sticky notes
- basket of persuasive texts

Academic Language / Important Vocabulary

- fact
- opinion
- persuasive
- argument

Continuum Connection

- Distinguish fact from opinion (p. 74)

Goal

Notice the difference between fact and opinion.

Rationale

When you teach students to evaluate evidence in a persuasive text as either fact or opinion, they can decide if the author's argument is believable to them.

Assess Learning

Observe students when they read and discuss persuasive texts. Notice if there is evidence of new learning based on the goal of this minilesson.

- Can students identify an author's argument?
- Are they able to sort the evidence as fact or opinion?
- Do they understand and use the terms *fact, opinion, persuasive,* and *argument*?

Minilesson

To help students think about the minilesson principle, use familiar persuasive texts to engage them in noticing the difference between fact and opinion. Here is an example.

- Show *Can We Save the Tiger?* Read the last two paragraphs on page 10, some facts from page 12 (especially the number of tigers left), and a few parts of page 14.

  What does the author describe on these pages?

- Record responses on a chart in separate columns. Sort into facts and opinion, but do not label the columns or discuss how you are sorting yet.

  What do you notice about the information in the second column? The third column?

  When an author teaches you, the pieces of information are called facts. Facts can be proved to be true.

- Label the second column *Facts*.

  When an author tells you what he or she is thinking about those facts, that is called opinion.

- Label the third column *Author's Opinion*.

Have a Try

Invite the students to notice and sort the facts and opinions in *One Well.*

- Read the last two paragraphs on page 23.

  What does the author share here? Are these facts or opinions?

- Record responses. Repeat with page 16.

Summarize and Apply

Summarize the learning and remind students to differentiate between facts and opinions.

Look at the chart. What do you need to think about when you read a persuasive text?

- Review the chart and write the principle at the top.

  Choose a persuasive text or essay from the basket to read today. Notice the facts and opinions the author provides. Be ready to share when we come back together.

Notice the difference between fact and opinion.

Title	Facts	Author's Opinion
Can we save the tiger?	• Fewer than 2,500 breeding adult tigers are left in the wild. • Tigers need a lot of space. • People kill tigers for their skin. • Tigers sometimes eat farm animals.	• Tigers are special. • Tigers are beautiful. • Tigers are fierce.
One Well	• There are more people so more water is needed. • The water we have now is all the water we will ever have. • We use water for cleaning, cooking, and drinking. • Water is used to produce electricity.	• We need to find a balance between the water we want and the water that is available.

Share

Following independent reading time, gather students together in the meeting area to talk about their reading.

What facts and opinions did the author share? Was the author's writing persuasive?

Extend the Lesson (Optional)

After assessing students' understanding, you might decide to extend the learning.

- As you read persuasive texts, discuss whether the author provides facts that support the argument and persuade the reader. Consider having students research some of the facts to confirm that they are true.
- **Writing About Reading** After reading a persuasive text, have students write in a reader's notebook an opinion the author gave and the facts that support the opinion.

RML 4
LA.U15.RML4

Reading Minilesson Principle
Notice the techniques authors use to persuade you.

Exploring Persuasive Texts

You Will Need

- several familiar persuasive texts, such as the following from Text Set: Caring for Our World:
  - *One Well* by Rochelle Strauss
  - *Can We Save the Tiger?* by Martin Jenkins
- chart paper prepared with sentences from *One Well* (pp. 19, 26) and *Can We Save the Tiger?* (pp. 12, 30, and 51)
- markers
- basket of familiar persuasive texts, letters, speeches, or simple editorials
- sticky notes in different colors
- document camera (optional)

Academic Language / Important Vocabulary

- persuade
- persuasion
- techniques

Continuum Connection

- Notice and think critically about a writer's word choice (p. 74)
- Recognize a writer's use of the techniques for persuasion in a persuasive text (p. 74)

Goal

Recognize a writer's use of the techniques of persuasion.

Rationale

When students read critically, they notice the techniques authors use in a persuasive text, learn about the craft of writing—which they may apply to their own persuasive writing—and are able to discuss the strength of an author's argument and evidence.

Assess Learning

Observe students when they read and discuss persuasive texts. Notice if there is evidence of new learning based on the goal of this minilesson.

- Can students identify techniques an author uses to persuade?
- Do they understand terms such as *persuade, persuasion,* and *techniques*?

Minilesson

To help students think about the minilesson principle, use familiar persuasive texts to engage them in noticing how authors persuade the reader. Here is an example:

- Show *One Well.*

  In this book, the author wants to persuade you to conserve water. Listen as I reread some sentences from this book.

- Read the first sentence on the prepared chart, or read it aloud from page 19.

  How is the author trying to persuade you with this sentence? What does she want you to think?

- Write the minilesson principle at the top of the chart and record responses.

  The author gives a rather surprising fact to persuade you of the importance of conserving and protecting water.

- Write *Provides facts* on a sticky note and attach it to the chart.
- Repeat the process with the second sentence in the first column, which is from page 26.

  What do you notice about this sentence? To whom is it addressed?

  The author speaks directly to you to make you part of the problem and the solution.

- Repeat the process with the last two sentences from *One Well* (p. 26).

Have a Try

Invite the students to talk with a partner about how the author tries to persuade readers in *Can We Save the Tiger?*

- Read each sentence on the chart.

  Turn and talk to your partner. What do you notice about the language the author uses? How does the author try to persuade you not to give up on saving tigers from extinction?

- Ask a few students to share. Label the techniques as before.

Notice the techniques authors use to persuade you.

Author's Words	Technique	Author's Words	Technique
"While there is a lot of water on the planet, we have access to less than 1 percent of it." (p. 19)	Provides facts	"Number of tigers left: Fewer than 2,500 breeding adults in the wild" (p. 12)	Provides facts
"...you too can protect the water in Earth's One Well." (p. 26)	Speaks directly to you	"And I think that would be a shame, don't you?" (p. 51)	Speaks directly to you
"Taking action to conserve water can help save the well." (p. 26)	Problem/ solution	"Now that everyone knows what the problem is, maybe something can be done about it." (p. 30)	Problem/ solution
"Water has the power to change everything." (p. 26)	Uses persuasive language		

Summarize and Apply

Summarize the learning and remind students to notice how authors try to persuade readers.

What are some techniques authors use to try to persuade you?

- Review the chart.

  Choose a persuasive text from this basket to read today. When you notice a technique the author uses to try to persuade you, mark it with a sticky note so you can share when we come back together.

Share

Following independent reading time, gather students in the meeting area to talk about persuasive texts.

What techniques did the author use to try to persuade you?

- Add new techniques to the chart.

Extend the Lesson (Optional)

After assessing students' understanding, you might decide to extend the learning.

- Discuss other techniques an author might use to persuade (personal experience, repetition, comparison, or addressing oppositions).
- **Writing About Reading** Have students write in a reader's notebook about a technique a writer uses to persuade and whether that technique is effective.

RML 5

LA.U15.RML5

Reading Minilesson Principle

Consider an author's qualifications and sources when you read a persuasive text.

Exploring Persuasive Texts

You Will Need

- several familiar persuasive texts, such as the following from Text Set: Caring for Our World:
  - *One Well* by Rochelle Strauss
  - *Cycle of Rice, Cycle of Life* by Jan Reynolds
  - *Can We Save the Tiger?* by Martin Jenkins
- chart paper and markers
- basket of persuasive texts

Academic Language / Important Vocabulary

- biographical
- persuade
- qualified
- evaluate
- sources

Continuum Connection

- Critically examine the quality or accuracy of the text, citing evidence for opinions (p. 74)

Goal

Evaluate an author's qualifications and sources when you read a persuasive text.

Rationale

When students apply critical thinking and research skills to their reading they can evaluate a writer's claims and begin to draw their own conclusions from persuasive texts.

Assess Learning

Observe students when they talk about persuasive texts. Notice if there is evidence of new learning based on the goal of this minilesson.

- Are students able to identify ways to check an author's qualifications and sources?
- Can they explain why evaluating qualifications and sources is important?
- Do they use language such as *biographical, persuade, qualified, evaluate,* and *sources*?

Minilesson

To help students understand how to evaluate an author's qualifications and sources when reading a persuasive text, use familiar texts in which the author tries to persuade the readers. Here is an example.

- Read the second paragraph of the acknowledgments in *One Well.*

  Why do you think the author included this in her acknowledgments?

  How does this help you to know the author is able–or qualified–to persuade you?

  The author listed the experts that she consulted to make sure the facts in her book are correct.

- Record responses on chart paper.
- Read the dedication, acknowledgments, sources, and additional sources in the front of *Cycle of Rice, Cycle of Life* and point out the websites listed at the back of the book. Repeat the inquiry process to determine that these are places to look to evaluate the author's qualifications and sources of information.

Have a Try

Invite the students to consider with a partner how to evaluate an author's qualifications and sources.

- Read "Find out more online" and the author's biography from *Can We Save the Tiger?*

  Turn and talk to your partner. Why did the author include this list of online resources? What do you learn about the author and his qualifications to write a book to persuade readers to help endangered species?

- Record responses on the chart.

Consider an author's qualifications and sources when you read a persuasive text.

Where can you look for an author's qualifications and sources?	How does this help you know an author is qualified to persuade you?
Biographical Information	Gives the author's experience and background in the topic.
Acknowledgments and Dedications	Describes expert researchers or organizations that reviewed the author's work and the facts the author used.
Other Sources: • Primary observations of others • Conversations with researchers • Nonfiction books • Websites • Videos/ Television / Radio news reports	You know where the information originated. You can read more to check if the author is correct.

Summarize and Apply

Summarize the learning and remind students to think about how readers consider an author's qualifications and sources.

How does the inclusion of additional resources in a persuasive text help you as a reader?

- Review the chart and write the principle at the top.

  Choose a persuasive text from the basket to read today. As you read, notice how the author shares her qualifications for writing the persuasive text. Be ready to share your thoughts with the class.

Share

Following independent reading time, gather students in the meeting area to talk about persuasive texts.

How do you know the author is qualified to write a persuasive text on the topic of the book you read today?

Extend the Lesson (Optional)

After assessing students' understanding, you might decide to extend the learning.

- Provide time for students to look at some of the online resources listed in the back of *Can We Save the Tiger?* as a way to confirm the author's claims.
- **Writing About Reading** Have students write in a reader's notebook about a persuasive text they have read, including how they know the author was qualified to write the text.

Exploring Persuasive Texts

Assessment

After you have taught the minilessons in this umbrella, observe students as they talk and write about their reading across instructional contexts: interactive read-aloud, independent reading, guided reading, shared reading, and book club. Use *The Literacy Continuum* (Fountas and Pinnell 2017) to guide the observation of students' reading and writing behaviors.

- What evidence do you have of new understandings related to persuasive texts?
    - Can students understand what the author is trying to persuade them to believe or do, and how?
    - Can they evaluate evidence the author provides to support their argument?
    - Are they talking about the difference between fact and opinion?
    - Are they evaluating an author's qualifications and sources?
    - Do they use vocabulary such as *persuade, evaluate, qualified, argument, opinion,* and *evidence*?
- In what other ways, beyond the scope of this umbrella, are students talking about persuasive texts?
    - Are students writing about persuasive texts?
    - Do they read and evaluate multiple sources on the same topic?

Use your observations to determine the next umbrella you will teach. You may also consult Minilessons Across the Year (pp. 61–64) for guidance.

Link to Writing

After teaching the minilessons in this umbrella, help students link the new learning to their own writing:

- Ask students to think of a topic about which they feel strongly. Invite them to write persuasively about the topic. Remind them that they should try to convince readers to believe or do something, provide evidence to support their arguments, include facts and opinions, and cite sources as a way to build their credibility. Students may use Analyzing Persuasive Writing to create an outline for their writing (visit resources.fountasandpinnell.com to download this resource).

Reader's Notebook

When this umbrella is complete, provide a copy of the minilesson principles (see resources.fountasandpinnell.com) for students to glue in the reader's notebook (in the Minilessons section if using *Reader's Notebook: Advanced* [Fountas and Pinnell 2011]), so they can refer to the information as needed.

Minilessons in This Umbrella

RML1	Biographies are alike in many ways.
RML2	The definition of biography is what is always true about it.
RML3	Biographers choose their subjects for a variety of reasons.
RML4	Biographers decide when to start and stop telling the story of the subject's life.
RML5	Biographers include details about the society and culture of the time in which the subject lived.
RML6	Biographers usually include the people who influenced the subject's life.
RML7	Biographers choose to include facts that reveal something important about the subject's personality traits and motivations.
RML8	Sometimes biographers include imagined scenes but base them on facts.
RML9	Think about how the subject's accomplishments have influenced life today.

Before Teaching Umbrella 16 Minilessons

During a genre study (pp. 39–41), students learn what to expect when reading in the genre, expand comprehension skills, notice distinguishing characteristics, and develop tools to navigate a variety of texts. Before beginning this genre study, students should read many biographies. Select books that are clear examples of biography, such as the following books from the *Fountas & Pinnell Classroom*™ *Interactive Read-Aloud Collection*.

Genre Study: Biography (Musicians)

Strange Mr. Satie by M. T. Anderson

I and I: Bob Marley by Tony Medina

Ella Fitzgerald by Andrea Davis Pinkney

The Legendary Miss Lena Horne by Carole Boston Weatherford

Esquivel! by Susan Wood

Achieving a Dream

Surfer of the Century by Ellie Crowe

Silent Star by Bill Wise

Long-Armed Ludy and the First Women's Olympics by Jean L. S. Patrick

Sixteen Years in Sixteen Seconds by Paula Yoo

Tallchief by Maria Tallchief with Rosemary Wells

As you read aloud and enjoy these texts together, help students

- notice things that are *always* and *often* true about biographies, and
- understand the choices a biographer makes when writing a biography.

Genre Study: Biography (Musicians)

Ella Fitzgerald by Andrea Davis Pinkney

Achieving a Dream

RML 1

LA.U16.RML1

Reading Minilesson Principle
Biographies are alike in many ways.

Studying Biography

You Will Need

- a variety of familiar biographies
- chart paper and markers
- basket of biographies
- sticky notes

Academic Language / Important Vocabulary

- biography
- genre
- characteristics
- subject

Continuum Connection

- Connect texts by a range of categories: e.g., content, message, genre, author/illustrator, special form, text structure, or organization (p. 73)
- Notice and understand the characteristics of some specific nonfiction genres: e.g., expository, narrative, procedural and persuasive texts, biography, autobiography, memoir, hybrid text (p. 73)

Goal

Notice and understand the characteristics of biography as a genre.

Rationale

When you teach students the characteristics of biographies, they will know what to expect when reading a story written by one person about another person's life.

Assess Learning

Observe students when they talk about biographies and notice if there is evidence of new learning based on the goal of this minilesson.

- Do students talk about the characteristics of biographies?
- Do they realize that characteristics either *always* or *often* occur in biographies?
- Are they using the terms *biography, genre, characteristics,* and *subject*?

Minilesson

To help students think about the minilesson principle, guide them to recognize the characteristics of biographies. Here is an example.

- Show the covers of multiple familiar biographies.

  In what ways are all these books alike?

- Record responses. For each suggestion, prompt the students to think about whether the similarities occur *always* or *often* in the books. Create separate columns on the chart for each category.
- Select a few of the biographies to discuss in greater detail by revisiting a few pages of text and illustrations.

  What else do you notice?

  Where should we add that information to the chart?

- Continue recording responses. The following prompts may be used as needed:
  - *What do you notice about the subject's accomplishments?*
  - *What types of things does the author focus on?*
  - *Why do you think the author chose this person to write about?*

Have a Try

Invite the students to talk in groups about the characteristics of the books.

- Provide each group with a biography.

  Think about what is written on the chart as you look through this book with your group. See how many things from the chart can be found in the book. Look for anything new to add to the chart.

- After time for discussion, ask if students found anything new that can be added to the chart.

Summarize and Apply

Summarize the learning by explaining that all the books they discussed were biographies. Remind them to think about what *always* or *often* occurs in biographies when they read one.

- Review the chart.

  Today choose a biography from the basket unless you are already reading one from the library. As you read, look at the chart to see which things you can find in the biography you are reading. If you notice something you want to remember, add a sticky note to the page. Bring the book when we meet so you can share.

Biography

Noticings:

Always	Often
• The author tells the story of another person's life or a part of it. • The author chooses facts to include about the person's life. • The author tells about the important things a person did or why the person is interesting. • The author gives an important message. • The author includes the setting and the people who influenced the person's life.	• The author tells about a person's life in the order it happened. • The author includes some imagined scenes and made-up dialogue but bases them on facts. • The author includes quotes by the person. • The author includes additional information at the end of the book (e.g., timelines). • The author includes photographs and illustrations. • Biographies are told like a story.

Share

Following independent reading time, gather students in the meeting area to talk about biographies.

What did you notice about the biography you read or started to read today?

Extend the Lesson (Optional)

After assessing students' understanding, you might decide to extend the learning.

- Have students record the titles of biographies they read on the Reading List page of a reader's notebook (see WAR.U1.RML2).
- Introduce students to the Genre Thinkmark for biography (to download this resource, see resources.fountasandpinnell.com). A Genre Thinkmark is a tool that guides students to notice certain characteristics of a genre in their reading. They can quickly note page numbers so they can share the information with classmates.

RML 2
LA.U16.RML2

Studying Biography

You Will Need

- several familiar biographies, such as the following from Text Set: Achieving a Dream:
  - *Silent Star* by Bill Wise
  - *Tallchief* by Maria Tallchief with Rosemary Wells
- biography noticings chart from RML1
- chart paper and markers
- basket of biographies

Academic Language / Important Vocabulary

- biography
- definition
- subject

Continuum Connection

- Understand that a biography is the story of a person's life written by someone else (p. 73)

Reading Minilesson Principle

The definition of biography is what is always true about it.

Goal

Construct a working definition for biography.

Rationale

When you teach students to construct a working definition of biography, they need to analyze examples of the genre and summarize the characteristics. Then they will know what to expect when they read in the genre. They will be able to revise and expand their understandings as they have new experiences with biographies.

Assess Learning

Observe students when they discuss biographies and notice if there is evidence of new learning based on the goal of this minilesson.

- Do students cooperate to create a working definition of biography?
- Are students talking about the definition of biography and able to tell what is true of all biographies?
- Do they use the terms *biography, definition,* and *subject*?

Minilesson

To help students think about the minilesson principle, engage them in constructing a working definition of biography. Here is an example.

- Discuss the characteristics of biography by revisiting the biography noticings chart.

  What do you know about biography?

  The definition of biography tells what is *always* true about books in this genre.

- On chart paper, write the words *A biography is*, leaving space for constructing a working definition.

  How could this sentence be finished in a way that describes all biographies? Think about the noticings chart. Turn and talk about that.

- After time for discussion, ask students to share. Use the ideas to construct a working definition and add it to the chart.
- Show the cover of *Silent Star* and show a few pages.

  Think about *Silent Star: The Story of Deaf Major Leaguer William Hoy*. Does it fit the definition of a biography?

- As students share, ask for text examples to show that it fits the definition.

Have a Try

Invite the students to talk with a partner about the definition of biography.

- Show the cover of *Tallchief* and revisit a few pages.

  Turn and talk about whether *Tallchief: America's Prima Ballerina* fits the definition of a biography.

- Ask a few volunteers to share their thinking. Have them point out examples from the book to show that it fits the definition.

Summarize and Apply

Summarize the learning and remind students to think about what is always true about biographies.

Today we created a definition of biography.

Choose a biography from the basket to read, unless you are already reading one from the library. Think about whether it fits the definition of biography. Bring the book when we meet so you can share.

Biography

A biography is a story about a person written by someone else.

Share

Following independent reading time, gather students in pairs to talk about their reading.

With a partner, share the pages you marked to show that the book fits the definition of biography.

Extend the Lesson (Optional)

After assessing students' understanding, you might decide to extend the learning.

- Do some online research with students to evaluate the accuracy and quality of the biographies the class has read (see LA.U14.RML6).

RML 3

LA.U16.RML3

Reading Minilesson Principle

Biographers choose their subjects for a variety of reasons.

Studying Biography

You Will Need

- several familiar biographies, such as the following:
  - *Surfer of the Century* by Ellie Crowe and *Sixteen Years in Sixteen Seconds* by Paula Yoo, from Text Set: Achieving a Dream
  - *I and I: Bob Marley* by Tony Medina, from Text Set: Genre Study: Biography (Musicians)
  - *Long-Armed Ludy* by Jean L. S. Patrick, from Text Set: Achieving a Dream
- chart paper and markers
- sticky notes
- basket of biographies

Academic Language / Important Vocabulary

- biography
- subject
- accomplished
- obstacles
- message

Continuum Connection

- Infer the purpose of a writer of a biography, autobiography, or memoir (p. 578)
- Discuss a writer's purpose in selecting a particular genre, topic, subject, or type of narrative structure (pp. 558, 567, 579)

Goal

Understand that biographers choose their subjects for a variety of reasons.

Rationale

When students think about why an author chooses the subject of a biography, they understand that the life of the subject is an important consideration in deciding whom to write about, and they begin to think about the biographer's craft.

Assess Learning

Observe students when they talk about biographies and notice if there is evidence of new learning based on the goal of this minilesson.

- Do students understand that a biographer carefully chooses a particular subject to write about?
- Are they discussing why a biographer chose a subject?
- Do they use the terms *biography, subject, accomplished, obstacles,* and *message*?

Minilesson

To help students think about the minilesson principle, engage them in a discussion about why a biographer chooses a particular subject. Here is an example.

- Show the cover of *Surfer of the Century* and share a few entries from the timeline at the back of the book.

  Why do you think the author decided to write about Duke Kahanamoku?

- On chart paper, write a sentence that makes a generalization based on the students' responses that includes one reason the author might have decided to write about the subject.
- The sentences created in class may look different than the sample chart because they will be based on your students' noticings. The important thing is that students are thinking about the reasons why an author chooses a subject.

  Now think about the subject of a different biography, *Sixteen Years in Sixteen Seconds: The Story of Sammy Lee.*

- Show the cover and read the last page.

  What do you think about what Sammy Lee did and why the author might have written a book about him?

- Add to the chart.
- Repeat the activity with *I and I: Bob Marley*.

Have a Try

Invite the students to talk with a partner about why a biographer chooses a particular subject.

- Show the cover of *Long-Armed Ludy*.

  Think about Ludy Godbold and what her accomplishments represent. Why was her life important to write about?

- After time for discussion, ask a few volunteers to share. Summarize their thinking on the chart.

Biographers choose their subjects for a variety of reasons.	
Title	Why the Author Chose the Subject
 Surfer of the Century	Duke accomplished something important.
 Sixteen Years in Sixteen Seconds	Sammy Lee overcame obstacles.
 Bob Marley cover	Bob Marley is interesting to read about.
 Long-Armed Ludy	Ludy Godbold's life sends a message.

Summarize and Apply

Summarize the learning and remind students to think about the reasons biographers choose a particular subject.

A biographer chooses a subject because she has accomplished something, has overcome obstacles, or is very interesting. An author often chooses a subject because his life sends a message.

- Add the principle to the chart.

  Choose a biography to read from the basket, unless you are already reading one from the library. Think about the subject's life and why the biographer might have decided to write about that person. Mark any pages you want to remember with sticky notes. Bring the book when we meet so you can share.

Share

Following independent reading time, gather students in small groups to talk about their reading.

Share with your group the reasons you think the author decided to write about the person in the biography you read.

Extend the Lesson (Optional)

After assessing students' understanding, you might decide to extend the learning.

- Hold a discussion about people students would like to write a biography about. Have them share the reasons they would choose that subject. If appropriate, have students plan and write a biography.

RML 4
LA.U16.RML4

Reading Minilesson Principle

Biographers decide when to start and stop telling the story of the subject's life.

Studying Biography

You Will Need

- several familiar biographies, such as the following:
  - *I and I: Bob Marley* by Tony Medina, from Text Set: Genre Study: Biography (Musicians)
  - *Long-Armed Ludy* by Jean L. S. Patrick, from Text Set: Achieving a Dream
- chart paper and markers
- sticky notes
- basket of biographies

Academic Language / Important Vocabulary

- biography
- biographer
- subject
- decisions

Continuum Connection

- Talk critically about what a writer does to make a topic interesting or important (p. 559)
- Think critically about how a writer does (or does not) make a topic interesting and engaging, and share opinions (pp. 569, 581)

Goal

Analyze the craft decisions the biographer makes in writing a biography.

Rationale

To fully understand the importance of a biography, students have to know that biographers make many decisions about what they write. Biographers choose to write about the parts of a subject's life that best support their purpose for writing.

Assess Learning

Observe students when they talk about biographies and notice if there is evidence of new learning based on the goal of this minilesson.

- Can students identify the different times in a subject's life that a biography can begin and end?
- Are they aware that a biographer makes choices when writing a biography?
- Do they understand the terms *biography, biographer, subject,* and *decisions*?

Minilesson

To help students think about the minilesson principle, engage them in a discussion about the decisions an author makes in writing a biography. Here is an example.

- Display a familiar biography, such as *I and I: Bob Marley,* and revisit the text and illustrations that show when the biographer begins and ends the story. For example, show the illustrations on page 3 and read a few lines from pages 2 and 4. Then show the illustration on page 32 and read a few words from page 31.

  At what points in Bob Marley's life did the biographer decide to begin and end this story about him?

- As students share, create a chart that shows where the story begins and ends.

  Why do you think the biographer made this decision?

- Add possible reasons for the biographer's decisions to the chart.
- Repeat the activity using *Long-Armed Ludy.*

  How do you think biographers make the decision about what period of time from a subject's life to write about?

  Usually a biographer chooses the most interesting or important part of the subject's life to write about.

Have a Try

Invite the students to talk in small groups about a biographer's decisions.

- Provide each group with a biography.

  Take a look at the biography and talk about what part of the subject's life the biographer included. Talk about why you think the biographer made that decision.

- After time for discussion, ask a few volunteers to share. Add to the chart.

Biographers decide when to start and stop telling the story of the subject's life.

Bob Marley

Begins: young boy ⟶ Ends: adult
The biographer writes about key events in the life of Bob Marley.

Ludy Godbold

Begins: 1917 (college) ⟶ Ends: 1922 (Olympics)
The book is about Ludy winning at the first Women's Olympics, so it focuses on the time she practiced in college to the time she won.

Summarize and Apply

Summarize the learning and remind students to think about a biographer's decisions when they read biographies.

What does the chart show you about biographers' writing choices?

- Add the principle to the top of the chart.

  Today when you read, choose a biography from the basket unless you are already reading one. As you read, notice the period of a subject's life that the biographer decided to write about. Bring the book when we meet so you can share.

Share

Following independent reading time, gather students in pairs.

Talk with your partner about the biography you read. When did the biographer decide to start telling the story of the subject's life? When did the biographer stop telling the story? Why do you think the biographer made those choices?

- Add a few new books to the chart.

Extend the Lesson (Optional)

After assessing students' understanding, you might decide to extend the learning.

- Discuss with students reasons that biographers choose to omit parts of a subject's life.
- Locate two or more biographies of the same person so that students can compare the decisions the biographers made in writing their books.

RML 5
LA.U16.RML5

Reading Minilesson Principle

Biographers include details about the society and culture of the time in which the subject lived.

Studying Biography

You Will Need

- several familiar biographies that have details about the time in which the subject lived, such as the following:
  - *The Legendary Miss Lena Horne* by Carole Boston Weatherford, from Text Set: Genre Study: Biography (Musicians)
  - *Long-Armed Ludy* by Jean L. S. Patrick, from Text Set: Achieving a Dream
  - *Strange Mr. Satie* by M. T. Anderson, from Text Set: Genre Study: Biography (Musicians)
- chart paper and markers
- sticky notes
- basket of biographies

Academic Language / Important Vocabulary

- biography
- biographer
- subject
- time period
- society
- culture

Continuum Connection

- Understand that biographies are often set in the past (p. 73)
- Notice how the writer reveals the setting in a biographical or historical text (p. 74)
- Infer the impact of the setting on the subject of a biography and the motives or reasons for the subject's decisions (pp. 557, 566, 578)

Goal

Understand why biographers include details about the society and culture of the time the subject lived.

Rationale

When students learn to think about the details about the time period that a biographer chooses to include, they learn to consider how culture and society affected the subject and subject's accomplishments.

Assess Learning

Observe students when they talk about biographies and notice if there is evidence of new learning based on the goal of this minilesson.

- Do students recognize the time period in which the subject of a biography lived?
- Are students talking about the significance of the details about the time period that the biographer chooses to include?
- Do they use the terms *biography, biographer, subject, time period, society,* and *culture*?

Minilesson

To help students think about the minilesson principle, engage them in a discussion about the way a time period influences the subject of a biography. Here is an example.

- Show a few pages of *The Legendary Miss Lena Horne* that reveal details of the time period.

  What did the author do to show the time period in which Lena Horne lived?

  Why do you think it is important that the author included information about the time period?

- As students offer suggestions, record their thinking on the chart.
- Show a few illustrations from *Long-Armed Ludy* that provide details about the time period.

  How did the author and illustrator provide information about the time period in which Ludy Godbold lived?

  Why is it important that you know about the society and culture at that time to understand her accomplishments?

- Record student responses.

Have a Try

Invite the students to talk with a partner about the significance of time-period details in a biography.

- Show a few illustrations from *Strange Mr. Satie*.

  Think about the details that the author included about the time and place in which Erik Satie lived. Turn and talk about why these details are important in a book about his life.

- After time for discussion, ask students to share. Add to the chart.

Biographers include details about the society and culture of the time in which the subject lived.		
Title and Subject	Details That Show Setting and Culture	Why is it important that the author included time-period details?
 Lena Horne	clothing hairstyles old photographs city background civil rights march	Horne spoke out for equality for African Americans at a time when they were not treated equally.
 Ludy Godbold	sports outfit school outfit hairstyle cars suitcases	Women were not included in major sports back then, but Ludy qualified for the first Women's Olympics.
 Erik Satie	top hats candle lamps old furniture French signs	Satie's music was too different for people at that time. Much later, people appreciated Erik Satie's music.

Summarize and Apply

Summarize the learning and remind students to think about the time-period facts in a biography when they read one.

Today we talked about why a biographer includes details about the time period in a biography.

- Add the principle to the chart.

  Choose a biography from the basket to read, unless you are already reading one from the library. Think about facts that the biographer included and why they are important. Mark any pages with sticky notes that give a clue. Bring the book when we meet so you can share.

Share

Following independent reading time, gather students in pairs to talk about biographies.

Share with your partner the biography you read. Talk about the reasons you think the author included facts about the time period and why those facts are important.

Extend the Lesson (Optional)

After assessing students' understanding, you might decide to extend the learning.

- Encourage students to write in a reader's notebook about why they think the author included specific facts and how those details are important in understanding the subject's life and accomplishments.

RML 6

LA.U16.RML6

Reading Minilesson Principle

Biographers usually include the people who influenced the subject's life.

Studying Biography

You Will Need

- several familiar biographies that include facts about people who influenced the lives of the subjects, such as the following:
  - *Ella Fitzgerald* by Andrea Davis Pinkney, from Text Set: Genre Study: Biography (Musicians)
  - *Sixteen Years in Sixteen Seconds* by Paula Yoo, from Tet Set: Achieving a Dream
- chart paper and markers
- basket of biographies
- sticky notes

Academic Language / Important Vocabulary

- biography
- biographer
- subject
- influenced
- inspiration

Continuum Connection

- Notice that a biography is built around significant events, problems to overcome, and the subject's decisions (pp. 558, 567, 579)

Goal

Understand and infer the influence of the subject's relationships.

Rationale

When students understand that people act in certain ways based on the influence of other people, they learn that the subject of a biography is a product of multiple factors. This enables students to extend the idea to their own lives in order to think about the ways that other people influence them.

Assess Learning

Observe students when they talk about biographies and notice if there is evidence of new learning based on the goal of this minilesson.

- Do students notice facts about people who influence a biography subject's life?
- Are students talking about the facts that a biographer chooses to include about a subject's inspiration?
- Do they understand the terms *biography, biographer, subject, influenced,* and *inspiration*?

Minilesson

To help students think about the minilesson principle, engage them in a discussion about how the subjects of biographies are influenced by others. Here is an example.

- Revisit pages 9–14 of *Ella Fitzgerald.*

  What details did the biographer include about Ella Fitzgerald and the people who influenced her?

  Often, the person who influences the subject is also an inspiration to the subject.

- As needed, discuss the meanings of *influenced* and *inspiration.*
- On a chart, write the title and subject of the biography and the name of the person who influenced the subject. Ask students to provide ideas for the chart.

  In what ways did Chick Webb influence or inspire Ella Fitzgerald?

- Add details to the chart about how the person influenced the subject.

  Why do you think the author included details about Chick Webb in a biography about Ella Fitzgerald?

Have a Try

Invite the students to talk with a partner about how and why a biographer includes facts about people who influenced a subject.

- Revisit pages 7–10 of *Sixteen Years in Sixteen Seconds.*

  Turn and talk about who influenced Sammy Lee's diving and how. Also talk about why you think the author decided to include this information in a biography about Sammy Lee.

- After time for discussion, ask a few volunteers to share. Add to the chart.

Biographers usually include the people who influenced the subject's life.

Title	Subject	WHO influenced the subject?	HOW did the person influence the subject?
Ella Fitzgerald	Ella Fitzgerald	Chick Webb	Brought her into his band Taught her a lot about music
Sixteen Years in Sixteen Seconds	Sammy Lee	Coach Ryan	Gave him great diving advice Made him work hard Let Sammy dig a hole in his yard to practice

Summarize and Apply

Summarize the learning and remind students to think about the reasons biographers include particular facts in a biography about who influenced the subject.

Today you talked about some of the facts a biographer includes about a subject. What did you learn?

- Add the principle to the chart.

  Choose a biography from the basket to read, unless you are already reading one from the library. Notice any facts about who influenced the subject and how that person influenced the subject. Mark any pages with sticky notes that give a clue. Bring the book when we meet so you can share.

Share

Following independent reading time, gather students in the meeting area to talk about biographies.

Did you notice facts about who influenced the subject of the biography you read and how that person influenced the subject? Share what you noticed.

Extend the Lesson (Optional)

After assessing students' understanding, you might decide to extend the learning.

- When you read aloud biographies, ask students to notice not only people but events that influenced the subject.
- Have students write in a reader's notebook about the people or events that influenced or inspired the subject of a biography.

RML 7
LA.U16.RML7

Reading Minilesson Principle
Biographers choose to include facts that reveal something important about the subject's personality traits and motivations.

Studying Biography

You Will Need

- several familiar biographies, such as the following from Text Set: Genre Study: Biography (Musicians):
  - *Esquivel!* by Susan Wood
  - *Ella Fitzgerald* by Andrea Davis Pinkney
- chart paper and markers
- basket of biographies
- sticky notes

Academic Language / Important Vocabulary

- biography
- biographer
- subject
- reveal
- personality traits
- motivations

Continuum Connection

- Notice that a biography is built around significant events, problems to overcome, and the subject's decisions (pp. 558, 567, 579)

Goal

Infer a subject's personality traits and motivations from the facts and details the biographer includes about the subject's life.

Rationale

When you teach students to think about what the facts in a biography reveal about a subject, they begin to think about the decisions a biographer makes about how to reveal what a subject is like.

Assess Learning

Observe students when they talk about biographies and notice if there is evidence of new learning based on the goal of this minilesson.

- Can students identify facts in a biography that reveal something about the subject?
- Are students talking about the decisions a biographer makes about which facts to include about the subject?
- Do they understand the terms *biography, biographer, subject, reveal, personality traits,* and *motivations*?

Minilesson

To help students think about the minilesson principle, engage them in a discussion about what the facts reveal about the subject of a biography. Here is an example.

- Show the cover of *Esquivel!* and revisit page 3.

  How would you describe Juan Garcia Esquivel, based on the information on this page?

  What examples does the biographer include that show you what Juan Garcia Esquivel was like?

- As students share their thinking, begin recording their responses to link personality traits and motivations with examples from the book. As needed, prompt the conversation so they use the terms *personality traits* and *motivations*. Then revisit page 4.

  What did you learn about Esquivel on this page?

  What do these facts show you about his personality traits and motivations?

- Add to chart.
- Revisit page 6 and a few more pages. Continue adding to the chart as students share their thinking.

Have a Try

Invite the students to talk with a partner about how a biographer shows the personality traits and motivations of a subject.

- Show the cover of *Ella Fitzgerald*. Revisit pages 4, 6, and 21.

 Turn and talk about the facts the biographer includes and what they reveal about Ella's personality traits and motivations.

- After time for discussion, ask students to share their thinking. Add to chart.

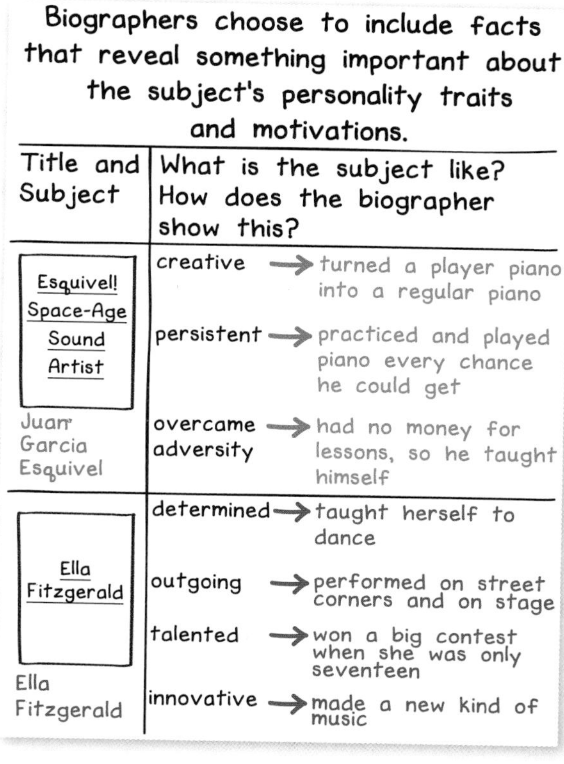

Summarize and Apply

Summarize the learning and remind students to think about what the facts in a biography show about the subject's personality traits and motivations.

 Biographers carefully choose the information they include in a biography to show what the subject is or was like.

- Add the principle to the chart.

 Choose a biography to read today unless you are already reading one from the library. Think about facts that the biographer includes and what the facts show about the subject. Mark any pages with sticky notes that you want to remember. Bring the book when we meet so you can share.

Share

Following independent reading time, gather students in the meeting area to talk about biographies.

 Share one or two facts that show something about the subject's personality traits and motivations.

Extend the Lesson (Optional)

After assessing students' understanding, you might decide to extend the learning.

- As you read other biographies with students, have them think about other things the facts in a biography reveal and why the biographer includes those facts.
- **Writing About Reading** Encourage students to use a reader's notebook to write about facts that a biographer includes in a biography and what those facts show about the subject.

RML 8
LA.U16.RML8

Reading Minilesson Principle
Sometimes biographers include imagined scenes but base them on facts.

Studying Biography

You Will Need

- several familiar biographies, such as the following:
  - *Strange Mr. Satie* by M. T. Anderson, from Text Set: Genre Study: Biography (Musicians)
  - *Silent Star* by Bill Wise, from Text Set: Achieving a Dream
- chart paper prepared ahead of time with headings *Title and Subject, Scene, Importance? Imagined?* and *Based on Facts?*
- markers
- sticky notes
- basket of biographies

Academic Language / Important Vocabulary

- biography
- biographer
- subject
- imagined
- facts
- authentic

Continuum Connection

- Talk critically about what a writer does to make a topic interesting or important (p. 559)
- Think critically about how a writer does (or does not) make a topic interesting and engaging, and share opinions (pp. 569, 581)

Goal

Analyze the craft decisions the biographer makes in writing a biography.

Rationale

It is important for students to understand that some scenes in biographies are imagined and that authors use them to convey information about the subject or to make the writing more interesting. When you teach students to think critically about the way a biographer sometimes uses imagined scenes in a biography, they understand the choices the biographer makes and deepen their thinking about an author's craft.

Assess Learning

Observe students when they talk about a biographer's decisions to include imagined scenes and notice if there is evidence of new learning based on the goal of this minilesson.

- Can students identify scenes that are imagined?
- Are students aware that a biographer makes decisions about what to include when writing a biography?
- Do they understand the terms *biography, biographer, subject, imagined, facts,* and *authentic*?

Minilesson

To help students think about the minilesson principle, help them recognize the imagined scenes a biographer includes. Here is an example.

- Revisit pages 19–20 of *Strange Mr. Satie.*

  Do you think Erik Satie really threw Suzanne out the window, and then she used acrobatic skills to land on her feet? Why or why not?

- As students share their thinking, begin filling in the chart with their responses.

  Do you think this scene was based on anything true about Erik Satie?

  Why do you think the biographer made the decision to include this scene?

  Why is the scene important to understanding Erik?

- Continue adding to chart.
- Show the author's note at the end of the book and talk about how biographers include some imagined scenes.

  Why is it important that imagined scenes in a biography are based on fact?

Have a Try

Invite the students to talk with a partner about a biographer's decisions.

- Read and show page 10 of *Silent Star*.

  Turn and talk about this scene. Have a conversation about whether this is exactly what William experienced or if it is imagined by the biographer. Think about if it feels authentic and why it is important to the biography.

- After time for discussion, ask several volunteers to share their thinking. Add to chart.

Sometimes biographers include imagined scenes but base them on facts.

Title and Subject	Scene	Importance	Imagined?	Based on Facts?
 Strange Mr. Satie Erik Satie	Satie threw Suzanne out the window and she used her acrobat skills to land on her feet. She left and never returned. (pp. 19-20)	Erik Satie had a bad temper and did things to push people he cared about away.	Yes. It seems unlikely that this actually happened.	Yes. Satie had a bad temper. This scene uses exaggeration to show Satie's personality.
 Silent Star William Hoy	William dreamed about being a major league baseball player (p. 10)	Baseball was very important to William.	Yes. The author does not know what he dreamed every night.	Yes. Baseball was very important to William, so he probably thought about it a lot.

Summarize and Apply

Summarize the learning and remind students to think about a biographer's decisions when they read biographies.

  What does the chart show you about biographers?

- Add the principle to the top of the chart.

  Today when you read, choose a biography from the basket unless you are already reading one from the library. Think about the scenes that the biographer includes. Place a sticky note on any pages you want to remember. Bring the book when we meet so you can share.

Share

Following independent reading time, gather students in the meeting area to talk about biographies.

  Who noticed the decisions the biographer made in a biography you read today? Share what you noticed.

- Add new ideas to the chart.

Extend the Lesson (Optional)

After assessing students' understanding, you might decide to extend the learning.

- Have students fill in a grid (see resources.fountasandpinnell.com) similar to the chart in this minilesson to compare biographies. They can glue the grid into a reader's notebook.

RML 9

LA.U16.RML9

Reading Minilesson Principle

Think about how the subject's accomplishments have influenced life today.

Studying Biography

You Will Need

- several familiar biographies, such as the following:
  - *Long-Armed Ludy* by Jean L. S. Patrick and *Silent Star* by Bill Wise, from Text Set: Achieving a Dream
  - *The Legendary Miss Lena Horne* by Carole Boston Weatherford, from Text Set: Genre Study: Biography (Musicians)
- chart paper and markers
- basket of biographies
- sticky notes

Academic Language / Important Vocabulary

- biography
- biographer
- subject
- accomplishments
- influenced

Continuum Connection

- Infer the importance of a subject's accomplishments (biography) (p. 73)
- Talk about why the subject of a biography is important or sets an example for others (pp. 559, 569, 581)

Goal

Infer ways the subject's accomplishments might have influenced life today.

Rationale

When students learn to infer the influence that a biography subject has had on life today, they think about how biographers choose their subjects and consider why biographies are written about certain people.

Assess Learning

Observe students when they talk about a subject's accomplishments and notice if there is evidence of new learning based on the goal of this minilesson.

- Can students identify the accomplishments of the subject of a biography?
- Are students able to infer the way that a subject's accomplishments have influenced life today?
- Do they understand the terms *biography, biographer, subject, accomplishments,* and *influenced*?

Minilesson

To help students think about the minilesson principle, engage them in a discussion about a subject's influence. Here is an example.

- Show the cover of *The Legendary Miss Lena Horne.*

  Think about this biography of Lena Horne. Why do you think the biographer chose Lena for a subject?

- Revisit a few parts of the book that show the impact she has had on life today. Discuss the meanings of *accomplishments* and *influenced*. Use the words in the conversation.

  What are Lena Horne's accomplishments?

  How has she influenced life today?

- As students respond, add their ideas to the chart.
- Show the cover of *Silent Star.*

  Now think about the biography of William Hoy. Why do you think the biographer wrote a book about him?

- Revisit a few parts of the book that show his influence.

  What are William Hoy's accomplishments?

  How have his accomplishments influenced life today?

- Add students' responses to the chart.

Have a Try

Invite the students to talk with a partner about how the subject of a biography has influenced life today.

- Show the cover of *Long-Armed Ludy*.

  Think about Ludy Godbold and how she has influenced life today. Turn and talk about that.

- After time for discussion, ask a few volunteers to share. Summarize their thinking on the chart.

Summarize and Apply

Summarize the learning and remind students to think about the influence that the subjects of biographies have on life today.

What did you learn to think about when you read a biography?

- Add the principle to the chart.

  Choose a biography to read from the basket unless you are already reading one from the library. Think about how the subject of the biography has influenced life today. Mark any pages with sticky notes that you want to remember. Bring the book when we meet so you can share.

Think about how the subject's accomplishments have influenced life today.

Title and Subject	How the Subject's Accomplishments Have Influenced Life Today
 Lena Horne	She paved the way for other African Americans to participate as equals in the entertainment industry. 
 William Hoy	He inspired other people with disabilities to compete in sports. He was an inspiration to all people, showing that we should follow our dreams. 
 Ludy Godbold	She was a role model for future female athletes. 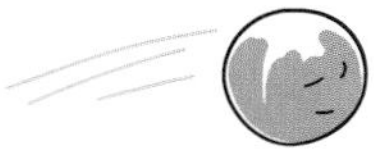

Share

Following independent reading time, gather students in small groups to talk about biographies.

Talk with your group about the ways that the subject of the biography you read has influenced life today.

Extend the Lesson (Optional)

After assessing students' understanding, you might decide to extend the learning.

- Have students fill in a grid (see resources.fountasandpinnell.com) similar to the one in this lesson to compare biographies. They can glue the grid into a reader's notebook.
- **Writing About Reading** Have students research someone who has had an influence on life today and then use a reader's notebook to make an outline for a biography they might write about that person.

Assessment

After you have taught the minilessons in this umbrella, observe students as they talk and write about biographies across instructional contexts: interactive read-aloud, independent reading and literacy work, guided reading, shared reading, and book club. Use *The Literacy Continuum* (Fountas and Pinnell 2017) to observe students' reading and writing behaviors.

- What evidence do you have of new understandings related to biographies?
  - Can students articulate the ways biographies are alike and create a definition of a biography?
  - Are they talking about the reasons a biographer chooses a subject to write about?
  - How well do they understand the decisions an author makes in writing a biography?
  - Can they discuss the influence of society and culture on a subject?
  - Can they identify the ways that a subject's accomplishments have influenced life today?
  - Do they use vocabulary terms such as *biography, biographer, subject, influence,* and *accomplishments*?
- In what other ways, beyond the scope of this umbrella, are students showing an interest in nonfiction genres?
  - Are students reading other types of nonfiction, such as expository nonfiction or persuasive texts?

Use your observations to determine the next umbrella you will teach. You may also consult Minilessons Across the Year (pp. 61–64) for guidance.

Read and Revise

After completing the steps in the genre study process, help students read and revise their definition of the genre based on their new understandings.

- **Before:** A biography is a story about a person written by someone else.
- **After:** A biography is the story of an interesting and often influential person and is written by someone else.

Reader's Notebook

When this umbrella is complete, provide a copy of the minilesson principles (see resources.fountasandpinnell.com) for students to glue in the reader's notebook (in the Minilessons section if using *Reader's Notebook: Advanced* [Fountas and Pinnell 2011]), so they can refer to the information as needed.

Noticing How Nonfiction Authors Choose to Organize Information

Umbrella 17

Minilessons in This Umbrella

RML1	Nonfiction authors tell information in chronological order or temporal order.
RML2	Nonfiction authors organize information into categories and subcategories.
RML3	Nonfiction authors organize information by comparing and contrasting two things.
RML4	Nonfiction authors organize information using cause and effect.
RML5	Nonfiction authors organize information by explaining the problem and solution.
RML6	Nonfiction authors organize information in several ways within the same book.

Before Teaching Umbrella 17 Minilessons

Read and discuss a variety of high-quality, engaging nonfiction books in which the authors have organized information in one or more ways (e.g., sequence, cause and effect, problem and solution). Use the following texts from the *Fountas & Pinnell Classroom™ Interactive Read-Aloud Collection* or choose nonfiction books that are familiar to your students and whose information is organized in different ways.

Genre Study: Expository Nonfiction

Birds: Nature's Magnificent Flying Machines by Caroline Arnold

Giant Squid: Searching for a Sea Monster by Mary Cerullo and Clyde F. E. Roper

The Cod's Tale by Mark Kurlansky

Caring for Our World

One Well: The Story of Water on Earth by Rochelle Strauss

Can We Save the Tiger? by Martin Jenkins

Understanding How Things Work

Skateboards by Patricia Lakin

Titanic: Disaster at Sea by Martin Jenkins

As you read aloud and enjoy these texts together, help students notice the different ways that authors organize information.

Genre Study: Expository Nonfiction

Giant Squid by Mary Cerullo and Clyde F. E. Roper

Caring for Our World

Understanding How Things Work

RML1

LA.U17.RML1

Reading Minilesson Principle

Nonfiction authors tell information in chronological order or temporal order.

Noticing How Nonfiction Authors Choose to Organize Information

You Will Need

- two or three familiar nonfiction books that include information organized in chronological or temporal order, such as the following:
    - *The Cod's Tale* by Mark Kurlansky, from Text Set: Genre Study: Expository Nonfiction
    - *Skateboards* by Patricia Lakin and *Titanic* by Martin Jenkins, from Text Set: Understanding How Things Work
- chart paper and markers

Academic Language / Important Vocabulary

- nonfiction
- author
- organize
- information
- chronological
- temporal

Continuum Connection

- Understand when a writer is telling information in a sequence (chronological order) (p. 74)
- Understand that a writer can tell about something that usually happens in the same order (temporal sequence) and something that happens in time order (chronological order) (p. 74)
- Notice a nonfiction writer's use of temporal and chronological sequence (p. 74)
- Notice language used to show chronological and temporal order (pp. 558, 568, 580)

Goal

Notice nonfiction authors' use of chronological and temporal sequence.

Rationale

When students are aware of chronological order, they better understand how a series of events unfolds over time as well as the relationships between the events. When they notice temporal sequence, they understand that certain processes always follow the same sequence of steps.

Assess Learning

Observe students when they read and talk about nonfiction books and notice if there is evidence of new learning based on the goal of this minilesson.

- Do students notice chronological and temporal sequences in nonfiction books?
- Do they use academic vocabulary, such as *nonfiction, author, organize, information, chronological,* and *temporal*?

Minilesson

To help students think about the minilesson principle, use familiar nonfiction books to engage them in noticing chronological order and temporal order. Here is an example.

- Show the cover of *The Cod's Tale* and read the title. Then read from page 17 (starting from "He left Iceland in about 982") to the end of page 18.

    What do you notice about how the information is organized?

    The author tells what Erik and Leif did in the order they did it. This is called chronological order.

- Record a definition and an example of chronological order on the chart paper.

    Which words in the text helped you figure out that the information is in chronological order?

- Record students' responses on chart paper.
- Show the cover of *Skateboards* and read the title. Then read pages 15–17.

    What does Jake do first? Then what does he do? What does he do after that?

- Record students' responses on the chart.

    What do you notice about how the information on these pages is organized?

    These pages tell the steps Jake follows *every* time he makes a skateboard. This is called a temporal sequence. How is a temporal sequence different from a chronological sequence?

- Write a definition of each type of sequence and add them to the chart.

Have a Try

Invite the students to talk with a partner about how the information is organized in *Titanic*.

- Show pages 24–25 of *Titanic*. Read aloud the headings and times (e.g., "Flooding Begins—11:50 p.m.").

  Turn and talk to your partner about how the information on these pages is organized.

- After students turn and talk, invite a few pairs to share their thinking.

  Is this a chronological or a temporal sequence? How do you know?

Nonfiction authors tell information in chronological order or temporal order.

Order/ Title	Definition	Signal Words	Example
Chronological Order  	Describes a series of events in the order they happened	then after a few years in [year] until	Erik and Leif left Iceland in 982. → They arrived in a new land. → Then they built a colony.
Temporal Order 	Describes the sequence in which something always/usually occurs (such as the steps in a process)	step 1, 2, 3, etc.	Step 1: He chooses strips of wood. Step 2: He examines each strip. Step 3: He sands the strips.

Summarize and Apply

Summarize the learning and remind students to notice how nonfiction books are organized.

What did you notice about how authors organize information in nonfiction books?

- Write the principle at the top of the chart.

  If you read a nonfiction book today, think about how the author organized the information. If you find an example of a chronological or a temporal sequence in your book, bring it to share when we come back together.

Share

Following independent reading time, gather students together in the meeting area to talk about their reading.

Did anyone find an example of a chronological or a temporal sequence today?

How could you tell?

Extend the Lesson (Optional)

After assessing students' understanding, you might decide to extend the learning.

- **Writing About Reading** Have students make a timeline of the events in a book that is organized in chronological order. If they read a book that describes a continuous sequence (such as a life cycle), have them make a cycle diagram.

RML 2

LA.U17.RML2

Reading Minilesson Principle

Nonfiction authors organize information into categories and subcategories.

Noticing How Nonfiction Authors Choose to Organize Information

You Will Need

- two familiar nonfiction books that have information organized into categories and, optionally, subcategories, such as the following:
  - *Birds* by Caroline Arnold, from Text Set: Genre Study: Expository Nonfiction
  - *Skateboards* by Patricia Lakin, from Text Set: Understanding How Things Work
- chart paper and markers

Academic Language / Important Vocabulary

- nonfiction
- author
- organize
- information
- category
- subcategory

Continuum Connection

- Notice information in texts that are organized in categories (p. 73)
- Notice a nonfiction writer's use of categories and subcategories to organize an informational text (expository) (p. 74)

Goal

Notice when nonfiction authors organize information into categories and subcategories.

Rationale

When students notice the organization of information into categories and subcategories, they are able to recognize relationships and make connections between different details. They are also better able to find information in nonfiction books and organize their own nonfiction texts.

Assess Learning

Observe students when they read and talk about nonfiction books and notice if there is evidence of new learning based on the goal of this minilesson.

- Do students notice when the information in a nonfiction book is organized into categories and subcategories?
- Do they use academic vocabulary, such as *nonfiction, author, organize, information, category,* and *subcategory*?

Minilesson

To help students think about the minilesson principle, use familiar nonfiction books to engage them in noticing categories and subcategories of information. Here is an example.

- Show the cover of *Birds* and read the title. Then read page 3.

  What is the topic of this whole book?

  What is the information on this page about?

- Turn to pages 8–9 and read the information under the heading Feathers.

  What is the information in this part of the book about?

  How did the author organize the information in this book?

  The author organized the information into categories, like "why birds fly" and "feathers."

- Point to each of the subheadings on pages 8–9 and read the information underneath them.

  What do you notice about how the author organized information in the category "feathers"?

  The author organized some of the information about feathers into smaller categories, called subcategories.

- Make a chart showing how the information on these pages is divided into categories and subcategories.

Have a Try

Invite the students to talk with a partner about how the information is organized in *Skateboards*.

- Show the cover of *Skateboards*. Read the headings on pages 6, 8, and 10.

  Turn and talk to your partner about how the author of this book organized her information.

- After students turn and talk, invite a few students to share their thinking.

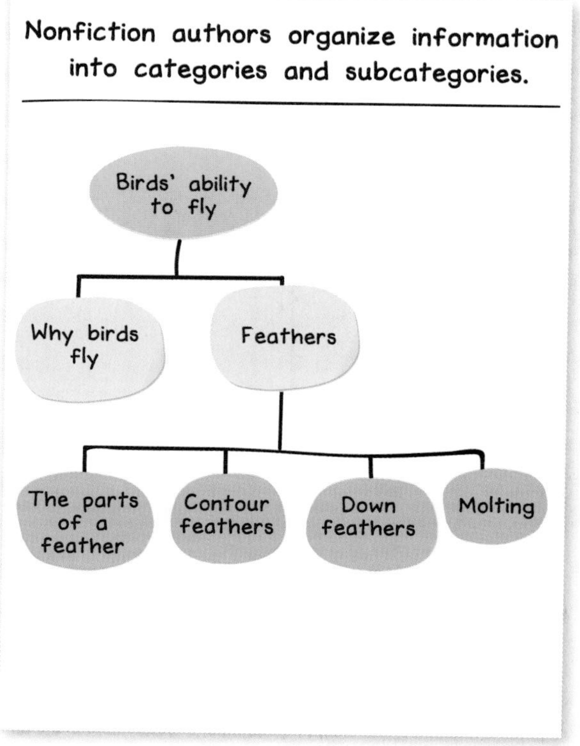

Nonfiction authors organize information into categories and subcategories.

Summarize and Apply

Summarize the learning and remind students to notice how nonfiction books are organized.

What did you notice about how nonfiction authors organize information?

- Write the principle at the top of the chart.

  If you read a nonfiction book today, think about how the author organized the information in your book. If the information in your book is organized into categories and subcategories, bring it to share when we come back together.

Share

Following independent reading time, gather students together in the meeting area to talk about their reading.

Did anyone read a nonfiction book that is organized into categories?

What categories of information were in your book?

Were any of those categories divided into subcategories?

Extend the Lesson (Optional)

After assessing students' understanding, you might decide to extend the learning.

- Teach a minilesson to show how the table of contents reflects the structure of the book (categories, subcategories).
- **Writing About Reading** Have students make or fill in a graphic organizer similar to this lesson's chart (visit resources.fountasandpinnell.com to download a graphic organizer) to show how the information in a nonfiction book is divided into categories and subcategories.

RML 3

LA.U17.RML3

Reading Minilesson Principle

Nonfiction authors organize information by comparing and contrasting two things.

Noticing How Nonfiction Authors Choose to Organize Information

You Will Need

- two familiar nonfiction books that contain examples of compare-and-contrast text structure, such as the following:
  - *Titanic* by Martin Jenkins, from Text Set: Understanding How Things Work
  - *Giant Squid* by Mary Cerullo and Clyde F. E. Roper, from Text Set: Genre Study: Expository Nonfiction
- chart paper and markers

Academic Language / Important Vocabulary

- nonfiction
- author
- organize
- information
- compare
- contrast

Continuum Connection

- Recognize and understand a writer's use of underlying text structures: e.g., description, cause and effect, sequence (chronological, temporal), compare and contrast, problem and solution, question and answer, combination (p. 74)

Goal

Notice when nonfiction authors organize information using a compare-and-contrast structure.

Rationale

When you teach students to recognize compare-and-contrast text structures, they are better able to acquire and understand information about how two things are alike or different. They also understand that nonfiction writers must make decisions about how best to present information.

Assess Learning

Observe students when they read and talk about nonfiction books and notice if there is evidence of new learning based on the goal of this minilesson.

- Do students notice compare-and-contrast structures in nonfiction books?
- Do they recognize words that signal a compare-and-contrast text structure?
- Do they use academic vocabulary, such as *nonfiction, author, organize, information, compare,* and *contrast*?

Minilesson

To help students think about the minilesson principle, use familiar nonfiction books to engage them in noticing compare-and-contrast text structures. Here is an example.

- Show the cover of *Titanic* and read the title. Read aloud the main text on pages 14–15.

  What do you notice about how the author organized information in this part of the book?

  The author compared and contrasted the first-, second-, and third-class passengers on the *Titanic*. What did you learn about how the passenger classes were different?

- Use students' responses to make a chart contrasting the first-, second-, and third-class passengers.

  Sometimes the author uses words to signal that information is being compared or contrasted. Listen for those words.

- Read the first column on the bottom of page 30.

  What other words can you think of that signal a comparison or a contrast?

- Write the words on a second sheet of chart paper.

Have a Try

Invite the students to talk with a partner about how the information is organized in *Giant Squid*.

- Read the information (including the caption) underneath the heading beginning "There is another gigantic squid" on page 30.

  Turn and talk to your partner about how the authors organized the information.

- After students turn and talk, invite a few students to share their thinking.

  Which word in the caption signaled that the authors were comparing and contrasting two things?

Nonfiction authors organize information by comparing and contrasting two things.

First Class	Second Class	Third Class
• Arrived just before the ship set sail • Many sent their luggage and servants in advance. • Many were wealthy Americans returning home.	• 240 passengers • Came on board by a different gangway than the third-class passengers	• Many were emigrants from Scandinavia. • Many were families who were trying to escape poverty. • They were checked by a team of doctors.

Summarize and Apply

Summarize the learning and remind students to notice how nonfiction books are organized.

What did you notice today about how nonfiction authors sometimes organize information?

- Write the principle at the top of the first chart.

  If you read a nonfiction book today, think about how the author organized the information in your book. Bring it to share when we come back together.

Signal Words for Comparing and Contrasting

both
same as
likewise
compared to
similar to
different from
but
however
on the other hand

Share

Following independent reading time, gather students together in the meeting area to talk about their reading.

Did anyone find an example of a compare-and-contrast text structure today?

What did the author of your book compare and contrast?

Extend the Lesson (Optional)

After assessing students' understanding, you might decide to extend the learning.

- **Writing About Reading** Have students make or fill in a Venn diagram (visit resources.fountasandpinnell.com) to show how a nonfiction author compares and contrasts two things. They can glue the diagram into a reader's notebook.

RML4

LA.U17.RML4

Reading Minilesson Principle

Nonfiction authors organize information using cause and effect.

Noticing How Nonfiction Authors Choose to Organize Information

You Will Need

- two familiar nonfiction books that contain examples of cause-and-effect text structure, such as the following:
  - *Titanic* by Martin Jenkins, from Text Set: Understanding How Things Work
  - *Can We Save the Tiger?* by Martin Jenkins, from Text Set: Caring for Our World
- chart paper and markers

Academic Language / Important Vocabulary

- nonfiction
- author
- organize
- information
- cause
- effect

Continuum Connection

- Recognize and understand a writer's use of underlying text structures: e.g., description, cause and effect, sequence (chronological, temporal), compare and contrast, problem and solution, question and answer, combination (p. 74)

Goal

Notice when nonfiction authors organize information using cause and effect.

Rationale

When you teach students to recognize cause-and-effect text structures, they are better able to understand causal relationships. They also understand that nonfiction writers must make decisions about how best to present information.

Assess Learning

Observe students when they read and talk about nonfiction books and notice if there is evidence of new learning based on the goal of this minilesson.

- Do students notice cause-and-effect structures in nonfiction books?
- Do they recognize words that signal a cause-and-effect relationship?
- Do they use academic vocabulary, such as *nonfiction, author, organize, information, cause,* and *effect*?

Minilesson

To help students think about the minilesson principle, use familiar nonfiction books to engage them in noticing cause-and-effect text structures. Here is an example.

- Show the cover of *Titanic* and read the title. Read from the last paragraph on page 29 through the first paragraph on page 30.

  What happened as a result of the *Titanic*'s sinking?

- Record students' responses on chart paper.

  What could you say about how the author organized information in this part of the book?

  The author organized information using cause and effect. He describes a cause–the *Titanic*'s sinking–and the effects of that cause. A cause is something that makes something else happen, and an effect is something that happens because of a cause.

- Reread the first and third sentences on page 30.

  Which words in these sentences signal that the author is describing a cause and its effects?

  What other words can you think of that signal a cause-and-effect relationship?

- Write the words on a second sheet of chart paper.

Have a Try

Invite the students to talk with a partner about how the information is organized in *Can We Save the Tiger?*

- Show the cover of *Can We Save the Tiger?* Read the title and page 20.

  Turn and talk about how the author organized the information on this page.

- After time for discussion, invite a few pairs to share their thinking. Record their responses on the chart.

Summarize and Apply

Summarize the learning and remind students to notice how nonfiction books are organized.

What did you notice today about how nonfiction authors sometimes organize information?

- Write the principle at the top of the first chart.

  If you read a nonfiction book today, think about how the author organized the information in your book. If you find a page or section that is organized using cause and effect, bring it to share when we come back together.

Share

Following independent reading time, gather students together in the meeting area to talk about their reading.

Did anyone find an example of information that is organized using cause and effect? What is the cause and what is the effect?

Extend the Lesson (Optional)

After assessing students' understanding, you might decide to extend the learning.

- Help students understand that something can be both a cause and an effect (if *X* causes *Y*, which then causes *Z*, then *Y* is both a cause and an effect).
- Teach students that one effect can have more than one cause and that one cause can lead to more than one effect.

Nonfiction authors organize information using cause and effect.

Cause (Something that makes something else happen)	Effect (Something that happens because of a cause)
The Titanic sank.	• Ships were fitted with more lifeboats. • Ship designs were modified. • The International Convention for the Safety of Life at Sea was created.
People brought the African land snail to the islands.	• The snails ate people's crops.

Signal Words for Cause and Effect

as a result
due to
so
since
therefore
if . . . then
consequence
led to
because

RML 5

LA.U17.RML5

Reading Minilesson Principle

Nonfiction authors organize information by explaining the problem and solution.

Noticing How Nonfiction Authors Choose to Organize Information

You Will Need

- two familiar nonfiction books that contain examples of a problem-and-solution text structure, such as the following from Text Set: Caring for Our World:
  - *Can We Save the Tiger?* by Martin Jenkins
  - *One Well* by Rochelle Strauss
- chart paper and markers

Academic Language / Important Vocabulary

- nonfiction
- author
- organize
- information
- problem
- solution

Continuum Connection

- Recognize and understand a writer's use of underlying text structures: e.g., description, cause and effect, sequence (chronological, temporal), compare and contrast, problem and solution, question and answer, combination (p. 74)

Goal

Notice when nonfiction authors organize information by explaining the problem and the solution.

Rationale

When you teach students to recognize problem-and-solution text structures, they are better able to acquire and understand information pertaining to problems and solutions. They also understand that nonfiction writers must make decisions about how best to present information.

Assess Learning

Observe students when they read and talk about nonfiction books and notice if there is evidence of new learning based on the goal of this minilesson.

- Do students notice problem-and-solution structures in nonfiction books?
- Do they use academic vocabulary, such as *nonfiction, author, organize, information, problem,* and *solution*?

Minilesson

To help students think about the minilesson principle, use familiar nonfiction books to engage them in noticing problem-and-solution structures. Here is an example.

- Show the cover of *Can We Save the Tiger?* Read the title and page 38.

  What problem did the author describe on this page?

  What was the solution to this problem?

- Write the problem and solution on chart paper.

  How did the author organize information on this page?

  The author organized information by explaining a problem and its solution.

  What words might authors use to let you know that they are writing about a problem and a solution?

- Write the words on a second sheet of chart paper.

Have a Try

Invite the students to talk with a partner about how the information is organized in *One Well.*

- Show the cover of *One Well* and read the title. Read page 26.

  Think about how the author organized information on this page by explaining a problem and its solution. What is the problem and what is the solution? Turn and talk to your partner about this.

- After students turn and talk, invite a few students to share their thinking. Record responses on the chart.

Nonfiction authors organize information by explaining the problem and solution.

PROBLEM	SOLUTION
The American bison was endangered.	• Ranchers started breeding bison. • Governments set up reserves for wild bison.
There is not enough clean water to go around.	• Use less water. • Reduce water pollution.

Summarize and Apply

Summarize the learning and remind students to notice how nonfiction books are organized.

What did you notice today about how nonfiction authors sometimes organize information?

- Write the principle at the top of the first chart.

  If you read a nonfiction book today, think about how the author organized the information in your book. If you find a section in your book that is organized using a problem-and-solution structure, bring it to share when we come back together.

Signal Words for Problem and Solution

problem
solution
question
answer
because
so that
difficulty
resolved
fixed

Share

Following independent reading time, gather students together in the meeting area to talk about their reading.

Did anyone find an example of problem-and-solution organization in the book you read today?

In the book you read, what is the problem and what is the solution?

Extend the Lesson (Optional)

After assessing students' understanding, you might decide to extend the learning.

- Have students write their own nonfiction texts that are organized using a problem-and-solution text structure.

RML 6
LA.U17.RML6

Reading Minilesson Principle
Nonfiction authors organize information in several ways within the same book.

Noticing How Nonfiction Authors Choose to Organize Information

You Will Need

- two familiar nonfiction books that contain multiple text structures, such as the following from Text Set: Understanding How Things Work:
  - *Titanic* by Martin Jenkins
  - *Skateboards* by Patricia Lakin
- chart paper and markers

Academic Language / Important Vocabulary

- organize
- information
- chronological order
- compare and contrast
- cause and effect

Continuum Connection

- Recognize and understand a writer's use of underlying text structures: e.g., description, cause and effect, sequence (chronological order, temporal order), compare and contrast, problem and solution, question and answer, combination (p. 74)

Goal

Understand that sometimes nonfiction authors use several different organizational structures within the same book.

Rationale

When students notice that nonfiction authors sometimes use several different organizational structures within the same book, they understand that nonfiction writers are constantly making decisions about how best to organize information and that different types of information are suited to different structures.

Assess Learning

Observe students when they read and talk about nonfiction books and notice if there is evidence of new learning based on the goal of this minilesson.

- Can students identify multiple organizational structures within a single nonfiction book?
- Do they use academic vocabulary, such as *organize, information, chronological order, compare and contrast,* and *cause and effect*?

Minilesson

To help students think about the minilesson principle, use familiar nonfiction books to engage them in noticing the variety of organizational structures writers use. Here is an example.

- Show the cover of *Titanic*.

  We have been talking about different ways that authors organize information in nonfiction books. What did you notice about how the author of *Titanic* organized his information?

- Record students' responses on chart paper. If necessary, revisit the specific pages that you discussed during previous minilessons (chronological order: pp. 24–25; compare and contrast: pp. 14–15; cause and effect: pp. 29–30) and ask students to notice how the information on these pages is organized.
- Show the cover of *Skateboards*.

  What did you notice about how the author of this book organized information?

- Record students' responses on the chart. Revisit pages 6–10 and 15–17 if necessary.

Have a Try

Invite the students to talk with a partner about how the information is organized in *Skateboards*.

- Read paragraphs 1–4 on page 10 of *Skateboards*.

  What's another way that the author of this book organized information? Turn and talk to your partner about what you noticed.

- After students turn and talk, invite a few students to share their thinking. Add responses to the chart. If needed, help students understand that the author organized the information on this page using a chronological sequence.

Nonfiction authors organize information in several ways within the same book.

	• Chronological order • Compare and contrast • Cause and effect
	• Temporal order • Categories • Chronological order

Summarize and Apply

Summarize the learning and remind students to notice how nonfiction books are organized.

What did you notice today about how nonfiction authors organize information in their books?

- Write the principle at the top of the chart.

  If you read a nonfiction book today, think about all the different ways the author organized the information in your book. Be ready to share your thinking when we come back together.

Share

Following independent reading time, gather students together in the meeting area to talk about their reading.

Who read a nonfiction book today?

In what ways is the information in your book organized?

Extend the Lesson (Optional)

After assessing students' understanding, you might decide to extend the learning.

- Make a list of signal words (see resources.fountasandpinnell.com) to post in the classroom for students to refer to when they are writing nonfiction.
- Have students fill in a graphic organizer (see resources.fountasandpinnell.com) to remind them of the text structures they have learned. They can glue the graphic organizer in a reader's notebook to refer to as needed.

Noticing How Nonfiction Authors Choose to Organize Information

Assessment

After you have taught the minilessons in this umbrella, observe students as they talk and write about their reading across instructional contexts: interactive read-aloud, independent reading, guided reading, shared reading, and book club. Use *The Literacy Continuum* (Fountas and Pinnell 2017) to observe students' reading and writing behaviors.

- What evidence do you have of new understandings related to organizational structures in nonfiction?
- Are students able to identify organizational structures (e.g., chronological, temporal, categories and subcategories, compare and contrast, cause and effect, problem and solution)?
- Do students understand that writers can organize information in multiple ways within the same text?
- Do they use academic language, such as *nonfiction*, *author*, *organize*, *information*, *chronological*, *temporal*, *category*, *compare*, *contrast*, *cause*, and *effect*?
- In what other ways, beyond the scope of this umbrella, are students talking about nonfiction?
    - Have they noticed that there are different genres of nonfiction?
    - Are they thinking about illustrations and graphics?
    - Are they using text features to find and gain information?

Use your observations to determine the next umbrella you will teach. You may also consult Minilessons Across the Year (pp. 61–64) for guidance.

Link to Writing

After teaching the minilessons in this umbrella, help students link the new learning to their own writing:

- Give students various opportunities to write their own nonfiction texts throughout the school year. Remind them of the different ways to organize nonfiction and discuss how to choose the most appropriate organizational structure for the topic.

Reader's Notebook

When this umbrella is complete, provide a copy of the minilesson principles (see resources.fountasandpinnell.com) for students to glue in the reader's notebook (in the Minilessons section if using *Reader's Notebook: Advanced* [Fountas and Pinnell 2011]), so they can refer to the information as needed.

Minilessons in This Umbrella

RML1	Read multiple sources of information about a topic.
RML2	Use multiple sources to answer a bigger question.
RML3	Read primary and secondary sources for information on a topic.
RML4	Notice and evaluate multiple points of view on the same topic.

Before Teaching Umbrella 18 Minilessons

The minilessons in this umbrella teach students how to synthesize information from multiple sources in order to arrive at a deeper understanding of a topic or an idea. Before teaching these minilessons, read and discuss engaging informational texts about a variety of high-interest topics with your students. Use the following texts from the *Fountas & Pinnell Classroom™ Interactive Read-Aloud Collection, Guided Reading Collection*, and *Independent Reading Collection* or choose nonfiction books from your classroom library.

Interactive Read-Aloud Collection

Hope and Resilience

Malala: A Brave Girl from Pakistan / Iqbal: A Brave Boy from Pakistan by Jeanette Winter

Caring for Our World

Rachel Carson and Her Book That Changed the World by Laurie Lawlor

Author Study: Andrea Davis Pinkney

Boycott Blues: How Rosa Parks Inspired a Nation by Andrea Davis Pinkney

Understanding How Things Work

Titanic: Disaster at Sea by Martin Jenkins

Guided Reading Collection

Malala the Brave by Joan Kane Nichols

Independent Reading Collection

Malala Yousafzai: Defender of Education for Girls by Kelly Spence

As you read aloud and enjoy these texts together, help students

- discuss information and big ideas in each text,
- synthesize information from multiple sources, and
- notice the author's point of view about the topic.

Interactive Read-Aloud
Hope and Resilience

Caring for Our World

Author Study: Andrea Davis Pinkney

Boycott Blues by Andrea Davis Pinkney

Understanding How Things Work

Guided Reading

Independent Reading

Section 2: Literary Analysis

RML 1

LA.U18.RML1

Reading Minilesson Principle

Read multiple sources of information about a topic.

Reading and Evaluating Multiple Sources

You Will Need

- three sources of information about a single topic, such as the following:
  - *Malala / Iqbal* by Jeanette Winter, from Text Set: Hope and Resilience
  - *Malala the Brave* by Joan Kane Nichols, from *Guided Reading Collection*
  - *Malala Yousafzai* by Kelly Spence, from *Independent Reading Collection*
- chart paper and markers
- highlighter

Academic Language / Important Vocabulary

- source
- multiple
- information
- topic
- nonfiction

Continuum Connection

- Think across texts to construct knowledge of a topic (p. 74)
- Notice and understand multiple points of view on the same topic (p. 74)
- Notice and evaluate the accuracy of the information presented in the text and across texts (p. 75)

Goal

Think across nonfiction texts to construct knowledge of a topic and to confirm accuracy of topic.

Rationale

When you teach students to read multiple sources of information about a topic, they learn more about the topic and develop their ability to synthesize information and judge its accuracy across sources. They learn that every resource is an incomplete source of information, and they begin to read nonfiction with a more critical eye.

Assess Learning

Observe students when they read and talk about nonfiction books and notice if there is evidence of new learning based on the goal of this minilesson.

- Can students explain why it is important to read multiple sources of information?
- Can they explain how each source added to or confirmed their learning about the topic?
- Do they use academic vocabulary, such as *source, multiple, information, topic,* and *nonfiction*?

Minilesson

To help students think about the minilesson principle, engage them in a discussion about considering multiple sources of information. Here is an example.

- Show the cover of *Malala/Iqbal* (*Malala* side) and read the title. Then read page 13.

  What do you learn about Malala from this page?

- Record students' responses on chart paper.

  Listen carefully as I read from another book about Malala. Think about how the information is the same or different.

- Read page 23 of *Malala the Brave*.

  What do you notice about the information on this page? How is it similar to the information in the other book? What new information do you learn?

- Record responses on the chart.

Have a Try

Invite the students to talk with a partner about how *Malala Yousafzai* adds to or contradicts their knowledge of Malala.

- Show the cover of *Malala Yousafzai* and read the title. Read pages 22–24.

  Turn and talk to your partner about how this source adds to or contradicts your learning about Malala.

- After students turn and talk, invite a few students to share their thinking. Record responses on the chart.

Read multiple sources of information about a topic.

Source	Information
Source 1: Malala/Iqbal	• Malala gave a speech on her 16th birthday. • She said, "One child, one teacher, one book, one pen, can change the world."
Source 2: Malala the Brave	• Malala gave a speech on her 16th birthday at the United Nations. • She said, "One child, one teacher, one book, one pen, can change the world." • There are more details about what she said in her speech.
Source 3: Malala Yousafzai	• Malala gave a speech on her 16th birthday at the United Nations in New York City. • She said, "One child, one teacher, one book, one pen, can change the world." • 400 people listened to her speech. • There are details about how Malala made a difference after her speech.

Summarize and Apply

Summarize the learning and remind students to read multiple sources of information.

What information is the same in all three books?

- Highlight the common information and point out that additional sources can provide more information.

  Reading multiple sources helps you gain an accurate and more complete understanding of the topic.

- Write the principle at the top of the chart.

  If you read a nonfiction book today, think about whether you'd like to learn more about the topic or confirm the information by reading additional sources. If so, look for another source of information about the topic. Ask me for help if you need it.

Share

Following independent reading time, gather students together in the meeting area to talk about reading multiple sources on the same topic.

Who found multiple sources of information about a topic today?

How did reading multiple sources add to or confirm your learning?

Extend the Lesson (Optional)

After assessing students' understanding, you might decide to extend the learning.

- Help students compare and contrast two sources of information about a topic. Discuss why the authors may have made different choices about what information to include or how to present it.

RML 2
LA.U18.RML2

Reading Minilesson Principle
Use multiple sources to answer a bigger question.

Reading and Evaluating Multiple Sources

You Will Need

- three nonfiction sources centered around a single topic or theme, such as the following:
  - *Malala / Iqbal* by Jeanette Winter, from Text Set: Hope and Resilience
  - *Rachel Carson and Her Book That Changed the World* by Laurie Lawlor, from Text Set: Caring for Our World
  - *Boycott Blues* by Andrea Davis Pinkney, from Text Set: Author Study: Andrea Davis Pinkney
- chart paper prepared with a research question about the sources listed above (e.g., *How can one person change the world?*)
- several other research questions and a collection of relevant sources for each one (see Summarize and Apply)
- markers

Academic Language / Important Vocabulary

- source
- nonfiction

Continuum Connection

- Think across texts to compare and expand understanding of content and ideas from academic disciplines: e.g., social responsibility, environment, climate, history, social and geological history, cultural groups (p. 74)

Goal

Use multiple sources of information to answer a research question.

Rationale

When you teach students to use multiple sources to answer a bigger question, they gain the ability to read nonfiction purposefully. They also develop the understanding that different nonfiction writers may approach the same theme or topic from different angles and that reading multiple sources promotes a more complete understanding of the theme or topic.

Assess Learning

Observe students when they read and talk about nonfiction books and notice if there is evidence of new learning based on the goal of this minilesson.

- Do students read multiple sources when they are trying to answer a research question?
- Can they explain how each source helps them answer the question?
- Do they use academic vocabulary, such as *source* and *nonfiction*?

Minilesson

To help students think about the minilesson principle, use familiar nonfiction books to engage them in thinking about how to use multiple sources to answer a bigger question. Here is an example.

Sometimes when you read multiple sources about a theme or topic, you may have a big question that you want to answer. Think about the question on the chart as I reread a couple of pages from *Malala / Iqbal*.

- Reread pages 12–13 of *Malala / Iqbal* (*Malala* side).

How does this book help you answer our question? What does it teach you about how one person can change the world?

- Record students' responses on chart paper.
- Show the cover of *Rachel Carson and Her Book That Changed the World* and read the title. Briefly flip through its pages to remind students of its content.

What does this book help you understand about how one person can change the world?

- Record responses on the chart.

Even though these two books are about different people, they both contribute an answer to our question.

Have a Try

Invite the students to talk with a partner about *Boycott Blues.*

- Show the cover of *Boycott Blues* and read the title. Then read pages 7–10.

  Turn and talk to your partner about how this source helps you answer our big question.

- After students turn and talk, invite a few pairs to share their thinking. Record responses on the chart.

  What can we conclude about how one person can change the world?

- Combine students' responses to create an agreed-upon class answer. Record it on the chart.

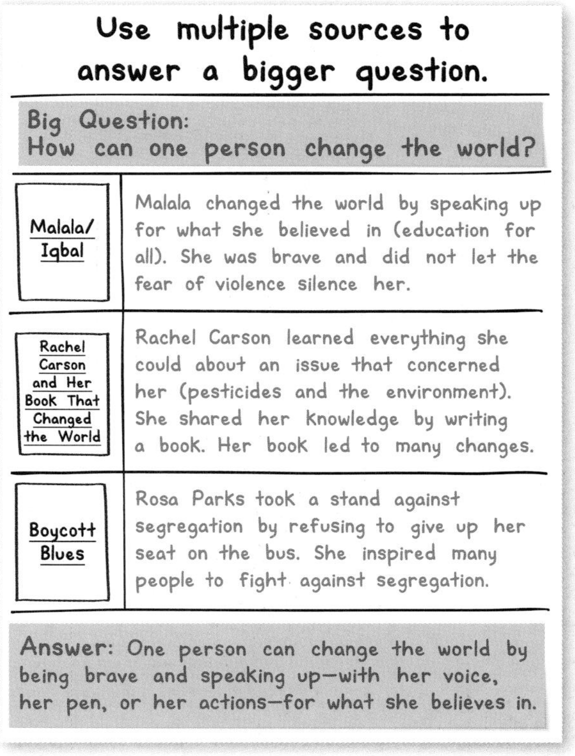

Use multiple sources to answer a bigger question.

Big Question: How can one person change the world?

Source	Notes
Malala/ Iqbal	Malala changed the world by speaking up for what she believed in (education for all). She was brave and did not let the fear of violence silence her.
Rachel Carson and Her Book That Changed the World	Rachel Carson learned everything she could about an issue that concerned her (pesticides and the environment). She shared her knowledge by writing a book. Her book led to many changes.
Boycott Blues	Rosa Parks took a stand against segregation by refusing to give up her seat on the bus. She inspired many people to fight against segregation.

Answer: One person can change the world by being brave and speaking up—with her voice, her pen, or her actions—for what she believes in.

Summarize and Apply

Summarize the learning for students.

How can using multiple sources help you answer a bigger question?

- Display a sheet of chart paper that lists several bigger questions. For example: *How can people work together to create change? How do people overcome adversity? How can we protect our planet? What rights and responsibilities do we have as citizens?* Provide a basket of resources to support each question.

  When you read today, think about one of these questions and read multiple sources to help you answer it. You can also come up with your own question and find your own sources.

Share

Following independent reading time, gather students together in the meeting area to talk about their reading.

What question did you think about today? How did reading multiple sources help you answer it?

Extend the Lesson (Optional)

After assessing students' understanding, you might decide to extend the learning.

- Have students write a research paper or an informational article. Have them define a research question. Then walk them through finding relevant sources, reading them and taking notes, organizing their information, and writing and editing.

RML 3

LA.U18.RML3

Reading Minilesson Principle

Read primary and secondary sources for information on a topic.

Reading and Evaluating Multiple Sources

You Will Need

- two or three familiar nonfiction books that contain examples of primary sources (e.g., photographs, journal entries, letters), such as the following:
    - *Malala the Brave* by Joan Kane Nichols, from *Guided Reading Collection*
    - *Titanic* by Martin Jenkins, from Text Set: Understanding How Things Work
- chart paper and markers

Academic Language / Important Vocabulary

- primary source
- secondary source
- information
- topic

Continuum Connection

- Notice primary and secondary sources of information when embedded in a text (p. 74)

Goal

Notice and use primary and secondary sources of information to learn about a topic.

Rationale

Studying primary sources allows students to engage directly with artifacts from the past and helps them develop critical thinking skills. Understanding the difference between primary and secondary sources helps students realize that the study of history reflects interpretations of past events and that those interpretations are constructed through the study and analysis of primary sources.

Assess Learning

Observe students when they read and talk about nonfiction books and notice if there is evidence of new learning based on the goal of this minilesson.

- Can students explain what primary and secondary sources are?
- Do they use academic vocabulary, such as *primary source, secondary source, information,* and *topic*?

Minilesson

To help students think about the minilesson principle, use familiar nonfiction books to discuss primary and secondary sources. Here is an example.

- Show the cover of *Malala the Brave* and read the title. Read the last paragraph on page 13 and the first paragraph on page 14. Then read the journal entry at the top of page 14.

    What do you notice about this part of the page?

    This is an actual entry that Malala wrote in her online diary. This journal entry is an example of a primary source. Does anyone know what a primary source is?

    A primary source is something written or recorded by someone who was directly involved in or witnessed a historical event. A journal entry is one example. What is the other primary source on this page?

    Photographs are also primary sources because they were taken by someone who was present at the event. What is another example of a primary source?

- Record students' responses on chart paper. If needed, offer a few more examples.

    Most of this book–all the parts that were written by the author, Joan Kane Nichols–is a secondary source. What do you think a secondary source is?

    A secondary source is written by someone who was not directly involved in the event. What are some examples of secondary sources?

- Record responses on the chart.

Have a Try

Invite the students to talk with a partner about *Titanic*.

- Show the cover and read the title. Then read the first section of page 20.

  Turn and talk to your partner about the primary and secondary sources on this page. What's a primary source, and what's a secondary source? How can you tell?

- After students turn and talk, invite a few students to share their thinking.

Read primary and secondary sources for information on a topic.

PRIMARY SOURCE	SECONDARY SOURCE
Written or recorded by someone who witnessed a historical event	Written by someone who did <u>not</u> witness the event
Examples: • Journal entries • Photographs • Letters • Interviews • Videos • Speeches • Memoirs/ autobiographies	Examples: • History books • Textbooks • News articles • Movies
 SATURDAY 3 JANUARY: I AM AFRAID "I had a terrible dream yesterday with military helicopters and the Taliban. I have had such dreams..."	Malala's first entry was called "I Am Afraid." In it, she told about her nightmares, about looking over her shoulder...

Summarize and Apply

Summarize the learning and remind students to read both primary and secondary sources.

- Write the principle at the top of the chart.

  Why is it important to read both primary and secondary sources when you research a historical topic?

  If you read a nonfiction book today, notice if your book includes any primary sources. If so, bring your book to share when we come back together.

Share

Following independent reading time, gather students together in the meeting area to talk about their reading.

Who found an example of a primary source in the book you read today?

What did the primary source help you understand about the topic?

Extend the Lesson (Optional)

After assessing students' understanding, you might decide to extend the learning.

- Discuss the benefits and drawbacks of both primary and secondary sources.
- When students write informational texts about historical events, encourage them to reference both primary and secondary sources. Help them find relevant, appropriate sources of each type. The Library of Congress is a good resource for primary sources.

RML 4

LA.U18.RML4

Reading Minilesson Principle

Notice and evaluate multiple points of view on the same topic.

Reading and Evaluating Multiple Sources

You Will Need

- two or three news articles (not editorials/opinion pieces) about the same event or topic from different sources; there should be clear differences in how the articles approach the subject, and at least one of them should contain evidence of a particular point of view (bias)
- chart paper and markers
- document camera (optional)
- sticky notes

Academic Language / Important Vocabulary

- sources
- point of view
- bias
- evaluate

Continuum Connection

- Relate important information and concepts in one text and connect to information and concepts in other texts (p. 73)

Goal

Notice and evaluate multiple sources for differing points of view.

Rationale

Teaching students how to recognize that every author has a point of view helps them understand that works of nonfiction, although based in fact, are not necessarily entirely objective and are influenced by the writer's background and attitude. This underscores the importance of reading multiple sources to gain a more complete understanding of a topic, event, or issue.

Assess Learning

Observe students when they read and talk about nonfiction and notice if there is evidence of new learning based on the goal of this minilesson.

- Do students understand that every author has a point of view?
- Do they use academic vocabulary, such as *sources, point of view, bias,* and *evaluate*?

Minilesson

To help students think about the minilesson principle, use news articles to help them notice and discuss varying points of view. Here is an example.

- Display side by side two of the articles you chose before class. Read them aloud.

  How do you think each author feels about the topic? How can you tell?

  The way an author feels about a topic is called a point of view. An author's point of view can influence how or what the author writes about the topic.

- Draw students' attention to evidence of the author's point of view, perhaps using the following prompts:
  - *What details are in one article but not in the other?*
  - *What do the titles reveal about how the authors feel about their topics?*
  - *What do you notice about the words the authors use to describe their topics? Are they positive or negative words?*
  - *What do you notice about the photos included with the articles?*
- Record students' responses on the chart.

  Sometimes an author has a strong point of view, which is reflected by the way the author writes. This is called bias. Be sure to get a balanced view of a topic by reading more than one source about it.

Have a Try

Invite the students to talk with a partner about how to evaluate an author's point of view.

Think about the discussion we just had. Turn and talk to your partner about some questions you can ask yourself to find out how an author feels about a topic?

- After time for discussion, create a chart of questions to guide students in determining bias in an article. Write the principle at the top.

Notice and evaluate multiple points of view on the same topic.

- Are certain details included or left out?
- Does the headline or title contain clues about how the writer feels about the topic?
- Does the author's choice of words reveal how he or she feels about the topic? (For example, "They took the diamond" vs. "They stole the diamond")
- What do you notice about the way the sentences are formed? (For example, "He made a mistake" vs. "Mistakes were made")
- What do you notice about the photographs? Do they show a person in a positive or negative way?

Summarize and Apply

Summarize the learning and remind students to evaluate sources for bias.

Why is it important to get more than one point of view when you read about a topic?

If you read a nonfiction book or article today, notice whether the author seems to have a particular point of view about or bias for or against someone or something. Make a note of any evidence of bias that you find, and be ready to share your thinking when we come back together.

Share

Following independent reading time, gather students together in the meeting area to talk about their reading.

Did anyone find any examples of bias today?

What examples did you find? What do those examples show about how the author feels about the topic?

Extend the Lesson (Optional)

After assessing students' understanding, you might decide to extend the learning.

- Discuss pairs of words with positive and negative connotations (e.g., *unique/strange, confident/arrogant, reached for/grabbed, in charge/pushy*). Help students notice how word choice reveals clues about a writer's point of view about a person or topic.

Assessment

After you have taught the minilessons in this umbrella, observe students as they talk and write about their reading across instructional contexts: interactive read-aloud, independent reading, guided reading, shared reading, and book club. Use *The Literacy Continuum* (Fountas and Pinnell 2017) to observe students' reading and writing behaviors.

- What evidence do you have of new understandings related to reading and evaluating multiple sources?
  - Do students understand why it's important to read multiple sources of information about a topic?
  - Do they read both primary and secondary sources, and can they differentiate between them?
  - Are they able to evaluate sources for bias?
  - Do they use terms such as *source, information, topic, bias*, and *evaluate*?
- In what other ways, beyond the scope of this umbrella, are students talking about nonfiction books?
  - Are they noticing different organizational structures in nonfiction?
  - Are they using text features to gain information?

Use your observations to determine the next umbrella you will teach. You may also consult Minilessons Across the Year (pp. 61–64) for guidance.

Link to Writing

After teaching the minilessons in this umbrella, help students link the new learning to their own writing:

- Remind students to read and evaluate multiple sources when they conduct research for writing their own informational texts. Encourage them to include both primary and secondary sources in their research, and remind them to evaluate the sources they use for bias.

Reader's Notebook

When this umbrella is complete, provide a copy of the minilesson principles (see resources.fountasandpinnell.com) for students to glue in the reader's notebook (in the Minilessons section if using *Reader's Notebook: Advanced* [Fountas and Pinnell 2011]), so they can refer to the information as needed.

Minilessons in This Umbrella

RML1	Authors use illustrations and graphics to help you understand bigger ideas.
RML2	Authors use infographics to show several kinds of information in a clear and interesting way.
RML3	The graphics and print are carefully placed in a nonfiction text to communicate ideas clearly.

Before Teaching Umbrella 19 Minilessons

Read and discuss high-quality, engaging nonfiction picture books that include illustrations and a variety of graphics, such as photographs, maps, diagrams, and infographics. Use the following books from the *Fountas & Pinnell Classroom™ Interactive Read-Aloud Collection* and *Guided Reading Collection* or choose nonfiction books with clear illustrations and graphics from your classroom library.

Interactive Read-Aloud Collection

Genre Study: Expository Nonfiction

Birds: Nature's Magnificent Flying Machines by Caroline Arnold

Giant Squid: Searching for a Sea Monster by Mary Cerullo and Clyde F. E. Roper

The Story of Salt by Mark Kurlansky

Understanding How Things Work

Mr. Ferris and His Wheel by Kathryn Gibbs Davis

Skateboards by Patricia Lakin

Titanic: Disaster at Sea by Martin Jenkins

Caring for Our World

One Well: The Story of Water on Earth by Rochelle Strauss

Guided Reading Collection

Dangerous Waters by Jacqueline Adams

As you read aloud and enjoy these texts together, help students

- notice and discuss illustrations and graphics and
- understand information and ideas conveyed through graphics.

Interactive Read-Aloud
Genre Study: Expository Nonfiction

Giant Squid by Mary Cerullo and Clyde F. E. Roper

Understanding How Things Work

Caring for Our World

Guided Reading

RML1

LA.U19.RML1

Reading Minilesson Principle

Authors use illustrations and graphics to help you understand bigger ideas.

Learning Information from Illustrations and Graphics

You Will Need

- two or three familiar nonfiction books that contain illustrations and graphics that help communicate bigger ideas and messages, such as the following:
  - *Birds* by Caroline Arnold, from Text Set: Genre Study: Expository Nonfiction
  - *Mr. Ferris and His Wheel* by Kathryn Gibbs Davis and *Titanic* by Martin Jenkins, from Text Set: Understanding How Things Work
- chart paper and markers

Academic Language / Important Vocabulary

- illustration
- graphic
- diagram
- graph
- nonfiction
- author

Continuum Connection

- Notice how illustrations and graphics help to communicate the writer's message (p. 75)

Goal

Understand that authors use graphics to help you understand bigger ideas and messages.

Rationale

Nonfiction authors use illustrations and graphics—such as diagrams, charts, and maps—to convey information visually and help communicate big ideas. When students understand how to acquire information from graphics in nonfiction books, they are better able to understand the author's big ideas or central messages.

Assess Learning

Observe students when they read and talk about nonfiction books and notice if there is evidence of new learning based on the goal of this minilesson.

- Can students explain how an illustration or graphic helps communicate a bigger idea?
- Do they use academic vocabulary, such as *illustration, graphic, diagram, graph, nonfiction,* and *author*?

Minilesson

To help students think about the minilesson principle, use familiar nonfiction books to engage them in a discussion about illustrations and graphics. Here is an example.

- Show the cover of *Birds*. Read the title and pages 4–5.

  What do you notice about the graphics, or images, on these pages?

  The graphic on the left is a diagram. A diagram shows the parts of something or how something works. What does this diagram show?

- Record students' responses on chart paper.

  The illustrations and the diagram on these pages show different parts inside a bird's body. Why do you think the author included these graphics?

  The author showed you not only what a bird's body looks like inside but how that body helps a bird fly.

- Record students' responses on the chart.
- Show the cover of *Mr. Ferris and His Wheel* and read the title. Read the caption for the water wheel on page 20 and display the illustration.

  What does this illustration show?

  What big idea about Mr. Ferris' thought process does the illustration help you understand?

- Record students' responses on the chart.

Have a Try

Invite the students to talk with a partner about *Titanic*.

- Show page 30 of *Titanic*. Read the "Survivors of the Titanic Disaster" sidebar. Show the graph and read and point to all of the numbers and labels.

  What kind of graphic is it? What big idea does it help you understand? Turn and talk to your partner about this.

- After students turn and talk, invite a few pairs to share their thinking. Record responses on the chart.

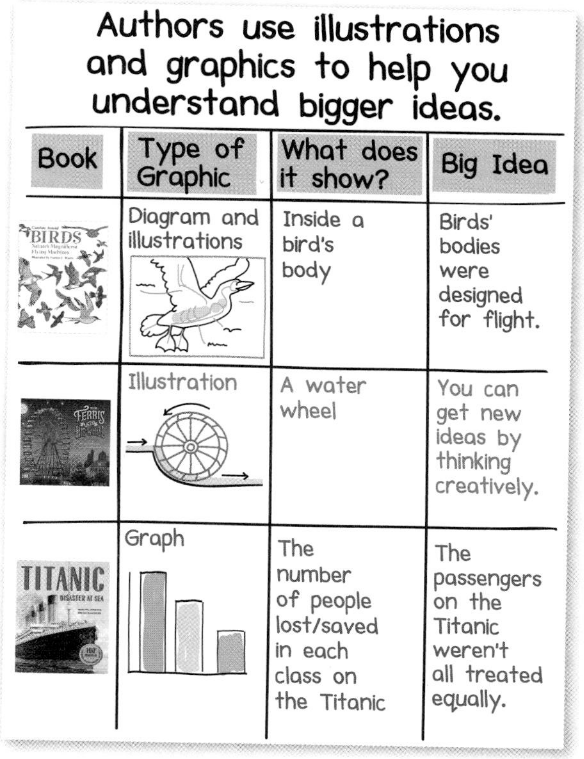

Authors use illustrations and graphics to help you understand bigger ideas.

Book	Type of Graphic	What does it show?	Big Idea
BIRDS	Diagram and illustrations	Inside a bird's body	Birds' bodies were designed for flight.
FERRIS	Illustration	A water wheel	You can get new ideas by thinking creatively.
TITANIC	Graph	The number of people lost/saved in each class on the Titanic	The passengers on the Titanic weren't all treated equally.

Summarize and Apply

Summarize the learning and remind students to notice illustrations and graphics in nonfiction books.

What did you learn about the reason nonfiction authors use illustrations and graphics?

Nonfiction authors often use illustrations and graphics to help you understand bigger ideas.

- Write the principle at the top of the chart.

  If you read a nonfiction book today, remember to notice, read, and think about the illustrations and graphics. If you find an example of a graphic that helps you understand a bigger idea, bring your book to share when we come back together.

Share

Following independent reading time, gather students together in the meeting area to talk about their reading.

Who found an example of an illustration or graphic that helped you understand a bigger idea?

What bigger idea did the graphic help you understand?

Extend the Lesson (Optional)

After assessing students' understanding, you might decide to extend the learning.

- When you read a nonfiction book with an interesting illustration or graphic during interactive read-aloud, discuss how it helps communicate a bigger idea.

RML2

LA.U19.RML2

Reading Minilesson Principle

Authors use infographics to show several kinds of information in a clear and interesting way.

Learning Information from Illustrations and Graphics

You Will Need

- two familiar nonfiction books that contain infographics, such as the following:
  - *Dangerous Waters* by Jacqueline Adams, from *Guided Reading Collection*
  - *One Well* by Rochelle Strauss, from Text Set: Caring for Our World
- chart paper and markers
- sticky notes
- document camera (optional)

Academic Language / Important Vocabulary

- infographic
- information
- nonfiction
- graphic
- author

Continuum Connection

- Understand that graphics provide important information (p. 75)
- Recognize and use information in a variety of graphics: e.g., photo and/or drawing with label or caption, diagram, cutaway, map with legend and scale, infographic (p. 75)

Goal

Understand that authors use infographics to show patterns and trends.

Rationale

In today's digital age, infographics are used more and more frequently to convey complex information in a clear and eye-catching way, both on websites and in print publications. When you teach students how to read infographics, they are better prepared to acquire information from the many infographics that they will inevitably encounter.

Assess Learning

Observe students when they read and talk about infographics and notice if there is evidence of new learning based on the goal of this minilesson.

- Do students notice and read infographics?
- Can they explain what they learned from an infographic?
- Do they use academic vocabulary, such as *infographic, information, nonfiction, graphic,* and *author*?

Minilesson

To help students think about the minilesson principle, help them notice the important information in infographics. Here is an example.

- Display the infographic from pages 6–7 of *Dangerous Waters*.

  What do you notice about this graphic?

- Read the text aloud, pointing to each text element as you read it.

  What did you notice about how I read this graphic? Where did I start?

  What idea does it help communicate?

  This is an infographic. How do the parts of the word help us know what it means? Let's look at the first part, *info*. What does *info* mean?

  Now let's look at the second part, *graphic*. What does *graphic* mean?

  Why do you think authors use infographics in their books?

- With students' input, label the different parts of the infographic.

Have a Try

Invite the students to talk with a partner about another infographic.

- Display the infographic from page 21 of *One Well*.

  Think about this infographic with your partner. Turn and talk about what you notice about this infographic and what you learned from it.

- After students turn and talk, invite a few pairs to share their thinking. Ask how they read the infographic, what they noticed about how the infographic displays information, and what they learned from it.

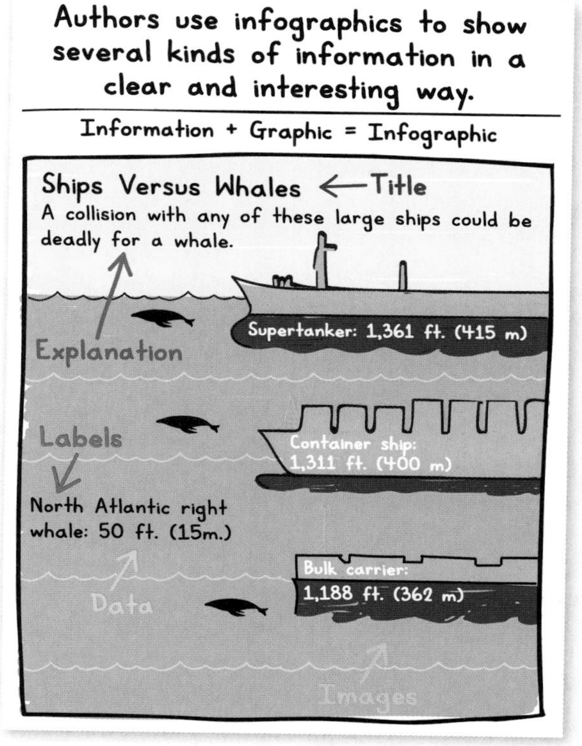

Authors use infographics to show several kinds of information in a clear and interesting way.

Information + Graphic = Infographic

Ships Versus Whales ←Title
A collision with any of these large ships could be deadly for a whale.
Explanation
Supertanker: 1,361 ft. (415 m)
Labels
Container ship: 1,311 ft. (400 m)
North Atlantic right whale: 50 ft. (15m.)
Data
Bulk carrier: 1,188 ft. (362 m)
Images

Summarize and Apply

Summarize the learning and remind students to read and think about infographics.

What did you learn about infographics today?

Why do you think authors use infographics? Why are they helpful?

- Write the principle at the top of the chart.

  If you read a nonfiction book today, notice if it has any infographics. If it does, be sure to look closely at them and think about all of the information they provide. If you find an example of an infographic, bring it to share when we come back together.

Share

Following independent reading time, gather students together in the meeting area to talk about their reading.

Who found an example of an infographic today?

- Form a small group around each student that found an infographic. Ask the students to share the information conveyed by the infographic.

Extend the Lesson (Optional)

After assessing students' understanding, you might decide to extend the learning.

- Find infographics that are engaging to and appropriate for your class and glue them on a chart so students can use them as models as they work in pairs or small groups to make their own infographics to convey information in their nonfiction writing about a science or social studies topic.

RML 3

LA.U19.RML3

Reading Minilesson Principle

The graphics and print are carefully placed in a nonfiction text to communicate ideas clearly.

Learning Information from Illustrations and Graphics

You Will Need

- two or three familiar nonfiction books that have pages with multiple graphics and text elements, such as the following:
  - *Giant Squid* by Mary Cerullo and Clyde F. E. Roper and *The Story of Salt* by Mark Kurlansky, from Text Set: Genre Study: Expository Nonfiction
  - *Skateboards* by Patricia Lakin, from Text Set: Understanding How Things Work
- chart paper and markers

Academic Language / Important Vocabulary

- graphics
- text
- nonfiction
- placed
- communicate

Continuum Connection

- Understand that graphics and text are carefully placed in a nonfiction text so that ideas are communicated clearly (p. 75)

Goal

Understand that graphics and print are carefully placed in a nonfiction text so that ideas are communicated clearly.

Rationale

When students think about how the graphics and print are placed in nonfiction books, they understand that they work together to communicate ideas. They also understand that people who work on creating books (e.g., editors, designers) need to make decisions about how best to place the graphics and the print.

Assess Learning

Observe students when they read and talk about nonfiction books and notice if there is evidence of new learning based on the goal of this minilesson.

- Can students infer why the graphics and print are placed on the page in a certain way?
- Do they use vocabulary such as *graphics, text, nonfiction, placed,* and *communicate*?

Minilesson

To help students think about the minilesson principle, engage them in a discussion about the placement of graphics and print. Here is an example.

- Show the cover of *Giant Squid* and read the title. Display pages 16–17 and read the text aloud, pointing to each section as you read it.

  What do you notice about how the graphics and the print are placed, or arranged, on these pages?

- As needed, prompt the conversation with further questions such as the following:
  - *Why is a squid's tail placed above the section titled "Ocean Detective on the Chase"?*
  - *Why is the print in this section shaped like a question mark? Why is there a magnifying glass? Why is the background in this section black?*
  - *Why is the print that says "ARCHITEUTHIS 'The Chief Squid'" placed here?*
- Show the cover of *The Story of Salt* and read the title. Read and display page 7.

  What do you notice about how the graphics and print are placed on this page?

  Why do you think they are placed in this way?

Have a Try

Invite the students to talk with a partner about the placement of graphics and text in *Skateboards*.

- Show the cover of *Skateboards* and read the title. Then read and display pages 22–23.

    Turn and talk to your partner about what you notice about how the graphics and print are placed on these pages. Why do you think they are placed in this way?

- After students turn and talk, invite a few pairs to share their thinking.

Summarize and Apply

Summarize the learning and remind students to notice the placement of graphics and print in nonfiction books.

> What did you notice today about the placement of the graphics and text in nonfiction books?

- Record students' responses on chart paper and write the principle at the top of the chart.

    If you read a nonfiction book today, notice how the graphics and text are placed on the pages, and think about why they might be placed in that way. If you find a page that has the graphics and print placed in an interesting way, bring your example to share when we come back together.

The graphics and print are carefully placed in a nonfiction text to communicate ideas clearly.

- Graphics are placed near the print that they relate to.

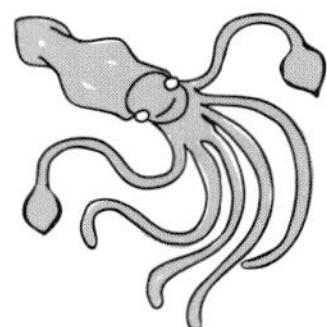

Words about a squid would be placed near a picture of a squid.

- The print may be placed in a certain shape to communicate an idea.

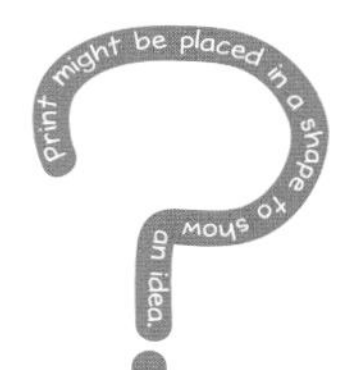

Print might be placed in a shape to show an idea.

- The graphics may be placed in a certain order to indicate a process or sequence.

Share

Following independent reading time, gather students together in the meeting area to talk about their reading.

> Did anyone find an example of a page in a nonfiction book that has the graphics and print placed in an interesting way?
>
> Why do you think the graphics and print are placed in that way?

Extend the Lesson (Optional)

After assessing students' understanding, you might decide to extend the learning.

- When students write their own nonfiction texts, encourage them to think about how best to place the print and graphics on a page. Teach them how to place graphics and print in interesting ways using word-processing or page-layout software.

Assessment

After you have taught the minilessons in this umbrella, observe students as they talk and write about their reading across instructional contexts: interactive read-aloud, independent reading, guided reading, shared reading, and book club. Use *The Literacy Continuum* (Fountas and Pinnell 2017) to observe students' reading and writing behaviors.

- What evidence do you have of new understandings related to learning information from illustrations and graphics?
  - Do students talk about what they learned from illustrations and other graphics in nonfiction books?
  - Can they explain how a graphic can communicate a bigger idea?
  - Do they know how to read infographics?
  - Can they infer why the graphics and print are placed a certain way?
  - Do they use academic language, such as *illustration, photograph, graphic, author, illustrator, diagram,* and *infographic*?
- In what other ways, beyond the scope of this umbrella, are students talking about nonfiction?
  - Have they noticed that there are different genres of nonfiction?
  - Are they noticing different ways that nonfiction authors organize information?

Use your observations to determine the next umbrella you will teach. You may also consult Minilessons Across the Year (pp. 61–64) for guidance.

Link to Writing

After teaching the minilessons in this umbrella, help students link the new learning to their own writing:

- Give students numerous opportunities to write their own nonfiction texts. Let them decide whether to include illustrations, photographs, infographics, or other types of graphics, and help them find or create relevant images. Remind them to use graphics that help the reader understand bigger ideas and to think about how to place the images on the page.

Reader's Notebook

When this umbrella is complete, provide a copy of the minilesson principles (see resources.fountasandpinnell.com) for students to glue in the reader's notebook (in the Minilessons section if using *Reader's Notebook: Advanced* [Fountas and Pinnell 2011]), so they can refer to the information as needed.

Minilessons in This Umbrella

RML1	Authors use headings and subheadings to help you understand the category of information.
RML2	Authors and illustrators use sidebars to emphasize or give additional information.
RML3	Authors include a table of contents and an index to help you find information.
RML4	Authors include a bibliography to show the resources used to find information for the book.

Before Teaching Umbrella 20 Minilessons

Before teaching this umbrella, you might find it helpful to teach Umbrella 14: Studying Expository Nonfiction and Umbrella 17: Noticing How Nonfiction Authors Choose to Organize Information. Additionally, be sure to read aloud and discuss a number of engaging, high-quality nonfiction books that include a variety of text and organizational features, such as headings and subheadings, sidebars, tables of contents, indexes, and bibliographies. Use the suggested examples from the *Fountas & Pinnell Classroom™ Interactive Read-Aloud Collection* and *Independent Reading Collection* or choose nonfiction books from your classroom library that have text and organizational features.

Interactive Read-Aloud Collection

Understanding How Things Work

Mr. Ferris and His Wheel by Kathryn Gibbs Davis

Titanic: Disaster at Sea by Martin Jenkins

Caring for Our World

One Well: The Story of Water on Earth by Rochelle Strauss

Genre Study: Expository Nonfiction

Giant Squid: Searching for a Sea Monster by Mary M. Cerullo and Clyde F. E. Roper

The Story of Salt by Mark Kurlansky

Independent Reading Collection

The Sinking of the Titanic by Matt Doeden

As you read aloud and enjoy these texts together, help students

- discuss the main idea of each page or section, and
- notice and use text features and organizational tools, such as headings and subheadings, sidebars, tables of contents, indexes, and bibliographies.

Interactive Read-Aloud

Understanding How Things Work

Caring for Our World

Genre Study: Expository Nonfiction

Giant Squid by Mary Cerullo and Clyde F. E. Roper

Independent Reading

RML1

LA.U20.RML1

Reading Minilesson Principle

Authors use headings and subheadings to help you understand the category of information.

Using Text Features to Gain Information

You Will Need

- two familiar nonfiction books that have headings, including at least one that has subheadings, such as the following:
  - *One Well* by Rochelle Strauss, from Text Set: Caring for Our World
  - *Giant Squid* by Mary M. Cerullo and Clyde F. E. Roper, from Text Set: Genre Study: Expository Nonfiction
- chart paper and markers
- document camera (optional)

Academic Language / Important Vocabulary

- nonfiction
- heading
- subheading
- category
- subcategory
- information

Continuum Connection

- Notice and use and understand the purpose of some organizational tools: e.g., title, table of contents, chapter title, heading, subheading (p. 75)

Goal

Notice, use, and understand the purpose of headings and subheadings.

Rationale

When students notice and read headings and subheadings, they know what the upcoming section will be about and are better prepared for the information they will encounter because they can call on related information they already know. Using the headings and subheadings may also help them consider how the author has organized the information.

Assess Learning

Observe students when they read and talk about nonfiction books and notice if there is evidence of new learning based on the goal of this minilesson.

- Can they describe the purpose of and physical differences between headings, subheadings, and body text (font size, color, capital letters, etc.)?
- Do they use academic language, such as *nonfiction, heading, subheading, category, subcategory,* and *information*?

Minilesson

To help students think about the minilesson principle, use familiar nonfiction texts to help students notice and discuss headings and subheadings. Here is an example.

- Display page 11 of *One Well*, using a document camera if possible. Point to the heading.

  How is the print at the top of the page different from the rest of the print on the page? Do you know what it is called?

  The large print at the top of the page is called the heading.

- Read the heading aloud and then the first paragraph.

  Why did the author use a heading?

- Display pages 28–29.

  Where is the heading on this page?

- Point to the subheadings.

  What do you notice about this print? Do you know what these are called?

- Read the Learn More and Educate Others subheading and the paragraph that follows it.

  Why did the author use subheadings?

  How are the subheadings different from the heading?

Have a Try

Invite the students to talk with a partner about the headings in *Giant Squid*.

- Show the cover of *Giant Squid*. Then display pages 22–23. Point to and read the heading.

  Turn and talk to your partner about what you think the information on these pages will be about and how you know.

- After time for discussion, invite a few students to share their thinking.

Summarize and Apply

Summarize the learning and remind students to read headings and subheadings.

- Ask students to summarize what they have learned about headings and subheadings. Use students' responses to make a chart summarizing their observations about headings and subheadings. Write the principle at the top.

  If you read a nonfiction book today, notice if it has headings and subheadings. If so, remember to read them and think about the information you'll find in the section.

Authors use headings and subheadings to help you understand the category of information.

Headings

Purpose	Appearance
• to help you find information in the book • to indicate what category of information is on the page or in the section • to show the organization of the information	• bigger than the main print on the page • may be a different color • may have capital letters

Subheadings

Purpose	Appearance
• to indicate what the paragraph or short section is about • to show how a category of information is divided into subcategories	• smaller than the heading • look different from the main print (might be bigger, bold, italics, etc.)

Share

Following independent reading time, gather students together in the meeting area to talk about their reading.

Who read a nonfiction book that included headings and subheadings today?

How did the headings and subheadings help you while you read?

Extend the Lesson (Optional)

After assessing students' understanding, you might decide to extend the learning.

- **Writing About Reading** Display a page from a nonfiction book that does not have headings. Have students work with a partner to write headings and subheadings for the page.

RML 2

LA.U20.RML2

Reading Minilesson Principle

Authors and illustrators use sidebars to emphasize or give additional information.

Using Text Features to Gain Information

You Will Need

- two familiar nonfiction books that have sidebars, such as the following:
  - *Titanic* by Martin Jenkins, from Text Set: Understanding How Things Work
  - *The Story of Salt* by Mark Kurlansky, from Text Set: Genre Study: Expository Nonfiction
- chart paper and markers
- document camera (optional)

Academic Language / Important Vocabulary

- author
- illustrator
- nonfiction
- sidebar
- information

Continuum Connection

- Gain new understandings from searching for and using information found in text body, sidebars, and graphics (p. 75)

Goal

Gain new understandings from the sidebar and understand how it is related to the information in the body of the text.

Rationale

When students know how to look for, read, and think about the highlighted or additional information provided in sidebars, they gain a fuller understanding of the topic of the book.

Assess Learning

Observe students when they read and talk about nonfiction books and notice if there is evidence of new learning based on the goal of this minilesson.

- Can students explain how the information in a sidebar relates to the information in the text body?
- Do they use academic vocabulary, such as *author, illustrator, nonfiction, sidebar,* and *information*?

Minilesson

To help students think about the minilesson principle, engage them in a discussion about the purpose of sidebars. Here is an example.

- Show the cover of *Titanic* and read the title. Then display, using a document camera if possible, pages 12–13. Read the body text and then one of the sidebars.

  How does this part of the page look different from the rest of the page?

  Does anyone know what this text feature is called?

  This is a sidebar. How does the sidebar relate to the information on the rest of the page?

  On this page, the author uses sidebars to give some statistics about the provisions and crew aboard the *Titanic*. These statistics don't quite fit in the main text, but this information adds interest and background. Sometimes, a writer might also use a sidebar to highlight or emphasize information.

- Turn to pages 14–15. Invite a volunteer to identify the sidebars on these pages. Then read aloud the first sidebar.

  Why did the author include sidebars on these pages?

Have a Try

Invite the students to talk with a partner about the sidebars in *The Story of Salt*.

- Display pages 20–21 from *The Story of Salt*. Read the text body followed by the sidebar.

  Why do you think the author put this information in a sidebar instead of in the body of the page? Turn and talk to your partner about what you think.

- After students turn and talk, invite a few students to share their thinking.

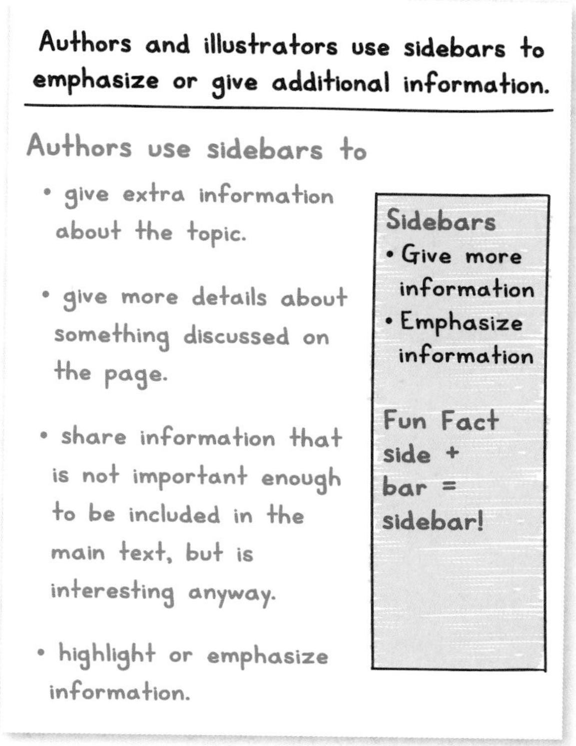

Authors and illustrators use sidebars to emphasize or give additional information.

Authors use sidebars to

- give extra information about the topic.
- give more details about something discussed on the page.
- share information that is not important enough to be included in the main text, but is interesting anyway.
- highlight or emphasize information.

Sidebars
- Give more information
- Emphasize information

Fun Fact
side + bar = sidebar!

Summarize and Apply

Summarize the learning and remind students to read sidebars.

Why do some nonfiction authors use sidebars in their books?

- Record students' responses on chart paper and write the principle at the top.

  When you read today, remember to read every part of the page, including the sidebars if your book has them. Think about how the information in the sidebars relates to the information in the rest of the book. Be ready to share your thinking when we come back together.

Share

Following independent reading time, gather students together in the meeting area to talk about their reading.

Who read a book that has sidebars?

What did you learn from the sidebars in your book? What did the information in the sidebars have to do with the rest of the book?

Extend the Lesson (Optional)

After assessing students' understanding, you might decide to extend the learning.

- Encourage students to include sidebars when they write their own nonfiction books.
- Teach a similar minilesson about the use of timelines in nonfiction books. Examples of books with a timeline include *The Story of Salt* and *The Cod's Tale*, both by Mark Kurlansky and both in Text Set: Genre Study: Expository Nonfiction.

RML 3

LA.U20.RML3

Using Text Features to Gain Information

You Will Need

- two familiar nonfiction books that have a table of contents and/or an index, such as the following:
  - *Giant Squid* by Mary M. Cerullo and Clyde F. E. Roper, from Text Set: Genre Study: Expository Nonfiction
  - *One Well* by Rochelle Strauss, from Text Set: Caring for Our World
- chart paper and markers
- document camera

Academic Language / Important Vocabulary

- nonfiction
- topic
- subtopic
- information
- index
- table of contents

Continuum Connection

- Notice and use and understand the purpose of some other text resources: e.g., glossary, index (p. 75)

Reading Minilesson Principle

Authors include a table of contents and an index to help you find information.

Goal

Notice, use, and understand the purpose of the table of contents and the index.

Rationale

When students know how to use a table of contents and an index, they are able to find information about a specific topic in a nonfiction book.

Assess Learning

Observe students when they read and talk about nonfiction books and notice if there is evidence of new learning based on the goal of this minilesson.

- Can students explain the similarities and differences between a table of contents and an index?
- Do they use academic vocabulary, such as *nonfiction, topic, subtopic, information, index,* and *table of contents*?

Minilesson

To help students think about the minilesson principle, use familiar nonfiction texts to discuss the information in tables of contents and indexes. Here is an example.

- Show the cover of *Giant Squid* and read the title. Then display the table of contents using a document camera.

  What do you know about this page?

- Guide students to talk about a table of contents: its purpose, its organization, its use. Then display the index and guide students in a similar discussion.
- Point to the entry for sperm whales.

  What do you notice about the words underneath *sperm whales*? What do they have to do with sperm whales?

  This index lists both topics and subtopics. Sperm whales are a topic in this book. This topic is divided into smaller subtopics, like what sperm whales eat and what their teeth are like. What do you notice about the order of the topics and subtopics in the index?

  The topics are listed in alphabetical order. The subtopics under each topic are also in alphabetical order. How is the index different from the table of contents?

Have a Try

Invite the students to talk with a partner about the index in *One Well*.

- Show the cover of *One Well* and read the title. Then project the index.

  What page would you go to if you wanted to read about the roots of plants? Look carefully at the index, and then turn and talk to your partner about what you think.

- After students turn and talk, invite a few pairs to share their thinking. If necessary, guide students to look under the *plants* entry for the *roots* subentry.

Authors include a table of contents and an index to help you find information.

Table of Contents	← Both →	Index
• Lists the sections or chapters in the book • Organizes the information in the order the sections/chapters appear in the book • Placed at the beginning of the book	• Help you find information • List topics in the book • Tell what page the topic is on	• Lists all of the topics and subtopics in the book • Organizes the information in alphabetical order • Placed at the end of the book

Summarize and Apply

Summarize the learning and remind students to use tables of contents and indexes.

- Have students summarize what they have noticed about the table of contents and the index. Use students' responses to make a chart to show similarities and differences. Write the principle at the top.

  If you read a nonfiction book today, notice if it has a table of contents or an index. If so, use it to find information in your book. Be ready to share how you used the table of contents or index when we come back together.

Share

Following independent reading time, gather students together in the meeting area to talk about their reading.

Who read a nonfiction book that has a table of contents or an index today?

How did you use the table of contents or index? How did it help you?

Extend the Lesson (Optional)

After assessing students' understanding, you might decide to extend the learning.

- During interactive read-aloud, model how to preview the table of contents before reading a book to have in mind what the book will be about.

RML 4

LA.U20.RML4

Reading Minilesson Principle

Authors include a bibliography to show the resources used to find information for the book.

Using Text Features to Gain Information

You Will Need

- two familiar nonfiction books that have a bibliography, such as the following:
  - *The Sinking of the Titanic* by Matt Doeden, from *Independent Reading Collection*
  - *Mr. Ferris and His Wheel* by Kathryn Gibbs Davis, from Text Set: Understanding How Things Work
- chart paper and markers
- document camera (optional)

Academic Language / Important Vocabulary

- author
- nonfiction
- resource
- information
- bibliography

Continuum Connection

- Notice and use and understand the purpose of some text resources outside the body (peritext): e.g., dedication, acknowledgments, author's note, illustrator's note, endpapers, foreword, prologue, pronunciation guide, footnote, epilogue, appendix, endnote, reference (p. 75)

Goal

Notice and understand the purpose of the bibliography.

Rationale

When students understand the purpose of the bibliography, they begin to understand the enormous amount of research that goes into writing a nonfiction book. They realize that the information in nonfiction books must be supported by other sources. They can also use the bibliography to verify information in a nonfiction book or do further reading about the topic.

Assess Learning

Observe students when they read and talk about nonfiction books and notice if there is evidence of new learning based on the goal of this minilesson.

- Can students explain the purpose of a bibliography?
- Do they use academic language, such as *author, nonfiction, resource, information,* and *bibliography*?

Minilesson

To help students think about the minilesson principle, use familiar nonfiction texts to engage them in a discussion about bibliographies. Here is an example.

- Show the cover of *The Sinking of the Titanic* and read the title. Then display the bibliography.

  What do you notice about this page?

  What is the purpose of this page?

  Do you know what it is called? What is included?

- Record students' responses on chart paper.

  This is a bibliography. A bibliography is a list of resources the author used to find information about the topic of the book. Resources are what an author uses to do research about a topic and might include books, scientific journals, or online articles and websites. When you talk about the item or place the author's information comes from, you call it a source. Let's take a closer look at some of the resources this author used.

- Point to a few different entries in the bibliography and read them aloud.

  What kinds of resources did this author use?

  What information does the author give about each resource?

- Record responses on the chart.

Have a Try

Invite the students to talk with a partner about the bibliography in *Mr. Ferris and His Wheel.*

- Show the cover of *Mr. Ferris and His Wheel* and read the title. Then display the bibliography.

  What do you notice about this bibliography? What kinds of resources did the author use? Turn and talk to your partner about what you notice.

- After time for discussion, invite a few pairs to share their thinking.

Summarize and Apply

Summarize the learning and remind students to notice bibliographies in nonfiction books.

Why do you think nonfiction authors sometimes include a bibliography in their books?

All the information in a nonfiction book must be accurate, so an author must show that the information came from a valid source.

- Write the principle at the top of the chart.

  If you read a nonfiction book today, notice if it has a bibliography. If it does, notice what resources the author used and think about how you might use the bibliography.

Authors include a bibliography to show the resources used to find information for the book.

- A bibliography is a list of the resources the author used.
- A bibliography lists different kinds of resources (books, websites, videos, etc.).
- The author gives the title, author, date, and other important information about each resource.
- You can read the resources in the bibliography to check if the information or quotes in the book are accurate.
- You can also read the resources to learn more about the topic.

Share

Following independent reading time, gather students together in the meeting area to talk about their reading.

Who read a book that has a bibliography?

What did you notice about the bibliography in your book?

Extend the Lesson (Optional)

After assessing students' understanding, you might decide to extend the learning.

- Teach students how to create a bibliography for their own nonfiction writing.
- Guide students to notice the list of books for further reading in some nonfiction books. Discuss how they are different from bibliographies (a list of books gives the reader more places to learn about the topic; a biography shows the books the author consulted).

Assessment

After you have taught the minilessons in this umbrella, observe students as they talk and write about their reading across instructional contexts: interactive read-aloud, independent reading, guided reading, shared reading, and book club. Use *The Literacy Continuum* (Fountas and Pinnell 2017) to guide the observation of students' reading and writing behaviors.

- What evidence do you have of new understandings related to students' use of text features to gain information?
  - Can students describe the purpose and appearance of headings and subheadings?
  - Can they explain what sidebars are used for?
  - Are they able to use a table of contents and an index to find information?
  - Do they understand the purpose of a bibliography?
  - Do they use academic language, such as *nonfiction, heading, subheading, information, sidebar, table of contents, index,* and *bibliography*?
- In what other ways, beyond the scope of this umbrella, are students talking about nonfiction books?
  - Have they noticed that there are different types of nonfiction books (e.g., biography, persuasive)?
  - Are they noticing different ways nonfiction books are organized?

Use your observations to determine the next umbrella you will teach. You may also consult Minilessons Across the Year (pp. 61–64) for guidance.

Link to Writing

After teaching the minilessons in this umbrella, help students link the new learning to their own writing:

- Encouraging students to use headings and subheadings in their writing will help them organize their writing. Suggest that they include extra information about the topic in sidebars. Encourage them to include a table of contents and/or an index to help readers find information. Teach them how to list their sources in a bibliography.

Reader's Notebook

When this umbrella is complete, provide a copy of the minilesson principles (see resources.fountasandpinnell.com) for students to glue in the reader's notebook (in the Minilessons section if using *Reader's Notebook: Advanced* [Fountas and Pinnell 2011]), so they can refer to the information as needed.

Understanding Realistic Fiction

Umbrella 21

Minilessons in This Umbrella

RML1	Realistic fiction stories could happen in real life.
RML2	Notice how realistic fiction writers reveal characters and make them seem real.
RML3	Evaluate whether the plot and story outcome of a realistic fiction story are believable.

Before Teaching Umbrella 21 Minilessons

Before teaching the minilessons in this umbrella, students should be familiar with realistic fiction as a genre and be able to recognize texts as realistic fiction and name some characteristics of the genre.

While reading realistic fiction as a class, notice and read any author's notes included in the books in order to gain a richer understanding of the stories.

Use the following books from the *Fountas & Pinnell Classroom™ Interactive Read-Aloud Collection* text sets or choose other realistic fiction texts with which your students are familiar.

Freedom

Wall by Tom Clohosy Cole

The Composition by Antonio Skármeta

Grit and Perseverance

Brian's Winter by Gary Paulsen

The Power of Knowledge

The Treasure Box by Margaret Wild

As you read aloud and enjoy these texts together, help students

- identify what makes them realistic fiction,
- think about what makes the settings, plots, and story outcomes realistic,
- recognize ways a writer reveals characters and makes them seem real, and
- consider whether everything that happens in a realistic fiction story is believable.

Freedom

The Composition by Antonio Skármeta

Grit and Perseverance

The Power of Knowledge

Section 2: Literary Analysis

RML 1

LA.U21.RML1

Reading Minilesson Principle

Realistic fiction stories could happen in real life.

Understanding Realistic Fiction

You Will Need

- two or three familiar realistic fiction texts, such as the following:
  - *Wall* by Tom Clohosy Cole and *The Composition* by Antonio Skármeta, from Text Set: Freedom
  - *The Treasure Box* by Margaret Wild, from Text Set: The Power of Knowledge
- chart paper and markers

Academic Language / Important Vocabulary

- realistic fiction
- character
- plot
- setting

Continuum Connection

- Understand when a story could happen in real life (realistic fiction) and when it could not happen in real life (traditional literature, fantasy) (p. 69)

Goal

Understand that a characteristic of realistic fiction is that the characters, plot, and setting could exist in real life.

Rationale

When students understand that the characters, plot, and setting in realistic fiction books seem real, they can engage with and make authentic personal connections to their reading.

Assess Learning

Observe students when they read and talk about realistic fiction. Notice if there is evidence of new learning based on the goal of this minilesson.

- Can students identify realistic fiction by evaluating the characters, plot, and setting?
- Are they using academic language, such as *realistic fiction, character, plot,* and *setting*?

Minilesson

To help students think about the minilesson principle, use familiar realistic fiction texts to engage students in thinking about how the characters, setting, and plot could exist in real life.

- Show *Wall* and review a few pages to remind students of the story.

  This book is realistic fiction. What makes this story realistic?

- Help students notice that realistic settings and characters are imagined by the author but could be real. As necessary, support the conversation with these prompts:
  - *What makes the characters seem real?*
  - *What happens in the story that could happen in real life?*
  - *Could the setting of the story be a real place?*
- Record responses on a chart.
- Repeat this process with *The Treasure Box*.

Have a Try

Invite the students to talk with a partner about what makes *The Composition* realistic fiction.

Turn and talk to a partner about the characters, plot, and setting of this book. How do you know this is realistic fiction?

- After students turn and talk, ask a few students to share, and record their responses on the chart.

Realistic fiction stories could happen in real life.

Book	Character	Plot	Setting
Wall	The main character has feelings: he misses his father and imagines being reunited.	A family is separated when the Berlin Wall is built in 1961.	Berlin, Germany, is a real place.
The Treasure Box	The main character is loyal to his father. He keeps his promise.	Peter's father dies while they are escaping the dangers of war. Peter must continue on without his father.	There are real war-torn cities today.
The Composition	The main character likes soccer and goes to school. He tries to understand the dictatorship in his country.	Pedro and his community struggle with the effects of a military dictatorship.	There are real countries ruled by dictators. You can go to soccer fields, stores, and schools.

Summarize and Apply

Summarize the learning and remind students to think about whether the characters, plot, and setting in a book seem real.

What did you notice today about realistic fiction books?

- Review the chart and write the principle at the top.

If you are reading a realistic fiction book today, think about what makes it seem real or true to life. Be prepared to share when we come back together.

Share

Following independent reading time, gather students together to share as a group.

Did you read a realistic fiction book today?

How do you know your book is realistic fiction?

Extend the Lesson (Optional)

After assessing students' understanding, you might decide to extend the learning.

- Introduce your students to Genre Thinkmarks for realistic fiction (visit resources.fountasandpinnell.com). A Genre Thinkmark is a tool that guides readers to note certain elements of a genre in their reading. They can quickly note the page numbers of parts of the book where they see evidence of the characteristics of realistic fiction and share it with others.
- Have students fill in a grid similar to the chart in this minilesson to compare realistic fiction stories they read (visit resources.fountasandpinnell.com).

RML 2

LA.U21.RML2

Reading Minilesson Principle

Notice how realistic fiction writers reveal characters and make them seem real.

Understanding Realistic Fiction

You Will Need

- two or three realistic fiction texts, such as the following:
  - *The Composition* by Antonio Skármeta, from Text Set: Freedom
  - *The Treasure Box* by Margaret Wild, from Text Set: The Power of Knowledge
- chart paper and markers
- sticky notes

Academic Language / Important Vocabulary

- realistic fiction
- character
- dialogue
- reveal

Continuum Connection

- Notice how a writer reveals characters and makes them seem real (p. 71)

Goal

Notice how realistic fiction writers reveal characters and make them seem real.

Rationale

When you teach students to notice how an author makes characters seem real in a realistic fiction text, it helps them to understand the characters better, make authentic personal connections to them, analyze the writer's craft, and learn how to reveal characters in their own writing.

Assess Learning

Observe students when they talk about realistic fiction. Notice if there is evidence of new learning based on the goal of this minilesson.

- Do students notice how an author reveals characters in realistic fiction texts?
- Can they discuss what makes a character seems real?
- Do they understand and use the terms *realistic fiction, character, dialogue,* and *reveal*?

Minilesson

To help students think about the minilesson principle, use familiar realistic fiction texts to help them think about how authors reveal characters and make them seem real. Here is an example.

- Show *The Composition.*

  The genre of this book is realistic fiction.

- Read the dialogue on the bottom of page 1.

  What do you notice about how the author reveals information about Pedro? How does that make Pedro seem real?

- As necessary, support the conversation with the following prompts:
  - *What do you notice about what Pedro says?*
  - *What does the author want you to think about Pedro?*
  - *How does the dialogue make Pedro seem real?*
- Record responses on a chart.

Have a Try

Invite the students to talk with a partner about how characters are revealed in *The Treasure Box*.

- Read the pages where Peter's father shows Peter the iron box and where Peter carries the box after his father's death.

  Turn and talk to your partner. What does the author want you to notice about Peter? How does this make Peter seem real?

- Have a few students share. Add responses to the chart.

Notice how realistic fiction writers reveal characters and make them seem real.

Book	Fictional Character	A Real Person
The Composition	Pedro asks many questions. Pedro plays soccer and makes a joke.	Real children ask questions when they don't understand something. Real kids play soccer and joke around with friends.
The Treasure Box	Peter thinks they have no treasure because there are no rubies, no silver, and no gold. Peter carries the iron box even when people tell him to leave it behind.	Real children may not understand that treasures don't have to cost a lot of money. A real child would want to keep his promise to a parent who has passed away.

Summarize and Apply

Summarize the learning and remind students to think about how an author reveals characters in a realistic fiction text.

What did you notice about how the authors told about, or revealed, the characters in the realistic fiction stories we looked at today?

- Review the chart and write the principle at the top.

  When you read today, choose a realistic fiction story if you are not already reading one. As you read, notice how the author reveals characters and makes them seem real. Mark spots with a sticky note. Be ready to share your noticings when we come back together.

Share

Following independent reading time, gather students together in the meeting area to talk about realistic fiction books.

Who would like to talk about the book you read?

Did the characters seem real? What did the author do to make the characters seem real?

Extend the Lesson (Optional)

After assessing students' understanding, you might decide to extend the learning.

- Ask students to notice other ways writers reveal characters to make them seem real, such as through characters' feelings and thoughts.
- **Writing About Reading** Have students use a character web (visit resources.fountasandpinnell.com) to keep track of characters' actions and dialogue that make them seem real.

RML 3
LA.U21.RML3

Reading Minilesson Principle

Evaluate whether the plot and story outcome of a realistic fiction story are believable.

Understanding Realistic Fiction

You Will Need

- two or three realistic fiction texts, such as the following:
  - *Wall* by Tom Clohosy Cole, from Text Set: Freedom
  - *Brian's Winter* by Gary Paulsen, from Text Set: Grit and Perseverance
- chart paper and markers

Academic Language / Important Vocabulary

- realistic fiction
- events
- plot
- ending
- believable
- evaluate

Continuum Connection

- Evaluate the logic and believability of the plot and its resolution (p. 70)

Goal

Evaluate the believability of a realistic fiction text.

Rationale

A key characteristic of realistic fiction is that, even though parts are imagined by the author, it has to be believable. When you teach students to read realistic fiction with this awareness, looking to see whether each part of the story seems real, you teach them to read critically.

Assess Learning

Observe students when they talk about realistic fiction. Notice if there is evidence of new learning based on the goal of this minilesson.

- Can students decide whether the elements of a realistic fiction story are believable or not?
- Are they thinking critically about realistic fiction stories?
- Can they use important language, such as *realistic fiction, events, plot, ending, believable,* and *evaluate*?

Minilesson

To help students think about the minilesson principle, use familiar realistic fiction texts to help them consider the believability of the plot and story outcomes. Here is an example.

- Hold up *Wall*, showing the illustrations, to remind students of what happens in the story.

  This book is realistic fiction. What happens in the story that you think could happen in real life?

- Record responses on a chart.

  Are there also parts of the plot that you don't believe could actually happen in real life? Why do you think that?

- Record responses on the chart.

  Do you believe the story outcome—the ending—could happen in real life? Why do you think that?

- Record responses on the chart.

  Why do you think the story outcome in a realistic fiction book should seem believable?

Have a Try

Invite the students to talk with a partner about the plot and story outcome of *Brian's Winter*.

What happens in *Brian's Winter* that is believable? Is there a part that is hard to believe? Talk about that.

- After they turn and talk, ask a few students to share. Record responses on the chart.

Summarize and Apply

Summarize the learning and remind students to evaluate the believability of the plot and story outcomes in a realistic fiction text.

A realistic fiction story has characters, a plot, a setting, and an outcome that could be real, but you may not always find the elements believable. You can think about—or evaluate—whether you think parts of the story are believable.

- Write the principle at the top of the chart.

Choose a realistic fiction book to read today. As you read, think about whether the plot and story outcome are believable. Be ready to share when we come back together.

Evaluate whether the plot and story outcome of a realistic fiction story are believable.

Book	What seems believable?	What seems unbelievable?
WALL	The boy worries about his father. He dreams of being reunited.	The boy digs a tunnel to get to the other side of the Berlin Wall. He doesn't get caught.
GARY PAULSEN BRIAN'S WINTER	Brian uses what he learned during the summer to survive the winter. Brian thinks about his loved ones.	Brian survives without any serious injuries or major struggles. He meets a helpful family just in time as he runs out of food.

Share

Following independent reading time, gather students together in the meeting area to talk about their reading.

Were the plot and outcome in the realistic fiction book you read today believable? Why or why not?

Extend the Lesson (Optional)

After assessing students' understanding, you might decide to extend the learning.

- If a plot or story outcome seems hard to believe, encourage students to look for notes or resources in the book that support the believability of the plot.
- Have students compare and contrast a plot or story outcome that is hard to believe in a realistic fiction text with the plot or ending of a fantasy book.
- **Writing About Reading** Have students write in a reader's notebook about a part of a realistic fiction story that is hard to believe, and how the author could have written the story to make it more believable.

Assessment

After you have taught the minilessons in this umbrella, observe students as they talk and write about their reading across instructional contexts: interactive read-aloud, independent reading, guided reading, shared reading, and book club. Use *The Literacy Continuum* (Fountas and Pinnell 2017) to guide the observation of students' reading and writing behaviors.

- What evidence do you have of new understandings related to realistic fiction?
  - Are students able to identify realistic fiction texts?
  - Can they explain how the characters, plots, and settings are realistic?
  - Do they notice how writers reveal characters and make them seem real?
  - Do they identify parts of the story that may not be as believable as other parts of the story, and can they explain their thinking?
  - Do they use terms such as *realistic fiction, character, setting, plot, believable, evaluate, reveal,* and *dialogue*?
- In what other ways, beyond the scope of this umbrella, are students talking about realistic fiction?
  - Are students writing about fiction texts?
  - Do they show interest in the writer's craft?

Use your observations to determine the next umbrella you will teach. You may also consult Minilessons Across the Year (pp. 61–64) for guidance.

Link to Writing

After teaching the minilessons in this umbrella, help students link the new learning to their own writing:

- When students write a realistic fiction story, remind them that the characters, plot, and setting must seem like they could occur in real life. Ask them to consider the details they include to reveal characters and make them seem real.

Reader's Notebook

When this umbrella is complete, provide a copy of the minilesson principles (see resources.fountasandpinnell.com) for students to glue in the reader's notebook (in the Minilessons section if using *Reader's Notebook: Advanced* [Fountas and Pinnell 2011]), so they can refer to the information as needed.

Minilessons in This Umbrella

RML1	Fantasy stories cannot happen but can be set in the real world or in a completely imagined world.
RML2	The characters in fantasy often represent the symbolic struggle of good and evil.
RML3	Fantasy stories often reveal a lesson or something true about the world.
RML4	Science fiction is a type of fantasy that involves technology and scientific advances.

Before Teaching Umbrella 22 Minilessons

Prior to teaching this series of minilessons, students should read and discuss a variety of fantasy books. While this umbrella focuses only on modern fantasy, students should also be experienced with traditional literature. Modern fantasy includes animal fantasy, low fantasy, high fantasy, and science fiction. While the lessons do not make these distinctions, if your students are ready to understand these differences between types of modern fantasy, you might choose to extend their understanding with more minilessons. Use the following books from *Fountas & Pinnell Classroom*™ collections or choose fantasy stories from the classroom library.

Interactive Read-Aloud Collection

Empathy

The Poet's Dog by Patricia MacLachlan

Writer's Craft

Black Dog by Levi Pinfold

Grit and Perseverance

Coraline by Neil Gaiman

Rikki-Tikki-Tavi by Rudyard Kipling

Problem Solving/Resourcefulness

Aliens Ate My Homework by Bruce Coville

Book Club Collection

Lowriders in Space by Cathy Camper

Independent Reading Collection

Found by Margaret Peterson Haddix

Guided Reading Collection

Transformed by Jacqueline Adams

As you read aloud and enjoy these texts together, help students to

- discuss what is unique about fantasy literature, and
- notice which elements *always* and *often* occur in fantasy stories.

Interactive Read-Aloud

Empathy

The Poet's Dog by Patricia MacLachlan

Writer's Craft

Grit and Perseverance

Coraline by Neil Gaiman

Rikki-Tikki-Tavi by Rudyard Kipling

Problem Solving/ Resourcefulness

Book Club

Independent Reading

Guided Reading

RML1

LA.U22.RML1

Reading Minilesson Principle

Fantasy stories cannot happen but can be set in the real world or in a completely imagined world.

Understanding Fantasy

You Will Need

- several familiar fantasy stories that have a variety of settings, such as the following:
  - *Black Dog* by Levi Pinfold, from Text Set: Writer's Craft
  - *Aliens Ate My Homework* by Bruce Coville, from Text Set: Problem Solving/ Resourcefulness
  - *Coraline* by Neil Gaiman, from Text Set: Grit and Perseverance
- chart paper and markers
- basket of fantasy stories
- sticky notes

Academic Language / Important Vocabulary

- fantasy
- genre
- setting
- real world
- imagined world

Continuum Connection

- Notice and understand the characteristics of some specific fiction genres: realistic fiction, historical fiction, folktale, fairy tale, fractured fairy tale, fable, myth, legend, epic, ballad, fantasy including science fiction, hybrid text (p. 69)

Goal

Notice and understand that a defining characteristic of fantasy is that the story could never happen in the real world.

Rationale

It is important for students to become aware that realistic elements coincide with fantasy elements in a fantasy story so that they don't spend time trying to grasp the reality of something fantastical. This enables them to engage fully with the story and understand the connection between setting, characters, and plot.

Assess Learning

Observe students when they read and discuss fantasy stories and notice if there is evidence of new learning based on the goal of this minilesson.

- Are students able to determine whether a setting is real or imagined?
- Can they discuss the interconnectedness of setting with characters and plot?
- Do they use the terms *fantasy, genre, setting, real world,* and *imagined world*?

Minilesson

To help students think about the minilesson principle, engage them in noticing both the real and unusual settings of familiar fantasy stories. Here is an example.

- Display some of the illustrations that show the setting of *Black Dog*.

  What do you know about the setting in the fantasy story *Black Dog*?

- Prompt the conversation so that students discuss that the setting is imagined but could be real.

  How is the setting important to the story?

- As students respond, begin a chart that shows which settings are real and which are imagined. Include a column of information about the importance of setting.

  Now think about the setting in another fantasy story, *Aliens Ate My Homework*. What do you know about the setting in this story? Is it real or imagined?

- Add to the chart.

Have a Try

Invite the students to talk with a partner about the setting in a fantasy story.

- Show the cover of *Coraline*.

  Think about the setting in *Coraline*. Turn and talk about which parts could be real and which are imagined. Also talk about how the setting is important to the story.

- After time for discussion, ask a few volunteers to share. Add to the chart.

Fantasy stories cannot happen but can be set in the real world or in a completely imagined world.

Title	Real/ Could Be Real	Imagined/Could Never Be Real	How is the setting important to the story?
Black Dog	The Hope family's house		The setting is a normal house, but a dog that grows has arrived, which is what the plot centers around. He is too big for the setting.
Aliens Ate My Homework	Rod's bedroom and school	The alien spaceship	Most of the settings seem normal, but aliens land in Rod's bedroom and go to his school.
Coraline	Coraline's flat in England	The house through the wall that looks just like hers but is different	The magic house causes Coraline to appreciate what she already has in her normal life.

Summarize and Apply

Summarize the learning and remind students to think about the unusual settings in fantasy stories.

What do you know about settings in fantasy stories?

- Add the principle to the chart.

  Today you can choose a fantasy story from the basket or continue a book you have already started. If you read a fantasy story, notice if all or part of the setting is unusual and whether it could happen in the real world or if it is imagined. Place a sticky note about setting on any pages that you want to remember. Bring the book when we meet so you can share.

Share

Following independent reading time, gather students in the meeting area to talk about their reading.

What did you notice about the setting in the book you read today? Tell whether your book's setting could exist in the real world or could only be imagined.

Extend the Lesson (Optional)

After assessing students' understanding, you might decide to extend the learning.

- As students encounter other fantasy stories (both modern fantasy and traditional literature), bring the setting to their awareness and have them think and talk about whether the setting could be real or if it is imagined.

RML 2

LA.U22.RML2

Reading Minilesson Principle

The characters in fantasy often represent the symbolic struggle of good and evil.

Understanding Fantasy

You Will Need

- several fantasy books that have clear examples of good and evil, such as the following:
  - *Coraline* by Neil Gaiman, from Text Set: Grit and Perseverance
  - *Rikki-Tikki-Tavi* by Rudyard Kipling, from Text Set: Grit and Perseverance
  - *Aliens Ate My Homework* by Bruce Coville, from Text Set: Problem Solving/ Resourcefulness
- chart paper and markers
- basket of fantasy stories
- sticky notes

Academic Language / Important Vocabulary

- fantasy
- genre
- symbols
- struggle
- good
- evil
- versus (vs.)

Continuum Connection

- Infer the significance of heroic or larger-than-life characters in fantasy who represent the symbolic struggle of good and evil. (p. 71)

Goal

Understand that the heroic and sometimes larger-than-life characters in fantasy represent the symbolic struggle between good and evil.

Rationale

When you teach students to notice the struggle of good versus evil in fantasy stories, they learn to recognize characteristics of the genre and think deeply about character traits and behavior.

Assess Learning

Observe students when they read and talk about fantasy stories and notice if there is evidence of new learning based on the goal of this minilesson.

- Are students able to recognize symbols of good and evil in fantasy stories?
- Do they use the terms *fantasy, genre, symbols, struggle, good,* and *evil,* and *versus (vs.)*?

Minilesson

To help students think about the minilesson principle, engage them in thinking about the struggle between good and evil in fantasy stories. Here is an example.

- Show the cover of *Coraline*.

  A symbol is one thing that stands for another. Think about the symbols of good and evil in *Coraline*. Turn and talk about that.

- After time for discussion, ask students to share their thinking. Support them to recognize that there are both good and bad characters, settings, and objects, and that the plot centers around the struggle between these good and bad forces.

  There are characters in *Coraline* that show good and evil. Which character could we draw in each section?

- Create a chart with sketches to represent good and evil characters.

  Now think about *Rikki-Tikki-Tavi*. Who are the main good and bad characters and what struggle do they have?

  Which characters show good and evil?

- As students respond, add to chart.

Have a Try

Invite the students to talk with a partner about characters that show the struggle of good and evil in fantasy.

- Show the cover of *Aliens Ate My Homework*.

    Turn and talk about good and evil in *Aliens Ate My Homework*. Who are the characters that show the struggle between those forces in this fantasy story?

- After time for discussion, ask students who could be drawn to represent good and evil and add to chart.

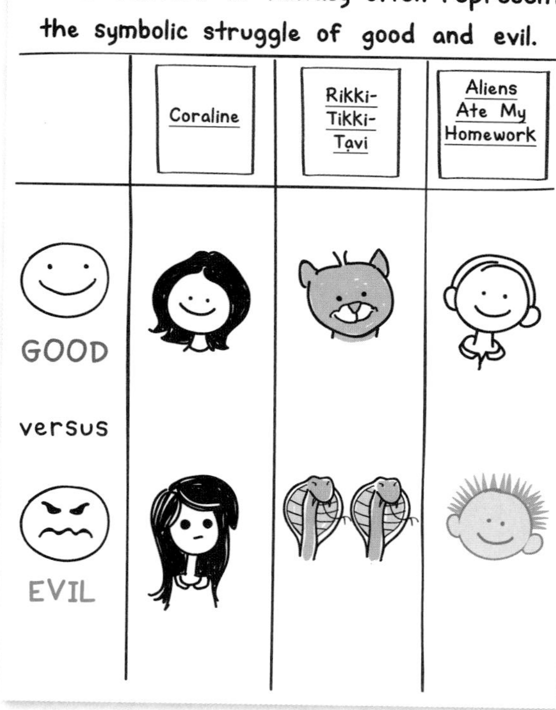

Summarize and Apply

Summarize the learning and remind students to think about the struggle of good and evil in fantasy books.

What did you notice about how good and evil are shown in fantasy books?

- Add the principle to the chart.

    Today you can choose a fantasy story from the basket or continue reading a fantasy book you have already started. Think about the struggle of good and evil and mark any pages with sticky notes that you want to remember. Bring the book when we meet so you can share.

Share

Following independent reading time, gather students in small groups.

Share with your group what you noticed about the struggle of good and evil in a fantasy book.

Extend the Lesson (Optional)

After assessing students' understanding, you might decide to extend the learning.

- Ask students to think about whether characters in the books discussed in this minilesson are all good or all bad, or whether some are a combination of those traits. Encourage them to think about how this idea applies to real life.

RML 3
LA.U22.RML3

Reading Minilesson Principle

Fantasy stories often reveal a lesson or something true about the world.

Understanding Fantasy

You Will Need

- several fiction stories that include a life lesson or universal truth, such as the following:
  - *Rikki-Tikki-Tavi* by Rudyard Kipling from Text Set: Grit and Perseverance
  - *The Poet's Dog* by Patricia MacLachlan, from Text Set: Empathy
  - *Black Dog* by Levi Pinfold, from Text Set: Writer's Craft
- chart paper and markers
- basket of fantasy stories

Academic Language / Important Vocabulary

- fantasy
- genre
- lesson
- universal truth
- reveal

Continuum Connection

- Understand that the messages or big ideas in fiction texts can be applied to their own lives or to other people and society. (p. 69)

Goal

Understand that the messages or big ideas in fantasy stories can be applied to their own lives or to other people and society.

Rationale

When students learn to identify the messages or big ideas in fantasy stories, they understand that these messages have a place in the real world: they lead to lessons students can apply to their own lives.

Assess Learning

Observe students when they read and talk about fantasy stories and notice if there is evidence of new learning based on the goal of this minilesson.

- Are students able to identify the message or big idea in a fantasy story?
- Can they apply a lesson or universal truth from a fantasy story to their own lives?
- Do they use the terms *fantasy, genre, lesson, universal truth,* and *reveal*?

Minilesson

To help students think about the minilesson principle, engage them in thinking about what lessons or truths are revealed in a fantasy story. Here is an example.

- Show the illustrations on pages 37–40 of *Rikki-Tikki-Tavi.*

  Think about the character Rikki-tikki-tavi and the big idea or message from this book. Turn and talk about that.

- After time for discussion, ask students to share. Encourage them to identify the lesson or universal truth that is revealed through Rikki-tikki-tavi's character. Add the book title and information to the first two columns of a three-column chart.

  What lesson can you learn from the message in *Rikki-Tikki-Tavi*?

  How can you apply it to your own life?

- Choose one or two responses to write in the third column.

  Now think about *The Poet's Dog*. What is the big idea or message in this story?

  How can that idea be applied to your own life?

- Create another row on the chart and add students' responses as they relate to *The Poet's Dog*.

Have a Try

Invite the students to talk with a partner about what a fantasy story reveals.

- Show the cover of *Black Dog*.

  What lesson or universal truth do you learn from *Black Dog*? How can it be applied to your own life? Turn and talk about that.

- After time for discussion, add students' ideas to the chart.

Fantasy stories often reveal a lesson or something true about the world.

Title	Lesson or Universal Truth	Connection to My Life
Rikki-Tikki-Tavi	Have courage even when you doubt yourself.	Try a new sport, even when I am afraid of being a beginner.
The Poet's Dog	Friends can help us deal with sad things in life.	Help my friends when they are feeling sad, and I know they will help me in return.
Black Dog	When you face your fears, you become less afraid.	Do things I am afraid of so they will become less scary.

Summarize and Apply

Summarize the learning and remind students to think about the big ideas in fantasy stories.

What did you learn about what fantasy stories reveal?

- Add the principle to the chart.

  When you read today, you can choose a fantasy story from the basket if you aren't already reading one. Think about what lesson you learn from reading the fantasy. Bring the book when we meet so you can share.

Share

Following independent reading time, gather students in the meeting area to talk about their reading.

Who noticed a lesson or universal truth in a fantasy story? Tell what you noticed.

Extend the Lesson (Optional)

After assessing students' understanding, you might decide to extend the learning.

- As students experience more fantasy stories, have them talk about whether multiple books have the same big idea or message. Have them compare and contrast the way that different fantasy authors reveal universal truths.

RML4
LA.U22.RML4

Reading Minilesson Principle

Science fiction is a type of fantasy that involves technology and scientific advances.

Understanding Fantasy

You Will Need

- several familiar science fiction stories, such as the following:
  - *Transformed* by Jacqueline Adams, from *Guided Reading Collection*
  - *Lowriders in Space* by Cathy Camper, from *Book Club Collection*
  - *Found* by Margaret Peterson Haddix, from *Independent Reading Collection*
- chart prepared for one of the books you are using, listing elements identifying it as science fiction
- markers and highlighter or highlighting tape
- basket of science fiction stories
- sticky notes

Academic Language / Important Vocabulary

- science fiction
- technology
- scientific advances
- futuristic
- aliens
- outer space

Continuum Connection

- Identify some elements of science fiction: technology or scientific advances, futuristic setting, time travel, aliens, or outer space. (p. 69)

Goal

Understand that science fiction is a type of fantasy that involves technology and scientific advances and often takes place in the future.

Rationale

When students understand that science fiction falls into the fantasy genre and includes technology and scientific advances, they learn to recognize a book as science fiction and know what to expect when reading.

Assess Learning

Observe students when they read and talk about science fiction and notice if there is evidence of new learning based on the goal of this minilesson.

- Are students able to recognize that a story is science fiction?
- Can students describe some of the elements of a science fiction story?
- Do they understand the terms *science fiction, technology, scientific advances, futuristic, aliens,* and *outer space*?

Minilesson

To help students think about the minilesson principle, engage them in thinking about science fiction. Here is an example.

- Show the cover of *Transformed* and the chart prepared with science fiction details about the book.

  Think about this book you know, *Transformed*. I have listed several ways to show that it is science fiction. Which words offer a clue that the story is science fiction?

  Aliens and future scientific technology are two characteristics of science fiction.

- Highlight the keywords *alien, technology,* and *future*.
- Show the cover of *Lowriders in Space*.

  Is *Lowriders in Space* science fiction? How do you know?

- After time for discussion, add responses to the chart.

  What keywords are on the chart that show that *Lowriders in Space* is science fiction?

- Ask a volunteer to highlight the words.

Have a Try

Invite the students to talk with a partner about what makes *Found* science fiction.

- Show the cover of *Found*.

  Turn and talk about how you know that *Found* is a science fiction story.

- After time for discussion, have two or three students share their thinking. Record responses as before.

Summarize and Apply

Summarize the learning and remind students to think about the elements of a science fiction story.

You learned that science fiction is a type of fantasy that has technology and scientific advances.

- Add the principle to the chart.

  Today choose a science fiction story if you aren't already reading one. Think about how you know it is science fiction and mark any pages you want to remember. Bring the book when we meet so you can share.

Science fiction is a type of fantasy that involves technology and scientific advances.

 Transformed: How Everyday Things Are Made by Bill Slavin	An alien is in a dog body. Technology is from the future.
 Lowriders in Space	The car is futuristic. There is lots of technology. The car goes into outer space.
 Margaret Peterson Haddix, The Missing: Found	There is time travel. Some events take place in the future.

Share

Following independent reading time, gather students in small groups.

In your group, talk about the science fiction book you read today and how you know it is science fiction.

Extend the Lesson (Optional)

After assessing students' understanding, you might decide to extend the learning.

- Assist students in searching online for science fiction short stories. Then compare and contrast the elements they notice in the stories.
- Ask the librarian to assist students in finding additional science fiction books to read.

Assessment

After you have taught the minilessons in this umbrella, observe students as they talk and write about their reading across instructional contexts: interactive read-aloud, independent reading, guided reading, shared reading, and book club. Use *The Literacy Continuum* (Fountas and Pinnell 2017) to guide the observation of students' reading and writing behaviors.

- What evidence do you have of new understandings related to fantasy?
- Do students understand that the setting in fantasy stories could take place in the real world or could be wholly imagined?
- Are students aware that the characters in fantasy often represent good and evil?
- Can they discuss the lesson or universal truth that is revealed in a fantasy story?
- Are they aware that one type of fantasy is science fiction and that it involves technology and scientific advances?
- Are they using the terms *real, imagined, good, evil, lesson, universal truth,* and *technology*?

- In what other ways, beyond the scope of this umbrella, are students talking about fantasy?
  - Are students able to talk about different types of fantasy books, such as animal fantasy, low fantasy, high fantasy, and traditional literature?

Use your observations to determine the next umbrella you will teach. You may also consult Minilessons Across the Year (pp. 61–64) for guidance.

Link to Writing

After teaching the minilessons in this umbrella, help students link the new learning to their own writing:

- Have students begin to plan and write a fantasy story of their own that incorporates the different elements in the fantasy genre.

Reader's Notebook

When this umbrella is complete, provide a copy of the minilesson principles (see resources.fountasandpinnell.com) for students to glue in the reader's notebook (in the Minilessons section if using *Reader's Notebook: Advanced* [Fountas and Pinnell 2011]), so they can refer to the information as needed.

Studying Legends

Umbrella 23

Minilessons in This Umbrella

RML1	Legends are alike in many ways.
RML2	The definition of a legend is what is always true about it.
RML3	Legends are about heroes and their accomplishments.
RML4	The subject of a legend can be a real or an imaginary person.
RML5	Legends often involve a quest.
RML6	Legends are often passed down over many years and are often connected to myths.
RML7	Legends are often told in poetic language.
RML8	The legend often shows what the culture values.

Before Teaching Umbrella 23 Minilessons

Genre study supports students in knowing what to expect when beginning to read a text in a genre. It helps students develop an understanding of the distinguishing characteristics of a genre and gives them the tools they need to navigate a variety of texts. There are six broad steps in the genre study process; they are detailed on pages 39–41. Prior to teaching this series of minilessons, make sure your students are familiar with the principles in Umbrella 22: Understanding Fantasy.

Because students must be familiar with multiple legends and other types of traditional literature before beginning a genre study, select books that are clear examples. Fantasy is classified as either traditional literature or modern fantasy, and legends are a type of traditional literature along with folktales, fables, fairy tales, epics, ballads, and myths. Examples of legends can be found in the following books from the *Fountas & Pinnell Classroom™ Interactive Read-Aloud Collection*; however, you can use legends from the classroom library.

Genre Study: Legends

John Henry by Julius Lester

The Kitchen Knight: A Tale of King Arthur by Margaret Hodges

Merlin and the Dragons by Jane Yolen

The Story of Jumping Mouse by John Steptoe

As you read aloud and enjoy these texts together, help students

- notice similarities between them,
- notice the traits of the characters, and
- make connections to their own lives.

Genre Study: Legends

The Story of Jumping Mouse by John Steptoe

RML 1

LA.U23.RML1

Reading Minilesson Principle

Legends are alike in many ways.

Studying Legends

You Will Need

- a collection of familiar legends
- chart paper with the headings *Legends* and *Noticings*, and sections for *Always* and *Often*
- markers

Academic Language / Important Vocabulary

- legend
- fantasy
- traditional literature
- characteristics

Continuum Connection

- Notice and understand the characteristics of some specific fiction genres: e.g., realistic fiction, historical fiction, folktale, fairy tale, fractured fairy tale, fable, myth, legend, epic, ballad, fantasy including science fiction, hybrid texts (p. 69)
- Understand when a story could happen in real life (realistic fiction) and when it could not happen in real life (traditional literature, fantasy) (p. 69)

Goal

Notice and understand the characteristics of legends.

Rationale

When students study legends as a genre through inquiry, they gain a deeper understanding both of individual stories and the genre as a whole. When they develop an understanding of legends, they will know what to expect when they encounter books of that genre (see pages 39–41 for more information about genre study.)

Assess Learning

Observe students when they talk about legends and notice if there is evidence of new learning based on the goal of this minilesson.

- Are students able to notice similarities between multiple examples of legends?
- Do they use the terms *legend, fantasy, traditional literature,* and *characteristics*?

Minilesson

To help students develop a list of characteristics of legends, choose legends that you have read aloud to use for an inquiry-based lesson. Here is an example.

- Have students sit in small groups and provide each group with several examples of legends. Groups can rotate the books so they have an opportunity to compare several examples.

  Think about the legends you know and the examples your group has. Talk with each other about how all legends are alike.

- Provide a few minutes for conversation.

  Now think of each of those ideas your group discussed. Which of those things occur *always* in legends, which occur *often*, and which occur *sometimes*?

- As students share, prompt the discussion as needed to help them identify whether characteristics occur *always*, *often*, or *sometimes* in legends. The following suggested prompts may be helpful:
  - *Who are legends about?*
  - *What types of things do the main characters do?*
  - *What types of things happen in legends?*
  - *What types of settings do you notice?*
  - *Does that* always, often, *or* sometimes *occur in the legends you know?*
- On chart paper, create a noticings chart and add student ideas.

Have a Try

Invite the students to talk with a partner about legends.

> Think about a book you are reading. Turn and talk about whether it is a legend and why or why not. Use the chart to talk about the characteristics of legends as you think about the book.

Summarize and Apply

Summarize the learning and remind students to think about the characteristics of legends.

> A legend is a type of fantasy story that fits into the traditional literature category. What else do you know about the characteristics of legends?

- Review the chart.

> Choose a legend to read today. Think about which of the characteristics on the chart occur in the book you read. Bring the book when we meet so you can share.

Legends

Noticings:

Always	Often
• Legends are handed down over many years. • They are about heroes and their accomplishments. • The hero might be an imaginary character or a real person whose qualities have been exaggerated.	The hero's qualities show what the culture values. Legends involve a quest. They have otherworldly heroes. They are written with a poetic language. Legends exaggerate the qualities of the hero. They are connected to myths. **Sometimes** Legends explain a mystery or phenomena.

Share

Following independent reading time, gather students in the meeting area to talk about their reading.

> Who read a legend today? Talk about which characteristics from the list you noticed in the book.

Extend the Lesson (Optional)

After assessing students' understanding, you might decide to extend the learning.

- Continue adding to the noticings chart as students read more examples of legends.

RML2
LA.U23.RML2

Reading Minilesson Principle

The definition of a legend is what is always true about it.

Studying Legends

You Will Need

- a familiar legend, such as *John Henry* by Julius Lester from Text Set: Genre Study: Legends
- the legends noticings chart from RML1
- chart paper and markers
- basket of legends

Academic Language / Important Vocabulary

- legend
- genre
- definition
- characteristics

Continuum Connection

- Notice and understand the characteristics of some specific fiction genres: e.g., realistic fiction, historical fiction, folktale, fairy tale, fractured fairy tale, fable, myth, legend, epic, ballad, fantasy including science fiction, hybrid text (p. 69)

Goal

Create a working definition of legends.

Rationale

When students construct a working definition of legends, they are able to identify and summarize the most important characteristics of the genre and to recognize other books they read that fit in the genre.

Assess Learning

Observe students when they talk about legends and notice if there is evidence of new learning based on the goal of this minilesson.

- Can students identify the characteristics of a legend?
- Are they able to identify whether a book fits the definition of a legend?
- Do they use the terms *legend, genre, definition,* and *characteristics*?

Minilesson

To help students think about the minilesson principle, guide them in constructing a working definition of a legend. Here is an example.

- Show the legends noticings chart and discuss the characteristics of a legend.

  What do you know about legends?

- Ask several volunteers to read the noticings aloud.

  Think about the ways legends are *always* alike. How does knowing how legends are *always* alike help you create a definition of a legend?

- Write *A legend is* on chart paper.

  Turn and talk about how you could finish this sentence to write a definition for all legends.

- After time for discussion, ask a few volunteers to share. Use the ideas to construct a working definition of a legend and write it on the chart paper.

Have a Try

Invite the students to talk with a partner about the definition of a legend.

- Show the cover of a legend, such as *John Henry*. Revisit a few pages as needed.

  Turn and talk about whether *John Henry* fits the definition you created for a legend.

- After time for discussion, ask students to share. Revise the working definition as needed.

Summarize and Apply

Summarize the learning and remind students to think about the definition of a legend.

Today we wrote a definition of a legend. As you learn more about legends, we can revise this definition.

- Add the principle to the chart.

  When you read today, choose a legend and think about how it fits the definition. Bring the book when we meet so you can share.

The definition of a legend is what is always true about it.

A legend is an imagined story about a hero.

Share

Following independent reading time, gather students in small groups to talk about legends.

Share with your group the legend you read today. How does it fit the definition of a legend? Talk about that.

Extend the Lesson (Optional)

After assessing students' understanding, you might decide to extend the learning.

- As you read other types of traditional literature during interactive read-aloud, compare and contrast another type of fantasy with what students have learned about legends. For example, talk about how characters are different in tall tales and legends.

RML 3
LA.U23.RML3

Reading Minilesson Principle
Legends are about heroes and their accomplishments.

Studying Legends

You Will Need

- several familiar legends, such as the following from Text Set: Genre Study: Legends:
  - *Merlin and the Dragons* by Jane Yolen
  - *The Story of Jumping Mouse* by John Steptoe
  - *The Kitchen Knight* by Margaret Hodges
- chart paper and markers
- labels to tape or glue to the chart: *Heroes, Accomplishments*
- sticky notes

Academic Language / Important Vocabulary

- legend
- hero
- accomplishments

Continuum Connection

- Notice and understand the characteristics of some specific fiction genres: e.g., realistic fiction, historical fiction, folktale, fairy tale, fractured fairy tale, fable, myth, legend, epic, ballad, fantasy including science fiction, hybrid text (p. 69)

Goal

Understand that legends are about heroes and their accomplishments.

Rationale

When students learn legends are about heroes and their accomplishments, they learn to pay close attention to characters, which helps them recognize which genre they are reading.

Assess Learning

Observe students when they read and talk about legends and notice if there is evidence of new learning based on the goal of this minilesson.

- Do students understand that legends are about heroes and their accomplishments?
- Are they using the terms *legend, hero,* and *accomplishments*?

Minilesson

To help students think about the minilesson principle, use familiar legends to engage them in a discussion about heroes and their accomplishments. Here is an example.

- Show the cover of *Merlin and the Dragons.*

  Who is the main character in this book?

  What are some important things that he did?

- Write students' responses in two unlabeled columns.
- Repeat the two questions for *The Story of Jumping Mouse.*

  What is a word for a person who does very brave and courageous deeds?

  The characters you have named are heroes. Their brave deeds were all completed successfully, so those deeds are called accomplishments.

- Add the labels for the two columns.

Have a Try

Invite the students to talk with a partner about legends.

- Show the cover of *The Kitchen Knight*.

  Is Sir Gareth a hero? What are his accomplishments? Turn and talk about that.

- After time for discussion, ask students to share ideas.

Summarize and Apply

Summarize the learning and remind students to think about heroes and their accomplishments as they read legends.

  You learned that legends are about heroes and their accomplishments.

- Add the principle to the chart.

  When you read today, choose a legend. As you read, think about who the heroes are in the story and what they accomplish. Mark any pages with sticky notes that show those things. Bring the book when we meet so you can share.

Legends are about heroes and their accomplishments.

	Hero	Accomplishments
Merlin and the Dragons	Merlin	• Guides evil Vortigern to the dragons • Keeps Arthur safe
	Uther	• Defeats Vortigern
The Story of Jumping Mouse	Jumping Mouse	• Helps many animals, like the bison who can't see
The Kitchen Knight	Sir Gareth	• Battles knights • Saves a princess

Share

Following independent reading time, gather students in small groups.

  In your group, share the legend you read today and talk about the heroes and their accomplishments.

Extend the Lesson (Optional)

After assessing students' understanding, you might decide to extend the learning.

- When you read a legend during interactive read-aloud, talk about the phrase *larger than life* as it relates to the heroes in legends and why people write stories about these larger-than-life characters.

RML 4
LA.U23.RML4

Reading Minilesson Principle

The subject of a legend can be a real or an imaginary person.

Studying Legends

You Will Need

- several familiar legends, such as the following from Text Set: Genre Study: Legends:
  - *Merlin and the Dragons* by Jane Yolen
  - *John Henry* by Julius Lester
- chart paper and markers
- sticky notes

Academic Language / Important Vocabulary

- legend
- subject
- imaginary
- real

Continuum Connection

- Identify elements of traditional literature and fantasy: e.g., the supernatural; imaginary and otherworldly creatures; gods and goddesses; talking animals, toys, and dolls; heroic characters; technology or scientific advances; time travel; aliens or outer space (p. 69)
- Understand when a story could happen in real life (realistic fiction) and when it could not happen in real life (traditional literature, fantasy) (p. 69)
- Express opinions about whether a character seems real (p. 71)

Goal

Understand that the subject of a legend can be imaginary or based on a real person.

Rationale

When students understand that the subjects of legends can be imaginary or based on real people, they are able to think deeply about the characters in legends and know what to expect when reading books in the genre.

Assess Learning

Observe students when they talk about and read legends and notice if there is evidence of new learning based on the goal of this minilesson.

- Do students recognize that legends can be about an imaginary hero or based on a real person's life?
- Do they use the terms *legend, subject, imaginary,* and *real*?

Minilesson

To help students think about the minilesson principle, use familiar legends to engage them in a discussion about whether the subject of a legend is imaginary or real. Here is an example.

- Show the cover of *Merlin and the Dragons*. Show the illustration of Arthur on page 1 and Emrys (Merlin) on page 5.

  Do you think that these boys really existed? Why or why not?

- As they have a conversation, guide students to understand that nobody really knows if these boys existed because the legend began so long ago. Record responses on chart paper.

  If Arthur and Merlin were real people, how would they have been different from the way they are described in the legend?

- Add ideas to the *Real or Imaginary*? column that show that if they were real, they could not have done things as described in the legend.
- Show the cover of *John Henry.*

  Now think about John Henry. Do you think he really existed? Why or why not?

- Read the first few lines of the foreword, which explains that nobody really knows if John Henry existed.

  What can we add to the chart about whether John Henry was real or imaginary?

- Add to chart.

Have a Try

Invite the students to talk with a partner about legends.

> Do you think it is important to know whether the subject of a legend is real or imaginary? Why or why not? Turn and talk about that.

- After time for discussion, have a few volunteers share their thinking.

Summarize and Apply

Summarize the learning and remind students that the subjects of legends can be real or imaginary.

- Review the chart and add the principle to the top.

> You may choose a legend to read today. If you do, notice if you can determine if the subject is real or imaginary. Mark any pages with sticky notes that give information about this and bring the book when we meet so you can share.

The subject of a legend can be a real or an imaginary person.

Title	Real or Imaginary?
	**Not sure** The magical things could not have happened, but maybe there was a real king named Arthur and a boy named Emrys.
	**Not sure** There might have been a real John Henry. If so, the things he did have been exaggerated for the story.

Share

Following independent reading time, gather students in pairs.

> Share with your partner the legend you read today. Talk about whether the subject is real or imaginary and how you know that.

Extend the Lesson (Optional)

After assessing students' understanding, you might decide to extend the learning.

- Encourage students to do some research about Merlin, Arthur, John Henry, or the subject of another legend to learn more about whether they were real people.
- Have students write a legend based on a real or imaginary person.

RML 5

LA.U23.RML5

Reading Minilesson Principle

Legends often involve a quest.

Studying Legends

You Will Need

- several familiar legends, such as the following from Text Set: Genre Study: Legends:
  - *The Story of Jumping Mouse* by John Steptoe
  - *The Kitchen Knight* by Margaret Hodges
  - *John Henry* by Julius Lester
- chart paper and markers
- sticky notes

Academic Language / Important Vocabulary

- legend
- quest

Continuum Connection

- Notice and understand the characteristics of some specific fiction genres: e.g., realistic fiction, historical fiction, folktale, fairy tale, fractured fairy tale, fable, myth, legend, epic, ballad, fantasy including science fiction, hybrid text (p. 69)
- Notice story outcomes that are typical of traditional literature (p. 69)
- Notice recurring themes or motifs in traditional literature and fantasy: e.g., struggle between good and evil, the hero's quest (p. 70)

Goal

Understand that legends often involve a quest.

Rationale

When students learn to recognize that legends often have a hero who goes on a journey or quest, they are able to identify books that fit in the genre and know what to expect when reading legends.

Assess Learning

Observe students when they talk about the characteristics of legends and notice if there is evidence of new learning based on the goal of this minilesson.

- Do students recognize that many legends have a quest or journey?
- Do they use the terms *legend* and *quest*?

Minilesson

To help students think about the minilesson principle, use familiar legends to provide an interactive lesson. Here is an example.

Turn and talk about what you know about quests.

- After time for a brief discussion, ask students to share ideas. Make sure students understand that a quest is a very long and hard journey to reach a goal.
- Show and read page 3 from *The Story of Jumping Mouse*.

  What can you say about the quest in this legend?

- Prompt the conversation as needed. For example:
  - *What is the goal of the mouse's journey?*
  - *Why is the mouse's quest important to the story?*
- Record responses on the chart paper.
- Show page 8 from *The Kitchen Knight*.

  What can you say about the quest in *The Kitchen Knight*?

  What is the goal of Sir Gareth's journey?

- Record responses.

Have a Try

Invite the students to talk with a partner about the quest in a familiar legend.

- Show the illustrations on pages 11–12 of *John Henry* and read the first two paragraphs on page 11.

  Turn and talk about John Henry's quest.

- After time for discussion, ask a few volunteers to share. Record responses.

Summarize and Apply

Summarize the learning and remind students to think about the quests in legends.

You have been talking about how legends often involve a quest.

- Add the principle to the chart.

  If you choose to read a legend today, notice if there is a quest and mark any pages with sticky notes that you want to remember. Bring the book when we meet so you can share.

Legends often involve a quest.

Title	Goal of the Quest
The Story of Jumping Mouse	To find the far-off land
The Kitchen Knight	To save a prisoner who is locked in a castle
John Henry	To make his way in the world as an adult

Share

Following independent reading time, gather students in the meeting area.

Who read a legend today that has a quest? Tell us about that.

Extend the Lesson (Optional)

After assessing students' understanding, you might decide to extend the learning.

- As students read other legends, ask them to describe the quest, or to look for a series of tasks or tests that the hero must complete. Ask them to talk about why the outcome of the quest, tasks, or tests is important to the story.
- Students might be interested to know that *quest* is from a Latin word that means "to ask, to seek" and is related to the word *question*.

RML 6

LA.U23.RML6

Reading Minilesson Principle

Legends are often passed down over many years and are often connected to myths.

Studying Legends

You Will Need

- a collection of familiar legends, such as the following from Text Set: Genre Study: Legends:
  - *Merlin and the Dragons* by Jane Yolen
  - *John Henry* by Julius Lester
  - *The Story of Jumping Mouse* by John Steptoe
- chart paper prepared with three columns headed *Title, Passed Down? How do you know?* and *Myth? How do you know?*
- sticky notes

Academic Language / Important Vocabulary

- legend
- passed down
- storytellers
- myths
- natural phenomena

Continuum Connection

- Notice and understand the characteristics of some specific fiction genres: e.g., realistic fiction, historical fiction, folktale, fairy tale, fractured fairy tale, fable, myth, legend, epic, ballad, fantasy including science fiction, hybrid text (p. 69)

Goal

Understand that legends are often passed down over many years and are often connected to myths.

Rationale

When students learn to recognize that legends are often passed down and/or connected to myths, they recognize characteristics of the genre that help them identify and understand legends.

Assess Learning

Observe students when they read and discuss legends and notice if there is evidence of new learning based on the goal of this minilesson.

- Do students understand that legends are often passed down over time?
- Are they able to identify parts of a legend that are connected to myths?
- Do they use the terms *legend, passed down, storytellers, myths,* and *natural phenomena*?

Minilesson

Use familiar legends to continue talking about their characteristics. Here is an example.

- Display the prepared chart. Be sure students understand the meaning of *passed down* and *myth*.

  What are some ways to know that a legend has been passed down over time by storytellers?

  A myth is a story that explains a natural phenomenon. What could you notice in a legend that shows it is connected to a myth?

- Support the conversation and encourage students to share their background knowledge.
- Show the cover of *Merlin and the Dragons* and then show and read pages 7–8.

  Turn and talk about *Merlin and the Dragons*. Was it passed down over time, and are there parts that are connected to a myth?

- After time for discussion, ask students to share their thinking and add responses to the chart.
- Show the cover of *John Henry* and then read selected portions of the notes at the beginning of the book that explain how the author and illustrator came to work on it.

  What should I write on the chart for this book?

Have a Try

Invite the students to talk about *The Story of Jumping Mouse.*

- Have students sit in groups and give each group a legend. Each group should have access to several sticky notes and a pencil.

  What do you remember about this story? Do you think it was passed down over time or connected to a myth? Turn and talk to a partner about that.

- Record responses on the chart.

Legends are often passed down over many years and are often connected to myths.

Title	Passed Down? How do you know?	Myth? How do you know?
Merlin and the Dragons	Yes King Arthur and Merlin stories have been told for years.	Yes Page 8 explains eclipses.
John Henry	Yes Foreword says that the story is based on a song from the 1800s.	No It is about a person who might have been real.
The Story of Jumping Mouse	Yes Copyright notice says that the story is based on another story.	No The story doesn't explain anything. It's just about the quest.

Summarize and Apply

Summarize the learning and remind students to think about the origins of a legend as they read.

Today you thought about whether a legend was passed down over time or connected to a myth.

- Add the principle to the chart.

  If you choose to read a legend today, think about whether it was passed down over time and/or connected to a myth. Bring the book when we meet so you can share.

Share

Following independent reading time, gather students in pairs to talk about their reading.

Who would like to talk about a legend you have read? Do you know if it was passed down or connected to a myth?

Extend the Lesson (Optional)

After assessing students' understanding, you might decide to extend the learning.

- **Writing About Reading** Have students write a new version of an old legend or have them write a legend that explains something that was misunderstood before modern science.

RML7

LA.U23.RML7

Reading Minilesson Principle

Legends are often told in poetic language.

Studying Legends

You Will Need

- familiar poetic legends, such as *Merlin and the Dragons* by Jane Yolen and *John Henry* by Julius Lester, from Text Set: Genre Study: Legends
- chart paper and markers

Academic Language / Important Vocabulary

- legend
- poetic
- ballad

Continuum Connection

- Notice and understand the characteristics of some specific fiction genres: e.g., realistic fiction, historical fiction, folktale, fairy tale, fractured fairy tale, fable, myth, legend, epic, ballad, fantasy including science fiction, hybrid text (p. 69)

Goal

Understand that legends often include poetic language.

Rationale

When students learn that legends are often told in poetic language, having originally taken the form of a poem or ballad, they understand the development of the legend and can interpret its meaning and importance.

Assess Learning

Observe students when they talk about and read legends and notice if there is evidence of new learning based on the goal of this minilesson.

- Do students recognize that the language of legends can be poetic?
- Do they use the terms *legend, poetic,* and *ballad?*

Minilesson

To help students think about the minilesson principle, use a familiar poetic legend to provide an interactive discussion. Here is an example.

- Show the cover of *Merlin and the Dragons*. Read the first paragraph and the last sentence on page 6, the beginning of Merlin's story.

  Is there any language here that sounds more like it came from a poem than from a story?

- Write examples on the chart.
- Show the cover of *John Henry* and the final page of print.

  What do you notice about the print on this page?

  The last few lines are written to look like a poem.

- Read the refrain with some rhythm so students can notice the poetic qualities. Introduce the word *poetic* and explain that poems and songs are written in poetic language.
- Review that the legend of John Henry is based on a ballad, a type of song, which explains why it has a songlike or poetic quality to the language.

Have a Try

Invite the students to talk with a partner about why a legend might have poetic language.

> Why do you think a legend might be told in poetic language? Turn and talk about that.

- After time for discussion, ask a few volunteers to share.

Summarize and Apply

Summarize the learning and remind students to think about whether a legend is poetic.

> You learned that sometimes, legends are told in poetic language.

- Add the principle to the chart.

> Today, you can choose to read a legend. Think about if any parts of the legend are told in poetic language. Bring the book when we meet so you can share.

Legends are often told in poetic language.

"Dark-haired he was"
"Dreams of dragons, dreams of stone"

"I got a rainbow RINGGGG! RINGGGG! Tied round my shoulder RINGGGG! RINGGGG!"

Share

Following independent reading time, gather students in the meeting area.

> Who found some poetic language in a legend today? Share your example.

Extend the Lesson (Optional)

After assessing students' understanding, you might decide to extend the learning.

- Find the original ballad about John Henry online and play it for the class. Discuss how it is similar to and different from the book by Julius Lester.

RML 8

LA.U23.RML8

Reading Minilesson Principle

The legend often shows what the culture values.

Studying Legends

You Will Need

- several familiar legends, such as the following from Text Set: Genre Study: Legends:
  - *The Story of Jumping Mouse* by John Steptoe
  - *Merlin and the Dragons* by Jane Yolen
  - *John Henry* by Julius Lester
- chart paper and markers
- sticky notes

Academic Language / Important Vocabulary

- legend
- culture
- values

Continuum Connection

- Extend understanding to fiction content that is beyond most students' immediate experience: e.g., customs and beliefs in different cultures, a wide range of settings (p. 70)

Goal

Understand that legends often reflect the values of the legend's culture of origin.

Rationale

When students learn to recognize that a legend often reflects the values of a culture, they begin to understand that legends help people gain knowledge about their shared history and build a community of shared values.

Assess Learning

Observe students when they talk about and read legends and notice if there is evidence of new learning based on the goal of this minilesson.

- Are students able to recognize that legends often reflect the values of a culture?
- Do they use the terms *legend, culture,* and *values*?

Minilesson

To help students think about the minilesson principle, use familiar legends to provide an interactive lesson. Here is an example.

- Show the cover of *The Story of Jumping Mouse.*

  Where does this story take place?

  What do you remember about how Magic Frog treated Jumping Mouse and Jumping Mouse treated the other animals?

  The story takes place outside in nature. Magic Frog and Jumping Mouse both help each other. Some of the other animals offer help to Jumping Mouse, too. This story is based on a Great Plains Indians legend. What do you learn from it about the culture of the Great Plains Indians and what they value?

- As needed, explain the meaning of *culture* and *values*. Record responses on the chart paper.

  Think about another book, *Merlin and the Dragons*. What do you know about the setting and what was important to the people in that culture?

- Revisit a few pages as needed to guide students to understanding. Add notes to the chart based on the conversation.

Have a Try

Invite the students to talk with a partner about legends.

- Show the cover of *John Henry* and revisit a few pages as needed.

  Think about the legend of John Henry. Turn and talk about the setting and what was important to the people of that time.

- After time for discussion, ask volunteers to share. Add to chart.

Book	Setting	Culture and Values
The Story of Jumping Mouse	Outside in nature	The Great Plains Indians seem to have valued nature and treating one another kindly.
Merlin and the Dragons	England long ago	Kings had all of the control, so royalty and power were very important. Magic was used to explain things people didn't understand.
John Henry	1800s, moving west in America	Building railroads was very important at that time. Hard-working and strong people were valued.

The legend often shows what the culture values.

Summarize and Apply

Summarize the learning and remind students to think about how a legend often reflects the values of a culture.

You learned that legends often show what is important to a culture. How does knowing that help you understand a legend better?

- Add the principle to the chart.

  If you choose to read a legend today, think about the cultural values as you read. Place sticky notes on pages that show the values. Bring the book when we meet so you can share.

Share

Following independent reading time, gather students together to talk about their reading.

Who would like to share your thoughts about the cultural values of the legend you read? Talk about how that helps you understand the legend better.

Extend the Lesson (Optional)

After assessing students' understanding, you might decide to extend the learning.

- As students read other legends, talk about why the legend was important to the people in the culture the legend is from. Encourage students to do research to help them identify what is important to the people in that culture and how the legend came to be.

Assessment

After you have taught the minilessons in this umbrella, observe students as they talk and write about their reading across instructional contexts: interactive read-aloud, independent reading, guided reading, shared reading, and book club. Use *The Literacy Continuum* (Fountas and Pinnell 2017) to guide the observation of students' reading and writing behaviors.

- What evidence do you have of new understandings related to legends?
    - Can students identify ways in which legends are alike?
    - Do students participate in constructing a working definition for legends?
    - Do they understand that legends are about heroes and their accomplishments?
    - Are they aware that a legend can be about an imaginary or a real person?
    - Can they talk about the quest in a legend?
    - Are they aware that legends are often passed down over time and sometimes are connected to myths?
    - Can they identify the poetic language in a legend?
    - Do they talk about how a legend is connected to the values of a culture?
    - Are they using the terms *legends, traditional literature, fantasy,* and *quest*?
- In what other ways, beyond the scope of this umbrella, are students talking about fiction books?
    - Are students interested in other types of fantasy?

Use your observations to determine the next umbrella you will teach. You may also consult Minilessons Across the Year (pp. 61–64) for guidance.

Read and Revise

After completing the steps in the genre study process, help students read and revise their definition of the genre based on their new understandings.

- **Before:** A legend is an imagined story about a hero.
- **After:** A legend is an imagined story about heroes and their accomplishments that has been handed down over time.

Reader's Notebook

When this umbrella is complete, provide a copy of the minilesson principles (see resources.fountasandpinnell.com) for students to glue in the reader's notebook (in the Minilessons section if using *Reader's Notebook: Advanced* [Fountas and Pinnell 2011]), so they can refer to the information as needed.

Minilessons in This Umbrella

RML1	Tall tales are alike in many ways.
RML2	The definition of a tall tale is what is always true about it.
RML3	Tall tales are a type of folktale.
RML4	Authors of tall tales use exaggeration throughout the story.
RML5	Authors of tall tales describe the unbelievable parts of the story as if they are factual or true.
RML6	The characters in tall tales do not change or develop.

Genre Study: Tall Tales

Before Teaching Umbrella 24 Minilessons

Genre study supports students in knowing what to expect when beginning to read a text in a genre. It helps students develop an understanding of the distinguishing characteristics of a genre and gives them the tools they need to navigate a variety of texts. There are six broad steps in a genre study, described on pages 39–41. Depending on your students' experience with fiction genres, you may want to teach LA.U6.RML3 before teaching the minilessons in this umbrella.

Because students must be familiar with multiple tall tales and other types of folktales before beginning a genre study, immerse them in books that are clear examples. Gather a basket of tall tales to have available during independent reading time. Folktales are a type of traditional literature along with fables, fairy tales, legends, epics, ballads, and myths (see p. 40). In addition to tall tales, other types of folktales include beast tales, cumulative tales, pourquoi tales, trickster tales, noodlehead tales, and realistic tales. Use the suggested tall tales from the *Fountas & Pinnell Classroom*™ *Interactive Read-Aloud Collection* or tall tales from the classroom library.

Genre Study: Tall Tales

Doña Flor: A Tall Tale About a Giant Woman with a Great Big Heart by Pat Mora
Swamp Angel by Anne Isaacs
Paul Bunyan by Steven Kellogg
Thunder Rose by Jerdine Nolen
Big Jabe by Jerdine Nolen

As you read aloud and enjoy these texts together, help students

- notice similarities between them,
- notice the traits of the characters, and
- make connections to their own lives.

RML 1
LA.U24.RML1

Reading Minilesson Principle

Tall tales are alike in many ways.

Studying Tall Tales

You Will Need

- a collection of familiar tall tales
- chart paper with a blank space at the top for a title, plus the heading *Noticings* and sections for *Always* and *Often*
- markers

Academic Language / Important Vocabulary

- tall tale
- folktale
- characteristics

Continuum Connection

- Understand that there are different types of texts and that they have different characteristics (p. 69)
- Notice and understand the characteristics of some specific fiction genres: e.g., realistic fiction, historical fiction, folktale, fairy tale, fractured fairy tale, fable, myth, legend, epic, ballad, fantasy including science fiction, hybrid texts (p. 69)

Goal

Notice and understand the characteristics of tall tales.

Rationale

When students study tall tales as a genre through inquiry, they gain a deeper understanding both of individual stories and the genre as a whole (see pages 39–41 for more information about genre study).

Assess Learning

Observe students when they talk about tall tales and notice if there is evidence of new learning based on the goal of this minilesson.

- Are students able to identify characteristics that define tall tales?
- Can students classify characteristics by determining whether they *always* or *often* occur in tall tales?
- Do they use the terms *tall tale, folktale,* and *characteristics*?

Minilesson

To help students think about the minilesson principle, use familiar tall tales to engage them in noticing the characteristics that define a tall tale. Here is an example.

- Have students sit in small groups and provide each group with several examples of a tall tale. Groups can rotate the books so they have an opportunity to compare several examples.

  Think about the tall tales you already know and your group's examples. Talk with your group about how all tall tales are alike.

- Provide a few minutes for conversation.

  Now think about what you noticed. Which of those things *always* occur in tall tales and which things *often* occur? Let's keep track on a chart.

- As students share, prompt the discussion as needed to help them identify whether certain characteristics occur always or often in tall tales. The following suggested prompts may be helpful:
  - *What are the characters like?*
  - *What types of events do you notice in tall tales?*
  - *What types of settings do you notice in tall tales?*
- On chart paper, create a noticings chart and add student ideas.

Have a Try

Invite the students to talk with a partner about tall tales.

> Think about a book you are reading. Compare it to the chart and decide if it is a tall tale or not. Turn and talk to your partner about that.

Summarize and Apply

Summarize the learning and remind students to think about the characteristics of tall tales.

> What do you notice about tall tales?

- Add the title *Tall Tales* to the chart.

> If you read a tall tale today, think about which of the characteristics on the chart you can find in it. Bring the book when we meet so you can share.

Share

Following independent reading time, gather students in the meeting area to talk about their reading.

> Who read a tall tale today? Talk about which characteristics from the list you noticed in the book.

Tall Tales

Noticings:

Always	Often
• Are a type of folktale, handed down over many years	• Describe how something came to be
• Have characters, settings, and events that are exaggerated	• Have characters that do not change or develop
• Tell about a person with extraordinary qualities and abilities	• Reflect something important about the culture or place they come from
• Describe unbelievable things as factual or true	

Extend the Lesson (Optional)

After assessing students' understanding, you might decide to extend the learning.

- Continue adding to the noticings chart as students read more examples of tall tales.
- **Writing About Reading** Have students write in a reader's notebook about the characteristics of a tall tale they have read.

RML 2

LA.U24.RML2

Reading Minilesson Principle

The definition of a tall tale is what is always true about it.

Studying Tall Tales

You Will Need

- a familiar tall tale, such as *Doña Flor* by Pat Mora, from Text Set: Genre Study: Tall Tales
- the tall tales noticings chart from RML1
- chart paper and markers

Academic Language / Important Vocabulary

- tall tale
- genre
- definition

Continuum Connection

- Notice and understand the characteristics of some specific fiction genres: e.g., realistic fiction, historical fiction, folktale, fairy tale, fractured fairy tale, fable, myth, legend, epic, ballad, fantasy including science fiction, hybrid texts (p. 69)

Goal

Construct a working definition of tall tales.

Rationale

When students construct a working definition of tall tales, they have to identify and summarize the most important characteristics of the genre. Using the definition, they will be able to recognize other books that fit the genre.

Assess Learning

Observe students when they talk about tall tales and notice if there is evidence of new learning based on the goal of this minilesson.

- Can students identify the characteristics of a tall tale?
- Are they able to identify whether a book fits the definition of a tall tale?
- Do they use the terms *tall tale, genre,* and *definition*?

Minilesson

To help students think about the minilesson principle, guide them in constructing a working definition of a tall tale. Here is an example.

- Show the tall tales noticings chart and discuss the characteristics of a tall tale.

  What do you know about tall tales?

- Ask several volunteers to read the noticings.

  Think about the ways tall tales are *always* alike. How does knowing how tall tales are *always* alike help you read a tall tale?

  Using what you know about tall tales, let's write a definition of tall tales. The definition will always be true about tall tales.

- Write *Tall tales are* on chart paper.

  Turn and talk about how you could finish this sentence to write a definition for all tall tales.

- After time for discussion, ask a few volunteers to share. Use the ideas to construct a working definition of a tall tale and write it on the chart paper.

Have a Try

Invite the students to talk with a partner about the definition of a tall tale.

- Show the cover of a tall tale, such as *Doña Flor*. Revisit a few pages as needed.

  Turn and talk about whether *Doña Flor* fits the definition we wrote for a tall tale.

- After time for discussion, ask students to share. Revise the working definition as needed.

Summarize and Apply

Summarize the learning and remind students to think about the definition of a tall tale.

What is always true about a tall tale?

If you read a tall tale today, think about whether it fits the definition. Bring the book when we meet so you can share.

Tall Tales

Tall tales are stories with a lot of exaggeration.

Share

Following independent reading time, gather students in the meeting area to talk about their reading.

Did the book you read today fit the definition of a tall tale? Talk about that.

Extend the Lesson (Optional)

After assessing students' understanding, you might decide to extend the learning.

- **Writing About Reading** Encourage students to write a tall tale of their own using the definition constructed in class.

RML3
LA.U24.RML3

Reading Minilesson Principle
Tall tales are a type of folktale.

Studying Tall Tales

You Will Need

- several familiar tall tales, such as the following from Text Set: Genre Study: Tall Tales:
  - *Thunder Rose* by Jerdine Nolen
  - *Paul Bunyan* by Steven Kellogg
  - *Doña Flor* by Pat Mora
- a variety of familiar folktales, such as beast tales, cumulative tales, pourquoi tales, trickster tales, noodlehead tales, and realistic tales
- chart paper prepared like the chart on the next page but without check marks and principle
- markers
- basket of folktales, including tall tales

Academic Language / Important Vocabulary

- tall tale
- folktale
- characteristics

Continuum Connection

- Notice and understand the characteristics of some specific fiction genres: e.g., realistic fiction, historical fiction, folktale, fairy tale, fractured fairy tale, fable, myth, legend, epic, ballad, fantasy including science fiction, hybrid texts (p. 69)

Goal

Understand that tall tales are a type of folktale.

Rationale

When students learn that tall tales fit within the broader category of folktales, they think more deeply about what characterizes certain types of literature. They begin to think about what all folktales have in common and also which characteristics distinguish tall tales from other folktales.

Assess Learning

Observe students when they categorize tall tales as a type of folktale and notice if there is evidence of new learning based on the goal of this minilesson.

- Are students familiar with the characteristics of tall tales and folktales?
- Can they identify why a tall tale is a type of folktale?
- Are they using academic vocabulary, such as *tall tale, folktale,* and *characteristic*?

Minilesson

To help students think about the minilesson principle, guide them to notice how tall tales and folktales are related. Here is an example.

- Before teaching this lesson, students should have had many experiences with tall tales and other types of folktales.
- Read aloud the characteristics on the prepared chart.

  We've been talking about tall tales, like *Thunder Rose* and *Paul Bunyan*. Keep those books in mind as you turn and talk to a partner about which of these characteristics are true for tall tales.

- After a few moments, ask volunteers to go to the prepared chart and put a check mark in the *Tall Tale* column for each characteristic that applies.

  You could say that all these characteristics are true of tall tales. Now think what you know about folktales, such as "Jack and the Beanstalk," "Goldilocks and the Three Bears," or the Anansi stories.

  Where would you put check marks in the *Folktales* column?

Have a Try

Invite the students to talk with a partner about tall tales.

- Have students compare *Doña Flor* with a familiar folktale, such as "Chicken Little," "The Little Red Hen," or a Coyote folktale.

  Where would you put check marks for these two stories?

- After time for discussion, ask several pairs to share.

Summarize and Apply

Summarize the learning and remind students to think about what they know about tall tales when they read one.

What does the chart show you about tall tales and folktales?

- Add the principle to the chart.

  When you read today, choose a book from this basket. Notice whether you are reading a folktale or, specifically, a tall tale. Bring the book when we meet so you can share.

Tall tales are a type of folktale.

Characteristic	Tall Tale	Folktale
Handed down over many years	✓	✓
Story is imagined	✓	✓
Characters, setting, and events are exaggerated	✓	
About a person with extraordinary qualities and abilities	✓	
Describes unbelievable things as factual or true	✓	

Share

Following independent reading time, gather students in small groups to share their books.

Share the book you read with your group. Talk about what kind of book it is and how you know.

Extend the Lesson (Optional)

After assessing students' understanding, you might decide to extend the learning.

- **Writing About Reading** Have students write about a tall tale they have read, explaining how they knew it was a tall tale.

RML4
LA.U24.RML4

Reading Minilesson Principle

Authors of tall tales use exaggeration throughout the story.

Studying Tall Tales

You Will Need

- several familiar tall tales, such as the following from Text Set: Genre Study: Tall Tales:
  - *Paul Bunyan* by Steven Kellogg
  - *Swamp Angel* by Anne Isaacs
  - *Doña Flor* by Pat Mora
- chart paper prepared with sketches that show an example of exaggeration from each tall tale
- markers

Academic Language / Important Vocabulary

- tall tale
- exaggeration

Continuum Connection

- Notice and understand the characteristics of some specific fiction genres: e.g., realistic fiction, historical fiction, folktale, fairy tale, fractured fairy tale, fable, myth, legend, epic, ballad, fantasy including science fiction, hybrid texts (p. 69)

Goal

Notice how authors use exaggeration throughout tall tales.

Rationale

When students learn to recognize exaggeration in tall tales, they become familiar with the characteristics of the genre and know what to expect when reading other tall tales.

Assess Learning

Observe students when they talk about and read tall tales and notice if there is evidence of new learning based on the goal of this minilesson.

- Are students able to identify examples of exaggeration in tall tales?
- Do they use the terms *tall tale* and *exaggeration*?

Minilesson

To help students think about the minilesson principle, use familiar tall tales to help them notice how exaggeration is used in tall tales. Here is an example.

- Display the prepared chart and the covers of the tall tales you used for the sketches, such as *Paul Bunyan*, *Swamp Angel*, and *Doña Flor*.

  Take a look at the sketches I made from tall tales that you know. Turn and talk about the sketches I have drawn and what they show.

- Allow students a few moments to think about the sketches and talk about what they represent.

  What do these sketches show about tall tales?

- Guide the conversation as needed so that students understand that the sketches from the tall tales show a character with extraordinary qualities and abilities. As needed, introduce the word *exaggeration* and explain what it means.

  I have drawn just one example of the exaggeration used to show the main character's extraordinary qualities and abilities. Think about other examples of exaggeration in the stories.

- Ask volunteers to share just one or two examples. Turn through the pages as needed to prompt student thinking. Add the word *exaggeration* beneath each sketch and record students' responses.

Have a Try

Invite the students to talk with a partner about examples of exaggeration in tall tales.

> What other examples of exaggeration are in these stories? Turn and talk to a partner about that.

- Ask several volunteers to share their ideas and record responses on the chart.

Summarize and Apply

Summarize the learning and remind students to think about exaggeration in tall tales.

> What characteristic of tall tales did you talk about today?

- Add the principle to the chart.

> If you read a tall tale today, notice examples of exaggeration. Bring the book when we meet so you can share.

Authors of tall tales use exaggeration throughout the story.

Paul Bunyan	Swamp Angel	Doña Flor

Exaggeration:	Exaggeration:	Exaggeration:
• way bigger than others • lifts cows • holds trees • plays with bears • digs a river	• builds a cabin with her hands • throws a bear to the sky • snores make trees fall	• grabs star • hugs wind • giant • birds build nests in her hair

Share

Following independent reading time, gather students together to talk about their reading.

> Who read a tall tale today? What exaggerations did you notice?

Extend the Lesson (Optional)

After assessing students' understanding, you might decide to extend the learning.

- **Writing About Reading** Have students add on to one of the tall tales they read by writing about new ways that the character might use her extraordinary qualities and abilities.

RML 5

LA.U24.RML5

Reading Minilesson Principle

Authors of tall tales describe the unbelievable parts of the story as if they are factual or true.

Studying Tall Tales

You Will Need

- several familiar tall tales, such as the following from Text Set: Genre Study: Tall Tales:
  - *Big Jabe* by Jerdine Nolen
  - *Thunder Rose* by Jerdine Nolen
- chart paper prepared with several sentences from tall tales
- markers
- sticky notes

Academic Language / Important Vocabulary

- tall tale
- unbelievable
- factual
- true

Continuum Connection

- Notice and understand the characteristics of some specific fiction genres: e.g., realistic fiction, historical fiction, folktale, fairy tale, fractured fairy tale, fable, myth, legend, epic, ballad, fantasy including science fiction, hybrid texts (p. 69)

Goal

Notice how the author makes unbelievable parts seem factual or true.

Rationale

When students learn to recognize that an author of a tall tale shows the unbelievable parts as true, they understand how the author brings humor and exaggeration into the tale. They gain a deeper understanding of and know what to expect when reading tall tales.

Assess Learning

Observe students when they talk about the characteristics of tall tales and notice if there is evidence of new learning based on the goal of this minilesson.

- Are students able to identify the unbelievable parts of a tall tale?
- Can students discuss the way that an author of a tall tale writes unbelievable parts of the story as if they are true?
- Do they use the terms *tall tale, unbelievable, factual,* and *true*?

Minilesson

To help students think about the minilesson principle, use familiar tall tales to engage students in a discussion about another characteristic of tall tales. Here is an example.

- Display the chart and the cover of *Big Jabe*.

  Take a look at the sentences from *Big Jabe* that I have written here.

- Read the sentences.

  What do you notice about the way the author has written these sentences?

- Guide the conversation as needed so that students understand that the author has written the unbelievable parts as if they are true. As students provide ideas, paraphrase and add to their ideas to encourage use of the words *unbelievable, factual,* and *true* in the conversation.

  How does it make a tall tale more enjoyable to read when an author writes in this way?

Have a Try

Invite the students to talk with a partner about tall tales.

- Show the cover of *Thunder Rose*.

  Notice the examples from *Thunder Rose* that I have included on the chart. Turn and talk about how the author described these parts of the story.

- After time for discussion, ask a few volunteers to share.

Authors of tall tales describe the unbelievable parts of the story as if they are factual or true.

"He could weed a whole field of soybeans before sunup, hoe the back forty by midday, and mend ten miles of fence by sunset."

"So much cotton was flying 'round that come morning, when the sun rose up, it couldn't shine through."

"At the age of five, Rose did a commendable job of staking the fence without a bit of help."

"She caught hold of a mass of clouds and squeezed them hard, real hard, all the while humming her song."

Summarize and Apply

Summarize the learning and remind students to think about the way an author of a tall tale writes unbelievable parts as if they are true.

You noticed examples of the way an author of a tall tale writes unbelievable parts as if they are factual or true.

- Add the principle to the chart.

  If you read a tall tale today, use a sticky note to mark any pages that show examples of an unbelievable part that is written as if it is factual or true. Bring the book when we meet so you can share.

Share

Following independent reading time, gather students in the meeting area to talk about their reading.

Who read a tall tale today? Share a part that shows an unbelievable event as if it were factual or true.

Extend the Lesson (Optional)

After assessing students' understanding, you might decide to extend the learning.

- **Writing About Reading** Encourage students to work with a partner to brainstorm ideas for tall tales. Have them make notes of different ways they could show an unbelievable event as if it were true.

RML 6

LA.U24.RML6

Reading Minilesson Principle

The characters in tall tales do not change or develop.

Studying Tall Tales

You Will Need

- several familiar tall tales, such as the following from Text Set: Genre Study: Tall Tales:
  - *Doña Flor* by Pat Mora
  - *Thunder Rose* by Jerdine Nolen
- chart paper and markers

Academic Language / Important Vocabulary

- tall tale
- character
- change
- develop

Continuum Connection

- Notice predictable or static characters (characters that do not change) as typical in traditional literature (p. 71)

Goal

Notice how the characters in tall tales are flat (i.e., they do not change or develop).

Rationale

Often, students spend time learning about how characters change from the beginning of a story to the end of a story. When they read tall tales, however, they need to know that the characters do not change. Students need to change their expectations when they read a tall tale.

Assess Learning

Observe students when they read and discuss tall tales and notice if there is evidence of new learning based on the goal of this minilesson.

- Do students understand that characters in tall tales do not change or develop?
- Do they use the terms *tall tale, character, change,* and *develop*?

Minilesson

To help students think about the minilesson principle, use familiar tall tales to engage students in a discussion about the nature of characters in tall tales. Here is an example.

- Show the cover of *Doña Flor*.

  Think about the character of Doña Flor as I revisit the beginning and the end of this story.

- Show and read the first two pages and the last two pages.

  What do you notice about who Doña Flor is at the beginning and who she is at the end of the book?

- As students discuss the character, prompt the conversation to help students think about the way that she does not change from the beginning to the end. Here are some suggested prompts:
  - *Using a few words, how would you describe the character at the beginning? At the end?*
  - *Has she changed who she is?*
  - *Has she developed or learned any lessons?*
  - *What examples from the story show you this?*

- As students provide ideas, write the title on chart paper and then write the description of Doña Flor at the beginning and the description of her at the end to show that she has not developed or changed.

Have a Try

Invite the students to talk with a partner about how a character in a tall tale does not change or develop.

- Show and read pages 3–4 and the last two pages of *Thunder Rose.*

  Think about Rose at the beginning and the end of this book. Even though she is a baby at the beginning, is she already the character who she will be throughout the story? Turn and talk about that.

- After time for a brief discussion, ask students to share ideas. Record responses on the chart.

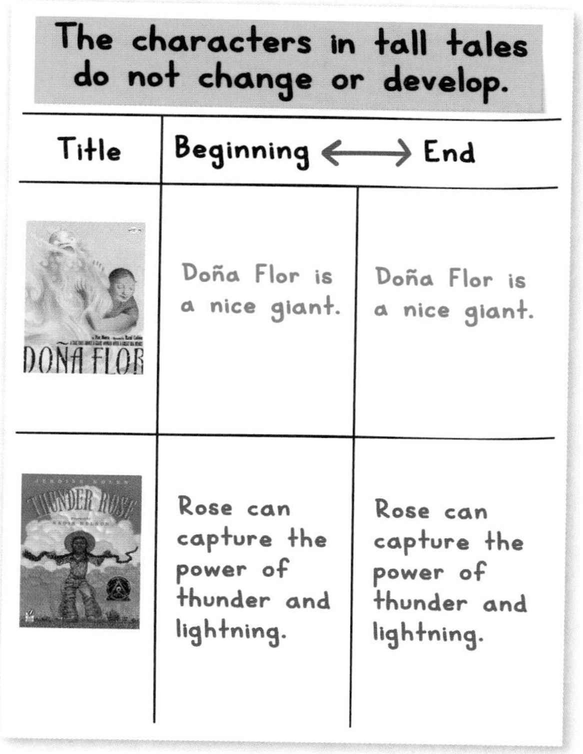

The characters in tall tales do not change or develop.

Title	Beginning	End
DOÑA FLOR	Doña Flor is a nice giant.	Doña Flor is a nice giant.
THUNDER ROSE	Rose can capture the power of thunder and lightning.	Rose can capture the power of thunder and lightning.

Summarize and Apply

Summarize the learning and remind students to think about how characters in tall tales do not change or develop.

What did you learn about characters in tall tales?

- Add the principle to the chart.

  If you read a tall tale today, think about the main character at the beginning and the end of the story and whether he changes or develops. Bring the book when we meet so you can share.

Share

Following independent reading time, gather students in the meeting area.

Who read a tall tale today? Share what you noticed about the main character.

Extend the Lesson (Optional)

After assessing students' understanding, you might decide to extend the learning.

- **Writing About Reading** Have students make a two-column chart to compare and contrast a character from a fiction story who changes and develops with a character from a tall tale who does not. Encourage the student to add specific examples from the story to explain their thinking.

Assessment

After you have taught the minilessons in this umbrella, observe students as they talk and write about their reading across instructional contexts: interactive read-aloud, independent reading, guided reading, shared reading, and book club. Use *The Literacy Continuum* (Fountas and Pinnell 2017) to guide the observation of students' reading and writing behaviors.

- What evidence do you have of new understandings related to tall tales?
    - Can students identify the ways in which tall tales are alike?
    - Do they understand the definition of a tall tale?
    - Do they understand that tall tales are a type of folktale?
    - Can students identify the exaggeration in a tall tale?
    - Are they aware that the unbelievable parts of a tall tale are described as being true?
    - Do they notice that the characters in tall tales do not change or develop?
    - Are they using the terms *tall tales, folktales, definition, exaggeration, unbelievable, factual,* and *develop*?
- In what other ways, beyond the scope of this umbrella, are students talking about fantasy?
    - Do students express an interest in other kinds of fantasy or fairy tales?

Use your observations to determine the next umbrella you will teach. You may also consult Minilessons Across the Year (pp. 61–64) for guidance.

Read and Revise

After completing the steps in the genre study process, help students read and revise their definition of the genre based on their new understandings.

- **Before:** Tall tales are stories with a lot of exaggeration.
- **After:** Tall tales are stories that are unbelievable but are described like they are factual and true.

Reader's Notebook

When this umbrella is complete, provide a copy of the minilesson principles (see resources.fountasandpinnell.com) for students to glue in the reader's notebook (in the Minilessons section if using *Reader's Notebook: Advanced* [Fountas and Pinnell 2011]), so they can refer to the information as needed.

Minilessons in This Umbrella

RML1	Historical fiction stories are alike in many ways.
RML2	The definition of historical fiction is what is always true about it.
RML3	The setting is important to the story in historical fiction.
RML4	Historical fiction is always imagined but may be based on real people, places, or events.
RML5	Historical fiction writers often use the language of the times in the dialogue.
RML6	Historical fiction writers use the past to give a message that can be applied today.

Before Teaching Umbrella 25 Minilessons

Genre study supports students in knowing what to expect when beginning to read a text in a genre. It helps students develop an understanding of the distinguishing characteristics of a genre and gives students the tools they need to navigate a variety of texts. There are six broad steps in the genre study process, and they are described on pages 39–41. Before engaging in genre study, students must read and discuss examples of the genre.

Prior to teaching this series of minilessons, read and discuss a variety of historical fiction stories that include diverse people, cultures, time periods, and circumstances. For this umbrella, it is important to select books that are clear examples of historical fiction, such as the following books from the *Fountas & Pinnell Classroom*™ *Interactive Read-Aloud Collection* text sets or suitable historical fiction books from your own library.

Genre Study: Historical Fiction

Baseball Saved Us by Ken Mochizuki

The Butterfly by Patricia Polacco

The Bracelet by Yoshiko Uchida

White Water by Michael S. Bandy and Eric Stein

Coming On Home Soon by Jacqueline Woodson

Freedom

Under the Quilt of Night by Deborah Hopkinson

As you read aloud and enjoy these texts together, help students

- notice similarities across them,
- think about whether characters, settings, and problems are based on actual historic events, and
- make connections between an author's message and their own lives.

Genre Study: Historical Fiction

Freedom

RML1
LA.U25.RML1

Studying Historical Fiction

You Will Need

- a collection of familiar historical fiction books, such as these from Text Set: Genre Study: Historical Fiction:
- *Baseball Saved Us* by Ken Mochizuki
- *The Butterfly* by Patricia Polacco
- *The Bracelet* by Yoshiko Uchida
- *White Water* by Michael S. Bandy and Eric Stein
- *Coming On Home Soon* by Jacqueline Woodson
- chart paper prepared with the headings *Historical Fiction* and *Noticings* and with sections for *Always* and *Often*
- a selection of books that are not historical fiction

Academic Language / Important Vocabulary

- historical fiction
- narrative structure
- characteristics

Continuum Connection

- Notice and understand the characteristics of some specific fiction genres: e.g., realistic fiction, historical fiction, folktale, fairy tale, fractured fairy tale, fable, myth, legend, epic, ballad, fantasy including science fiction, hybrid text (p. 69)

Reading Minilesson Principle

Historical fiction stories are alike in many ways.

Goal

Notice and understand the characteristics of historical fiction.

Rationale

When students study the historical fiction genre through inquiry, they gain a deeper understanding both of individual stories and the genre as a whole. When they develop an understanding of historical fiction, they will know what to expect when they encounter books of that genre (see pages 39–41 for information about genre study).

Assess Learning

Observe students when they read and talk about historical fiction. Notice if there is evidence of new learning based on the goal of this minilesson.

- Do students notice similarities across historical fiction stories?
- Are they able to identify which things *always* occur and which things *often* occur in historical fiction?
- Do they understand the terms *historical fiction, narrative structure*, and *characteristics*?

Minilesson

To help students think about the minilesson principle, choose historical fiction stories that you have read aloud, and engage the students in noticing the characteristics across the texts. Here is an example.

- Have students sit in small groups. Provide each group with an example of a familiar historical fiction text. As needed, groups can rotate the books so they have an opportunity to compare several examples.

  Think about the historical fiction books we have read in class, the example you have in your group, and others you may have read on your own. Talk with your group about how the historical fiction books are all alike.

- After time to turn and talk, ask students to think and share by having a conversation about the ways historical fiction texts are *always* alike and *often* alike. The following prompts may be helpful:
  - *What have you noticed about the characters, settings, plots, and narrative structures?*
  - *When do the stories take place?*
  - *What type of dialogue have you noticed?*
  - *Does that* always *or* often *occur in historical fiction?*
- Record students' noticings on the prepared chart.

Have a Try

Invite the students to talk in a small group about historical fiction.

- Hand each group of three or four students a book, some historical fiction and some not.

  Talk with your group about whether the book is historical fiction. Why do you think that? Look back at the chart and talk about each of the categories as they relate to the book.

Summarize and Apply

Summarize the learning and remind students to think about the characteristics of historical fiction.

Today we created a list of the characteristics of historical fiction. You decided which characteristics *always* occur in historical fiction and which characteristics *often* occur.

When you read today, think about whether the book you are reading is historical fiction. If it is, bring it when we meet so you can share.

Historical Fiction

Noticings:

Always	Often
• Stories are imagined but take place in the real world. • They have characters, plots, and settings (narrative structures). • The stories focus on problems and issues of life in the past.	• The characters, plot, and setting are usually believable. • The stories are often based on real people or events from the past. • The stories are often connected to the author's own personal experiences. • Authors often use the language of the time in the dialogue.

Share

Following independent reading time, gather students together in the meeting area to talk about their reading.

Who read a historical fiction book today? How did you know the genre?

Extend the Lesson (Optional)

After assessing students' understanding, you might decide to extend the learning.

- Continue to add to the noticings chart as students read more historical fiction stories and notice more about the genre.
- Introduce students to Genre Thinkmarks for historical fiction (visit resources.fountasandpinnell.com to download this resource). A Genre Thinkmark is a tool that guides readers to note certain elements of a genre in their reading. They can quickly note the page numbers of parts of the book where they see evidence of the characteristics of historical fiction and share it with others.

RML 2

LA.U25.RML2

Reading Minilesson Principle

The definition of historical fiction is what is always true about it.

Studying Historical Fiction

You Will Need

- a familiar historical fiction story, such as *The Butterfly* by Patricia Polacco, from Text Set: Genre Study: Historical Fiction
- the historical fiction noticings chart from RML1
- chart paper and markers

Academic Language / Important Vocabulary

- historical fiction
- genre
- definition

Continuum Connection

- Notice and understand the characteristics of some specific fiction genres: e.g., realistic fiction, historical fiction, folktale, fairy tale, fractured fairy tale, fable, myth, legend, epic, ballad, fantasy including science fiction, hybrid text (p. 69)

Goal

Create a working definition of historical fiction.

Rationale

When you help students create a working definition of historical fiction, you help them summarize the most important characteristics of the genre. Over time, the definition can be revised as students experience additional examples of historical fiction.

Assess Learning

Observe students when they think and talk about the characteristics of historical fiction. Notice if there is evidence of new learning based on the goal of this minilesson.

- Can students describe the characteristics of historical fiction?
- Can they determine whether a particular book fits the genre?
- Do they use language such as *historical fiction*, *genre*, and *definition*?

Minilesson

Guide students in constructing a definition of historical fiction from the RML1 noticings chart. Here is an example.

- Review the noticings chart created during RML1.

  We created a list of the ways that historical fiction stories are alike.

- Ask one or more students to read the noticings.

  Look at the ways that historical fiction stories are *always* alike and think about a definition for historical fiction. What is always true about historical fiction?

- Write *Historical fiction stories are* on chart paper.

  Think about how you could finish this sentence to create a definition for all books in the historical fiction genre. Turn and talk about that.

- After time for discussion, ask students to share. Assist students in adding to the ideas of classmates to collaboratively construct a definition. Using students' ideas, write a definition on the chart.

Have a Try

Invite the students to talk with a partner about whether a familiar historical fiction book, such as *The Butterfly*, fits the definition.

- Show the cover of the book and revisit a few pages as necessary.

  Turn and talk about whether *The Butterfly* fits the definition of historical fiction.

- After time for discussion, ask several students to share their thinking. Encourage them to refer back to the chart as they offer their explanations.

Historical Fiction

Historical fiction stories are made-up stories that take place in the past and tell about something in history.

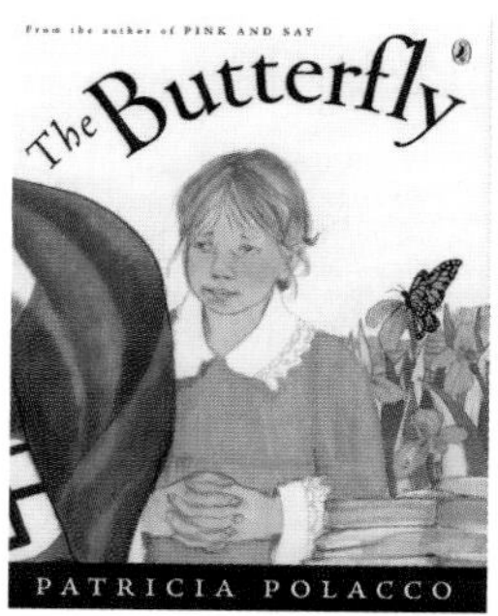

Summarize and Apply

Summarize the learning and remind students to think about characteristics of historical fiction as they read historical fiction stories.

Today you helped write a definition that describes the genre of historical fiction.

Choose a fiction book to read today and think about whether it fits the definition of historical fiction. If it does, bring the book to share when we meet.

Share

Following independent reading time, gather students in the meeting area to talk about their reading.

Who read a book today that fits the definition of historical fiction? Tell a little bit about the book and the characteristics that make you think it is historical fiction.

Extend the Lesson (Optional)

After assessing students' understanding, you might decide to extend the learning.

- Lead a discussion about similarities and differences between historical fiction and realistic fiction.
- Historical fiction writers do a lot of research to write about something that took place during a specific time period. When you read a historical fiction book during interactive read-aloud, take time to talk about what the author needed to know to write the book and how the author might have found that information.

RML 3
LA.U25.RML3

Reading Minilesson Principle

The setting is important to the story in historical fiction.

Studying Historical Fiction

You Will Need

- several familiar historical fiction books, such as the following from Text Set: Genre Study: Historical Fiction:
  - *The Butterfly* by Patricia Polacco
  - *The Bracelet* by Yoshiko Uchida
  - *White Water* by Michael S. Bandy and Eric Stein
- chart paper and markers

Academic Language / Important Vocabulary

- historical fiction
- setting
- plot
- characters

Continuum Connection

- Infer the importance of the setting to the plot of the story in realistic and historical fiction and fantasy (p. 70)

Goal

Infer the importance of the setting to the plot of the story in historical fiction.

Rationale

When students understand the importance of setting in historical fiction stories, they begin to think about the ways that writers create a sense of authenticity and the ways that setting drives characters and plot, developing their understanding of an author's craft.

Assess Learning

Observe students when they read and talk about historical fiction books. Notice if there is evidence of new learning based on the goal of this minilesson.

- Do students understand the importance of setting in historical fiction books?
- Are they able to analyze the connection between the setting and the plot?
- Do they use academic language, such as *historical fiction*, *setting*, *plot*, and *characters*?

Minilesson

To help students think about the minilesson principle, use familiar historical fiction stories to demonstrate how they can think about the setting and its importance to the plot. Here is an example.

- Show the illustration of Monsieur Marks being taken away by Nazi soldiers in *The Butterfly*.

  When does this story take place?

- Record responses on a chart.

  Why is it important that this story takes place in France during the Nazi German occupation?

- As students share ideas, engage them in a conversation about the importance of setting in historical fiction. The following prompts may be helpful:
  - *How does the setting affect the plot?*
  - *How does the setting affect what the characters do and say?*
  - *Would the events in this story be as likely to occur in a different time and place? Why not?*

  Now think about the setting in another familiar historical fiction book, *The Bracelet*.

- Show the illustration of the Bay Bridge. Repeat the questions above about the setting and its importance. Record responses on the chart.

Have a Try

Invite the students to talk with a partner about the setting in a historical fiction book.

- Show the illustration of Michael and a boy drinking from different water fountains in *White Water*.

  Turn and talk with a partner about the setting in this historical fiction book. When does it take place? How does the setting impact the plot?

- After time for discussion, ask a few students share. Add to the chart.

The setting is important to the story in historical fiction.

Book	Setting	Why is it important to the plot?
 The Butterfly (Patricia Polacco)	Nazi Germany's occupation of France →	Monique discovers that her mother has been helping Jews hide from the Nazis.
 the bracelet	California during World War II →	Emi and her family are sent to a prison camp for Japanese Americans.
 White Water	1962, segregation-era South →	Michael decides to take a risk and drinks from the "white" fountain.

Summarize and Apply

Summarize the learning and remind students to think about how setting impacts plot in historical fiction.

What does the chart show about the setting in historical fiction stories?

- Review the chart and add the principle to the top.

  If you read a historical fiction book today, think about how the setting is important to the plot. Bring the book with you when we meet so you can share.

Share

Following independent reading time, gather students in the meeting area to talk about their reading.

Did anyone read a historical fiction book today?

Tell about the setting. Why is it important to the plot?

Extend the Lesson (Optional)

After assessing students' understanding, you might decide to extend the learning.

- Have students work with partners to conduct research about the setting of historical fiction books they read. Invite students to share their findings with the class.
- **Writing About Reading** Have students write in a reader's notebook about the setting of a historical fiction book and how the setting impacts the plot. Encourage them to write about how the plot would be different if the setting were different.

RML 4

LA.U25.RML4

Reading Minilesson Principle

Historical fiction is always imagined but may be based on real people, places, or events.

Studying Historical Fiction

You Will Need

- several familiar historical fiction books, such as the following from Text Set: Genre Study: Historical Fiction:
  - *The Butterfly* by Patricia Polacco
  - *White Water* by Michael S. Bandy and Eric Stein
  - *Baseball Saved Us* by Ken Mochizuki
- chart paper and markers
- basket of historical fiction books

Academic Language / Important Vocabulary

- historical fiction
- characters
- setting
- imagined

Continuum Connection

- Notice and understand the characteristics of some specific fiction genres: e.g., realistic fiction, historical fiction, folktale, fairy tale, fractures fairy tale, fable, myth, legend, epic, ballad, fantasy including science fiction, hybrid text (p. 69)

Goal

Understand that historical fiction is always imagined but may be based on real people, places, and events.

Rationale

When students recognize that historical fiction stories are always imagined but that they may be based on real people, places, and events, they are better able to connect to the characters, places, and events as they evaluate the authenticity of historical fiction books they read.

Assess Learning

Observe students when they read and talk about historical fiction stories. Notice if there is evidence of new learning based on the goal of this minilesson.

- Do students recognize that historical fiction stories are imagined but that they may be based on real people, places, or events?
- Can they distinguish between the imagined and the real people, places, and events?
- Do they use language such as *historical fiction*, *characters*, *setting*, and *imagined*?

Minilesson

To help students think about the minilesson principle, use familiar historical fiction stories to engage them in a discussion of what is imagined and what is real. Here is an example.

- Show the cover of *The Butterfly*.

  In this historical fiction book, what do you know about the main characters, setting, and events?

- Read the first three paragraphs of the Author's Note.

  Which parts of the story are imagined, and which parts are based on real people or real events?

  What is real about the setting?

- Record responses on a chart.

  Think about another historical fiction book, *White Water*.

- Read the Authors' Note.

  What is real and what is imagined about the characters, setting, and events?

- Add responses to the chart.

  Why do authors base historical fiction stories on real characters, places, and events?

Have a Try

Invite the students to talk with a partner about whether another historical fiction book is based on real people, places, or events.

- Show *Baseball Saved Us.*

  Turn and talk with a partner about whether this historical fiction book is based on real people, places, or events. What evidence do you have?

- After time for discussion, read the Author's Note. Ask students to share their thinking, and add to the chart.

Historical fiction is always imagined but may be based on real people, places, or events.

Book	Real People	Real Place	Real Event
 The Butterfly	• Marcelle Solliliage • Monique • Sevrine	• France	• French citizens helped Jews escape the Nazis
 White Water	• Michael • Michael's grand-mother	• Michael's home	• Racial segregation
 Baseball Saved Us	• Japanese Americans	• Internment camps in American desert, 1942-1945	• Japanese Americans were forced to live separately from other Americans

Summarize and Apply

Summarize the learning and remind students to think about whether a historical fiction book they read is based on real people, places, or events.

Look at the chart. What did you learn today about historical fiction stories?

- Add the principle to the top of the chart.

  When an author includes an author's note or there is additional information included on the back of the book or the book jacket, be sure to read it. These sections help you know which parts of the story are real and which parts are imagined.

  You may want to choose a historical fiction book from this basket today. If you do, think about whether the people, places, and setting are real or imagined. Bring the book with you when we meet so you can share.

Share

Following independent reading time, gather students in the meeting area to talk about their reading.

Who read a historical fiction book today?

Tell what parts were based on real people, places, or events.

Extend the Lesson (Optional)

After assessing students' understanding, you might decide to extend the learning.

- Have students fill in a Historical Fiction Evidence from Text chart (visit resources.fountasandpinnell.com to download this resource) to record page numbers and historical evidence in books they read. Once they fill in the chart, they can glue it into a reader's notebook.

RML 5

LA.U25.RML5

Reading Minilesson Principle

Historical fiction writers often use the language of the times in the dialogue.

Studying Historical Fiction

You Will Need

- several familiar historical fiction books, such as the following:
  - *Baseball Saved Us* by Ken Mochizuki and *Coming On Home Soon* by Jacqueline Woodson, from Text Set: Genre Study: Historical Fiction
  - *Under the Quilt of Night* by Deborah Hopkinson, from Text Set: Freedom
- chart paper and markers

Academic Language / Important Vocabulary

- historical fiction
- dialogue
- racist
- derogatory
- authentic

Continuum Connection

- Notice a writer's use of regional or historical vocabulary or features of dialect included for literary effect (p. 71)

Goal

Understand that historical fiction writers often use language of the times in the dialogue to make the text feel authentic.

Rationale

When you teach students to recognize and analyze dialogue and language in historical fiction stories, they are able to evaluate the authenticity of a writer's voice and think about how language helps create the setting.

Assess Learning

Observe students when they read and talk about historical fiction books. Notice if there is evidence of new learning based on the goal of this minilesson.

- Do students recognize when dialogue in historical fiction stories is different from the way we speak today and why an author might use this kind of language?
- Do they use language such as *historical fiction*, *dialogue*, *racist*, *derogatory*, and *authentic*?

Minilesson

To help students think about the minilesson principle, use familiar historical fiction stories to help students notice the dialogue and language. Here is an example.

- Show *Baseball Saved Us* and read the dialogue on the third to last page of text.

  Would you hear that kind of dialogue today? Why do you think that?

  Why do you think the writer included that kind of dialogue?

- Create and add to a chart that reflects the discussion and students' thinking.

  Now listen to dialogue from another historical fiction book.

- Show *Coming On Home Soon* and read the dialogue on the first page.

  What do you notice about the dialogue?

  What was the author's purpose in deciding to use this dialogue?

- Add responses to the chart.

Have a Try

Invite the students to talk with a partner about dialogue in a historical fiction book.

- Show *Under the Quilt of Night*. Read the dialogue on the page titled *Traveling*.

  Turn and talk with a partner. What does the dialogue on this page tell you about the time period?

- After time for discussion, ask students to share. Add to the chart.

Historical fiction writers often use the language of the times in the dialogue.

Book	Time Period	Dialogue	How does the language help you understand the time period?
 Baseball Saved Us	• 1942-1945 • World War II	• Racist language	• It includes a derogatory term that is not acceptable today.
 Coming On Home Soon	• World War II	• Commonly used language during the time but considered racist today • ". . . since all the <u>men</u> are off <u>fighting</u> in the war."	• It includes terminology that is not acceptable today. • At that time, women did not fight in wars, but now they do.
 Under the Quilt of Night	• 1850s • pre-Civil War	• "Your <u>master</u> and <u>his men</u> are close behind!"	• <u>Master</u> and <u>his men</u> refer to slavery.

Summarize and Apply

Summarize the learning and remind students to think about how an author uses dialogue to make a historical fiction story feel authentic.

What do you understand about how writers of historical fiction use dialogue in their stories?

- Review the chart and add the principle to the top.

  As you read historical fiction, notice how the author uses dialogue and language in a way that is authentic for the time period. If you read historical fiction today, bring the book with you when we meet so you can share.

Share

Following independent reading time, gather students together in the meeting area to talk about historical fiction.

Did anyone notice authentic dialogue or language in a historical fiction book today? Share what you noticed.

Extend the Lesson (Optional)

After assessing students' understanding, you might decide to extend the learning.

- Students may use the Historical Fiction Noticing Details chart (visit resources.fountasandpinnell.com to download this resource) to list what they notice about the setting, people, events, and language as they read historical fiction books. Once they fill in the chart, they can glue it into a reader's notebook.
- **Writing About Reading** Have students write in a reader's notebook what they notice about dialogue in a historical fiction book. Have them compare and contrast the time period's language and today's language.

RML 6
LA.U25.RML6

Reading Minilesson Principle

Historical fiction writers use the past to give a message that can be applied today.

Studying Historical Fiction

You Will Need

- several familiar historical fiction books, such as the following from Text Set: Genre Study: Historical Fiction:
  - *Baseball Saved Us* by Ken Mochizuki
  - *The Butterfly* by Patricia Polacco
  - *White Water* by Michael S. Bandy and Eric Stein
- chart paper and markers

Academic Language / Important Vocabulary

- historical fiction
- message
- apply

Continuum Connection

- Understand that the messages or big ideas in fiction texts can be applied to their own lives or to other people and society (p. 69)

Goal

Understand that the messages in historical fiction can be applied to their own lives, to other people's lives, or to society today.

Rationale

When you teach students to notice and think about the messages in historical fiction books, they understand that events that happened in the past affect how we live our lives in the present. You may want to teach LA.U8.RML1 before this lesson to ensure students understand how to notice the author's message.

Assess Learning

Observe students when they read and talk about historical fiction books. Notice if there is evidence of new learning based on the goal of this minilesson.

- Are students able to identify the author's message(s) in historical fiction books?
- Can they explain how these messages are applied to their own lives?
- Do they use language such as *historical fiction*, *message*, and *apply*?

Minilesson

To help students think about the minilesson principle, guide students to infer the author's message and think about how the message applies to life today. Here is an example.

- Show *Baseball Saved Us* and read the first page.

  What message about this time in history do you think the author is trying to share with you? Turn and talk about that.

- After time for discussion, ask students to share their thinking. Use students' responses to create a chart.

  Do you think this message applies to your own life today? How?

- Add to the chart.
- Next, show *The Butterfly* and read the page with the illustration of Sevrine and Monique going to the cellar, starting with "'My mother and father.'"

  What do you think the author's message is (or messages are) on this page? Do you think the message applies to your life today? How?

- Add to the chart.

Have a Try

Invite the students to talk with a partner about the message in another historical fiction story.

- Show *White Water* and read the last page of the story.

  Turn and talk with a partner. What do you think the author's message is (or messages are) about this time in history? Does it apply to your life today?

- After time for discussion, ask students to share. Add to the chart.

Historical fiction writers use the past to give a message that can be applied today.

Title	Author's Message, Related to a Time in History	How the Message Applies Today
 Baseball Saved Us	• It was wrong to treat Japanese Americans badly.	• Don't assume things about people. • Treat everyone fairly.
 The Butterfly	• It took courage for French citizens to help Jewish people during the Nazi occupation.	• Stand up for what is right. • Find ways to help those around you who are in need.
 White Water	• People should not have been made to think they weren't good enough because of their skin.	• Do not judge people based on skin color or other outward appearances. • Believe in yourself. Don't let anything stop you from achieving your goals.

Summarize and Apply

Summarize the learning and remind students to think about how the message in a historical fiction book might be applied to their own lives.

What does the chart show you about historical fiction?

- Add the principle to the top of the chart.

  As you read historical fiction, notice the author's message and how it relates to the time period and your own life. If you read historical fiction today, bring the book with you when we meet so you can share.

Share

Following independent reading time, gather students together in the meeting area to talk about their reading.

Who read a historical fiction book today? Did you notice the message? How does it apply to your life today? Share your thinking.

Extend the Lesson (Optional)

After assessing students' understanding, you might decide to extend the learning.

- As students read more historical fiction books, have them notice any recurring themes or messages. Continue to have them think about how these messages might apply to life today.
- **Writing About Reading** Have students write in a reader's notebook about the message in a historical fiction book and the supporting details that help them recognize that message.

Assessment

After you have taught the minilessons in this umbrella, observe students as they talk and write about their reading across instructional contexts: interactive read-aloud, independent reading, guided reading, shared reading, and book club. Use *The Literacy Continuum* (Fountas and Pinnell 2017) to observe students' reading and writing behaviors.

- What evidence do you have of new understandings related to historical fiction?
  - Do students recognize how historical fiction stories are alike?
  - Do they understand that historical fiction is always imagined but that it can be based on real characters, settings, and events?
  - Do they recognize when writers use language of the historical time period in the dialogue?
  - Can students identify the author's message and how it can be applied to their own lives?
  - Do they use language such as *historical fiction*, *narrative structure*, *setting*, *characteristics*, *genre*, *definition*, *dialogue*, *authentic*, and *message*?
- In what other ways, beyond the scope of this umbrella, are students talking about books?
  - Do they show interest in reading other kinds of books that take place in the past, such as biographies?

Use your observations to determine the next umbrella you will teach. You may also consult Minilessons Across the Year (pp. 61–64) for guidance.

Read and Revise

After completing the steps in the genre study process, help students read and revise their definition of the genre based on their new understandings.

- **Before:** Historical fiction stories are made-up stories that take place in the past and tell about something in history.
- **After:** Historical fiction stories are made up by the author but have characters, events, and settings that could be real. They take place in the past.

Reader's Notebook

When this umbrella is complete, provide a copy of the minilesson principles (see resources.fountasandpinnell.com) for students to glue in the reader's notebook (in the Minilessons section if using *Reader's Notebook: Advanced* [Fountas and Pinnell 2011]), so they can refer to the information as needed.

Minilessons in This Umbrella

RML1	Writers use poetic or descriptive language to help you understand the setting.
RML2	Evaluate the significance of the setting in a story.
RML3	Evaluate the believability of the setting in fantasy books.
RML4	Evaluate the authenticity of the setting in historical and realistic fiction.

Before Teaching Umbrella 26 Minilessons

Read aloud and discuss engaging realistic fiction, historical fiction, and modern fantasy stories that take place in a variety of locations and time periods. Include books that take place in both real and imagined places. As much as possible, choose books in which the setting is central to the story. Read aloud books in which the setting is richly described with poetic or descriptive language. Use the following books from the *Fountas & Pinnell Classroom™ Interactive Read-Aloud Collection* text sets or choose books from your classroom library in which setting has an effect on the characters or plot.

Exploring Literary Language

Sequoia by Tony Johnston

If You're Not from the Prairie by David Bouchard

Family

Morning on the Lake by Jan Bourdeau Waboose

Grit and Perseverance

Rikki-Tikki-Tavi by Rudyard Kipling

Coraline by Neil Gaiman

Problem Solving/Resourcefulness

Destiny's Gift by Natasha Anastasia Tarpley

Writer's Craft

Black Dog by Levi Pinfold

Exploring Rights and Citizenship

The Day Gogo Went to Vote by Elinor Batezat Sisulu

As you read aloud and enjoy these texts together, help students

- talk about when and where the story takes place,
- notice whether the setting is real or imagined,
- notice and discuss poetic or descriptive language that describes the setting, and
- discuss the importance of the setting to the plot and characters.

Exploring Literary Language

Sequoia by Tony Johnston

Family

Grit and Perseverance

Rikki-Tikki-Tavi by Rudyard Kipling

Problem Solving/ Resourcefulness

Writer's Craft

Exploring Rights and Citizenship

The Day Gogo Went to Vote by Elinor Batezat Sisulu

RML 1
LA.U26.RML1

Reading Minilesson Principle

Writers use poetic or descriptive language to help you understand the setting.

Thinking About the Setting in Fiction Books

You Will Need

- several familiar fiction books that include poetic or descriptive language about the setting, such as the following from Text Set: Exploring Literary Language:
  - *Sequoia* by Tony Johnston
  - *If You're Not from the Prairie* by David Bouchard
- chart paper and markers
- fiction books students are reading
- basket of familiar fiction books
- sticky notes

Academic Language / Important Vocabulary

- fiction
- setting
- poetic language
- descriptive language

Continuum Connection

- Notice and understand long stretches of descriptive language important to understanding setting and characters (p. 71)
- Notice when a fiction writer use poetic or descriptive language to show the setting, appeal to the five senses, or convey human feelings such as loss, relief, or anger (p. 71)

Goal

Notice and understand the poetic or descriptive language used to show the setting.

Rationale

Poetic and descriptive language helps readers visualize and understand settings. When you guide students to think about how authors use this type of language, they develop an appreciation for and understanding of how writers construct believable settings. They can also use this knowledge in their own fiction writing.

Assess Learning

Observe students when they talk about setting and notice if there is evidence of new learning based on the goal of this minilesson.

- Are students able to identify poetic and descriptive language?
- Can students understand the information about setting that an author tries to convey through language?
- Do they use the terms *fiction, setting, poetic language,* and *descriptive language*?

Minilesson

To help students think about the minilesson principle, engage them in a discussion of an author's use of poetic and descriptive language to describe the setting. Here is an example.

> As I revisit a few pages from *Sequoia*, think about the setting and what the author wants you to hear, see, feel, or smell.

- Read page 7 from *Sequoia* without showing the illustration.

  > What did you notice?
  >
  > What mental image do you form about the time and place?
  >
  > What are some of the words that the author uses to describe the setting?

- Continue the conversation, reading page 29 without showing the illustration.

  > What words does the author use to give clues about the setting?
  >
  > What does the author want you to know about this setting?

- Record examples of poetic and descriptive language and students' responses on chart paper.
- Repeat the activity by reading page 8 from *If You're Not from the Prairie* and continuing the conversation.
- Add to the chart.

Have a Try

Invite the students to talk with a partner about setting.

- Have each student bring a fiction book they are reading or have them choose one from the basket.

  Think about whether an author uses descriptive or poetic language to help you know about the setting. With your partner, look through a fiction book and see if you notice any examples.

- After students turn and talk, invite a few students to share their thinking.

Writers use poetic or descriptive language to help you understand the setting.

	The Writer's Words	What the Words Show
Sequoia	"He listens to beetles scratch, to woodpeckers tap, to firs converse in wind." (page 7)	• what animals and plants sound like in the forest • personification—"He" is the tree, and the trees are having a conversation. • can feel the wind on my face as if I am really there
	"He tells of golden grizzles—gone. He tells of olden forests—gone." (page 29)	• shows what is missing in the setting, or how it used to be • shows a change in environment • shows how the sequoia trees have been around a long time
If You're Not from the Prairie	"Our cold winds of winter cut right to the core, Hot summer wind devils can blow down the door . . ." (page 8)	• change in season • severity of weather • extremes in weather, from hot to cold to wind

Summarize and Apply

Summarize the learning and remind students to notice poetic and descriptive language.

How would you describe the language writers use to help you understand the setting?

- Write the principle at the top of the chart.

  If you read a fiction book today, notice if the writer uses poetic or descriptive language to help you understand the setting. If so, put a sticky note on an example and bring your book to share when we come back together.

Share

Following independent reading time, gather students together in the meeting area to talk about their reading.

Who found an example of poetic or descriptive language that describes a setting today?

Read the description and explain how it helped you understand the setting.

Extend the Lesson (Optional)

After assessing students' understanding, you might decide to extend the learning.

- **Writing About Reading** Have students write in a reader's notebook about how an author uses poetic and descriptive language to help them understand a story's setting. They should include specific examples of the language and explain the effect of each example.

RML 2
LA.U26.RML2

Reading Minilesson Principle
Evaluate the significance of the setting in a story.

Thinking About the Setting in Fiction Books

You Will Need

- several familiar fiction texts, such as the following:
  - *Morning on the Lake* by Jan Bourdeau Waboose, from Text Set: Family
  - *Rikki-Tikki-Tavi* by Rudyard Kipling, from Text Set: Grit and Perseverance
- chart paper and markers
- realistic fiction or fantasy stories students are reading
- basket of familiar realistic fiction and fantasy stories
- sticky notes

Academic Language / Important Vocabulary

- setting
- plot
- fiction

Continuum Connection

- Infer the importance of the setting to the plot of the story in realistic and historical fiction and fantasy (p. 70)
- Evaluate the significance of the setting in the story (p. 70)

Goal

Evaluate the significance of the setting in the story.

Rationale

When you teach students to think about the importance of the setting in a story and to evaluate its significance, they understand that the setting is not an arbitrarily chosen time and place and that it has to make sense with the story. They develop an understanding of universal truths and ideas that are shaped by time and place.

Assess Learning

Observe students when they talk about setting and notice if there is evidence of new learning based on the goal of this minilesson.

- Are students able to identify the setting in a realistic fiction or fantasy story?
- Can they infer the importance of the setting to the plot?
- Are students able to evaluate the significance of the setting?
- Do they use the terms *setting, plot,* and *fiction*?

Minilesson

To help students think about the minilesson principle, engage them in thinking about and evaluating the significance of the setting in a realistic fiction or fantasy story. Here is an example.

- Revisit several pages that provide details about the setting from a familiar realistic fiction story, such as *Morning on the Lake*. For example, to show time, revisit the first sentence on page 1 and the illustration on the last page; to show place, revisit pages 4 and 19–20.

  What can you say about where and when this story takes place?

  How does the author show you the setting?

- Begin a chart and add the title and setting.
- Engage the students in a conversation that guides them to discuss the significance of the setting to the plot and also to evaluate whether the setting matters. Students' responses may vary, but be sure students have evidence to support their opinions. Here are some suggested prompts:
  - *Does it matter where and when the story takes place? Why do you think that?*
  - *Would the story be different if the setting changed? How?*
- Record whether the setting is important to the story (yes or no).
- Repeat the activity with a fantasy story, such as *Rikki-Tikki-Tavi*.

Have a Try

Invite the students to talk with a partner about the significance of setting and evaluate whether the setting matters.

- Have each student bring a realistic fiction or fantasy story they are reading or have them choose one from the basket.

  Think about where and when a story takes place. Turn and talk about the importance of the setting. Find specific examples from the story and tell your partner why the setting matters to the plot or why it doesn't matter.

- After time for discussion, ask students to share their thinking.

  Some stories could happen anywhere or anytime, but other stories could happen only in a particular setting. These are things to think about as you read fiction stories.

Evaluate the significance of the setting in a story.

Title	Setting	Important to the story?	Why or why not?
Morning on the Lake	Where: an area in the Northern wilderness with a lake When: one day in recent times from morning to night	No	• A reader anywhere can relate to spending quality time with a family member. • Learning about a family's history could happen anyplace or anytime.
Rikki-Tikki-Tavi	Where: a family's house and yard in India	Yes	• The animals (mongoose, cobra, tailorbird) all live in India.
	When: not too long ago	No	• The time period does not really matter to the story because it could be 100 years ago, today, or 100 years from now.

Summarize and Apply

Summarize the learning and remind students to think about the setting and its significance.

What did you learn about setting?

- Add the principle to the chart.

  If you read a fiction book today, think about the significance of the setting and whether the setting matters to the story. Mark pages you want to remember with a sticky note. Bring the book when we meet so you can share.

Share

Following independent reading time, gather students in small groups. Ensure that at least one member of each group read a realistic fiction or fantasy story today.

Share what you noticed about the significance of the setting.

Extend the Lesson (Optional)

After assessing students' understanding, you might decide to extend the learning.

- You can expand on this idea by having students think about the significance of the setting in historical fiction books (see LA.U25.RML3).

RML 3
LA.U26.RML3

Reading Minilesson Principle

Evaluate the believability of the setting in fantasy books.

Thinking About the Setting in Fiction Books

You Will Need

- several familiar fantasy books, such as the following:
  - *Coraline* by Neil Gaiman, from Text Set: Grit and Perseverance
  - *Black Dog* by Levi Pinfold, from Text Set: Writer's Craft
- chart paper and markers
- sticky notes

Academic Language / Important Vocabulary

- fantasy
- setting
- believable

Continuum Connection

- Evaluate the authenticity of the writer's presentation of the setting (p. 70)

Goal

Evaluate the believability of the setting in fantasy books.

Rationale

When students think about the believability of the setting in a fantasy book, they develop critical thinking skills and begin to evaluate the ways authors develop setting. Whether a fantasy story is set in a realistic world or a fantasy world, the characters and plot need to be believable within the setting. This lesson could also be taught as part of Umbrella 22: Understanding Fantasy.

Assess Learning

Observe students when they discuss setting in fantasy stories and notice if there is evidence of new learning based on the goal of this minilesson.

- Do students discuss whether a setting is believable within the parameters of the story?
- Do they use the terms *fantasy, setting,* and *believable*?

Minilesson

To help students think about the minilesson principle, engage them in thinking about the believability of a fantasy setting. Here is an example.

As I revisit a few pages from *Coraline*, think about the setting. Notice the world that the author has created and decide whether the things that happen make sense in the fantasy world of this story.

- Revisit a few parts of the story that relate to setting, such as pages 25, 33, 45, and 69.

  What details do you notice that show the setting?

- Record their examples on a chart.

  Think about the setting of this fantasy. Does the author make the setting believable within the fantasy? Why or why not?

  What does the writer do to get you to believe that the things that happen in this setting make sense?

- As students have a conversation, record their responses on the chart. Guide their understanding so they realize that believability of a setting is related to the context of the particular fantasy story. As readers, they make decisions as to whether an author successfully causes a reader to suspend disbelief.

Have a Try

Invite the students to talk with a partner about the believability of a fantasy setting.

- Revisit a few pages from *Black Dog*, such as pages 6, 15–16, and 17–18.

  What is the setting of this story? Does the author make it believable within the fantasy world he has created? Why or why not? Turn and talk about that.

- After students turn and talk, ask students to share ideas. Add to the chart.

Evaluate the believability of the setting in fantasy books.

Title	Setting Details	How does the writer make the setting believable?
Coraline	• The other house looks almost the same as her own house but with some odd differences. (pp. 25, 33) • Coraline goes back and forth between the fantasy world and the real world. (p. 45) • "It was so familiar—that was what made it feel so truly strange." (p. 69)	• The other house is part of her real house so it almost seems believable that it could exist. • The details make it seem it could be real, but creepy things happen. • The fantasy is slowly discovered, so it feels like it's really happening.
Black Dog	• The house has some normal parts that seem a little old. A giant eye is looking in. (p. 6) • The bridge, birdhouses, winter trees, and frozen lake are normal. (pp. 15–16) • The playground has normal swings but very strange looking slides. (pp. 17–18)	• Some details look like they could be real, while others are strange but believable. • Small details, like the birdhouses, make you feel like this could be a real place, but make-believe things happen. • The whole setting feels odd, so it makes sense that the giant dog comes out of the strange slides.

Summarize and Apply

Summarize the learning and remind students to notice settings when they read fantasy stories.

Today you learned it's important that the things that happen to the characters make sense in the author's fantasy world.

- Add the principle to the top of the chart.

  If you read a fantasy book today, notice if the setting is believable and mark any pages you want to remember. Bring the book when we come back together so you can share.

Share

Following independent reading time, gather students together in the meeting area to talk about their reading.

Who read a fantasy story today?

What is the setting of the book you read? Was it believable? Why or why not?

Extend the Lesson (Optional)

After assessing students' understanding, you might decide to extend the learning.

- **Writing About Reading** Have students write in a reader's notebook about the setting in a fantasy story. They should identify the time and place of the setting and write about whether the setting is believable and why or why not.

RML 4
LA.U26.RML4

Reading Minilesson Principle

Evaluate the authenticity of the setting in historical and realistic fiction.

Thinking About the Setting in Fiction Books

You Will Need

- several familiar historical and realistic fiction books, such as the following:
  - *The Day Gogo Went to Vote* by Elinor Batezat Sisulu, from Text Set: Exploring Rights and Citizenship
  - *Destiny's Gift* by Natasha Anastasia Tarpley, from Text Set: Problem Solving/ Resourcefulness
- chart paper prepared with two columns: *Historical Fiction* and *Realistic Fiction*
- markers
- six sticky notes, each labeled *Authentic*
- historical fiction or realistic fiction books students are reading
- basket of historical fiction and realistic fiction books
- sticky notes

Academic Language / Important Vocabulary

- historical fiction
- realistic fiction
- setting
- authenticity

Continuum Connection

- Evaluate the authenticity of the writer's presentation of the setting (p. 70)

Goal

Evaluate the authenticity of the setting in historical and realistic fiction.

Rationale

When students think about the authenticity of a historical or realistic fiction setting, they develop critical thinking skills and begin to evaluate the ways authors and illustrators reveal the setting. This lesson could also be taught when you teach minilessons on realistic fiction or historical fiction.

Assess Learning

Observe students when they talk about the authenticity of setting in historical and realistic fiction stories and notice if there is evidence of new learning based on the goal of this minilesson.

- Can students make connections between the setting and the characters and plot in historical fiction or realistic fiction?
- Are students able to evaluate the authenticity of a setting?
- Do they use the terms *historical fiction, realistic fiction, setting,* and *authenticity*?

Minilesson

To help students think about the minilesson principle, engage them in thinking about the authenticity of a historical and realistic setting. Here is an example.

- Revisit a few pages from *The Day Gogo Went to Vote* that show setting (see chart for examples). Start by showing pages 5–6.

  When an author and illustrator get the setting right for the characters and events of a story, the setting is authentic. Do you think the setting on these pages is authentic?

- Place one of the labeled sticky notes next to the page numbers.

  What details does the author or the illustrator include to make the setting historically accurate?

- Record students' responses in the first column of the chart. Then repeat the process for a couple of other examples in *The Day Gogo Went to Vote*.
- Repeat the process, this time using an example of realistic fiction, *Destiny's Gift*.

  Do you think the setting is authentic?

  What details does the author or the illustrator include to make the setting realistic and appropriate for the story?

Have a Try

Invite the students to talk with a partner about the setting of a realistic or historical fiction book.

- Have students bring a realistic or historical fiction book they are reading or choose one from the basket.

  Think about the setting in a realistic or historical fiction book. How does the author or illustrator create an authentic setting? Turn and talk about that.

- After students turn and talk, ask several volunteers to share what they noticed about the authenticity of the setting.

Evaluate the authenticity of the setting in historical and realistic fiction.

Historical Fiction — *The Day Gogo Went to Vote*	Realistic Fiction — *Destiny's Gift*
Pages 7–8 **Authentic** • April 26–28, 1994 were real dates for voting in South Africa.	Pages 1–2 **Authentic** • Characters have modern clothing. • The store looks like a town or city that could be real.
Page 12 **Authentic** • An old clock and no computer make the home seem real for the time and place.	Page 16–18 **Authentic** • Cordless phone, TV, and newspapers are all real things.
Page 19 **Authentic** • An ultraviolet machine was used to make sure no one voted twice.	Page 19–20 **Authentic** • Looks like a neighborhood that could exist today. • Characters have a block party in a neighborhood that could be real.

Summarize and Apply

Summarize the learning and remind students to notice settings when they read realistic and historical fiction.

What did you learn about the settings in historical and realistic fiction stories?

- Add the principle to the top of the chart.

  If you read a historical or realistic fiction book today, think about the setting. Notice if the author created an authentic setting and why or why not. Mark pages you want to remember with a sticky note and bring the book when we come together again.

Share

Following independent reading time, gather students together in the meeting area to talk about their reading.

Who read a realistic or historical fiction book today?

What is the setting of the book you read? What details did the author use to create an authentic setting?

Extend the Lesson (Optional)

After assessing students' understanding, you might decide to extend the learning.

- **Writing About Reading** Have students write in a reader's notebook an evaluation of the setting in a realistic or historical fiction book. They should identify the time and place of the setting and describe the details used by the author or illustrator to make the setting authentic.

Thinking About the Setting in Fiction Books

Assessment

After you have taught the minilessons in this umbrella, observe students as they talk and write about their reading across instructional contexts: interactive read-aloud, independent reading, guided reading, shared reading, and book club. Use *The Literacy Continuum* (Fountas and Pinnell 2017) to observe students' reading and writing behaviors.

- What evidence do you have of new understandings related to setting?
- Are students able to identify where and when a story takes place?
- Do students recognize when a writer uses poetic or descriptive language to give the reader information about time and place?
- Are they talking about the impact of setting on characters and plot?
- Are they able to evaluate a text for the believability and authenticity of a setting?
- Are they using terms such as *setting, poetic language, descriptive language, believable,* and *authenticity*?

- In what other ways, beyond the scope of this umbrella, are students talking about fiction?
  - Can students identify the elements of plot in a fiction text?
  - Are they discussing the ways that authors develop characters?

Use your observations to determine the next umbrella you will teach. You may also consult Minilessons Across the Year (pp. 61–64) for guidance.

Link to Writing

After teaching the minilessons in this umbrella, help students link the new learning to their own writing:

- Give students numerous opportunities throughout the school year to write their own stories. Encourage them to plan the setting before they start writing. Some students may benefit from drawing the setting before writing about it. Remind them to think about how the setting will influence the story's characters and action. Encourage them to use poetic or descriptive language.

Reader's Notebook

When this umbrella is complete, provide a copy of the minilesson principles (visit resources.fountasandpinnell.com) for students to glue in the reader's notebook (in the Minilessons section if using *Reader's Notebook: Advanced* [Fountas and Pinnell 2011]), so they can refer to the information as needed.

Minilessons in This Umbrella

RML1	The plot usually includes a beginning, a problem, a series of events, a high point, a solution, and an ending.
RML2	Sometimes stories have more than one problem.
RML3	Writers use flashbacks, flash-forwards, or a story-within-a-story.
RML4	Notice a writer's use of plots and subplots.
RML5	Use what you know to predict what will happen next or at the end of the story.
RML6	Writers end stories in a variety of ways.

Before Teaching Umbrella 27 Minilessons

Read and discuss a variety of high-quality fiction books that vary in types of characters, setting, and plot and that include a clearly defined problem, high point, and solution. The minilessons in this umbrella use the following books from the *Fountas and Pinnell Classroom* ™ *Interactive Read-Aloud Collection*; however, you can use any fiction books you have available in the classroom that have the characteristics listed above.

Grit and Perseverance

Rikki-Tikki-Tavi by Rudyard Kipling

Freedom

Under the Quilt of Night by Deborah Hopkinson

Wall by Tom Clohosy Cole

Family

Keeping the Night Watch by Hope Anita Smith

The Power of Knowledge

The Storyteller by Evan Turk

The Treasure Box by Margaret Wild

Hope and Resilience

Sami and the Time of the Troubles by Florence Parry Heide and Judith Heide Gilliland

Let the Celebrations Begin! by Margaret Wild

Empathy

The Crane Girl by Curtis Manley

Conflict Resolution

The Lion Who Stole My Arm by Nicola Davies

As you read aloud and enjoy these texts together, help students

- think about the problem and solution in the story,
- notice the events in the story, and
- summarize the story and include the problem, events, high point, solution, and ending.

Grit and Perseverance

Rikki-Tikki-Tavi by Rudyard Kipling

Freedom

Family

Keeping the Night Watch by Hope Anita Smith

The Power of Knowledge

Hope and Resilience

Empathy

Conflict Resolution

The Lion Who Stole My Arm by Nicola Davies

RML1

LA.U27.RML1

Reading Minilesson Principle

The plot usually includes a beginning, a problem, a series of events, a high point, a solution, and an ending.

Understanding Plot

You Will Need

- several familiar fiction books, such as the following:
  - *Rikki-Tikki-Tavi* by Rudyard Kipling, from Text Set: Grit and Perseverance
  - *Under the Quilt of Night* by Deborah Hopkinson, from Text Set: Freedom
- chart paper with a graphic organizer prepared with the labels: *Beginning, Problem, Event (several), High Point, Solution, Ending*
- markers
- sticky notes
- basket of fiction books

Academic Language / Important Vocabulary

- plot
- events
- problem
- solution
- high point
- narrative text structure

Continuum Connection

- Recognize and discuss aspects of narrative structure (beginning, series of events, high point of the story, problem, resolution, ending) (p. 70)

Goal

Notice and understand that the plot is a sequence of events in a story, including a beginning, problem, high point, solution, and ending.

Rationale

When students understand that the plot is what happens in a story, they can understand how the story works as a whole, follow events, and think about cause and effect. When students learn to expect that stories have a beginning, a problem, a series of events, a high point, a solution to the problem, and an ending, they understand how stories are constructed and can attend to the individual parts.

Assess Learning

Observe students when they talk about the plot in fiction stories and notice if there is evidence of new learning based on the goal of this minilesson.

- Are students aware that plot is what happens in a story?
- Can they identify the beginning, problem, events, high point, solution, and ending?
- Are they able to chronologically summarize a story and include the important elements of plot?
- Do they understand the terms *plot, events, problem, solution, high point,* and *narrative text structure*?

Minilesson

To help students think about the minilesson principle, engage them in thinking about narrative text structure. Here is an example.

- Show the prepared chart paper.

  What do you notice about this organizer?

- As needed, guide students to talk about the elements of narrative text structure. If students are unfamiliar with the term *high point*, ensure that they understand that it is the most exciting part of the story and that it leads to the solution of the problem.

  Think about *Rikki-Tikki-Tavi*. If I want to add details from this story that show each of the plot features, what could I add? Let's start with the beginning and talk about what happens in the same sequence as it happens in the story.

- As students provide ideas, add sticky notes to the chart.
- Ask a volunteer to read the chart, including each label and the details from the story written next to the label.

Have a Try

Invite the students to talk with a partner about the elements of narrative text structure.

> What would you write in the organizer to show the narrative text structure of *Under the Quilt of Night*? Turn and talk about that.

- After time for discussion, ask a few students to share. You can add sticky notes (use a different color sticky note or marker) for this story to the chart if it will be helpful for your students.

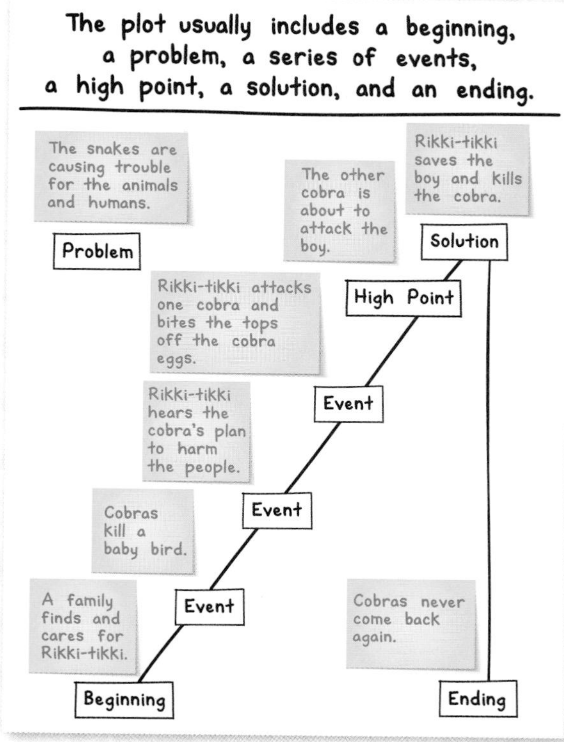
The plot usually includes a beginning, a problem, a series of events, a high point, a solution, and an ending.
The snakes are causing trouble for the animals and humans.
Problem
The other cobra is about to attack the boy.
Rikki-tikki saves the boy and kills the cobra.
Solution
Rikki-tikki attacks one cobra and bites the tops off the cobra eggs.
High Point
Rikki-tikki hears the cobra's plan to harm the people.
Event
Cobras kill a baby bird.
Event
A family finds and cares for Rikki-tikki.
Event
Cobras never come back again.
Beginning
Ending

Summarize and Apply

Summarize the learning and remind students to think about narrative text structure when they read fiction stories.

> What do you know about plot?

- Add the principle to the chart.

> Today you can choose a fiction story from the basket or continue one that you are already reading. Think about the parts of the story and mark pages with sticky notes that show these parts. Bring the book when we meet so you can share.

Share

Following independent reading time, gather students in small groups to talk about plot.

> In your group, talk about the parts of a story you noticed when you read today. Look back at the chart and see how many you can include. If you have not finished the book, you will probably not know about every part yet.

Extend the Lesson (Optional)

After assessing students' understanding, you might decide to extend the learning.

- Have students make or fill in a graphic organizer (see resources.fountasandpinnell.com) about the plot of a story. They can glue the organizer into a reader's notebook.

RML2
LA.U27.RML2

Reading Minilesson Principle
Sometimes stories have more than one problem.

Understanding Plot

You Will Need

- several familiar fiction books that have more than one problem, such as the following:
  - *The Treasure Box* by Margaret Wild, from Text Set: The Power of Knowledge
  - *Wall* by Tom Clohosy Cole, from Text Set: Freedom
  - *The Lion Who Stole My Arm* by Nicola Davies, from Text Set: Conflict Resolution
- chart paper and markers
- sticky notes
- basket of fiction stories with multiple problems

Academic Language / Important Vocabulary

- plot
- problem
- solution
- narrative text structure

Continuum Connection

- Follow a complex plot with multiple events, episodes, or problems (p. 70)

Goal

Understand that stories can have more than one problem.

Rationale

When students understand that some stories have more than one problem, they learn how to follow the plot in more complex works of fiction and understand the connection between each problem and the overall story and solution.

Assess Learning

Observe students when they read and discuss plot and notice if there is evidence of new learning based on the goal of this minilesson.

- Are students able to identify more than one problem in a story?
- Can they discuss the relationship between the different problems?
- Do they use the terms *plot, problem, solution,* and *narrative text structure*?

Minilesson

To help students think about the minilesson principle, engage them in thinking about the problems in a fiction story. Here is an example.

> Think about *The Treasure Box* and the problems faced by Peter. What problems does he have?

- Guide the students to understand that the characters face multiple problems. Use these prompts as needed.
  - *What is the main problem of the story?*
  - *What are some other problems Peter faces while trying to solve the main problem?*
- As students identify the main problems, write their responses on chart paper.

> Think about another fiction story, *Wall*. What is the main problem in the story?
>
> What is another problem in the story?

- Add responses to the chart.

> Usually, the main problem is presented at the beginning of the story and solved at the end. Other problems sometimes happen as the main character attempts to solve the main problem.

Have a Try

Invite the students to talk with a partner about a story with multiple problems.

- Show the cover of a book with multiple problems, such as *The Lion Who Stole My Arm*.

  Turn and talk about the main problem and the other problems Pedru faces.

- After time for discussion, ask a few students to share their thinking.

Summarize and Apply

Summarize the learning and remind students to think about multiple problems in stories.

What do you know about problems in stories?

- Add the principle to the chart.

  Today choose a fiction story from the basket or continue one that you are already reading. Think about whether you notice multiple problems and mark any pages with sticky notes that you want to remember. Bring the book when we meet so you can share.

Sometimes stories have more than one problem.

	Main Problem	Other Problems
The Treasure Box	Peter and his father must flee their home during a war.	Peter's father dies. Peter has to leave his treasure box behind.
Wall	When the wall was built, the boy's dad was stuck on the other side.	A soldier halts the boy and his mother as they head for the tunnel.
The Lion Who Stole My Arm	Pedru lost his arm to a lion and wants to get revenge.	The other children treat him differently. Pedru has trouble writing with one hand.

Share

Following independent reading time, gather students in small groups to talk about the problems in the books they read.

Talk about whether you noticed multiple problems in the book you read today and what they were. Share specific examples from the book.

Extend the Lesson (Optional)

After assessing students' understanding, you might decide to extend the learning.

- Have students make or fill in a graphic organizer (see resources.fountasandpinnell.com) about stories with more than one problem. They can glue the graphic organizer into a reader's notebook.
- **Writing About Reading** As students write their own fiction stories, have them think about whether the main character might have more than one problem and how they could weave the problems together.

RML 3
LA.U27.RML3

Reading Minilesson Principle

Writers use flashbacks, flash-forwards, or a story-within-a-story.

Understanding Plot

You Will Need

- several familiar fiction books that have flashbacks, flash-forward, or a story-within-a-story, such as the following:
  - *Sami and the Time of the Troubles* by Florence Parry Heide and Judith Heide Gilliland, from Text Set: Hope and Resilience
  - *The Storyteller* by Evan Turk, from Text Set: The Power of Knowledge
  - *The Crane Girl* by Curtis Manley, from Text Set: Empathy
  - *Let the Celebrations Begin!* by Margaret Wild, from Text Set: Hope and Resilience
- chart paper and markers
- highlighter or highlighting tape
- sticky notes

Academic Language / Important Vocabulary

- plot
- present
- flashback
- flash-forward
- story-within-a-story

Continuum Connection

- Recognize when the writer uses literary devices such as flashback and story-within-a-story to structure the text (p. 70)

Goal

Recognize when writers use literary devices such as flashbacks, flash-forwards, and story-within-a-story.

Rationale

When students recognize that sometimes an author uses a flashback (a scene within a story that takes place at an earlier time), a flash-forward (a scene within a story that takes place in the future), or a story-within-a-story (a story within the main story), they are better able to follow the plot in more complex and longer texts.

Assess Learning

Observe students when they read and talk about fiction stories and notice if there is evidence of new learning based on the goal of this minilesson.

- Do students understand that sometimes authors use a flashback, a flash-forward, or a story-within-a-story?
- Do they use the terms *plot, present, flashback, flash-forward,* and *story-within-a-story*?

Minilesson

To help students think about the minilesson principle, engage them in noticing when and why authors use flashbacks, flash-forwards, and a story-within-a-story. Here is an example.

- Read page 2 of *Sami and the Time of the Troubles.*

  What is happening to Sami in this story?

- Revisit the sections of text and illustrations on pages 25–28 that refer to the day long ago when Sami was younger and the children marched.

  What is happening in this part of the story?

  Why do you think the authors decided to take a break from the present time in the story to insert a flashback into the story?

  Sometimes an author will include a flashback as a way to give the reader some information to explain the characters' actions or to show a difference between the way things are now and the way things were in the past.

- Create a chart to show which part of the story shows the present time in the story and which part takes a break from it.
- Continue the conversation and chart with several other examples, such as the example of a story-within-a-story in *The Storyteller* and the flash-forward in *The Crane Girl.*

Have a Try

Invite the students to talk with a partner about a flashback, flash-forward, or story-within-a-story.

- Review a few pages of *Let the Celebrations Begin!*

  Are there parts of this story that take a break from the present time in the story? Turn and talk about that.

- After time for discussion, ask students to share. Add responses to the chart.

Writers use flashbacks, flash-forwards, or a story-within-a-story.

Title	Present Time in the Story	Break from the Present Time
 Sami and the Time of the Troubles	Sami and his family hide from the bombs.	The flashback is to a day when children marched in the streets.
 The Storyteller	The boy is very thirsty.	In a story-within-a-story, a bluebird that has lived for thousands of years finds water for a family.
 The Crane Girl	The crane, disguised as a girl, helps the family by making silk from her feathers.	The flash-forward is to a time when the cranes live together and raise their crane children.
 Let the Celebrations Begin!	The people are living in a war camp.	The flashback is to a time when Miriam was happily eating a chicken leg.

Summarize and Apply

Summarize the learning and remind students to notice when a story takes a break from the present time of the story.

How does an author fill in story details that happen in a different time or place?

- Add the principle to the chart.

  Today choose a fiction story from the basket or continue one that you are already reading. Think about whether there is a break from the present time of the story and mark pages with sticky notes that show that. Bring the book when we meet so you can share.

Share

Following independent reading time, gather students in the meeting area to talk about variations in the plot structures of the books they read.

Did anyone read a book in which the author included a flashback, flash-forward, or story-within-a-story? Share what you noticed.

Extend the Lesson (Optional)

After assessing students' understanding, you might decide to extend the learning.

- **Writing About Reading** Have students make or fill in a graphic organizer (see resources.fountasandpinnell.com) about flashbacks. They can glue the organizer into a reader's notebook to record other examples they notice as they read fiction stories.

RML 4
LA.U27.RML4

Reading Minilesson Principle

Notice a writer's use of plots and subplots.

Understanding Plot

You Will Need

- several familiar fiction books that include subplots, such as the following:
  - *Keeping the Night Watch* by Hope Anita Smith, from Text Set: Family
  - *The Lion Who Stole My Arm* by Nicola Davies, from Text Set: Conflict Resolution
- chart paper and markers
- fiction books students are reading

Academic Language / Important Vocabulary

- main plot
- plotline
- subplot
- minor plot

Continuum Connection

- Recognize a writer's use of plots and subplots (p. 70)

Goal

Recognize a writer's use of plots and subplots.

Rationale

When students learn to identify a main plot and subplots in a fictions story, they are better able to follow more complex, longer texts, and can think deeply about how the subplot relates to the main plot.

Assess Learning

Observe students when they read and discuss fiction stories and notice if there is evidence of new learning based on the goal of this minilesson.

- Are students able to identify a plot and a subplot in a fiction story?
- Do they recognize and use the terms *main plot, plotline, subplot,* and *minor plot*?

Minilesson

To help students think about the minilesson principle, engage them in thinking about a plot and subplots. Here is an example.

- Show the cover of *Keeping the Night Watch.*

  Think about the plot of *Keeping the Night Watch*, which includes a beginning, a problem, a series of events, a high point, a solution, and an ending. Turn and talk about the plot of this story.

- After discussion, ask volunteers to share. Work with students to summarize the main plot and then to list the events that make up the plot. Record on the chart paper.

  The events that make up the plot are called the plotline. Sometimes, stories have a subplot, which is a side story. It is also called a minor plot, and it continues alongside the main plot. The subplot also has its own plotline. Think about the subplot as I revisit one part from the book.

- Read pages 54–55.

  How would you describe the subplot?

  What is the minor plotline, or the events that make up the subplot?

- Add to chart.
- If students need additional practice, repeat the activity with another familiar story that has subplots.

  Why do you think the author includes this subplot? How is it connected to the main plot line?

Have a Try

Invite the students to talk with a partner about a plot, plot lines, and subplots.

- Show the cover of *The Lion Who Stole My Arm*.

  Turn and talk about the main plot and the subplot of this story. Remember that both the main plot and the subplot have a storyline, or plot line.

- After time for discussion, ask a few volunteers to share. Guide the conversations so students recognize that the *main plot* involves Pedru and his family getting revenge on the lion that bit off Pedru's arm and the *subplot* involves Pedru adjusting to living with one arm and using drawing as a way to work through it.

Notice a writer's use of plots and subplots. — Keeping the Night Watch

Main Plot Summary:	Subplot Summary:
C.J. is angry and struggling to forgive his father when his father leaves home for a while.	C.J. and Maya like each other, but they are nervous around each other.
Main Plotline:	**Minor Plotline:**
• C.J. ignores his father. • C.J. tries to help his sister through the adjustment. • C.J. starts to come around and talk to his dad. • C.J. asks his dad to sign his field trip permission slip. • C.J. follows his dad around the house secretly. • C.J. accepts that his dad made a mistake, but that they are still a family.	• C.J. is caught off guard when he suddenly likes Maya. • C.J. is very nervous to call Maya and struggles to talk. • C.J. wants to go on the field trip with Maya. • C.J. pulls away from best friend Preacher because he prefers spending time with Maya. • C.J. and Maya are both nervous around each other when they walk home from school. • C.J. tries to figure out how to be a boyfriend now.

Summarize and Apply

Summarize the learning and remind students to think about plots, plot lines, and subplots in fiction stories they are reading.

You learned that sometimes authors include both a main plot and subplots.

- Add the principle to the chart.

  Today choose a fiction story from the basket or continue one that you are already reading. Look for the main plot and notice whether there are any subplots. Bring the book when we meet so you can share.

Share

Following independent reading time, gather students in the meeting area to talk about plots and subplots.

Who would like to share a story you read that has both a plot and a subplot? Tell us what you noticed.

Extend the Lesson (Optional)

After assessing students' understanding, you might decide to extend the learning.

- As students encounter other books with subplots, guide them to clarify the main plot, main plot line, and the minor plot line and to think and talk about their interconnection. Examples from the *Independent Reading Collection* include *The Penderwicks at Point Mouette* and *Yang the Third and Her Impossible Family*.

RML 5

LA.U27.RML5

Reading Minilesson Principle

Use what you know to predict what will happen next or at the end of the story.

Understanding Plot

You Will Need

- independent reading books that students have selected
- chart paper and markers

Academic Language / Important Vocabulary

- predict
- evidence
- outcome
- plot
- setting
- characters

Continuum Connection

- Make predictions on an ongoing basis during and after reading (based on progress of the plot, characteristics of the setting, attributes of the characters, actions of the characters) (p. 70)

Goal

Predict what will happen next in a story and the outcome of the plot.

Rationale

When students learn to assess what they know about characters, setting, and plot to make predictions, they begin to understand motivation and to apply understandings to their own lives.

Assess Learning

Observe students when they make predictions about fiction stories and notice if there is evidence of new learning based on the goal of this minilesson.

- Do students apply what they know so far when making predictions?
- Are they using text evidence to support their predictions?
- Do they use the terms *predict, evidence, outcome, plot, setting,* and *characters*?

Minilesson

To help students think about the minilesson principle, engage them in making predictions. Here is an example.

- Ask students to bring a familiar fiction book that they are reading independently but have not yet finished.

  Think about the book you are reading right now. Based on what you know so far, what do you predict will happen next?

  What evidence from the book makes you think that?

- Ask one volunteer to share. Then, continue the conversation with that same student. As needed, prompt the conversation to help the student think about the book in different ways to find text evidence for his prediction.
  - *What do you know about the main character so far?*
  - *What has happened in the plot?*
  - *What are the characteristics of the setting?*
  - *What do you think will happen at the end?*
- As the student shares, make a list on chart paper of general strategies for making predictions.
- Have one or two additional students share their predictions. Continue adding to the chart.

Have a Try

Invite the students to talk with a small group about predictions.

> In your group, share a prediction about the book you are reading. Discuss evidence from the book that helped you make that prediction.

- After time for discussion, ask several students to share. Continue adding to the chart.

Use what you know to predict what will happen next or at the end of the story.

What might help make predictions?

- The progress of the plot
- Hints from the story
- Setting characteristics
- Character traits
- Character relationships
- Actions of characters
- Words of characters
- Thoughts of characters

Summarize and Apply

Summarize the learning and remind students to think about what might happen next in a story.

> What did you learn about making predictions?

- Add the principle to the chart.

> When you read today, notice if one of your predictions was correct. You can also make a new prediction based on information you get from reading. Bring the book when we meet so you can share.

Share

Following independent reading time, gather students in the meeting area to talk about their predictions.

> Who found the outcome of a prediction you made? Did you make any new predictions? Talk about that.

- As students share, add any new strategies for making predictions to the chart.

Extend the Lesson (Optional)

After assessing students' understanding, you might decide to extend the learning.

- **Writing About Reading** Have students make or fill in a graphic organizer about making predictions (see resources.fountasandpinnell.com). They can glue the organizer into their reader's notebook.

RML 6
LA.U27.RML6

Reading Minilesson Principle

Writers end stories in a variety of ways.

Understanding Plot

You Will Need

- several familiar fiction books with different types of endings, such as the following:
  - *Under the Quilt of Night* by Deborah Hopkinson, from Text Set: Freedom
  - *Sami and the Time of the Troubles* by Florence Parry Heide and Judith Heide Gilliland, from Text Set: Hope and Resilience
  - *The Crane Girl* by Curtis Manley, from Text Set: Empathy
  - *The Treasure Box* by Margaret Wild, from Text Set: The Power of Knowledge
- chart paper prepared with two columns, the first column filled in with book titles
- markers
- basket of familiar fiction books

Academic Language / Important Vocabulary

- ending
- predictable
- message
- ambiguous
- circular

Continuum Connection

- Follow plots that have particular patterns, such as circular plots or parallel plots (p. 70)
- Recognize and appreciate an ambiguous ending of a fiction text (p. 71)

Goal

Notice the different ways writers craft endings to their stories.

Rationale

Authors choose from several types of endings for their stories: predictable (plot events point toward the ending), ambiguous (it's unclear what will happen after the story ends), circular (the story ends where it started), and unexpected (a surprise ending). When students recognize that writers make decisions about how to end a story, they are able to think deeply about a writer's craft and think of possibilities for ways to conclude their own stories.

Assess Learning

Observe students when they read and discuss fiction stories and notice if there is evidence of new learning based on the goal of this minilesson.

- Are students talking about the different ways that writers choose to end fiction stories?
- Do they use the terms *ending, predictable, message, ambiguous,* and *circular*?

Minilesson

To help students think about the minilesson principle, engage them in thinking about story endings. Here is an example.

- Read the beginning page and ending page of *Under the Quilt of Night.*

  How would you describe the way the book ends?

- As students talk about the ending, guide the conversation so they understand that the ending was somewhat predictable because the title hints at protection for people escaping slavery. Fill in the chart the type of ending for this book.
- Read the first and last pages of text in *Sami and the Time of the Troubles.*

  What do you notice about the way this story begins and ends?

  What do the authors leave you thinking about?

  This ending is circular because Sami ended up right back where he started. It is also ambiguous because we don't really know what will happen to Sami and his family or if they will survive the bombings.

- Add to the chart. Continue the activity with several more books that have different types of endings, such as *The Crane Girl* and *The Treasure Box.*

Have a Try

Invite the students to talk with a partner about the choices that writers make about story endings.

> Take a look at the chart and think about the different ways a writer can end a story. Have you read any other stories that end in one of these ways? Turn and talk about that.

- After a brief time for discussion, ask a few volunteers to share. Record titles on the chart.

Writers end stories in a variety of ways.

Title	Kind of Ending
 Under the Quilt of Night	predictable
 Sami and the Time of the Troubles	ambiguous circular
 The Crane Girl	unexpected
 Grandma's Tree (Treasure Box)	circular

Summarize and Apply

Summarize the learning and remind students to think about how a writer chooses to end a story.

> What do you know about the endings of fiction books?

- Add the principle to the chart.

> If you finish a book today, notice how the author ended the book and think about why the author might have decided to end it that way. Bring the book when we meet so you can share.

Share

Following independent reading time, gather students in small groups to talk about how the authors ended the stories they read.

> If you finished a book today or if you have finished one recently, talk about how it ended. Tell your group why you think the author decided to end the story in that way.

Extend the Lesson (Optional)

After assessing students' understanding, you might decide to extend the learning.

- **Writing About Reading** Have students use a reader's notebook to analyze the ending of a book. Have them write about how the story ended and whether they feel the ending was satisfying.

Assessment

After you have taught the minilessons in this umbrella, observe students as they talk and write about their reading across instructional contexts: interactive read-aloud, independent reading, guided reading, shared reading, and book club. Use *The Literacy Continuum* (Fountas and Pinnell 2017) to observe students' reading and writing behaviors.

- What evidence do you have of new understandings related to plot?
    - Can students identify the parts of narrative text structure that make up the plot?
    - Can they recognize when a story has more than one problem?
    - Are they aware of when a writer is using a flashback, a flash-forward, or a story-within-a-story?
    - Can they identify the plot and any subplots?
    - Are they able to use what they know to make predictions while reading?
    - Can they discuss the different ways that writers conclude stories?
    - Are they using academic language, such as *plot, problem, beginning, events, high point, ending, flashbacks, flash-forwards, story-within-a-story, plot line, subplot,* and *predict*?
- In what other ways, beyond the scope of this umbrella, are students talking about fiction?
    - Are students interested in reading different genres of fiction?

Use your observations to determine the next umbrella you will teach. You may also consult Minilessons Across the Year (pp. 61–64) for guidance.

Link to Writing

After teaching the minilessons in this umbrella, help students link the new learning to their own writing:

- Encourage students to use a variety of plot features as they write their own fiction stories.

Reader's Notebook

When this umbrella is complete, provide a copy of the minilesson principles (see resources.fountasandpinnell.com) for students to glue in the reader's notebook (in the Minilessons section if using *Reader's Notebook: Advanced* [Fountas and Pinnell 2011]), so they can refer to the information as needed.

Understanding Characters' Feelings, Motivations, and Intentions

Umbrella 28

Minilessons in This Umbrella

RML1	Notice what the characters think, say, and do to understand how they are feeling.
RML2	Notice what the characters say and do to understand their relationships.
RML3	Think about what characters really want.

Before Teaching Umbrella 28 Minilessons

Read and discuss books with characters whose feelings can be observed through their words and through the illustrations, as well as books with a variety of settings and diversity of characters. Students should be reading fiction books during independent reading, or fiction books should be available. The minilessons in this umbrella use the following books from the *Fountas and Pinnell Classroom* ™ *Interactive Read-Aloud Collection*; however, you can use any fiction books you have available in the classroom that have the characteristics listed above.

Freedom

The Composition by Antonio Skármeta

Empathy

The Crane Girl by Curtis Manley

The Power of Knowledge

The Treasure Box by Margaret Wild

Hope and Resilience

Sami and the Time of the Troubles by Florence Parry Heide and Judith Heide Gilliland

Family

The Way a Door Closes by Hope Anita Smith

Conflict Resolution

Shooting at the Stars: The Christmas Truce of 1914 by John Hendrix

As you read aloud and enjoy these texts together, help students

- notice characters' thoughts, words, and actions, and
- think about how a character's thoughts, words, and actions show how the character feels about himself and others.

Freedom

The Composition by Antonio Skármeta

Empathy

The Power of Knowledge

Hope and Resilience

Family

The Way a Door Closes by Hope Anita Smith

Conflict Resolution

RML1

LA.U28.RML1

Reading Minilesson Principle

Notice what the characters think, say, and do to understand how they are feeling.

Understanding Characters' Feelings, Motivations, and Intentions

You Will Need

- several familiar fiction books that have characters with clear feelings, such as the following:
  - *The Composition* by Antonio Skármeta, from Text Set: Freedom
  - *The Crane Girl* by Curtis Manley, from Text Set: Empathy
- chart paper and markers
- sticky notes

Academic Language / Important Vocabulary

- feelings
- thoughts
- words
- actions
- motivations
- intentions

Continuum Connection

- Infer characters' traits, intentions, feelings, and motivations as revealed through thought, dialogue, behavior, and what others say or think about them (p. 70)

Goal

Infer characters' feelings as revealed through thought, dialogue, and behavior.

Rationale

When students learn to infer characters' feelings, motivations, and intentions, they learn to relate to characters and deepen their comprehension of the text.

Assess Learning

Observe students when they talk about characters and notice if there is evidence of new learning based on the goal of this minilesson.

- Are students able to connect a character's thoughts, words, and actions with that character's feelings?
- Do they use evidence from the text to make inferences about a character's feelings?
- Do they use the terms *feelings, thoughts, words, actions, motivations,* and *intentions*?

Minilesson

To help students think about the minilesson principle, engage them in thinking about a character's feelings. Here is an example.

- Read the first paragraph on page 3 of *The Composition*.

  What do you notice about how Pedro is feeling in this part of the book?

  What makes you think that?

- As needed, prompt the conversation to help students identify that Pedro is feeling confident as a soccer player because he feels like he is in a stadium receiving applause for being the neighborhood soccer star.
- Begin a chart to note student responses about Pedro's feelings.

  Think about how Pedro might be feeling as I read another part of the story.

- Read page 16.

  How is Pedro feeling now? How do his words help you know this?

- Add responses to the chart. Read Pedro's letter on page 31.

  How is Pedro feeling? How does writing this letter show you how Pedro is feeling?

Have a Try

Invite the students to talk with a partner about how a character feels.

Think about how Hiroko might be feeling as I read a few parts from *The Crane Girl.*

- Read and show the illustrations from pages 9–10 and 27–28, and then read the haiku on page 29.

Turn and talk about how Hiroko might be feeling during these parts of the book and how you know.

- After time for discussion, ask students to share. Add responses to the chart.

Notice what the characters think, say, and do to understand how they are feeling.

Title	How is the character feeling?	How do you know?
The Composition Pedro	confident concerned aware protective loyal	Thoughts Pedro feels like he's in a soccer stadium getting lots of applause. Words Pedro asks his parents questions about what he hears on the radio. Actions Pedro writes a letter for his school assignment but does not write down that his parents listen to the radio.
The Crane Girl Hiroko	appreciative content loyal in love unselfish	Actions Hiroko smiles and plays with Yasuhiro. Words Hiroko tells Yasuhiro that she plucked her own feathers because Yasuhiro saved her life and she wanted to be with him. Thoughts and Actions Hiroko thinks that Yasuhiro could not love a crane, so she leaves.

Summarize and Apply

Summarize the learning and remind students to think about the feelings of the characters when they read fiction stories.

How can you figure out how a character is feeling?

- Add the principle to the chart.

If you read a fiction book today, think about how a character might be feeling and how the author shows you that. Mark any pages you want to remember with sticky notes. Bring the book when we meet so you can share.

Share

Following independent reading time, gather students in the meeting area to discuss characters' feelings.

Who noticed how a character is feeling in a fiction story? What evidence did the author include to help you understand the character's feelings?

Extend the Lesson (Optional)

After assessing students' understanding, you might decide to extend the learning.

- If appropriate for your students, you may also provide a lesson on inferring what a character feels by noticing what other characters say or think about him.

RML2

LA.U28.RML2

Reading Minilesson Principle

Notice what the characters say and do to understand their relationships.

Understanding Characters' Feelings, Motivations, and Intentions

You Will Need

- several familiar fiction books with easily identifiable character relationships, such as the following:
  - *The Way a Door Closes* by Hope Anita Smith, from Text Set: Family
  - *Sami and the Time of the Troubles* by Florence Parry Heide and Judith Heide Gilliland, from Text Set: Hope and Resilience
  - *The Treasure Box* by Margaret Wild, from Text Set: The Power of Knowledge
- chart paper and markers
- sticky notes

Academic Language / Important Vocabulary

- character
- relationships
- dialogue
- behavior
- inference

Continuum Connection

- Infer relationships between characters as revealed through dialogue and behavior (p. 71)

Goal

Infer relationships between characters as revealed through dialogue and behavior.

Rationale

When students learn to make inferences about how characters feel about each other from what they say and do, they deepen comprehension of the text and build empathy.

Assess Learning

Observe students when they talk about character relationships and notice if there is evidence of new learning based on the goal of this minilesson.

- Are students discussing the relationships characters have in fiction stories?
- Do students identify text evidence showing how a character's words and actions show their relationships?
- Do they use the terms *character, relationships, dialogue, behavior,* and *inference*?

Minilesson

To help students think about the minilesson principle, engage them in thinking about character relationships. Here is an example.

Listen to the words and notice the illustrations on these pages from *The Way a Door Closes.*

- Read and show pages 28–29.

What do you notice about how the characters feel about each other?

What evidence does the author include in the story to help you understand the relationship between C.J. and his grandmother?

- As students respond, create a chart with a column for the title, a column for students' inferences about character relationships, and a column for text evidence. Add students' ideas to the chart.

Now think about the characters' relationships in another book, *Sami and the Time of the Troubles.*

- Read and show pages 9–10.

What clues do Sami's words and actions give about his relationship with his grandfather?

- Add to the chart.

Have a Try

Invite the students to talk with a partner about how characters feel about each other.

- Read and show pages 11–14 in *The Treasure Box*.

  Think about the relationship between Peter and his father in *The Treasure Box*. Turn and talk about how Peter's words and actions show his relationship with his father and how they feel about each other.

- After time for discussion, ask students to share ideas. Add to chart.

Notice what the characters say and do to understand their relationships.

Title	Relationships	How do you know?
The Way a Door Closes	Grandmomma is very supportive and caring to C.J. C.J. counts on his grandmother and leans on her.	Grandmomma holds C.J.'s hands when he needs it. Grandmomma makes a joke when C.J. loses his temper, instead of getting angry.
Sami and the Time of the Troubles	Grandfather cares about Sami and the family and keeps them safe. He supports Sami by helping him learn. Sami trusts his grandfather.	Sami thinks about what Grandfather is trying to teach him. Grandfather patiently waits until Sami learns an important lesson.
The Treasure Box	Peter is loyal to his father and loves him very much. Peter's father cares about him and trusts him.	Peter's father shares a very special book with Peter about their people's history. Peter stays by his father's side and keeps his promise to take care of the special treasure.

Summarize and Apply

Summarize the learning and remind students to think about characters' relationships when they read fiction stories.

How can you learn about characters' relationships when you read a story?

- Add the principle to the chart.

  If you read a fiction book today, think about the relationships between characters and what they show about how the characters might feel about one another. Mark any pages with sticky notes that you want to remember. Bring the book when we meet so you can share.

Share

Following independent reading time, gather students in the meeting area to talk about characters' relationships.

Who noticed the way an author or an illustrator gives you clues about how characters feel about each other? Talk about that and share any pages that would be helpful to explain your thinking.

Extend the Lesson (Optional)

After assessing students' understanding, you might decide to extend the learning.

- Have students make or fill in a graphic organizer about characters' relationships (visit resources.fountasandpinnell.com). They can glue the organizer into a reader's notebook to record other examples they notice as they read more fiction stories.

RML 3

LA.U28.RML3

Reading Minilesson Principle

Think about what characters really want.

Understanding Characters' Feelings, Motivations, and Intentions

You Will Need

- several familiar fiction books, such as the following:
  - *Sami and the Time of the Troubles* by Florence Parry Heide and Judith Heide Gilliland, from Text Set: Hope and Resilience
  - *The Crane Girl* by Curtis Manley, from Text Set: Empathy
  - *Shooting at the Stars* by John Hendrix, from Text Set: Conflict Resolution
- chart paper and markers
- sticky notes

Academic Language / Important Vocabulary

- character
- motivations
- dialogue
- behavior

Continuum Connection

- Infer characters' traits, intentions, feelings, and motivations as revealed through thought, dialogue, behavior, and what others say or think about them (p. 70)

Goal

Infer characters' motivations as revealed through dialogue and behavior.

Rationale

Learning to notice evidence in a story about what a character wants shows the character's motivation behind her words and actions. Often, determining a character's motivations enables students to fully understand the problem and solution.

Assess Learning

Observe students when they talk about characters' motivations and notice if there is evidence of new learning based on the goal of this minilesson.

- Are students talking about the ways that a character's words and actions indicate his motivations?
- Can they identify text evidence that supports their opinions about characters' motivations?
- Do they use the terms *character, motivations, dialogue,* and *behavior*?

Minilesson

To help students think about the minilesson principle, engage them in thinking about character motivation. Here is an example.

- Show the cover of *Sami and the Time of the Troubles.*

  What do you think Sami really wants? What motivates him?

  What examples from the story help you know his motivations?

- As needed, revisit a few pages of the text and draw attention to illustrations to support students' thinking, such as pages 11–12, 14, and 25. Encourage students to identify specific examples of dialogue and actions to show Sami's motivations.
- Using students' responses, create a chart that shows Sami's motivations. Include a few specific examples from the story.

  You can identify the main problem in the story when you notice what a character really wants.

  Now think about Hiroko and Yasuhiro in *The Crane Girl.* As I revisit a few pages, think about what they really want by noticing what they say and do.

- Revisit pages as needed, such as pages 9–12 and 28–32.

  What did you notice?

- Add to the chart.

Have a Try

Invite the students to talk with a partner about characters' motivations.

- Revisit a few pages of the text and point out illustrations in *Shooting at the Stars*, such as pages 6 and 21–22.

  Turn and talk about what the British soldier really wants.

- After time for discussion, ask students to share. Add ideas to the chart.

Think about what characters really want.

Title	What Characters Do and Say	What the Characters Want
	• Sami imagines life before the war and says someday he will have that again. • Sami tells Amir that this war will not last forever so they will not need their own guns. • Sami silently stares at the ceiling, afraid of the next bomb.	• Sami wants to be safe and have life how it was before the war.
	• Hiroko and Yasuhiro share chores and play together. • Yasuhiro shares with Hiroko about life before his mom died. • Hiroko harms herself by plucking feathers to make silk. • Yasuhiro calls after Hiroko. • Yasuhiro says he will come with her because they will be together.	• Hiroko wants to help Yasuhiro and to be with him. • Yasuhiro wants to help Hiroko and be with her. • Yasuhiro loves Hiroko more than money.
	• The soldier writes about how miserable he is. • The soldier trades some of his buttons for a belt buckle from a German soldier and they laugh together. • He writes a letter to his mom describing Christmas Eve and what it meant to him.	• The British soldier wants to enjoy life, be alive, and celebrate holidays. • The British soldier wants peace and to relate to enemies as humans. He doesn't want to kill.

Summarize and Apply

Summarize the learning and remind students to think about what the characters really want.

You talked about what characters really want. How does this help you understand the story?

- Add the principle to the chart.

  As you read fiction, think about what a character really wants and how an author shows you that. If you are reading fiction today, mark any pages with sticky notes that you want to remember. Bring the book when we meet so you can share.

Share

Following independent reading time, gather students in small groups. Be sure each group has at least one member who read fiction today.

Share what you noticed about what a character really wants. Show the pages that helped you know that.

Extend the Lesson (Optional)

After assessing students' understanding, you might decide to extend the learning.

- **Writing About Reading** Have students use a reader's notebook to write about the connection between a character's motivations and the problem in the story. Encourage them to use evidence from the text to show their thinking.

Understanding Characters' Feelings, Motivations, and Intentions

Assessment

After you have taught the minilessons in this umbrella, observe students as they talk and write about their reading across instructional contexts: interactive read-aloud, independent reading, guided reading, shared reading, and book club. Use *The Literacy Continuum* (Fountas and Pinnell 2017) to observe students' reading and writing behaviors.

- What evidence do you have of new understandings related to characters' feelings, motivations, and intentions?
    - Are students able to understand how a character feels by noticing what the character thinks, says, and does?
    - Can they determine a character's relationships with other characters by noticing what the character does and says?
    - Do they think about a character's motivations?
    - Are they using the terms *characters, feelings, motivations, intentions,* and *relationships*?
- In what other ways, beyond the scope of this umbrella, are students demonstrating an understanding of characters?
    - Do students talk about the ways that a character's traits are revealed through what the character does, thinks, and says?

Use your observations to determine the next umbrella you will teach. You may also consult Minilessons Across the Year (pp. 61–64) for guidance.

Link to Writing

After teaching the minilessons in this umbrella, help students link the new learning to their own writing:

- As students write their own fiction stories, encourage them to reveal information about how a character feels, what the character wants, and what the character intends through the use of dialogue.

Reader's Notebook

When this umbrella is complete, provide a copy of the minilesson principles (see resources.fountasandpinnell.com) for students to glue in the reader's notebook (in the Minilessons section if using *Reader's Notebook: Advanced* [Fountas and Pinnell 2011]), so they can refer to the information as needed.

Understanding a Character's Traits and Development

Umbrella 29

Minilessons in This Umbrella

RML1	Behaviors, thoughts, and dialogue show a character's traits.
RML2	Primary and secondary characters play different roles in the story.
RML3	Characters can be complex individuals.
RML4	Characters change because of the things that happen to them.

Before Teaching Umbrella 29 Minilessons

Read and discuss books with characters whose traits can be determined by behaviors, thoughts, and dialogue. Include books with both primary and secondary characters, complex characters, and clear example of characters who change. The minilessons in this umbrella use the following books from the *Fountas and Pinnell Classroom* ™ *Interactive Read-Aloud Collection*; however, you can use any fiction books you have available in the classroom that have the characteristics listed above.

Freedom

Under the Quilt of Night by Deborah Hopkinson

The Composition by Antonio Skármeta

Hope and Resilience

Sami and the Time of the Troubles by Florence Parry Heide and Judith Heide Gilliland

Grit and Perseverance

Rikki-Tikki-Tavi by Rudyard Kipling

Family

The Raft by Jim LaMarche

The Way a Door Closes by Hope Anita Smith

Conflict Resolution

Shooting at the Stars: The Christmas Truce of 1914 by John Hendrix

As you read aloud and enjoy these texts together, help students

- talk about a character's traits,
- notice that sometimes good characters make mistakes,
- identify the way a character changes, and
- talk about whether they feel empathy toward a character.

Freedom

The Composition by Antonio Skármeta

Hope and Resilience

Grit and Perseverance

Rikki-Tikki-Tavi by Rudyard Kipling

Family

The Way a Door Closes by Hope Anita Smith

Conflict Resolution

RML1

LA.U29.RML1

Reading Minilesson Principle

Behaviors, thoughts, and dialogue show a character's traits.

Understanding a Character's Traits and Development

You Will Need

- several familiar fiction stories with well-developed characters, such as the following:
  - *Sami and the Time of the Troubles* by Florence Parry Heide and Judith Heide Gilliland, from Text Set: Hope and Resilience
  - *Under the Quilt of Night* by Deborah Hopkinson, from Text Set: Freedom
- chart paper and markers
- fiction books students are reading
- basket of fiction books
- sticky notes

Academic Language / Important Vocabulary

- character
- trait
- evidence
- behavior
- thought
- dialogue

Continuum Connection

- Infer characters' traits, intentions, feelings, and motivations as revealed through thought, dialogue, behavior, and what others say or think about them (p. 70)

Goal

Infer characters' traits as revealed through their behaviors, dialogue, and inner thoughts.

Rationale

When students connect a character's behavior, thoughts, and dialogue to the character's traits, they have a deeper comprehension of the story and develop empathy for the characters.

Assess Learning

Observe students when they talk about characters in fiction stories and notice if there is evidence of new learning based on the goal of this minilesson.

- Do students notice the behavior, thoughts, and dialogue of characters?
- Are they able to analyze what an author reveals about a character's traits?
- Do they use the terms *character, trait, evidence, behavior, thought,* and *dialogue*?

Minilesson

To help students think about the minilesson principle, guide them to notice how authors reveal characters' traits in their stories. Here is an example.

- Revisit a few pages from *Sami and the Time of the Troubles* that show Sami's traits. For example, you might share when Sami reflects on happier times (pp. 2–3), when he goes outside to clean up from the bombing (p. 17), and when he talks to Grandpa about marching (p. 31).

  Think about Sami's personality. What would you say about Sami's character traits?

  How do you know what Sami is like?

  Do any of the behaviors, thoughts, or dialogue of the other characters help you know about Sami's traits?

- As students have a conversation, create a chart with students' responses. Add the traits that students suggest using sticky notes.
- Support students' thinking by guiding them to notice Sami's behavior, thoughts, and dialogue that reveal his traits.

  Now think about the girl who is escaping slavery in *Under the Quilt of Night*. What helps you understand her character traits?

- Guide the conversation, adding students' responses about character traits and text evidence to the chart.

Have a Try

Invite the students to talk with a partner about character traits.

- Students can bring the fiction book they are currently reading or they can choose a fiction book from the basket.

  Think about the traits of a character in the fiction book. What behaviors, actions, and dialogue does the author include to help you know what the character is like? Turn and talk about that.

Behaviors, thoughts, and dialogue show a character's traits.

Title and Character	Trait	Evidence
 Sami and the Time of the Troubles	reflective	Sami thinks about happy times in the past.
	responsible	Sami goes outside to help clean up after the bombing.
	loyal	Grandpa believes in Sami and trusts him to become an activist. Sami tells Grandpa that he will do this.
	resilient	Even though Sami's dad was killed, Sami is a survivor and believes in the future.
 Under the Quilt of Night	brave	The girl leads the way.
	trustworthy	The others follow her and trust in her to be in front.
	determined	She says she will make her steps quiet and run where nobody will find her.
	patient	She waits silently when she really wants to dance and sing.

Summarize and Apply

Summarize the learning and remind students to think about a character's traits when they read a fiction book.

How do you learn the traits of a character in a story?

- Add the principle to the chart.

  If you are reading a fiction book, think about the behavior, thoughts, and dialogue that help you know about a character's traits. Mark any pages that you want to remember with a sticky note. Bring the book when we meet so you can share.

Share

Following independent reading time, gather students in small groups. Be sure each group has at least one person who read a fiction book.

Did you notice a character's traits and how the author revealed those traits? Talk to your group about that.

Extend the Lesson (Optional)

After assessing students' understanding, you might decide to extend the learning.

- Provide a lesson that shows that a character in a series often has the same traits in multiple books, such as Anastasia in *Anastasia Krupnik*, *Anastasia Again!* and *Anastasia at Your Service*.
- **Writing About Reading** Have students make or fill in a graphic organizer about character traits (see resources.fountasandpinnell.com). They can glue the organizer into a reader's notebook.

RML 2
LA.U29.RML2

Reading Minilesson Principle

Primary and secondary characters play different roles in the story.

Understanding a Character's Traits and Development

You Will Need

- several familiar fiction texts that have both primary and secondary characters, such as the following:
  - *Rikki-Tikki-Tavi* by Rudyard Kipling, from Text Set: Grit and Perseverance
  - *Sami and the Time of the Troubles* by Florence Parry Heide and Judith Heide Gilliland, from Text Set: Hope and Resilience
- chart paper and markers
- highlighter or highlighting tape
- sticky notes

Academic Language / Important Vocabulary

- primary character
- secondary character
- role

Continuum Connection

- Infer characters' traits, intentions, feelings, and motivations as revealed through thought, dialogue, behavior, and what others say or think about them (p. 70)

Goal

Understand that primary and secondary characters play different roles in the story.

Rationale

When students learn to notice how secondary characters can reveal information about the primary character, they gain a deeper understanding of all characters and think about the choices a writer makes when creating them and determining their roles.

Assess Learning

Observe students when they talk about characters and notice if there is evidence of new learning based on the goal of this minilesson.

- Can students identify which characters are primary and which are secondary in a fiction text?
- Are they able to recognize what a secondary character reveals about a primary character?
- Do they use the terms *primary character, secondary character,* and *role*?

Minilesson

To help students think about the minilesson principle, engage them in thinking about the roles of primary and secondary characters. Here is an example.

- Show the cover of *Rikki-Tikki-Tavi.*

  In *Rikki-Tikki-Tavi*, who is the main character? How do you know?

  In fiction stories, the main character is called the primary character and the other characters are called secondary characters.

- Revisit a few pages of text and illustrations that show Rikki-tikki's interactions with the humans and the other animals.

  Let's name some of the secondary characters.

  What do the humans and the other animals reveal about Rikki-tikki?

- As students respond, begin a chart that lists the primary and secondary characters. Write what the secondary characters reveal about the primary, or main, character and include details from the story. Use a highlighter to identify what the secondary characters show about Rikki-tikki.

  What is the role of the secondary characters?

  What do you think was the author's purpose in including the humans and the other animals in the story?

Have a Try

Invite the students to talk with a partner about primary and secondary characters.

- Briefly revisit a few pages from *Sami and the Time of the Troubles* that show the interactions between Sami and his grandfather.

  Turn and talk about who is the primary character and who is a secondary character. What does the secondary character reveal about the primary character?

- After time for discussion, ask students to share their thinking. Add to the chart.

Primary and secondary characters play different roles in the story.

Book	Primary Character	Secondary Characters	What do secondary characters reveal about the primary character?
Rikki-Tikki-Tavi	Rikki-tikki	the humans and the other animals	We only know the humans through how they interacted with Rikki-tikki. They allowed him to come into their house and the boy's bed and said that he saved their lives. The humans show that Rikki-tikki is trustworthy and loyal. Darzee sang when Nag died, but Rikki-tikki knew that Nagaina's eggs would hatch. The birds show how Rikki-tikki is a leader.
Sami and the Time of the Troubles	Sami	Grandpa	Grandpa talked to Sami about serious issues and guided Sami to understand that he must become an activist. Grandpa shows that Sami is trustworthy, protective, and loyal.

Summarize and Apply

Summarize the learning and remind students to think about the role of primary and secondary characters.

What did you learn about characters?

- Add the principle to the chart.

  If you are reading a fiction book today, think about the role of the primary and secondary characters and mark any pages you want to remember with a sticky note. Bring the book when we meet so you can share.

Share

Following independent reading time, gather students in small groups. Ensure that at least one member of each group read a fiction book.

Share what you noticed about the role of primary and secondary characters in a fiction book.

Extend the Lesson (Optional)

After assessing students' understanding, you might decide to extend the learning.

- **Writing About Reading** Have students describe the role of a secondary character in a story. Remind them to use examples from the story to back up their statements.

RML 3

LA.U29.RML3

Reading Minilesson Principle

Characters can be complex individuals.

Understanding a Character's Traits and Development

You Will Need

- several familiar fiction stories with complex characters, such as the following:
  - *The Way a Door Closes* by Hope Anita Smith, from Text Set: Family
  - *Shooting at the Stars* by John Hendrix, from Text Set: Conflict Resolution
  - *The Raft* by Jim LaMarche, from Text Set: Family
- chart paper and markers
- highlighter
- sticky notes

Academic Language / Important Vocabulary

- character
- complex
- mistake

Continuum Connection

- Recognize that characters can have multiple dimensions: e.g., can be good but make mistakes, can change (p. 70)

Goal

Recognize that characters can have multiple dimensions.

Rationale

When students recognize that characters can be complex and that good characters can make mistakes, they learn to connect the lives of the characters to their own lives and learn that good people sometimes make mistakes.

Assess Learning

Observe students when they discuss characters and notice if there is evidence of new learning based on the goal of this minilesson.

- Are students talking about the different aspects of a character's personality?
- Do they recognize that making a mistake does not necessarily mean that a character is bad?
- Do they use the terms *character, complex,* and *mistake*?

Minilesson

To help students think about the minilesson principle, engage them in a discussion about what makes a character complex. Here is an example.

- Revisit pages 44–46 in *The Way a Door Closes* when C.J. is rude to his mom. Stop reading after he walks out the front door on page 46.

  Think about C.J. What do you think of the way he acted during this part of the story? Does treating his mom this way make him a bad person? Turn and talk about that.

- After time for a brief discussion, continue reading to the end of page 47.

  What kind of character is C.J.?

- As needed, support the conversation by helping students recognize that C.J. is a good person but acted wrongly when he was rude to his mom. He felt hurt by his dad's leaving, so he acted poorly but then apologized.

  How could we describe the way that C.J. is a complex character?

- On chart paper, record students' ideas. Highlight words that emphasize the character's complexity.
- Repeat the discussion about a character from another book, such as the soldier in *Shooting at the Stars*.

Have a Try

Invite the students to talk with a partner about a good character who makes a mistake.

- Revisit a section of *The Raft* that shows Nicky having a bad attitude, such as some text and illustrations from pages 1–11.

  Turn and talk about what Nicky did that shows you the kind of character he is.

- After time for discussion, ask a few students to share ideas. Add to the chart.

Characters can be complex individuals.

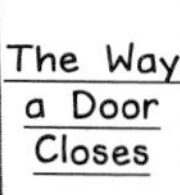

C.J. was rude to his mom and ran away. He felt sad because his dad had left and he was acting out because of that. He came home and apologized to his mom and cried.

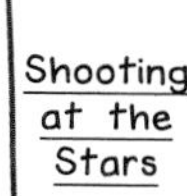

The soldiers were enemies and they hated each other and felt they were different. But, after spending Christmas Eve together, they realized they were all humans, not just soldiers, and they didn't really want to kill each other.

Nicky was rude to his grandma and had a bad attitude about everything. The author revealed that he was only acting that way because he was bored and lonely. After he found a raft and learned to enjoy nature, he was kind to Grandma and became positive.

Summarize and Apply

Summarize the learning and remind students to think about the complexity of characters when they read fiction stories.

Today you learned that characters are not just one way or another. They are complex.

- Add the principle to the chart.

  If you are reading a fiction book today, think about whether a good character does something wrong or makes a mistake. Mark any pages that you want to remember with a sticky note. Bring the book when we meet so you can share.

Share

Following independent reading time, gather students in the meeting area.

Did anyone notice a good character who does something wrong or makes a mistake? Talk about that and share any pages that support your thinking.

Extend the Lesson (Optional)

After assessing students' understanding, you might decide to extend the learning.

- **Writing About Reading** Have students write in a reader's notebook about the complexity of a character in a story they have read. They might note how the character changed from the beginning of the story to the end of the story or how the character exhibited different sides to his personality.

RML 4
LA.U29.RML4

Reading Minilesson Principle

Characters change because of the things that happen to them.

Understanding a Character's Traits and Development

You Will Need

- several familiar fiction books with characters who change as a result of story events, such as the following:
  - *The Composition* by Antonio Skármeta, from Text Set: Freedom
  - *The Raft* by Jim LaMarche, from Text Set: Family
- chart paper and markers
- sticky notes

Academic Language / Important Vocabulary

- character change
- events
- traits

Continuum Connection

- Notice character change and infer reasons from events of the plot (p. 71)

Goal

Notice character changes and infer reasons from events of the plot.

Rationale

When students think about the way events cause a character to change, they deepen their understanding of both character and plot.

Assess Learning

Observe students when they talk about character change and notice if there is evidence of new learning based on the goal of this minilesson.

- Are students able to identify the events that cause a character to change?
- Do they infer the way a character changes?
- Do they use the terms *character change, events,* and *traits?*

Minilesson

To help students think about the minilesson principle, engage them in a discussion about how and why a character changes. Here is an example.

- Revisit several parts of *The Composition* that show Pedro's lack of awareness about the dictatorship at the beginning and his awareness at the end of the book, such as pages 1, 8–9, 17, and 32.

  How is Pedro different at the beginning of the book from the way he is at the end of the book?

  What happened? Turn and talk about what events caused him to change.

- After time for discussion, ask students to share their thinking. Prompt the conversation as needed by revisiting parts of the book to help them identify specific events that caused Pedro to change.
- On chart paper, use student ideas to create a timeline that shows Pedro at the beginning, lists the events that caused him to change, and shows how he changed at the end.

  Why do you think the author included each of these facts in the story?

  Why might the author have thought about how he wanted Pedro to change before he wrote about the events?

Have a Try

Invite the students to talk with a partner about why and how characters change.

- Briefly revisit the text and illustrations of *The Raft* that show Nicky when he first went to Grandma's house, the events that caused him to change, and how he is at the end.

  Turn and talk about how Nicky changed and why.

- After time for discussion, ask students to share ideas and add to the chart.

Characters change because of the things that happen to them.

Title and Character	The Character at the Beginning	What happened?	How the Character Changed
The Composition	Pedro had no idea about the dictatorship or dangers to his family.	Pedro saw Daniel's dad taken away. Pedro was given a school assignment to talk about family activities. Pedro talked to Juan and learned that Juan's father was also taken away.	Pedro showed awareness and maturity about the dangers of General Perdomo and the soldiers.
The Raft	Nicky was a city kid who needed TV and friends for entertainment. He had a negative attitude about going to Grandma's house.	Nicky arrived at Grandma's house and did chores. He found a raft. Grandma introduced him to the fun in nature.	Nicky was a river rat like Grandma and also an artist. He appreciated nature. He found ways to entertain himself.

Summarize and Apply

Summarize the learning and remind students to think about the events that caused a character to change, and the ways the character changed because of those events.

You talked about how and why a character changes in fiction stories.

- Add the principle to the chart.

  If you are reading a fiction book, think about whether a character changed. Mark any pages you want to remember with a sticky note. Bring the book when we meet so you can share.

Share

Following independent reading time, gather students in the meeting area to share what they noticed about characters that changed.

What did you notice about how and why a character changed? Talk about what you noticed and share any pages that support your thinking.

Extend the Lesson (Optional)

After assessing students' understanding, you might decide to extend the learning.

- During interactive read-aloud, talk with students about events that effect a change in the character. Discuss how such events are integral to moving the plot along.

Assessment

After you have taught the minilessons in this umbrella, observe students as they talk and write about their reading across instructional contexts: interactive read-aloud, independent reading, guided reading, shared reading, and book club. Use *The Literacy Continuum* (Fountas and Pinnell 2017) to observe students' reading and writing behaviors.

- What evidence do you have of new understandings related to characters?
    - Are students able to identify a character's traits by thinking about behavior, thoughts, and dialogue?
    - Do they understand that primary and secondary characters can have different purposes in the story?
    - Are they talking about the complexity of some characters?
    - Can they recognize when a character changes because of story events?
    - Are they using the terms *character, traits, development, behavior, thoughts, dialogue, primary, secondary, complex,* and *change*?
- In what other ways, beyond the scope of this umbrella, are students demonstrating an understanding of characters?
    - Are students talking about the decisions an author makes in creating a character?

Use your observations to determine the next umbrella you will teach. You may also consult Minilessons Across the Year (pp. 61–64) for guidance.

Link to Writing

After teaching the minilessons in this umbrella, help students link the new learning to their own writing:

- Encourage students to plan for writing their own fiction stories by thinking and making notes about how they want a character's traits revealed in the story.

Reader's Notebook

When this umbrella is complete, provide a copy of the minilesson principles (see resources.fountasandpinnell.com) for students to glue in the reader's notebook (in the Minilessons section if using *Reader's Notebook: Advanced* [Fountas and Pinnell 2011]), so they can refer to the information as needed.

Minilessons in This Umbrella

RML1	Think critically about whether a character is believable and authentic.
RML2	Evaluate whether characters behave in ways consistent with the setting of the book.
RML3	Evaluate whether the writer makes you feel empathy for a character.

Before Teaching Umbrella 30 Minilessons

Read and discuss books with characters and settings that are complex and diverse. Discuss empathy as it relates to characters and also as it relates to the students' own lives. The minilessons in this umbrella use the following books from the *Fountas and Pinnell Classroom™ Interactive Read-Aloud Collection*; however, you can use any fiction books you have available in the classroom that have the characteristics listed above.

Grit and Perseverance

Rikki-Tikki-Tavi by Rudyard Kipling

Family

The Raft by Jim LaMarche

Conflict Resolution

Shooting at the Stars: The Christmas Truce of 1914 by John Hendrix

Freedom

Under the Quilt of Night by Deborah Hopkinson

The Composition by Antonio Skármeta

Empathy

The Crane Girl by Curtis Manley

As you read aloud and enjoy these texts together, help students

- think about whether characters are believable,
- talk about how a character would behave based on the place and time period, and
- talk about whether they feel empathy for a character.

Grit and Perseverance

Family

Conflict Resolution

Freedom

The Composition by Antonio Skármeta

Empathy

RML 1

LA.U30.RML1

Reading Minilesson Principle

Think critically about whether a character is believable and authentic.

Thinking Critically About Characters

You Will Need

- several familiar realistic fiction and fantasy stories, such as the following:
  - *The Raft* by Jim LaMarche, from Text Set: Family
  - *Rikki-Tikki-Tavi* by Rudyard Kipling, from Text Set: Grit and Perseverance
  - *Shooting at the Stars* by John Hendrix, from Text Set: Conflict Resolution
- chart paper and markers
- two colors of sticky notes

Academic Language / Important Vocabulary

- character
- conditions
- believable
- authentic
- critically

Continuum Connection

- Think critically about the authenticity and believability of characters and their behavior, dialogue, and development (p. 71)

Goal

Think critically about the authenticity and believability of characters and their behavior and dialogue.

Rationale

When students think about the authenticity of characters, they develop critical thinking skills and begin to evaluate the ways authors develop characters.

Whether a character is authentic is relative to the parameters of the world created by the author, regardless of whether it is a realistic or a fantasy setting. This lesson could also be taught as part of U21: Understanding Realistic Fiction or U22: Understanding Fantasy.

Assess Learning

Observe students when they talk about character authenticity and notice if there is evidence of new learning based on the goal of this minilesson.

- Do students discuss whether a character's behavior is believable within the story?
- Are they able to analyze whether dialogue seems real?
- Do they understand the terms *character, conditions, believable, authentic,* and *critically*?

Minilesson

To help students think about the minilesson principle, engage them in thinking about the authenticity of characters. Here is an example.

- Revisit pages 1, 7, and 11 of *The Raft*.

  Think about what Nicky says and how he acts. How would you describe him?

  Do you know anyone or any other characters that might act like him in the same situation?

- As students share ideas, introduce the terms *believable* and *authentic*.
- Create a chart with one column to show whether a character is authentic and another column for evidence from the text. Ask a few volunteers to talk about whether Nicky is authentic, and then have the volunteers write *yes* or *no* on a sticky note and add it to the chart. In the next column, write text examples.
- Repeat the process with *Rikki-Tikki-Tavi*.

  Think about *Rikki-Tikki-Tavi*. Is Rikki-tikki believable? Why or why not?

Have a Try

Invite the students to talk with a partner about whether a character is believable.

> Think about the young British soldier in *Shooting at the Stars.* Was he believable and authentic within the setting of World War I? What about the soldiers who sang carols? Turn and talk about that.

- After time for discussion, ask a few volunteers to add sticky notes to the chart. Ask others to share text examples and write their examples on the chart.

Think critically about whether a character is believable and authentic.

Title	Are the characters believable and authentic?	Why or why not?
The Raft	Yes	• A kid leaving home would feel sad and upset the way Nicky felt. He seems real.
	No	• It seems fake that he loved nature so suddenly and became excited.
Rikki-Tikki-Tavi	Yes	• Rikki-tikki acted like a loyal hero. The way he talked to the birds feels real. The things he did to save everyone matches his personality.
	Yes	• It somehow feels normal that a mongoose was planning to save everyone from the cobras.
Shooting at the Stars	Yes	• The letter sounded like how a son would write to his mom back then.
	No	• The soldiers who sang carols seem real because both sides celebrated Christmas, but it doesn't seem likely they would have put up Christmas trees and traded things.

Summarize and Apply

Summarize the learning and remind students to think about whether fiction characters are authentic.

> You talked about whether characters are authentic based on the conditions of the story.

- Add the principle to the chart.

> If you read a fiction book today, think about whether the characters are authentic and how the author shows you that. Mark pages that you want to remember with a sticky note. Bring the book when we meet so you can share.

Share

Following independent reading time, gather students in small groups. Make sure at least one student in each group read a fiction book.

> With your group, talk about what you noticed about characters when you read today. Were they authentic within the conditions of the story? What makes you think that?

Extend the Lesson (Optional)

After assessing students' understanding, you might decide to extend the learning.

- **Writing About Reading** Have students think critically about the authenticity of characters in fiction books they have read by using a reader's notebook to write about their noticings. Encourage them to include text examples to support their thinking.

RML 2

LA.U30.RML2

Reading Minilesson Principle

Evaluate whether characters behave in ways consistent with the setting of the book.

Thinking Critically About Characters

You Will Need

- several fiction stories with a variety of settings and genres, such as the following:
  - *The Raft* by Jim LaMarche, from Text Set: Family
  - *Under the Quilt of Night* by Deborah Hopkinson, from Text Set: Freedom
  - *The Crane Girl* by Curtis Manley, from Text Set: Empathy
- chart paper prepared with labeled columns: *Genre, Questions About the Setting, Example*
- markers
- fiction books students are reading
- basket of familiar fiction books
- sticky notes

Academic Language / Important Vocabulary

- character
- behave
- consistent
- setting
- genre

Continuum Connection

- Evaluate the consistency of characters' actions within a particular setting (p. 71)

Goal

Evaluate the consistency of characters' actions within a particular setting.

Rationale

When students evaluate whether characters are speaking and behaving in ways that are consistent with the setting, they are thinking deeply about the author's craft and developing critical thinking skills.

Assess Learning

Observe students when they talk about characters and notice if there is evidence of new learning based on the goal of this minilesson.

- Can students think critically about the genre and setting by discussing whether characters speak and behave in ways that are consistent with the setting of the story?
- Do they use the terms *character, behave, consistent, setting,* and *genre*?

Minilesson

To help students think about the minilesson principle, engage them in thinking about whether characters speak and behave in ways consistent with the setting. Here is an example.

- Revisit a few pages from *The Raft.*

  What do you know about the genre and setting of *The Raft?*

  Do you think Nicky talks and acts like a kid living today who has to go alone to his grandma's house for the summer? Why or why not?

- As students share ideas, begin to fill in the chart.

  What type of questions about a realistic fiction book could you ask yourself when you are deciding whether a character behaves and talks in a way that is consistent with the setting?

- Add to the chart, prompting the conversation as needed. Explain and use the term *consistent* as needed.
- Repeat the activity with a historical fiction book, such as *Under the Quilt of Night* and a fantasy book, such as *The Crane Girl.*

  Why is it important for the characters to talk and behave in ways that are consistent with the time and place of the story?

Have a Try

Invite the students to talk with a partner about whether characters are consistent with the setting.

- Have students bring a fiction book they are reading or choose a familiar fiction story from the basket and sit with a partner.

  Turn and talk about whether the characters speak and behave in a way that is appropriate for the setting of a fiction book. Think about the genre and which questions from the chart might help you answer.

- After time for discussion, ask students to share ideas. Add new questions to the chart.

Evaluate whether characters behave in ways consistent with the setting of the book.

Genre	Questions About Setting	Example
Realistic Fiction 	Do I know someone who acts like this? Could I imagine this happening today?	I could imagine a boy being sad and lonely when he is away from home and not used to nature.
Historical Fiction 	What was happening during that time? How would characters need to behave to live at that time?	The girl was fighting for her life and could be killed or hurt. Her worries seem real and it's believable that she was scared but brave.
Fantasy 	What kind of fantasy world is it? What is necessary to survive in the fantasy world?	Yasuhiro and Hiroko lived in a world where magic things happened. People could turn into cranes and cranes could turn into people. It was believable that Yasuhiro wanted to be a crane because he loved Hiroko.

Summarize and Apply

Summarize the learning and remind students to think about whether characters are consistent with the setting.

What did you learn today about characters?

- Add the principle to the chart.

  If you read a fiction book today, think about whether the characters behave in a way that is consistent with the setting. Mark pages that you want to remember with sticky notes. Bring the book when we meet so you can share.

Share

Following independent reading time, gather students in the meeting area.

Were the characters in your book consistent with the setting of the story? What questions did you ask to think about that when you read?

Extend the Lesson (Optional)

After assessing students' understanding, you might decide to extend the learning.

- **Writing About Reading** Ask students to write in a reader's notebook their opinions about whether a character in a fiction book acts in a way that is consistent within the setting.

RML 3
LA.U30.RML3

Reading Minilesson Principle

Evaluate whether the writer makes you feel empathy for a character.

Thinking Critically About Characters

You Will Need

- several familiar fiction stories, such as the following:
  - *Under the Quilt of Night* by Deborah Hopkinson and *The Composition* by Antonio Skármeta, from Text Set: Freedom
  - *Shooting at the Stars* by John Hendrix, from Text Set: Conflict Resolution
- chart paper and markers
- fiction books students are reading
- basket of fiction books
- two colors of sticky notes

Academic Language / Important Vocabulary

- character
- empathy

Continuum Connection

- Assess the extent to which a writer makes readers feel empathy or identify with characters (p. 71)

Goal

Evaluate whether the writer makes you feel empathy for a character.

Rationale

When students recognize that an author can use techniques to cause a reader to feel empathy toward a character, they think more deeply about the author's craft and learn how ideas gained from reading can be applied to their own lives. The more empathy students feel toward characters, the more engaged they will be in their reading.

Assess Learning

Observe students when they talk about whether they feel empathy for characters and notice if there is evidence of new learning based on the goal of this minilesson.

- Can students recognize when they feel empathy for a character?
- Do they talk about the techniques used by a writer to create empathy?
- Do they use the terms *character* and *empathy*?

Minilesson

To help students think about the minilesson principle, engage them in thinking about whether a writer makes them feel empathy for a character. Here is an example.

- Turn through a few pages of *Under the Quilt of Night.*

  Think about the girl who is escaping slavery in *Under the Quilt of Night*. Do you think the author is successful in getting you to know what it would be like to experience the same things as she did? Turn and talk about that.

- Allow students time for discussion, and add the title and main character's name to the chart.
- Ask one student to share his thinking.

  Did the author make you feel empathy? Write *Yes* or *No* on a sticky note and place the sticky note on the chart next to the character's name.

- After the student places the sticky note on the chart, have a conversation about his thinking. Add an example from the story to the chart, along with his thoughts on why the author did or did not create a feeling of empathy.
- Repeat the activity with characters from other books, such as Pedro from *The Composition* and the British soldier from *Shooting at the Stars.*

  What techniques do you notice these authors using to try to make you feel empathy for the characters?

Have a Try

Invite the students to talk with a partner about whether the author causes them to feel empathy for a character.

- Have students bring a fiction book they are reading or choose a familiar fiction story from the basket and sit with a partner.

  Turn and talk about whether the author makes you feel empathy for a character. Share examples from the book that make you feel that way.

Evaluate whether the writer makes you feel empathy for a character.

Title and Character	Do you feel empathy?	Examples	Why or why not?
Under the Quilt of Night the girl	Yes	"My cuts sting, my bites itch. I'm hungry all the time."	"I felt empathy. The words made me picture how the girl was feeling and I could understand." —Jamal
The Composition Pedro	No	"Daniel owns the store now. Maybe he will give me some candy."	"Pedro seemed so clueless about everything going on around him. It didn't make sense. I did not care about him." —Abraham
Shooting at the Stars British soldier	Yes	"We spend most of our time and energy trying to stay dry and warm."	"The description of how muddy and cold it was made me feel like I was there and I felt bad for the soldier." —Leila
	Yes	"Then came a voice followed by great laughter from their trench."	"I could imagine being that soldier at war and suddenly hearing Christmas music. I felt happy like the soldier." —Miguel

Summarize and Apply

Summarize the learning and remind students to think about whether they feel empathy for characters in fiction stories.

You talked about whether authors caused you to feel empathy for some characters. What did you notice?

- Add the principle to the top of the chart.

  If you read a fiction book today, think about whether the author makes you feel empathy for any of the characters. Mark any pages you want to remember with a sticky note. Bring the book when we meet so you can share.

Share

Following independent reading time, gather students in the meeting area.

Did anyone read about a character for whom you felt empathy? Share what you noticed and tell what the author did to try to make the reader feel empathy for a character.

Extend the Lesson (Optional)

After assessing students' understanding, you might decide to extend the learning.

- Have students share examples of when they believe the author wanted the reader to care about a character but was not successful. Ask them to talk about how the author could have written the story in a different way that would have caused them to care more about the character.

Assessment

After you have taught the minilessons in this umbrella, observe students as they talk and write about their reading across instructional contexts: interactive read-aloud, independent reading, guided reading, shared reading, and book club. Use *The Literacy Continuum* (Fountas and Pinnell 2017) to observe students' reading and writing behaviors.

- What evidence do you have of new understandings related to characters?
  - Are students talking about whether a character is authentic?
  - Can they analyze whether characters behave in ways that are true to the setting?
  - Do they notice whether they feel empathy for a character?
  - Are they using the terms *character, believable, authentic, setting,* and *empathy*?
- In what other ways, beyond the scope of this umbrella, are students talking about characters?
  - Do students notice a character's traits and feelings by thinking about what the text evidence reveals?

Use your observations to determine the next umbrella you will teach. You may also consult Minilessons Across the Year (pp. 61–64) for guidance.

Link to Writing

After teaching the minilessons in this umbrella, help students link the new learning to their own writing:

- Encourage students to think about ways to create authenticity in their own writing.

Reader's Notebook

When this umbrella is complete, provide a copy of the minilesson principles (see resources.fountasandpinnell.com) for students to glue in the reader's notebook (in the Minilessons section if using *Reader's Notebook: Advanced* [Fountas and Pinnell 2011]), so they can refer to the information as needed.

Minilessons in This Umbrella

RML1	Writers choose the narrator and the point of view of the story.
RML2	Sometimes writers change the narrator and the perspective of the story.
RML3	Sometimes writers show the perspective of more than one character.

Before Teaching Umbrella 31 Minilessons

The minilessons in this umbrella introduce students to some of the different ways authors experiment with narrator (who is telling the story), point of view (the angle from which the reader views the story), and perspective (a character's attitude toward or way of seeing something). Before teaching these minilessons, read aloud and discuss a variety of engaging fiction books with different kinds of narrators and points of view (first person and third person). Include stories that clearly show the differing perspectives of characters and stories in which the narrator and/or perspective changes. Use the following books from the *Fountas & Pinnell Classroom™ Interactive Read-Aloud Collection* and *Independent Reading Collection* or choose appropriate fiction books from your classroom library.

Interactive Read-Aloud Collection

Facing the Unknown

The Village That Vanished by Ann Grifalconi

King of the Sky by Nicola Davies

Grit and Perseverance

Rikki-Tikki-Tavi by Rudyard Kipling

Nim and the War Effort by Milly Lee

Brian's Winter by Gary Paulsen

Exploring Literary Language

Sequoia by Tony Johnston

Independent Reading Collection

Same Sun Here by Silas House

As you read aloud and enjoy these texts together, help students notice and discuss

- who is telling the story,
- whether the story is told from a first-person or third-person point of view,
- whose perspective the narrator focuses on,
- any changes in the narrator or perspective, and
- differing perspectives of different characters.

Interactive Read-Aloud

Facing the Unknown

Grit and Perseverance

Rikki-Tikki-Tavi by Rudyard Kipling

Nim and the War Effort by Milly Lee

Exporing Literary Language

Sequoia by Tony Johnston

Independent Reading

RML 1

LA.U31.RML1

Reading Minilesson Principle

Writers choose the narrator and the point of view of the story.

Analyzing Perspective and Point of View

You Will Need

- two or three familiar fiction books with different kinds of narrators and points of view, such as the following:
  - *King of the Sky* by Nicola Davies, from Text Set: Facing the Unknown
  - *Brian's Winter* by Gary Paulsen, from Text Set: Grit and Perseverance
  - *Sequoia* by Tony Johnston, from Text Set: Exploring Literary Language
- chart paper and markers

Academic Language / Important Vocabulary

- narrator
- first-person point of view
- third-person point of view

Continuum Connection

- Notice the narrator of a text and notice a change in narrator and perspective (p. 71)

Goal

Notice the narrator and point of view of the story.

Rationale

An author chooses the narrator (the person telling the story) and the point of view, or the angle from which the story is told (e.g., first person, third-person omniscient, third-person limited). The author's choices regarding the narrator and the point of view influence how the story is told, including which details are included and omitted. Noticing the narrator and point of view helps students understand that there are multiple sides to a story and that the author must make decisions about how to tell it.

Assess Learning

Observe students when they read and talk about books and notice if there is evidence of new learning based on the goal of this minilesson.

- Can students identify the narrator and the point of view of a story?
- Do they use academic vocabulary, such as *narrator*, *first-person point of view*, and *third-person point of view*?

Minilesson

To help students think about the minilesson principle, use familiar fiction books to help students notice the writer's choice of narrator and point of view. Here is an example.

- Show the cover of *King of the Sky* and read the title. Then read pages 1–6.

  Who is the narrator of this story? How can you tell?

- Record students' responses on chart paper.

  A young boy is the narrator. You can tell because he uses pronouns like *I*, *my*, and *me*. This is called first-person point of view. We see the story unfold as the boy sees it, and we know only what the narrator knows. The story is told from the boy's point of view.

- Show *Brian's Winter* and read the title. Then read page 5.

  Who is the narrator? How do you know?

  This story has a third-person narrator. A third-person narrator is usually not a character in the story but knows what is going on. Pronouns like *he*, *she*, and *they* let you know that the story is told in the third person.

- Record responses on the chart.

  The narrator tells about what Brian does and how he feels about what is happening, but the narrator is not a character in the story.

Have a Try

Invite the students to talk with a partner about the narrator and the point of view in *Sequoia*.

- Read pages 1–6 from *Sequoia*.

  Turn and talk to your partner about what you notice about the narrator and the point of view in this story. Who is telling the story? From what point of view is the narrator telling it?

- After students turn and talk, invite a few students to share their thinking. Record responses on the chart.

Writers choose the narrator and the point of view of the story.

Book	Narrator and Point of View	Evidence
King of the Sky	• A young boy • First-person point of view	• "reminded me of home" • "my house"
Brian's Winter	• Unnamed narrator • Third-person point of view	• "Brian didn't realize what was in store." • "He had never thought he would be here this long."
Sequoia	• Unnamed narrator • Third-person point of view	• "He watches the grove below slowly fill with light."

Summarize and Apply

Summarize the learning and remind students to notice the narrator and the point of view when they read fiction.

What did you learn about narrators and points of view?

- Write the principle at the top of the chart.

  If you read fiction today, notice the narrator and the point of view of your story. Be ready to share what you noticed when we come back together.

Share

Following independent reading time, gather students together in the meeting area to talk about narrators and point of view.

If you read a fiction book today, think about the narrator of the story.

What did you notice about the point of view from which your story is told?

Extend the Lesson (Optional)

After assessing students' understanding, you might decide to extend the learning.

- Discuss the advantages and disadvantages of first- and third-person point of view. Ask students to infer why an author would choose one or the other.
- If you feel your students are ready for it, you may want to discuss the difference between third-person-limited point of view and third-person-omniscient point of view.
- Use shared writing to rewrite a story (or part of a story) that is told from third-person point of view as first-person point of view or vice versa.

RML 2
LA.U31.RML2

Reading Minilesson Principle

Sometimes writers change the narrator and the perspective of the story.

Analyzing Perspective and Point of View

You Will Need

- two familiar fiction books in which the narrator and/or perspective changes, such as the following:
  - *Same Sun Here* by Silas House, from *Independent Reading Collection*
  - *The Village That Vanished* by Ann Grifalconi, from Text Set: Facing the Unknown
- chart paper and markers

Academic Language / Important Vocabulary

- narrator
- perspective
- fiction

Continuum Connection

- Notice the narrator of a text and notice a change in narrator and perspective (p. 71)

Goal

Notice when a writer changes the narrator and perspective of the story.

Rationale

A character's perspective is shaped by the character's life experiences and is the lens through which he or she views the world. It is different from, though related to, point of view. When students notice a change in the narrator or perspective of a story, they understand that there are multiple sides to every story and that the author must make decisions about how to tell the story.

Assess Learning

Observe students when they read and talk about fiction books and notice if there is evidence of new learning based on the goal of this minilesson.

- Do students notice changes in the narrator or perspective?
- Do they use academic vocabulary, such as *narrator*, *perspective*, and *fiction*?

Minilesson

To help students think about the minilesson principle, use familiar fiction books to discuss changes in narrator or perspective. Here is an example.

- Show the cover of *Same Sun Here* and read the title. Then read pages 4–5.

  Who is the narrator in this part of the book?

  From what point of view is she telling the story?

  Meena is a first-person narrator. We learn about her perspective from reading what she says about her life. Her perspective is shaped by her experiences and is how she views the events in the story.

- Read the first two paragraphs on page 12.

  What do you notice about the narrator and perspective in this part of the book? What has changed? What has stayed the same?

- Record responses on chart paper.

  Now the narrator is River. He is also a first-person narrator. The narrator in this book changes back and forth between Meena and River. In River's chapters, we see events from River's perspective.

- Show the cover of *The Village That Vanished* and read the title. Then read the first three lines on page 1.

  Who is the narrator of this book?

  What do you notice about how the narrator is telling the story? Whose perspective is being shown?

Have a Try

Invite the students to talk with a partner about the narrator and perspective in *The Village That Vanished.*

- Read pages 30–35 of *The Village That Vanished.*

  Who is the narrator in this part of the book?

  Whose perspective does the narrator show in this part of the book?

  Turn and talk to your partner about whether the narrator and the perspective stay the same or change in this story.

- After students turn and talk, invite a few students to share their thinking. Record responses on the chart. If necessary, help students understand that the narrator remains the same throughout the whole story but shows the perspective of different characters.

Sometimes writers change the narrator and the perspective of the story.

Book	Narrator	Whose perspective?
 Same Sun Here	• First-person narrator: sometimes Meena, sometimes River	• Sometimes Meena's • Sometimes River's
 The Village That Vanished	• Unnamed third-person narrator	• Sometimes Abikanile's • Sometimes the slavers'

Summarize and Apply

Summarize the learning and remind students to notice changes in the narrator and perspective.

What did you notice about the narrator and perspective in the books we looked at today?

- Write the principle at the top of the chart.

  If you read fiction today, think about the narrator and perspective of your story. If the narrator or perspective changes at any point in your book, bring it to share when we come back together.

Share

Following independent reading time, gather students together in the meeting area to talk about perspective in the books they read.

Did anyone read a story in which the narrator or perspective changes?

How did the narrator or perspective change in your story?

Extend the Lesson (Optional)

After assessing students' understanding, you might decide to extend the learning.

- Discuss why authors sometimes change the narrator and/or the perspective in a story.
- **Writing About Reading** Have students rewrite or tell a familiar story from a different character's perspective.

RML 3

LA.U31.RML3

Reading Minilesson Principle

Sometimes writers show the perspective of more than one character.

Analyzing Perspective and Point of View

You Will Need

- two or three familiar fiction books that have characters with differing perspectives, such as the following from Text Set: Grit and Perseverance:
  - *Rikki-Tikki-Tavi* by Rudyard Kipling
  - *Nim and the War Effort* by Milly Lee
- chart paper and markers

Academic Language / Important Vocabulary

- primary character
- secondary character
- perspective

Continuum Connection

- Notice the narrator of a text and notice a change in narrator and perspective (p. 71)

Goal

Notice how the writer shows different perspectives through primary and secondary characters.

Rationale

When students notice and think about the perspectives of multiple characters in a story, they gain a deeper understanding of the characters' personalities and motivations. They also develop their understanding of the bigger idea that in real life every person has his own perspective, or way of viewing the world. Understanding different perspectives helps students develop empathy.

Assess Learning

Observe students when they read and talk about fiction books and notice if there is evidence of new learning based on the goal of this minilesson.

- Can students compare the perspectives of two or more characters in a story?
- Do they use academic vocabulary, such as *primary character, secondary character,* and *perspective*?

Minilesson

To help students think about the minilesson principle, use familiar fiction books to help students notice different perspectives. Here is an example.

- Show the cover of *Nim and the War Effort* and read the title.

  Who is the main character in this story?

  Nim is the main, or primary, character in this story. Primary character is another way to say main character. Who are the other characters in this story?

  The other characters in the story are called secondary characters.

  What does Nim do in this story to help the war effort?

- Read pages 30–32.

  How does Nim feel about winning the newspaper drive?

  Does Nim's grandfather see the situation the same way she does, or does he have a different perspective on it?

  How is his perspective different?

  Why are their perspectives different?

- Record students' responses on chart paper.

Have a Try

Invite the students to talk with a partner about perspective in *Rikki-Tikki-Tavi*.

- Show the cover of *Rikki-Tikki-Tavi* and read the title. Then read the last paragraph of page 16 and the first paragraph of page 18.

  Turn and talk to your partner about how Rikki-tikki's perspective is different from Teddy's mother's perspective.

- After students turn and talk, invite a few pairs to share their thinking. Record their responses on the chart.

Sometimes writers show the perspective of more than one character.

Book	Situation	Primary Character	Secondary Character
Nim and the War Effort	Nim wins the newspaper drive.	Nim is proud and excited. She wants to prove herself to be an American.	Nim's grandfather is mad at her for coming home late and worrying her family. He is very traditional.
Rikki-Tikki-Tavi	Rikki-tikki kills a snake.	Rikki-tikki doesn't see what the big deal is.	Teddy's mother is proud of Rikki-tikki for having "saved Teddy's life."

Summarize and Apply

Summarize the learning and remind students to notice differing perspectives.

What did you notice about characters' perspectives today?

- Write the principle at the top of the chart.

  If you read fiction today, think about the perspectives of different characters. How do they see things differently? Be ready to share your thinking when we come back together.

Share

Following independent reading time, gather students together in the meeting area to talk about perspective in the books they read.

Who read a fiction book today?

What did you notice about the perspectives of the characters in your story?

Extend the Lesson (Optional)

After assessing students' understanding, you might decide to extend the learning.

- Discuss *why* different characters in a story have different perspectives. Help students build their understanding of the different factors that can influence a person's perspective (e.g., culture, religion, age, personal experiences).

Assessment

After you have taught the minilessons in this umbrella, observe students as they talk and write about their reading across instructional contexts: interactive read-aloud, independent reading, guided reading, shared reading, and book club. Use *The Literacy Continuum* (Fountas and Pinnell 2017) to observe students' reading and writing behaviors.

- What evidence do you have of new understandings related to perspective and point of view?
    - Can students identify the narrator of a story?
    - Can they identify whether a story is told from a first- or third-person point of view?
    - Can they identify whose perspective the narrator focuses on?
    - Do they notice when a writer changes the narrator and/or perspective?
    - Can they explain how two characters' perspectives differ?
    - Do they use academic vocabulary, such as *narrator*, *perspective*, and *point of view*?
- In what other ways, beyond the scope of this umbrella, are students talking about fiction books?
    - Are students thinking critically about characters?
    - Are they noticing the elements of plot development?

Use your observations to determine the next umbrella you will teach. You may also consult Minilessons Across the Year (pp. 61–64) for guidance.

Link to Writing

After teaching the minilessons in this umbrella, help students link the new learning to their own writing:

- When students write their own stories, remind them to think carefully about the narrator, point of view, and characters' perspectives before they begin writing.
- Have students write the same story from the point of view of two or more characters.

Reader's Notebook

When this umbrella is complete, provide a copy of the minilesson principles (see resources.fountasandpinnell.com) for students to glue in the reader's notebook (in the Minilessons section if using *Reader's Notebook: Advanced* [Fountas and Pinnell 2011]), so they can refer to the information as needed.

Section 3 Strategies and Skills

The Strategies and Skills minilessons are designed to bring a few important strategic actions to temporary, conscious attention so that students can apply them in their independent reading. By the time students participate in these minilessons, they should have engaged these strategic actions successfully in guided reading lessons as they continue to strengthen in-the-head literacy processing systems. These lessons reinforce effective and efficient reading behaviors.

3 Strategies and Skills

Minilessons in This Umbrella

RML1	Break a multisyllable word between consonants but keep consonant digraphs together.
RML2	Break a multisyllable word after the vowel if the syllable has a long vowel sound and after the consonant if the syllable has a short vowel sound.
RML3	Break a multisyllable word between vowels.
RML4	Break a multisyllable word before the consonant and *le*.
RML5	Remove the prefix or suffix to take apart a word.
RML6	Look for a part of the word that can help.

Before Teaching Umbrella 1 Minilessons

Most of the word work you do with your students will take place during small-group guided reading or a separate word study lesson. However, there are minilessons that may serve as reminders and be helpful to the whole class. They can be taught any time you see a need among your students. Before teaching these minilessons, make sure students know terms such as *syllable, word part, consonant*, and *vowel*. Students must also be able to recognize consonant digraphs, prefixes, and suffixes. Use the examples that are provided in these minilessons or choose sentences with multisyllable words from texts your students are reading. Use two- and three-syllable words and unknown words as examples of each principle.

RML 1
SAS.U1.RML1

Reading Minilesson Principle

Break a multisyllable word between consonants but keep consonant digraphs together.

Solving Multisyllable Words

You Will Need

- word cards: *number, insect, cricket, quarter, fraction, laughing, mushroom, tablet, culture, adverb, bleachers, emphasis, advantage, company, withdraw, checkers, weather*
- chart paper and markers

Academic Language / Important Vocabulary

- consonant
- consonant digraph
- syllable

Continuum Connection

- Recognize and use syllables in words with the VCCV pattern (syllable juncture): e.g., *ber/ry, both/er, dis/may, hel/met* (p. 384)

Goal

Learn to break multisyllable words between consonants, keeping consonant diagraphs together.

Rationale

Students need to know how to break multisyllable words apart to read new words more efficiently, to write words accurately, and to know where to break words at the end of a line when writing by hand. Two-syllable words with medial consonants are broken between the two consonants, except when the consonants form a digraph (e.g., *th, sh*). Then the word is broken after the digraph.

Assess Learning

Observe students when they solve unknown words. Notice if there is evidence of new learning based on the goal of this minilesson.

- Do students know to break apart unknown words into syllables to read them?
- Do they understand the terms *consonant, consonant digraph,* and *syllable*?

Minilesson

To help students practice determining where to break multisyllable words with medial consonants, use examples of words that have medial consonants and medial consonant digraphs. Here is an example.

- Show the word card for *number*. Have students tap the word and tell where to break it. Write the word on the left side of the chart and draw a slash between the two syllables (*num/ber*).
- Repeat with the word *insect*.

  What do you notice about where the words are broken?

  Both words are broken between the consonants in the middle.

- Show the word card for *cricket*. Have students tap the word and note the number of syllables. Start a column on the right side of the chart. Write the word and draw a slash between the syllables (*crick/et*).
- Continue showing the word cards, having students tap the syllables, and writing the words in the appropriate column on the chart: *quarter, fraction, laughing, mushroom, tablet, culture, adverb, bleachers, emphasis, advantage, company.*

  What do you notice about the words in the left-hand column? Where are they broken?

  What do you notice about the words in the right-hand column? What do you notice about how to break them?

Have a Try

Invite the students to break apart words with medial consonants and consonant digraphs.

- Show the word card for *withdraw.*

  Turn and talk to your partner about where you would break this word.

- Write (or have a volunteer write) the word on the chart and draw a slash between the syllables. Repeat with *checkers and weather*.

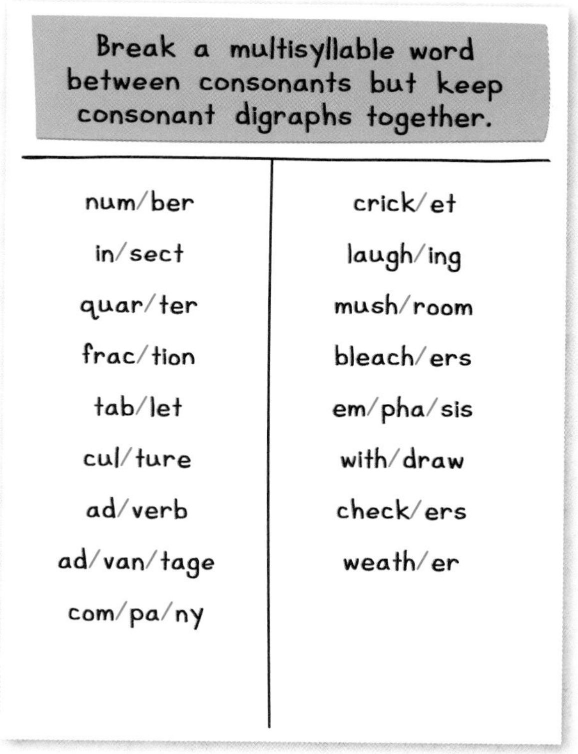

Summarize and Apply

Summarize the learning and remind students to break words apart between two consonants and keep consonant digraphs together.

Look at the chart. What do you notice about where to break apart words when they have consonants in the middle?

- Write the principle at the top of the chart.

  If you come to a new word when you read today, break it apart to read it, and be prepared to share when we come back together.

Break a multisyllable word between consonants but keep consonant digraphs together.

num/ber	crick/et
in/sect	laugh/ing
quar/ter	mush/room
frac/tion	bleach/ers
tab/let	em/pha/sis
cul/ture	with/draw
ad/verb	check/ers
ad/van/tage	weath/er
com/pa/ny	

Share

Following independent reading time, gather students together in the meeting area to talk about how they read unknown words.

Did anyone come to a new word while reading? What did you do?

Extend the Lesson (Optional)

After assessing students' understanding, you might decide to extend the learning.

- During shared writing, model how to write multisyllable words by saying them slowly, listening for the parts, and writing one part at a time.

RML 2
SAS.U1.RML2

Reading Minilesson Principle

Break a multisyllable word after the vowel if the syllable has a long vowel sound and after the consonant if the syllable has a short vowel sound.

Solving Multisyllable Words

You Will Need

- word cards: *humid, global, comet, hazard, nation, radish, closet, galaxy, pronoun, fragrant, resident, microwave, cucumber, volcano, ambulance, agency*
- chart paper and markers

Academic Language / Important Vocabulary

- long vowel sound
- short vowel sound
- multisyllable
- syllable

Continuum Connection

- Break a word into syllables to decode manageable units: e.g., *re/mem/ber, hos/pi/tal, be/fore, de/part/ment* (p. 387)

Goal

Learn where to break apart multisyllable words with long vowel sounds and words with short vowel sounds.

Rationale

Students learn to take words apart and write multisyllable words accurately by listening for syllable breaks. Two-syllable words are generally broken after the vowel if the first syllable has a long vowel sound (open syllable) and after the consonant if the first syllable has a short vowel sound (closed syllable).

Assess Learning

Observe students when they solve unknown words. Notice if there is evidence of new learning based on the goal of this minilesson.

- Do students listen for the vowel sound in the first syllable so they know where to break a word apart?
- Do they use the language *long vowel sound, short vowel sound, multisyllable,* and *syllable*?

Minilesson

To help students apply the minilesson principle, engage them in listening for where to break apart multisyllable words. Here is an example.

- Show the word card for *humid*. Have students tap the word to note the number of syllables. Write the word on the left side of the chart and draw a slash between the two syllables (*hu/mid*).
- Repeat with the word *global* (*glo/bal*).

  What do you notice about where the words are broken? What vowel sound do you hear in the first syllable?

  Break the words after the vowel.

- Show the word card for *comet*. Have students tap the syllables and tell where to break the word. Start a new column on the right. Write the word and draw a slash between the syllables (*com/et*).
- Continue showing word cards and having students tap the syllables and tell where to break each word. Write the words in the correct column on the chart: *hazard, nation, radish, closet, galaxy, pronoun, fragrant, resident, microwave.*

Have a Try

Invite the students to break apart multisyllable words that have both open and closed syllables.

- Show the word card for *cucumber*.

  Turn and talk to your partner about where you would break this word.

- Write (or have a volunteer write) the word on the chart and draw a slash between the syllables. Repeat the process with *volcano, ambulance*, and *agency*.

Break a multisyllable word after the vowel if the syllable has a long vowel sound and after the consonant if the syllable has a short vowel sound.

hu/mid	com/et	cu/cum/ber
glo/bal	haz/ard	vol/ca/no
na/tion	rad/ish	am/bu/lance
pro/noun	clos/et	a/gen/cy
fra/grant	gal/ax/y	
mi/cro/wave	res/i/dent	

Summarize and Apply

Summarize the learning and remind students to break a word after the vowel if the syllable has a long vowel sound and after the consonant if the syllable has a short vowel sound.

Look at the chart. What do you notice about where the words are broken?

- Guide students to notice that when a syllable has a long vowel sound, the syllable ends with the vowel. When the syllable has a short vowel sound, the syllable usually ends with a consonant. Write the principle at the top of the chart.

  When you read today, if you get to a new word, you may need to break it in a couple of different places and try each vowel sound to find out which one is correct. Be prepared to share when we come back together.

Share

Following independent reading time, gather students together in the meeting area to talk about how they solve unknown words.

Did anyone come to a word you didn't know? What did you do?

Extend the Lesson (Optional)

After assessing students' understanding, you might decide to extend the learning.

- Challenge students to break the word *project*, which can be pronounced two different ways and, therefore, divided into syllables two different ways, into syllables (*proj/ect, pro/ject*).
- During shared writing, model how to write multisyllable words by saying them slowly, listening for the parts, and writing one part at a time.

RML3
SAS.U1.RML3

Reading Minilesson Principle
Break a multisyllable word between vowels.

Solving Multisyllable Words

You Will Need

- word cards: *triumph, riot, quiet, chaos, fluent, client, violin, denial, media, cereal, cardiac, defiant, hideous, scientific*
- chart paper and markers

Academic Language / Important Vocabulary

- vowel
- syllable

Continuum Connection

- Break a word into syllables to decode manageable units: e.g., *re/mem/ber, hos/pi/tal, be/fore, de/part/ment* (p. 387)
- Recognize and use syllables in words with the VV pattern: e.g., *gi/ant, ru/in, sci/ence* (p. 384)

Goal

Learn to take apart a multisyllable word between vowels.

Rationale

Students learn to take words apart and write multisyllable words accurately by listening for syllable breaks. In some words, the syllable break comes between two vowels, as in the word *ruin*.

Assess Learning

Observe students when they solve unknown words. Notice if there is evidence of new learning based on the goal of this minilesson.

- Do students break unknown words into parts?
- Do they break multisyllable words into parts between two vowel sounds if the first syllable is an open syllable (long vowel sound)?
- Are they using the terms *vowel* and *syllable*?

Minilesson

To help students think about the minilesson principle, engage them in a demonstration of breaking apart words between vowels. Here is an example.

- Show the word card for *triumph*. Have students tap the syllables and tell where to break the word. Write the word on the chart paper and draw a slash between the syllables (*tri/umph*).
- Repeat with the word *riot* (*ri/ot*).

  What do you notice about where each word is broken?

- Continue showing the word cards, having students tap the syllables and tell where to break it. Write each word on the chart: *quiet, chaos, fluent, client, violin, denial, media, cereal, cardiac, defiant.*

Have a Try

Invite the students to break apart the words *hideous* and *scientific* with a partner.

> Turn and talk to your partner about where to break the word *hideous*.

- Write (or have volunteers write) the word on the chart and draw a slash between each syllable. Repeat with the word *scientific*.

Break a multisyllable word between vowels.

tri/umph
ri/ot
qui/et
cha/os
flu/ent
cli/ent
vi/o/lin
de/ni/al
me/di/a
cer/e/al
car/di/ac
de/fi/ant
hid/e/ous
sci/en/tif/ic

Summarize and Apply

Summarize the learning and remind students to break new multisyllable words apart between vowels.

> Look at the chart. What can you say about where the words are broken?

- Write the principle at the top of the chart. Make sure students understand that when two vowels combine to make a sound (a vowel digraph, such as *ou*), the vowels stay together (*house*, *cou/pon*).

> When you read today, if you come to a new multisyllable word, you may need to break the word between the vowels. Be prepared to share when we come back together.

Share

Following independent reading time, gather students together in the meeting area to talk about breaking words apart.

> Did anyone come to a word you didn't know? What did you do?

Extend the Lesson (Optional)

After assessing students' understanding, you might decide to extend the learning.

- During shared writing, model how to write multisyllable words by saying them slowly, listening for the parts, and writing one part at a time.

RML 4

SAS.U1.RML4

Reading Minilesson Principle

Break a multisyllable word before the consonant and *le*.

Solving Multisyllable Words

You Will Need

- word cards: *scramble, sparkle, shuffle, startle, stable, tangle, nimble, portable, dismantle, adorable, tentacle, bicycle, accessible*
- chart paper and markers

Academic Language / Important Vocabulary

- consonant
- syllable

Continuum Connection

- Recognize and use consonant + *le* syllables—syllables that contain a consonant followed by the letters *le*: e.g., *a/ble, ea/gle, scram/ble, tem/ple* [p. 384]

Goal

Learn to break multisyllable words apart before the consonant and *le*.

Rationale

Students learn to take multisyllable words apart and write them accurately by listening for the syllable breaks. Students learn that in most words that end with *le*, the syllable is broken before the consonant and *le*.

Assess Learning

Observe students when they take apart unknown words ending with a consonant and *le*. Notice if there is evidence of new learning based on the goal of this minilesson.

- Do students break unknown words into parts when word solving?
- Do they know to break multisyllable words before the consonant and *le*?
- Are they using the terms *consonant* and *syllable*?

Minilesson

To help students think about the minilesson principle, engage them in a demonstration of breaking apart words ending with a consonant and *le*. Here is an example.

- Show the word card for *scramble*. Have students tap the syllables and tell where to break the word. Write the word on the chart paper and draw a slash between the syllables (*scram/ble*).
- Repeat the process with *sparkle* (*spar/kle*).

  What do you notice about where each word is broken?

  Break the word before the consonant and *le*.

- Repeat this process with these words: *shuffle, startle, stable, tangle, nimble, portable, dismantle, adorable,* and *tentacle*.

  When you get to a word you don't know, break it before the consonant and *le* to help you read the word.

Have a Try

Invite the students to break apart the words *bicycle* and *accessible* with a partner.

- Show the word card for *bicycle*.

  Turn and talk to your partner about where to break the word *bicycle*.

- Write (or have a volunteer write) the word on the chart and draw slashes between the syllables. Repeat with *accessible*.

Summarize and Apply

Summarize the learning and remind students to break new words apart before the consonant and *le*.

Look at the chart. What do you notice about where the words are broken?

When you get to a word you don't know, break it before the consonant and *le* to help you read the word.

- Write the principle at the top.

  When you read today, if you come to a new word, break it apart to help you read it. Be ready to share when we come back together.

Break a multisyllable word before the consonant and le.

scram/ble
spar/kle
shuf/fle
star/tle
sta/ble
tan/gle
nim/ble
por/ta/ble
dis/man/tle
a/dor/a/ble
ten/ta/cle
bi/cy/cle
ac/ces/si/ble

Share

Following independent reading time, gather students together in the meeting area to talk about word solving.

Did anyone come to a word you didn't know? What did you do? Did you have to try more than one way of breaking apart the word?

Extend the Lesson (Optional)

After assessing students' understanding, you might decide to extend the learning.

- Challenge students to break apart the words *crackle* (*crack/le*) and *knuckle* (*knuck/le*). In these words, the letters *ck* form a consonant digraph, which cannot be broken apart.
- During shared writing, model how to write multisyllable words by saying them slowly, listening for the parts, and writing one word at a time.

RML5

SAS.U1.RML5

Reading Minilesson Principle

Remove the prefix or suffix to take apart a word.

Solving Multisyllable Words

You Will Need

- chart paper prepared with two columns, the first column filled in: *improper*, *flexible*, *recover*, *government*, *monotone*, *multiplayer*, *entertainment*, *heroic*
- sticky note or index card
- markers

Academic Language / Important Vocabulary

- prefix
- suffix
- base word

Continuum Connection

- Recognize and use word parts to solve an unknown word and understand its meaning: e.g., *conference*—prefix *con-* ("with or together"), Latin root *fer* ("to bring" or "to carry"), suffix *-ence* ("state of" or "quality of") (p. 387)

Goal

Learn to take off the prefix or suffix to solve multisyllable words.

Rationale

When you teach students to take multisyllable words apart by removing the prefix or suffix and reading the base word, they can problem solve words more efficiently and keep their attention on meaning.

Assess Learning

Observe students when they take apart unknown words with a prefix or suffix. Notice if there is evidence of new learning based on the goal of this minilesson.

- Do students break apart words between the base word and the prefix or suffix?
- Are they using the terms *prefix*, *suffix*, and *base word*?

Minilesson

To help students think about the minilesson principle, engage them in a demonstration of removing a prefix or suffix to identify the base word. Here is an example.

- Display the premade chart and read the first word. Use a sticky note or an index card to cover the prefix (*im*). Read the base word (*proper*) and then reveal the prefix. Read the whole word to make sure it sounds right and looks right.

  What did you notice about where I broke the word *improper*? Where did I break the word?

- Prompt the students to say that you removed the prefix, read the base word, and then added the prefix back onto the word and read the whole word. Write on the chart how you broke apart the word. You may wish to point out that a prefix or suffix can have more than one syllable.
- Repeat this process with the word *flexible* to illustrate how to remove a suffix to read a new word. Then continue in the same way for the remaining words: *recover*, *government*, *monotone*, *multiplayer*, *entertainment*, *heroic*.

  You can remove the suffix so you can read the base word and then the whole word.

Have a Try

Invite the students to break apart the words that have a prefix or a suffix.

- Write *predictable* and *disrespect* on the chart.

  Turn and talk to your partner about how to break apart these words.

- Write (or have volunteers write) the words on the chart and draw a slash between each syllable.

Summarize and Apply

Summarize the learning and remind students to solve new words by removing the prefix or suffix or both.

Look at the chart. What do you notice about how the words were broken?

When you come to a word you don't know, look for a prefix or suffix (or both) to remove so that you can read the word.

Remove the prefix or suffix to take apart a word.

improper	im/proper
flexible	flex/ible
recover	re/cover
government	govern/ment
monotone	mono/tone
multiplayer	multi/player
entertainment	entertain/ment
heroic	hero/ic
predictable	predict/able
disrespect	dis/respect

- Write the principle at the top of the chart.

  When you read today, if you come to a new word, break it into parts to help you read it. Be ready to share when we come back together.

Share

Following independent reading time, gather students together in the meeting area to talk about word solving.

Did anyone come to a word you didn't know? What did you do?

Extend the Lesson (Optional)

After assessing students' understanding, you might decide to extend the learning.

- Challenge students to break apart words that have both prefixes and suffixes (e.g., *un/predict/able, dis/respect/ful*).
- During shared writing, model how to write multisyllable words by saying them slowly, listening for the parts, and writing one word at a time.

RML 6
SAS.U1.RML6

Reading Minilesson Principle
Look for a part of the word that can help.

Solving Multisyllable Words

You Will Need

- chart paper prepared with two columns, the first column filled in: *formations, massive, controversy, population, specialization, expression*
- sticky note or index card
- markers
- highlighter

Academic Language / Important Vocabulary

- word
- word part

Continuum Connection

- Use known word parts (some are words) to solve unknown larger words: e.g., *in/into, can/canvas; us/crust* (p. 386)

Goal

Search for and use familiar parts of a word to help solve the word.

Rationale

When you teach students to notice parts of a word they already know, you increase their efficiency in reading unknown words in continuous text, allowing them to improve fluency and focus on meaning.

Assess Learning

Observe students when they take apart unknown words. Notice if there is evidence of new learning based on the goal of this minilesson.

- Do students use known word parts to solve words?
- Are they using the terms *word* and *word part*?

Minilesson

To help students think about the minilesson principle, engage them in a demonstration of using known word parts to read a new word. Here is an example.

- Display the prepared chart. Read the first word, *formations*.

  I'm not sure what this word is, but I see part of the word that I know how to say.

- Use a sticky note or an index card to cover the less familiar part of the word (*ations*). Say the known part of the word (*form*) and highlight it on the chart. Reveal the rest of the word, sound it out, and then say the whole word to make sure it looks right and sounds right.

  What did I do to read the word *formations*?

  When you come to a word you don't know, look for a part or parts of the word you do know how to say.

- Repeat this process with the words *massive, controversy,* and *population*.

Have a Try

Invite the students to break apart the words *specialization* and *expression* with a partner by looking for a part they know.

Turn and talk to your partner. What could these words be?

- Ask a student to highlight the part of the word they know on the chart.

Summarize and Apply

Summarize the learning and remind students to look for a part of the word that can help.

Look at the chart. How can you read a word you don't know?

- Write the principle at the top.

When you read today, if you come to a word you aren't sure of, look to see if there is a part that can help. Be prepared to share when we come back together.

Look for a part of the word that can help.

formations	form / ations
massive	mass / ive
controversy	con / troversy
population	pop / ulation
specialization	special / ization
expression	express / ion

Share

Following independent reading time, gather students together in the meeting area to talk about word solving.

Did anyone come to a word you didn't know? Was there a part you did know that could help?

How else can you read a word that is unfamiliar to you?

Extend the Lesson (Optional)

After assessing students' understanding, you might decide to extend the learning.

- During guided and independent reading, remind students that they might have to try more than one way to read an unfamiliar word.

Assessment

After you have taught the minilessons in this umbrella, observe students as they talk and write about their reading across instructional contexts: interactive read-aloud, independent reading, guided reading, shared reading, and book club. Use *The Literacy Continuum* (Fountas and Pinnell 2017) to guide the observation of students' reading and writing behaviors.

- What evidence do you have of new understandings related to solving multisyllable words?
  - Are students flexible about applying ways to take apart words?
  - Can they use known parts to solve words?
  - Do they remove the prefix or suffix to find the base word or use a part they know that can help?
  - Are they using language such as *syllable*, *base word*, *prefix*, *suffix*, *consonant digraph*, and *vowel sound*?
- In what other ways, beyond the scope of this umbrella, are students talking about their reading?
  - Do students need help navigating difficult texts?
  - Do they read digital texts in a productive way?

Use your observations to determine the next umbrella you will teach. You may also consult Minilessons Across the Year (pp. 61–64) for guidance.

Link to Writing

After teaching the minilessons in this umbrella, help students link the new learning to their own writing:

- When engaging in shared writing and independent writing, refer to resources you have in the room, such as a word wall, to make connections between known words and new words.
- When engaging in shared writing, demonstrate how slow articulation of unknown words in writing relates to solving unknown words in reading.

Reader's Notebook

When this umbrella is complete, provide a copy of the minilesson principles (see resources.fountasandpinnell.com) for students to glue in the reader's notebook (in the Minilessons section if using *Reader's Notebook: Advanced* [Fountas and Pinnell 2011]), so they can refer to the information as needed.

Minilessons in This Umbrella

RML1	A writer defines a word within the text to help you understand it.
RML2	A writer uses a word in the sentence that is similar or opposite in meaning to the word you don't know.
RML3	A writer gives an example to help you understand the meaning of a word.
RML4	Word parts help you understand what a word means.
RML5	Greek and Latin roots help you understand what a word means.

Before Teaching Umbrella 2 Minilessons

Although most of the teaching of solving words while reading happens during small-group instruction, there are some lessons that are worth presenting to the whole class. Once you teach these minilessons, you can follow them up in more detail when you meet with guided reading groups. For the minilessons in this umbrella, use books with strong examples of context-supported vocabulary. Look for books that define unknown words within the sentence or the paragraph; use synonyms, antonyms, or examples to clarify meaning; and contain words with prefixes, suffixes, and Greek and Latin roots.

Use the following books from the *Fountas & Pinnell Classroom*™ *Interactive Read-Aloud Collection* text sets or choose other books that have strong contextual support for vocabulary.

Genre Study: Expository Nonfiction

Giant Squid: Searching for a Sea Monster by Mary Cerullo and Clyde F. E. Roper

The Cod's Tale by Mark Kurlansky

Team Moon: How 400,000 People Landed Apollo 11 on the Moon by Catherine Thimmesh

Birds: Nature's Magnificent Flying Machines by Caroline Arnold

Author/Illustrator Study: Ted and Betsy Lewin

Gorilla Walk

As you read aloud and enjoy these texts together, guide students to notice how the author helps the reader learn the meaning of new words through context.

Genre Study: Expository Nonfiction

Giant Squid by Mary Cerullo and Clyde F. E. Roper

Author/Illustrator Study: Ted and Betsy Lewin

RML 1

SAS.U2.RML1

A writer defines a word within the text to help you understand it.

Using Context and Word Parts to Understand Vocabulary

You Will Need

- two or three books that contain new or unfamiliar vocabulary, such as the following from Text Set: Genre Study: Expository Nonfiction:
  - *Giant Squid* by Mary Cerullo and Clyde F. E. Roper
  - *The Cod's Tale* by Mark Kurlansky
  - *Birds* by Caroline Arnold
- chart paper prepared with sentences from the chosen texts
- markers and highlighters

Academic Language / Important Vocabulary

- define
- sentence
- paragraph

Continuum Connection

- Derive the meaning of words from the context of a sentence, paragraph, or the whole text (p. 75)

Goal

Understand that sometimes a writer tells the meaning of a word in the sentence, the paragraph, or elsewhere in the book.

Rationale

Students who notice when a writer gives the definition of a challenging word are better able to understand the ideas in the text because they can figure out the meaning of the vocabulary.

Assess Learning

Observe students when they use context to understand vocabulary. Notice if there is evidence of new learning based on the goal of this minilesson.

- Can students use context from the sentence, the paragraph, or elsewhere in the text to derive the meaning of an unfamiliar word?
- Are they using language such as *define*, *sentence*, and *paragraph*?

Minilesson

To help students think about how to learn the meaning of new or unfamiliar words, engage them in noticing how writers define challenging words. Here is an example.

- Display the cover of *Giant Squid* and the prepared chart paper. Read the example sentence.

  What is a naturalist?

  How do the authors of this book help you understand what the word *naturalist* means?

- Highlight the words *people who study nature* on the chart.
- Turn to the glossary in the back of the book.

  What is this page for?

  Sometimes an author includes a glossary to explain the meanings of words that may be unfamiliar to the reader and that are important to the topic. A glossary is another way to find out the meaning of a word.

- Show the cover of *The Cod's Tale* and read the title. Turn to page 9 and read the second paragraph.

  The author doesn't give the definition of *greedy*, so how can you figure out what it means?

- Highlight context clues on the chart.

Have a Try

Invite the students to talk with a partner about the meaning of another word.

- Show the cover of *Birds*. Read the example sentence on the chart.

  Turn and talk to your partner about how the author of this book helps you understand what the word *glides* means.

- If students need more clues, read the rest of page 18. After time for discussion, invite a few students to share their thinking. Highlight the clues they mention on the chart.

A writer defines a word within the text to help you understand it.

Giant Squid	"In the 1700s and 1800s, many captains of whaling ships were amateur naturalists—people who study nature." (p. 6)
The Cod's Tale	"The cod spends its life swimming with its big mouth wide open, trying to swallow whatever will fit... Almost any bait or object, even a fish-shaped piece of lead, can attract a cod. The cod's greedy appetite makes it easy to catch." (p. 9)
Birds	"Once a bird is in the air, it can often go for long distances without flapping at all. It simply spreads its wings and glides. The wings still provide lift while gliding, but without flapping, the bird will gradually sink to the ground." (p. 18)

Summarize and Apply

Summarize the learning and remind students to look for the meaning of unfamiliar words in the sentence, the paragraph, or elsewhere in the text.

Where do authors offer help to figure out what challenging words mean?

- Write the principle at the top of the chart.

  If you come across a word you don't understand while you're reading today, look carefully to see if the author defines it somewhere in the sentence, the paragraph, or elsewhere in the book. Sometimes you need to read beyond the word to figure out what it means.

Share

Following independent reading time, gather students together in the meeting area to discuss how they figured out the meaning of an unfamiliar word.

Did anyone learn a new word from the book you read today?

How did you figure out the meaning?

Extend the Lesson (Optional)

After assessing students' understanding, you might decide to extend the learning.

- During interactive read-aloud, model how to derive the meaning of a new word.
- During individual reading conferences, make sure students know that there is more than one way to figure out what a word means while they are reading.

RML 2

SAS.U2.RML2

Reading Minilesson Principle

A writer uses a word in the sentence that is similar or opposite in meaning to the word you don't know.

Using Context and Word Parts to Understand Vocabulary

You Will Need

- two or three books that contain new or unfamiliar vocabulary, such as the following from Text Set: Genre Study: Expository Nonfiction:
  - *Giant Squid* by Mary Cerullo and Clyde F. E. Roper
  - *The Cod's Tale* by Mark Kurlansky
  - *Birds* by Caroline Arnold
- chart paper prepared with sentences from the chosen texts
- markers and highlighters

Academic Language / Important Vocabulary

- synonym
- antonym

Continuum Connection

- Recognize and use synonyms (words that have almost the same meaning): e.g., *mistake/error, high/tall, desperately/frantically* (p. 383)
- Use connections between or among words that mean the same or almost the same to solve an unknown word: e.g., *damp, wet* (p. 387)

Goal

Understand that writers sometimes use synonyms or antonyms within a sentence to explain the meaning of a word.

Rationale

When students know how to use context clues, including synonyms and antonyms, to determine the meanings of unfamiliar words, they are better able to learn new vocabulary when they read independently.

Assess Learning

Observe students when they use context to understand vocabulary. Notice if there is evidence of new learning based on the goal of this minilesson.

- Can students use synonyms and antonyms to help them understand the meaning of an unfamiliar word?
- Do they understand the terms *synonym* and *antonym*?

Minilesson

To help students think about the minilesson principle, engage them in using synonyms and antonyms to determine the meanings of unfamiliar words. Here is an example.

- Show the cover of *Giant Squid* and the prepared chart paper. Turn to page 5 and read the heading and the first paragraph.

  What clues in the first paragraph help you figure out what the word *colossal* means?

  Sometimes an author uses a synonym—a word that means the same or almost the same thing as another word—to help explain what an unfamiliar word means. *Colossal* and *gigantic* are synonyms.

- Highlight the word *gigantic* on the chart.
- Show the cover of *The Cod's Tale*. Read the example sentence on the chart.

  How does the author help you understand what the word *settlements* means?

  It says that they did *not* have settlements, though they *did* have camps–so settlements and camps must be different things. I know that summer camps are places where people live for a short period of time, so settlements must be places where people live for a long time. The word *though* alerts you to something that is the opposite of or different from what was just said. Knowing that settlements are not like camps helps you understand the word's meaning.

- Highlight the word *camps*.

Have a Try

Invite the students to talk with a partner about the meaning of another word.

- Show the cover of *Birds*. Read the example sentences on the chart.

  Turn and talk to your partner about how the author of this book helps you understand what the word *migrate* means.

- After students turn and talk, invite a few pairs to share their thinking. If needed, point out that the author uses both a synonym and an antonym to illustrate what this word means. Highlight *stay* and *travel*.

A writer uses a word in the sentence that is similar or opposite in meaning to the word you don't know.

Giant Squid	"A Creature of Colossal Size Without warning, a gigantic, twisting tentacle bursts out of a dark sea." (p. 5)
The Cod's Tale	"They built no settlements, though they did have camps in the summer where whale fat was cooked into oil. . ." (p. 22)
Birds	"Some birds stay in one place year-round. Others travel, or migrate, with the seasons." (p. 24)

Summarize and Apply

Summarize the learning and remind students to use synonyms and antonyms to determine the meanings of unfamiliar words when they read.

How do authors sometimes help you figure out what challenging words mean?

- Write the principle at the top of the chart.

  If you come across a word you don't understand as you read today, see if the author includes a synonym or antonym to help you understand what the word means.

Share

Following independent reading time, gather students together in the meeting area to discuss how they figured out the meaning of an unfamiliar word.

Did anyone learn a new word from the book you read today?

How did you figure out what it means?

Extend the Lesson (Optional)

After assessing students' understanding, you might decide to extend the learning.

- During interactive read-aloud, model how to use synonyms and antonyms to derive the meaning of unfamiliar words.
- During individual reading conferences, make sure students know that there is more than one way to figure out what a word means.

RML 3
SAS.U2.RML3

Using Context and Word Parts to Understand Vocabulary

You Will Need

- two or three books that contain new or unfamiliar vocabulary, such as the following:
  - *Birds* by Caroline Arnold and *Giant Squid* by Mary Cerullo and Clyde F. E. Roper, from Text Set: Genre Study: Expository: Nonfiction
  - *Gorilla Walk* by Ted and Betsy Lewin, from Text Set: Author/Illustrator Study: Ted and Betsy Lewin
- chart paper prepared with sentences from the chosen texts
- markers and highlighters

Academic Language / Important Vocabulary

- example

Continuum Connection

- Derive the meaning of words from the context of a sentence, paragraph, or the whole text (p. 75)

Reading Minilesson Principle

A writer gives an example to help you understand the meaning of a word.

Goal

Understand that sometimes writers use examples to show the meaning of a word.

Rationale

When students learn multiple ways to solve unknown words, they are able to learn new vocabulary independently, read more fluently, and maintain comprehension of the text. Learning to use examples in the text to help determine the meaning of an unfamiliar word is another tool students can use.

Assess Learning

Observe students when they use context to understand vocabulary. Notice if there is evidence of new learning based on the goal of this minilesson.

- Do students use examples in the text to help them determine the meanings of unfamiliar words?
- Do they understand the term *example*?

Minilesson

To help students think about the minilesson principle, engage them in using examples to determine the meanings of unfamiliar words. Here is an example.

- Show the cover of *Birds* and the prepared chart paper. Read the example sentence.

  What do you think the word *barriers* means?

  What clues in the sentence helped you figure out what it means?

  The writer gives examples of different kinds of natural barriers: mountains, deserts, rivers, and oceans.

- Highlight the words *such as mountains, deserts, rivers, and oceans* on the chart.
- Show the cover of *Giant Squid* and read the example sentence on the chart.

  The writers say that the word *mollusks* means "soft-bodied animals." How else do the authors help you understand what this word means? What other clues do they give you?

  The authors name some examples of mollusks: snails, squids, and periwinkles.

- Highlight *snails*, *squids*, and *periwinkles* on the chart.

Have a Try

Invite the students to talk with a partner about the meaning of another word.

- Show the cover of *Gorilla Walk* and read the example on the chart.

  Turn and talk to your partner about what the term *nonvocal communications* means. Then talk about how you were able to figure out its meaning.

- After time for discussion, invite a few students to share their thinking. Highlight the examples on the chart.

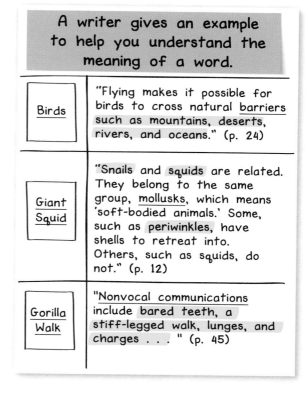

A writer gives an example to help you understand the meaning of a word.

Birds	"Flying makes it possible for birds to cross natural barriers such as mountains, deserts, rivers, and oceans." (p. 24)
Giant Squid	"Snails and squids are related. They belong to the same group, mollusks, which means 'soft-bodied animals.' Some, such as periwinkles, have shells to retreat into. Others, such as squids, do not." (p. 12)
Gorilla Walk	"Nonvocal communications include bared teeth, a stiff-legged walk, lunges, and charges . . . " (p. 45)

Summarize and Apply

Summarize the learning and remind students to use examples to determine the meanings of unfamiliar words.

  How does a writer sometimes help you figure out what a challenging word means?

- Write the principle at the top of the chart.

  If you come across a word you don't understand as you read today, see if the author includes any examples to help you understand what the word means.

Share

Following independent reading time, gather students together in the meeting area to discuss how they figured out the meaning of an unfamiliar word.

  Did anyone use examples to figure out what a word means today?

Extend the Lesson (Optional)

After assessing students' understanding, you might decide to extend the learning.

- During interactive read-aloud, model how to use examples to derive the meaning of unfamiliar words.
- During individual reading conferences, make sure students know that there is more than one way to figure out what a word means.

RML 4

SAS.U2.RML4

Word parts help you understand what a word means.

Using Context and Word Parts to Understand Vocabulary

You Will Need

- two or three books that contain new or unfamiliar vocabulary, such as the following from Text Set: Genre Study: Expository Nonfiction:
    - *Giant Squid* by Mary Cerullo and Clyde F. E. Roper
    - *The Cod's Tale* by Mark Kurlansky
    - *Birds* by Caroline Arnold
- chart paper prepared with sentences from the chosen texts
- markers

Academic Language / Important Vocabulary

- prefix
- suffix
- base word

Continuum Connection

- Understand and discuss the concept of prefixes and suffixes and recognize their use in determining the meaning of some English words (p. 384)
- Recognize and use word parts to solve an unknown word and understand its meaning: e.g., *conference*—prefix *con-* ("with or together"), Latin root *fer* ("to bring" or "to carry"), suffix *-ence* ("state of" or "quality of") (p. 387)

Goal

Understand that word roots, base words, suffixes, and prefixes can be used to determine the meaning of a word.

Rationale

When students know to look at the parts of a word (e.g., prefix, suffix, base word, word root) to solve for meaning, they can problem solve more efficiently and keep their attention on the overall meaning of a text.

Assess Learning

Observe students when they use word parts to understand unfamiliar words. Notice if there is evidence of new learning based on the goal of this minilesson.

- Do students look for known word parts when they encounter unfamiliar words?
- Can they identify the base word or word root and its prefix and/or suffix?
- Are they using language such as *prefix, suffix,* and *base word*?

Minilesson

To help students think about the minilesson principle, engage them in using word parts to determine the meanings of unfamiliar words. Here is an example.

- Read the first sentence on the chart from *Giant Squid* and underline the word *uncharted*.

    What do you think the word *uncharted* means? If you're not sure, look closely and see if you recognize any parts of the word.

- Show how the word can be broken down into the prefix (*un-*), base word (*chart*) and the suffix (*-ed*).

    Sometimes you can figure out what an unfamiliar word means by looking for parts that you do know. The prefix *un-* at the beginning of the word means "not." The base word in the middle, *chart*, is something that is written down. The suffix at the end, *-ed*, means that it happened in the past. Seas that were *uncharted* might be seas that have not been written down, or mapped.

- Continue in a similar manner with the words *spiderlike* and *plentiful*.

Have a Try

Invite the students to talk with a partner about the meaning of another word.

- Read the final sentence on the chart. Underline the word *flightless*.

  Turn and talk to your partner about what you think the word *flightless* means. Remember to look for parts of the word that you recognize.

- After students turn and talk, invite a few students to share how they determined the meaning of the word. Record responses on the chart.

Summarize and Apply

Summarize the learning and remind students to use word parts to determine the meanings of unfamiliar words.

- Review the chart and write the principle at the top.

  If you come across a word you don't know as you read today, look for parts of the word that you recognize and see if you can use them to figure out what the word means.

Word parts help you understand what a word means.

Giant Squid	"When the seas were still largely uncharted, sailors and fishermen told stories like this about a mythic monster of the deep. Norwegian sailors described a spiderlike creature as big as an island." (p. 5)	un / chart /ed not charted/ mapped spider / like like a spider
The Cod's Tale	"Today, cod are no longer plentiful . . ." (p. 7)	plenti / ful existing in great numbers
Birds	"So does the kakapo, a flightless New Zealand parrot." (p. 10)	flight / less without flight, cannot fly

Share

Following independent reading time, gather students together in the meeting area to discuss how they figured out the meaning of an unfamiliar word.

Did anyone use word parts to figure out what a word means today?

Extend the Lesson (Optional)

After assessing students' understanding, you might decide to extend the learning.

- Support this behavior in guided or independent reading. From the *Fountas & Pinnell Prompting Guide, Part 1, for Oral Reading and Early Writing* (Fountas and Pinnell 2009), use prompts, such as the following:
  - *Look at the prefix.*
  - *Look at the suffix.*
  - *Do you see a part that might help you?*

RML 5
SAS.U2.RML5

Greek and Latin roots help you understand what a word means.

Using Context and Word Parts to Understand Vocabulary

You Will Need

- books that have words with Greek or Latin roots, such as the following from Text Set: Genre Study: Expository Nonfiction:
  - *Birds* by Caroline Arnold
  - *Giant Squid* by Mary Cerullo and Clyde F. E. Roper
  - *Team Moon* by Catherine Timmesh
- markers and chart paper prepared with sentences

Academic Language / Important Vocabulary

- root

Continuum Connection

- Understand and discuss the concept of Greek and Latin roots and recognize their use in determining the meanings of some English words (p. 384)
- Recognize and use Latin roots to solve an unknown word and determine its meaning: e.g., the Latin root *cred*, meaning "believe," in the word *credible*, meaning "capable of being believed" or "believable" (p. 387)
- Recognize and use Greek roots to solve an unknown word and determine its meaning: e.g., the Greek root *graph*, meaning "write," in the word *autograph*, meaning "the writing of one's name" (p. 387)

Goal

Understand that knowledge of Greek and Latin roots can be used to figure out what a word means.

Rationale

Many words in the English language stem from Greek or Latin. Exposing students to and teaching them a variety of Greek and Latin roots supports them in independently solving unfamiliar vocabulary.

Assess Learning

Observe students when they use Greek or Latin roots to understand unfamiliar words. Notice if there is evidence of new learning based on the goal of this minilesson.

- Do students determine the meanings of unfamiliar words by using their knowledge of Greek and Latin roots?
- Do they understand the word *root*?

Minilesson

To help students think about the minilesson principle, engage them in using Greek and Latin roots to determine the meanings of unfamiliar words. Here is an example.

- Read the first sentence on the chart from *Birds* and underline the word *maximum*.

  What do you notice about the word *maximum*? Is there a word part that you know?

  Do you know any other words that have the word part *max*?

  Many English words have roots that originally came from Latin or Greek. *Max* is a word root that comes from Latin and means "greatest." Some English words, like *maximum*, *maximize*, and *maximal* were created by adding suffixes to this Latin root.

- Record notes and examples about the Latin root *max* on the chart.
- Read the example sentence from *Giant Squid* on the chart.

  Specimens contains the Latin root *spec*, which means "see" or "look at." What do you think the word *specimens* means?

  What other words do you know that contain the root *spec*?

- Record responses on the chart.

Have a Try

Invite the students to talk with a partner about the meaning of another word.

- Read the third example sentence on the chart. Underline the word *astronauts*.

  Astro is a Greek root meaning "star," and *naut* is a Greek root meaning "sailor." Turn and talk to your partner about why it makes sense that these two roots were combined to make the word *astronaut*.

- After students turn and talk, invite a few students to share their thinking. Ask students to list other words that contain these Greek roots and record them on the chart.

Greek and Latin roots help you understand what a word means.

Birds	"Soaring birds have large wings for maximum lift." (p. 17) Meaning: greatest, most Latin root: max, meaning "greatest" Other words: maximize, maximal, climax
Giant Squid	"Soon specimens of all kinds of squids arrived at the Smithsonian for Clyde to examine. . ." (p. 20) Meaning: an example of something to look at closely Latin root: spec/spect, meaning "see" Other words: spectacle, perspective, inspect
Team Moon	". . . there was enough oxygen to keep the astronauts alive for just one day." (p. 51) Meaning: people trained to fly a spacecraft Greek roots: astro, meaning "star"; naut, meaning "sailor" Other words: astronomy, asterisk; nautical, aeronaut

Summarize and Apply

Summarize the learning and remind students to use Greek and Latin roots to determine the meanings of unfamiliar words.

- Review the chart and write the principle at the top.

  If you come across a word you don't know as you read today, look for parts of the word that you recognize and see if you can use them to figure out what the word means.

Share

Following independent reading time, gather students together in the meeting area to discuss with a partner how they solved unfamiliar words in their reading.

Did anyone recognize a root in a word from your reading today?

What other words have the same root?

Extend the Lesson (Optional)

After assessing students' understanding, you might decide to extend the learning.

- Teach additional Greek and Latin roots when you lead word study lessons (download a list from resources.fountasandpinnell.com).

Assessment

After you have taught the minilessons in this umbrella, observe students as they talk and write about their reading across instructional contexts: interactive read-aloud, independent reading, guided reading, shared reading, and book club. Use *The Literacy Continuum* (Fountas and Pinnell 2017) to guide the observation of students' reading and writing behaviors.

- What evidence do you have of new understandings related to using context to understand vocabulary?
    - Can students use context clues from a sentence, a paragraph, or elsewhere in a text to derive the meaning of unfamiliar words?
    - Can they use synonyms or antonyms to help them understand the meaning of unfamiliar words?
    - Do they use word parts (word roots, base words, suffixes, prefixes, Greek and Latin roots) to help them determine the meaning of unfamiliar words?
    - Are they using academic language, such as *synonym*, *antonym*, *prefix*, *suffix*, and *root*?
- In what other ways, beyond the scope of this umbrella, are students using strategies and skills to understand what they read?
    - Do students know how to break apart words?
    - Are they able to monitor their comprehension while reading difficult texts?

Use your observations to determine the next umbrella you will teach. You may also consult Minilessons Across the Year (pp. 61–64) for guidance.

Link to Writing

After teaching the minilessons in this umbrella, help students link the new learning to their own writing:

- When students write independently, encourage them to think about how they can help their readers understand unfamiliar words.

Reader's Notebook

When this umbrella is complete, provide a copy of the minilesson principles (see resources.fountasandpinnell.com) for students to glue in the reader's notebook (in the Minilessons section if using *Reader's Notebook: Advanced* [Fountas and Pinnell 2011]), so they can refer to the information as needed.

Minilessons in This Umbrella

RML1	Writers use connecting words to add on to an idea.
RML2	Writers use connecting words to show the passage of time or to sequence something.
RML3	Writers use connecting words to show cause and effect.
RML4	Writers use connecting words to show a different or opposite point of view.

Before Teaching Umbrella 3 Minilessons

Connectives are words and phrases that help readers understand the relationships between and among ideas in a text. Easy texts have very simple connectives like *and*, *or*, and *but*. As students read more complex texts, they will begin to encounter more sophisticated connectives, many of which are rare in everyday oral language, for example, *nevertheless, as a result,* or *consequently*. Overlooking connectives in a text, however, can lead to a misunderstanding of the ideas the writer is presenting. A list of connecting words and phrases can be found in the appendix for grammar, usage, and mechanics in *The Literacy Continuum* (Fountas and Pinnell 2017, 642–644) and in online resources (see specific minilessons).

Read and discuss books with a variety of connectives. The minilessons in this umbrella use the following books from the *Fountas & Pinnell Classroom™ Interactive Read-Aloud Collection* text sets; however, you can choose any books from your classroom library.

Genre Study: Expository Nonfiction

Giant Squid: Searching for a Sea Monster by Mary Cerullo and Clyde F. E. Roper

The Cod's Tale by Mark Kurlansky

The Story of Salt by Mark Kurlansky

Understanding How Things Work

Titanic: Disaster at Sea by Martin Jenkins

As you read aloud and enjoy these texts together, help students notice how the author has used connecting words to show the relationships between and among ideas.

Genre Study: Expository Nonfiction

Giant Squid by Mary Cerullo and Clyde F. E. Roper

Understanding How Things Work

RML 1
SAS.U3.RML1

Reading Minilesson Principle

Writers use connecting words to add on to an idea.

Understanding Connectives

You Will Need

- a familiar book that uses a variety of connectives to add on to ideas, such as *Titanic* by Martin Jenkins from Text Set: Understanding How Things Work
- chart paper prepared with example sentences from the chosen book
- a highlighter

Academic Language / Important Vocabulary

- connecting words

Continuum Connection

- Understand (when listening) some sophisticated connectives (words that link ideas and clarify meaning) that are used in written texts but do not appear often in everyday oral language: e.g., *although, however, meantime, meanwhile, moreover, otherwise, therefore, though, unless, until, whenever, yet* (p. 72)

Goal

Learn connectives that are used to add on to an idea.

Rationale

When students notice connectives that writers use to add on to an idea, they think about the relationships between details and ideas and better understand the text.

Assess Learning

Observe students when they talk about connecting words. Notice if there is evidence of new learning based on the goal of this minilesson.

- Do they understand the purpose of connecting words?
- Can students identify connecting words that add on to an idea?
- Do they use the term *connecting words*?

Minilesson

To help students think about the minilesson principle, engage them in noticing connecting words and phrases that writers use to add on to ideas. Here is an example.

- Show the cover of *Titanic* and display the prepared chart paper. Read the first example.

  What does the author tell you about in the first sentence?

  What extra information does he give about this idea in the second sentence?

  What word or phrase does he use to connect these two sentences?

- Highlight the phrase *In fact*.
- Read the first part of the second example sentence (stop when you get to the semicolon).

  What is the main idea of this part of the sentence?

- Read the rest of the sentence.

  How does the second part of the sentence relate to the first part?

  The second part gives more information about why many third-class passengers didn't make it onto the lifeboats. It adds on to the idea presented in the first part. Which word connects the two parts of the sentence?

- Highlight the word *besides*.

  In fact and *besides* are connecting words. They connect ideas and details together. Writers use different kinds of connecting words for different reasons. The author uses these connecting words to add information to an idea.

Have a Try

Invite the students to talk with a partner about connecting words or phrases that add on to an idea.

- Read the third example.

  Turn and talk to your partner about how the author uses a connecting word or phrase in these sentences.

- After time for discussion, invite a few students to share their thinking. Highlight *What's more.*

Writers use connecting words to add on to an idea.

"Naturally, the question of the number of lifeboats was raised. In fact, several people expressed the view that even if there had been many more lifeboats, not everyone would necessarily have been saved." (p. 29)

"The lifeboats were on the boat deck, reserved for first- and second-class, and many third-class passengers would have been reluctant to go up there without permission; besides, the layout of the ship was confusing." (p. 30)

"At least some of the possible routes were apparently blocked for some time by locked gates. What's more, many of the third-class passengers understood little or no English and would have found it difficult to grasp what was going on until it was too late." (p. 30)

Summarize and Apply

Summarize the learning and remind students to notice connecting words that are used to add on to an idea.

Why do writers use connecting words and phrases like *in fact*, *besides*, and *what's more*?

- Write the principle at the top of the chart.

  When you read today, notice how the author of your book uses connecting words to add on to ideas. Be ready to share an example from your book when we come back together.

Share

Following independent reading time, gather students together in the meeting area to talk about connecting words.

Turn and talk to your partner about how the author of your book uses connecting words to add on to ideas. Share an example.

Extend the Lesson (Optional)

After assessing students' understanding, you might decide to extend the learning.

- Point out connectives during interactive read-aloud. Talk with the students about how connectives help make writing more smooth and fluent in addition to linking ideas.
- Provide a list of connectives that are used to add on to an idea (e.g., *in fact, besides, what's more, moreover, specifically, furthermore, in addition, also, for example*; see also *The Literacy Continuum*, pp. 642–644, and resources.fountasandpinnell.com), which students can use as a resource when they do their own writing. Add to the list as students discover new connectives in their reading.

RML 2

SAS.U3.RML2

Reading Minilesson Principle

Writers use connecting words to show the passage of time or to sequence something.

Understanding Connectives

You Will Need

- a familiar book that uses a variety of connectives to show the passage of time, such as *The Cod's Tale* by Mark Kurlansky, from Text Set: Genre Study: Expository Nonfiction
- chart paper prepared with example sentences from the chosen book
- a highlighter

Academic Language / Important Vocabulary

- connecting words
- sequence

Continuum Connection

- Understand (when listening) some sophisticated connectives (words that link ideas and clarify meaning) that are used in written texts but do not appear often in everyday oral language: e.g., *although, however, meantime, meanwhile, moreover, otherwise, therefore, though, unless, until, whenever, yet* (p. 72)

Goal

Notice how writers use connecting words to show the passage of time or to sequence something.

Rationale

When students pay attention to connecting words that show the passage of time (e.g., *meanwhile, yet, finally, later*), they better understand sequences and series of events.

Assess Learning

Observe students when they talk about connecting words. Notice if there is evidence of new learning based on the goal of this minilesson.

- Can students identify connecting words that show the passage of time or sequence something?
- Do they use the terms *connecting words* and *sequence*?

Minilesson

To help students think about the minilesson principle, engage them in noticing connecting words and phrases that show the passage of time or sequence something. Here is an example.

- Show the cover of *The Cod's Tale* and display the prepared chart paper. Read the first example. Point out and highlight the words *At first* and *After*.

  What do these words help you understand?

  At first and *after* are connecting words that help you understand the passage of time in a cod's life cycle. What other words in this paragraph show the passage of time?

- Highlight the words *Days later*.

Have a Try

Invite the students to talk with a partner about connecting words that show the passage of time or sequence something.

- Read aloud the second example on the chart.

  What connecting words does the author use in this sentence to show when something happened? Turn and talk to your partner about this.

- After students turn and talk, invite a few students to share their thinking. Highlight *until* and *when*.

Writers use connecting words to show the passage of time or to sequence something.

"At first they eat phytoplankton, creatures so small that they appear not as individual animals, but as a cloud in the water. After a few days of eating, the cod are large enough to eat the slightly bigger zooplankton. Days later, still not an inch long, they are large enough to eat krill." (p. 11)

"Many historians did not believe that the Vikings had been to North America, until 1960, when the remains of eight Viking-built turf houses. . . were found in Newfoundland. . ." (p. 19)

Summarize and Apply

Summarize the learning and remind students to notice connecting words that show the passage of time or sequence something.

Why do writers use connecting words and phrases like *at first, after, days later, until,* and *when*?

- Write the principle at the top of the chart.

  When you read today, notice how the author of your book uses connecting words to show the passage of time or to sequence something. Be ready to share an example from your book when we come back together.

Share

Following independent reading time, gather students together in the meeting area to talk about connecting words.

Who would like to share an example they found of a connecting word or phrase that shows the passage of time or sequences something?

Extend the Lesson (Optional)

After assessing students' understanding, you might decide to extend the learning.

- Provide a list of connectives that are used to show the passage of time or to sequence something (e.g., *at first, after, later, until, when, meantime, meanwhile, whenever, yet, eventually, finally, ultimately, then, as soon as, during;* see also *The Literacy Continuum,* pp. 642–644, and resources.fountasandpinnell.com), which students can use as a resource when they do their own writing. Continue adding to the list as students discover new connectives in their reading.

RML3

SAS.U3.RML3

Reading Minilesson Principle

Writers use connecting words to show cause and effect.

Understanding Connectives

You Will Need

- a familiar book that uses a variety of connecting words to show cause and effect, such as *The Story of Salt* by Mark Kurlansky, from Text Set: Genre Study: Expository Nonfiction
- chart paper prepared with example sentences from the chosen book
- a highlighter

Academic Language / Important Vocabulary

- connecting words
- cause
- effect

Continuum Connection

- Understand (when listening) some sophisticated connectives (words that link ideas and clarify meaning) that are used in written texts but do not appear often in everyday oral language: e.g., *although, however, meantime, meanwhile, moreover, otherwise, therefore, though, unless, until, whenever, yet* (p. 72)

Goal

Learn connectives that show cause and effect.

Rationale

When students notice connecting words that show cause and effect, they understand that the author is explaining a cause-and-effect relationship and better understand the ideas in the text.

Assess Learning

Observe students when they talk about connecting words. Notice if there is evidence of new learning based on the goal of this minilesson.

- Can students identify connecting words that show cause and effect?
- Do they understand and use the terms *connecting words*, *cause*, and *effect*?

Minilesson

To help students think about the minilesson principle, engage them in noticing connecting words that show cause and effect. Here is an example.

- Show the cover of *The Story of Salt* and display the prepared chart paper. Read the first example.

  Why did the author rinse the crystals off the rock with water?

  The author is describing a cause and an effect in these sentences. The cause is the rock starting to look like white salt, and the effect is that he rinses the crystals off. What connecting word does the author use in the second sentence to show that he's explaining an effect?

- Highlight the word *So*.
- Read the second example.

  Why doesn't it take much time to boil this water into salt? What is the cause?

  What connecting word does the author use to show that he's explaining a cause?

- Highlight the word *Because*.

Have a Try

Invite the students to talk with a partner about connecting words that show cause and effect.

- Read the third example.

  Why did having a good supply of salt help people have a thriving international trade?

  Turn and talk to your partner about what connecting word the author uses to show that he's explaining an effect.

- After students turn and talk, invite a few pairs to share their thinking. Highlight *Hence*, and explain that this is a connecting word (meaning "for this reason") that students might see in writing but rarely hear in conversation.

Writers use connecting words to show cause and effect.

"My beautiful pink rock was starting to look like white salt and that seemed very ordinary. So I rinsed the crystals off the rock with water." (p. 4)

"Because this water is usually saltier than the ocean, it does not take as much time or fuel to boil it into salt." (p. 10)

"In fact, food preserved in salt could be taken hundreds or thousands of miles away to be traded or sold. Hence, when people had a good supply of salt, they could also have a thriving international trade. (p. 17)

Summarize and Apply

Summarize the learning and remind students to notice connecting words that are used to show cause and effect.

Why do writers use connecting words like *so*, *because*, and *hence*?

- Write the principle at the top of the chart.

  When you read today, notice if the author of your book uses connecting words to show cause and effect. If you find an example, bring it to share when we come back together.

Share

Following independent reading time, gather students together in the meeting area to talk about connecting words.

Did anyone find an example of a connecting word that shows cause and effect?

Extend the Lesson (Optional)

After assessing students' understanding, you might decide to extend the learning.

- Provide a list of connectives that are used to show cause and effect (e.g., *so, because, hence, as a result, consequently, for, as a consequence;* see also *The Literacy Continuum*, pp. 642–644, and resources.fountasandpinnell.com) for students to use as a resource for their own writing.

RML 4

SAS.U3.RML4

Reading Minilesson Principle

Writers use connecting words to show a different or opposite point of view.

Understanding Connectives

You Will Need

- a familiar book that uses a variety of connecting words to show a different point of view, such as *Giant Squid* by Mary Cerullo and Clyde F. E. Roper, from Text Set: Genre Study: Expository Nonfiction
- chart paper prepared with example sentences from the chosen book
- a highlighter

Academic Language / Important Vocabulary

- connecting words
- point of view

Continuum Connection

- Understand (when listening) some sophisticated connectives (words that link ideas and clarify meaning) that are used in written texts but do not appear often in everyday oral language: e.g., *although, however, meantime, meanwhile, moreover, otherwise, therefore, though, unless, until, whenever, yet* (p. 72)

Goal

Learn connectives that show a different or opposite point of view.

Rationale

When students notice connecting words that show a different or opposite point of view, they understand that the author is describing contrasting ideas and better understand the ideas in the text.

Assess Learning

Observe students when they talk about connecting words. Notice if there is evidence of new learning based on the goal of this minilesson.

- Can students identify connecting words that show a different or opposite point of view?
- Do they understand and use the terms *connecting words* and *point of view*?

Minilesson

To help students think about the minilesson principle, engage them in noticing connecting words that show a different or opposite point of view. Here is an example.

- Show the cover of *Giant Squid* and display the prepared chart paper. Read the first example.

  What word do the authors use in this sentence to show that they are about to explain a different point of view?

  The authors use the connecting word *but* to show two points of view. On the one hand, Clyde Roper has decided to dedicate himself to studying this squid. *But* on the other hand, it will be very difficult for him to do so.

- Highlight the word *but*.
- Read the second example.

  Why do the authors use the word *despite* in this sentence?

  The authors use the connecting word *despite* to show two opposite ideas or points of view. They explain that even though some people might think giant squids attack ships, this is actually not true.

- Highlight the word *Despite*.

Have a Try

Invite the students to talk with a partner about connecting words that show a different or opposite point of view.

- Read the third example.

  Turn and talk to your partner about what connecting word the authors use to show that they are showing two different points of view.

- After time for discussion, invite a few students to share their thinking. Highlight the word *Although*.

Writers use connecting words to show a different or opposite point of view.

Giant Squid

"Clyde Roper decided to dedicate himself to studying this secretive squid . . . but how would he study a creature that was so difficult to find?" (p. 16)

"Despite the stories of giant squid attacking ships, scientists have learned that these beasts rarely emerge from their home." (p. 12)

"Although not nearly as large as the other big squids, it has a reputation as a vicious killer." (p. 27)

Summarize and Apply

Summarize the learning and remind students to notice connecting words that show a different or opposite point of view.

Why do writers use connecting words like *despite*, *but*, and *although*?

- Write the principle at the top of the chart.

  When you read today, notice if the author of your book uses connecting words to show a different or opposite point of view. If you find an example, bring it to share when we come back together.

Share

Following independent reading time, gather students together in the meeting area to talk about connecting words.

Who found an example of a connecting word that shows a different or opposite point of view?

Extend the Lesson (Optional)

After assessing students' understanding, you might decide to extend the learning.

- Provide a list of connectives that are used to show a different or opposite point of view (e.g., *despite, but, although, however, on the other hand, otherwise, whereas;* see also *The Literacy Continuum*, pp. 642–644, and resources.fountasandpinnell.com) for students to use as a resource for their own writing.

Assessment

After you have taught the minilessons in this umbrella, observe students as they talk and write about their reading across instructional contexts: interactive read-aloud, independent reading, guided reading, shared reading, and book club. Use *The Literacy Continuum* (Fountas and Pinnell 2017) to guide the observation of students' reading and writing behaviors.

- What evidence do you have of new understandings related to understanding connectives?
    - Do students notice connecting words and phrases that show relationships between and among ideas?
    - Can they talk about how authors use connecting words to add on to an idea?
    - Do they understand how writers use connecting words to indicate the passage of time, or a sequence, as well as cause and effect?
    - Can they discuss how authors use connecting words to write about a different or opposite point of view?
    - Do they understand and use academic language, such as *connecting words, sequence, cause, effect*, and *point of view*?
- In what other ways, beyond the scope of this umbrella, are students using connecting words?
    - Do students use a variety of connecting words in their weekly letters about reading?

Use your observations to determine the next umbrella you will teach. You may also consult Minilessons Across the Year (pp. 61–64) for guidance.

Link to Writing

After teaching the minilessons in this umbrella, help students link the new learning to their own writing:

- Encourage students to use a wide variety of connecting words in their own writing. Display lists of various types of connecting words in the classroom.

Reader's Notebook

When this umbrella is complete, provide a copy of the minilesson principles (see resources.fountasandpinnell.com) for students to glue in the reader's notebook (in the Minilessons section if using *Reader's Notebook: Advanced* [Fountas and Pinnell 2011]), so they can refer to the information as needed.

Minilessons in This Umbrella

RML1	Notice how the author wants you to read the sentence.
RML2	Make your reading sound smooth and interesting.
RML3	Use your voice to reflect the tone of the text you are reading.

Before Teaching Umbrella 4 Minilessons

Read aloud and discuss books with a variety of punctuation marks and print features, such as commas, ellipses, dashes, colons, and italics. Include books that contain a wide array of ways that authors convey meaning, such as through tone. Use a variety of large books, small books projected with a document camera, posters, and examples of poetry or shared writing—anything large enough for students to see the print. Your primary focus is first to support the meaning and enjoyment of the text before focusing on reading the text fluently. For this umbrella, use these suggested books from the *Fountas & Pinnell Classroom™ Interactive Read-Aloud Collection* text sets, or you can use books or student writing samples from your classroom.

Facing the Unknown

The Village That Vanished by Ann Grifalconi

The Lamp, the Ice, and the Boat Called Fish by Jacqueline Briggs Martin

Exploring Literary Language

Sequoia by Tony Johnston

If You're Not from the Prairie . . . by David Bouchard

Hoops by Robert Burleigh

Grit and Perseverance

Rikki-Tikki-Tavi by Rudyard Kipling

Freedom

Under the Quilt of Night by Deborah Hopkinson

As you read aloud and enjoy these texts together, help students

- notice the punctuation and font styles in sentences,
- think about how to make their voices sound when they read aloud,
- read fluently and with expression, and
- read in a way that represents the intentions of the writer.

Facing the Unknown

Exploring Literary Language

Sequoia by Tony Johnston

Grit and Perseverance

Rikki-Tikki-Tavi by Rudyard Kipling

Freedom

RML1

SAS.U4.RML1

Reading Minilesson Principle

Notice how the author wants you to read the sentence.

Maintaining Fluency

You Will Need

- several familiar books with a variety of punctuation marks and font styles, such as the following:
  - *The Village That Vanished* by Ann Grifalconi, from Text Set: Facing the Unknown
  - *Sequoia* by Tony Johnston, from Text Set: Exploring Literary Language
- chart paper prepared with the punctuation in red
- markers
- books students are reading independently or a basket of books
- document camera (optional)

Academic Language / Important Vocabulary

- fluency
- punctuation
- dialogue
- ellipses
- dash
- italics

Continuum Connection

- Recognize and reflect punctuation with the voice: e.g., period, question mark, exclamation point, dash, comma, ellipses, when reading in chorus or individually (p. 146)
- Recognize and reflect variations in print with the voice (e.g., italics, bold type, special treatments, font size) when reading in chorus or individually (p. 146)

Goal

Understand how voice changes reflect punctuation and font style in a sentence.

Rationale

When students adjust their voices for punctuation marks and font styles in order to read the way the writer intended, they begin to interpret text, gain confidence as readers, and improve fluency.

Assess Learning

Observe students when they read aloud. Notice if there is evidence of new learning based on the goal of this minilesson.

- Do students' voices reflect the punctuation and font styles in sentences they read aloud?
- Are they using the terms *fluency, punctuation, dialogue, ellipses, dash,* and *italics*?

Minilesson

To help students think about the minilesson principle, engage them in noticing how to change the voice to reflect the writer's intention. Here is an example.

- Show pages 3–4 from *The Village That Vanished.*

  Notice what my voice does as I read the words aloud the way the author intended.

- Read the print, emphasizing voice changes for the period, question mark, exclamation mark, commas, italics, parentheses, quotation marks, and words in larger font.

  What did you notice about my voice when I came to the punctuation marks?

- Write students' suggestions on the prepared chart. Define any vocabulary that is new to students. Show the print with the ellipses (p. 5) and colon (p. 10).

  What punctuation marks do you notice in these sentences?

- Read the sentences, emphasizing how your voice sounds when you come to the ellipses and colon. Ask students what they noticed and add to the chart.
- Display the poem on page 19 from *Sequoia.* Model fluent reading for the poem. Then display the notes page at the end of the book and read the first three sentences in the second paragraph.

  What did you notice about my voice when I read the print written as a poem with dashes and the notes to the reader with a semicolon?

- Add responses to the chart.

Have a Try

Invite the students to practice fluency with a partner.

- Have students sit in pairs with books that they are reading or have them choose books from a basket.

  Choose a few sentences or pages to read to your partner. Think about the way the author wants you to read and make your voice change when you come to a punctuation mark or a different font style.

- After a few minutes, ask several students to share what they noticed. Add any new ideas to the chart.

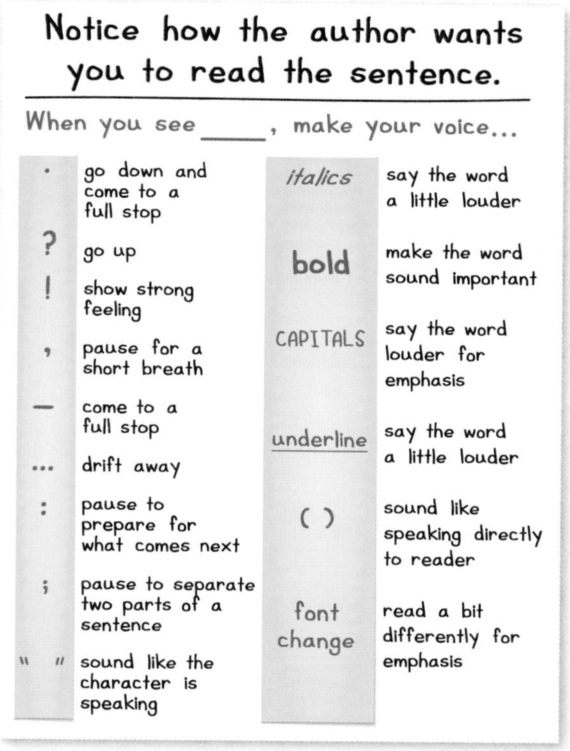

Notice how the author wants you to read the sentence.

When you see ____, make your voice...

.	go down and come to a full stop	*italics*	say the word a little louder
?	go up	**bold**	make the word sound important
!	show strong feeling	CAPITALS	say the word louder for emphasis
,	pause for a short breath	underline	say the word a little louder
—	come to a full stop	( )	sound like speaking directly to reader
...	drift away	font change	read a bit differently for emphasis
:	pause to prepare for what comes next		
;	pause to separate two parts of a sentence		
" "	sound like the character is speaking		

Summarize and Apply

Summarize the learning and remind students to notice punctuation marks and font styles when they read.

Writes use punctuation and special print to let you know how they want their words to be read aloud.

- Add the principle to the chart.

  Today when you read, notice different punctuation or font styles and practice how your voice should sound when you read them. Bring the book when we meet so you can share.

Share

Following independent reading time, gather students in small groups to read aloud to one another.

In your group, read aloud one or more sentences in which you noticed how the author wants you to read the sentence. Show how the author wants your voice to sound.

Extend the Lesson (Optional)

After assessing students' understanding, you might decide to extend the learning.

- Point out, as appropriate, that italics and boldface do not always mean that a word should be read with emphasis. For example, titles (e.g., book, movie) and foreign words are set in italics to set them apart from the surrounding print. Headings and glossary words are often in boldface.
- Have the students engage in a readers' theater activity to practice speaking the way an author intends.

RML 2
SAS.U4.RML2

Reading Minilesson Principle
Make your reading sound smooth and interesting.

Maintaining Fluency

You Will Need

- several familiar books with a variety of punctuation marks, font styles, and dialogue, such as the following:
  - *If You're Not from the Prairie . . .* by David Bouchard, from Text Set: Exploring Literary Language
  - *Rikki-Tikki-Tavi* by Rudyard Kipling, from Text Set: Grit and Perseverance
- chart paper and markers
- books students are reading independently or a basket of books
- document camera (optional)

Academic Language / Important Vocabulary

- voice
- fluency
- phrasing
- smooth
- emphasis
- expression

Continuum Connection

- Adjust the voice to reflect dialogue in the body of the text (p. 145)
- Read orally with integration of all dimensions of fluency (e.g., pausing, phrasing, word stress, intonation, and rate) alone and while maintaining unison with others (p. 145)

Goal

Learn how to integrate pausing, phrasing, stress, intonation, and rate to demonstrate fluent reading.

Rationale

When students know how to use rising and falling tones, pitch, volume, and rate to integrate all dimensions of fluency, their oral reading will sound smooth. This will also transfer to silent reading, resulting in better understanding and more enjoyment. When students read sentences with proper phrasing so that their reading sounds like talking, they can reflect on the author's meaning and increase their understanding of the text.

Assess Learning

Observe students when they read aloud and notice if there is evidence of new learning based on the goal of this minilesson.

- Are students integrating all aspects of fluent reading?
- Do they understand the terms *voice, fluency, phrasing, smooth, emphasis,* and *expression*?

Minilesson

To help students think about the minilesson principle, engage them in noticing the characteristics of fluent reading. Here is an example.

- Show page 16 from *If You're Not from the Prairie . . . .*

  Listen to my voice and notice how it changes as I read this page.

- Read the page with appropriate rate, expression, pausing, and stress.

  What did you notice about how I made my reading sound smooth and interesting?

- As students respond, make a list on chart paper.

  Let's look at another page in this book. I will read the page first. Then we will read it again together so you can make your voice sound the same.

- Show and read page 20. After reading the page, ask students to join in as you read a second time.

  What did you notice about what our voices did when we read this page?

- Read page 9 from *Rikki-Tikki-Tavi*. After reading, ask students to describe the way your voice changed when you read the dialogue and came to other punctuation marks.
- Continue adding student ideas to the chart.

Have a Try

Invite the students to practice fluency with a partner.

- Have students sit in pairs with books they are reading or have them choose books from a basket.

  Choose a few sentences or pages to read to your partner. Think about the way the author wants you to read and make your voice change when you come to a punctuation mark or a font style.

- A couple of students can also practice reading dialogue, using page 3 from *Rikki-Tikki-Tavi*.
- After a few minutes, ask several students to share what they noticed. Add any new ideas to the chart.

Make your reading sound smooth and interesting.

- make your voice volume louder or softer
- make your voice go up or down
- read with expression
- stress the words appropriately
- read with rhythm
- use the right speed
- sound smooth like you are talking
- read phrases together
- pause or stop the right amount of time
- sound like the character

Summarize and Apply

Summarize the learning and remind students to make their reading sound smooth and interesting.

Today you noticed that when you read, you can change your voice in ways to make your reading sound smooth and interesting.

- Add the principle to the chart. Then review the list on the chart.

  When you read aloud, make your voice sound smooth and interesting. Think about that when you read today. Bring your book when we meet so you can share.

Share

Following independent reading time, gather students in pairs to read aloud to one another.

Choose a page from the book you read today to read to your partner. Make your reading sound smooth and interesting.

Extend the Lesson (Optional)

After assessing students' understanding, you might decide to extend the learning.

- Provide professional models of fluency by playing recordings of books (e.g., audiobooks) or inviting members of a community acting group to read aloud to your class.
- To encourage fluent and expressive reading, have students rehearse and present a readers' theater script.

RML3

SAS.U4.RML3

Reading Minilesson Principle
Use your voice to reflect the tone of the text you are reading.

Maintaining Fluency

You Will Need

- several familiar books that provide good examples of tone, such as the following:
  - *The Lamp, the Ice, and the Boat Called Fish* by Jacqueline Briggs Martin, from Text Set: Facing the Unknown
  - *Under the Quilt of Night* by Deborah Hopkinson, from Text Set: Freedom
  - *Hoops* by Robert Burleigh from Text Set: Exploring Literary Language
- chart paper and markers
- books students are reading independently or a basket of books

Academic Language / Important Vocabulary

- fluency
- tone
- reflect
- word choice
- formal
- informal

Continuum Connection

- Understand the role of the voice in communicating meaning in readers' theater, choral reading, songs, and poetry (p. 152)

Goal

When reading aloud, reflect the tone of the text in the voice.

Rationale

When students learn to adjust their voices to indicate the tone that the author wishes to convey, they can reflect on the author's meaning. They will begin to do this when reading silently, resulting in deeper comprehension and more enjoyment.

Assess Learning

Observe students when they read aloud. Notice if there is evidence of new learning based on the goal of this minilesson.

- Do students' voices reflect tone when they read aloud?
- Are they using the terms *fluency, tone, reflect, word choice, formal,* and *informal*?

Minilesson

To help students think about the minilesson principle, engage them in noticing how to reflect tone. Here is an example.

> As I revisit a few pages from *The Lamp, the Ice, and the Boat Called Fish,* think about how my voice changes.

- Read page 3, using an informal, hopeful yet melancholy tone, and then read page 17, changing your voice from detached while reading the part in italics to a little more connected while reading the remainder of the page.

> The attitude, view, or feeling that the author conveys through careful word choice is tone. In addition to specific words, the way I read the text aloud expresses the author's tone.
>
> What statement could you make about the author's tone in this book?

- Prompt the conversation as needed to support students' understanding of tone:
  - *Thinking about word choice, is the author conveying a formal or informal tone?*
  - *What do you notice about the characters, setting, details, and language choice that helps you identify the author's attitude toward the subject?*
  - *What do you notice about any changes in tone in different parts of the book?*
- Begin a chart and add students' noticings about the way you read to convey tone.
- Repeat the activity with different examples, such as pages 6 and 22 from *Under the Quilt of Night* and pages 11–13 from *Hoops.*
- Add responses to the chart.

Have a Try

Invite the students to practice with a partner reading in a way that reflects tone.

- Have students sit in pairs with books that they are reading or have them choose books from a basket.

  Choose a few sentences or pages to read to your partner. Think about the way the author wants you to read and make your voice change to match the intended tone.

- After a few minutes, ask several students to share how they changed their voices to reflect tone.

Use your voice to reflect the tone of the text you are reading.

Title	Author's Tone	How should the words be read to convey tone?
 *The Lamp, the Ice, and the Boat Called Fish*	Grandmother speaking: • informal • hopeful yet melancholy	Gently, slightly sadly, a little slowly
	Facts about cracks in the ice in italics: • formal • detached	Seriously, in a straightforward way, in a detached voice
	facts about the house: formal, but more connected	With a little more connection but still factual
 *Under the Quilt of Night*	When she begins to run: • informal • confident	In a self-assured, strong voice
	When they are caught: • informal • fearful	With concern, in a hushed voice
 *Hoops*	Informal confident, pensive, focused, stealthy	Rhythmic Changing pace with the game

Summarize and Apply

Summarize the learning and remind students to think about how to convey tone when they read.

When you read aloud, think about the tone conveyed by the author and use your voice to express that tone.

- Add the principle to the chart.

  Today when you read, notice tone and practice how your voice should sound to convey tone. Bring the book when we meet so you can share.

Share

Following independent reading time, gather students in small groups to read aloud to one another.

In your group, read aloud one or more sentences in which you noticed the tone. Show how the author wants your voice to sound.

Extend the Lesson (Optional)

After assessing students' understanding, you might decide to extend the learning.

- Encourage students to identify the tone in a variety of books and to practice reading aloud in a voice that conveys the tone.

Assessment

After you have taught the minilessons in this umbrella, observe students as they talk and write about their reading across instructional contexts: interactive read-aloud, independent reading, guided reading, shared reading, and book club. Use *The Literacy Continuum* (Fountas and Pinnell 2017) to observe students' reading and writing behaviors.

- What evidence do you have of new understandings related to fluency?
    - Are students reading and responding appropriately to punctuation when they read aloud?
    - Do they adjust their voices when appropriate while reading aloud words in italics or all capital letters?
    - Do they integrate the various elements of fluency, such as pausing, phrasing, word stress, intonation, and rate when they read aloud?
    - Do they notice dialogue and try to read the way the character would say it?
    - Are students able to identify tone and read aloud using the author's intended tone?
    - Do they use terms such as *fluency, punctuation, dialogue, expression* and *tone*?
- In what other ways, beyond the scope of this umbrella, are students demonstrating fluency?
    - Are students using a confident and enthusiastic voice when they speak in front of others, for example, when they give a book talk?

Use your observations to determine the next umbrella you will teach. You may also consult Minilessons Across the Year (pp. 61–64) for guidance.

Link to Writing

After teaching the minilessons in this umbrella, help students link the new learning to their own writing:

- Have students use dialogue in their writing. Encourage them to think about how the character would say it and then write it that way.

Reader's Notebook

When this umbrella is complete, provide a copy of the minilesson principles (see resources.fountasandpinnell.com) for students to glue in the reader's notebook (in the Minilessons section if using *Reader's Notebook: Advanced* [Fountas and Pinnell 2011]), so they can refer to the information as needed.

Minilessons in This Umbrella

RML1	Tell about the theme and plot in an organized way to summarize a fiction story.
RML2	Tell about the important events to summarize a biography or memoir.
RML3	Tell the big idea and how the most important information is organized to summarize an informational text.

Before Teaching Umbrella 5 Minilessons

The minilessons in this umbrella do not need to be taught consecutively; rather, you can teach them in conjunction with relevant Literary Analysis minilessons. A summary of any text includes the most important details or information plus the message or lesson that the author is trying to convey.

Use the texts from the *Fountas & Pinnell Classroom™ Interactive Read-Aloud Collection* text sets listed below, or choose books from your classroom library to support students in learning to summarize their reading. Read and discuss fiction texts with characters, settings, clear problems and solutions, and a message. Read and discuss informational texts with a variety of underlying text structures.

Grit and Perseverance

Nim and the War Effort by Milly Lee

Rikki-Tikki-Tavi by Rudyard Kipling

Genre Study: Biography (Musicians)

The Legendary Miss Lena Horne by Carole Boston Weatherford

I and I: Bob Marley by Tony Medina

Genre Study: Expository Nonfiction

The Cod's Tale by Mark Kurlansky

Giant Squid: Searching for a Sea Monster by Mary Cerullo and Clyde F. E. Roper

As you read aloud and enjoy these texts together, help students

- notice and discuss the events that shaped the life of a character in a fiction text or a subject in a biography,
- think about the message or lesson the author is trying to convey,
- understand what makes the subject of a biography notable, and
- notice the important information and the underlying text structures presented in an informational text.

Grit and Perseverance

Nim and the War Effort by Milly Lee

Rikki-Tikki-Tavi by Rudyard Kipling

Genre Study: Biography (Musicians)

Genre Study: Expository Nonfiction

Giant Squid by Mary Cerullo and Clyde F. E. Roper

RML1
SAS.U5.RML1

Reading Minilesson Principle

Tell about the theme and plot in an organized way to summarize a fiction story.

Summarizing

You Will Need

- two familiar fiction books, such as the following from Text Set: Grit and Perseverance:
  - *Nim and the War Effort* by Milly Lee
  - *Rikki-Tikki-Tavi* by Rudyard Kipling
- chart paper prepared with a summary of *Nim and the War Effort*
- chart paper and markers

Academic Language / Important Vocabulary

- summary
- summarize
- character
- setting
- plot
- theme

Continuum Connection

- Tell a summary of a text after hearing it read (p. 69)
- Present an organized oral summary that includes the setting (if important), significant plot events including climax and resolution, main characters and supporting characters, character change (where significant) and the theme or lesson (fiction) (pp. 555, 565, 576)
- Include the problem and its resolution in a summary of a text (p. 70)

Goal

Tell about the theme and the important events of a text in a sequence, including the characters, setting, problem, and solution.

Rationale

When summarizing a fiction text, students must organize details about the characters, setting, plot, and theme in a logical sequence. This helps readers remember what they read and think about the most important parts of the story.

Assess Learning

Observe students when they summarize fiction texts. Notice if there is evidence of new learning based on the goal of this minilesson.

- Can students deliver an oral summary of a fiction text that tells about the theme and the important events of the story in a logical sequence?
- Can students distinguish between essential and nonessential information when they give a summary?
- Are they using language such as *summary*, *summarize*, *character*, *setting*, *plot*, and *theme*?

Minilesson

To help students think about summarizing fiction books, engage them in noticing the characteristics of a summary. Here is an example.

- Read aloud the written summary of *Nim and the War Effort.*

  What do you notice about the information in my summary of *Nim and the War Effort*?

  What parts of the story did I include?

  What else did I include in my summary?

  What didn't I include?

- Record students' responses on chart paper.

  When you tell the most important parts of a story, you summarize it, or give a summary. A summary is short but gives enough information so someone can understand what the story is mainly about. You need to organize the information so the summary makes sense. What did you notice about how I organized the information in my summary?

Have a Try

Invite the students to summarize *Rikki-Tikki-Tavi* with a partner.

> One of you will give a summary of *Rikki-Tikki-Tavi* to your partner. If you are listening to your partner give a summary, notice what information is in it.

- If time allows, ask one or two students to share their summaries with the class. Invite other students to share what they noticed.

Summarize and Apply

Summarize the learning and invite students to prepare an oral summary of a book.

> What should you tell in the summary of a fiction book?

- Review the chart, adding any additional ideas. Write the principle at the top of the chart.

> Today, think about how you would summarize the last fiction book you finished reading. Be prepared to give a summary of that book to a partner when we come back together.

Share

Following independent reading time, gather pairs of students together in the meeting area to share their summaries.

> Give a summary to your partner of the last fiction book you read.
>
> What did you notice about your partner's summary?

Summary

Nim and the War Effort
by Milly Lee

This story takes place in San Francisco in 1943. The main character, Nim, is a Chinese American girl who wants to win her school's newspaper drive to help the war effort. A boy named Garland taunts her and tells her that an "American" is going to win the contest. Determined to prove that she is the American who is going to win, Nim ventures out of Chinatown to find newspapers. Through Nim's determination to win the newspaper drive and prove that she is a real American, this story explores themes of culture, identity, and family.

Tell about the theme and plot in an organized way to summarize a fiction story.

What to Include in a Story Summary

- Title and author
- Main character(s)
- Setting
- Problem and solution
- Important events in the plot
- Ending
- Theme(s)

Extend the Lesson (Optional)

After assessing students' understanding, you might decide to extend the learning.

- During guided reading lessons and individual conferences, ask students to summarize the book they have just read.
- **Writing About Reading** After students have demonstrated the ability to deliver a strong oral summary, ask them to write a summary in a reader's notebook (see WAR.U5.RML3).

RML 2
SAS.U5.RML2

Reading Minilesson Principle

Tell about the important events to summarize a biography or memoir.

Summarizing

You Will Need

- two familiar biographies or memoirs, such as the following from Text Set: Genre Study: Biography (Musicians):
  - *The Legendary Miss Lena Horne* by Carole Boston Weatherford
  - *I and I: Bob Marley* by Tony Medina
- chart paper prepared with a summary of *The Legendary Miss Lena Horne*
- chart paper and markers

Academic Language / Important Vocabulary

- biography
- summary
- subject

Continuum Connection

- Tell a summary of a text after hearing it read (p. 73)
- Present a concise, organized oral summary that includes all important information (pp. 555, 565, 576)

Goal

Tell the important events in chronological order to summarize a biography or memoir.

Rationale

A biography or memoir often follows a chronological or narrative structure. Learning how to summarize a biography helps students learn to summarize other texts with a narrative structure. This lesson can also be used to help students summarize narrative nonfiction.

Assess Learning

Observe students when they summarize a biography or memoir. Notice if there is evidence of new learning based on the goal of this minilesson.

- Can students give an organized oral summary of a biography or memoir?
- Can they distinguish between essential and nonessential details?
- Are they using language such as *biography*, *summary*, and *subject*?

Minilesson

To help students think about the minilesson principle, engage them in noticing the important characteristics of a summary of a biography. Here is an example.

- Read the written summary of *The Legendary Miss Lena Horne*.

  What do you notice about the way I told you about this biography? What information did I include?

- Record responses on chart paper.

  What did you notice about how I organized the information in my summary?

  My summary is of a biography, but a summary of a memoir would be similar in content and organization.

Have a Try

Invite students to summarize *I and I: Bob Marley* with a partner.

One of you will give a summary of *I and I: Bob Marley* to your partner. If you are listening to your partner give a summary, notice what information is in it.

- If time allows, ask a student to share a summary with the class. Invite other students to share what they noticed.

Summarize and Apply

Summarize the learning and invite students to prepare an oral summary of a biography.

What should you tell in the summary of a biography or memoir?

- Review the chart, adding any additional ideas. Write the principle at the top.

When you read today, read a biography or memoir or think about the last one you read. Be prepared to tell a summary of the book when we come back together.

Share

Following independent reading time, gather students together in the meeting area to share their summaries.

- Choose two or three students to share a summary of a biography or memoir with the class.

Summary

The Legendary Miss Lena Horne
by Carole Boston Weatherford

Singer, dancer, and actress Lena Horne was born in New York City in 1917. As a teenager, she began to sing and dance onstage. She quickly became successful and started to tour. As she toured the country, she faced discrimination. Nevertheless, she became an international star. Lena's story is one of determination and courage. Today, she is remembered not only for her incredible talent but also for breaking down racial barriers and refusing to be treated as a second-class citizen.

Tell about the important events to summarize a biography or memoir.

What to Include in the Summary of a Biography

- Title and author
- The subject of the book
- Why the subject is important
- Where and when the subject lived
- The important events in order
- Problems the subject encountered and how they were solved
- The author's message

Extend the Lesson (Optional)

After assessing students' understanding, you might decide to extend the learning.

- Use this lesson as a model for teaching students to summarize narrative nonfiction.
- During guided reading lessons and individual conferences, ask students to summarize a biography or memoir.
- **Writing About Reading** After students have demonstrated the ability to deliver a strong oral summary of a biography or memoir, ask them to write a summary in a reader's notebook (see WAR.U5.RML3).

RML 3

SAS.U5.RML3

Reading Minilesson Principle

Tell the big idea and how the most important information is organized to summarize an informational text.

Summarizing

You Will Need

- two familiar informational texts, such as the following from Text Set: Genre Study: Expository Nonfiction:
  - *The Cod's Tale* by Mark Kurlansky
  - *Giant Squid* by Mary Cerullo and Clyde F. E. Roper
- chart paper prepared with a summary of *The Cod's Tale*
- chart paper and markers

Academic Language / Important Vocabulary

- summarize
- summary

Continuum Connection

- Tell a summary of a text after hearing it read (p. 73)
- Present a concise, organized oral summary that includes all important information (pp. 555, 565, 576)
- Present a logically organized oral summary that includes information expressing the main idea or larger message and reflects the overall structure (expository or narrative) as well as important underlying structures: e.g., description, cause and effect, chronological sequence, temporal sequence, categorization, comparison and contrast, problem and solution, question and answer (nonfiction) (pp. 555, 565, 576)

Goal

Tell a summary of the most important information and ideas in an informational book and reflect the overall structure (expository or narrative) as well as important underlying structures.

Rationale

When you teach students how to summarize an informational book, you help them organize and clearly articulate the most important information in the book. This also helps them learn and notice a variety of informational text structures, such as categorical, descriptive, and compare and contrast.

Assess Learning

Observe students when they summarize informational texts. Notice if there is evidence of new learning based on the goal of this minilesson.

- Can students distinguish between essential and nonessential information when summarizing?
- Can they notice the underlying text structure of an informational text?
- Are they using academic language, such as *summarize* and *summary*?

Minilesson

To help students think about the minilesson principle, engage them in noticing the important characteristics of a summary of an informational book. Here is an example.

- Read the written summary of *The Cod's Tale*.

  What do you notice about the information I shared?

  What did I include in my summary?

- Record responses on chart paper.

  A summary does not tell everything in a book–only enough important information to give someone an idea of what the book is about. What did you notice about how I organized the information in my summary?

Have a Try

Invite students to summarize *Giant Squid* with a partner.

> One of you will give a summary of *Giant Squid* to your partner. If you are listening to your partner give a summary, notice what information is in it.

- If time allows, ask one or two students to share their summaries with the class. Invite other students to share what they noticed.

Summarize and Apply

Summarize the learning and invite students to prepare an oral summary of an informational book.

- Review the chart, adding any additional ideas. Write the principle at the top.

> When you read today, read an informational book or think about the last one you read. Be prepared to tell a summary of the book when we come back together.

Share

Following independent reading time, gather students in pairs in the meeting area to share their summaries.

> Share your summary with a partner.

- After students turn and talk, invite two or three students to share with the class.

Extend the Lesson (Optional)

After assessing students' understanding, you might decide to extend the learning.

- During guided reading lessons and individual conferences, ask students to summarize an informational book.
- **Writing About Reading** After students have demonstrated the ability to deliver a strong oral summary of an informational book, ask them to write a summary in a reader's notebook (see WAR.U5.RML3).

Summary

The Cod's Tale
by Mark Kurlansky

The Cod's Tale tells how the cod fits into human history. It traces in chronological order how the cod affected various groups of people in history—from the Vikings to the Basques to the Pilgrims. In addition to tracing the history of the cod, the book also provides information about the cod's characteristics, life cycle, and habitat. It ends in the present day, explaining that there are fewer and fewer fish in our seas. It urges readers to consider what may happen if overfishing continues.

Tell the big idea and how the most important information is organized to summarize an informational text.

What to Include in the Summary of an Informational Book

- The title and author
- The topic
- The most important information
- How the book is organized
- The main message or big idea

Assessment

After you have taught the minilessons in this umbrella, observe students as they talk and write about their reading across instructional contexts: interactive read-aloud, independent reading, guided reading, shared reading, and book club. Use *The Literacy Continuum* (Fountas and Pinnell 2017) to guide the observation of students' reading and writing behaviors.

- What evidence do you have of new understandings related to summarizing?
    - Can students articulate clear, well-organized summaries of fiction, informational, and biographical texts?
    - Are they able to distinguish between essential and nonessential information?
    - Do they use academic language, such as *summary, summarize, character, setting, theme, plot, biography,* and *subject*?
- In what other ways, beyond the scope of this umbrella, are students talking about fiction and nonfiction books?
    - Have students begun to notice and discuss underlying text structures in nonfiction?
    - Do they notice and comment on text features in nonfiction books?
    - Are they noticing elements of author's craft in fiction books?

Use your observations to determine the next umbrella you will teach. You may also consult Minilessons Across the Year (pp. 61–64) for guidance.

Link to Writing

After teaching the minilessons in this umbrella, help students link the new learning to their own writing:

- Have students write mini-summaries to attach to some books in the classroom library to help other students choose a book they will enjoy reading.

Reader's Notebook

When this umbrella is complete, provide a copy of the minilesson principles (see resources.fountasandpinnell.com) for students to glue in the reader's notebook (in the Minilessons section if using *Reader's Notebook: Advanced* [Fountas and Pinnell 2011]), so they can refer to the information as needed.

Minilessons in This Umbrella

RML1	Prepare for reading by using the text features and resources.
RML2	Be persistent when you read a difficult text.
RML3	Notice when you don't understand what you're reading and take action.
RML4	Read short sections and stop to think about what the author is saying.

Before Teaching Umbrella 6 Minilessons

The minilessons in this umbrella are intended to encourage students to use a variety of effective techniques when approaching texts that are difficult for them to read. You will not only address focus and persistence but also teach students to monitor their comprehension.

Unlike other minilessons in this book, these minilessons do not rely on previously read texts. Instead, provide real-world examples of texts that are likely to be difficult for your students, such as material from disciplinary reading. Expose students to reading materials that are beyond their instructional levels and that can be enlarged (written on chart paper or projected). Examples include practice testing booklets, online informational material and directions, scientific articles, textbooks, and primary source documents. The texts should be tailored to your group of students and what they find difficult, so readings will vary from class to class.

Introduce, read, and discuss a variety of texts that your students may find difficult. When you do,

- discuss what the text is about,
- demonstrate how to reread and check if a word makes sense, sounds right, and looks right,
- model how to keep track of who is speaking,
- think about the important information and details when you read,
- show how to stop and reread if something is confusing, and
- read short sections and then stop and think about what the author is trying to say.

RML1

SAS.U6.RML1

Reading Minilesson Principle

Prepare for reading by using the text features and resources.

Monitoring Comprehension of Difficult Texts

You Will Need

- a sample of texts that may be difficult for your students and that include at least some of these text features: titles, headings, an introduction, a summary, graphics, and key words
- chart paper and markers
- document camera (optional)
- basket of texts (e.g., books, magazines, articles) that may be difficult for your students and that include a variety of text features

Academic Language / Important Vocabulary

- difficult
- techniques
- text features
- resources

Continuum Connection

- Notice and use and understand the purpose of some organizational tools: e.g., title, table of contents, chapter title (p. 72)
- Notice and use and understand the purpose of some organizational tools: e.g., title, table of contents, chapter title, heading, subheading (p. 75)

Goal

Navigate a difficult text by previewing the title and headings, graphics, introduction, and summary.

Rationale

Teach students to use text features and resources to preview a difficult text so that they have a way to begin to peel back the layers to find the meaning. They will benefit from knowing that navigating a difficult text usually requires more than one pass.

Assess Learning

Observe students when they navigate difficult texts and notice if there is evidence of new learning based on the goal of this minilesson.

- Can students identify text features and resources to use in navigating difficult text?
- Do they understand the terms *difficult, techniques, text features,* and *resources*?

Minilesson

To help students think about the minilesson principle, engage them in generating a list of text features and resources to use when navigating difficult texts. Here is an example.

- Display a text that has a variety of text features (e.g., title, headings, graphics) that can be used to determine what the text is about.

  If you need to read a difficult text, what text features on the page can help you get information that will help you? What do you notice on this page that might help you understand what you will be reading about?

- Guide students to identify key features, such as the title, headings, and illustrations. As students name them, begin a list on chart paper.

  Some texts have an introduction or a summary, which is short to read and gives you a general idea of what the text will be about.

- Continue showing examples of difficult texts that include a variety of text features, such as headings, an introduction, a summary, graphics, illustrations, and key words. As students identify each, add to the list on the chart. The following prompts may be useful:
  - *What features of this text give you a clue about what you are reading?*
  - *What do you notice about the introduction?*
  - *How does the author identify key words?*
  - *How could you get to know key words that are unfamiliar?*
  - *How does a summary help you understand what you are reading?*

Have a Try

Provide each pair of students with a nonfiction book or article.

Talk with your partner about where you can look to find out what the book (or article) is about.

- After time for brief discussion, ask a few pairs to share what they found.

Summarize and Apply

Summarize the learning and remind students to use text features and resources.

- Review the chart and add the principle to the top.

When you read today, choose a text from the basket that may be difficult for you to read. Look for text features and resources. Bring the text when we meet so you can share.

Prepare for reading by using the text features and resources.

- Title
- Headings
- Introduction
- Graphics and illustrations
- Key words
- Summary

Share

Following independent reading time, gather students in small groups.

In your group, share what you read today and talk about text features or resources that helped you understand what you read.

Extend the Lesson (Optional)

After assessing students' understanding, you might decide to extend the learning.

- Continue to support techniques for approaching difficult texts during guided reading or independent reading time. From *Fountas & Pinnell Prompting Guide, Part 2, for Comprehension: Thinking, Talking, and Writing* (Fountas and Pinnell 2009), use prompts such as the following:
  - *What does the (title, dust jacket, back cover, illustrations, chapter headings, dedication, opening page) tell you about the book?*
  - *What print features does the book have (cartoons, speech bubbles, headings, special fonts)?*
  - *What can you learn from these features?*
  - *What kind of illustrations and graphics are included (photographs, drawings, diagrams, cross-sections, maps, sidebars)?*

RML 2

SAS.U6.RML2

Reading Minilesson Principle

Be persistent when you read a difficult text.

Monitoring Comprehension of Difficult Texts

You Will Need

- a sample of texts that may be difficult for your students, with highlighting and notes to assist with comprehension
- chart paper and markers
- sticky notes
- document camera (optional)
- basket of texts that are difficult for students

Academic Language / Important Vocabulary

- difficult
- techniques
- persistent
- focused

Continuum Connection

- Notice and ask questions when meaning is lost or understanding is interrupted (pp. 69, 73)

Goal

Use techniques to stay focused and persistent when reading.

Rationale

When you teach students ways to access the content of a difficult text, you help them persist in reading that text. They learn it is normal to sometimes encounter texts that are difficult but that there are ways to unlock the meaning.

Assess Learning

Observe students when they approach difficult texts and notice if there is evidence of new learning based on the goal of this minilesson.

- Are students able to generate a list of ways to approach difficult texts?
- Do they try more than one way to stay focused when reading a difficult text?
- Do they understand the terms *difficult, techniques, persistent,* and *focused*?

Minilesson

To help students think about the minilesson principle, engage them in constructing a list of techniques to help them stay focused when navigating difficult texts. Here is an example.

- Ahead of time, choose a text that is beyond the instructional level of most of your students. Prepare highlighting, notes in the margins, and/or attach sticky notes.

  How do you feel when you read something that is very difficult?

  One of the things I do before I read something that is really hard is think about what I already know and what I want to know about the topic.

- Start a chart by listing things to do before reading.

  Let's look at this topic. What are some things you might want to learn or be interested in finding out about this topic?

- Show the prepared document and have a brief conversation about the topic.

  Here is something that is difficult to read. I have done some things to help me stay focused and persistent. What do you notice that I have done?

- As students provide ideas, continue the list with techniques that can be used while reading. Prompt the conversation as needed.

Have a Try

Invite the students to talk with a partner about navigating difficult texts.

> What do you do to read something difficult? Turn and talk about that.

- After time for discussion, ask students to share. Add new ideas to the chart.

Summarize and Apply

Summarize the learning and remind students to stay focused and persistent when reading something that is difficult.

> When you read something difficult, it is important to stick with it and try different techniques. That means that you are focused and persistent.

- Add the principle to the chart.

> When you read today, choose something that may be difficult for you to read. Try using one or more of the techniques we talked about before and during reading. Bring what you read when we meet so you can share.

Be persistent when you read a difficult text.

Before Reading

- Think about what you know about the topic before reading.
- Think about what you want to learn or find out.
- Think about what you wonder.

While Reading

- Use a highlighter to mark important words, phrases, or sentences.
- Write a note in the margin on the page.
- Add sticky notes.
- Reread a sentence or paragraph.
- Don't give up.

Share

Following independent reading time, gather students together to talk about their reading.

> Who would like to share what you read today and talk about what you did to help yourself understand it?

Extend the Lesson (Optional)

After assessing students' understanding, you might decide to extend the learning.

- Continue to support techniques for approaching difficult texts during guided reading or independent reading time. From *Fountas & Pinnell Prompting Guide, Part 2, for Comprehension: Thinking, Talking, and Writing* (Fountas and Pinnell 2009), use prompts such as the following:
    - *What do you know about the genre that might help you?*
    - *What do you think the writer will teach you about ____________?*
    - *How does that fit with what you know?*
    - *What questions do you still have?*
    - *What confused you?*

RML 3
SAS.U6.RML3

Reading Minilesson Principle

Notice when you don't understand what you're reading and take action.

Monitoring Comprehension of Difficult Texts

You Will Need

- a sample of texts that are difficult for most students (e.g., a challenging novel, a scientific or technology article, or a medical journal)
- chart paper and markers
- document camera (optional)

Academic Language / Important Vocabulary

- techniques
- take action
- reread
- key vocabulary

Continuum Connection

- Notice and ask questions when meaning is lost or understanding is interrupted (pp. 69, 73)

Goal

Self-monitor and self-correct by rereading, finding the meaning of key vocabulary, and reading on to gain more information.

Rationale

When you teach students to notice when they do not understand what they are reading by self-monitoring, they learn to self-correct by rereading, reading on, and/or looking up key vocabulary to gain meaning.

Assess Learning

Observe students when they read difficult text and notice if there is evidence of new learning based on the goal of this minilesson.

- Do students notice when they do not understand what they are reading?
- Are they able to stop and take action when they do not comprehend a difficult text?
- Do they understand the terms *techniques, take action, reread,* and *key vocabulary*?

Minilesson

To help students think about the minilesson principle, engage them in thinking about the actions that support comprehension. Here is an example.

Sometimes, you will come to a part of a book that doesn't make sense or that is difficult for you to understand.

- Display an example of difficult reading material. Read aloud the first paragraph or a difficult section with good momentum and no explanations.

Did you understand what I read?

I read that quickly. Sometimes you realize that you are reading too quickly to understand what the author is writing about. What can you do if that happens?

- As students provide ideas, make a list on chart paper.

It's important to notice when you don't understand what you are reading. The first thing to do is stop. Then you can try some different actions to work out the meaning.

Have a Try

Invite the students to talk with a partner about noticing when they don't understand what they are reading and how they can take action.

> We made a list of some things you can do when you don't understand what you are reading. Can you think of any others? Turn and talk about that.

- After time for brief discussion, ask if students have ideas to add to the chart.

Summarize and Apply

Summarize the learning and remind students to notice when they don't understand what they are reading and to take action.

- Review the chart and add the principle to the top.

> When you read today, if you come to a part you don't understand, try one or more of the actions that are listed on the chart. Bring your reading when we meet so you can share.

Notice when you don't understand what you're reading and take action.

TAKE ACTION

- Slow down.
- Reread the part slowly.
- Read ahead to see if the meaning is clarified.
- Find key words in the glossary or other source.
- Think about what the whole book is about and how the information fits.

Share

Following independent reading time, gather students in small groups.

> In your group, share what you read today and talk about what you did to help you understand what you read.

Extend the Lesson (Optional)

After assessing students' understanding, you might decide to extend the learning.

- Continue to support techniques for approaching difficult texts during guided reading or independent reading. From *Fountas & Pinnell Prompting Guide, Part 2, for Comprehension: Thinking, Talking, and Writing* (Fountas and Pinnell 2009), use prompts such as the following:
  - *Does that make sense?*
  - *Were there parts where you wanted to slow down and think more?*
  - *What do you think the author meant when she said ____________?*
  - *How do the illustrations enhance your understanding of the topic?*

RML4
SAS.U6.RML4

Reading Minilesson Principle

Read short sections and stop to think about what the author is saying.

Monitoring Comprehension of Difficult Texts

You Will Need

- prepared chart paper or projected document showing text that may be difficult for your students
- chart paper and markers
- document camera (optional)
- sticky notes
- basket of texts that may be difficult for your students

Academic Language / Important Vocabulary

- actions
- section
- summarize

Continuum Connection

- Tell a summary of a text after hearing it read (pp. 69, 73)

Goal

Read short sections and think about what the author is saying.

Rationale

When students learn to stop and think about what an author is saying while reading difficult material, they begin to remember what they read, organize the information, and increase comprehension. In content-area studies and research, they will likely encounter difficult texts.

Assess Learning

Observe students when they encounter difficult text and notice if there is evidence of new learning based on the goal of this minilesson.

- Do they read a short section and then think about what the author is trying to say?
- Do they understand the terms *actions, section,* and *summarize*?

Minilesson

To help students think about the minilesson principle, engage them in a discussion about how to read a short section of a difficult text and then pause to think about what the author is trying to say.

- Show or project an example of text that is difficult for students.

  When you read something that is difficult to understand, there are different actions that you can take to be sure you understand what you are reading.

- Read a short section and then stop and ask the students what the author is trying to say. Briefly summarize the section with them. Add the summary on a sticky note next to the text that was summarized.
- Read another short portion of the text. Then stop and repeat the process.
- Engage students in a discussion about what they noticed about the technique you used.
- Help students conclude that when they read a short section and pause to think about what they read, they can assure good understanding.

Have a Try

Show or project another difficult text.

With a partner, take turns reading a short section aloud and then think and talk about what the author is trying to say.

Summarize and Apply

Summarize the learning and remind students to read a short section of a difficult text and think about what an author is trying to say.

What can you do to help yourself when reading something that is difficult?

- Add the principle to the chart.

When you read today, choose something that is very difficult for you. When you come to a part you don't understand, read a short section and then think about what the author is trying to say. Bring the text when we meet so you can share.

Read short sentences and stop to think about what the author is saying.

Phantom Limbs Here's what we've learned from mapping the somatosensory cortex: our brains are hardwired for two legs and feet, two arms and hands, and so on. Even someone born without a hand has a cortex location for it.	All our limbs are connected to the brain.
The fact that an amputated hand can't send sensory information to the brain might seem obvious, but the brain is hardwired to receive sensory data from two hands. When one hand is no longer there, the brain must do some rewiring.	This must be why people feel a limb that is no longer there.

Share

Following independent reading time, gather students in pairs.

With your partner, talk about any actions you took that helped you understand what you read.

Extend the Lesson (Optional)

After assessing students' understanding, you might decide to extend the learning.

- Continue to support effective actions for monitoring comprehension during guided reading or independent reading. From *Fountas & Pinnell Prompting Guide, Part 2, for Comprehension: Thinking, Talking, and Writing* (Fountas and Pinnell 2009), use prompts such as the following:
  - *What is the author really trying to say?*
  - *Why did the author say ____________? What are some of the most important ideas?*
  - *Did the writer compare (and contrast) anything?*
  - *Why did the author decide to use italics (use a graphic text form, use free verse)?*
  - *What does the author want you to know about?*
  - *What kinds of words and language did the writer use?*

Monitoring Comprehension of Difficult Texts

Assessment

After you have taught the minilessons in this umbrella, observe students as they talk and write about their reading across instructional contexts: interactive read-aloud, independent reading, guided reading, shared reading, and book club. Use *The Literacy Continuum* (Fountas and Pinnell 2017) to guide the observation of students' reading and writing behaviors.

- What evidence do you have of new understandings related to monitoring comprehension of difficult texts?
  - Do students persist and stay focused when reading a difficult text?
  - Are they using text features and resources when reading?
  - Do students notice when they do not understand what they are reading and take action?
  - Do they stop and think about what an author is trying to say?
  - Do they understand the terms *difficult, techniques, persistent, focused, text features, resources, reread, take action,* and *summarize*?
- In what other ways, beyond the scope of this umbrella, are students talking about ways to monitor comprehension of difficult texts?
  - Are students engaging in conversations about difficult texts and providing support and ideas to classmates as they read text that is beyond their instructional level?

Use your observations to determine the next umbrella you will teach. You may also consult Minilessons Across the Year (pp. 61–64) for guidance.

Reader's Notebook

When this umbrella is complete, provide a copy of the minilesson principles (see resources.fountasandpinnell.com) for students to glue in the reader's notebook (in the Minilessons section if using *Reader's Notebook: Advanced* [Fountas and Pinnell 2011]), so they can refer to the information as needed.

Minilessons in This Umbrella

RML1	Search efficiently and effectively for information on the internet.
RML2	Evaluate whether you have found the information you need.
RML3	Stay focused while reading on the internet.
RML4	Evaluate the credibility of the source of the information you read on the internet.
RML5	Evaluate whether a website presents one perspective or multiple perspectives.

Before Teaching Umbrella 7 Minilessons

With the constant explosion of new technologies, children and teenagers spend more and more time reading in digital environments. A 2015 report by Common Sense Media (https://www.commonsensemedia.org/sites/default/files/uploads/research/census_researchreport.pdf, 21) found that eight- to twelve-year-old children spend about two and a half hours per day using digital media (e.g., computers, tablets, and smart phones) outside of school. Although the growth of digital technologies offers myriad benefits to children and adults alike, it also presents a number of challenges. Reading in digital environments requires a different set of skills than reading print publications. Students need teaching to show them how to effectively find the information they need, how to evaluate its relevance and credibility, and how to stay focused while doing so.

Before teaching the minilessons in this umbrella, determine how and when your students will have access to digital devices during the school day, and put structures in place for ensuring that they can use them safely. You might, for example, have students use a child-friendly search engine or give them lists of safe, trustworthy websites about different topics. Be sure to give your students numerous opportunities to use digital technology in different ways and for different purposes.

RML1

SAS.U7.RML1

Reading Minilesson Principle

Search efficiently and effectively for information on the internet.

Reading in Digital Environments

You Will Need

- a computer or tablet with internet access (connected to a projector, if possible)
- chart paper and markers
- a list of possible questions for students to research on the internet (see Summarize and Apply)

Academic Language / Important Vocabulary

- internet
- website
- information
- search engine
- keywords

Continuum Connection

- Use different strategies to increase the effectiveness of your searches including keywords, advanced search engine filters, and symbols (p. 354)
- Locate websites that fit one's needs and purpose (p. 354)

Goal

Use different search techniques to increase the effectiveness of searches, including keywords, search engine filters, and symbols.

Rationale

Many students understand the basics of searching for information on the internet but often find it challenging to find the information they actually need. When students are armed with a toolkit of effective searching techniques—for example, using filters and symbols, knowing how to phrase inquiries, knowing how to perform multistep searches—they are more likely to find the information they need (for more resources on effective searching techniques, visit a website such as *Common Sense* [commonsense.org].

Assess Learning

Observe students when they search for information on the internet and notice if there is evidence of new learning based on the goal of this minilesson.

- Do students know how to phrase search inquiries?
- Do they use and understand the terms *internet*, *website*, *information*, *search engine*, and *keywords*?

Minilesson

Engage students in a discussion about how to search for information on the internet. This lesson assumes the use of Google as a search engine.

- Display Google (or another search engine) on a projector or large screen.

  The internet is a wonderful resource, but there is so much information that it can be hard to find exactly what you're looking for. What are some of the problems or challenges you've had?

- Make a list of students' responses on chart paper.
- Then discuss each problem one by one, inviting students to offer possible solutions. Add solutions to the chart in a second column.

  These are all great ideas. Now let's do a search together. I want to learn about the *Titanic*.

- Search for the word *Titanic*.

  The search engine found 131 million websites about the *Titanic*! I need to think about what exactly I want to find out. I'm interested in the *Titanic* because I recently read a book about it, and I still have some questions that weren't answered by the book. For example, I would like to know who designed the *Titanic*. What do you think I should search for?

- Search for *who designed the* Titanic.

  One of the top results is "Who designed the *Titanic*?" It says that the *Titanic* was designed by three men, and it gives information about each one of them. This result gives me exactly the information I'm looking for.

Have a Try

Invite the students to talk with a partner about another search inquiry.

> Turn and talk to your partner about how you can find out whether more people live in Alabama or Utah. What can I search for to find this information?

- If necessary, explain that some topics need to be broken down into multiple steps. Demonstrate searching for *Utah population* and then doing the same for Alabama.

Search efficiently and effectively for information on the internet.

Problem	Solution
I don't know what to write in the search box.	• Type only the most important keywords.
I can't find what I'm looking for.	• Is there another way to say what you're looking for? Use synonyms. • Make your search terms more specific or less specific.
I don't know how to spell the thing I'm looking for.	• Don't worry about spelling. The search engine can often guess what word you mean, even if you spell it wrong!
I want to search for words in an exact order.	• Use quotation marks if you want to find websites that have your keywords in the same order. "with liberty and justice for all"
The results are about something completely different from what I'm looking for.	• Use a minus sign (-) in front of words you want to exclude. If you are looking for websites about the Milky Way—the galaxy, not the chocolate bar—type this: milky way -chocolate
The websites are too hard to read—they're for adults.	• Type the word kids after your search terms to find websites that are for kids. Declaration of Independence kids

Summarize and Apply

Summarize the learning and remind students to use these tips and techniques when searching for information on the internet.

- Ask students to summarize what they learned today. Write the principle at the top of the chart.
- Have students practice these search techniques. Give them a list of possible topics/questions to search for. For example: *What important events happened in this month one hundred years ago? When and where was the first vice president of the United States born? What does the biggest animal in the world eat?*

Share

Following independent reading time, gather students together in the meeting area to talk about their search techniques and results.

> What information did you search for? What techniques did you use to find the information you needed? What did you find out?

Extend the Lesson (Optional)

After assessing students' understanding, you might decide to extend the learning.

- Share additional techniques for searching for information on the internet. For example, you might talk about Google image search, show students how to narrow down results by date, or show them how to search for results within a particular website.

RML 2

SAS.U7.RML2

Reading Minilesson Principle

Evaluate whether you have found the information you need.

Reading in Digital Environments

You Will Need

- a computer or tablet with internet access (connected to a projector, if possible)
- chart paper and markers

Academic Language / Important Vocabulary

- internet
- website
- information
- evaluate
- search engine

Continuum Connection

- Locate websites that fit one's needs and purpose (p. 354)
- Identify the purpose of a website (p. 354)

Goal

Evaluate whether you have found the appropriate information after doing a search.

Rationale

When students are able to evaluate whether they have found the information they need after conducting an internet search, they spend more time reading relevant, interesting information and less time searching for information or going off-task.

Assess Learning

Observe students when they search for information on the internet and notice if there is evidence of new learning based on the goal of this minilesson.

- Can students choose a result that is likely to be relevant?
- Do they understand and use the terms *internet, website, information, evaluate,* and *search engine*?

Minilesson

To help students think about the minilesson principle, engage them in a demonstration and discussion about how to evaluate search results. Here is an example.

- Display Google (or another search engine) on a projector or large screen.

  Today I'm going to search on the internet for information about endangered animals. I'm going to search for *how can people help endangered animals*.

- Think aloud as you choose a result to click on.

  I see a result that says "10 Easy Things You Can Do to Save Endangered Species." Below the result and the web address, Google shows a few sentences from the website. I really think this website will have the information I'm looking for. What did you notice about how I chose which search result to click on?

- Record students' responses on chart paper. Click on the search result you chose and think aloud as you evaluate the source for relevancy.

  I want to make sure that it has the information I need, so I'm going to skim the website.

- Read aloud and point to any important words or phrases, subheadings, and text features.

  This website has what I need, so I'm going to read the whole page closely. What did you notice about what I did after I chose a website to click on?

- Record responses on the chart.

Have a Try

Invite the students to evaluate the relevancy of a website with a partner.

Now I would like to find out about what food sharks eat.

- Search for *shark food*. Click on a search result that is *not* relevant (e.g., a website about sharks *as* food).

Does this website have the information I need? Turn and talk to your partner about what you think.

This website clearly doesn't have the information I need, so I'm not going to waste my time reading the whole website. I need to go back to my search results and choose another website.

Summarize and Apply

Summarize the learning and remind students to evaluate the relevancy of search results.

What should you do if you determine that a website doesn't have what you need?

- Add any new insights to the chart and write the principle at the top.

If you use the internet today, think about a topic that you would like to learn about or a question that you'd like to have answered. Evaluate whether you have found the information you need.

Evaluate whether you have found the information you need.

1. Decide which website to click on.

- Check out the web address/source. (Is it a website that you've heard of before?)
- Read the titles.
- Read the short description, especially the words in bold.
- Click on the website that seems most likely to have the information you need.

2. Evaluate whether the website you clicked on has the information you need.

- Skim the website (look for titles, subheadings, text features, and key words and phrases).
- If it seems to have the information you need, read the website closely.
- If it doesn't, go back to your search results and choose another website.

Share

Following independent reading time, gather students together in the meeting area to talk about how they evaluated their search results.

Who searched for information on the internet today?

How did you evaluate whether the websites you found had the information you needed?

Extend the Lesson (Optional)

After assessing students' understanding, you might decide to extend the learning.

- Teach students how to recognize advertisements/sponsored links in search engine results and explain that they should generally be avoided.

RML 3
SAS.U7.RML3

Reading Minilesson Principle
Stay focused while reading on the internet.

Reading in Digital Environments

You Will Need

- chart paper and markers

Academic Language / Important Vocabulary

- internet
- website
- information
- link
- focused

Continuum Connection

- Use a variety of digital resources such as websites, public and subscription-based databases, e-books, and apps to locate, evaluate, and analyze literary and informational content (p. 354)

Goal

Stay focused on one thing at a time and be aware of hyperlinks that link to different content.

Rationale

With practically an endless array of links, videos, advertisements, and other distractions, websites offer an optimal environment for distracted reading. When students are aware of this potential and know techniques for staying focused while reading on the internet, they are less likely to be easily distracted, and they spend more time doing in-depth reading.

Assess Learning

Observe students when they use the internet and notice if there is evidence of new learning based on the goal of this minilesson.

- How well do students stay focused while reading on the internet?
- Do they understand and use the terms *internet, website, information, link,* and *focused*?

Minilesson

To help students think about the minilesson principle, engage them in a discussion about staying focused while reading on the internet.

- To introduce the idea of distracted reading online, use the following example or an authentic example from your personal experience.

  You can learn a lot of interesting information by reading on the internet, but sometimes it is difficult to stay focused. For example, once I was searching online to learn about World War I, but I ended up reading current news [or substitute personal example]. Has something like this ever happened to any of you?

  One thing that helps me stay focused is to make sure I always have a purpose for being online. For example, one day my purpose might be to learn about gardening. If I find myself getting tempted to click on a link, I'll ask myself, "Will this link help me learn more about gardening?" If the answer is no, I won't click on it.

  What are some other techniques you might use to stay focused?

- Record students' responses on chart paper.
- Note: Some web browsers offer a "reader view" feature, which strips away all the clutter—images, advertisements, links, etc.—from a website, making it easier to focus on reading. If you have such a feature on your classroom devices, show students how to use it, and add it to the chart.

Have a Try

Invite the students to talk with a partner about how to stay focused while reading on the internet.

Turn and talk to your partner about staying focused while reading online. You might talk about problems you've had, which of these ideas you would like to try, or any other ideas you have for staying focused.

- After time for discussion, invite several students to share their thinking. Add any new ideas to the list.

Stay focused while reading on the internet.

- Always have a purpose, or reason, for using the internet. Don't click on links that won't help you with that purpose.
- Read or skim the whole website first before deciding what links to click on next.
- Use the "reader view" option on the web browser.
- Try to have only one tab open at a time.
- Take notes about what you are reading.

Summarize and Apply

Summarize the learning and remind students to stay focused while reading on the internet.

What did you learn today about how to stay focused while reading on the internet?

- Write the principle at the top of the chart.

If you use the internet today, remember to stay focused on what you're reading. If you find it difficult to stay focused, review the chart we made and try some of these ideas.

Share

Following independent reading time, gather students together in the meeting area to share how they stayed focused while reading on the internet.

Who read on the internet today?

What techniques did you use to stay focused?

Extend the Lesson (Optional)

After assessing students' understanding, you might decide to extend the learning.

- Display the chart in the technology area of your classroom. Revisit it from time to time, and add new ideas that come up.
- Teach a minilesson about how to take notes while reading on the internet.

RML4
SAS.U7.RML4

Reading Minilesson Principle
Evaluate the credibility of the source of the information you read on the internet.

Reading in Digital Environments

You Will Need

- a computer or tablet with internet access (connected to a projector, if possible)
- chart paper and markers

Academic Language / Important Vocabulary

- internet
- website
- information
- credibility
- source

Continuum Connection

- Determine when a website was last updated (p. 354)
- Be alert to an author's point of view, examine for bias, and validate the author's authority on the topic through multiple sources (p. 354)

Goal

Evaluate the credibility of sources of the information read on the internet.

Rationale

When you teach students how to evaluate the credibility of internet sources, they are more likely to access and acquire accurate information. Additionally, the ability to critically evaluate information will serve them in all aspects of their lives, whether they are reading print or digital publications or are engaged in discussions, and will help them develop into thoughtful and critical members of society.

Assess Learning

Observe students when they read information on the internet and notice if there is evidence of new learning based on the goal of this minilesson.

- Do students evaluate the credibility of the websites they read on the internet?
- Can they explain how to evaluate the credibility of a website?
- Do they understand and use the terms *internet, website, information, credibility,* and *source*?

Minilesson

To help students think about the minilesson principle, model evaluating the credibility of a website. Here is an example.

- Display Google (or another search engine). Search for *Rosa Parks* (or another topic of your choice).

  Today I want to learn more about Rosa Parks. I searched for her name on the internet, and I found these results. I want to make sure I choose a credible, or trustworthy, source that will give me accurate information about her. Which of these results do you think are credible, or trustworthy? What makes you think that?

- If necessary, guide students to notice any results from well-known, credible publications. Click on one of them.

  What are some other things you would want to check to find out if this site is credible?

- Guide students to understand how to check the author's credentials, bibliography, and date updated (if available).

Have a Try

Invite the students to talk with a partner about how to evaluate the credibility of a website.

> What did we think about when we evaluated the credibility of a website? What questions did we ask ourselves? Turn and talk to your partner about this.

- After time for discussion, invite several students to share their thinking. Use their responses to make a chart.

Evaluate the credibility of the source of the information you read on the internet.

- Who created this website?
- Are they a trusted source (for example, a government agency, a university, or a major publication)? Web addresses that end in **.gov** or **.edu** are usually trustworthy.
- Who is the author?
- Is the author an expert on the topic?
- Does the author list the sources (a bibliography)?
- When was the website last updated? Is the information current?

Summarize and Apply

Summarize the learning and remind students to evaluate the credibility of internet sources.

> What did you learn today about how to evaluate the credibility of a website?
>
> Why is it important to think about whether a website is credible?

- Write the principle at the top of the chart.

> If you use the internet today, think about what you would like to read about and search for information on the topic. Remember to evaluate the credibility of the websites you find.

Share

Following independent reading time, gather students together in the meeting area to share how they evaluated the credibility of internet sources.

> Who searched for information on the internet today?
>
> How did you evaluate the credibility of the websites you found?

Extend the Lesson (Optional)

After assessing students' understanding, you might decide to extend the learning.

- Involve students in creating and maintaining running lists of trusted internet sources about various topics. Display the lists in your classroom's technology area.

RML 5

SAS.U7.RML5

Reading Minilesson Principle

Evaluate whether a website presents one perspective or multiple perspectives.

Reading in Digital Environments

You Will Need

- a computer or tablet with internet access (connected to a projector, if possible)
- two student-friendly web articles about the same topic: one that presents a single perspective and one that presents multiple perspectives. For example, you might use an opinion piece in favor of school uniforms and another article that explains the pros and cons of school uniforms. Unless the articles are very short, choose in advance key sentences or paragraphs to read aloud.
- a web article about a different topic
- chart paper and markers

Academic Language / Important Vocabulary

- internet
- website
- perspective
- evaluate

Continuum Connection

- Determine whether a website presents one perspective or multiple perspectives (p. 354)

Goal

Evaluate whether a website presents one perspective or multiple perspectives.

Rationale

When students are able to evaluate whether a website presents one perspective or multiple perspectives, they are less likely to indiscriminately believe everything they read on the internet–or elsewhere. They understand that an author's perspective influences what information is included, and they begin to develop the ability to evaluate information analytically and forge their own perspectives.

Assess Learning

Observe students when they read information on the internet and notice if there is evidence of new learning based on the goal of this minilesson.

- Can students evaluate whether a website presents one perspective or multiple perspectives?
- Do they understand and use the terms *internet, website, perspective,* and *evaluate*?

Minilesson

To help students think about the minilesson principle, engage them in a demonstration and discussion about how to evaluate whether a website presents one or more perspectives. Here is an example.

- Display the single-perspective web article.
- Read the title of the article and a few important passages from throughout the article that clearly show the author's perspective on the topic.

  What is this website about?

  How an author feels about a topic is her perspective. What is the author's perspective on school uniforms? How can you tell?

  Does the author give any reasons why school uniforms might be a bad thing?

  Does this website present one perspective or multiple perspectives about school uniforms?

- Display the multiple-perspective web article. Read the title and then a few select passages that discuss multiple perspectives.

  How do you think the author of this article feels about school uniforms?

  What reasons does the author give to support school uniforms?

  What reasons does she give for why uniforms may be a bad thing?

  Does this website give one perspective or multiple perspectives about school uniforms?

Have a Try

Invite the students to talk with a partner about another web article.

- Display the third web article. Read the title and a few important passages.

  Does this website present one perspective or multiple perspectives about the topic? Turn and talk to your partner about this. Be sure to explain your thinking.

- After students turn and talk, invite a few pairs to share their thinking.

Summarize and Apply

Summarize the learning and remind students to evaluate whether websites present one or multiple perspectives.

How can you tell if a website presents only one perspective on a topic or an issue?

How can you tell if a website presents multiple perspectives?

- Use students' responses to make a chart. Write the principle at the top.

  If you use the internet today, think about a topic or an issue that you would like to learn more about. Search for websites about that topic, and remember to evaluate whether each website you read presents one or multiple perspectives.

Evaluate whether a website presents one perspective or multiple perspectives.

One Perspective	• It is obvious how the author feels about the topic. • The author tells you that something is either GOOD or BAD (or right or wrong). • The author only gives reasons and evidence for ONE side of an issue. • The title tells you how the author feels.
Multiple Perspectives	• The title tells you what the website is about, but it doesn't tell you how the author feels. • You don't necessarily know how the author personally feels about the topic. • The author gives reasons and evidence for BOTH sides of an issue.

Share

Following independent reading time, gather students together in the meeting area to discuss how they evaluated websites.

Who searched for information on the internet today?

How did you determine whether a website presented one perspective or multiple perspectives?

Extend the Lesson (Optional)

After assessing students' understanding, you might decide to extend the learning.

- Explicitly discuss how an author's perspective on a topic influences how they write about it and what information they choose to include and omit.
- Discuss why it is important to read multiple perspectives about a topic or an issue not just online but in print as well.

Reading in Digital Environments

Assessment

After you have taught the minilessons in this umbrella, observe students as they use the internet. Use *The Literacy Continuum* (Fountas and Pinnell 2017) to guide the observation of students' reading and writing behaviors.

- What evidence do you have of new understandings related to reading in digital environments?
  - Are students able to use search engines effectively? If their initial search fails to yield relevant results, are they able to revise their search strategy?
  - Are they able to evaluate whether they have found the information they need?
  - Do they stay focused while reading on the internet?
  - Do they evaluate the credibility of internet resources?
  - Can they evaluate whether a website presents one perspective or multiple perspectives?
  - Do they understand and use terms such as *internet, information, source, website, link, search engine, evaluate,* and *perspective*?

Use your observations to determine the next umbrella you will teach. You may also consult Minilessons Across the Year (pp. 61–64) for guidance.

Link to Writing

After teaching the minilessons in this umbrella, help students link the new learning to their own writing:

- If you have your students conduct online research for writing projects, remind them to use the skills they learned from this umbrella. Teach them how to record the sources they use to avoid plagiarizing.

Reader's Notebook

When this umbrella is complete, provide a copy of the minilesson principles (see resources.fountasandpinnell.com) for students to glue in the reader's notebook (in the Minilessons section if using *Reader's Notebook: Advanced* [Fountas and Pinnell 2011]), so they can refer to the information as needed.

Section 4 Writing About Reading

Throughout the year, students will respond to what they read in a reader's notebook. These lessons help students use this important tool for independent literacy learning and make it possible for them to become aware of their own productivity, in the process building self-efficacy. All opportunities for writing about reading support the students in thinking about texts and articulating their understandings.

4 Writing About Reading

Minilessons in This Umbrella

RML1	Collect your thinking in your reader's notebook.
RML2	Record each book you read on your reading list.
RML3	Keep a tally of the kinds of books you read.
RML4	Follow the guidelines to help you do your best reading and writing work.

Before Teaching Umbrella 1 Minilessons

The minilessons in this umbrella are intended to introduce *Reader's Notebook: Advanced* (Fountas and Pinnell 2011) to your students; however, if you do not have it, a plain notebook can be used instead. The goal of a reader's notebook is for students to have a consistent place to collect their thinking about their reading (see pp. 52–53 for more on using a reader's notebook).

Students will do most of their writing about reading in a reader's notebook during the time set aside for independent reading and writing. To establish routines for that time, teach MGT.U2.RML2. For this umbrella, use the following books from the *Fountas & Pinnell Classroom™ Independent Reading Collection* or any other books from your classroom library.

Independent Reading Collection

The Science of a Tornado by Linda Cernak

Jacques Cousteau: Conserving Underwater Worlds by John Zronik

Independent Reading

Reader's Notebook

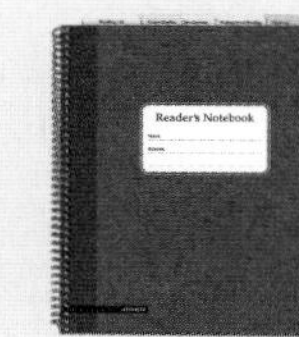

RML1
WAR.U1.RML1

Reading Minilesson Principle

Collect your thinking in your reader's notebook.

Introducing a Reader's Notebook

You Will Need

- a reader's notebook for each student (if using a plain notebook, set up tabbed sections for Reading List, Genre Studies, Minilessons, Writing About Reading, and Glossary)
- chart paper prepared with a five-column chart
- markers

Academic Language / Important Vocabulary

- reader's notebook
- reading list
- genre studies
- minilessons
- writing about reading
- glossary

Continuum Connection

- Form and express opinions about a text in writing and support those opinions with rationales and evidence (pp. 201, 204)
- Compose notes, lists, letters, or statements to remember important information about a text (pp. 200, 203)

Goal

Understand that a reader's notebook is a special place to collect thinking about books read.

Rationale

Students need numerous opportunities to respond to reading in different forms. A reader's notebook is a special place for them to keep a record of their reading lives and to share their thinking about books they have read.

Assess Learning

Observe students when they use a reader's notebook and notice if there is evidence of new learning based on the goal of this minilesson.

- Do students understand the purpose of a reader's notebook and of each section?
- Do they understand the terms *reader's notebook, reading list, genre studies, minilessons, writing about reading*, and *glossary*?

Minilesson

Give each student a reader's notebook and introduce them to the contents and purpose of the notebook. This lesson uses *Reader's Notebook: Advanced* (Fountas and Pinnell 2011).

> You each have your own reader's notebook, which you will use throughout the school year. Take a few minutes to look through it and see what you notice.
>
> What do you notice about the reader's notebook? What do you think you will do with it?

- Draw students' attention to the tabs at the top of the reader's notebook.

> The reader's notebook has five sections, and you can use the tabs to find each one. Open your notebook to the yellow tab that says Reading List.
>
> What do you think you will write in this section?
>
> What information will you record about each book?

- Record students' responses in the first column of the chart, under the heading *Reading List*.
- Continue in a similar manner with the four remaining sections (Genre Studies, Minilessons, Writing About Reading, and Glossary).
- You might also wish to have students look at the different ways they will write about their reading on the Forms for Writing About Reading page and the Suggestions for Writing About Reading page in the Writing About Reading section.

Have a Try

Invite the students to talk with a partner about the reader's notebook.

Turn and talk to your partner about what you will do in your reader's notebook.

- After time for discussion, invite a few pairs to share their thinking. Confirm their understanding of the reader's notebook and clear up any misconceptions that may have arisen.

Summarize and Apply

Summarize the learning and remind students to collect their thinking about their reading in a reader's notebook.

Why do you think it's a good idea to use a reader's notebook?

- Write the principle at the top of the chart.

After you read today, turn to the Writing About Reading section in your reader's notebook and write a few sentences or a paragraph about what you are thinking about the book. Be ready to share what you wrote when we come back together.

Collect your thinking in your reader's notebook.

Reading List	Genre Studies	Minilessons	Writing About Reading	Glossary
A list of books you have read (title, author, genre, etc.)	What you have noticed about different genres	The minilesson principles and notes about minilessons	Your thinking about books you have read (letters, summaries, lists, etc.)	Definitions of important terms related to reading and writing

Share

Following independent reading time, gather students together in the meeting area to talk about what they wrote.

What did you write about today in your reader's notebook?

Extend the Lesson (Optional)

After assessing students' understanding, you might decide to extend the learning.

- Have students personalize the covers of their reader's notebooks.
- Have students establish a place to store their reader's notebooks in their personal book boxes (see MGT.U2.RML3).

RML 2
WAR.U1.RML2

Introducing a Reader's Notebook

You Will Need

- two books, such as the following from *Independent Reading Collection:*
  - *The Science of a Tornado* by Linda Cernak
  - *Jacques Cousteau: Conserving Underwater Worlds* by John Zronik
- chart paper prepared to look like the reading list in *Reader's Notebook: Advanced* (Fountas and Pinnell 2011) and partially filled in with a few books
- markers
- a reader's notebook for each student

Academic Language / Important Vocabulary

- reader's notebook
- reading list
- title
- author
- genre
- response

Continuum Connection

- Record in Reader's Notebook the titles, authors, illustrators, genre of texts read independently, and dates read (pp. 200, 203)

Reading Minilesson Principle

Record each book you read on your reading list.

Goal

Learn to record the book title, author, genre, the level of challenge the book provided, and the date it is completed in the reader's notebook.

Rationale

Recording a list of books they have read helps students remember those they have read and enjoyed. It also helps them remember which books they found difficult or did not enjoy, and those examples help them make better reading choices and develop self-awareness as readers.

Assess Learning

Observe students when they use a reader's notebook and notice if there is evidence of new learning based on the goal of this minilesson.

- Do students understand the purpose of the reading list and how to use it?
- Do they understand the terms *reader's notebook, reading list, title, author, genre,* and *response*?

Minilesson

To help students think about the minilesson principle, engage them in a demonstration and discussion about how to fill in the reading list in a reader's notebook. Here is an example.

- Direct students to find the yellow tab that says Reading List. Then tell them to turn to the white page titled Reading List, and give them a couple of minutes to look over the page.

  What will you write on this page in your reader's notebook?

- Display the prepared chart.

  What do you notice about how I listed a few books on my reading list? What information did I provide about each one?

  What do you think the letters *TL*, *F*, and *RF* mean?

- Direct students' attention to the Reading Requirements page on the front of the yellow tab and point out the genre codes. Hold up *The Science of a Tornado.*

  If I were going to read this book today, how would I record it on my reading list? What do you think I should write first?

- Demonstrate filling in the columns marked #, *Title*, and *Author*.

  What will I write on my list when I've finished reading it?

- Discuss the columns marked *Genre Code*, *Date Completed*, and *One-Word Response* and demonstrate filling them in.

Have a Try

Invite the students to talk with a partner about how to record books.

- Display the cover of *Jacques Cousteau: Conserving Underwater Worlds*.

  If I decide to read this book next, how should I list it on my reading list? Turn and talk to your partner about what I should do.

- After students turn and talk, invite a few students to share their thinking. Add the number, title, and author to the chart.

Record each book you read on your reading list.

#	Title	Author	Genre Code	Date Completed	One-Word Response
1	Tales from the Odyssey	Mary Pope Osborne	TL	9/10	Challenging
2	George's Marvelous Medicine	Roald Dahl	F	9/14	Hilarious
3	The Red Pencil	Andrea Davis Pinkney	RF	9/22	Sad
4	The Science of a Tornado	Linda Cernak	I	9/27	Interesting
5	Jacques Cousteau: Conserving Underwater Worlds	John Zronik			

Summarize and Apply

Summarize the learning and remind students to list the books they read on their reading list.

Why is it a good idea to keep a list of the books you read in your reader's notebook?

- Write the principle at the top of the chart.

  When you read today, write the title and author of the book you're reading on your reading list. When you finish reading it, fill in the rest of the information.

Share

Following independent reading time, gather students together in the meeting area to discuss their reading lists.

What did you read today?

How did you record that book on your reading list? What information did you write?

Extend the Lesson (Optional)

After assessing students' understanding, you might decide to extend the learning.

- Invite students to look at their reading lists and notice whether they are reading all one type of book or whether they are reading a variety of genres.

RML 3
WAR.U1.RML3

Reading Minilesson Principle

Keep a tally of the kinds of books you read.

Introducing a Reader's Notebook

You Will Need

- six realistic fiction books
- two biographies
- chart paper prepared with the Reading Requirements page from *Reader's Notebook: Advanced* (Fountas and Pinnell 2011), filled in with the specific reading requirements you have chosen for your students (the requirements given in this lesson are merely intended as examples)
- markers

Academic Language / Important Vocabulary

- reader's notebook
- genre
- requirement
- realistic fiction
- biography

Continuum Connection

- Record in Reader's Notebook the titles, authors, illustrators, genre of texts read independently, and the dates read (pp. 200, 203)

Goal

Keep track of how many books are read in a particular genre in the reader's notebook.

Rationale

When students read books from a variety of genres (and keep track of their progress), they become well-rounded readers. Reading books outside of their preferred genres allows students to step outside the comfort zone and expand their reading interests, literary and general knowledge, and vocabulary.

Assess Learning

Observe students when they use a reader's notebook and notice if there is evidence of new learning based on the goal of this minilesson.

- Do students keep a tally of the genres of the books they have read?
- Do they use the terms *reader's notebook, genre, requirement, realistic fiction,* and *biography*?

Minilesson

To help students think about the minilesson principle, demonstrate how to tally books on the Reading Requirements page of a reader's notebook (adjust to fit your specific reading requirements). Here is an example.

- Display the prepared chart.

  The title of this page in the reader's notebook is Reading Requirements. What is a requirement?

- Point to the numbers in the column labeled *Requirement*.

  What do you think these numbers mean?

- Point to the tally column.

  What do you think you'll write in this column?

- Point to a pile of six realistic fiction books.

  Here are six realistic fiction books that I plan to read. After I read the first one, I'll write one mark here.

- Demonstrate tallying the books on the chart, pausing after making the first four marks.

  After I read the fifth book, I'll make a mark that goes through the first four marks. After I read the sixth book, I will make a new mark that is separate from the first five. When I have read a lot of realistic fiction books, I will be able to count them easily by counting by fives.

Have a Try

Invite the students to talk with a partner about how to tally books.

- Display two biographies.

  Turn and talk to your partner about how to tally these books on the Reading Requirements page.

- After students turn and talk, invite a volunteer to share his or her thinking. Add two tally marks to the row for biography and authobiography.

Reading Requirements
Total Books: 40

Requirement	Genre	Tally
5	(RF) Realistic Fiction	~~IIII~~ I
2	(HF) Historical Fiction	
5	(TL) Traditional Literature	
5	(F) Fantasy	
2	(SF) Science Fiction	
3	(B) Biography/ Autobiography	//
	(M) Memoir	
5	(I) Informational	
1	(P) Poetry	
1	(H) Hybrid	

Summarize and Apply

Summarize the learning and remind students to tally the kinds of books they read.

> This year you will read books from many different genres, but most of the books you read can be from any genre you like.
>
> Today, read any book you like and notice what genre it is. When you finish reading it, make a tally mark on your Reading Requirements page next to the genre of the book.

Share

Following independent reading time, gather students together in the meeting area to discuss their Reading Requirements pages.

> What did you write on your Reading Requirements page today?

Extend the Lesson (Optional)

After assessing students' understanding, you might decide to extend the learning.

- You may want to talk with each student individually about personal reading requirements.
- Review students' tallies regularly to make sure they are on track to meet the requirements and are reading a variety of books.

RML 4
WAR.U1.RML4

Reading Minilesson Principle

Follow the guidelines to help you do your best reading and writing work.

Introducing a Reader's Notebook

You Will Need

- chart paper and markers

Academic Language / Important Vocabulary

- reader's notebook
- guidelines

Continuum Connection

- Listen with attention during instruction, and respond with statements and questions (p. 339)

Goal

Learn and/or develop the guidelines for working together in the classroom.

Rationale

When you teach students to follow guidelines, they are better equipped to do their best work. You might have students review the established guidelines in *Reader's Notebook: Advanced* (Fountas and Pinnell 2011) or construct their own. When students play an active role in developing guidelines, they take ownership of them.

Assess Learning

Observe students during literacy work and notice if there is evidence of new learning based on the goal of this minilesson.

- Do students follow the guidelines established during this minilesson?
- Do they use and understand the terms *reader's notebook* and *guidelines*?

Minilesson

If you have *Reader's Notebook: Advanced*, you can read and discuss the guidelines printed on the inside front cover or you may choose to develop guidelines with your students, as demonstrated in the lesson below. If you construct the guidelines with your students, provide a copy of the guidelines for them to glue into their reader's notebooks after the lesson.

- Divide students into small groups.

  You have been learning about what to do when it's time to read and write independently and how to use a reader's notebook. Today we're going to make a list of guidelines for that time. What are guidelines?

  A guideline is a rule or suggestion about how something should be done. Talk with your group about what you should all agree to do so that you can do your best work.

- After time for discussion, invite each group to share their thinking. Record their responses on chart paper. If needed, prompt students with questions such as the following:
  - *What should you do when it's independent reading time?*
  - *What kind of voice should you use when you and others are reading?*
  - *What kind of voice should you use when you are working with a teacher?*
  - *What should you do if you give a book a good chance but you're still not enjoying it?*
  - *What should you do each time you start a new book?*
  - *What should you think about while you're reading?*

Have a Try

Invite the students to talk with a partner about the guidelines.

> Turn and talk to your partner about anything else you think we should add to our guidelines.

- After time for discussion, invite several students to share their thinking. Add any new guidelines to the list, if appropriate.

Summarize and Apply

Summarize the learning and remind students to follow the guidelines for literacy work.

> Today we made a list of guidelines for independent reading. Why is it important to follow these guidelines?

- Direct students to look at the guidelines inside the front cover of *Reader's Notebook: Advanced* or provide copies of the guidelines on the chart for students to glue into a plain notebook.

> When you are reading or writing on your own today, be sure to follow the guidelines we created together. If you think of anything else that you'd like to add to the guidelines, bring your ideas to share when we come back together.

Guidelines to Help You Do Your Best Reading and Writing Work

1. Read a book or write down your thoughts about your reading.
2. Work silently so that you and your classmates can do your best thinking.
3. Use a soft voice when conferring with a teacher.
4. Choose books that you think you'll enjoy and abandon books that aren't working for you after you've given them a good chance.
5. List the book information when you begin reading and record the date and a one-word response when you finish the book.
6. Think about the genre of the book you are reading and what you notice.
7. Always do your best work.

Share

Following independent reading time, gather students together in the meeting area to talk about the guidelines.

> How did the guidelines help you do your best thinking today?
>
> Does anyone have anything to add to our guidelines?

Extend the Lesson (Optional)

After assessing students' understanding, you might decide to extend the learning.

- Revisit the list of guidelines with your students from time to time to see how they are working and to decide whether they need to be revised.

Assessment

After you have taught the minilessons in this umbrella, observe students as they talk and write about their reading across instructional contexts: interactive read-aloud, independent reading, guided reading, shared reading, and book club. Use *The Literacy Continuum* (Fountas and Pinnell 2017) to guide the observation of students' reading and writing behaviors.

- What evidence do you have of new understandings related to using a reader's notebook?
    - Do students understand the purpose of a reader's notebook?
    - Do they understand the purpose of each section?
    - Do they record the title, author, and date completed of the books they read on the reading list?
    - How well do they keep a tally of the kinds of books they have read?
    - Do they follow the guidelines for working during the time for independent reading and writing?
    - Do they use the terms *reader's notebook, reading list, writing about reading*, and *genre*?
- What other parts of the reader's notebook might you have the students start using based on your observations?

Use your observations to determine the next umbrella you will teach. You may also consult Minilessons Across the Year (pp. 61–64) for guidance.

Reader's Notebook

When this umbrella is complete, provide a copy of the minilesson principles (see resources.fountasandpinnell.com) for students to glue in the reader's notebook (in the Minilessons section if using *Reader's Notebook: Advanced* [Fountas and Pinnell 2011]), so they can refer to the information as needed.

Minilessons in This Umbrella

RML1	Make a list of the books you want to read.
RML2	Keep a tally of the kinds of writing about reading that you use in your notebook.
RML3	Take minilesson notes in your reader's notebook so you can refer to information you need.
RML4	Write about the genres you study.
RML5	Use the glossary as a tool to support your writing about reading.

Before Teaching Umbrella 2 Minilessons

Before teaching the minilessons in this umbrella, teach the minilessons in Umbrella 1: Introducing a Reader's Notebook to introduce your students to the purpose and structure of *Reader's Notebook: Advanced* (Fountas and Pinnell 2011). If you do not have it, a plain notebook can be used instead (see pp. 52–53). It would also be helpful to have taught the minilessons in Umbrella 3: Living a Reading Life in Section One: Management. The minilessons in this umbrella do not have to be taught consecutively; instead, each one may be taught when it is relevant to the work students are doing in the classroom. However, before students begin to use a reader's notebook, they should have read and discussed a variety of high-quality books, such as those listed below from the *Fountas & Pinnell Classroom™ Interactive Read-Aloud Collection*, and participated in several writing lessons incorporating shared writing.

Genre Study: Biography (Musicians)

Strange Mr. Satie: Composer of the Absurd by M. T. Anderson

I and I: Bob Marley by Tony Medina

Ella Fitzgerald: The Tale of a Vocal Virtuosa by Andrea Davis Pinkney

As you read aloud and discuss books together, help students

- talk about books they want to read and share their reasons for their choices,
- notice the characteristics of different genres, and
- write about their reading in different ways.

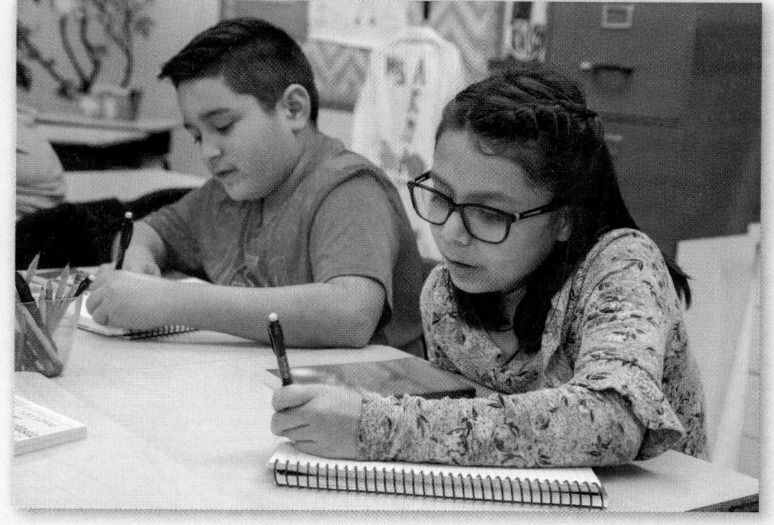

Genre Study: Biography (Musicians)

Ella Fitzgerald by Andrea Davis Pinkney

Reader's Notebook

RML1

WAR.U2.RML1

Reading Minilesson Principle

Make a list of the books you want to read.

Using a Reader's Notebook

You Will Need

- a reader's notebook for each student (if using a plain reader's notebook, create copies of a Books to Read chart)
- chart paper prepared to look like the Books to Read page from *Reader's Notebook: Advanced* (Fountas and Pinnell 2011)
- a few books from your classroom library that your students might enjoy reading independently
- markers

Academic Language / Important Vocabulary

- reader's notebook
- title
- author
- list

Continuum Connection

- Record in Reader's Notebook the titles, authors, illustrators, genre of texts read independently, and dates read (pp. 200, 203)

Goal

Create and maintain a list of books to read in the future.

Rationale

When students keep a list of the books they would like to read, they are better able to make good book choices, and they develop an identity as a reader in a community of readers where books are recommended and shared.

Assess Learning

Observe students when they talk and write about books they want to read and notice if there is evidence of new learning based on the goal of this minilesson.

- Do students add books to the Books to Read list?
- Do they use vocabulary such as *reader's notebook, title, author,* and *list*?

Minilesson

To help students think about the minilesson principle, discuss ways to choose books and how to keep a list of books to read in a reader's notebook. Here is an example.

- Direct students to turn to the Books to Read chart on the back of the yellow tab in the reader's notebook.

  What do you notice about this page? What do you think you'll write on it?

  You will make a list of books that you want to read on this page. Can anyone think of a book that you would like to read?

  You will be learning about many different ways to learn about great books to read.

- Invite a volunteer to name a book that she would like to read.

  ____________ wants to read ____________. How could she record this book on her Books to Read list? What should she write and where?

- Demonstrate writing the title, author, and genre code on the prepared chart.

  What should she do when she has finished reading the book?

- Demonstrate adding a check mark to the Check When Completed column.

Have a Try

Invite the students to start their own Books to Read lists.

> Listen carefully as I tell you about a few books from our classroom library, and think about whether you would like to read each book.

- Give a brief book talk about a few books from your classroom library. Allow time between talks for students to add the books to their Books to Read list, if they would like to do so.

> If there is another book that you would like to read, feel free to add it to your list.

Books to Read

Title	Author	Genre	Check When Completed
Bridge to Terabithia	Katherine Paterson	F	✓

Summarize and Apply

Summarize the learning and remind students to add books they would like to read to their Books to Read list.

> Why is it a good idea to keep a list of books that you want to read? When you read today, you may want to start reading one of the books on your list. You can also add books to the list whenever you learn about one you would like to read. Bring your list to share when we come back together.

Share

Following independent reading time, gather students together in the meeting area to discuss their Books to Read lists.

> Did anyone read one of the books on your Books to Read list or add a new book to your list? Which book?

Extend the Lesson (Optional)

After assessing students' understanding, you might decide to extend the learning.

- Refer to students' Books to Read lists during individual reading conferences to help them plan what to read next.
- Remind students of ways they can find out about good books to read (see MGT.U3.RML1).

RML2

WAR.U2.RML2

Reading Minilesson Principle

Keep a tally of the kinds of writing about reading that you use in your notebook.

Using a Reader's Notebook

You Will Need

- chart paper resembling the Forms for Writing About Reading page in *Reader's Notebook: Advanced* (Fountas and Pinnell 2011)
- markers
- document camera (optional)

Academic Language / Important Vocabulary

- writing about reading
- tally

Goal

Learn how to keep a tally of the different forms of writing about reading.

Rationale

When you teach students to keep a tally of the kinds of writing they do, they are more likely to write about their reading in a wide variety of ways. It would be best to help students do the recording and tallying after each form of writing is introduced (see Umbrella 5 in this section).

Assess Learning

Observe students when they keep track of the kinds of writing they do and notice if there is evidence of new learning based on the goal of this minilesson.

- Do students keep a tally of the kinds of writing about reading they used?
- Do they use and understand the terms *writing about reading* and *tally*?

Minilesson

To help students think about the minilesson principle, demonstrate how to tally forms of writing in a reader's notebook. Discuss only the forms of writing that you have already introduced to your students. Here is an example.

- Display the prepared chart paper or project the Forms for Writing About Reading page from *Reader's Notebook: Advanced*.

  What do you notice about this page? What do you think you will write on this page in your reader's notebook?

  This page lists some of the different ways to write about reading. Which of these kinds of writing have you used before?

- Based on students' responses, point to one kind of writing (e.g., book recommendation) on the list and read its definition.

  What does the third column in the chart tell you?

  The third column gives the definition of each type of writing. It also describes each type of writing.

- Point to the first column and read the heading, *Tally*.

  What will you write in this column?

  In this column, keep a tally of the different kinds of writing you use. Who remembers how to keep a tally?

- If necessary, review (or teach) how to keep a tally and count tally marks (see WAR.U1.RML3).

Have a Try

Invite the students to enter tally marks for the kinds of writing they have used.

> If you have already used any of these types of writing about reading in your reader's notebook this year, add a tally mark on your list.

- Invite a volunteer to demonstrate how to add a tally mark next to one kind of writing about reading.

Forms for Writing About Reading

Tally	Kind of Writing	Definition
	Summary	a few sentences that tell the most important information
I	Book Recommendation	writing that gives another reader some information and advice on a book
	Book Review	an opinion and analysis that includes comments on the quality of a book and gives another reader advice
	Poem	a poetic piece that responds to a book (characters, setting, story events)
	Blog	a blend of the term "web log," a blog has entries of comments, descriptions of events, or other information

Summarize and Apply

Summarize the learning and remind students to keep track of the kinds of writing they use.

> What did you learn how to do today in your reader's notebook?
>
> If you write about your reading today, remember to make a tally mark next to the kind of writing that you use.

Share

Following independent reading time, gather students together in the meeting area to talk about their writing about reading.

> Who wrote about your reading today?
>
> What kind of writing did you use?
>
> How did you keep track of it in your reader's notebook?

Extend the Lesson (Optional)

After assessing students' understanding, you might decide to extend the learning.

- You will need to decide which forms of writing about reading are appropriate for your students. After teaching each new form of writing, read aloud its definition on the Forms for Writing About Reading page and remind students to keep track of the kinds of writing they use.

RML 3
WAR.U2.RML3

Reading Minilesson Principle

Take minilesson notes in your reader's notebook so you can refer to information you need.

Using a Reader's Notebook

You Will Need

- a chart from a recently taught minilesson or the principles from a recently taught umbrella (see **resources.fountasandpinnell.com**) plus added notes
- chart paper and markers
- a reader's notebook for each student

Academic Language / Important Vocabulary

- reader's notebook
- minilesson
- principle
- information
- notes

Goal

Keep minilesson notes in a reader's notebook to refer to when needed.

Rationale

When students keep information from previous minilessons, they are better able to remember what they learned and to use and build on that knowledge. At the end of each minilesson, have students copy the minilesson principle into a reader's notebook and make notes. Or you can download the minilesson principles for students to glue in the Minilessons section (see resources.fountasandpinnell.com).

Assess Learning

Observe students when they use the Minilessons section of the reader's notebook and notice if there is evidence of new learning based on the goal of this minilesson.

- Do students neatly write (or glue) the minilesson principles into the Minilessons section of the reader's notebook and add notes?
- Do they understand the terms *reader's notebook, minilesson, principle, information,* and *notes*?

Minilesson

Teach students how to take notes about minilessons in the reader's notebook and engage them in a discussion about how and when they might use them. Here is an example.

- Direct students to turn to the Minilessons section (gray tab) of the reader's notebook. Have them read the page silently.

  What will you write in this section of your reader's notebook?

- Display a chart from a recently taught minilesson.

  When we have minilessons, we usually make a chart together about what you are learning. Often I write the minilesson principle at the top. The principle tells the important understanding you need to learn.

  At the end of each minilesson, you will have the chance to take notes in your reader's notebook about what you learned. Watch what I do.

- On a separate sheet of chart paper, copy the minilesson principle from the chart and write a few notes about the minilesson underneath it (e.g., examples of books, important terms and definitions).

  What did you notice about the notes I wrote about the minilesson?

  Because you will put all your minilesson notes in the same section, you will always know where to find them if you need to remember what you have learned.

Have a Try

Invite the students to talk with a partner about when and why they might use their notes from previous minilessons.

> The gray tab in the reader's notebook says "You can look back at what you learned when you need to." When might you need to look back at the information from a minilesson? Turn and talk about when you might do this and why.

- After students turn and talk, invite several to share.

Summarize and Apply

Summarize the learning and remind students to take notes about minilessons in the Minilessons section to refer to as needed.

> Let's make a chart to help you remember what you learned from this minilesson. What do you think we should put on our chart?

- After writing the chart with students' input, write the principle at the top.

> Now take a few minutes to make notes about what you learned from this minilesson in your reader's notebook. Then read a book! Bring your notes to share when we come back together.

Share

Following independent reading time, gather students together in the meeting area to talk about their notes.

> What did you write in your reader's notebook about today's minilesson?
>
> How might your notes help you in the future?

Understanding Fiction and Nonfiction Genres

There are different genres of fiction books.
fantasy, realism, realistic fiction, historical fiction

There are different genres of nonfiction books.
expository, biography, memoir

There are several types of traditional literature.
folktales, fairy tales, tall tales

Take minilesson notes in your reader's notebook so you can refer to information you need.

- Write the minilesson principles in the Minilessons section of your reader's notebook.
- If you want to, write some examples or notes to help you better remember the information.
- Reread the principles and notes when you need to.

Extend the Lesson (Optional)

After assessing students' understanding, you might decide to extend the learning.

- If students are not up to writing the principles and notes for each umbrella, download the page of minilesson principles for each umbrella (see resources.fountasandpinnell.com) and have students glue it into a reader's notebook.

RML4
WAR.U2.RML4

Reading Minilesson Principle

Write about the genres you study.

Using a Reader's Notebook

You Will Need

- charts from a recently taught genre studies umbrella (e.g., LA.U16.RML1 and RML2)
- chart paper resembling the Genre Studies form in *Reader's Notebook: Advanced* (Fountas and Pinnell 2011)
- markers
- two or three familiar biographies, such as these from Text Set: Genre Study: Biography (Musicians):
  - *Strange Mr. Satie* by M. T. Anderson
  - *I and I: Bob Marley* by Tony Medina
  - *Ella Fitzgerald* by Andrea Davis Pinkney
- a reader's notebook for each student

Academic Language / Important Vocabulary

- reader's notebook
- genre
- definition
- examples
- noticings

Continuum Connection

- Record the titles, authors, and genres of books to recommend (pp. 200, 203)

Goal

Write a working definition of the genre, book examples, and noticings about the characteristics of the genre.

Rationale

When students take notes about the genres they study, they are more likely to remember what they noticed and learned about the genre.

Assess Learning

Observe students when they write about genres in a reader's notebook and notice if there is evidence of new learning based on the goal of this minilesson.

- Can students write a working definition, noticings, and book examples for each genre they study in their reader's notebook?
- Do they understand the terms *reader's notebook, genre, definition, examples,* and *noticings*?

Minilesson

This minilesson should be taught immediately or shortly after finishing a genre studies umbrella. The following example references biography (Umbrella 16: Studying Biography in Section Two: Literary Analysis), but you can adapt the lesson to fit a genre your students have studied.

- Direct students to turn to the back of the orange Genre Studies tab in the reader's notebook.

  What do you think you will write in this section of your reader's notebook?

- Display a genre definition chart from a recently taught genre studies umbrella. Also display the prepared chart and several biographies.

  We've been studying biographies lately. I want to take some notes about biographies so I can remember what I've learned. What should I write on the line at the top of the Genre Studies page?

- Demonstrate writing the name of the genre on the line at the top of the enlarged page.

  What should I write in the Working Definition section?

- Copy the definition from the definition chart onto the Genre Studies form. Then display the noticings chart from the genre studies umbrella.

  What should I write in the Noticings section?

- Copy the noticings from the noticings chart onto the Genre Studies form.

Have a Try

Invite the students to talk with a partner about examples of the genre.

> Turn and talk to your partner about what we should write in the Book Examples section of the page. What are some examples of biographies that we have read?

- After students turn and talk, invite a few students to share their thinking. Add book examples to the chart.

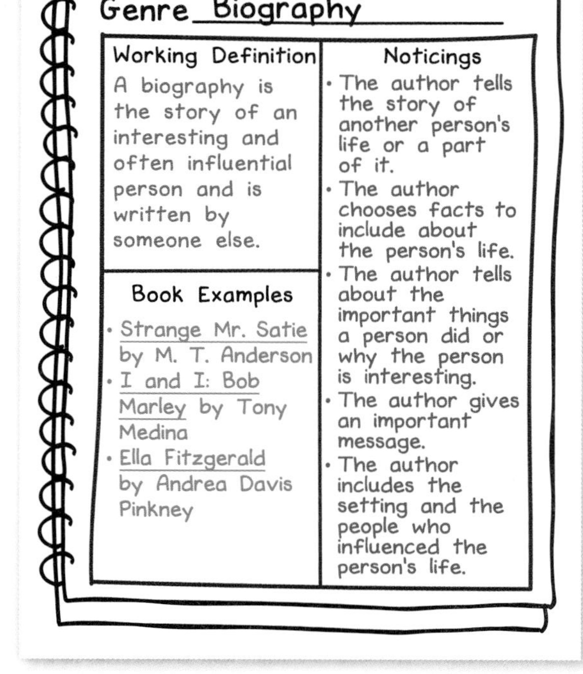

Summarize and Apply

Summarize the learning and remind students to write about the genres they study.

> Why is it a good idea to write about the genres you study in your reader's notebook?
>
> Before you read today, take a few minutes to copy our notes about biographies onto the first blank page in the Genre Studies section of your reader's notebook. You can also make a note of anything else you've noticed about biographies or about any other specific biographies that you've read. Bring your reader's notebook to share when we come back together.

Share

Following independent reading time, gather students together in the meeting area to discuss their notes.

> What did you write about biographies in your reader's notebook today?

Extend the Lesson (Optional)

After assessing students' understanding, you might decide to extend the learning.

- At the end of each subsequent genre studies minilesson, give students time to make notes about their learning in a reader's notebook.

RML 5

WAR.U2.RML5

Reading Minilesson Principle

Use the glossary as a tool to support your writing about reading.

Using a Reader's Notebook

You Will Need

- chart paper and markers
- a reader's notebook for each student

Academic Language / Important Vocabulary

- reader's notebook
- glossary
- term
- definition

Goal

Use the glossary as a tool to support writing about reading.

Rationale

When students are familiar with literary terms, they can communicate their ideas about what they read more clearly and precisely. *Reader's Notebook: Advanced* [Fountas and Pinnell 2011] includes a glossary of literary terms, which students can use to remind themselves of this language.

Assess Learning

Observe students when they write about their reading and notice if there is evidence of new learning based on the goal of this minilesson.

- Do students understand the purpose of the glossary and know how to use it?
- Do they understand the terms *reader's notebook, glossary, term,* and *definition*?

Minilesson

Discuss the Glossary of Terms in *Reader's Notebook: Advanced* and engage students in using the glossary to revise a prepared piece of writing. Here is an example.

- Direct students to turn to the Glossary of Terms section (blue tab) of the reader's notebook. Give them a few minutes to review this section silently.

  What do you notice about this section of the reader's notebook?

- Guide students to notice that the glossary contains definitions of genres, literary terms, and different text structures.

  When and why might you use this section? How might it be helpful?

- Record students' responses on the chart paper.
- Ask students to read the definitions of a few of the genres listed in the glossary (e.g., biography, historical fiction, legend).

  How might these definitions be a helpful resource?

- Record students' responses on the chart.
- Repeat the same process, drawing students' attention to the parts of the glossary that address text structure.

Have a Try

Invite the students to further explore the glossary with a partner.

> Find one or two literary terms that are either new to you or that you need clarified. Talk with your partner about the terms you find.

- After students turn and talk, invite a few to share what they discovered.

> Are there any other ways that the glossary might be helpful for you?

- Record additional ideas on the chart.

Use the glossary as a tool to support your writing about reading.

Ways to Use the Reader's Notebook Glossary

- Make sure you understand a literary term.
- Look up literary terms to use in letters about reading.
- Check the definition of a genre.
- Use the genre definitions to make sure you use the right genre code on the reading list.
- Check the spelling of literary terms.

Summarize and Apply

Summarize the learning and remind students to use the glossary as a tool to support their writing about reading.

> Today you learned how you can use the glossary as a tool to support your writing about reading.

- Write the principle at the top of the chart.

> After you read today, write about your reading in your reader's notebook. Use the literary terms you have learned when appropriate. If you need help remembering a term, use the glossary.

Share

Following independent reading time, gather students together in the meeting area to talk about their writing about reading.

> Did anyone use the glossary in the reader's notebook when you wrote about your reading today?
>
> How did the glossary help you?

Extend the Lesson (Optional)

After assessing students' understanding, you might decide to extend the learning.

- During literary analysis lessons, you might have students highlight terms in the glossary as they are introduced.
- When doing shared writing, model using the glossary to look up literary terms.

Assessment

After you have taught the minilessons in this umbrella, observe students as they talk and write about their reading across instructional contexts: interactive read-aloud, independent reading, guided reading, shared reading, and book club. Use *The Literacy Continuum* (Fountas and Pinnell 2017) to guide the observation of students' reading and writing behaviors.

- What evidence do you have of new understandings related to using the reader's notebook?
    - Are students continuing to add to the list of books they want to read?
    - Do they keep a tally of the forms of writing about reading they have used?
    - Do they take notes about minilessons in reader's notebooks and refer to them when appropriate?
    - Do they take notes about the genres they study?
    - Do they use the glossary to support their writing about reading?
    - Do they use the terms *title, author, list, minilesson*, *genre*, and *tally*?
- Based on your observations, what other ways might you have your students write about reading in a reader's notebook?

Use your observations to determine the next umbrella you will teach. You may also consult Minilessons Across the Year (pp. 61–64) for guidance.

Reader's Notebook

When this umbrella is complete, provide a copy of the minilesson principles (see resources.fountasandpinnell.com) for students to glue in the reader's notebook (in the Minilessons section if using *Reader's Notebook: Advanced* [Fountas and Pinnell 2011]), so they can refer to the information as needed.

Minilessons in This Umbrella

RML1	Share your thinking about your reading in a letter.
RML2	Respond to the teacher's questions to you when you write your next letter.
RML3	Know the qualities of a strong letter about your reading.

Before Teaching Umbrella 3 Minilessons

Writing letters about reading is an authentic way for students to discuss texts with another reader. We suggest having each student write one letter about reading each week. We believe it is important that their writing is read by you and that you provide a response, so you will need to develop a management system for receiving and responding to the letters. You might have all students turn in a reader's notebook on one day each week (e.g., Friday), or we suggest that you stagger the due dates for four or five students each day so you can provide regular responses to their thinking without being overwhelmed by a large stack. If responding every week is difficult, consider every-other-week responses (see pp. 53–55 for more about letters about reading and the reading-writing connection).

To teach the minilessons in this umbrella, we suggest having everyone write a letter so they can apply these understandings as the minilessons are taught. Sometimes students will start a new letter; other times they will work on a letter in progress.

To teach the minilessons in this umbrella, use letters that you have written as a model. For mentor texts, use the books from the *Fountas & Pinnell Classroom™ Interactive Read-Aloud Collection* text sets listed below or choose books from your own classroom library.

Conflict Resolution

Desmond and the Very Mean Word by Archbishop Desmond Tutu and Douglas Carlton Abrams

Thirty Minutes Over Oregon: A Japanese Pilot's World War II Story by Marc Tyler Nobleman

The Power of Knowledge

Richard Wright and the Library Card by William Miller

Empathy

Mrs. Katz and Tush by Patricia Polacco

As you read aloud and enjoy these texts together, help students

- think, talk, and express opinions about texts,
- discuss the author's message, and
- mark interesting parts of their reading that they want to include in a letter.

Conflict Resolution

The Power of Knowledge

Empathy

Reader's Notebook

RML 1
WAR.U3.RML1

Reading Minilesson Principle

Share your thinking about your reading in a letter.

Writing Letters to Share Thinking About Books

You Will Need

- chart paper prepared with a letter about a book that you recently read aloud to your students, such as one of the following:
  - *Desmond and the Very Mean Word* by Archbishop Desmond Tutu and Douglas Carlton Abrams, from Text Set: Conflict Resolution
  - *Richard Wright and the Library Card* by William Miller, from Text Set: The Power of Knowledge
- chart paper and markers
- a reader's notebook for each student

Academic Language / Important Vocabulary

- opinion
- genre
- summary
- message
- evidence
- support

Continuum Connection

- Compose notes, lists, letters, or statements to remember important information about a text (p. 200)
- Form and express opinions about a text in writing and support those opinions with rationales and evidence (pp. 201, 204)

Goal

Understand some of the different ways to share thinking about books in a letter and how to provide evidence for that thinking.

Rationale

In this minilesson, students will learn how to share their thoughts about their reading by writing a letter and to support their statements with evidence from the text or personal experience. This will help them to read more closely and think critically about what they are reading.

Assess Learning

Assess students' letters. Notice if there is evidence of new learning based on the goal of this minilesson.

- Can students share various kinds of thinking about their reading in their letters?
- Do they provide evidence from the text and/or personal experience?
- Do they understand and use terms in their letters such as *opinion*, *genre*, *summary*, *message*, *evidence*, and *support*?

Minilesson

To help students think about the minilesson principle, use a letter as a model to help students learn about the kind of thinking they can share in their letters and how to provide evidence for one's thinking. Here is an example.

- Display the prepared letter.

  Today, I will share my thinking about a book you all know in a letter I wrote to you. First of all, notice what is at the very beginning and the very end of my letter. These parts are called the date, the greeting (or salutation), and the closing.

- Read the letter aloud.

  What do you notice about what I wrote in my letter? What kinds of things did I write about?

- Record students' responses on chart paper under the heading *Ways to Share Thinking*. Generalize the responses if they are overly specific. Point out parts of the letter, such as a personal opinion, characters' names, and the setting.

  Whenever you share your thinking about a book, you need to provide evidence, or proof, for your thinking. When you provide evidence, give specific details from the book or from your own life to show why you think something. What evidence did I give you to support my thinking?

- Point out the evidence from the book and from your personal experience.

  What do you notice about the punctuation for the evidence?

  If you copy the exact words from a book, use quotation marks. You should also put the page number that you got them from, if the book has page numbers.

Have a Try

Invite the students to talk with a partner about what they might include in a letter about their reading.

Turn and talk about what you could write in a letter about *Richard Wright and the Library Card*.

- Explain that students can write about what they talked about. Relate their ideas to the chart and add new ideas.

Summarize and Apply

Summarize the learning and remind students to share their thinking about books in their letters.

Today, start writing a letter about *Richard Wright and the Library Card* in your reader's notebook. Use the chart for ideas of what to include in your writing. Remember to provide evidence for your thinking in your letter. Use my letter as a model. Bring your reader's notebook when we come back together.

November 14

Dear Class,

The book Desmond and the Very Mean Word made a strong impression on me. A group of boys yelled a very mean word at Desmond, a young boy in South Africa. Father Trevor encouraged Desmond to think about forgiveness. Father Trevor said, "When you forgive someone, you free yourself from what they have said or done. It's like magic." (p. 18) I understand how Desmond felt because I can think of a time when it was hard for me to forgive someone.

The authors want us to think about how forgiving someone makes us free because they wrote that Desmond felt free. If my feelings are hurt, I will try to forgive.

Your teacher,
Mrs. Schultz

Ways to Share Thinking

- Give a well-organized short summary (title, characters, setting, problem, solution).
- Tell what you notice about the illustrations.
- Tell what you learned about the characters and how they changed.
- Give opinions about the book.
- Tell the author's message.
- Explain how the book reminds you of something in your life, another book, or something in the world.
- Describe the setting and why it's important.
- Give interesting examples of the author's writing.
- Pose questions or wonderings.
- Provide evidence for your thinking, including quotes.

Share

Following independent reading time, gather students together in the meeting area to talk about their letters.

Who would like to read aloud your letter about *Richard Wright and the Library Card*? It's okay if you haven't finished writing. You'll have a chance to work on it later.

Extend the Lesson (Optional)

After assessing students' understanding, you might decide to extend the learning.

- There is a list of starter ideas in the Writing About Reading section of *Reader's Notebook: Advanced* (Fountas and Pinnell 2011) that students can refer to if they need help deciding what to write about.
- Have students highlight examples of evidence in their own letters.

RML 2

WAR.U3.RML2

Reading Minilesson Principle

Respond to the teacher's questions to you when you write your next letter.

Writing Letters to Share Thinking About Books

You Will Need

- chart paper prepared with a pair of letters between teacher and student about a book that you have recently read, such as *Thirty Minutes Over Oregon* by Marc Tyler Nobleman, from Text Set: Conflict Resolution
- highlighters
- a reader's notebook for each student

Academic Language / Important Vocabulary

- respond
- dialogue

Continuum Connection

- Follow a topic and add to a discussion with comments on the same topic (p. 339)

Goal

Understand that letters about reading are an ongoing conversation with the teacher.

Rationale

When you teach students to respond to the questions you have asked them, they begin to understand that the purpose of writing letters about reading is to engage in an ongoing discussion about books with another reader. This minilesson should ideally be taught when students have already written at least two letters and have received two responses back from you. Make sure that you include at least one question in each of your responses.

Assess Learning

Assess students' letters. Notice if there is evidence of new learning based on the goal of this minilesson.

- Do students write thoughtful responses to the questions you have asked them?
- Do they understand the terms *respond* and *dialogue*?

Minilesson

To help students think about the minilesson principle, use a sample letter to demonstrate how to respond to your questions in their responses to your letters. Here is an example.

- Show the cover of *Thirty Minutes Over Oregon*.

  We read and talked about *Thirty Minutes Over Oregon* together recently. Carlos shared his thinking about the book in a letter. This is what I wrote back to him.

- Display and read aloud the first letter.

  What do you notice about this letter?

- Ask a volunteer to come up and highlight the questions in the letter.

  What do you think Carlos might write in his next letter?

- Help students understand that they should answer any questions that you pose in your letter. Then read the second letter.

  Every time you write a letter to me about your reading, I will write a letter back to you. Sometimes, I will ask you questions in my letter. It's important that you read my questions, think about them, and respond to them in your letter back to me. Our letters will be a dialogue, or conversation, about books.

Have a Try

Invite the students to think about how they will respond to questions in the letters you write to them.

- Direct students to open their reader's notebooks to the most recent letter that you wrote to them.

  As you read my letter to you, look for questions and highlight them.

  Now turn and talk to your partner about one question that you found in my letter and how you might answer it.

Summarize and Apply

Summarize the learning and remind students to respond to your questions in their letters.

When you write a letter today or later this week, be sure to read my letter, highlight any questions I asked, and respond to the questions. Today you can either start a new letter or work on a letter you have started.

Share

Following independent reading time, gather students together in the meeting area to talk about their letters.

Who wrote a letter today and would like to share how you responded to my questions?

Extend the Lesson (Optional)

After assessing students' understanding, you might decide to extend the learning.

- Increase the complexity of your questions as students demonstrate the ability to respond thoughtfully to them. For example, in the beginning you might ask simple questions such as "What did you like about the book?" whereas later on you might ask questions like "Why do you think the main character did that?"
- Teach students to keep the conversation about books going by having them ask *you* questions when they write their letters.

November 14

Dear Carlos,

I thought Thirty Minutes Over Oregon was an interesting story, too. In your letter you wrote about Nobuo receiving the invitation to visit Oregon for the Memorial Day festival. I was surprised he was invited to the festival! He did try to bomb their state. Why do you think Nobuo accepted the invitation? How did he feel about going back to Oregon? What makes you think that?

After the students from Brookings visited Japan, Nobuo said, "The war is finally over for me." What did he mean? Why do you think he said that?

Your teacher,

Mrs. Schultz

November 24

Dear Mrs. Schultz,

I was kind of surprised they invited him to Oregon, too. I think Nobuo wanted to go to Oregon because he wanted to apologize for bombing their country. The book said he brought his sword to Oregon. If they accepted his apology, he would give them the sword. If they didn't accept, he said he would commit suicide. That makes me think he was nervous about the reaction of the Americans.

I think Nobuo said that the war was finally over because the people from two different countries had come together. Both sides of the war were able to share and accept one another's country.

From,

Carlos

RML 3
WAR.U3.RML3

Reading Minilesson Principle

Know the qualities of a strong letter about your reading.

Writing Letters to Share Thinking About Books

You Will Need

- chart paper prepared with a strong student-written letter about a book that you recently read aloud, such as *Mrs. Katz and Tush* by Patricia Polacco, from Text Set: Empathy
- chart paper and markers
- a reader's notebook for each student

Academic Language / Important Vocabulary

- qualities
- evidence

Continuum Connection

- Write in a way that speaks directly to the reader (p. 292)
- Show enthusiasm and energy for the topic (p. 292)
- Understand that a writer can learn to write effective business letters by studying the characteristics of examples (p. 286)

Goal

Identify the qualities of a strong letter, including content and conventions.

Rationale

When students can identify what makes a letter strong and assess letters against those standards, they are able to think more deeply about the books they read and communicate their thinking clearly in their letters. Note: This minilesson should be taught after students have written at least three letters about their reading.

Assess Learning

Assess students' letters. Notice if there is evidence of new learning based on the goal of this minilesson.

- Can students identify the qualities of a strong letter?
- Do they include these qualities when writing their own letters?
- Do they understand the terms *qualities* and *evidence*?

Minilesson

To help students think about the minilesson principle, use a prepared letter example to engage students in a discussion about the qualities of a strong letter. Here is an example.

- Display the prepared letter and read it aloud.

  Here's a letter a student wrote that shows her best thinking. What makes it a strong letter?

- Invite student responses. If necessary, prompt students with questions such as these:
  - *How does she share her thinking about the text?*
  - *What makes this letter interesting to read?*
  - *Does her letter make sense?*
  - *How does she let you know what she was reading?*
  - *Does it have all the parts of a letter?*
  - *Does she give you an idea about what the author is like?*
  - *Does her writing sound like talking?*
- Use the students' noticings to create a list of qualities of a strong letter on chart paper. This will serve as a checklist for students to use when they write their next letter.

Have a Try

Invite the students to talk with a partner about one of their own reader's notebook letters.

> Look at the last letter you wrote or one you are working on. What makes it strong? Are there parts that could be improved? Share these thoughts with a partner.

- When students have finished sharing with their partners, ask a few to share their thoughts with the class. Add new ideas to the chart.

Summarize and Apply

Summarize the learning and remind students to refer to the checklist when assessing their own letters.

> Today you thought about the qualities of a strong letter. Look through the letters you have written. Which one shows your best thinking? What makes it strong? Bring your letter with you to share when we come back together.

Share

Following independent reading time, gather students together in the meeting area to talk about their letters.

> Turn and talk to a partner about the letter you chose. What parts show your best thinking? What makes this a strong letter?

Extend the Lesson (Optional)

After assessing students' understanding, you might decide to extend the learning.

- Invite students to write a few sentences or a paragraph telling what makes the letter they chose strong.
- Use the form called Assessment of Letters in Reader's Notebook (p. 55) to assess your students' letters (visit resources.fountasandpinnell.com to download the resource).

December 4

Dear Mrs. Schultz,

I read Mrs. Katz and Tush by Patricia Polacco. When I first started reading this book I wondered why a young boy and an older lady would spend time together. I don't think I would have fun spending time with an older person. At first, I thought Larnel was just being polite. As I continued reading, guess what? I found that the two enjoyed spending time together and even had some things in common! They both enjoyed cats and Larnel enjoyed Mrs. Katz's cooking. They talked about all kinds of things. I was surprised to find out that Larnel's family had a similar history to Mrs. Katz's family.

I think the author wanted us to think about how even when two people seem very different, they might find that they have some things in common.

Your student,
Charlotte

Qualities of a Strong Letter

- ✓ Is enjoyable to read
- ✓ Includes information about the book: title and author
- ✓ Makes sense
- ✓ Uses letter format: date, greeting, closing
- ✓ Has evidence from the book or personal experience
- ✓ Sometimes uses a quote from the book
- ✓ Is neat and easy to read
- ✓ Shows best spelling and punctuation
- ✓ Shares the parts of the text you enjoyed or found interesting
- ✓ Sounds like talking
- ✓ Asks questions you have about the book
- ✓ Provides responses to the teacher's questions

Assessment

After you have taught the minilessons in this umbrella, observe students as they talk and write about their reading across instructional contexts: interactive read-aloud, independent reading, guided reading, shared reading, and book club. Use *The Literacy Continuum* (Fountas and Pinnell 2017) to guide the observation of students' reading and writing behaviors.

- What evidence do you have of new understandings related to writing letters about reading?
    - Do students write a letter about their reading each week?
    - Do they include evidence from the text or personal experience to support their thinking?
    - Are they making their letters interesting by writing with voice and including genuine thoughts and reactions to the text?
    - Are they consistently responding to questions in their letters?
    - Can they identify the qualities of a strong letter?
    - Do they use terms such as *quality, evidence,* and *respond* when they talk about their letters about reading?
- In what other ways, beyond the scope of this umbrella, are students writing about books?
    - Are students using other forms of writing to share their thinking about books?
    - Are they writing about longer chapter books over the course of several letters?

Use your observations to determine the next umbrella you will teach. You may also consult Minilessons Across the Year (pp. 61–64) for guidance.

Reader's Notebook

When this umbrella is complete, provide a copy of the minilesson principles (see resources.fountasandpinnell.com) for students to glue in the reader's notebook (in the Minilessons section if using *Reader's Notebook: Advanced* [Fountas and Pinnell 2011]), so they can refer to the information as needed.

Using Graphic Organizers to Share Thinking About Books

Minilessons in This Umbrella

RML1	Use a diagram to show cause and effect.
RML2	Use an outline to show the main topic of a book and its subtopics.
RML3	Use a web to show how ideas are connected.
RML4	Use a Venn diagram to compare and contrast books.
RML5	Use a grid to organize, analyze, and compare information.

Before Teaching Umbrella 4 Minilessons

Graphic organizers can reveal the structure of a piece of writing and assist in examining the content. These minilessons may be taught in any order that coordinates with relevant Literary Analysis minilessons. For a description of graphic organizers appropriate for grade 5, see page 198 in *The Literacy Continuum* (Fountas and Pinnell 2017).

The students should think and talk about the concepts before they write about them. Use books from the complete *Fountas & Pinnell Classroom* ™ *Interactive Read-Aloud Collection* text sets listed below, including the specific titles listed. Or, choose high-quality fiction and nonfiction books from your classroom library.

Author Study: Andrea Davis Pinkney

Sit-In

Martin and Mahalia

Illustrator Study: Duncan Tonatiuh

Funny Bones

Pancho Rabbit and the Coyote

Author/Illustrator Study: Demi

Confucius

The Emperor's New Clothes

Genre Study: Expository Nonfiction

The Cod's Tale by Mark Kurlansky

Empathy

Mrs. Katz and Tush by Patricia Polacco

My Man Blue by Nikki Grimes

The Crane Girl by Curtis Manley

Achieving a Dream

Sixteen Years in Sixteen Seconds by Paula Yoo

Silent Star by Bill Wise

Genre Study: Tall Tales

Paul Bunyan by Steven Kellogg

Thunder Rose by Jerdine Nolen

As you read aloud and enjoy these texts together, help students notice the underlying text structures, such as topics and subtopics, cause and effect, and comparison and contrast.

Author Study: Andrea Davis Pinkney

Illustrator Study: Duncan Tonatiuh

Author/Illustrator Study: Demi

Expository Nonfiction

Empathy

Achieving a Dream

Tall Tales

RML1

WAR.U4.RML1

Reading Minilesson Principle

Use a diagram to show cause and effect.

Using Graphic Organizers to Share Thinking About Books

You Will Need

- several familiar books that have clear examples of cause and effect, such as the following from Text Set: Achieving a Dream:
  - *Sixteen Years in Sixteen Seconds* by Paula Yoo
  - *Silent Star* by Bill Wise
- two pieces of chart paper prepared with cause-and-effect diagrams
- baskets of short fiction and nonfiction books that have clear examples of cause and effect
- a copy of a cause-and-effect diagram for each student (optional)
- To download the following online resource for this lesson, visit **resources.fountasandpinnell.com:** Cause-and-Effect Diagram

Academic Language / Important Vocabulary

- reader's notebook
- graphic organizer
- diagram
- cause and effect

Continuum Connection

- Write about the connections among texts by topic, theme, major ideas, authors' styles, and genres (pp. 200, 203)

Goal

Use a diagram to show cause and effect.

Rationale

Using a diagram to show cause and effect provides a visual representation of a common underlying structural pattern. This lesson provides a model that can be used to teach students to make graphic organizers to show other structural patterns. Students will benefit from understanding underlying text structures in nonfiction books before you teach this minilesson (see Umbrella 17: Noticing How Nonfiction Authors Choose to Organize Information in Section Two: Literary Analysis).

Assess Learning

Observe students when they make diagrams to show cause and effect and notice if there is evidence of new learning based on the goal of this minilesson.

- Are students able to determine cause and effect in books they read?
- Are they using the terms *reader's notebook, graphic organizer, diagram,* and *cause and effect*?

Minilesson

To help students think about the minilesson principle, use familiar nonfiction texts to help them think about cause and effect. Here is an example.

- Display one of the prepared cause-and-effect diagrams.

  What do you notice about this graphic organizer? How might it be used?

- Show the cover of *Sixteen Years in Sixteen Seconds* and briefly review the story.

  Sammy dreamed of being an Olympic athlete from a young age.

- Write a brief version of this on the *Effect* side of the chart.

  What events caused him to feel this way? How would you describe that cause in just a few words?

- Add student responses to the *Cause* section of the chart.

  What other events in the book can you trace back to a cause?

- As students provide responses, help them form their thoughts into just a few words that will fit in the *Cause* and *Effect* boxes on the chart.

  In what ways might this cause-and-effect diagram be helpful?

Have a Try

Invite the students to talk with a partner about using a graphic organizer to show cause and effect.

- Display a blank cause-and-effect diagram alongside *Silent Star*.

  Turn and talk to your partner about how to fill in a graphic organizer for *Silent Star*.

- As needed, review a few key pages from the story to highlight cause and effect before students turn and talk. After time for discussion, create a cause-and-effect diagram using students' ideas.

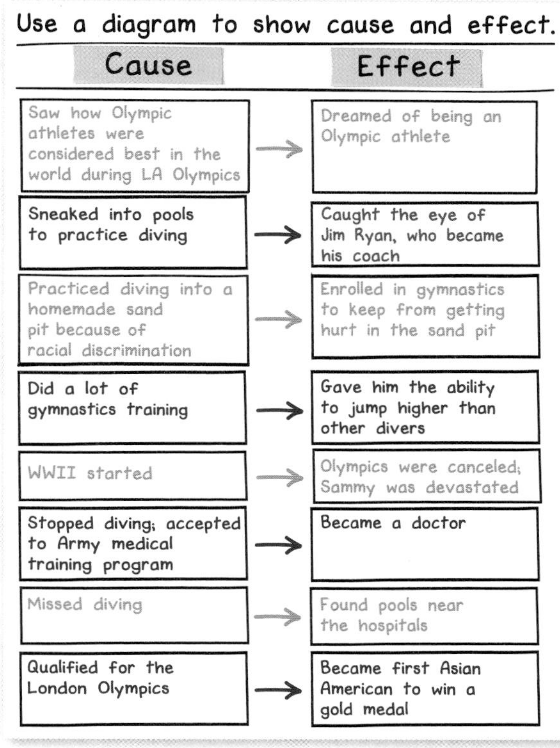

Use a diagram to show cause and effect.
Cause
Effect
Saw how Olympic athletes were considered best in the world during LA Olympics
Dreamed of being an Olympic athlete
Sneaked into pools to practice diving
Caught the eye of Jim Ryan, who became his coach
Practiced diving into a homemade sand pit because of racial discrimination
Enrolled in gymnastics to keep from getting hurt in the sand pit
Did a lot of gymnastics training
Gave him the ability to jump higher than other divers
WWII started
Olympics were canceled; Sammy was devastated
Stopped diving; accepted to Army medical training program
Became a doctor
Missed diving
Found pools near the hospitals
Qualified for the London Olympics
Became first Asian American to win a gold medal

Summarize and Apply

Summarize the learning and remind students to think about how to use a graphic organizer to show cause and effect.

You learned that you can use a diagram to show cause and effect.

- Add the principle to the chart.
- Provide baskets of fiction and nonfiction books that have clear examples of cause and effect. Provide a copy of the Cause-and-Effect Diagram for students to glue in a reader's notebook or have them make their own.

  With a partner, choose a book from the baskets to read. Work together to fill in a cause-and-effect diagram. Bring your notebook when we meet so you can share.

Share

Following independent reading time, match up sets of partners to make groups of four.

Share with your group the cause-and-effect diagram you made.

Extend the Lesson (Optional)

After assessing students' understanding, you might decide to extend the learning.

- Use a similar graphic organizer to make a problem-and-solution chart for a familiar fiction or nonfiction text.
- **Writing About Reading** Once students have completed a cause-and-effect diagram for a book, have them use it to write about the book.

RML 2
WAR.U4.RML2

Reading Minilesson Principle
Use an outline to show the main topic of a book and its subtopics.

Using Graphic Organizers to Share Thinking About Books

You Will Need

- one or more familiar books that can be used to create an outline, such as *The Cod's Tale* by Mark Kurlansky, from Text Set: Genre Study: Expository Nonfiction
- chart paper prepared with the first section (I) of an outline
- markers
- basket of nonfiction books, some of which are organized by related topics

Academic Language / Important Vocabulary

- reader's notebook
- graphic organizer
- outline
- main topic
- subtopics

Continuum Connection

- Write an outline by providing summaries of information learned using headings and subheadings that reflect a text's overall structure and simple categories (p. 204)
- Outline the main topic of a book and its subtopics (p. 204)
- Recognize that informational texts may present a larger topic with many subtopics (p. 74)

Goal

Create an outline with headings and subheadings that reflect the organization of a text.

Rationale

When students learn to use an outline, they learn to identify the main topic and subtopics of a nonfiction book, which reveals the organization of the text.

Assess Learning

Observe students when they talk about and create outlines and notice if there is evidence of new learning based on the goal of this minilesson.

- Can they use and create an outline to show the main topic of a book and its subtopics?
- Are they using the terms *reader's notebook, graphic organizer, outline, main topic,* and *subtopics*?

Minilesson

To help students think about the minilesson principle, engage students in a discussion about how to make an outline. Here is an example.

- Before teaching this lesson, students should have read a variety of nonfiction books and discussed different nonfiction text structures, especially categorical (i.e., topics and subtopics). Depending on the experience of your students, you might want to adjust the number of entries to vary from those shown in the example.
- Display the prepared chart and the cover of *The Cod's Tale* by Mark Kurlansky.

  What do you notice about the book and the chart? How are they related?

  What I have written on the chart is called an outline. I wrote the outline to help me remember the information in *The Cod's Tale.*

- Draw students' attention to section I.

  This is called roman numeral one (I). What do you notice about what I wrote and how I wrote it in this section?

- Guide students to understand that topics are listed from larger to smaller and organized with roman and arabic numerals and sometimes uppercase and lowercase letters. The information is listed very briefly, not in complete sentences.

  If I were to continue the outline by writing about the Vikings and the Basques, what could I write next?

- If needed, explain that a different topic would start with roman numeral II and continue with the same type of organization as shown on the chart.

Have a Try

Invite the students to talk with a partner about using an outline.

> Turn and talk with your partner about how you could use an outline.

Summarize and Apply

Summarize the learning and remind students to use an outline to show the main idea and subtopics.

> Today you learned that an outline is useful for showing the main idea and subtopics from a book. Sometimes a book has headings. How might headings help you outline a book?

- Add the principle to the top of the chart.

> Today when you read, choose a nonfiction book to read with a partner. Work together to create an outline of the topics and subtopics of the book (or part of the book) that could be added to your reader's notebook. Bring your outline and the book you used when we meet.

Use an outline to show the main topic of a book and its subtopics.

The Cod's Tale

I. Description of cod
  A. Atlantic cod once plentiful and valuable, now threatened
  B. Appearance and appetite
    1. Can be more than 3 feet long
    2. Greedy appetite, so easy to catch
  C. Life cycle
    1. Must lay millions of eggs for species to survive
    2. Few eggs grow to adulthood
  D. Where they live
    1. Continental shelves
    2 Between North America and Europe
  E. Enemies
    1. Seals
    2. People

Share

Following independent reading time, match up sets of partners to make groups of four.

> As you share the outline you created with your group, talk about the decisions you made about what to include in the outline and how to organize it.

Extend the Lesson (Optional)

After assessing students' understanding, you might decide to extend the learning.

- Use different nonfiction examples to create more expanded outlines with students, including the various outline subsections.
- **Writing About Reading** Encourage students to create an outline in a reader's notebook to show the main topic and subtopics within one book, such as a biography or other nonfiction book.

RML3

WAR.U4.RML3

Reading Minilesson Principle

Use a web to show how ideas are connected.

Using Graphic Organizers to Share Thinking About Books

You Will Need

- several familiar books that have connected ideas, such as these from Text Set: Empathy:
  - *Mrs. Katz and Tush* by Patricia Polacco
  - *My Man Blue* by Nikki Grimes
  - *The Crane Girl* by Curtis Manley
- chart paper prepared with a blank web graphic organizer
- markers
- a copy of a web for each student (optional)
- To download the following online resource for this lesson, visit **resources.fountasandpinnell.com:** Web

Academic Language / Important Vocabulary

- reader's notebook
- graphic organizer
- web
- compassion
- connected

Continuum Connection

- Write about connections among texts by topic, theme, major ideas, authors' styles, and genres (pp. 200, 203)
- Use graphic organizers such as webs to show how a nonfiction writer puts together information related to the same topic or subtopic (p. 204)

Goal

Learn how to use webs as a graphic organizer to connect information within a text or across texts.

Rationale

When students learn to create a web as a way to connect ideas within or across texts, they learn to pay attention to common ideas both in books and in their own lives. This lesson provides a model for how you can teach students to use a graphic organizer to connect ideas.

Assess Learning

Observe students when they talk about webs to connect ideas and notice if there is evidence of new learning based on the goal of this minilesson.

- Do students participate in creating a web to connect ideas within or between books?
- Are students using the terms *reader's notebook, graphic organizer, web, compassion,* and *connected*?

Minilesson

To help students think about the minilesson principle, use familiar texts to help students create a web that connects an idea across several books. Here is an example.

- Display the blank web and a variety of books with a common theme, such as compassion (e.g., *Mrs. Katz and Tush, My Man Blue,* and *The Crane Girl*).

  One element all of these books have in common is compassion.

- Write the word *compassion* in the center bubble.

  What does *compassion* mean?

  What is an example of compassion from *Mrs. Katz and Tush*?

- As students provide examples, build the web by writing the title and a few words about the compassion example in one of the web bubbles. Help students revise their wording to include only a few words describing the idea of compassion in the story.
- Repeat the question with *My Man Blue* and *The Crane Girl.*

Have a Try

Invite the students to talk with a partner about creating a web to connect ideas.

- Show the covers of the example books again.

  What other elements of these books could you record in a web? Turn and talk about that.

- After time for discussion, ask a few volunteers to share ideas. Add responses to the web.

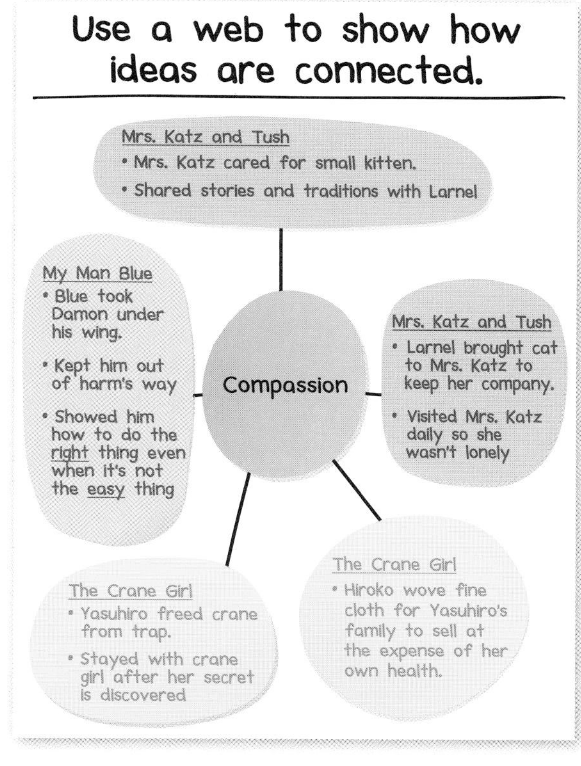

Summarize and Apply

Summarize the learning and remind students to think about how to use a web to connect ideas.

Today you learned that you can use a web to connect ideas in different books.

- Add the principle to the chart. Then provide a copy of a web that students can fill out and glue into a reader's notebook or have them draw their own webs.

  You talked with a partner about other elements of these books you could write in a web. Choose one of those ideas and fill in a web about that. Bring your web when we meet to share.

Share

Following independent reading time, gather students in the meeting area. Ask a few students to share.

Who would like to share the web you made?

Extend the Lesson (Optional)

After assessing students' understanding, you might decide to extend the learning.

- Encourage students to use webs in other ways to show how ideas in fiction and nonfiction books are connected (e.g., connect nonfiction topics or subtopics in one or more books, create a character traits web, use a web to connect themes across several texts).
- **Writing About Reading** Once students have completed a web, have them write about their noticings of how the information is connected.

RML 4
WAR.U4.RML4

Reading Minilesson Principle

Use a Venn diagram to compare and contrast books.

Using Graphic Organizers to Share Thinking About Books

You Will Need

- two familiar fiction books for comparing and contrasting, such as *Paul Bunyan* by Steven Kellogg and *Thunder Rose* by Jerdine Nolen, from Text Set: Genre Studies: Tall Tales
- chart paper prepared with a blank Venn diagram
- markers
- a copy of a Venn diagram for each student (optional)
- To download the following online resource for this lesson, visit **resources.fountasandpinnell.com:** Venn Diagram

Academic Language / Important Vocabulary

- graphic organizer
- genre
- Venn diagram
- compare and contrast

Continuum Connection

- Notice and write about an author's use of underlying structural patterns to organize information and sometimes apply the same structure to writing nonfiction texts: description, temporal sequence, question and answer, cause and effect, chronological sequence, compare and contrast, problem and solution, categorization (p. 205)

Goal

Use a Venn diagram to compare and contrast books.

Rationale

When students create a Venn diagram to compare and contrast books, they notice similarities and differences across texts. This lesson provides a model for teaching students to use a graphic organizer to compare and contrast genres.

Assess Learning

Observe students when they create a Venn diagram and notice if there is evidence of new learning based on the goal of this minilesson.

- Are students able to compare and contrast two books?
- Can they create a Venn diagram to compare and contrast two texts?
- Do they use the terms *graphic organizer, genre, Venn diagram*, and *compare and contrast*?

Minilesson

To help students understand how to use a Venn diagram, engage them in a demonstration of comparing two books. Here is an example.

- Show the prepared chart paper.

  What do you know about this type of graphic organizer?

- As students respond, ensure that they understand that a Venn diagram is used to compare and contrast two things.
- Show *Paul Bunyan* and *Thunder Rose*.

  These books have some similarities and some differences. What are some features of the two books that are different?

- Revisit a few pages of each book (e.g., the covers and the Author's Note in *Thunder Rose*) as needed to prompt students' thinking.
- List students' ideas in the outer sections of the Venn diagram.

  Notice that I wrote items that are only true about *Paul Bunyan* on one side of the diagram and items that are only true about *Thunder Rose* on the other side. What items do you think will go in the overlap of the circles?

Have a Try

Invite the students to talk with a partner about completing a Venn diagram.

Turn and talk about what information could be written in the center of the Venn diagram.

- After time for discussion, ask students for ideas. Add ideas to the chart.

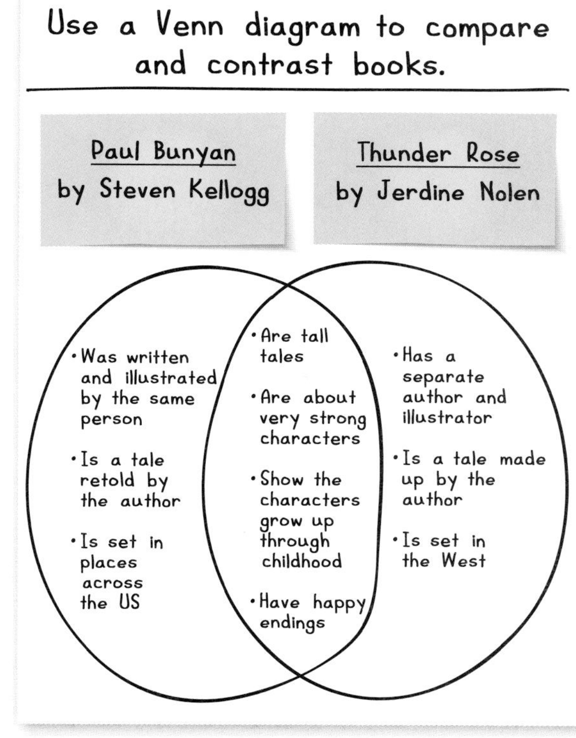
Use a Venn diagram to compare and contrast books.
Paul Bunyan by Steven Kellogg
Thunder Rose by Jerdine Nolen
• Was written and illustrated by the same person
• Is a tale retold by the author
• Is set in places across the US
• Are tall tales
• Are about very strong characters
• Show the characters grow up through childhood
• Have happy endings
• Has a separate author and illustrator
• Is a tale made up by the author
• Is set in the West

Summarize and Apply

Summarize the learning and remind students that they can use a Venn diagram to compare and contrast ideas.

Today you learned that a Venn diagram can be used to compare and contrast books.

- Add the principle to the top of the chart.
- Provide students with a copy of the Venn Diagram graphic organizer that they can glue in a reader's notebook or have them make their own.

Today when you read, choose two books to read with a partner. Work with your partner to fill in a Venn diagram. For example, you could compare and contrast genres, characters, or settings. Bring your diagram when we meet so you can share.

Share

Following independent reading time, match up sets of partners to make groups of four.

Share the Venn diagram that you made.

Extend the Lesson (Optional)

After assessing students' understanding, you might decide to extend the learning.

- Encourage students to use a Venn diagram to compare and contrast other ideas, such as the way a topic is presented in a fiction and nonfiction book, how two characters in a fiction story are similar and different, or how two animals from an expository text are similar and different.
- **Writing About Reading** Have students use the information in the Venn diagram to write about *Paul Bunyan* and *Thunder Rose* in a reader's notebook.

RML 5

WAR.U4.RML5

Reading Minilesson Principle

Use a grid to organize, analyze, and compare information.

Using Graphic Organizers to Share Thinking About Books

You Will Need

- several familiar books with clearly identifiable illustrator techniques, such as the following:
  - *Sit-In* and *Martin and Mahalia* by Andrea Davis Pinkney, from Text Set: Author Study: Andrea Davis Pinkney
  - *Funny Bones* and *Pancho Rabbit and the Coyote* by Duncan Tonatiuh, from Text Set: Illustrator Study: Duncan Tonatiuh
  - *Confucius* and *The Emperor's New Clothes* by Demi, from Text Set: Author/Illustrator Study: Demi
- chart paper prepared with a grid that has the headings *Illustrator*, *Medium*, and *Notable Characteristics*
- markers
- a reader's notebook for each student
- a copy of the Comparison Grid for each student (optional)
- To download the following online resource for this lesson, visit **resources.fountasandpinnell.com:** Comparison Grid

Academic Language / Important Vocabulary

- reader's notebook
- grid
- graphic organizer
- medium
- notable characteristics

Continuum Connection

- Write about connections among texts by topic, theme, major ideas, authors' styles, and genres (pp. 200, 203)

Goal

Use a grid to organize, analyze, and compare information across texts.

Rationale

When students learn how to use a grid to compare books, they learn to look closely at texts and compare characteristics across texts. This lesson provides a model for teaching students to use a graphic organizer to organize, analyze, and compare illustrator techniques. Make sure students have read a variety of fiction books with strong illustrative support and understand how to identify and discuss an illustrator's techniques before teaching this lesson.

Assess Learning

Observe students when they talk about and use grids and notice if there is evidence of new learning based on the goal of this minilesson.

- Are students able to use a grid to organize, analyze, and compare information from different books?
- Do they understand the terms *reader's notebook, graphic organizer, notable characteristics, grid,* and *medium*?

Minilesson

To help students think about the minilesson principle, use familiar texts to demonstrate how to use a grid to organize, analyze, and compare information (in this case, illustration styles) across texts. Here is an example.

- Show the grid that you started before class.

  What do you think I can use this grid for?

- As students respond, engage them in a discussion about grids so that they understand what should be written in each section of the grid and how the grid will help them consider the illustrator's medium and notable characteristics from several books.
- Show the covers of *Sit-In* and *Martin and Mahalia*.

  How can we fill in this grid for the illustrator Brian Pinkney?

- Ask volunteers to make suggestions. Briefly revisit any pages necessary to help students identify the multiple illustration techniques. As students provide ideas, fill in the sections of the grid.
- Show the covers of *Funny Bones* and *Pancho Rabbit and the Coyote*.

  Now let's fill in this grid for the illustrator Duncan Tonatiuh using these two books.

Have a Try

Invite the students to talk with a partner about adding a third illustrator to the grid.

- Show the covers of *Confucius* and *The Emperor's New Clothes*.

  Turn and talk to your partner about what would go in the grid for the illustrator Demi, using these two books as examples.

- After time for a brief discussion, ask students to share. Add to grid.

Use a grid to organize, analyze, and compare information.

Illustrator	Medium	Notable Characteristics
Brian Pinkney	• scratchboard • bright paint	• bright colors contrast with heavy, black brushstrokes to show movement and detail • fills page with color • characters are typically the focus
Duncan Tonatiuh	• hand drawn • collaged digitally	• characters have similar hands, ears, eyes, and expressions • inspired by pre-Columbian art, called "Mixtec codex" • earthy colors • texture created by collage
Demi	• gold leaf • calligraphy • paint • ink	• inspired by traditional Chinese drawings • parts seem to wander out of the drawing • elaborate details and textures • bold borders

Summarize and Apply

Summarize the learning and remind students to try using a grid in a reader's notebook.

You can use a grid like the one we made on the chart to think about several books together.

- Add the principle to the chart. Then provide a copy of the Comparison Grid graphic organizer for students to glue into a reader's notebook or have them make their own.

Choose a fiction book to read today. Label two columns *Medium* and *Notable Characteristics*, just like on the chart, and then fill in one row of the grid about the illustrations in your book. Bring the book and your reader's notebook when we meet so you can share.

Share

Following independent reading time, gather students in small groups.

Share the grid you started in your reader's notebook. Talk about how the illustrations your group looked at are similar and different.

Extend the Lesson (Optional)

After assessing students' understanding, you might decide to extend the learning.

- **Writing About Reading** When students have completed a grid, have them write about what they notice.
- **Writing About Reading** Encourage students to create grids (see resources.fountasandpinnell.com) to compare other aspects of fiction and nonfiction books.

Assessment

After you have taught the minilessons in this umbrella, observe students as they talk and write about their reading across instructional contexts: interactive read-aloud, independent reading, guided reading, shared reading, and book club. Use *The Literacy Continuum* (Fountas and Pinnell 2017) to guide the observation of students' reading and writing behaviors.

- What evidence do you have of new understandings related to graphic organizers?
  - Can students use a grid to represent ideas from books?
  - Are they able to create an outline to organize ideas from fiction and nonfiction books?
  - Can they create a web to show how ideas from books are connected?
  - Do they use a Venn diagram to compare and contrast books?
  - Are they able to use a diagram to show cause and effect and other underlying text structures?
  - Do they use academic vocabulary, such as *reader's notebook, graphic organizer, grid, outline, web, cause and effect,* and *Venn diagram*?
- In what other ways, beyond the scope of this umbrella, are students using a reader's notebook?
  - Are students thinking about other ways to use a reader's notebook to write about fiction and nonfiction?
  - Do they use a reader's notebook to share opinions about their reading?

Use your observations to determine the next umbrella you will teach. You may also consult Minilessons Across the Year (pp. 61–64) for guidance.

Reader's Notebook

When this umbrella is complete, provide a copy of the minilesson principles (see resources.fountasandpinnell.com) for students to glue in the reader's notebook (in the Minilessons section if using *Reader's Notebook: Advanced* [Fountas and Pinnell 2011]), so they can refer to the information as needed.

Introducing Different Genres and Forms for Responding to Reading

Minilessons in This Umbrella

RML1	Your writing about your reading shows your thinking about it.
RML2	A storyboard shows the significant events in a story.
RML3	A summary of a book gives the important information.
RML4	A written sketch of the subject of a biography is a short description of his or her traits with supporting evidence.
RML5	A short write shows your quick thinking about a book.
RML6	Two-column writing shows your response to a phrase or quote from a book.

Before Teaching Umbrella 5 Minilessons

Students need to be familiar with using a reader's notebook (see Umbrella 1: Introducing a Reader's Notebook in this section). They should be thinking and talking about concepts before they write about them, so consider teaching these minilessons alongside relevant Literary Analysis minilessons that expand opportunities for reflecting about books.

Use these texts from the *Fountas & Pinnell Classroom* ™ *Interactive Read-Aloud Collection* and *Independent Reading Collection* or choose high-quality books from your classroom library.

Interactive Read-Aloud Collection

Family

Morning on the Lake by Jan Bourdeau Waboose

The Way a Door Closes by Hope Anita Smith

Empathy

The Poet's Dog by Patricia MacLachlan

Freedom

The Composition by Antonio Skármeta

Achieving a Dream

Silent Star: The Story of Deaf Major Leaguer William Hoy by Bill Wise

Tallchief: America's Prima Ballerina by Maria Tallchief with Rosemary Wells

Caring for Our World

One Well: The Story of Water on Earth by Rochelle Strauss

Can We Save the Tiger? by Martin Jenkins

Writer's Craft

Eliza's Freedom Road by Jerdine Nolen

Firebird by Misty Copeland

Independent Reading Collection

Roller Girl by Victoria Jamieson

Interactive Read-Aloud

Family

The Way a Door Closes by Hope Anita Smith

Empathy

The Poet's Dog by Patricia MacLachlan

Freedom

The Composition by Antonio Skármeta

Achieving a Dream

Caring for Our World

Writer's Craft

Independent Reading

Reader's Notebook

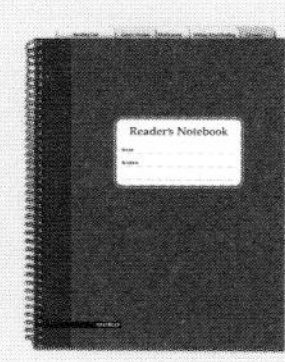

RML 1

WAR.U5.RML1

Reading Minilesson Principle

Your writing about your reading shows your thinking about it.

Introducing Different Genres and Forms for Responding to Reading

You Will Need

- chart paper and markers
- a reader's notebook for each student

Academic Language / Important Vocabulary

- reader's notebook
- brainstorm

Continuum Connection

- Have topics and ideas for writing in a list or notebook (p. 297)

Goal

Brainstorm a list of the different types of thinking you might share about books.

Rationale

When you teach students to think about the many ways they can write about books, they learn how to use writing as a tool to think more deeply about their reading. They reflect on common themes, messages, settings, and similar characteristics of literature. These understandings help them apply ideas and messages to their own lives, and they develop their understandings of writer's craft in a variety of genres.

Assess Learning

Observe students when they think and talk about writing about reading and notice if there is evidence of new learning based on the goal of this minilesson.

- Do students participate in brainstorming ideas for what they can write about their reading in a reader's notebook?
- Are they able to select an idea from the list to use for writing about a book they are reading?
- Do they use the terms *reader's notebook* and *brainstorm*?

Minilesson

To help students think about the minilesson principle, engage them in brainstorming ideas for writing about reading in a reader's notebook. Here is an example.

- Each student should have a reader's notebook to use during this lesson. If students have been keeping notes about reading or about minilessons in a reader's notebook, they can refer to those notes during the brainstorming portion of the lesson.

  When you talk about books, you share your thinking about books. You can also share your thinking by writing about what you read. Turn and talk about some different ideas you have for what you can think and write about in response to the books you read.

- Allow students a few moments to think or to refer to any notes they have about minilessons in the reader's notebook.
- As students share ideas, begin a list on chart paper.
- As needed, prompt the conversation to generate new categories of ideas. If you are using *Reader's Notebook: Advanced* (Fountas and Pinnell 2011), the Writing About Reading section has suggested ideas to help with the brainstorming session.

Have a Try

Invite the students to talk with a partner about the list of ways to write about reading in a reader's notebook.

> Look at the list of ideas for writing about your reading. Which ideas will you use? Do you have any ideas we didn't list? Turn and talk about that.

- After time for a brief discussion, ask a few students to share. Add any new ideas to the chart.

Your writing about your reading shows your thinking about it.

- The genre and its characteristics
- How the setting and characters support the genre
- Whether the main character is the narrator and how this affects the story
- Whether the characters are believable
- What you learned about the time period
- Whether the setting could be a place that exists
- The author's point of view
- The kind of research done to write the book
- What the story makes you want to know more about
- Whether there are twists or turns that surprised you
- How the events and action created tension in the story
- How the illustrations support the genre
- Your thoughts and feelings about the author's stated or implied message

Summarize and Apply

Summarize the learning and remind students to use writing about their reading as a way to reflect on books.

> Today we made a list of different ways you can write about your reading in your reader's notebook.

- Review the ideas on the chart.

> Today share your thinking by writing about the book you are reading. You may want to use some of the ideas from the list. Bring your reader's notebook and the book when we meet so you can share.

- If you are using *Reader's Notebook: Advanced* (Fountas and Pinnell 2011), have students write in the Writing About Reading section. If students are using another notebook, have them use a dedicated section of the notebook.

Share

Following independent reading time, gather students in small groups.

> Share with your group what you wrote in your reader's notebook. Did you use one of the ideas on the list, or did you write about something different?

Extend the Lesson (Optional)

After assessing students' understanding, you might decide to extend the learning.

- Keep the list posted and add to it as students experience new minilessons or as they generate new ideas for writing about reading. Encourage them to try new ideas from the list instead of repeating the same types of writing responses. Your feedback to their writing will also expand the possibilities.
- Remind students to keep a tally of the kinds of writing about reading they use (see WAR.U2.RML2).

RML 2
WAR.U5.RML2

Introducing Different Genres and Forms for Responding to Reading

You Will Need

- an example of a graphic novel (e.g., *Roller Girl* by Victoria Jamieson from *Independent Reading Collection*), or another book written in storyboard format (optional)
- several familiar books that have easy-to-follow events, such as the following from Text Set: Family:
  - *Morning on the Lake* by Jan Bourdeau Waboose
  - *The Way a Door Closes* by Hope Anita Smith
- chart paper and markers
- document camera (optional)
- a reader's notebook for each student

Academic Language / Important Vocabulary

- storyboard
- panel
- plot
- events

Continuum Connection

- Draw or sketch to represent or remember the content of a text and provide a basis for discussion or writing (p. 200)
- Represent a longer series of events from a text through drawing and writing (p. 200)
- Make notes or write descriptions to help remember important details about plot (p. 201)

Reading Minilesson Principle

A storyboard shows the significant events in a story.

Goal

Create a storyboard to represent the significant events in a plot.

Rationale

When students identify the most important events in stories and write about them in a sequential way, they recognize the pattern in narratives and are able to think deeply about the elements of plot. Storyboards provide an opportunity for students to use images to communicate their thinking about a book.

Assess Learning

Observe students when they create a storyboard and notice if there is evidence of new learning based on the goal of this minilesson.

- Are students able to identify and sequence the most important events in a plot?
- Can they create a storyboard that shows the events from a book they read?
- Are they using the terms *storyboard, panel, plot,* and *events*?

Minilesson

To help students think about the minilesson principle, guide them in creating a storyboard to show the plot events from a familiar book. Here is an example.

- If you have a comic book, graphic novel, or other book written in storyboard format, show a page.

  What do you notice about the format of this story?

- As needed, assist with the conversation so that students notice that each event is in a box (panel), there are pictures and just a few words, and the events go in order.

  This is similar to what is called a storyboard. A storyboard shows pictures of the important events in a story and has just a few words for each panel. Storyboards are often used to plan how to film a movie because they tell something about each main event that the director wants to show.

- Show the cover and review some pages of *Morning on the Lake*. As needed, guide them to think of which main events to show in a storyboard. The following prompts may be helpful:
  - *Which events from this story could be included in a storyboard?*
  - *How would you show the first event?*
  - *What could go in the next panel?*
- As students provide ideas, begin sketching panels to show events from the beginning, the middle, and the end of the story.

Have a Try

Invite the students to talk with a partner about how to create a storyboard using a familiar book.

> What would go in the first few panels of a storyboard to show the action in *The Way a Door Closes*? Turn and talk about that.

Summarize and Apply

Summarize the learning and remind students to think about the most important events as they read.

> Today you learned how to create a storyboard to show the important events in a story.

- Add the principle to the chart.

> Make a storyboard for the last fiction book you read. Bring the book and your storyboard when we meet so you can share.

- To make the drawing easier, you might want to give students an unlined sheet of paper the size of the page in the reader's notebook to glue in when finished.

A storyboard shows the significant events in a story.
It is so quiet that I am afraid to breathe.
In time, wisdom will come.

Share

Following independent reading time, gather students in pairs to share their storyboards.

> Share your storyboard. If you are not finished, tell your partner what you will put in the next few panels, or ask for ideas if you are unsure about what to draw next.

Extend the Lesson (Optional)

After assessing students' understanding, you might decide to extend the learning.

- Have students create storyboards for other types of books that have a narrative structure (e.g., autobiography, biography, memoir, narrative nonfiction).

RML3

WAR.U5.RML3

Reading Minilesson Principle

A summary of a book gives the important information.

Introducing Different Genres and Forms for Responding to Reading

You Will Need

- several fiction books that are good examples for writing a summary, such as the following:
  - *The Poet's Dog* by Patricia MacLachlan, from Text Set: Empathy
  - *The Composition* by Antonio Skármeta, from Text Set: Freedom
- chart paper prepared with a book summary
- chart paper and markers
- a reader's notebook for each student

Academic Language / Important Vocabulary

- reader's notebook
- summary

Continuum Connection

- Select and include appropriate and important details when writing a summary of a text (p. 200)
- Write summaries that include important details about setting (p. 201)
- Write summaries that include the story's main problem and how it is resolved (p. 201)
- Write summaries that include important details about characters (p. 201)

Goal

Write a brief summary of the most important information in a fiction text, including the characters, setting, and the problem and solution (when applicable).

Rationale

When students write a summary, they learn to think about the elements of fiction stories or nonfiction books and the big ideas in them. This is different from a retelling that gives most of the information. Prior to teaching this lesson, students need a good understanding of plot and summarizing (see Umbrella 27: Understanding Plot in Section Two: Literary Analysis and Umbrella 5: Summarizing in Section Three: Strategies and Skills).

Assess Learning

Observe students when they write summaries and notice if there is evidence of new learning based on the goal of this minilesson.

- Can students write a concise summary of a book they have read?
- Do they use the terms *reader's notebook* and *summary*?

Minilesson

To help students think about the minilesson principle, engage them in an inquiry-based lesson about writing a summary. Here is an example.

- Display the prepared summary and the cover of *The Poet's Dog*.

  I have written a summary of *The Poet's Dog.* What information do you notice I included in the summary?

- As students respond, prompt the conversation as needed so they notice the typical contents of a summary of a book: title and author, main characters, setting, problem, resolution, and the author's message, theme, or big idea.
- Record responses on chart paper.

  In what order did I write the information?

  What are some things from the book that I did *not* include in my summary?

  Why do you think I did not include that information?

  What is the difference between retelling and summarizing?

Have a Try

Invite the students to talk with a partner about writing a summary.

- Show *The Composition* and turn through a few pages.

  What would you include in a summary of *The Composition*? Turn and talk about that.

- After a brief time for discussion, ask students to share ideas.

Summarize and Apply

Summarize the learning and remind students to think about how they would summarize what they are reading.

- Review the chart about summaries. Add the principle to the chart.

  Try writing a summary of a book in your reader's notebook. You can write a summary of *The Composition*, or you can write about a book you recently finished reading. Bring your reader's notebook when we meet so you can share.

Share

Following independent reading time, gather students in pairs to share their summaries.

Share with your partner the summary you wrote. When you are the listener, look at our chart and notice whether the summary includes *only* the important information. Then talk about that when your partner is finished.

Extend the Lesson (Optional)

After assessing students' understanding, you might decide to extend the learning.

- Guide students in writing a summary for a familiar nonfiction book. This will be challenging since they must focus on the big ideas with only a few very important supporting facts.

Summary

The Poet's Dog

The narrator in The Poet's Dog by Patricia MacLachlan is a dog named Teddy. Teddy can talk, but only poets and children understand him. Teddy rescues two lost children from a snowstorm. As they wait in a cabin in the woods, Teddy tells stories of his life with Sylvan, a poet who had rescued and cared for him until he died. The children's parents find them, and they take Teddy with them to his new home. This story shows that your life continues after the death of a loved one, and you carry that person with you in your new life.

A summary of a book gives the important information.

- Gives only important information
  - Title and author
  - Main characters
  - Setting
  - Problem and resolution
  - Author's message, theme, or big idea
- Tells information in order

RML 4

WAR.U5.RML4

Introducing Different Genres and Forms for Responding to Reading

You Will Need

- several familiar biographies, such as the following from Text Set: Achieving a Dream:
  - *Silent Star* by Bill Wise
  - *Tallchief* by Maria Tallchief with Rosemary Wells
- chart paper and markers
- a reader's notebook for each student

Academic Language / Important Vocabulary

- reader's notebook
- written sketch

Continuum Connection

- Write about why an author might choose to write a story or to write about a topic (p. 203)

Reading Minilesson Principle

A written sketch of the subject of a biography is a short description of his or her traits with supporting evidence.

Goal

Write a sketch of the subject of a biography.

Rationale

When students write a sketch of the subject of a biography, they have to think about how the author portrays the subject and gain insight into why the author chose to write about the subject. Sometimes creating a drawing of the subject first can start their thinking. Before teaching this lesson, be sure students have learned about biographies (see Umbrella 16: Studying Biography in Section Two: Literary Analysis).

Assess Learning

Observe students when they write a sketch of the subject of a biography and notice if there is evidence of new learning based on the goal of this minilesson.

- Can students write a sketch of the subject of a biography that accurately reflects how the author depicts the subject?
- Are students using the terms *reader's notebook* and *written sketch*?

Minilesson

To help students think about the minilesson principle, engage them in thinking about what information to include in a written sketch. Here is an example.

- Show the cover of *Silent Star*.

  A written sketch is a brief paragraph that helps someone get to know the subject of a biography or a character. Think about what you know about William Hoy from reading *Silent Star: The Story of Deaf Major Leaguer William Hoy*. Turn and talk about what he is like and how he does things.

- Provide a moment for discussion.

  Let's work together to write a sketch of William. What information should be included in the paragraph?

- As students provide ideas, write a brief sketch. As you write, help students stay focused on the traits of the subject and evidence of those traits.

  What do you notice about what we wrote?

- Read the written sketch. Then, engage students in an analysis of the written sketch. Prompt students to understand that a good written sketch will tell not only something about a subject's physical traits, but also personality traits. A good written sketch includes text evidence.

  This is just one example of a written sketch. When you write your own sketch, you will make your own choices about what to include.

Have a Try

Invite the students to talk with a partner about information for a written sketch of the subject of a biography.

- Show the cover of *Tallchief*.

  What might you include in a sketch of Maria Tallchief, using what you learned about her in *Tallchief: America's Prima Ballerina*? Turn and talk about that.

- After time for a brief discussion, ask students to share ideas.

A written sketch of the subject of a biography is a short description of his or her traits with supporting evidence.

Silent Star

William Hoy, the subject of the biography Silent Star: The Story of Deaf Major Leaguer William Hoy, is one of the top baseball players of all time. What is most remarkable is that he was deaf. As a boy, he loved baseball. He was friendly and worked hard at all he did, as shown by the care with which he fixed and made shoes while working in a shoemaker's shop. He was resourceful and generous, and he even saved enough to buy the entire shop. He also built a baseball diamond where he let teenagers play. He was recruited by a coach and ignored people who believed a deaf person couldn't play baseball. He broke records and barriers in baseball. After retiring, he became a successful dairy farmer.

Summarize and Apply

Summarize the learning and remind students to create a written sketch in a reader's notebook.

- Review the written sketch.

  Today, create a written sketch in a reader's notebook. You can use one of the subjects we discussed (William Hoy or Maria Tallchief), or you can choose someone from a biography you are reading. Bring your reader's notebook when we meet so you can share.

Share

Following independent reading time, gather students in groups of three to share their written sketches.

With your group, share the written sketch you wrote. Talk about the choices you made.

Extend the Lesson (Optional)

After assessing students' understanding, you might decide to extend the learning.

- Have students write a character sketch using a familiar fiction book and include a drawing of the character. Encourage students to be sure that details in the written sketch and drawing go beyond just physical traits so a person reading the sketch and looking at the drawing can determine other qualities about the character.

RML5
WAR.U5.RML5

Reading Minilesson Principle

A short write shows your quick thinking about a book.

Introducing Different Genres and Forms for Responding to Reading

You Will Need

- several books that are good examples for doing a short write, such as the following from Text Set: Caring for Our World:
  - *One Well* by Rochelle Strauss
  - *Can We Save the Tiger?* by Martin Jenkins
- chart paper and markers
- document camera (optional)
- a reader's notebook for each student

Academic Language / Important Vocabulary

- short write

Continuum Connection

- Understand writing as a vehicle to communicate something the writer thinks (p. 297)

Goal

Use a short write to share and deepen thinking about a book.

Rationale

When you teach students to do a short write, they learn how to share their thinking about a variety of aspects of their reading quickly.

Assess Learning

Observe students when they write to share their thinking and notice if there is evidence of new learning based on the goal of this minilesson.

- Can students do a short write to share their thinking?
- Do they use the term *short write*?

Minilesson

To help students think about the minilesson principle, provide a demonstration of how to do a short write. Then have students talk about what they notice. Here is an example.

- Show the cover of *One Well*. On chart paper, begin a short write about the book. Write the title and author. Show the pages before the first page and model your thinking as you write.

  Let's see. One thing I really loved about this book was the way the author caught my attention right away and made me want to read. I think I will start my short write by writing about that.

- Show a few more pages of the book.

  This is a persuasive book, so I would like to include a critique of how persuasive the author is. I really felt persuaded by the author's position about conserving water, so I am going to write about that.

- Continue with the short write, modeling your thinking and writing aloud.

  What do you notice about my short write?

- Guide students to notice that a short write is quick thinking in response to something they have read and that it can be about anything, though it should have a clear point.

Have a Try

Invite the students to talk with a partner about doing a short write.

- Show the cover of *Can We Save the Tiger?*

  Think about doing a short write about *Can We Save the Tiger?* You want to focus on whether the author succeeds in persuading you of the importance of working to save endangered species. What would you write? Turn and talk about that.

- After time for a brief discussion, ask a few volunteers to share.

A short write shows your quick thinking about a book.

One Well: The Story of Water on Earth
by Rochelle Strauss

The author hooked my interest right from the start! Her first sentence made me want to read more about how all water on Earth is connected.

The purpose of this book is to persuade readers to be conscientious when using water and not waste it. Did I feel convinced after reading that I should help to conserve water? Yes! The author organizes the book in a way that shows how everything on Earth needs water, which puts a strain on fresh water resources. In my opinion, the author is successful in expressing concern about water by combining facts with an interesting writing style and detailed drawings.

Summarize and Apply

Summarize the learning and remind students to do a short write in a reader's notebook.

You can do a short write to share your quick thinking about any book.

Today, do a short write about *Can We Save the Tiger?* Bring your notebook when we meet so you can share.

Share

Following independent reading time, gather students in pairs to share their writing.

Share your short write with a partner. Take turns reading to each other.

Extend the Lesson (Optional)

After assessing students' understanding, you might decide to extend the learning.

- **Writing About Reading** Encourage students to use the Suggestions for Writing About Reading page in *Reader's Notebook: Advanced* (Fountas and Pinnell 2011) for other short write ideas (also available from resources.fountasandpinnell.com). Examples include whether the illustrations or photographs successfully enhance the topic of a nonfiction book; aspects of the author's or illustrator's craft; how the author builds suspense; what thoughts, dialogue, and behaviors reveal about a character; how the setting affects the plot; how the author uses time in the story; or what could be changed about the book to increase your enjoyment of the story.

RML 6
WAR.U5.RML6

Reading Minilesson Principle

Two-column writing shows your response to a phrase or quote from a book.

Introducing Different Genres and Forms for Responding to Reading

You Will Need

- several familiar books that have memorable phrases and/or quotes, such as the following from Text Set: Writer's Craft:
  - *Eliza's Freedom Road* by Jerdine Nolen
  - *Firebird* by Misty Copeland
- chart paper prepared with two columns
- markers
- a reader's notebook for each student
- document camera (optional)

Academic Language / Important Vocabulary

- phrase
- quote

Continuum Connection

- Draw and write about connections between the ideas in texts and students' own life experiences (p. 200)

Goal

Use a double-column entry with a phrase or quote from a text in the left column and responses in the right column.

Rationale

When students learn to respond to a phrase, quote, or question from their reading, they learn to express their responses to reading in a clear, organized way and to think deeply about language they encounter while reading.

Assess Learning

Observe students when they write responses to phrases, quotes, or questions and notice if there is evidence of new learning based on the goal of this minilesson.

- Can students write a response to an important phrase or quote?
- Are they using the terms *phrase* and *quote*?

Minilesson

To help students think about the minilesson principle, engage them in a discussion of how to respond to phrases, quotes, or questions that they encounter as they read. Here is an example.

> Sometimes when you read, you find a phrase or quote that stands out to you in some way. You might want to write about it in a way that helps you explore your thinking. Here's a sentence from *Eliza's Freedom Road* that I think is beautiful and interesting.

- Read aloud the two sentences that begin "Today I have only" from *Eliza's Freedom Road* and write it in the left-hand column.
- In the second column, write a response to the phrase, reading aloud as you write.

> Turn and talk about my writing. What do you notice?

- After a brief discussion, ask a few volunteers to share.

> If you were writing a response to these sentences, what would you write?

- Add a few ideas from students to the right-hand column.

> Responding to this sentence helped me appreciate the author's writing even more. Writing about something is a way to think about it.

Have a Try

Invite the students to respond to a phrase, quote, or question from a book.

- Show or project page 1 from *Firebird*. Draw students' attention to the quote "the space between you and me is longer than forever."

  Think about this quote. What is your reaction to it? In your reader's notebook, write a quick response to this quote.

- After students have had a few minutes to write a response, ask a few volunteers to share.

Two-column writing shows your response to a phrase or quote from a book.

Eliza's Freedom Road
by Jerdine Nolen

"Today I have only my mother's memory and the stories she would tell. This makes me feel as if a deep well inside me cannot be filled." (page 15)	I picture someone whose heart feels empty and feels deeply sad. While Eliza can think about her mother, she cannot see or talk with her because she is no longer alive. This quote really hit me hard because I could imagine that empty feeling. It really made me connect with Eliza when I read it. The figurative language is very powerful because I imagine Eliza's emptiness.

Summarize and Apply

Summarize the learning and remind students to use a reader's notebook to write responses to phrases and quotes.

- Review the idea of creating two columns to respond to phrases or quotes.

  Today, choose a phrase or quote that you like from the book you are reading. Make a two-column chart in your reader's notebook. Write the title of the book and the author at the top. Write the phrase or quote in the left column and write your response in the right column. Bring your reader's notebook and the book you used to our class meeting.

Share

Following independent reading time, gather students in groups of three to share what they wrote.

Share your quote or phrase and your response with your group.

Extend the Lesson (Optional)

After assessing students' understanding, you might decide to extend the learning.

- **Writing About Reading** Encourage students to respond to other types of language they notice (e.g., poetic language, memorable words, beautiful language, sensory details) in a two-column format.

Introducing Different Genres and Forms for Responding to Reading

Assessment

After you have taught the minilessons in this umbrella, observe students as they talk and write about their reading across instructional contexts: interactive read-aloud, independent reading, guided reading, shared reading, and book club. Use *The Literacy Continuum* (Fountas and Pinnell 2017) to guide the observation of students' reading and writing behaviors.

- What evidence do you have of new understandings related to responding to reading?
    - Are they able to create a storyboard to represent significant events in a story?
    - Do they write concise summaries of fiction books?
    - Are they able to write a sketch of the subject of a biography?
    - Can they do a short write about a book?
    - Can they respond in writing to an important phrase, quote, or question from a book?
    - Are they using the terms *reader's notebook, brainstorm, storyboard, summary, written sketch, short write, response,* and *opinion*?
- In what other ways, beyond the scope of this umbrella, are students responding to reading?
    - Are students using readers' notebooks in a variety of new ways?

Use your observations to determine the next umbrella you will teach. You may also consult Minilessons Across the Year (pp. 61–64) for guidance.

Reader's Notebook

When this umbrella is complete, provide a copy of the minilesson principles (see resources.fountasandpinnell.com) for students to glue in the reader's notebook (in the Minilessons section if using *Reader's Notebook: Advanced* [Fountas and Pinnell 2011]), so they can refer to the information as needed.

Minilessons in This Umbrella

RML1	Make an advertisement for a book.
RML2	Write a book review.
RML3	Make a persuasive poster based on an opinion you developed from reading.

Before Teaching Umbrella 6 Minilessons

The minilessons in this umbrella introduce students to different ways to write persuasively about their reading. We recommend that you teach Umbrella 15: Exploring Persuasive Texts in Section 2: Literary Analysis before teaching this umbrella. For these minilessons, use the following books from the *Fountas & Pinnell Classroom™ Interactive Read-Aloud Collection* or choose books from your classroom library.

Understanding How Things Work

Skateboards by Patricia Lakin

Problem Solving/Resourcefulness

Green City: How One City Survived a Tornado and Rebuilt for a Sustainable Future by Allan Drummond

The Soda Bottle School: A True Story of Recycling, Teamwork, and One Crazy Idea by Seño Laura Kutner and Suzanne Slade

As you read aloud and enjoy these and other texts together, help students express their opinions about the topics discussed in the books and the books themselves.

Understanding How Things Work

Problem Solving/ Resourcefulness

RML1

WAR.U6.RML1

Reading Minilesson Principle

Make an advertisement for a book.

Writing About Reading to Persuade

You Will Need

- a model advertisement that you have made about a book with which your students are familiar, such as *Skateboards* by Patricia Lakin, from Text Set: Understanding How Things Work (see example on the following page)
- a book that you have read aloud recently with your class
- chart paper and markers

Academic Language / Important Vocabulary

- advertisement
- persuade

Continuum Connection

- Understand how the purpose of the writing influences the selection of genre (p. 294)

Goal

Make an advertisement that tells about a text in an attention-getting or persuasive way.

Rationale

When students make book advertisements, they learn that there are genres that are better suited for certain purposes. Students also have the opportunity to express their opinions about books in persuasive and creative ways.

Assess Learning

Observe students when they create book advertisements and notice if there is evidence of new learning based on the goal of this minilesson.

- Can students create persuasive book advertisements?
- Do they understand the terms *advertisement* and *persuade*?

Minilesson

To help students think about the minilesson principle, use a book advertisement that you have created to engage them in noticing the characteristics of this type of persuasive writing. Here is an example.

- Display the book advertisement that you created before class.

  After I read *Skateboards* by Patricia Lakin, I created a book advertisement for it. What do you think a book advertisement is? What is the purpose of a book advertisement?

  The purpose of a book advertisement is to persuade other people to read the book. What does *persuade* mean?

  Take a close look at my book advertisement. What do you notice about it? What information did I include?

- Record students' noticings on chart paper.

  Is this advertisement an effective way to persuade you to read the book? What makes it effective (or not effective)?

Have a Try

Invite the students to talk with a partner about how to make a book advertisement.

- Show the cover of a book that you have read aloud recently with your class.

  If you were to make a book advertisement for this book, what would you put on it? What would you write about this book? Turn and talk to your partner about your ideas.

- After students turn and talk, invite a few pairs to share their thinking. Add new ideas to the chart.

Make an advertisement for a book.

From award-winning author Patricia Lakin...

Learn how Jake Eshelman makes one-of-a-kind skateboards by hand

"By the end of this book, you, too, will be as big a fan of skateboards as Jake Eshelman is. Totally engaging!" —Mr. Forina

Made by Hand
Skateboards
by Patricia Lakin

"If you've got wheels under your feet, you can **fly**."

- Book title and author
- The book cover
- What the book is about
- A quote from a positive review of the book
- An attention-getting quote from the book
- The author's credentials

Summarize and Apply

Summarize the learning and invite students to make a book advertisement.

What is one way you can persuade someone to read a book?

- Write the principle at the top of the chart.

  Today, make a book advertisement for a book that you have read recently and enjoyed. Think about what would appeal to someone who would like the book. Bring your book advertisement to share when we come back together.

Share

Following independent reading time, gather students together in the meeting area to share their book advertisements.

Share your book advertisement with your partner. Discuss what you notice about each other's advertisements and what makes them persuasive.

Extend the Lesson (Optional)

After assessing students' understanding, you might decide to extend the learning.

- Share with students an assortment of official book advertisements. Invite them to discuss what they notice and whether the advertisements are effective.

RML2

WAR.U6.RML2

Reading Minilesson Principle

Write a book review.

Writing About Reading to Persuade

You Will Need

- an assortment of book reviews from various sources about both fiction and nonfiction children's books
- a book that you have read aloud recently with your class
- chart paper and markers

Academic Language / Important Vocabulary

- book review
- opinion
- evidence

Continuum Connection

- Form and express opinions about a text in writing and support those opinions with rationales and evidence (p. 201)

Goal

Write a book review.

Rationale

When students write book reviews, they think critically about the books they read, express their opinions in writing, and support their opinions with rationales and evidence.

Assess Learning

Observe students when they write book reviews and notice if there is evidence of new learning based on the goal of this minilesson.

- Do students write effective book reviews?
- In their book reviews, do students express opinions about a book and support those opinions with rationales and evidence?
- Do they understand the terms *book review*, *opinion*, and *evidence*?

Minilesson

To help students think about the minilesson principle, provide them with several examples of book reviews and engage them in noticing the characteristics of book reviews. Here is an example.

- Divide students into small groups. Give each group several short book reviews.

  Take a look at the book reviews I gave you, and see what you notice about them. Discuss what you notice about book reviews with your group.

- After students have had time to read and discuss the book reviews within their groups, use several questions such as the following to elicit their noticings:
  - *What is a book review?*
  - *Why do people write book reviews?*
  - *What did the writers write about in their book reviews?*
  - *What kinds of opinions did the writers of the reviews express?*
  - *How did they support their opinions?*
- After time for discussion, ask students to list what to write in a book review. Record students' ideas on chart paper.

  How do you think someone prepares for writing a book review?

- Help students understand that the writer of a book review must read a book several times and think about who the audience is for the book.

Have a Try

Invite the students to talk with a partner about what they would write in a book review.

- Show the cover of a book that you have read aloud recently with your class.

  If you were to write a a review of this book, what would you write? What opinions would you give? Turn and talk to your partner to share your thinking.

- After time for discussion, invite a few students to share their thinking with the class.

Summarize and Apply

Summarize the learning and invite students to write a book review.

What can you write to persuade someone to agree with your opinion of a book?

- Write the principle at the top of the chart.

  Today, write a book review about the last book that you finished reading. Remember to support your opinions with reasons and evidence. Bring your book review to share when we come back together.

Write a book review.

Book Reviews

- Give the title and author of the book.
- Briefly tell what the book is about.
- Give the writer's opinions about the book.
- Give reasons and evidence for opinions.
- Say both positive and negative things about the book.
- Tell whether or not the writer recommends the book.
- Give the book a rating (for example, 5 out of 5 stars).

Share

Following independent reading time, gather students together in the meeting area to share their book reviews.

Share your book review with your partner. Discuss what you notice about each other's reviews, and give your partner feedback about what they did well and what could be improved in their review.

Extend the Lesson (Optional)

After assessing students' understanding, you might decide to extend the learning.

- Give students numerous opportunities to write book reviews throughout the school year. Have students share their book reviews with each other and use each other's reviews as a means for choosing new books to read.
- Look at book reviews online for books with which students are familiar. Discuss what makes the reviews persuasive—or not.

RML 3

WAR.U6.RML3

Reading Minilesson Principle

Make a persuasive poster based on an opinion you developed from reading.

Writing About Reading to Persuade

You Will Need

- a model persuasive poster that you have made about the topic of a book that your students are familiar with, such as *Green City* by Allan Drummond, from Text Set: Problem Solving/Resourcefulness (see example on the following page)
- a different nonfiction book that you have read aloud recently with your class, such as *The Soda Bottle School* by Seño Laura Kutner and Suzanne Slade, from Text Set: Problem Solving/Resourcefulness
- chart paper and markers
- materials for poster making (poster board, markers, etc.)

Academic Language / Important Vocabulary

- persuasive
- opinion

Continuum Connection

- Express opinions about facts or information learned (p. 203)

Goal

Make a persuasive poster that reflects an opinion about a topic.

Rationale

When students create persuasive posters based on their reading, they think deeply about the topic of a book they have read, develop an opinion about that topic, and gain confidence in sharing their opinion with others.

Assess Learning

Observe students when they create persuasive posters and notice if there is evidence of new learning based on the goal of this minilesson.

- Do students create persuasive posters based on opinions they developed from reading?
- Do they understand the terms *persuasive* and *opinion*?

Minilesson

To help students think about the minilesson principle, use a persuasive poster that you have created to engage them in noticing the characteristics of this type of writing. Here is an example.

- Display the cover of *Green City* alongside the persuasive poster that you created before class.

    Reading *Green City* helped me realize how important it is to go green. I think that we all have an important role to play in protecting our planet. After reading this book and thinking a lot about the idea of going green, I decided to make a persuasive poster to share my opinion with others. What do you think a persuasive poster is?

    What do you notice about my persuasive poster?

    What am I trying to persuade people to do?

    Do you think that my poster is persuasive? Will it convince people to agree with my point of view? If not, what could I do differently to make it more persuasive?

Have a Try

Invite the students to talk with a partner about how to make a persuasive poster.

- Show the cover of *The Soda Bottle School*.

  Think about an opinion that you have about the topic of this book. How could you make a persuasive poster to get people to agree with your opinion? What would you write on your poster? Turn and talk to your partner about your ideas.

- After students turn and talk, invite a few students to share their thinking.

Summarize and Apply

Summarize the learning and invite students to make a persuasive poster.

What is something you can do to persuade people to agree with your opinion?

- Write the principle at the top of the chart.

  Today, make a persuasive poster about an opinion that you developed from reading a book. Bring your poster to share when we come back together.

Make a persuasive poster based on an opinion you developed from reading.

Earth's resources will not last forever.

Do your part to save our planet

Tips for Going Green:

- Walk, ride your bike, or take public transportation whenever possible.
- Turn off lights and electronics when you're not using them.
- Create less waste. Recycle as much as possible.
- Take shorter showers.
- Use reusable bags instead of plastic bags when you go shopping.

It's not too late to make a difference!

Go Green Today!

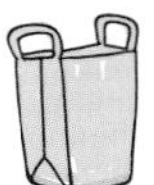

Share

Following independent reading time, gather students together in the meeting area to share their posters.

Who would like to share your persuasive poster?

What choices did you make and why?

Extend the Lesson (Optional)

After assessing students' understanding, you might decide to extend the learning.

- Have students express their opinions developed through reading in other written formats (e.g., a persuasive pamphlet).

Assessment

After you have taught the minilessons in this umbrella, observe students as they talk and write about their reading across instructional contexts: interactive read-aloud, independent reading, guided reading, shared reading, and book club. Use *The Literacy Continuum* (Fountas and Pinnell 2017) to observe students' reading and writing behaviors.

- What evidence do you have of new understandings related to writing about reading to persuade?
    - Can students make an advertisement for a book that tells about it in an attention-getting or persuasive way?
    - Can they write a review of a book and support their opinions about the book with evidence?
    - Can they make a persuasive poster based on an opinion they developed through reading?
    - Do they understand and use vocabulary such as *advertisement*, *review*, *persuasive*, and *opinion*?
- In what other ways, beyond the scope of this umbrella, might you have your students write about their reading?

Use your observations to determine the next umbrella you will teach. You may also consult Minilessons Across the Year (pp. 61–64) for guidance.

Reader's Notebook

When this umbrella is complete, provide a copy of the minilesson principles (see resources.fountasandpinnell.com) for students to glue in the reader's notebook (in the Minilessons section if using *Reader's Notebook: Advanced* [Fountas and Pinnell 2011]), so they can refer to the information as needed.

Minilessons in This Umbrella

RML1	Write a diary entry from the perspective of a character.
RML2	Create a poem in response to your reading.
RML3	Write an interview to tell about the subject of a biography.
RML4	Write a readers' theater script based on a book.

Before Teaching Umbrella 7 Minilessons

The minilessons in this umbrella introduce students to different ways to respond creatively to reading in writing. Before teaching this umbrella, make sure that your students have had experience writing about their reading in a variety of ways. For the model responses in these minilessons, use the following books from the *Fountas & Pinnell Classroom™ Interactive Read-Aloud Collection* or choose high-quality, engaging books from your classroom library.

Hope and Resilience

Home to Medicine Mountain by Chiori Santiago

Grit and Perseverance

Rikki-Tikki-Tavi by Rudyard Kipling

Nim and the War Effort by Milly Lee

Genre Study: Biography (Musicians)

The Legendary Miss Lena Horne by Carole Boston Weatherford

As you read aloud and enjoy these texts together, help students talk about what they learned from the books and/or share their emotional responses.

Hope and Resilience

Grit and Perseverance

Genre Study: Biography (Musicians)

RML 1
WAR.U7.RML1

Reading Minilesson Principle

Write a diary entry from the perspective of a character.

Responding Creatively to Reading

You Will Need

- a model diary entry that you have written in response to a book your students are familiar with, such as *Nim and the War Effort* by Milly Lee, from Text Set: Grit and Perseverance
- chart paper and markers

Academic Language / Important Vocabulary

- perspective
- diary entry
- character

Goal

Write a diary entry from the perspective of a character.

Rationale

Writing a diary entry from the perspective of a fictional character helps students connect with characters on a deeper level and better understand their emotions and motivations. This minilesson should be taught when students already have a good understanding of perspective and point of view. We recommend teaching Umbrella 31: Analyzing Perspective and Point of View in Section 2: Literary Analysis before this minilesson.

Assess Learning

Observe students when they write a diary entry from the perspective of a character and notice if there is evidence of new learning based on the goal of this minilesson.

- Can students write a diary entry from the perspective of a fictional character?
- Do they understand the terms *perspective*, *diary entry*, and *character*?

Minilesson

To help students think about the minilesson principle, use a diary entry that you have written from the perspective of a character to engage them in noticing the characteristics of this type of written response. Here is an example.

After I read *Nim and the War Effort*, I wanted to better understand Nim's feelings about what happened to her in the story. So I decided to write a diary entry from her perspective. What do you think it means to write a diary entry from the perspective of a character?

- Display and read aloud the diary entry that you wrote before class.
- Use questions such as the following to elicit students' noticings:
  - *What do you notice about my diary entry?*
  - *How can you tell that this is a diary entry?*
  - *How did I begin and end my diary entry?*
  - *How can you tell which character's perspective I wrote this entry from?*
  - *How can you tell that I read the story that the diary entry is about?*
  - *What kinds of things did I write about in my diary entry?*
  - *What does this diary entry help you understand about the character?*
- Annotate the diary entry with students' noticings.

To write from a character's perspective, you have to think about who the character is and what the character's life and experiences are like.

Have a Try

Invite the students to talk with a partner about writing a diary entry from the perspective of a character.

> If you were writing a diary entry from the perspective of Nim, what else might you include in your entry? What other details, thoughts, or feelings could you write about? Turn and talk to your partner about your ideas.

- After time for discussion, invite a few students to share their thinking.

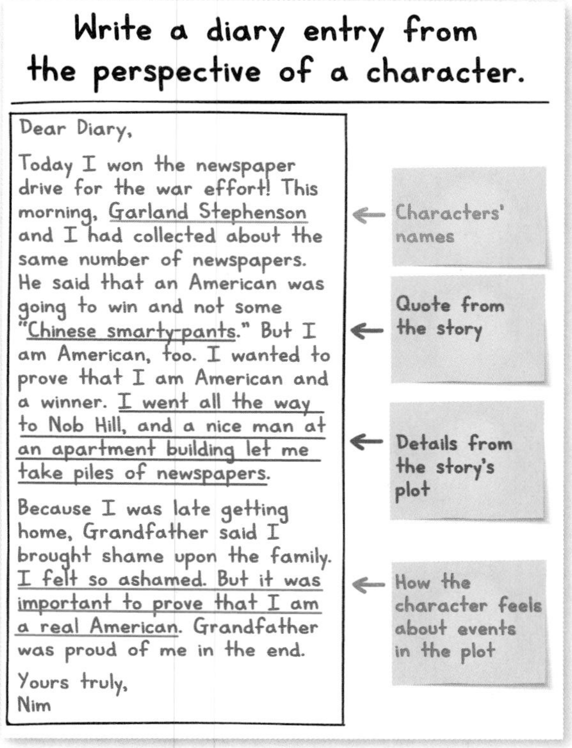

Write a diary entry from the perspective of a character.

Dear Diary,

Today I won the newspaper drive for the war effort! This morning, Garland Stephenson and I had collected about the same number of newspapers. He said that an American was going to win and not some "Chinese smarty-pants." But I am American, too. I wanted to prove that I am American and a winner. I went all the way to Nob Hill, and a nice man at an apartment building let me take piles of newspapers.

Because I was late getting home, Grandfather said I brought shame upon the family. I felt so ashamed. But it was important to prove that I am a real American. Grandfather was proud of me in the end.

Yours truly,
Nim

← Characters' names
← Quote from the story
← Details from the story's plot
← How the character feels about events in the plot

Summarize and Apply

Summarize the learning and invite students to write a diary entry from the perspective of a character in a reader's notebook.

> How can writing a diary entry from the perspective of a character help you better understand the character?

- Write the principle at the top of the chart.

> When you read today, choose a fiction book. Then write a diary entry from the perspective of a character in your story. Bring your diary entry to share when we come back together.

Share

Following independent reading time, gather students together in the meeting area to share their diary entries.

> Who would like to read aloud the diary entry you wrote today?
>
> How did writing a diary entry help you better understand the story you read?

Extend the Lesson (Optional)

After assessing students' understanding, you might decide to extend the learning.

- Have students write two (or more) diary entries about the same event in a story—each from the perspective of a different character.

RML 2

WAR.U7.RML2

Reading Minilesson Principle

Create a poem in response to your reading.

Responding Creatively to Reading

You Will Need

- a model poem that you have written in response to a book your students are familiar with, such as *Home to Medicine Mountain* by Chiori Santiago, from Text Set: Hope and Resilience (see example poem on the following page)
- chart paper and markers

Academic Language / Important Vocabulary

- poem
- response

Continuum Connection

- Write a poetic text in response to prose text, either narrative or informational (p. 289)

Goal

Create a poem in response to reading.

Rationale

Writing poems in response to reading gives students the opportunity to express their own personal emotional response to a book. It also strengthens their understanding of the characteristics of poetry.

Assess Learning

Observe students when they write poems in response to reading and notice if there is evidence of new learning based on the goal of this minilesson.

- Do students write poems in response to their reading?
- Do their poems refer to specific details from the book?
- Do they understand the terms *poem* and *response*?

Minilesson

To help students think about the minilesson principle, use a poem that you have written in response to a book to engage them in noticing the characteristics of this type of written response. Here is an example.

- Display the poem that you prepared before class.

  After I read *Home to Medicine Mountain*, I decided to write a poem in response to my reading. Listen carefully as I read my poem aloud, and see what you notice about it.

- Read the poem aloud. Then use questions such as the following to prompt students' thinking about the poem:
  - *What do you notice about how I wrote a poem in response to my reading?*
  - *How can you tell that this is a poem?*
  - *How can you tell that I wrote this poem in response to* Home to Medicine Mountain?
  - *What do you notice about the lines in my poem?*
  - *What do you notice about the words?*
- Annotate the poem with students' noticings.

Have a Try

Invite the students to talk with a partner about writing a poem in response to reading.

> Take a moment to think about what book you might like to write a poem in response to. Then turn and talk to your partner about what book you would write about and why.

- After students turn and talk, invite a few students to share their thinking with the class.

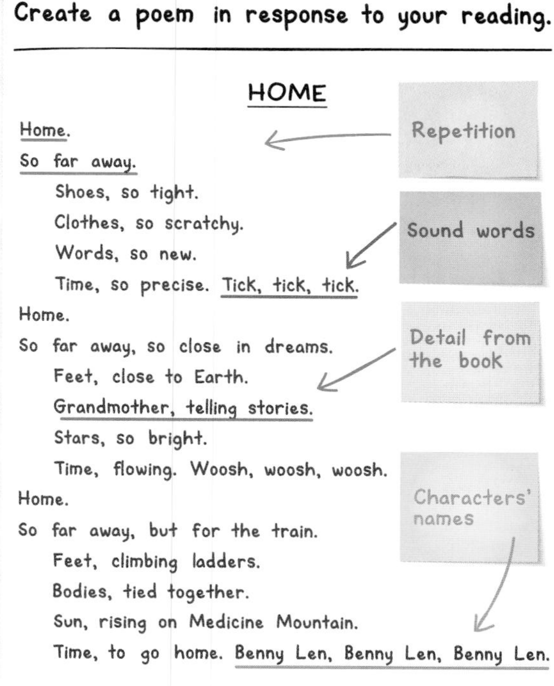

Create a poem in response to your reading.
HOME
Home.
So far away.
Shoes, so tight.
Clothes, so scratchy.
Words, so new.
Time, so precise. Tick, tick, tick.
Home.
So far away, so close in dreams.
Feet, close to Earth.
Grandmother, telling stories.
Stars, so bright.
Time, flowing. Woosh, woosh, woosh.
Home.
So far away, but for the train.
Feet, climbing ladders.
Bodies, tied together.
Sun, rising on Medicine Mountain.
Time, to go home. Benny Len, Benny Len, Benny Len.
Repetition
Sound words
Detail from the book
Characters' names

Summarize and Apply

Summarize the learning and invite students to write a poem in response to their reading.

> What did you learn today about how to write a poem in response to your reading?
>
> Why is it a good idea to write a poem in response to a book you read?

- Write the principle at the top of the chart.

> Today, take some time to write a poem in response to your reading. You might write a poem in response to the book you read today or another book that you've read recently. Bring your poem to share when we come back together.

Share

Following independent reading time, gather students together in the meeting area to share their poems.

> Who would like to read aloud the poem you wrote in response to your reading today?

Extend the Lesson (Optional)

After assessing students' understanding, you might decide to extend the learning.

- Give students numerous opportunities to share their poems with each other and give and receive feedback.

RML 3

WAR.U7.RML3

Reading Minilesson Principle

Write an interview to tell about the subject of a biography.

Responding Creatively to Reading

You Will Need

- a model interview that you have (partially) written about a biography your students are familiar with, such as *The Legendary Miss Lena Horne* by Carole Boston Weatherford, from Text Set: Genre Study: Biography (Musicians)
- chart paper prepared with part of an interview with an author (see blue print on chart)
- markers

Academic Language / Important Vocabulary

- interview
- subject
- biography

Continuum Connection

- Infer the importance of a subject's accomplishments (biography) (p. 73)

Goal

Write an interview with the author to provide information about the subject of a biography.

Rationale

Writing an interview with the author about the subject of a biography allows students to consolidate and summarize the key ideas and details in the biography.

Assess Learning

Observe students when they write interviews to tell about the subject of a biography and notice if there is evidence of new learning based on the goal of this minilesson.

- Can students write an interview to tell about the subject of a biography?
- Are their interviews in the correct format?
- Do their interviews accurately summarize key points from the biography?
- Do they understand the terms *interview*, *subject*, and *biography*?

Minilesson

To help students think about the minilesson principle, use an interview that you have written about the subject of a biography to engage students in noticing the characteristics of this type of written response. Here is an example.

- Display the interview that you started before class.

  After I read *The Legendary Miss Lena Horne*, I decided to write about Lena Horne. I wrote an interview with the author, Carole Boston Weatherford. I imagined the interview responses, but I used information from the book. I also did some research about Lena Horne. Take a few minutes to silently read what I wrote.

- Use questions such as the following to elicit students' noticings about the interview:
  - *What do you notice about what I wrote?*
  - *What do you think* Q *and* A *stand for?*
  - *What kind of writing is this?*
  - *What is the purpose of an interview?*
  - *What kind of information did I give about Lena Horne?*

Have a Try

Invite the students to talk with a partner about the answer to the final question in the interview.

I need you to help me finish writing this interview. I wrote the final question, but not the final answer. How could we answer the question "Why was Lena Horne important?" Turn and talk to your partner about what you think.

- After students turn and talk, invite a few pairs to share their thinking. Use their responses to write an answer to the final question.

Summarize and Apply

Summarize the learning and invite students to write an interview about the subject of a biography.

What did you learn how to write today?

Why is it a good idea to write an interview to tell about the subject of a biography?

- Write the principle at the top of the chart.

When you read today, choose a biography. Then, write an interview to tell about the subject of the biography. Write at least three questions and three answers. Bring your interview to share when we come back together.

Write an interview to tell about the subject of a biography.

Q: Why did you write about Lena Horne?

A: Lena Horne was amazing! She was an actress, singer, and civil rights activist.

Q: What was Lena Horne's childhood like?

A: She was born in New York City in 1917. Her mother was an actress, and her father was a street hustler. Lena spent some of her childhood traveling in the South and some of it living in Brooklyn. Her grandmother helped raise her. Lena loved reading, singing, and dancing.

Q: How did segregation affect Lena Horne?

A: Lena had to enter some southern theaters through a "colored entrance," and some restaurants and hotels refused to serve her.

Q: Why was Lena Horne important?

A: She fought hard against segregation and refused to be treated as a second-class citizen. She showed the world that all people can achieve their dreams if they persevere.

Share

Following independent reading time, gather students together in the meeting area to share their interviews.

Who would like to share your interview?

- Choose a volunteer and read (or have another student read) the interview with the volunteer so that two voices are heard.

Extend the Lesson (Optional)

After assessing students' understanding, you might decide to extend the learning.

- Have students research the subject of a biography and write an interview as if with the subject.

RML4
WAR.U7.RML4

Reading Minilesson Principle
Write a readers' theater script based on a book.

Responding Creatively to Reading

You Will Need

- a familiar fiction book that is well suited to being adapted into a readers' theater script, such as *Rikki-Tikki-Tavi* by Rudyard Kipling, from Text Set: Grit and Perseverance
- chart paper and markers

Academic Language / Important Vocabulary

- readers' theater
- script
- character
- dialogue

Continuum Connection

- Use organization in writing that is related to purpose and genre (letters, essays) (p. 291)
- Read writing aloud to help think critically about voice (p. 293)

Goal

Write a readers' theater script based on a book.

Rationale

When students write a readers' theater script based on a book, they have to determine the most important events and dialogue in the story, adapt them into a new form, and make sure that the dialogue sounds the way the characters would say it. This helps them to gain a better understanding of the story and to better connect with it.

Assess Learning

Observe students when they write readers' theater scripts and notice if there is evidence of new learning based on the goal of this minilesson.

- Can students write readers' theater scripts based on stories they have read?
- Do they understand the terms *readers' theater*, *script*, *character*, and *dialogue*?

Minilesson

To help students think about the minilesson principle, use shared writing to write the beginning of a readers' theater script based on a familiar book. Here is an example.

Today we're going to write a readers' theater script. What do you think a readers' theater script is?

Readers' theater is a way to enjoy a story through speaking and listening. Each reader holds a script and reads aloud the dialogue, or lines, of one of the characters in the story. The readers' theater script that we are going to write today will be based on *Rikki-Tikki-Tavi*. As I read the beginning of this story, listen carefully and think about how we could write a readers' theater script based on part of this book.

- Show the cover of *Rikki-Tikki-Tavi* and then revisit pages 1–3.

Which characters speak in this part of the story?

Besides Teddy and his mother and father, who else should be a speaker in our script? Who is telling the story?

- Record the speakers' names, including the narrator, on chart paper.

How should we begin our script? Which character should speak first? What should the character say?

- Use students' suggestions to write the first line of dialogue. Then continue in a similar manner with the rest of this section of the story. Emphasize to students that a readers' theater script is not an exact copy of the book. Writers must decide what details to include, what to leave out, and how to adapt the text to be spoken aloud so that it sounds the ways the characters would speak.

Have a Try

Invite the students to help revise the script by hearing it read aloud.

- Choose four students to read the script aloud.

  A readers' theater script is to be read out loud. As you read it, the rest of us will listen to see if the dialogue sounds right or whether it should be changed.

- After students read the script, ask for suggestions to make the dialogue sound even better.

Summarize and Apply

Summarize the learning and invite students to start working on a readers' theater script.

What did you learn how to write today?

What does a readers' theater script need to include?

- Write the principle at the top of the chart.
- Divide students into small groups.

  Today you're going to start writing a readers' theater script with your group. First, choose what book you're going to write a script for. Then start planning how you will write it. Think about who the speakers are, how they should sound, and the most important events in the plot. If you have time, you can begin writing the dialogue.

Write a readers' theater script based on a book.

The Rescue of Rikki-Tikki-Tavi
Adapted from Rikki-Tikki-Tavi by Rudyard Kipling
Parts: Narrator, Teddy, Teddy's mother, and Teddy's father

Narrator:	One day, a mongoose in India got washed out of his burrow by a flood. He held onto a floating stick, and when he awoke an English family was looking over him.
Teddy:	Here's a dead mongoose. We should have a funeral for him.
Mother:	No, let's take him in. Perhaps he isn't really dead.
Narrator:	They took the mongoose into their house, wrapped him in a blanket, and warmed him over a fire. Once he was warm, he ran all around the table and jumped on the boy's shoulders.
Father:	Don't be scared, Teddy. That's his way of making friends.
Teddy:	It tickles!
Mother:	Is he so tame because we helped him?
Father:	All mongooses are like that. Let's give him something to eat.

Share

Following independent reading time, gather students together in the meeting area to discuss their scripts.

- Invite each group to share the progress they have made on their script.

  What book are you going to write a script for? How are you going to write it?

Extend the Lesson (Optional)

After assessing students' understanding, you might decide to extend the learning.

- Help students finish writing their readers' theater scripts. When they have finished, have each group perform their script for the rest of the class.

Assessment

After you have taught the minilessons in this umbrella, observe students as they talk and write about their reading across instructional contexts: interactive read-aloud, independent reading, guided reading, shared reading, and book club. Use *The Literacy Continuum* (Fountas and Pinnell 2017) to observe students' reading and writing behaviors.

- What evidence do you have of new understandings related to responding creatively to reading?
    - Can students write a diary entry from the perspective of a character?
    - Do they write poems in response to their reading?
    - Can they write interviews to tell what they learned from a biography?
    - Do they know how to adapt a book into a readers' theater script?
    - Do they use terms such as *perspective, diary entry, character, interview, subject, biography, readers' theater, dialogue*, and *script*?
- In what other ways, beyond the scope of this umbrella, might you have your students write about their reading?

Use your observations to determine the next umbrella you will teach. You may also consult Minilessons Across the Year (pp. 61–64) for guidance.

Readers' Notebook

When this umbrella is complete, provide a copy of the minilesson principles (see resources.fountasandpinnell.com) for students to glue in the reader's notebook (in the Minilessons section if using *Readers' Notebook: Advanced* [Fountas and Pinnell 2011]), so they can refer to the information as needed.

Glossary

adventure/adventure story A contemporary realistic or historical fiction or fantasy text that presents a series of exciting or suspenseful events, often involving a main character taking a journey and overcoming danger and risk.

affix A letter or group of letters added to the beginning or end of a base or root word to change its meaning or function (e.g., *prefix* or *suffix*).

alphabet book/ABC book A book that helps children develop the concept and sequence of the alphabet by pairing alphabet letters with pictures of people, animals, or objects with labels related to the letters.

animal fantasy A modern fantasy text geared to a very young audience in which animals act like people and encounter human problems.

animal story A contemporary realistic or historical fiction or fantasy text that involves animals and that often focuses on the relationships between humans and animals.

assessment A means for gathering information or data that reveals what learners control, partially control, or do not yet control consistently.

beast tale A folktale featuring animals that talk.

behaviors Actions that are observable as children read or write.

biography A biographical text in which the story (or part of the story) of a real person's life is written and narrated by another person. Biography is usually told in chronological sequence but may be in another order.

bold/boldface Type that is heavier and darker than usual, often used for emphasis.

book and print features (as text characteristics) The physical attributes of a text (for example, font, layout, and length).

categorization A structural pattern used especially in nonfiction texts to present information in logical categories (and subcategories) of related material.

cause and effect A structural pattern used especially in nonfiction texts, often to propose the reasons or explanations for how and why something occurs.

character An individual, usually a person or animal, in a text.

chronological sequence An underlying structural pattern used especially in nonfiction texts to describe a series of events in the order they happened in time.

closed syllable A syllable that ends in a consonant: e.g., *lem*-on.

compare and contrast A structural pattern used especially in nonfiction texts to compare two ideas, events, or phenomena by showing how they are alike and how they are different.

comprehension (as in reading) The process of constructing meaning while reading text.

concrete poetry A poem with words (and sometimes punctuation) arranged to represent a visual picture of the idea the poem is conveying.

conflict In a fiction text, a central problem within the plot that is resolved near the end of the story. In literature, characters are usually in conflict with nature, with other people, with society as a whole, or with themselves. Another term for conflict is *problem*.

consonant digraph Two consonant letters that appear together and represent a single sound that is different from the sound of either letter: e.g., *sh*ell.

cumulative tale A story with many details repeated until the climax.

dialogue Spoken words, usually set off with quotation marks in text.

directions (how-to) A procedural nonfiction text that shows the steps involved in performing a task. A set of directions may include diagrams or drawings with labels.

elements of fiction Important elements of fiction include narrator, characters, plot, setting, theme, and style.

elements of poetry Important elements of poetry include figurative language, imagery, personification, rhythm, rhyme, repetition, alliteration, assonance, consonance, onomatopoeia, and aspects of layout.

endpapers The sheets of heavy paper at the front and back of a hardback book that join the book block to the hardback binding. Endpapers are sometimes printed with text, maps, or designs.

English language learners People whose native language is not English and who are acquiring English as an additional language.

epic A traditional tale or long narrative poem, first handed down orally and later in writing. Usually an epic involves a journey and a set of tasks or tests in which the hero triumphs. Generally the nature of the deeds and attributes of the hero have grown and become exaggerated over time.

essay An analytic or interpretive piece of expository writing with a focused point of view, or a persuasive text that provides a body of information related to a social or scientific issue.

expository text A nonfiction text that gives the reader information about a topic. Expository texts use a variety of text structures, such as compare and contrast, cause and effect, chronological sequence, problem and solution, and temporal sequence. Seven forms of expository text are categorical text, recount, collection, interview, report, feature article, and literary essay.

fable A folktale that demonstrates a useful truth and teaches a lesson. Usually including personified animals or natural elements such as the sun, fables appear to be simple but often convey abstract ideas.

factual text See *informational text.*

family, friends, and school story A contemporary realistic or historical fiction text focused on the everyday experiences of children of a variety of ages, including relationships with family and friends and experiences at school.

fantasy A fiction text that contains elements that are highly unreal. Fantasy as a category of fiction includes genres such as animal fantasy and science fiction.

fiction Invented, imaginative prose or poetry that tells a story. Fiction texts can be organized into the categories realism and fantasy. Along with nonfiction, fiction is one of two basic genres of literature.

figurative language Language that imaginatively compares two objects or ideas to allow the reader to see something more clearly or understand something in a new way. An element of a writer's style, figurative language changes or goes beyond literal meaning. Two common types of figurative language are metaphor (a direct comparison) and simile (a comparison that uses *like* or *as*).

flash-forward A literary device in which the action moves suddenly into the future to relate events that have relevance for understanding the present.

flashback A literary device in which the action moves suddenly into the past to relate events that have relevance for understanding the present.

fluency In reading, this term names the ability to read continuous text with good momentum, phrasing, appropriate pausing, intonation, and stress. In word solving, this term names the ability to solve words with speed, accuracy, and flexibility.

folktale A traditional fiction text about a people or "folk," originally handed down orally from generation to generation. Folktales are usually simple tales and often involve talking animals. Fables, fairy tales, beast tales, trickster tales, tall tales, realistic tales, cumulative tales, noodlehead tales, and pourquoi tales are some types of folktales.

font In printed text, the collection of type (letters) in a particular style.

form A kind of text that is characterized by particular elements. Mystery, for example, is a form of writing within the realistic fiction genre. Another term for form is *subgenre*.

fractured fairy tale A retelling of a familiar fairy tale with characters, setting, or plot events changed, often for comic effect.

free verse A type of poetry with irregular meter. Free verse may include rhyme, alliteration, and other poetic sound devices.

friendly letter In writing, a functional nonfiction text usually addressed to friends and family that may take the form of notes, letters, invitations, or e-mail.

genre A category of written text that is characterized by a particular style, form, or content.

graphic feature In fiction texts, graphic features are usually illustrations. In nonfiction texts, graphic features include photographs, paintings and drawings, captions, charts, diagrams, tables and graphs, maps, and timelines.

graphic text A form of text with comic strips or other illustrations on every page. In fiction, a story line continues across the text; illustrations, which depict moment-to-moment actions and emotions, are usually accompanied by dialogue in speech balloons and occasional narrative description of actions. In nonfiction, factual information is presented in categories or sequence.

haiku An ancient Japanese form of non-rhyming poetry that creates a mental picture and makes a concise emotional statement.

high-frequency words Words that occur often in the spoken and written language (for example, *the*).

humor/humor story A realistic fiction text that is full of fun and meant to entertain.

hybrid/hybrid text A text that includes at least one nonfiction genre and at least one fiction genre blended in a coherent whole.

illustration Graphic representation of important content (for example, art, photos, maps, graphs, charts) in a fiction or nonfiction text.

imagery The use of language—descriptions, comparisons, and figures of speech—that helps the mind form sensory impressions. Imagery is an element of a writer's style.

independent writing Texts written by children independently with teacher support as needed.

infer (as a strategic action) To go beyond the literal meaning of a text; to think about what is not stated but is implied by the writer.

infographic An illustration—often in the form of a chart, graph, or map—that includes brief text and that presents and analyzes data about a topic in a visually striking way.

informational text A nonfiction text in which a purpose is to inform or give facts about a topic. Informational texts include the following genres: biography, autobiography, memoir, and narrative nonfiction, as well as expository texts, procedural texts, and persuasive texts.

interactive read-aloud An instructional context in which students are actively listening and responding to an oral reading of a text.

interactive writing A teaching context in which the teacher and students cooperatively plan, compose, and write a group text; both teacher and students act as scribes (in turn).

intonation The rise and fall in pitch of the voice in speech to convey meaning.

italic (italics) A typestyle that is characterized by slanted letters.

label A written word or phrase that names the content of an illustration.

layout The way the print and illustrations are arranged on a page.

legend In relation to genre, this term names a traditional tale, first handed down orally and later in writing, that tells about a noteworthy person or event. Legends are believed to have some root in history, but the accuracy of the events and people they describe is not always verifiable. In relation to book and print features, this term names a key on a map or chart that explains what symbols stand for.

limerick A type of rhyming verse, usually surprising and humorous and frequently nonsensical.

limited point of view A method of storytelling in which the narrator knows what one character is thinking and feeling. The narrator may relate the actions of many characters but will not move between the points of view of different characters in a given scene or story.

literary essay An expository text that presents ideas about a work (or works) of literature in a formal, analytical way.

lyrical poetry A songlike type of poetry that has rhythm and sometimes rhyme and is memorable for sensory images and description.

main idea The central underlying idea, concept, or message that the author conveys in a nonfiction text. Compare to *theme, message*.

maintaining fluency (as a strategic action) Integrating sources of information in a smoothly operating process that results in expressive, phrased reading.

making connections (as a strategic action) Searching for and using connections to knowledge gained through personal experiences, learning about the world, and reading other texts.

meaning One of the sources of information that readers use (MSV: meaning, language structure, visual information). Meaning, the semantic system of language, refers to meaning derived from words, meaning across a text or texts, and meaning from personal experience or knowledge.

memoir A biographical text in which a writer takes a reflective stance in looking back on a particular time or person. Usually written in the first person, memoirs are often briefer and more intense accounts of a memory or set of memories than the accounts found in biographies and autobiographies.

mentor texts Books or other texts that serve as examples of excellent writing. Mentor texts are read and reread to provide models for literature discussion and student writing.

message An important idea that an author conveys in a fiction or nonfiction text. See also *main idea, theme*.

modern fantasy Fantasy texts that have contemporary content. Unlike traditional literature, modern fantasy does not come from an oral tradition. Modern fantasy texts can be divided into four more specific genres: animal fantasy, low fantasy, high fantasy, and science fiction.

monitoring and self-correcting (as a strategic action) Checking whether the reading sounds right, looks right, and makes sense, and solving problems when it doesn't.

mood The emotional atmosphere communicated by an author in his or her work, or how a text makes readers feel. An element of a writer's style, mood is established by details, imagery, figurative language, and setting. See also *tone*.

myth A traditional narrative text, often based in part on historical events, that explains human behavior and natural events or phenomena such as the seasons and the earth and sky.

narrative nonfiction Nonfiction texts that tell a story using a narrative structure and literary language to make a topic interesting and appealing to readers.

narrative text A category of texts in which the purpose is to tell a story. Stories and biographies are kinds of narrative.

narrative text structure A method of organizing a text. A simple narrative structure follows a traditional sequence that includes a beginning, a problem, a series of events, a resolution of the problem, and an ending. Alternative narrative structures may include devices, such as flashback or flash-forward, to change the sequence of events or have multiple narrators.

narrator The teller of the story of a text. The term *point of view* also indicates the angle from which the story is told, usually the first person (the narrator is a character in the story) or the third person (the unnamed narrator is not a character in the story).

nonfiction Prose or poetry that provides factual information. According to their structures, nonfiction texts can be organized into the categories of narrative and nonnarrative. Along with fiction, nonfiction is one of the two basic genres of literature.

nonnarrative text structure A method of organizing a text. Nonnarrative structures are used especially in three genres of nonfiction—expository texts, procedural texts, and persuasive texts. In nonnarrative nonfiction texts, underlying structural patterns include description, cause and effect, chronological sequence, temporal sequence, categorization, compare and contrast, problem and solution, and question and answer. See also *organization, text structure*, and *narrative text structure*.

open syllable A syllable that ends in a vowel sound: e.g., *ho*-tel.

oral tradition The handing down of literary material—such as songs, poems, and stories—from person to person over many generations through memory and word of mouth.

organization The arrangement of ideas in a text according to a logical structure, either narrative or nonnarrative. Another term for organization is *text structure*.

organizational tools and sources of information A design feature of nonfiction texts. Organizational tools and sources of information help a reader process and understand nonfiction texts. Examples include table of contents, headings, index, glossary, appendix, about the author, and references.

peritext Decorative or informative illustrations and/or print outside the body of the text. Elements of the peritext add to aesthetic appeal and may have cultural significance or symbolic meaning.

personification A figure of speech in which an animal is spoken of or portrayed as if it were a person, or in which a lifeless thing or idea is spoken of or portrayed as a living thing. Personification is a type of figurative language.

perspective How the characters view what is happening in the story. It is shaped by culture, values, and experience. See also *narrator* and *point of view*.

persuasive text A nonfiction text intended to convince the reader of the validity of a set of ideas—usually a particular point of view.

picture book An illustrated fiction or nonfiction text in which pictures work with the text to tell a story or provide information.

plot The events, action, conflict, and resolution of a story presented in a certain order in a fiction text. A simple plot progresses chronologically from start to end, whereas more complex plots may shift back and forth in time.

poetry Compact, metrical writing characterized by imagination and artistry and imbued with intense meaning. Along with prose, poetry is one of the two broad categories into which all literature can be divided.

point of view The angle from which a fiction story is told, usually the first person (the narrator is a character in the story; uses the pronouns *I*, *me*) or the third person (an unnamed narrator is not a character in the story; uses the pronouns *he*, *she*, *they*). See also *narrator*, *third-person limited point of view*, and *third-person omniscient point of view*.

pourquoi tale A folktale intended to explain why things are the way they are, usually having to do with natural phenomena.

predicting (as a strategic action) Using what is known to think about what will follow while reading continuous text.

prefix A group of letters placed in front of a base word to change its meaning: e.g., *pre*plan.

principle A generalization that is predictable.

print feature In nonfiction texts, print features include the color, size, style, and font of type, as well as various aspects of layout.

problem See *conflict*.

problem and solution A structural pattern used especially in nonfiction texts to define a problem and clearly propose a solution. This pattern is often used in persuasive and expository texts.

procedural text A nonfiction text that explains how to do something. Procedural texts are almost always organized in temporal sequence and take the form of directions (or "how-to" texts) or descriptions of a process.

prompt A question, direction, or statement designed to encourage the child to say more about a topic.

Prompting Guide, Part 1 A quick reference for specific language to teach for, prompt for, or reinforce effective reading and writing behaviors. The guide is organized in categories and color-coded so that you can turn quickly to the area needed and refer to it as you teach (Fountas and Pinnell 2012).

punctuation Marks used in written text to clarify meaning and separate structural units. The comma and the period are common punctuation marks.

purpose A writer's overall intention in creating a text, or a reader's overall intention in reading a text. To tell a story is one example of a writer's purpose, and to be entertained is one example of a reader's purpose.

question and answer A structural pattern used especially in nonfiction texts to organize information in a series of questions with responses. Question-and-answer texts may be based on a verbal or written interview, or on frequently arising or logical questions about a topic.

reader's notebook A notebook or folder of bound pages in which students write about their reading. A reader's notebook is used to keep a record of texts read and to express thinking. It may have several different sections to serve a variety of purposes.

readers' theater A performance of literature—i.e., a story, a play, or poetry—read aloud expressively by one or more persons rather than acted.

realistic fiction A fiction text that takes place in contemporary or modern times about believable characters involved in events that could happen. Contemporary realistic fiction usually presents modern problems that are typical for the characters, and it may highlight social issues.

repetition Repeated words or phrases that help create rhythm and emphasis in poetry or prose.

resolution/solution The point in the plot of a fiction story when the main conflict is solved.

rhyme The repetition of vowel and consonant sounds in the stressed and unstressed syllables of words in verse, especially at the ends of lines.

rhythm The regular or ordered repetition of stressed and unstressed syllables in poetry, other writing, or speech.

searching for and using information (as a strategic action) Looking for and thinking about all kinds of content to make sense of a text while reading.

self-correcting Noticing when reading doesn't make sense, sound right, or look right, and fixing it when it doesn't.

sequence See *chronological sequence* and *temporal sequence*.

series A set of books that are connected by the same character(s) or setting. Each book in a series stands alone, and often books may be read in any order.

setting The place and time in which a fiction text or biographical text takes place.

shared reading An instructional context in which the teacher involves a group of students in the reading of a particular big book to introduce aspects of literacy (such as print conventions), develop reading strategies (such as decoding or predicting), and teach vocabulary.

shared writing An instructional context in which the teacher involves a group of students in the composing of a coherent text together. The teacher writes while scaffolding children's language and ideas.

short write A sentence or paragraph that students write at intervals while reading a text. Students may use sticky notes, notepaper, or a reader's notebook to write about what they are thinking, feeling, or visualizing as they read. They may also note personal connections to the text.

sidebar Information that is additional to the main text, placed alongside the text and sometimes set off from the main text in a box.

small-group reading instruction The teacher working with children brought together because they are similar enough in reading development to teach in a small group; guided reading.

solving words (as a strategic action) Using a range of strategies to take words apart and understand their meanings.

sources of information The various cues in a written text that combine to make meaning (for example, syntax, meaning, and the physical shape and arrangement of type).

speech bubble A shape, often rounded, containing the words a character or person says in a cartoon or other text. Another term for *speech bubble* is *speech balloon.*

stance How the author feels about a topic; the author's attitude.

story A series of events in narrative form, either fiction or nonfiction.

story within a story A structural device occasionally used in fiction texts to present a shorter, self-contained narrative within the context of the longer primary narrative. See also *plot.*

strategic action Any one of many simultaneous, coordinated thinking activities that go on in a reader's head. See *thinking within, beyond, and about the text.*

stress The emphasis given to some syllables or words.

structure One of the sources of information that readers use (MSV: meaning, language structure, visual information). Language structure refers to the way words are put together in phrases and sentences (syntax or grammar).

style The way a writer chooses and arranges words to create a meaningful text. Aspects of style include sentence length, word choice, and the use of figurative language and symbolism.

subgenre A kind of text that is characterized by particular elements. See also *form.*

suffix A group of letters added at the end of a base word or word root to change its function or meaning: e.g., hand*ful*, hope*less*.

summarizing (as a strategic action) Putting together and remembering important information and disregarding irrelevant information while reading.

syllable A minimal unit of sequential speech sounds composed of a vowel sound or a consonant-vowel combination. A syllable always contains a vowel or vowel-like speech sound: e.g., *pen-ny.*

tall tale A folktale that revolves around a central legendary character with extraordinary physical features or abilities. Tall tales are characterized by much exaggeration.

temporal sequence An underlying structural pattern used especially in nonfiction texts to describe the sequence in which something always or usually occurs, such as the steps in a process. See also *procedural text* and *directions (how-to).*

text structure The overall architecture or organization of a piece of writing. Another term for text structure is *organization.* See also *narrative text structure* and *nonnarrative text structure.*

theme The central underlying idea, concept, or message that the author conveys in a fiction text. Compare to *main idea.*

thesis a statement, proposition, or theory that is put forward as a premise to be maintained or proved, often by argument; the main idea or claim of an essay or nonfiction text.

thinking within, beyond, and about the text Three ways of thinking about a text while reading. Thinking *within* the text involves efficiently and effectively understanding what is on the page, the author's literal message. Thinking *beyond* the text requires making inferences and putting text ideas together in different ways to construct the text's meaning. In thinking *about* the text, readers analyze and critique the author's craft.

third-person omniscient point of view A method of storytelling in which the narrator knows what all characters are thinking and feeling. Omniscient narrators may move between the points of view of different characters in a given scene or story.

thought bubble A shape, often rounded, containing the words (or sometimes an image that suggests one or more words) a character or person thinks in a cartoon or other text. Another term for *thought bubble* is *thought balloon.*

tone An expression of the author's attitude or feelings toward a subject reflected in the style of writing. For instance, a reader might characterize an author's tone as ironic or earnest. Sometimes the term *tone* is used to identify the mood of a scene or a work of literature. For example, a text might be said to have a somber or carefree tone. See also *mood.*

tools As text characteristics, parts of a text designed to help the reader access or better understand it (table of contents, glossary, headings). In writing, references that support the writing process (dictionary, thesaurus).

topic The subject of a piece of writing.

traditional literature Stories passed down in oral or written form through history. An integral part of world culture, traditional literature includes folktales, tall tales, fairy tales, fables, myths, legends, epics, and ballads.

trickster tale A folktale featuring a clever, usually physically weaker or smaller, animal who outsmarts larger or more powerful animals.

understandings Basic concepts that are critical to comprehending a particular area of content.

visual information One of three sources of information that readers use (MSV: meaning, language structure, visual information). *Visual information* refers to the letters that represent the sounds of language and the way they are combined (spelling patterns) to create words; visual information at the sentence level includes punctuation.

wordless picture book A form in which a story is told exclusively with pictures.

writing Children engaging in the writing process and producing pieces of their own writing in many genres.

writing about reading Children responding to reading a text by writing and sometimes drawing.

Credits

Cover image from *Ada's Violin* by Susan Hood, illustrated by Sally Wern Comport. Text copyright © 2016 Susan Hood. Illustrations copyright © 2016 Sally Wern Comport. Reprinted with the permission of Simon & Schuster Books for Young Readers, an imprint of Simon & Schuster Children's Publishing Division. All rights reserved.

Cover image from *Aliens Ate My Homework* by Bruce Coville. Text copyright © 1993 Bruce Coville. Illustrations copyright © 1993 Katherine Coville. Reprinted with the permission of Aladdin Books, an imprint of Simon & Schuster Children's Publishing Division. All rights reserved.

Cover image from *Amina's Voice* by Hena Khan. Copyright © 2017 Hena Khan. Reprinted with the permission of Simon & Schuster Books for Young Readers, an imprint of Simon & Schuster Children's Publishing Division. All rights reserved.

Cover image from *Anastasia at Your Service*. Copyright © 1982 by Lois Lowry. Reprinted with permission of Houghton Mifflin Harcourt.

Cover image from *Balarama* written and illustrated by Ted and Betsy Lewin. Copyright © 2009 Ted and Betsy Lewin. Permission arranged by Lee & Low Books, Inc., New York, NY 10016.

Cover image from *Baseball Saved Us* by Ken Mochizuki, illustrated by Dom Lee. Copyright © 1993 Ken Mochizuki and Dom Lee. Permission arranged by Lee & Low Books Inc., New York, NY 10016.

Cover image from *Big Jabe* by Jerdine Nolen, illustrated by Kadir Nelson. Text copyright © 2000 by Jerdine Nolen. Illustrations copyright © 2000 by Kadir Nelson. Used by permission of Harper Collins, Inc.

Cover image from *Birds: Nature's Magnificent Flying Machines* Text copyright © 2003 Caroline Arnold. Illustrations copyright © 2003 Patricia J. Wynne. Used with permission by Charlesbridge Publishing, Inc. 85 Main Street Watertown, MA 02472. (617) 926-0329. www.charlesbridge.com. All rights reserved.

Cover image from *Black Dog*. Copyright © 2011 Levi Pinfold. Reproduced by permission of the publisher, Candlewick Press, Somerville, MA.

Cover image from *Bluffton: My Summers with Buster Keaton*. Copyright © 2013 Matt Phelan. Reproduced by permission of the publisher, Candlewick Press, Somerville, MA.

Cover image from *Can We Save The Tiger?* Text copyright © 2011 Martin Jenkins. Illustrations copyright © 2011 Vicky White. Reproduced by permission of the publisher, Candlewick Press, Somerville, MA, on behalf of Walker Books, London.

Cover image from *Confucius: Great Teacher of China* written and illustrated by Demi. Copyright © 2018 Demi. Permission arranged by Lee & Low Books, Inc., New York, NY 10016.

Cover image from *The Crane Girl* by Curtis Manley, illustrated by Lin Wang. Copyright © 2017 Curtis Manley and Lin Wang. Permission arranged by Lee & Low Books, Inc., New York, NY 10016.

Cover image from *Cycle of Rice, Cycle of Life: A Story of Sustainable Farming* written and illustrated by Jan Reynolds. Copyright © 2009 Jan Reynolds. Permission arranged by Lee & Low Books, Inc., New York, NY 10016.

Cover image from *Danza* by Duncan Tonatiuh. Text and illustration copyright © 2017 Duncan Tonatiuh. Used by permission of Abrams, an imprint of Harry N. Abrams, Inc. New York. All rights reserved.

Cover image from *Dark Emperor & Other Poems of the Night.* Text copyright © 2010 by Joyce Sidman. Illustrations copyright © 2010 by Rick Allen. Reprinted with permission of Houghton Mifflin Harcourt.

Cover image from *Deadly!* Text copyright © 2012 Nicola Davies. Illustrations copyright © 2012 Neal Layton. Reproduced by permission of the publisher, Candlewick Press, Somerville, MA, on behalf of Walker Books, London.

Cover image from *Desmond And The Very Mean Word.* Text copyright © 2013 Desmond M. Tutu. Illustrations copyright © 2013 A. G. Ford. Reproduced by permission of the publisher, Candlewick Press, Somerville, MA.

Cover image from *Destiny's Gift* by Anastasia Tarpley, illustrated by Afjoa J. Burrowes. Copyright © 2010 Anastasia Tarpley and Adjoa J. Burrowes. Permission arranged by Lee & Low Books, Inc., New York, NY 10016.

Cover image from *Elephant Quest* written and illustrated by Ted and Betsy Lewin. Copyright © 2000 Ted and Betsy Lewin. Permission arranged by Lee & Low Books, Inc., New York, NY 10016.

Cover image from *Eliza's Freedom Road* by Jerdine Nolen. Copyright © 2011 Jerdine Nolen. Reprinted with the permission of Paula Wiseman Books, an imprint of Simon & Schuster Children's Publishing Division. All rights reserved.

Cover image from *The Emperor's New Clothes* by Demi. Copyright © 2000 Demi. Reprinted with the permissions of Margaret K. McElderry, an imprint of Simon & Schuster Children's Publishing Division. All rights reserved.

Cover image from *Encounter.* Text copyright © 1992 by Jane Yolen. Illustrations copyright © 1992 by David Shannon. Reprinted with permission of Houghton Mifflin Harcourt.

Cover image from *Esquivel! Space-Age Sound Artist.* Text copyright © 2016 Susan Wood. Illustrations copyright © 2016 Duncan Tonatiuh. Used with permission by Charlesbridge Publishing, Inc., 85 Main Street Watertown, MA 02472. (617) 926-0329. www.charlesbridge.com. All rights reserved.

Cover image from *Finding the Music* by Jennifer Torres, illustrated by Alexis Romay. Copyright © 2015 Jennifer Torres and Alexis Romay. Permission arranged by Lee & Low Books, Inc., New York, NY 10016.

Cover image from *Flora & Ulysses*. Text copyright © 2013 Kate DiCamillo. Illustrations copyright © 2013 Keith Campbell. Reproduced by permission of the publisher, Candlewick Press, Somerville, MA.

Cover image from *Found* by Margaret Peterson Haddix. Copyright © 2008 Margaret Peterson Haddix. Reprinted with permission of Simon & Schuster Books for Young Readers, an imprint of Simon & Schuster Children's Publishing Division. All rights reserved.

Cover image from *Funny Bones* by Duncan Tonatiuh. Text and illustration copyright © 2015 Duncan Tonatiuh. Used by permission of Abrams, an imprint of Harry N. Abrams, Inc. New York. All rights reserved.

Cover image from *The Gift-Giver*. Copyright © 1980 by Joyce Hansen. Reprinted with permission of Clarion Books, an imprint of Houghton Mifflin Harcourt.

Cover image from *Gorilla Walk* written and illustrated by Ted and Betsy Lewin. Copyright © 1999 Ted and Betsy Lewin. Permission arranged by Lee & Low Books, Inc., New York, NY 10016.

Cover image from *Green City: How One City Survived a Tornado and Rebuilt For a Sustainable Future* by Allan Drummond. Text copyright © 2016 by Allan Drummond. Reprinted by permission of Farrar, Straus and Giroux Books for Young Readers. All Rights Reserved.

Cover image from *A Handful of Stars* by Cynthia Lord. Copyright © 2015 Cynthia Lord. Reprinted by permission of Scholastic, Inc.

Cover image from *Home to Medicine Mountain* by Chiori Santiago, illustrated by Judith Lowry. Copyright © 2002 Chiori Santiago and Judith Lowry. Permission arranged by Lee & Low Books, Inc., New York, NY 10016.

Cover image from *Hoops*. Text copyright © 1997 by Robert Burleigh. Illustrations copyright © 1997 by Stephen T. Johnson. Reprinted with permission of Houghton Mifflin Harcourt.

Cover image from *I and I: Bob Marley* by Tony Medina, illustrated by Joshua J. Watson. Copyright © 2009 Tony Medina and Joshua J. Watson. Permission arranged by Lee & Low Books, Inc., New York, NY 10016.

Cover image from *If You're Not from the Prairie...* by David Bouchard with images by Henry Ripplinger. Text copyright © 1995 David Bouchard. Illustrations copyright © 1995 Henry Ripplinger. Reprinted with the permission of Atheneum Books for Young Readers, an imprint of Simon & Schuster Children's Publishing Division. All rights reserved.

Cover image from *Incredible African-American Jazz Musicians* by Stephen Feinstein. Copyright © 2013 Stephen Feinstein. Reprinted by permission of Enslow Publishers.

Cover image from *Ira's Shakespeare Dream* by Glenda Armand, illustrated by Floyd Cooper. Copyright © 2015 Glenda Armand and Floyd Cooper. Permission arranged by Lee & Low Books, Inc., New York, NY 10016.

Cover image from *Jacques Cousteau: Conserving Underwater Worlds* by John Zronik. Text Copyright © 2007 John Zronik. Reprinted by permission of Crabtree Publishing Company.

Cover image from *King Of The Sky*. Text copyright © 2017 Nicola Davies. Illustrations copyright © 2017 Laura Carlin. Reproduced by permission of the publisher, Candlewick Press, Somerville, MA, on behalf of Walker Books, London.

Cover image from *The Kitchen Knight: The Tale of King Arthur* by Margaret Hodges, illustrated by Trina Schart Hyman. Text copyright © 1990 Margaret Hodges. Illustrations copyright © 1990 Trina Schart Hyman. Reproduced by arrangement with Holiday House, Inc.

Cover image from *The Lamp, the Lice, and the Boat Called Fish*. Text copyright © 2001 by Jacqueline Briggs Martin. Illustrations and illustrator's note copyright © 2001 by Beth Krommes. Reprinted with permission of Houghton Mifflin Harcourt.

Cover image from *The Legendary Miss Lena Horne* by Carole Boston Weatherford, illustrated by Elizabeth Zunon. Text copyright © 2017 Carole Boston Weatherford. Illustrations copyright © 2017 Elizabeth Zunon. Reprinted with the permissions of Atheneum Books for Young Readers, an imprint of Simon & Schuster Children's Publishing Division. All rights reserved.

Cover image from *Let The Celebrations Begin!* Text copyright © 1991, 2013 Margaret Wild. Illustrations copyright © 1991, 2013 Julie Vivas. Reproduced by permission of the publisher, Candlewick Press, Somerville, MA, on behalf of Walker Books, Australia.

Cover image from *Long-Armed Ludy and the First Women's Olympics*. Text copyright © 2017 Jean L. S. Patrick. Illustrations copyright © 2017 Adam Gustavson. Used with permission by Charlesbridge Publishing, Inc. 85 Main Street Watertown, MA 02472. (617) 926-0329. www.charlesbridge.com. All rights reserved.

Cover image from *Look Up! Bird-Watching in Your Own Backyard*. © 2013 by Annette LeBlanc Cate. Reproduced by permission of the publisher, Candlewick Press, Somerville, MA.

Cover image from *Lowriders in Space* by Cathy Campe, illustrated by Raul the Third. Text copyright © 2014 Cathy Camper. Illustrations copyright © 2014 Raul the Third. Used with permission of Chronicle Books LLC, San Francisco. Visit ChronicleBooks.com.

Cover image from *Malala, a Brave Girl from Pakistan/Iqbal, a Brave Boy from Pakistan* by Jeannette Winter. Copyright © 2014 Jeanette Winter. Reprinted with the permission of Beach Lane Books, an imprint of Simon & Schuster Children's Publishing Division. All rights reserved.

Cover image from *Morning on the Lake* by Jan Bourdeau Waboose, illustrated by Karen Reczuch. Copyright © 1997 Jan Bourdeau Waboose and Karen Reczuch. Used by permission of Kids Can Press, Toronto.

Cover image from *Mr. Ferris and His Wheel.* Text copyright © 2014 by Kathryn Gibbs Davis. Jacket and interior illustrations copyright © 2014 by Gilbert Ford. Title Page Lettering © 2014 by Joel Felix. Reprinted with permission of Houghton Mifflin Harcourt.

Cover image from *One Well* written by Rochelle Strauss, illustrated by Rosemary Woods. Cover illustration © 2007 Rosemary Woods. Used by permission of Kids Can Press, Toronto.

Cover image from *Pancho Rabbit And The Coyote* by Duncan Tonatiuh. Text and illustration copyright © 2013 Duncan Tonatiuh. Used by permission of Abrams, an imprint of Harry N. Abrams, Inc. New York. All rights reserved.

Cover image from *Paul Bunyan* by Steven Kellogg. Copyright © 1984 Steven Kellogg. Used by permission of HarperCollins Publishers.

Cover image from *Rachel Carson and Her Book That Changed the World* by Laurie Lawlor. Copyright © 2014 Laurie Lawlor. Reproduced by arrangement with Holiday House, Inc.

Cover image from *The Raft* by Jim Lamarche. Copyright © 2000 Jim LaMarche. Used by permission of HarperCollins Publishers. This selection may not be re-illustrated without written permission of HarperCollins.

Cover image from *Richard Wright and the Library Card* by William Miller, illustrated by Gregory Christie. Copyright © 1997 William Miller and Gregory Christie. Permission arranged by Lee & Low Books, Inc., New York, NY 10016.

Cover image from *Same Sun Here.* Text copyright © 2011 Silas House and Neela Vaswani. Jacket illustration copyright © 2012 Andrea Dezso. Reproduced by permission of the publisher, Candlewick Press, Somerville, MA.

Cover image from *Sami and the Time of the Troubles.* Text copyright © 1992 by Florence Parry Heide and Judith Heide Gilliland. Illustrations copyright © 1992 by Ted Lewin. Reprinted with permission of Clarion Books, an imprint of Houghton Mifflin Harcourt.

Cover image from *Save Me a Seat* by Sarah Weeks and Gita Varadarajan. Copyright © 2016 Sarah Weeks and Gita Varadarajan. Reprinted by permission of Scholastic, Inc.

Cover image from *The School Story* by Andrew Clements. Text copyright © 2001 Andrew Clements. Reprinted with the permission of Atheneum Books for Young Readers, an imprint of Simon & Schuster Children's Publishing Division. All rights reserved.

Cover image from *The Science of a Tornado* by Linda Cernak. Copyright © 2016 Linda Cernak. Reprinted by permission of Sleeping Bear Press.

Cover image from *Seeker of Knowledge: The Man Who Deciphered Egyptian Hieroglyphs.* Copyright © 2000 by James Rumford. Reprinted with permission of Houghton Mifflin Harcourt.

Cover image from *Shooting At The Stars* by John Hendrix. Text and illustration copyright © 2014 John Hendrix. Used by permission of Abrams, an imprint of Harry N. Abrams, Inc. New York. All rights reserved.

Cover image from *Silent Star: The Story of Deaf Major Leaguer William Hoy* by Bill Wise, illustrated by Adam Gustavson. Copyright © 2012 Bill Wise and Adam Gustavson. Permission arranged by Lee & Low Books, Inc., New York, NY 10016.

Cover image from *The Sinking of the Titanic* by Matt Doeden. Copyright © 2005 Capstone. All rights reserved.

Cover image from *Sixteen Years in Sixteen Seconds* by Paula Yoo, illustrated by Dom Lee. Copyright © 2005 Paula Yoo and Dom Lee. Permission arranged by Lee & Low Books, Inc., New York, NY 10016.

Cover image from *Skateboards* by Patricia Lakin. Text copyright © 2017 Simon & Schuster. Reprinted with the permission of Aladdin, an imprint of Simon & Schuster Children's Publishing Division. All rights reserved.

Cover image from *The Soda Bottle School* by Suzanne Slade and Laura Kutner, illustrated by Aileen Farragh. Copyright © 2016 Suzanne Slade, Laura Kutner, and Aileen Farragh. Reprinted by permission of Tilbury House Publishers, Thomaston, Maine.

Cover image from *Song of the Water Boatman*. Text copyright © 2005 by Joyce Sidman. Illustrations copyright © 2005 by Beckie Prange. Reprinted with permission of Houghton Mifflin Harcourt.

Cover image from *The Storyteller* by Evan Turk. Copyright © 2016 Evan Turk. Reprinted with the permission of Atheneum Books for Young Readers, an imprint of Simon & Schuster Children's Publishing Division. All rights reserved.

Cover image from *Strange Mr. Satie*. Text copyright © 2016 M. T. Anderson. Illustrations copyright © 2016 Patra Mathers. Reproduced by permission of the publisher, Candlewick Press, Somerville, MA.

Cover image from *Surfer of the Century* by Ellie Crowe, illustrated by Richard Waldrep. Copyright © 2007 Ellie Crowe and Richard Waldrep. Permission arranged by Lee & Low Books, Inc., New York, NY 10016.

Cover image from *Tales from the Odyssey, Part 1* by Mary Pope Osborne. Cover illustration © 2010 James Bernardin. Reprinted by permission of Disney Hyperion Books, an imprint of Disney Book Group, LLC. All rights reserved.

Cover image from *Team Moon: How 400,000 People Landed* Apollo 11 *on the Moon*. Copyright © 2006 by Catherine Thimmesh. Reprinted with permission of Houghton Mifflin Harcourt.

Cover image from *Technology: Cool Women Who Code* by Andi Diehn, illustrated by Lena Chandhok. Copyright © 2015 Andi Diehn and Lena Chandhok. Reprinted by permission of Nomad Press LLC. All rights reserved.

Cover image from *Thirty Minutes Over Oregon: A Japanese Pilot's World War II Story.* Text copyright © 2018 by Mare Tyler Nobleman. Illustrations copyright © 2018 by Melissa Iwai. Reprinted with permission of Clarion Books, an imprint of Houghton Mifflin Harcourt.

Cover image from *This Is Just To Say: Poems of Apology and Forgiveness.* Text copyright © 2007 by Joyce Sidman. Illustrations copyright © 2007 by Pamela Zagarenski. Reprinted with permission of Houghton Mifflin Harcourt.

Cover image from *Thunder Rose.* Text copyright © 2003 by Jerdine Nolen. Illustrations copyright © 2003 by Kadir Nelson. Reprinted with permission of Houghton Mifflin Harcourt.

Cover image from *Titanic.* Text copyright © 2007 Martin Jenkins. Illustrations copyright © 2007 Brian Sanders. Reproduced by permission of the publisher, Candlewick Press, Somerville, MA, on behalf of Walker Books, London.

Cover image from *Top to Bottom Down Under* written and illustrated by Ted and Betsy Lewin. Copyright © 2005 Ted and Betsy Lewin. Permission arranged by Lee & Low Books, Inc., New York, NY 10016.

Cover image from *The Treasure Box.* Text copyright © 2013 Margaret Wild. Illustrations copyright © 2013 Freya Blackwood. Reproduced by permission of the publisher, Candlewick Press, Somerville, MA.

Cover image from *Under The Quilt Of Night* by Deborah Hopkinson, illustrated by James E. Ransome. Text copyright © 2002 Deborah Hopkinson. Illustrations copyright © 2002 James E. Ransome. Reprinted with the permission of Atheneum Books for Young Readers, an imprint of Simon & Schuster Children's Publishing Division. All rights reserved.

Cover image from *Wall.* Copyright © 2014 Tom Clohosy Cole. Reproduced by permission of the publisher, Candlewick Press, Somerville, MA.

Cover image from *White Water.* Text copyright © 2011 Michael S. Bandy and Eric Stein. Illustrations copyright © 2011 Shadra Strickland. Reproduced by permission of the publisher, Candlewick Press, Somerville, MA.

Cover image from *Winter Bees & Other Poems of the Cold.* Text copyright © 2014 by Joyce Sidman. Illustrations copyright © 2014 by Rick Allen. Reprinted with permission of Houghton Mifflin Harcourt.

Cover image from *The Year of the Three Sisters.* Copyright © 2015 Andrea Cheng. Illustrations copyright © 2015 by Patrice Barton. Reprinted with permission of Houghton Mifflin Harcourt.